POST-THEORY

*Reconstructing
Film Studies*

studies in film

General Editors

David Bordwell
Donald Crafton
Vance Kepley, Jr.
Kristin Thompson, Supervising Editor

Post-Theory: Reconstructing Film Studies
Edited by David Bordwell and Noël Carroll

*Shared Pleasures: A History of Movie Presentation
in the United States*
Douglas Gomery

*Lovers of Cinema: The First American Film
Avant-Garde, 1919–1945*
Edited by Jan-Christopher Horak

*The Wages of Sin: Censorship and the
Fallen Woman Film, 1928–1942*
Lee Jacobs

Settling the Score: Music and the Classical Hollywood Film
Kathryn Kalinak

Patterns of Time: Mizoguchi and the 1930s
Donald Kirihara

POST-THEORY
Reconstructing Film Studies

Edited by

DAVID BORDWELL
and
NOËL CARROLL

The University of Wisconsin Press

The University of Wisconsin Press
114 North Murray Street
Madison, Wisconsin 53715

3 Henrietta Street
London WC2E 8LU, England

Printed in the United States of America

Library of Congress Cataloging-in-Publication Data
Post-theory: reconstructing film studies/
edited by David Bordwell and Noël Carroll.
582 pp.   cm. — (Wisconsin studies in film)
Includes bibliographical references and index.
ISBN 0-299-14940-4 (cloth: alk. paper). — ISBN 0-299-14944-7 (pbk.: alk. paper)
1. Motion pictures.   I. Bordwell, David.   II. Carroll, Noël (Noël E.)   III. Series.
PN1994.P6565   1996
791.43—dc20   95-37052

CONTENTS

CONTRIBUTORS

JOSEPH ANDERSON and BARBARA ANDERSON have written several articles on film theory. Joseph Anderson's book *The Reality of Illusion: An Ecological Approach to Cognitive Film Theory* is forthcoming from Southern Illinois University Press.

TINO BALIO is Professor of Film in the Communication Arts Department at the University of Wisconsin–Madison. His most recent book is *Grand Design: Hollywood as a Modern Motion Picture Enterprise, 1930–1939,* published by Charles Scribner's Sons as volume 5 of the History of the American Cinema series.

DAVID BORDWELL is Jacques Ledoux Professor of Film Studies in the Communication Arts Department at the University of Wisconsin–Madison. His books include *The Cinema of Eisenstein* (Harvard University Press, 1993) and, with Kristin Thompson, *Film History: An Introduction* (McGraw-Hill, 1994).

VIRGINIA LORING BROOKS is Professor of Film at Brooklyn College. She is both a scholar and a filmmaker.

NOËL CARROLL is Monroe C. Beardsley Professor of the Philosophy of Art at the University of Wisconsin–Madison. He is the author of *Philosophical Problems of Film Theory* (Princeton University Press, 1988), *Mystifying Movies* (Columbia University Press, 1988), and *The Philosophy of Horror* (Routledge, 1990). He is also widely published in the philosophy of the arts.

DONALD CRAFTON is Professor of Film in the Communication Arts Department at the University of Wisconsin–Madison. He has directed the Wisconsin Center for Film and Theater Research and has written on the history and aesthetics of animated film. His study of Hollywood talkies is forthcoming as volume 4 of Scribner's History of the American Cinema series.

GREGORY CURRIE is Professor of Philosophy and Head of the School of Arts at Flinders University, Adelaide, Australia. His *Image and Mind: Film, Philosophy and Cognitive Science* will be published by Cambridge University Press in 1995. He is currently working on a study of the imagination.

CYNTHIA A. FREELAND is Associate Professor of Philosophy and Director of Women's Studies at the University of Houston. She has published widely on topics in ancient philosophy and aesthetics, and is the coeditor, with Thomas Wartenberg, of *Philosophy and Film* (Routledge, 1995).

RICHARD J. GERRIG is Associate Professor of Psychology at the State University of New York at Stony Brook. He is the author of *Experiencing Narrative Worlds* (Yale University Press, 1993).

DOUGLAS GOMERY is a professor at the University of Maryland, and is currently at work on an economic analysis of the contemporary mass media.

METTE HJORT is Associate Professor of English at McGill University. She is the author of *The Strategy of Letters* (Harvard University Press, 1993), and the editor of *Rules and Conventions* (Johns Hopkins University Press, 1992).

JULIAN HOCHBERG is Centennial Professor Emeritus in Psychology at Columbia University. He is a member of the National Academy of Science and the American Academy of Arts and Sciences. He is the author of *Perception* (Prentice-Hall, 1987) and numerous articles on the psychology of perception.

VANCE KEPLEY, JR., is Professor of Film in the Department of Communication Arts at the University of Wisconsin–Madison. He is the author of *In the Service of the State: The Cinema of Alexander Dovzhenko* (University of Wisconsin Press, 1986) and numerous essays on film history and Soviet cinema.

DONALD KIRIHARA is an assistant professor at the University of Arizona, where he teaches film history, criticism, and theory. He is the author of *Patterns of Time: Mizoguchi and the 1930s* (University of Wisconsin Press, 1992).

JERROLD LEVINSON is Professor of Philosophy at the University of Maryland. His books include *Music, Art, and Metaphysics* (Cornell University Press, 1990), *Work and Oeuvre and Other Essays* (Cornell University Press, 1996), and a forthcoming monograph, *Apprehending Music*. He is also the author of a number of articles in metaphysics.

FLO LEIBOWITZ is Professor of Philosophy at Oregon State University. Her most recent article is "David Hume and Francis Hutcheson on the Pleasures of Tragedy," to appear in *Hutcheson, Past and Present: Tricentennial Essays.*

PAISLEY LIVINGSTON is Professor of English at McGill University. His publications include *Literature and Rationality: Ideas of Agency in Theory and Fiction* (Cambridge University Press, 1991), *Literary Knowledge: Humanistic Inquiry and the Philosophy of Science* (Cornell University Press, 1988), and *Ingmar Bergman and the Rituals of Art* (Cornell University Press, 1982).

RICHARD MALTBY is Research Professor in Media Studies Sheffield Hallam University. The author of *Harmless Entertainment: Hollywood and the Ideology of Consensus* (Scarecrow, 1983) and, with Ian Craven, *Hollywood Cinema: An Introduction* (Blackwell's, 1995), he is completing a study of self-regulation and the political institutions of American cinema.

ALEX NEILL is a lecturer in philosophy at the University of St. Andrews, Scotland. He writes mainly on issues in aesthetics and the philosophy of mind.

JAMES PETERSON is the author of *Dreams of Chaos, Visions of Order: Understanding the American Avant-Garde Cinema* (Wayne State University Press, 1994). He has a Ph.D. in film studies from the University of Wisconsin–Madison.

CARL PLANTINGA, Associate Professor of Film at Hollins College, has published on the nonfiction film, film and psychology, and film theory.

DEBORAH A. PRENTICE is Associate Professor of Psychology at Princeton University, where she holds the Laurence S. Rockefeller preceptorship in the Center for Human Values. She has published articles and chapters in the *Journal of Personality and Social Psychology, Psychological Bulletin, Psychological Science,* and the *Annual Review of Psychology.*

STEPHEN PRINCE teaches at Virginia Tech. He is the author of *The Warrior's Camera: The Cinema of Akira Kurosawa* (Princeton, 1991) and *Visions of Empire: Political Imagery in Contemporary American Film* (Praeger, 1992).

JEFF SMITH has published articles in *Cinema Journal* and *The Velvet Light Trap.* He completed his Ph.D. in film studies at the University of Wisconsin–Madison with a dissertation on Hollywood film music of the 1960s.

MURRAY SMITH is Lecturer in Film Studies at the University of Kent at Canterbury (U.K.) and author of *Engaging Characters: Fiction, Emotion, and the Cinema* (Oxford: Clarendon Press, 1995).

MICHAEL WALSH is a doctoral candidate in film studies at the University of Wisconsin–Madison.

INTRODUCTION

Our title risks misleading you. Is this book about the end of film theory? No. It's about the end of Theory, and what can and should come after.

What we call Theory is an abstract body of thought which came into prominence in Anglo-American film studies during the 1970s. The most famous avatar of Theory was that aggregate of doctrines derived from Lacanian psychoanalysis, Structuralist semiotics, Post-Structuralist literary theory, and variants of Althusserian Marxism. Here, unabashedly, was Grand Theory—perhaps the first that cinema studies has ever had. The Theory was put forth as the indispensible frame of reference for understanding all filmic phenomena: the activities of the film spectator, the construction of the film text, the social and political functions of cinema, and the development of film technology and the industry.

Several essays in this volume directly address the problems of the Theory as it developed into the 1980s. The two introductions that follow attempt to place it in historical context and to criticize the conceptions of theorizing that it promotes. And all the essays in the volume show that solid research can proceed without appeal to the doctrines once held to form the basis of all proper reflection about cinema. In particular, the essays here demonstrate that film research can proceed sans psychoanalysis. Indeed, if there is an organizing principle to the volume, it is that solid film scholarship can proceed without employing the psychoanalytic frameworks routinely mandated by the cinema studies establishment.

Some film writers have polemically portrayed the only alternative to Theory as a mindless, low-level "empiricism" which simply digs up facts. This has always been a false option: we need not choose between practicing Lacanianism and compiling a filmography. The scholarly work of the last ten years has shown that one robust rival to Theory is a middle-range inquiry that moves easily from bodies of evidence to more general arguments and implications. This piecemeal, problem-driven reflection and research is as far from data shuffling as it is from the ethereal speculations of Grand Theory.

Thus the essays in this volume pose concrete questions and focus on specific problems. In what ways, asks Paisley Livingston, can we usefully understand the concept of character in film narrative? In studying the evidence for the popularity of *The Jazz Singer,* Don Crafton seeks to understand how we may determine a film's reception. Mette Hjort asks how we may best describe the sense of national identity that is at stake in contemporary Danish films.

The results of these and the other essays are theories, by any reasonable definition—general hypotheses about how best to explain a definite phenomenon, argued as proposed answers to a specific question.

This is, indeed, as it should be. What is coming after Theory is not another Theory but theor*ies* and the activity of *theorizing*. A theory of film defines a problem within the domain of cinema (defined nondogmatically) and sets out to solve it through logical reflection, empirical research, or a combination of both. *Theorizing* is a commitment to using the best canons of inference and evidence available to answer the question posed. The standards ought to be those of the most stringent philosophical reasoning, historical argument, and sociological, economic, and critical analysis we can find, in film studies or elsewhere (even in science).

In his introductory essay, Noël Carroll expands this case for localized theories and rigorous dialectical theorizing. David Bordwell's introductory essay addresses the continuities between "subject-position" theory of the 1970s and "culturalism," of the 1980s, seeking to suggest ways in which theorizing became replaced by the vagaries of Grand Theory. Similarly, Michael Walsh's study of Fredric Jameson's conception of postmodern cinema brings to light contradictions and vaguenesses in this influential candidate for Theory.

You will note that many of the articles in this volume are highly argumentative. That tendency derives from the editors' conviction that inquiry is dialectical and that criticism is a fundamental ingredient of research. This view is explicitly defended with respect to theory in Carroll's introductory piece, but the position is echoed throughout the volume in many articles, some of which are primarily critical of prevailing positions in the field. These articles are not simply offered as ground clearing in this or that area of research. The critical tone of much of this volume is introduced in the hope of encouraging the field of cinema studies to become more dialectical than we presently find it.

Although several of the articles in the anthology are primarily critical of certain aspects of contemporary film research, most combine the criticism of existing positions and theories with the construction and development of new perspectives. Thus the bulk of the essays in *Post-Theory* exemplify the ways in which the act of theorizing can combine the criticism of existing positions with positive argument. For example, Douglas Gomery attacks several myths about the history of film and its relation to other mass media, in the course of a defense of the idea that economically, film has long been anything but a distinct medium. Cynthia Freeland's comparably wide-ranging examination of feminist accounts of the horror film opens a path to the gender-ideology account she advocates. In the course of exploring various ways in which a viewer might understand a brief transition in *Casablanca*, Richard Maltby brings to light a series of common misunderstandings of how Hollywood operated. Donald Kirihara's argument for a more supple, subtle history of Japanese film style necessarily invokes broadly held misconceptions as well as the work of previous researchers.

Several other essays pursue this dialectical strategy of theorizing. Murray Smith points up the myriad problems with the Brechtianism of 1970s Theory before proposing that a more nuanced account of the spectator's relation to characters is feasible. Stephen Prince brings to light difficulties in translating psychoanalytic film theory into the concrete terms of actual film viewing, at the same time that he fields some alternatives from social science research. Jeff Smith argues against the idea that Hollywood film music goes "unheard" and suggests a more plausible prototype for film scoring. Jerrold Levinson reviews the difficulties in assigning nondiegetic music to a narrative agency; he then goes on to propose his own solution to the problem.

Similarly, Noël Carroll analyzes the myriad problems besetting arguments that documentary film cannot reliably transmit information about the world. Also in the domain of documentary, Carl Plantinga examines ways in which the concept of a "rhetoric" has been misleading and proposes a new understanding of the problem. Vance Kepley's account of spectatorial reception is couched as a specific reply to Baudry's influential conception of the "apparatus," while Flo Leibowitz's exploration of melodramatic appeals engages critically with accounts proposed by psychoanalytic feminists.

To commit oneself to letting a variety of middle-level theories compete in the field; to accept the constraints of theorizing rather than paraphrasing chunks of Theory—these decisions mean that the essays in this volume do not commit themselves to a single doctrine. While united in their turning away from Theory, they cannot be assembled into a homogeneous doctrine.

It is an anthologist's cliché to emphasize the disagreements among contributors. Even anthologies of Theory stress the disparities that riddle their pages. But the divergences among writers in this collection are significant in a way that is fresh to contemporary film studies. By accepting the challenge of middle-level theory, our contributors have also undertaken to think things through anew. Consequently, distinctly varied notions of film narrative, of historical significance, and of the relation of audiences and texts run through these essays. There are even sharp disagreements. One pair of psychologists, Julian Hochberg and Virginia Brooks, propose a psychophysical model of filmic perception that is at odds with the Gibsonian perspective developed by another duo, Joseph Anderson and Barbara Anderson. And the latter pair's conception of cinematic illusion is tacitly challenged by the philosophical arguments of Gregory Currie. There is no Party Line here, not even the general one that might be found in an anthology on film and psychoanalysis, or film and postmodernism.

The absence of a Party Line is also reflected in the fact that a number of essays in the volume proceed to construct their own positions without issuing denunciations of theory. That is, these authors pursue their research projects without reference—critical or otherwise—to current versions of Theory. How, asks Tino Balio, may we rationally reconstruct the goals of the managers of a marginal film studio who wanted to grow during the 1930s? Richard Gerrig and Deborah Prentice examine the ways in which spectators respond to filmic fictions and propose a new theory of how "participation" may be understood. Julian Hochberg and Virginia Brooks examine the preconditions for filmic perception and some likely candidates for mentalistic explanations.

If our essays converge on any area, it might be said to occur with respect to "cognitivism." In turning from psychoanalytic doctrines, several of our authors move toward cognitive explanations of filmic reception. But cognitivism in this sense is not a Theory. A casual perusal of work in the field of cognitive science—linguistics, anthropology, psychology, aesthetics, and philosophy of mind—will reveal vivid and irreconcilable differences.

We think that cognitivism is best characterized as a stance. A cognitivist analysis or explanation seeks to understand human thought, emotion, and action by appeal to processes of mental representation, naturalistic processes, and (some sense of) rational agency. But in the process of studying these matters, rather sharp differences emerge: "Soft," body-oriented cognitivism clashes with AI (artificial intelligence) cognitivism; serialist and syntactic hypotheses line up against Parallel Distributed Processing theories; reductive materialists argue with functionalists; Chomskyan accounts are criticized by anti-Chomskyan ones. Like feminism, cognitivism is not so much a Theory as a perspective which includes diametrically opposed theories.

Such oppositions emerge in our collection. Alex Neill's arguments about the mechanisms of filmic empathy contrast sharply with those of "engagement" proposed by Murray Smith. James Peterson's account of avant-garde comprehension strategies runs counter to the cognitivist hypotheses of Hochberg and Brooks. And the "cognitivist" strain running through the essays by Bordwell, Livingston, Leibowitz, and Plantinga is plainly quite varied.

Moreover, it needs to be stressed that though a number of the articles in this volume are cognitivist, the volume itself is not a primer in cognitivism. For many of the articles in this anthology are not concerned with film comprehension, but with historical or economic matters. The unifying principle in this book is that all the research included exemplifies the possibility of scholarship that is not reliant upon the psychoanalytic framework that dominates film academia. Cognitivism fits that bill; but so do the historical studies of Balio and Crafton.

The reader should also be warned that not only is psychoanalysis absent from this text. There is also much less film interpretation between the covers of this book than is typical in cinema studies. The primary reason for this revolves around the fact that many of the articles are theoretical and, as such, usually make reference to individual films briefly and use them to illustrate theoretical points. Whereas most academic film books nowadays are packed with intricate interpretations of individual films, most pieces here refer to particular films only in order to substantiate or illuminate theoretical claims or to flesh out larger narratives. In fact, as the reader might expect, the de-emphasis of dazzling readings of particular films is an intentional gambit on the part of the editors—one undertaken for the purpose of indicating that there are more approaches to film research than the one film/one article format.

Throughout this anthology, the commitment has been to introduce new approaches to cinema. In order to do this, decades of sedimented dogma need to be broken down and swept away and the spirit of critical thinking renewed. It is our conviction that after Theory the most fruitful work will represent theories and theorizing; problem-driven research and middle-level scholarship; responsible, imaginative, and lively inquiry. Pursuing this agenda can reconstruct film studies.

PART ONE

STATE OF
THE ART

As the title of this volume indicates, the editors suppose that film studies is at a historical juncture which might be described as the waning of Theory. In this context, we have attempted to assemble a body of writing that we hope suggest promising lines of research for the future. However, in order to help readers understand our concerns with present problems in cinema studies and our recommendations about prospects for new directions in film research, we thought that it would be appropriate to begin this anthology by stating forthrightly our assessments of the current state of the art.

David Bordwell's piece is an overview of the field. After briefly sketching developments before the 1970s which led to the consolidation of the institution of cinema studies, Bordwell attempts to delineate two major trends in film research that have dominated cinema studies for nearly two decades. He refers to these as subject-position theory and culturalism. According to Bordwell, these approaches are examples of "Grand Theories" insofar as each attempts to subsume the study of film under generally encompassing schemes that were developed to explain society, language, and psychology.

Furthermore, Bordwell notes that, though subject-positioning theory and culturalism are often presented as antitheses, they, in fact, share a surprising number of premises and biases. Indeed, he argues that the transition of practitioners of subject positioning theory to cultural studies can be explained by the fact that the two trends are far more alike than is often suggested in the current literature.

As might be anticipated, Bordwell's criticisms of the value of both subject positioning theory and culturalism are detailed and intense. In their stead, he advocates what he calls middle-level research, and he concludes his essay by reviewing a range of the kinds of middle-level research programs, some of which are represented in subsequent essays in this volume, which he believes promise fruitful areas of inquiry for the future of cinema scholarship.

Noël Carroll's somewhat personal and anecdotal essay is both broader and narrower than Bordwell's. It is narrower in that it focuses only on film theory rather than film studies in general; it is broader in that it situates the issues it discusses in terms of themes that are pertinent for humanistic studies and philosophy in general.

1

Carroll's central question concerns the prospects for film theory. Before introducing the framework for film theory that he advocates, Carroll begins by examining what he maintains are five major impediments to film theory. These include: a conception of film theory as monolithic; the conflation of film theory and film interpretation; the prevalence of political correctness; ad hominem jeremiads against so-called formalists; and a bias against truth talk amongst contemporary film theorists.

In contrast to contemporary film theory and its aspirations (delusions?) of "grandeur," Carroll recommends what he calls "piecemeal theorizing," an approach which often coincides with what Bordwell might regard as middle-level research. Carroll also defends the indispensability of dialectical argumentation for film theory and he attempts to illustrate the kind of dialectical confrontation that he has in mind by restaging, in an abbreviated form, the debate between those who advocate the cognitivist stance in film theory and those who advocate psychoanalytic film theory.

Though these overview essays introduce the present volume, it should be stressed that they do not represent a party line. These essays advance the opinions of their respective authors. They should not be mistaken as a creed that unites all the authors in this volume. Undoubtedly, many of our contributors would want to demur from, if not criticize, Bordwell and Carroll in these essays. Indeed, we're not even sure that Bordwell and Carroll wholly agree with each other, though rather than point up the disagreements, we leave it to the reader to search them out.

Contemporary Film Studies and the Vicissitudes of Grand Theory

David Bordwell

What we now call "film studies" has existed for barely thirty years. During the mid-1960s film courses proved to be attractive humanities options throughout North American colleges and universities. Young professors of literature or philosophy, themselves often movie buffs, launched courses on Shakespeare and film or on humanistic ideas in Ingmar Bergman, Satyajit Ray, and Akira Kurosawa. American studies began treating films as indices to social currents of a period. A mass art had found a home in mass education.

Since then, in the United States and Canada, then in Great Britain and Scandinavia, most recently in France and Germany, film theory and history came to be part of the academy. More university presses published books on film, while the number of journals expanded. There is now a "field" of film studies, if not a full-fledged academic discipline.

This field has hosted many schools of thought, and a comprehensive survey is out of the question here. Instead, I sketch some leading ideas that have informed the development of film studies in the U.S. academic setting. After reviewing some important pre-1970s developments, I try to delineate two large-scale trends of thought: subject-position theory and culturalism. These, I believe, have exercised the greatest influence over the last twenty-five years. I review their presuppositions and trace some changes and continuities.

Subject-position theory and culturalism are both "Grand Theories" in that their discussions of cinema are framed within schemes which seek to describe or explain very broad features of society, history, language, and psyche. By contrast, there has been a third, more modest trend which tackles more localized film-based problems without making such overarching theoretical commitments. A discussion of this "middle-level" research concludes the essay.

One caveat before I begin. Most accounts of film theory identify more specific schools of thought than the currents I shall trace. A standard account would discuss the 1970s as a period which saw the emergence of film-based semiotics, psychoanalysis, textual analysis, and feminism. The late 1980s would be seen as bringing to the fore Post-Structuralism, postmodernism, multiculturalism, and "identity politics," such as gay/lesbian/queer studies and subaltern studies. In this essay, these influential movements are situated within the three overarching trends I pick out. For instance, I take academic feminism to be a perspective within which scholars critically examine aspects of women's lives within social orders (notably patriarchal ones). From the standpoint I propose here, we can identify feminist versions of subject-position theory, feminist inflections of culturalism, and feminist projects within the middle-level research tradition. Similarly, questions of postcolonial identity can be studied from any of the three standpoints.

Admittedly, situating these developments within broader intellectual trends risks losing some of their nuance and specificity. The compensating advantage is the possibility of tracing conceptual affinities and historical connections among the various approaches.

Backstory: Authorship

In 1970 academic film studies was a small, disreputable area. A bright undergraduate could read all of the important English-language film books over summer vacation. Film history was treated largely as the development of "film language," as represented by canonized films. Film criticism—never called "textual analysis"—was largely interpretive and judgmental, emphasizing plot, character, and theme. And for English speakers film theory was still largely the province of the "classical" theorists: Arnheim and Eisenstein were still names to conjure with, and Bazin's essays had only recently been translated.

The reigning conceptual framework was auteurism. The young critics of *Cahiers du cinéma* had argued for an aesthetic of personal expression in cinema, and postwar "art cinema" in Europe and the emergence of major Hollywood directors during the 1950s gave impetus to the auteur line. Throughout the world the auteur initiative won the day. Like Soviet montage theory before it, it changed the face of film theory, criticism, and historiography. Henceforth most film journalism and film scholarship would concentrate upon directors and the distinctive world each body of work manifested.[1] In the 1970s, even commercial filmmakers picked up the intertextual referencing and homages that had been common practices amongst the French New Wave directors.[2]

In a wider perspective, however, auteur theory represented an interregnum in some key arguments about cinema that had been conducted for the previous fifty years. Cinema had been discussed along two lines: as a new art, and as a political and cultural force characteristic of modern mass society. Bazin and the critics of *Cahiers du cinéma* can be seen as severing ties both with the medium-specificity arguments of the 1920s aesthetic and with the left-wing political agenda of much film culture since the late 1920s. At the same time, though, the auteur line intensified one premise that underpinned much of the traditional aesthetic, formulated in 1926 by Iris Barry: "It is obvious that, as regards any one particular film, the director is the man of destiny, the one supremely important person." [3] Andrew Sarris's version of what he called "the auteur theory" set itself against the left-wing orientation of montage theory and much sociological research.

Around 1970, however, with the emergence of academic film studies, the humanistic version of auteurism began to come under attack. There was a new theoretical ambitiousness, largely the creation of French Structuralism. This diffuse intellectual movement was gaining force on the continent and in English-speaking countries during the late 1960s. Claude Lévi-Strauss's was among the first Structuralist work translated, and the Structuralist semiology of Christian Metz became more widely known in Anglo-American film circles at the same period.

Structuralism could also be seen as having a socially critical dimension, particularly when applied to the products of mass culture. The English translation of Roland Barthes' *Mythologies* offered a Structuralism with a human face—disrespectful of bourgeois ideology, bent on showing how the mass media disguise cultural artifice as nature. Ever since, teachers have used advertisements and television programs as primers for teaching students about signifiers and signifieds, codes and connotations.

Structuralist theories offered a way for a new generation—many allied to political movements of the 1960s—to distinguish itself from its auteurist predecessors. In addition, the very idea of Theory attracted young people with a taste for abstract ideas. Students from French, philosophy, and comparative literature discovered that they could study things in film departments that were still controversial elsewhere. And of course, as an intellectual movement, Structuralism's cachet within the university milieu made it appropriate for a discipline still seeking academic credentials.

As would happen again and again, a good deal of the persuasiveness of this theory came not from abstract reasoning and argument—that is, theorizing—but rather from its application to particular bodies of films. Although French critics proposed versions of Structuralist stylistics, the most influential ideas were set to work in the well-established modes of interpretive commentary. A group of critics around London's British Film Institute created an "auteur Structuralism" that revealed binary oppositions in Luchino Visconti, Don Siegel, John Ford, and Howard Hawks. [4] Other British critics produced mildly Structuralist studies of Westerns and gangster films. [5]

Perhaps most lastingly influential was a Structuralist interpretive model which treated film as akin to myth and ritual. According to Lévi-Strauss, myth functions to translate a contradiction in social life, such as that between life and death, into symbolic terms—say, agriculture and warfare. Myth resolves these oppositions by finding a term which mediates between them—in my example, hunting as a middle ground between agriculture and war. The notion that a film offers an imaginary resolution of binary alternatives became a staple of academic criticism. For example, Thomas Schatz argues that like myth, Hollywood genres are social rituals replaying key cultural contradictions. The emphasis which Hollywood filmmakers place upon the resolution of the narrative indicates the importance of key thematic oppositions, such as man/woman, individual/community, work/play, order/anarchy. In order to resolve these contradictions, a mediating figure arises.[6] Arguably, this binary approach to interpreting narrative structure is the most enduring legacy of "cine-structuralism."

Film Studies: 1975–1995

Structuralism in its pure state was to prove a fairly ephemeral phenomenon in the United States. By the mid-1970s, certain streams of thought were merging into an aggregate of doctrines that became self-consciously "contemporary film theory"—often known as film theory *tout court*.[7]

New Left Review, Screen, Camera Obscura, and publications issued by the British Film Institute spread ideas from Althusserian Marxism, Lacanian psychoanalysis, Metzian semiotics, and textual analysis among English-speaking film academics. During the early and mid-1970s, French film theorists began teaching in international programs, and their courses turned many U.S. and British students into emissaries of the new ideas. This activity coincided with a broadening of the influence of Barthes, Jacques Lacan, Jacques Derrida, Michel Foucault, and other *maîtres à pensers* in Anglo-American intellectual life generally. More indigenous currents, most notably feminism, incorporated these ideas, as in Juliet Mitchell's *Psychoanalysis and Feminism* (1974). The dissemination of Post-Structuralist ideas was assisted by numerous explications and, crucially, by the 1973 translation of J. Laplanche and J.-B. Pontalis's reference book *The Language of Psychoanalysis*.[8]

As usual, the results of such activities displayed considerable variety. Still, there is a common core. The "New Film Theory" can usefully be understood as asking this question: What are the social and psychic functions of cinema? In order to answer this, film theorists built conceptions of cinema upon some basic assumptions about social organization and psychic activity. These assumptions in turn rested upon conceptions of the "subject" in language and social activity.

According to most such theorizing, the subject is neither the individual person nor an immediate sense of one's identity or self. It is rather a category of knowing defined by its relation to objects and to other subjects. Subjectivity is not the human being's personal identity or personality; it is unavoidably social. It is not a pre-given consciousness; it is acquired. Subjectivity is constructed through representational systems.

In this frame of reference, the biological individual becomes a subject by virtue of having its inherent needs organized, gratified, and repressed by the processes of representation. The individual's drives are reconfigured as mental representations (wishes or desires) and then either repressed or channeled into socially acceptable patterns. The subject is thus split. Any social action requires a conscious agent who acts and speaks from a coherent position; but according to Lacan this unity is purchased through acquiescence to two psychic registers: the Imaginary, in which the subject finds visual representations of its postulated unity and bodily integrity; and the Symbolic, that register which creates difference and cultural law. Althusser extends the idea of representation to ideology, a process which appeals to the unified subjectivity underpinning conscious agency. Ideology may also appeal to unconscious processes by promising the impossible: gratification of desire in the Symbolic, fulfillment of drives in alienated identity.

At the same time, subjectivity is always in process and fluctuating. To Freud's suggestion that the unconscious emerges in dreams, slips of the tongue, jokes, bungled actions, or neurotic symptoms, Lacan adds that the repression enforced by cultural systems of representation is threatened at every point by eruptions of the unconscious. In every social act the subject's unitary position must be reconstructed moment by moment. Subjects are not merely addressed at a single instant; they are maintained over time.

From something like this set of presuppositions came the new pronouncements about cinema during the 1970s and much of the 1980s. Film was held to be a semiotic system, representing the world in texts by means of conventional codes. As a semiotic system, cinema could be considered to engage the spectator as a split subject, initiating a process in which conscious and unconscious interact.

This interaction was explained in somewhat varying ways. For Stephen Heath, cinema channels desire by offering identifications through sight—the register of the Imaginary—but controlled by the structuring and differentiating operations of the Symbolic. For Christian Metz, cinematic codes direct the scopophilic drive and create an identification with the camera and with the viewer's self as a transcendental, purely perceiving subject. For Laura Mulvey, classical cinema mobilizes scopophilia through voyeurism, fetishism, and narcissism. In another variant, known since as "apparatus theory," the cinema elicits a regression to an infantile sense of wholeness analogous to that yielded by what Lacan called the Mirror Stage. This is that emblematic period in the infant's development when she or he recognizes, or rather misrecognizes, him- or herself in the mirror and thus begins to define the ego narcissistically, as a unified and visible body.[9]

In these various ways, dominant cinema—Hollywood and its counterparts—was seen to gratify desire by offering socially acceptable satisfactions through cinematic codes and enunciative practices. Most theorists believed that the process fulfilled ideological purposes. Through film technology, through narrative structure, through "enunciative" processes, and through

particular sorts of representations (for example, those of women), cinema
constructs subject positions as defined by ideology and the social formation.
As one theorist puts it: "Ideology is definable as exactly the process whereby
human subjectivity takes on the outward appearance of wholeness and unity,
and furthermore . . .—in relation specifically to cinema—one of the central
ideological operations of dominant cinema is precisely the positioning of the
viewing subject as apparently unitary." [10] According to this theory, alternative
and oppositional filmmaking tries to block Imaginary identifications, to offer
alternative identifications (for example, films of "feminine writing"), and to
"deconstruct" the ideological underpinnings of dominant cinema.

Such in rough outline seems to me the "subject-position theory" of the
mid-1970s. It did not go unchallenged, but on the whole it was perceived to
be the cutting edge of film studies. While its effect on historical research was
slight, it had an immediate impact upon practical criticism. Throughout the
1970s and 1980s, film academics applied this theoretical framework to films
from a wide variety of periods and nations.

Ironically, soon after American academics launched this enterprise, Lacanian film theory fell out of favor in its homeland. [11] (Why? My Parisian informants refuse to say.) In the Anglophone countries, psychoanalytic approaches
continue to exercise some influence, particularly in projects with affinities to
literary criticism. [12] On the whole, though, most contemporary film scholars
act as if the subject-position view collapsed during the 1980s under the on-
slaught of new trends.

By and large the objections did not seize upon logical flaws. For instance,
film theorists could have objected that constituting a subject through recognition required that a prior cognition, and hence a prior state of subjecthood,
had already taken place: only if the individual has a conception of itself as
subject can it *recognize* that in a representation. [13] Similarly, to accept the Lacanian conception of psychic unity as a valid account of one's own subjectivity
must involve the *mis*recognition that, according to Lacan, accompanies all
acts of self-awareness. This creates an infinite regress. "The 'I' which analyzes
the perfidy of the 'I,'" notes Kate Soper, "must itself be a traitor to the
truth." [14]

Film theorists seldom interrogated subject-position theory on this terrain.
The objections were far more pragmatic. Feminists and leftists began arguing
that this theory provided no satisfactory account of how social actors could
criticize and resist ideology. There was, it was often said, no room for
"agency" in a framework in which ideological representations so thoroughly
determined subjectivity. [15] Postmodernists argued that the unified self purportedly produced by the "apparatus" was a fiction; in the contemporary
world, multiple and split subjectivity was everyone's lot.

Subject-position theory also fell victim to the charge of ahistoricality. Before 1970, there were virtually no works of film history in English which could
measure up to the standards set by historians in other fields. Slowly, this situ-

ation began to change. Though often attacked as empiricist and positivist, this new historical work could not be ignored. As a result, one of the key polemical thrusts of the 1980s was the effort to "historicize" theory.

The most pervasive result of these criticisms was the culturalist trend. The word "culture" has become to 1990s academe what Toyotas have become for the automobile market, but the term is unavoidable. Theorists began to substitute it for "ideology" and "society." "Culture" came to cover virtually all spheres of social activity, particularly those which orthodox Marxism would have considered part of the "superstructure."

Inquiry into cinema's cultural dimensions was not itself very novel. The interest in the ideological effects of cinema displayed by subject-position theory can itself be seen as a resurgence of pre-1950s controversies around film's socially manipulative uses. And "culture" was very much on the agenda in earlier decades. Not only Kracauer, Benjamin, and Brecht were interested in film's relation to culture; so too were Gilbert Seldes, Ruth Benedict, Margaret Mead, and Gregory Bateson. In the auteur camp, Sarris and certain members of the *Movie* group broached such issues. Moreover, the French journal *Positif* joined a version of auteur aesthetics to a vigorously Surrealist anarcho-leftism. Although the emergence of film studies as an academic discipline tended to rely upon auteurist principles, it also reinvigorated inquiry into the cultural and political functions of the medium. Henry Nash Smith's influential study of the myth of the American West, *Virgin Land,* furnished a prototype for a cultural approach to the Western, and critics in Britain and the United States explored the mass appeals and social traditions of other genres.[16]

The culturalism of contemporary film studies is, however, more self-consciously theoretical. In contrast to subject-position theory, it holds that pervasive cultural mechanisms govern the social and psychic functions of cinema.

One can roughly distinguish three strands of culturalist theory. There is what we might call Frankfurt School culturalism, which holds that enlightenment thought and industrial society have transformed public and private life over the last two centuries. Writers in this tradition postulate a change in social experience wrought by commodification, market relations, and other processes associated with modernity. This trend takes its cue from Benjamin, Kracauer, Jürgen Habermas, and Oskar Negt.

Postmodernism constitutes a second culturalist strand. Postmodernist thinkers presume that contemporary life is characterized by the dominance of multinational capital and by a corresponding fragmentation—pleasurable or alienated—of experience. In examining film, postmodernists focus upon the capacity of mass media to generate endless diverting spectacle. The postmodernist trend is probably crystallized for humanities scholars in the writings of Fredric Jameson, at once a critic of postmodernism and an influential explicator.

Probably the most influential version of culturalism is that known as Cultural Studies. On this account, culture is a site of struggle and contestation amongst different groups. A culture is conceived as a network of institutions, representations, and practices which produce differences of race, ethnic heritage, class, gender/sexual preference, and the like. These differences are centrally involved in the production of meaning. As one Cultural Studies handbook puts it:

> Culture is seen as the sphere in which class, gender, race, and other inequities are naturalized and represented in forms which sever (as far as possible) the connection between these and economic and political inequalities. Conversely, culture is also the means by and through which various subordinate groups live and resist their subordination.[17]

Cultural Studies, postmodernism, and Frankfurt School culturalism all bid to rival subject-position theory by offering equally foundational accounts of knowing and acting. The culturalist typically treats social agents as participating in many activities; an agent's identity is accordingly constituted in and through the overlap of diverse social practices. Moreover, according to most culturalist views, people are not "duped" by the Symbolic. Their subjectivity is not wholly constituted by representation; they are not always locked into a static subject position; they are much freer agents than subject-position theory allows.

Social practices, culturalists also suggest, are comprehensible only in historical terms. But the versions of history proposed are not the "grand narratives" of most academic tradition. Instead, "microhistories" trace the discourses and practices of agents at certain moments—at the hinge points of modernity, or in the course of our postmodernity, or at moments in which subcultures struggle with dominant culture.

The culturalist trend has sought to distinguish itself from subject-position theory by emphasizing that the object of study is not *texts* (dominant, oppositional, or whatever) but instead the *uses* made of texts. Hence culturalists of all stripes promote reception studies, whereby audiences are often held to appropriate films for their cultural agendas. Indeed, within the Cultural Studies position, notions of subversive films have given way to conceptions of resistant readers. Rather than locating diverse meanings in texts, the culturalist can locate them amongst audiences. Resisting readers can be read. And the reading of such readers can itself be "historicized" through consideration of advertising campaigns, exhibition circumstances, and the multifarious discourses that circulate through a culture.

In the United States, culturalism emerged when subject-position theory fell under attack by the literary "post-structuralism" of Derrida and the late Barthes. Given a strong momentum by feminism, gay/lesbian/bisexual groups, the unorthodox left, postmodernist aesthetics, and multicultural movements, the culturalist trend has become a central force in Anglo-American intellectual circles. Virtually every area of the humanities now nurtures its own culturalist wing. Culturalism became a component in what the American press dubbed "political correctness," and neoconservative ideologues have fastened upon it, somewhat desperately, as part of the agenda said to be pushed by "tenured radicals."

What enabled the culturalist trend to be so speedily assimilated? The success of subject-position theory had acclimated film scholars to the need for Grand Theory, and culturalism offered plausible candidates. It too rests its conclusions about media texts and activities upon a broader account of society, thought, and meaning.

At the same time, culturalism probably came as something of a relief. Its theory is generally less intricate and philosophically ambitious than its predecessor. Granted, Adorno and Habermas are not exactly beach reading; but most culturalist theories, particularly those on offer from British thinkers, are far more relaxed and user-friendly than subject-position theory. Given a forced choice, who would not rather peruse Raymond Williams than Lacan, or Baudrillard's *America* instead of Kristeva's *Révolution du langage poétique?* Culturalism's closeness to "cultural commentary" as practiced in journalism and belletristic essays renders it attractive, accessible, and highly teachable.

Both subject-position theory and culturalism put themselves forward as critically engaged doctrines: in demystifying power relations as manifested in popular media, they claim to offer tools for dismantling unjust social systems. Yet advocates at Cultural Studies can lay claim to a more practical politics. Subject-position theorists are vulnerable to accusations of left-wing pessimism. Proponents of 1970s Theory argued that any efforts for social change had to reckon with the ways in which semiotic systems have "always already" created obedient subjects. For example, feminists were urged to understand how, within patriarchy, Imaginary identifications maintain sexual difference. Feminists were encouraged to adopt the sexists Freud and Lacan strategically, as analysts of patriarchy. This theory, articulated in the wake of lost battles of the 1960s, was more diagnostic than prescriptive.[18] It arose at a period when explaining why revolutions fail had a higher priority than showing how successful rebellion might occur.

Cultural Studies is also committed to social change, but it offers a more positive program. The everyday activities of ordinary people are said to be complex negotiations with the forces they confront. And in their strategies of appropriating popular texts, audiences are often said to be reading against the grain in a far more effective way than library-bound academics. Furthermore, subject-position theory carries an ineradicable whiff of elitism, while culturalism is, at least in many variants, proudly populist. To many proponents, political engagement through avant-garde films seems far more implausible than down-to-earth accounts of how "real people" read mass media. Doubtless culturalism instilled in media academics a sense of empowerment. By studying movies and TV shows one could purportedly contribute to political struggles on behalf of the disadvantaged.

Culturalism attracted followers for a simpler reason as well. By the mid-1980s subject-position theory had become sterile through repetition. The theory proposed that certain non-obvious mechanisms—semiotic, ideological, and psychic—produce discriminable effects. And the theory posited a narrow set of causes or functions: this film or that television show always converted the Imaginary into the Symbolic or positioned the individual as a knowing and desiring subject. Everything else was details. Many culturalists object to this "totalizing" explanatory machinery.

The success of culturalism came in part from its swing toward more open, dispersed, and nonlinear accounts than subject-position theorists could countenance. One major culturalist writes that the theory "conceptualizes culture as interwoven with all social practices; and those practices, in turn, as a common form of human activity: sensuous human praxis, the activity through which men and women make history."[19] This breadth not only gives culturalism a large-scale object of study, underwriting its status as Grand Theory; it also gives the critic, theorist, or historian a wide range of materials to search through in producing case studies or microhistories.

For example, another writer has suggested that we think not in terms of this or that film but rather of a "cinematic event"—all institutions, activities, texts, and agents that might pertain to cinema. Both film production and reception open out "onto an infinite cultural space. . . . The cinema event is constituted by a continuing interchange, neither beginning nor ending at any specific point."[20] The idea of "interchange" here seems to include cause, effect, function, and purpose. Now this view can be criticized as simply restating the humanist's uninformative truism that everything is connected to everything else. But it has the institutional advantage of validating a huge variety of research projects.

In practice culturalists limit their projects—notably by using race/class/gender as a heuristic for ranking causal factors, or by tacitly applying intuitive principles of functional explanation. Still, one reason that contemporary film studies seems pluralistic is that culturalism allows people to study virtually any period and find lots of things going on there. And these revelations—funny and bizarre anecdotes; breath-catching remarks made by naïve historical agents; vivid examples of decentered spectacle, antihegemonic resistance, or the shocks of modernity—exude a charm that the more ascetic and text-centered subject-position theory lacked.

Continuities: Doctrinal Premises

There is another reason that versions of culturalism have won so many adherents, and this is worth exploring in more detail. Because of culturalism's explicit disagreements with subject-position theory, it is easily taken as a distinct break. Yet culturalism also attracted followers because in many respects it continues the program of subject-position theory.

Most obviously, many of the scholars practicing culturalist theory and interpretation once subscribed to the subject-position accounts. "I'm moving more into Cultural Studies" has become a cliché of the conference coffeeshop. Accordingly, we ought to expect some continuities between the two perspectives. Scholars who change their opinions do not typically revise their convictions from top to bottom. An intellectual trend that wishes to gain adherents will appeal to common ground—shared presuppositions and habitual practices.

Consider too the overlapping bibliographies. Saussure, Lévi-Strauss, the Barthes of *Mythologies,* and other sources of high-church Structuralism are still required reading for culturalists. Furthermore, some writers acknowledge the links between 1970s theory and the culturalist trend by trying to synthesize them. These efforts usually include reminders of the important gains made by Lacanian psychoanalysis or Metzian semiotics.[21]

Above all, there are deep continuities of doctrine and practice. In this section I will concentrate on four of the former; in the next, four of the latter. Sometimes we will see subject-position claims diluted and relaxed in their culturalist form, but there remain important, if tacit, agreements.

1. Human practices and institutions are in all significant respects socially constructed. The subject-position theorist believes that social structures superimpose historically defined categories upon human beings, thus "constructing" subjects in representation and social practice. Similarly, the culturalist takes social life and the agents who live it as "constructed" in some sense, although the causal networks are complicated: Culture is a social construction by its agents; at the same time, social processes construct culture; and social subjects are themselves constructs of culture.

Constructivism of this stripe, traceable at least as far back as Nietzsche, saturates the humanities. This premise often has a relativistic tinge, since some thinkers hold that, because social life is culturally constructed, all thought and social customs are indefinitely variable and so in some sense arbitrary.

Yet a strong version of cultural constructivism is self-refuting. If all systems of thought are culturally constructed, so is the theory of cultural construction. How, therefore, can it claim that its insights are any more reliable or valid than any other theory's? More pointedly: How can the intellectual argue that the activities of others are culturally constructed while arrogating to him- or herself a position that purportedly escapes this? A parallel argument attaches a relativistic rider. If beliefs are relative to a culture, then belief in relativism must be relative to our culture; but then that doctrine cannot claim true insights into the beliefs, relative or not, of other cultures. As far as I can tell, no film theorists have addressed the self-contradictions haunting the radical constructivist premise.

A radical constructivism is also empirically limiting. Universal or cross-cultural regularities can play important roles in our explanation of human action. It seems likely that scholars simply ignore cross-cultural features of

cinema because they worry that this would necessarily commit them to biological or "essentialist" causes. But this worry is groundless (as I try to show
in my essay in this volume). And it is ironic that most film academics, who like
most humanists harbor a deep suspicion of the social sciences, actually share
with many social scientists the assumption that human behavior is almost
completely shaped by its environment. This premise leads to exaggerating the
differences among individuals, groups, and cultures and to avoiding inquiry
into the areas of convergence.[22]

*2. Understanding how viewers interact with films requires a theory of subjec-
tivity.* Central to "1975 Film Theory" is the idea that the individual is constructed as a subject, both socially and epistemically. The subject is, most obviously, a role in the social system—worker, owner of property, intellectual—
and the subject's "position" may be understood in relation to the class
struggle. More radical is the thesis that the subject is also constructed as a
knowing entity situated before a putatively objective reality. In this sense, to
become a subject is to gain the capacity to undergo experiences and entertain
beliefs.

The target here is the so-called Cartesian subject, purportedly conceived as
the fully self-aware seat of indubitable knowledge. Lacan claimed that the
Cartesian ego was a product of a specific historical moment, and that it was
challenged by Freud's discovery of the unconscious. Freud showed that the
ego (*moi*, or "I") was achieved only through repression. To secure this point
on the philosophical level, Lacan "ontologized" Freud by treating the ego
not simply as a *psychic* agency but as a component of the *philosophical* category
of the subject.[23] Subjectivity, produced in the relationship between the drives
and the Imaginary and Symbolic domains, was a precondition for psychic activity, and a conflicted precondition at that. The ego, as a unified self-
conscious agent, was only part of the "split" subject, predicated upon a fundamental lack.

Althusser went on to claim that certain social institutions (Ideological State
Apparatuses) create ideologies which construct and maintain a sense of subjective unity and self-consciousness, reaffirming belief in the unity of the self
and the possibility of acting voluntarily. Ideology thus manifests itself in representational systems which "position" subjects. Representation creates the
very ground of knowledge and experience.

It may seem curious that culturalism would inherit such an esoteric merger
of antirationalist philosophy, unorthodox psychoanalysis, and the frequently
changing views of an official philosopher of the French Communist Party. Yet
the subject of the subject persists. This is, I think, largely because most theorists conflate the category of the *subject* with that of the *individual*. For purist
adherents of 1975 theory, the subject is a category that enables knowledge,
experience, and identity to occur within signifying practices—even if that
knowledge is duplicitous and that experience rests upon repression or regres-

sion. The subject is the ground which renders meaning, difference, and pleasure possible. By contrast, the individual or person is an entity capable of entering the condition of subjecthood.[24]

But this stringent view rarely comes through writings in the vein of 1975
theory. The very term *subject position* encouraged most writers to treat the
subject as an agent—you, me, a character, the camera—which can occupy a
site. Also, the demands of syntax, which make the epistemic or psychoanalytic
subject also the "subject" of a sentence, imply that the subject is an individuated agent. And so throughout the corpus of subject-position theory one can
find an equivocation between the subject conceived as the philosophical/
psychoanalytic/ideological *ground* of knowledge or experience and the subject conceived as *the one who* knows and experiences—author, character, analyst, theorist, or any other personified agent. Thus after declaring that "the
subject is determined by signifiers," Kaja Silverman claims that "the connections which are productive of meaning can only be made in the mind of the
subject."[25]

The notion of subject-as-individual has underwritten culturalist writing as
well. One critic asserts that *Salaam Bombay!* works to "produce the Indian
subject in terms dictated by the representational codes of the West."[26] The
ensuing argument considers how characters and their world are represented.
Similarly, Thomas Waugh proposes that in gay narrative films one can locate
an "invisible subject" behind the camera—the producer and spectator—as
well as visible subjects in types representing gay characters (ephebe, queen,
artist, etc.).[27] At the theoretical level, culturalists' conception of the subject
have proven surprisingly "Cartesian," or even pre-Cartesian.[28]

By treating subjects as conscious individuals who can assume roles, culturalists can reaffirm a key component of their theory: the social agent's freedom.
For example, the postmodern theorist Jim Collins proposes that "the activity
of the subject is as important as activity *on* the subject, whereas previous
conceptions of the subject have emphasized only the latter. Due to the bom-
bardment of conflicting messages the individual subject *must* be engaged in
processes of selection and arrangement."[29] A subject-position purist, if there
are any left, could reply that only if one were already positioned *as* a subject
of ideology—that is, already constituted as an instance of self-conscious experience—could one grasp, select, and arrange incoming messages. A critic
indifferent to either conception of the subject could simply point out that the
notion that the agent exercises choice within constraints is nothing but a truism of social theory.

3. The spectator's response to cinema depends upon identification. For the
subject-position theorist, this view entails the belief that all communication,
being an interplay of subject and other, requires something like identification
to take place. This occurs both in language and in perception. Lacan stresses
that identification is the basis of subjectivity, since the "I" is graspable only in

and through the other. The Mirror Stage, in which the infant forms a rough version of the ego through seeing his or her reflection, is the first step toward this other-based identification. Following Lacan, 1975 Film Theory held that socially structured regimes of meaning, known as the Symbolic domain, reinforce and govern Imaginary identification. In the Althusserian doctrine, ideology constructs the subject as a locus of unintelligibility by an Imaginary "interpellation" or hailing ("You there!") and by a concomitant naturalization of what is represented.

According to this view, pictorial systems interpellate subjects by organizing vision so as to elicit a transparent and unproblematic "seeing." This pure perception is the source of the illusion of the all-perceiving subject which structuralists believe that idealist and phenomenological philosophy celebrated. In fact, however, such a subjectivity is purportedly homologous with the Imaginary identification and misrecognition that Lacan identified in the Mirror Stage. It is this Imaginary identification with a point of coherence that guarantees the illusion of reality and of a fully present subject.

Supposedly, then, cinema's "positioning" of a subject is predicated upon a series of identifications—with characters, the camera, a transcendental subject, or a unified subject position itself. At the limit, broached in Metz's conception of filmic "enunciation," there is the claim that in identifying with the filmic *histoire* rather than the enunciatory *discours*, the spectator is under the illusion that she or he is actually creating the film. One psychoanalytic feminist remarks: "It is not so easy for the fiction reader to believe that he/she is creating the text as it is for the cinema spectator to believe that he/she is producing the images on the screen."[30] Throughout subject-position theory, identification is conceived in this extreme, and extremely implausible, way. (If spectators really believed they produced movie images, they would not pay money to enter theaters.)

For the adherent of Cultural Studies, identification has been a more straightforward concept. In grasping features of race, class, gender, or other subcultural attributes, the spectator identifies with the figures on the screen or the cultural allegiances offered by the film. For instance, John Fiske suggests that some women who watch female characters thereby engage in active identification. In this process, the spectator is involved in "completing the meaning of character or incident from his or her knowledge of him- or herself. The viewer is less a subject of the dominant ideology and more in control of the process of identification and thus of his or her own meanings."[31] Once again, the self-misrecognizing subject of 1975 Film Theory has become an active, self-conscious social agent.

Inherited from earlier film criticism (auteur critics pointed out how Hitchcock made us "identify" with characters), the notion of identification remains unclarified in both subject-position and culturalist work. I watch a film. If I sympathize with a character, or empathize with her; if I see things from her optical point of view, or discover the contents of her mind, or share her range and depth of knowledge, or agree with her attitudes, judgments, and values; if I entertain the thought of what I might do in her situation, or trace the overlap of her and my beliefs, or simply wish her efforts to be successful for reasons of my own—in all these cases, the critic will say that I identify with the character. One could argue, as Noël Carroll and Murray Smith have, that in trying to cover such a variety of cases the concept is simply too vague and equivocal.[32] There is no reason to expect that all these spectatorial activities have similar causes or functions.

More recently, feminist theorists have drawn on the Freudian concept of fantasy to argue that identification needs to be recognized as multiple. On this account, men can identify with female characters, women can identify with males, humans can identify with animals, and so on.[33] This common-sensical conclusion, hardly news to traditional literary theory, does not keep the theoretical bill from falling due. The theorist must still clarify what iden-tification *is* and why we need the concept in order to explain the effects of cinema.

At least one feminist theorist has suggested that the spectator can identify not only with characters but with "the entire scene, or the narrative itself."[34] We must therefore conceive the possibility that a spectator is identifying with "the entire scene" of Monument Valley in a John Ford landscape. But then no response to a film's world would *not* be identificatory. And, as if the con-cept were not already stretched thin enough, subject-position theorists qualify all these character-targeted processes as "secondary identification" (Metz's recasting of Freud's term), as opposed to a "primary identification" with the agency by which we gain access to the film's world. According to this view, the spectator "identifies" with the representing instance—the camera, the narration, the narrator, even the author. Again, though, exactly why all pro-cesses of representation should be lumped under the concept "identification" remains obscure.

4. Verbal language supplies an appropriate and adequate analogue for film. On the subject-positioning view, language is the prime instance of a representa-tional system. As an abstract system of categories and rules (what Saussure calls *langue*), language presents a closed structure, establishing meaning through difference. Thus the individual finds subjecthood within the opposi-tions set out by a given *langue* (male/female, father/mother). But in its ac-tive aspect (*parole*), language also creates and maintains subjectivity. The act of speaking assigns subject positions through certain privileged terms (*I/you, here/there*). Notoriously, Lacan recruited such Structuralist ideas to his ver-sion of psychoanalysis. He asserted that the laws of the unconscious are asso-ciative principles which are analogous to linguistic processes: condensation is a form of metaphor, displacement is a form of metonymy. "The unconscious is structured like a language."

Language, as the principal means of structuring subjectivity, becomes a model for all symbolic systems. Subject-position theorists accordingly treated cinema as analogous to language in its structure and effects. Its "codes" vary across the history of the medium. An individual text becomes analogous to an instance of *parole,* and film scholars developed the idea of "enunciation," a process that inscribes into the text subject positions for addresser and addressee.

Most variants of culturalism continue to subscribe to semiotic premises, and Cultural Studies is frequently committed to the radical conventionalist position often ascribed to Saussure. Stuart Hall's essay "Encoding/Decoding," a locus classicus of culturalism, asserts the linguistic analogy: "televisual discourse" is "subject to all the complex formal 'rules' by which language signifies." [35] This claim is sweeping enough (*all* the rules of language? honorifics? subject/verb agreement? the formation of plurals?), but Hall goes still further and asserts that highly habituated decoding has masked those rules from us. We take the sign for the thing: "[Naturalization] leads us to think that the visual sign for 'cow' actually *is* (rather than *represents*) the animal, cow." [36] If this is true, then people react with surprising equanimity when they find tiny cows grazing inside their TV sets.

As Hall's article indicates, what *langue* and *parole* have been for subject-position theory, "discourse" has been for culturalism—the term through which any work in any medium can be understood. A particular film offers a text or discourse; a group of films constitutes one too. The language analogy is attractive because it allows critics to apply protocols of literary interpretation, a central inspiration for both subject-position theory and culturalism. Most film scholars have still not become comfortable with analyzing the visual and aural aspects of films. They prefer instead those aspects which lend themselves to traditional literary commentary—plot, character, and dialogue. Reception studies, which concentrate upon the "discourses" around a film—principally and inevitably, critical reviews—likewise avoid exploring medium-specific factors.

Despite three decades of work in film semiotics, however, those who claim that cinema is an ensemble of "codes" or "discourses" have not yet provided a defense of why we should consider the film medium, let alone perception and thought, as plausibly analogous to language.

Continuities: Reasoning Routines

Not only doctrinal premises bridge the subject-position/culturalist divide. I would argue that at least four protocols of theory-making—not "methods" but habits of mind, routines of reasoning—also run through film studies of the last three decades.

1. Top-down inquiry. Most contemporary film writers appear to believe that theory, criticism, and historical research ought to be doctrine-driven. During the 1970s, film researchers held that no theory of cinema could be valid unless anchored in a highly explicit theory of society and the subject. The culturalist turn has intensified this demand. Rather than formulating a question, posing a problem, or trying to come to grips with an intriguing film, the writer often takes as the central task the proving of a theoretical position by adducing films as examples. From the theory the writer moves to the particular case. Lévi-Straussian analyses of the Western, feminist conceptions of the body in film, Jamesonian accounts of the postmodernity of *Blade Runner*—again and again research is seen chiefly as "applying" a theory to a particular film or historical period.

The difficulty here is that just as one swallow doesn't make a summer, a lone case cannot establish a theory. When theory projects downward to the datum, the latter becomes an illustrative example. The result may have rhetorical force, as vivid examples often do, but because of the underdetermination of theories by data, a single instance is not particularly strong evidence.

The sources drawn upon by top-down inquiry have remained surprisingly consistent since the late 1960s. The books and journals, seminars and symposia which promulgated semiotics, Structuralism, Post-Structuralism, Lacanian psychoanalysis, and Althusserian Marxism were based principally in France, and it was as "ideas from France"[37] that they entered Anglo-American film culture. Comparatively indigenous developments, such as feminism, were strongly influenced by French theory. To this day, contesting orthodoxy often comes down to picking different Parisians to back. A 1993 book that denounces psychoanalytic film theory as "a religious cult" and "utterly bankrupt" goes on to explain: "Rejecting Freud and Lacan, I draw instead upon a variety of theoretical sources: Benjamin, Bataille, Blanchot, Foucault, Deleuze, and Guattari."[38] The *maîtres à penser* bump into one another in the pages of film books far more often than on the Boulevard St.-Michel.

Why this reliance on Parisian sources? The 1960s had already created a widespread Francophilia amongst film intellectuals. Auteurism had initiated a tradition of borrowing from the French; Sarris alerted a generation to *Cahiers* and Bazin. And of course from *Hiroshima mon amour* to *Weekend* French directors were seen as perhaps the prime source of politically and aesthetically challenging films. Moreover, departments of comparative literature were important conduits of the new theory into the United States, and cinéphiliac professors, in the course of transmitting current Parisian ideas, promoted French theory as paramount. Finally, in the effort to win academic respectability, film scholars could best show their work to have significance if there were a powerful theory backing it up. Auteurism was a connoisseurship that required a staggering knowledge of particular films. In an academic context, such knowledge could seem mere buffery, so auteur studies could not fully justify studying movies "seriously." An analysis of Hitchcock that purported to demonstrate a theory of signification or the unconscious was more worthy of academic attention than an analysis of recurring authorial motifs.

Culturalism has continued the reliance upon French ideas. The postmod-

ern strain marks its indebtedness to Lyotard, Baudrillard, and the like. Those
in debt to the Birmingham Centre also draw heavily upon Foucault and Bourdieu. Even the Frankfurt School wing, in many respects opposed to Francophilia, has been known to integrate aspects of French theory.

Is it necessary to point out that French intellectual life inclines its celebrities
to bold, even caricatural positions and quick turnarounds? French humanistic
thought is celebrity- and fashion-driven to a degree uncommon in Anglophone countries. With no apparent irony, a middlebrow Parisian weekly can
run a special issue, "French Thought Today," adorning its cover with a
picture of Rodin's thinker leaning against the Louvre's pyramid and an-
nouncing articles on "The Keywords," "The Schools and Circles," "The
New Themes," "Who Thinks What?" and "A Who's Who of 45 Leading
Men."[39] One sociologist has pointed out that this solemnly self-regarding
frivolity is a response to the social conditions of intellectual work in France.[40]

Borrowing so heavily from continental theory also poses the problem of
inadvertent narrowness. Since relatively few film scholars expertly read the
relevant European languages in which these theorists write, contemporary
film studies depends heavily upon translations. But German sociology and
psychology of film, East European film theory, and Italian and Scandinavian
semiology have gone untranslated, and so contemporary Anglo-American
film studies has taken little note of them. Compared to other scholarly disciplines, film studies has been notably provincial.

Even with respect to the most favored nations, peculiar time lags appear.
Film studies can't really be called trendy, because by the time film scholars
spot a trend, it has passed out of fashion on its home ground. Structuralism,
in decline after 1967 in France, captivated American humanists for decades; a
noteworthy instance is Jameson's circling of the Greimassian square.[41] Although Barthes' 1950s essays on myth are largely pre-Structuralist, they were
not translated into English until 1972; they rapidly became founding texts for
both subject-position adherents and culturalists. Mikhail Bakhtin's *Rabelais
and His World* was introduced to a Parisian public in 1966; his influence in
Anglo-American film studies follows from the translations and commentaries
generated by Slavists in the 1980s. While Parisian intellectuals were discovering the Gulag Archipelago and disavowing Althusser, Anglo-American intellectuals were reading *Reading Capital*. While Lacan was unraveling Borro-
mean knot theory, Anglophones were burrowing into his writings of the
1950s and early 1960s. Now, when Parisian film academics are working
principally on what can only be called traditional film aesthetics, Americans
are reading Baudrillard, Irigary, Bourdieu, and other 1970s-era thinkers. If
American academics really want to be au courant, they should be embracing
liberal humanism, the latest discovery sweeping the City of Light.[42]

Whatever its sources, doctrine-driven thinking discourages a careful analysis of problems and issues. It encourages a more or less contingent search for
second-hand ideas. Professors commonly advise confused students: "Why

don't you use so-and-so at this point in your analysis?" Many film scholars find it more congenial to read the latest translation of a French master (or to turn to the latest Routledge précis) than to engage in research or reflect on questions for themselves.

At worst this technology spins out into mere appeal to authority. The pronouncements of Lacan, Althusser, Baudrillard, *et cie* are often simply taken on faith. Walter Benjamin's McLuhanite assumption that the organization of human sense modes "is determined not only by nature but by historical circumstances as well" is offered on the basis of extremely scanty evidence;[43] yet Frankfurt-influenced studies of early cinema routinely presuppose this idea in claiming that modernity altered human perception.

Still, top-down application has succeeded partly because it can be taught. Graduate students are encouraged to go beyond any writer's explicit case to probe what she or he takes for granted. Once the student keeps probing, and particularly if she or he reads associatively and metaphorically, she or he can arrive at very general assumptions—not only about film but about the nature of existence, of social life, of the mind and history. Often these assumptions are remarkably banal ones, or they do not affect the specific arguments of the text; nevertheless, students are encouraged to make them overt. People thereby come to believe that in order to say something about a particular problem one must be perfectly transparent and explicit about all one's most fundamental beliefs; for these are held to determine everything one could say about the issue at hand. Put another way: What could make people think that they *needed* a highly elaborated theory of ideology or culture in order to talk enlighteningly about a particular film or historical process? Partly, I suggest, an institutional routine which posited that every argument rested upon some larger assumptions about just such matters.

2. Argument as Bricolage. The top-down theorizing of 1975 Theory drew from widely diverse intellectual traditions—not only the triumvirate of Marx, Freud, and Saussure, but also Vico, Hegel, Heidegger, Husserl, and a host of others. Far from being a coherent system, this Grand Theory was a patchwork of ideas, any of which might be altered or removed when "recent developments," as they were usually called, threw it into question. The result was what Jonathan Rée has dubbed the *nouveau mélange*.[44]

Although culturalists sometimes attack the particular sources of subject-position theory, culturalism is just as eclectic in its inspiration. Any manual of Cultural Studies provides instances. Graeme Turner, for example, presents a bricolage of Propp, Lévi-Strauss, Todorov, Mulvey, and Will Wright, treating them all as contributing to the Cultural Studies perspective on narrative.[45]

Turner's enterprise is emblematic in another way. In assembling his theory of narrative, he does not mention that Propp and Lévi-Strauss declared their theories incommensurable. Yet such incompatibilities risk making any synthesis incoherent. It is likewise difficult to reconcile Lévi-Strauss's insistence on innate categories of human thinking with the idea that subjectivity is imposed from without. Lacan's recasting of Jakobson's linguistics is at least as extensive as Althusser's recasting of Lacan. A term drawn from the Russian Formalist tradition can be found alongside an invocation of the Hegelian concept of the Other. The Look passes from Kojève to Sartre to Lacan to film theory, each time rethematized.[46] The risk of selectively borrowing pieces of theories is that the scholar may miss exactly those portions of one source that contradict the assumptions of others.

But this eclecticism has its limits—what might be called, in the spirit of subject-position theory, its repressed. The subject-position framework proved highly selective—indeed, arbitrary—in assembling its theories. Film scholars characteristically cite Althusser for his account of Ideological State Apparatuses, ignoring his urge to demarcate a "science." Theorists highlight Lacan on the Imaginary and the Symbolic, while his discussions of the Real, let alone his baffling excursions into topology and knot theory, are ignored.[47]

Similarly, it is surprising that theorists who assign language a key role in determining subjectivity have almost completely ignored the two most important contemporary developments in linguistic theory: Chomsky's Transformational Generative Grammar and his Principles-and-Parameters theory. The silence is plainly strategic. Chomsky argues that language structure is in major respects biological and that central features of language involve not cultural variations but universal regularities. One could not hold that language imposes a culturally constructed notion of subjectivity upon the biological individual if there were good reason to believe that linguistic structure is part of human biological endowment. Yet no film theorist has mounted an argument for *why* the comparatively informal theories of Saussure, Émile Benveniste, or Bakhtin are superior to the Chomskyan paradigm.[48] For over two decades film theorists have made pronouncements about language without engaging with the major theoretical rival to their position.

3. Associational Reasoning. Psychoanalytic theorist Guy Rosolato is talking with film theorist Raymond Bellour. Rosolato remarks that in order to speak in detail of a film, he would have to analyze it on a stop-motion viewer. Bellour replies: "Do you mean to say that if one cannot re-view a film in this way, it practically does not exist?" Later Bellour comments that some of cinema's formal processes induce affect, and he takes the flashback as an example.

> No matter what the flashback actually recounts, by its very nature it provokes an extremely violent emotional shock through the mere fact that it points to the past. One of my friends had a slightly disturbed relation to his past at one point and flashbacks had an almost automatic effect on him; one could say that it was their form itself that made him cry.[49]

Presumably the interlocutors mean us to take the conversation seriously. (After all, they published it.) Yet the discussion is unintelligible because the connections among ideas meet no canons of reasonable inference. Rosolato says that a film must be examined closely in order to be discussed with precision; what grounds are there for Bellour's remarkable conclusion that perhaps therefore the film does not exist? Bellour claims to have had a friend who wept during flashbacks; why should Bellour infer that flashbacks necessarily provoke violent emotional upheavals in everyone? [50]

The game of tag played with ideas in this dialogue exemplifies another habit of mind prevalent in film studies. Both subject-position theorists and culturalists tend to shy away from inductive, deductive, and abductive reasoning. They rely upon remarkably unconstrained association.

Since analyzing the flow of an argument takes a little time, I summon only one illustrative example. Joan Copjec begins an essay on *Double Indemnity*[51] by asserting that there is "something unsatisfying" (168) about the insurance investigator Keyes's invocation of actuarial statistics in explaining why he doubts that the death of Diedrichson was a suicide. The spectator who does not find Keyes's intuition problematic will block Copjec's argument at the start, but let's assume that others share her unease. She goes on to ask: "How is it that an appeal to statistics can be taken as a devastating argument? . . . What, in the final analysis, do numbers have to do with detection?" (168) These two questions are not the same, since the first bears upon the evidentiary grounds for an argument, while the second poses a much broader range of possible relations between "numbers" (not just statistics) and "detection" (not an argument). Already an association of ideas (statistics → numbers, argument → detection) is ruling the critic's interpretation.

Copjec finds the answer in the origins of detective fiction. (Why the relation of statistics to argument, or numbers to detection, can best be discovered through a search for origins is not explained.) Copjec proposes "linking" detective fiction to "the advent of rationalism" (168). This is a very elastic link, since Copjec identifies rationalism with Descartes, who died in 1650, and most historians date the modern detective story from the 1840s. Moreover, Descartes relies on a purely deductive method, whereas Sherlock Holmes and other sleuths employ induction (not, as Copjec astonishingly asserts, a priori ideas [169]).

Copjec forges another link—that between the emergence of detective fiction and an unprecedented production of statistics, "an avalanche of numbers" (169). But she does not establish any causal connection between the publication of Poe's tales and the rise of statistical methods. Instead, she relies on metaphorical associations. The rise of statistical bureaucracies created "modern nations as large insurance companies"—a mnemonic "linkage" to *Double Indemnity* (170). Statistics made citizens more aware of the incidence of murder (another associative linkage to *Double Indemnity*). And statistics made people believe in the calculability of risk. Copjec concludes that the detective story is a product of statistical calculation. "The nineteenth century's fictional belief in the solvability of crime was specifically a mathematical

expectation. . . . Before statistics this sort of expectation was strictly impossible, and so, I would argue, was detective fiction" (170).

No line of reasoning has even begun to establish this dazzling claim. Even
if detective fiction was created out of statistical procedures, that contingent
fact does not support the inference that detective fiction was impossible
(let alone *strictly* impossible) before that. Moreover, detective fiction virtually
never employs statistical reasoning. And in any case there are earlier fictions
presupposing that a crime is soluble; The Strange Case of Oedipus Rex comes
to mind.[52]

The article goes on assembling concepts in the same associative fashion.
The toting up of information in the detective story calls forth Foucauldian
concepts of surveillance and disciplinary power, which in turn bring to mind
a recent study of the rise of the realist novel. The linkages involve not causality
or entailment but connotation and likeness. ("Here we may stop to note a
certain similarity between the rationalist project and that of new historicism,"
171.) Copjec concludes that detection "constitutes the very people with
which [sic] it comes into contact." Detective fiction is "linked" to statistical
sorting; and in counting people, statistics "created them. Beneath the categories actual people came into being" (171). If detection and numerical categories can bring actual people into being, the laws of genetics will need drastic
revision.

The example illustrates how the associationist reasoning of contemporary
film theory can create a bricolage of parallels, interpretive leaps, and nifty but
unsupported conclusions. Such associational thinking meshes smoothly with
the juggling of terms, names, and references encouraged by the bricolage
strategy.

4. The Hermeneutic Impulse. The urge to "apply" theory, as well as the demand that theory be specific and accessible, led Anglo-American writers to
interpret films as instantiations of theoretical categories and propositions.
Many examples show this process at work. Ever since the 1960s, interpretation has been central to academic film studies, and both theoretical and historical work have been subordinated to it. Now, as in the days of authorship
and before, most of film studies consists of critical commentary on individual
films.

For subject-position theory, the turn to top-down applications was perhaps
inevitable. Expressing a disdain for "empiricism," theorists resisted those
skeptics who sought, say, to challenge Lacan's account of subject formation
by pointing to evidence from studies in child development. This resistance is
partly a consequence of many academic humanists' hostility to and ignorance
of scientific research.[53] But the refusal to supply confirmatory evidence is also
characteristic of contemporary film theory's wholesale recasting of Freud.

For example, in a recent exposition of subject-position theory, Sandy

Flitterman-Lewis asserts that Freud's metapsychology is a "conceptual model" that "defies empirical verification."[54] Yet Freud writes of his metapsychology:

> It must not be supposed that these very general ideas are presuppositions upon which the work of psychoanalysis depends. On the contrary, they are its latest conclusions and are "open to revision." Psycho-analysis is founded securely upon the observation of the facts of mental life; and for that very reason its theoretical superstructure is still incomplete and subject to constant alteration.[55]

Freud makes his metapsychology speculative, non-foundational, and open to empirical disconfirmation. Flitterman-Lewis turns his speculations into presuppositions for the study of subject-positioning in film and then claims that these foundations are resolutely nonempirical.

She goes still further beyond Freud in declaring: "Once the unconscious and its mechanisms are seen to establish the fundamental discontinuity of psychic life, there can never be absolute certainty about empirical observation" (135). First, note that the reference to "absolute certainty" is a red herring. No serious researcher in any domain claims absolute certainty for observations. (In chapter 2 Noël Carroll provides further discussion.) Second, as Freud's passage indicates, he would certainly not assert that psychoanalysis makes observation uncertain. After all, he thought he was founding a medical science: diagnosing a patient's symptoms and arriving at a cure depend, he says, upon "observation of the facts of mental life."[56]

Film theorists, however, had no patients to worry about, so they could easily declare subject-position theory invulnerable to empirical objection. Theory was henceforth to be written as bricolage of other theories, never breaking out of the charmed circle of associative linkages and recent developments. But what to write? The most common course was simply to compose expositions of subject-position doctrines. The apparently endless résumés of the thoughts of Lacan, Metz, Oudart, Mulvey, and so on attest to the attractiveness of this option. Alternatively, one could logically dissect the theoretical claims of subject-position theory. Since this is a difficult task, we should not be surprised that the amount of "pure theory" written during the 1970s is quite small.

Most film academics pursued a somewhat different option. Subject-position theory generated a huge number of interpretations of individual films. Elsewhere I have suggested that film critics utilized theoretical ideas in ways that conform to the traditions of literary interpretation.[57] Moreover, the idea of using the theory to "read" films has its precedents in the subject-position tradition itself. Freud occasionally applied psychoanalysis to literary texts, and Sartre used literary examples to illuminate his philosophical points. Most tellingly, whereas Freud characteristically based his arguments upon data taken from clinical or personal experience, Lacan frequently illustrated his doctrines with detailed commentary on literary texts. With such encouragement, it should be no surprise that the bulk of subject-position work has concerned itself with "applying theory" in the act of interpretation.

By this process, subject-position theorists made interpretation a substitute for the empirical dimension they had cast out. For most scholars, a theory gained plausibility when it yielded a fresh reading of a film. Subject-position theory probably could not have won so many adherents if it had not shown that it could be "applied."

The culturalist trend has also been resolutely hermeneutic. Sometimes it is a matter of reading viewers rather than texts, as when Cultural Studies adherents undertake quasi-ethnographic interpretation of audiences. At other moments the culturalist will gather journalistic reviews and interpret them as evidence of "reading formations" or reception processes.[58] And often the culturalist view is no less text-centered than subject-position theory, generating readings that are substantially indistinguishable from the sort of commentary that became commonplace in the 1970s. One essay in Cultural Studies offers a quite traditional symptomatic reading of the gilded woman in *Goldfinger*'s title sequence: "At once sexually alluring and rewarding, as desirable as the gold of the title song, and finally laid on her back, in the ultimate demonstration of Bond's phallic power, she is at the same time deeply troubling and threatening to Bond in containing, within her body, the castrating threat represented by Goldfinger."[59] Similarly, Miriam Hansen's discussion of Griffith's *Intolerance* identifies Cyrus as the phallus, treats Babylon's fall as a "fissure of the ego," and claims that Griffith's editing "turned the father's sword against himself and performed something like a metaphorical self-castration."[60] Once more, culturalism is often closer to subject-position theory than adherents acknowledge.

Must a theory prove its validity through interpretations of particular films? There is no reason to think so, as Carroll argues in the essay which follows. Do the theories yield the interpretations as entailments? I have tried to show elsewhere that when interpreting films, critics follow a set of craft-like reasoning routines which do not depend on any abstract theory.[61] But clearly practitioners believe that by engaging in concrete "readings" they are somehow supporting the theory. (Significantly, no published interpretation has ever *disproven* the candidate theory.) Indeed, interpretations often function as allegories or figurations of the theory from which they issue.

Middle-Level Research

Subject-position theory and culturalism constitute Grand Theories. Each rests upon several substantive premises about the nature of society, history, mind, and meaning. Each of these premises can be traced back to nineteenth-century intellectual traditions.[62] Concrete interpretations of films and filmic contexts are thought to flow from these Theories, instantiating the processes already provided for in the abstract doctrines.

During the rise of subject-position theory and culturalism, another trend came to the fore. Closer to traditional academic scholarship, this tendency has concentrated on in-depth research. This "middle-level" research asks questions that have both empirical and theoretical import. That is, and contrary to many expositors of Grand Theory, being empirical does not rule out being theoretical.[63]

The most established realms of middle-level research have been empirical studies of filmmakers, genres, and national cinemas. This tradition has been enriched by gay/lesbian, feminist, minority, and postcolonialist perspectives. Researchers have begun to bring to light films, filmmakers, and Third World cinemas long ignored by orthodox film history.[64] A wider corpus of films and new information about particular film cultures have also complicated and nuanced the questions which film theorists ask. For example, the relation between African films and indigenous traditions of oral storytelling is a paradigm case of a researchable middle-level problem.[65]

Other examples belong to the historiographic trends that emerged in the mid-1970s and led to a wave of "revisionist" work in the 1980s. Film history as a scholarly pursuit is of even more recent vintage than film theory and criticism. Although book-length film histories were published from the 1920s onward, most were based on secondary sources and small bodies of films. The most useful histories were written by film aficionados, archivists, and independent scholars.[66] And most volumes of film history were nation-based or worldwide surveys rather than in-depth, monographic works.

The move by film studies into the academy during the late 1960s provided conditions for more systematic scholarly work. Young academics had often had some training in historiographic research, and professional historians became more interested in working in cinema as well. This influx of new researchers came at a time when archivists and librarians (often themselves with some training in history and cinema) began to recognize the value of films and film-related documents. Major sets of papers were microfilmed. Important film collections became more open to researchers. By the 1980s, many archives allowed researchers to view films on editing machines. European archives became more hospitable. Film scholars began to realize the importance of trade journals and newspapers, court cases, and other print materials generated around the film trade. Recall that Georges Sadoul and Jean Mitry wrote their massive histories from personal libraries and clipping files, and you will appreciate the vistas that academic support opened up to the young film historians of the 1970s.

Many sorts of "new film history" emerged at the period. One offered an unprecedentedly well-supported examination of the business aspects of the movie industry. Since most of the primary documents available in collections related to Hollywood cinema, there began to appear systematic studies of the structure and conduct of motion picture companies. How, these researchers asked, did economic forces and principles of management affect the institutions of film production, distribution, and exhibition? The answers began to show the importance of vertically integrating the companies, owning real estate, assimilating new technologies, dividing labor, and strategizing for a worldwide market.[67] These research programs continue to bear fruit, often by extension to other nations' industries.[68]

Another set of questions involved practices of film exhibition. Historians began to reconstruct what cinema was like in Manhattan or Chicago neighborhoods.[69] Instructors taught historiographic method by assigning students the task of writing histories of local exhibition.[70] Debates arose about the composition of early film audiences and the prevalence of women spectators in sustaining certain genres.

Other researchers renewed interest in the stylistic history of cinema. Since the 1920s, one model of the "evolution of film language" had ruled most discussions. The history of cinema was linked to an unfolding realization of the power of "film syntax," from Méliès, Porter, and Griffith to German Expressionism, the Soviet classics, and the international avant-garde. By developing cutting, close views, optical transformations, and camera movement, silent cinema had supposedly mastered a specifically cinematic storytelling. Bazin and his contemporaries in the *nouvelle critique* had argued against this view, but their advocacy of Jean Renoir, Orson Welles, and the Neorealists served chiefly to widen the canon, not to press historians to rethink the standard story.[71]

During the late 1960s, however, the growing reputation of the contemporary avant-garde suggested that the development toward narrative continuity was only one path cinema might have taken. Warhol made Lumière's static camera more interesting; Ken Jacobs's *Tom, Tom the Piper's Son* (1969), a reworking of an American Mutoscope and Biograph film, revealed the richness of "primitive" scenography. Archives and venturesome film distributors offered a broader corpus of work than ever before. Now Porter looked less innovative; Griffith looked atypical; and the Japanese cinema of the 1930s became of major importance.[72] Since the mid-1970s, historians of style have brought to light more fine-grained and complicated histories of cinematic technique.[73] Research projects on the development of lighting and staging, the emergence of sound film, and wide-screen aesthetics have all been made possible by ingenious exploitation of archival holdings.[74] The study of avant-garde cinema has particularly benefited from critics and historians who have posed researchable questions about film style.[75]

Because all these varieties of middle-level research are problem- rather than doctrine-driven, scholars can combine traditionally distinct spheres of inquiry. Middle-level questions can cut across traditional boundaries among film aesthetics, institutions, and audience response. Lea Jacobs has investigated how

Hollywood's internal censorship mechanisms produced negotiated representations of women at the level of image and narrative.[76] In particular, the massive international inquiry into pre-1920 cinema has generated questions which treat industry, audience, narrative, and style together.

This burst of revisionist film historiography is not the only sign of the emergence of middle-level research. What Noël Carroll calls "piecemeal theory" forms a comparable strategy: building theories not of subjectivity, ideology, or culture in general but rather of particular phenomena. (These, upon inspection, always turn out to be difficult enough to understand.) Thus, for example, several philosophers of art have launched inquiry into horror, suspense, emotional expressivity, genres, and specific questions of feminism.[77] Monographic studies of point of view, genres, and kindred phenomena have already yielded distinct positions and fruitful debates.[78] Film narratology is another thriving middle-level area.[79] Specific hypotheses about spectatorial activity have offered challenges to the terms underpinning both the subject-position model and culturalism.[80]

On all these fronts, the middle-level tradition of scholarship has made significant progress. Perhaps the strongest testimony to the power of these research programs is the extent to which subject-position adherents and culturalists have recruited the findings for their own purposes.[81] The significant issue, however, seems to me whether these established schools of thought can enter the *theoretical* and *methodological* debates broached by revisionist history and piecemeal theorizing.

To get specific: Middle-level research programs have shown that an argument can be at once conceptually powerful and based in evidence without appeal to theoretical bricolage or association of ideas. Moreover, these programs have demonstrated that you can do a lot with films besides interpreting them. In particular, we do not need to understand a film by projecting onto it the semantic fields "privileged" by this or that theory. Most important, the middle-level research programs have shown that *you do not need a Big Theory of Everything to do enlightening work in a field of study.* Contrary to what many believe, a study of United Artists' business practices or the standardization of continuity editing or the activities of women in early film audiences need carry *no* determining philosophical assumptions about subjectivity or culture, *no* univocal metaphysical or epistemological or political presumptions—in short, no commitment to a Grand Theory.

Literary studies, art history, musicology, and many other disciplines within the humanities developed rich research traditions before Grand Theory intervened. Film studies had hardly begun in-depth inquiry when subject-position theorists and culturalists gained supremacy. Had imaginative historians and rigorous theorists not ignored charges of "positivism" and "empiricism," we would not have most of the promising avenues that currently lie open. In the Post-Theory era, sharply focused, in-depth inquiry remains our best bet for producing the sort of scholarly debate that will advance our knowledge of cinema. Grand Theories will come and go, but research and scholarship will endure.

NOTES

I am grateful to Noël Carroll, Kirstin Thompson, and Paisley Livingston for their comments upon drafts of this essay.

1. There were, however, efforts to argue for the screenwriter as auteur. These arguments in the United States replayed debates that had already surfaced in Germany in the 1910s and 1920s and in France during the 1940s.

2. See Noël Carroll, "The Future of Allusion: Hollywood in the Seventies (and Beyond)," *October* 20 (Spring 1982): 51–81.

3. Iris Barry, *Let's Go to the Movies* (New York: Payson and Clarke, 1926), p. 197.

4. See Geoffrey Nowell-Smith, *Visconti* (Garden City, N.Y.: Doubleday, 1968); Peter Wollen, *Signs and Meaning in the Cinema* (Bloomington: Indiana University Press, 1969); Alan Lovell, *Don Siegel: American Cinema* (London: British Film Institute, 1975).

5. Jim Kitses, *Horizons West* (Bloomington: Indiana University Press, 1969); Colin McArthur, *Underworld USA* (New York: Viking, 1972).

6. See Schatz, *Hollywood Genres* (New York: Random House, 1981), pp. 30–32.

7. For example, although the title of Robert Lapsley and Michael Westlake's *Film Theory: An Introduction* (New York: St. Martin's, 1988) promises an introduction to all of film theory, it discusses only subject-position theory.

8. Without Laplanche and Pontalis's compact definitions and citation of relevant passages in Freud and Lacan, humanists would not have been able to absorb psychoanalytic doctrine so quickly. This 1966 book is still taken as an authoritative guide to Lacan's ideas, despite his harsh falling-out with its authors. See Elisabeth Roudinesco, *Jacques Lacan & Co.: A History of Psychoanalysis in France, 1925–1985*, trans. Jeffrey Mehlman (Chicago: University of Chicago Press, 1990), pp. 290, 312–16.

9. See, respectively, Stephen Heath, "Film and System: Terms of Analysis," *Screen* 16, 1 (Spring 1975): 7–77; 16, 2 (Summer 1975): 91–113; Christian Metz, *The Imaginary Signifier: Psychoanalysis and the Cinema,* trans. Celia Britton et al. (Bloomington: Indiana University Press, 1982); Laura Mulvey, "Visual Pleasure and Narrative Cinema," in *Visual and Other Pleasures* (Bloomington: Indiana University Press, 1989), pp. 14–26; and Jean-Louis Baudry, "Ideological Effects of the Basic Cinematographic Apparatus," in *Narrative, Apparatus, Ideology,* ed. Philip Rosen (New York: Columbia University Press), pp. 286–98.

10. Annette Kuhn, *Women's Pictures: Feminism and Cinema* (London: Routledge, 1982), p. 47.

11. Strangely, what has persisted within Parisian film theory has been something all but forgotten in Anglo-American circles—1966 semiotics. In 1975 a book called *Cinéma et production de sens* (Roger Odin; Paris: Armand Colin, 1990) would have been deeply psychoanalytic; the nineties version dwells upon Metz's *Grande Syntagmatique.* Metz's last work, *L'Énonciation impersonnel ou le site du film* (Paris: Klincksieck, 1991) likewise ignores psychoanalysis, subject-positioning, apparatus theory, and the like. Other books on film theory, in series published by Nathan and Hachette, produce summaries of semiotic and narratological doctrine for student consumption.

For the rest, most theoretical works produced in France seem to be in that vein of belletristic musing which Barthes popularized.

12. See Joan Copjec, "The Anxiety of the Influencing Machine," *October* 23 (Winter 1982): 43–59; Kaja Silverman, *The Acoustic Mirror: The Female Voice in Psychoanalysis and Cinema* (Bloomington: Indiana University Press, 1988); *Everything You Always Wanted to Know about Lacan (But Were Afraid to Ask Hitchcock)*, ed. Slavoj Žižek (London: Verso, 1992).

13. This point was made in Paul Hirst, "Althusser and the Theory of Ideology," *Economy and Society* 5, 4 (November 1976): 385–412.

14. Kate Soper, *Humanism and Anti-Humanism* (La Salle, Ill.: Open Court, 1986), p. 130.

15. This point was broached as a logical, rather than a pragmatic, objection by Noël Carroll in *Mystifying Movies: Fads and Fallacies in Contemporary Film Theory* (New York: Columbia University Press, 1988), pp. 75–78.

16. See John Cawelti, "The Concept of Formula in the Study of Popular Literature," *Journal of Popular Culture* 3, 3 (Winter 1969): 381–90, and *Six-Guns and Society* (Bowling Green: Popular Press, 1971); Lawrence Alloway, "The Iconography of the Movies," *Movie* 7 (February–March 1963): 4–5; Colin McArthur, "Genre and Iconography" (British Film Institute Education Department seminar paper, 27 March 1969).

17. Tim O'Sullivan et al., *Key Concepts in Communication and Cultural Studies*, 2d ed. (London: Routledge, 1994), p. 71.

18. See, for example, Keith Reader, *Intellectuals and the Left in France since 1968* (New York: St. Martin's, 1987), pp. 39–43; Sunil Khilnani, *Arguing Revolution: The Intellectual Left in Postwar France* (New Haven: Yale University Press, 1993), pp. 109–117; Tony Judt, *Marxism and the French Left: Studies on Labour and Politics in France, 1830–1981* (Oxford: Clarendon Press, 1986), pp. 192–196.

19. Stuart Hall, "Cultural Studies: Two Paradigms," in *Media, Culture, and Society: A Critical Reader* (Richard Collins et al. (London: Sage, 1986), p. 39.

20. Rick Altman, "General Introduction: Cinema as Event," in *Sound Theory Sound Practice*, ed. Rick Altman (New York: Routledge, 1992), p. 4.

21. For example, a recurrent theme of Judith Mayne's *Cinema and Spectatorship* (New York: Routledge, 1993) is the demand that any adequate theory of the film spectator take psychoanalysis into account (e.g., pp. 59, 70, 77). Yet Mayne nowhere gives reasons *why* psychoanalysis must be a component in any such theory. She contrasts psychoanalysis with cultural theories and cognitive theories (in the process, misdescribing the latter), but instead of refuting the competing claims by means of psychoanalysis, she simply restates the superiority of psychoanalysis to all rivals. It is odd, then, that Mayne's particular readings of films in chapters 6 and 7 do not rely upon psychoanalytic concepts. Can only those who swear allegiance to psychoanalysis choose to discard it?

22. For a detailed discussion of the social science model of human plasticity, see John Tooby and Leda Cosmides, "The Psychological Foundations of Culture," in *The Adapted Mind: Evolutionary Psychology and the Generation of Culture*, ed. Jerome H. Barkow, Leda Cosmides, and John Tooby (New York: Oxford University Press, 1992), pp. 19–136.

23. "The psychoanalytic experience runs its course entirely on the relationship of subject to subject, signifying in effect that it retains a dimension which is irreducible to any psychology considered as an objectification of certain properties of the individual." Cited in Bice Benvenuto and Roger Kennedy, *The Works of Jacques Lacan: An Introduction* (New York: St. Martin's, 1986), p. 101. On Lacan's running together of philo-

sophical and psychological conceptions of the subject, see David Macy's excellent *Lacan in Contexts* (London: Verso, 1988), pp. 89–93. Within film studies, Noël Carroll was, I think, the first to argue that Freud's claims about the empirical subject of consciousness do not confute any metaphysical claims about personal unity or identity. See *Mystifying Movies*, pp. 73–83.

24. Stephen Heath argues against the equating of subject and individual in "The Turn of the Subject," *Ciné-Tracts* 2, 3/4 (Summer/Fall 1979): 33–36. Interestingly, he traces the confusion back to Althusser. It might also be seen in Lacan, who exploits an equivocation: the traditional psychoanalytic conception of the subject as the person undergoing treatment, and the philosophical sense of the subject as consciousness or thinking entity.

25. *The Subject of Semiotics* (New York: Oxford, 1983), p. 19.

26. Poonam Arora, "The Production of Third World Subjects for First World Consumption: *Salaam Bombay* and *Parama*," in *Multiple Voices in Feminist Film Criticism*, ed. Diane Carson, Linda Dittmar, and Janice R. Welsch (Minneapolis: University of Minnesota Press, 1994), p. 294.

27. Thomas Waugh, "The Third Body: Patterns in the Construction of the Subject in Gay Male Narrative Film," in *Queer Looks: Perspectives on Lesbian and Gay Film and Video*, ed. Martha Gever, John Greyson, and Pratibha Parmar (London: Routledge, 1993), pp. 141–61.

28. According to a popular handbook of Cultural Studies, the subject is "the thinking subject; the site of consciousness"; consciousness is in turn defined as "awareness of situations, images, sensations, or memories" (Tim O'Sullivan et al., *Key Concepts*, pp. 309, 57). Another British theorist defines cultural studies as being about "the historical forms of consciousness or subjectivity" (Richard Johnson, "The Story So Far: And Further Transformations?" in *Introduction to Contemporary Cultural Studies*, ed. David Punter [London: Longman, 1986], p. 280).

29. Jim Collins, *Uncommon Cultures: Popular Culture and Post-Modernism* (London: Routledge, 1989), p. 144.

30. E. Ann Kaplan, "Introduction: From Plato's Cave to Freud's Screen," in *Psychoanalysis and Cinema*, ed. E. Ann Kaplan (New York: Routledge, 1990), p. 10.

31. John Fiske, *Television Culture* (London: Methuen, 1987), p. 171.

32. See Noël Carroll, *The Philosophy of Horror; or, Paradoxes of the Heart* (New York: Routledge, 1990), pp. 88–96; and Murray Smith, *Engaging Characters* (Oxford: Oxford University Press, 1995).

33. See Elizabeth Cowie, "Fantasia," *m/f* 9 (1984): 70–71.

34. Constance Penley, "Feminism, Psychoanalysis, and Popular Culture," in *Cultural Studies*, ed. Lawrence Grossberg, Cary Nelson, and Paula Treichler (New York: Routledge, 1992), p. 490.

35. "Encoding/Decoding," in Stuart Hall et al., *Culture, Media, Language: Working Papers in Cultural Studies, 1972–79* (London: Hutchinson, 1980), p. 129.

36. Ibid., p. 132.

37. I refer to *Ideas from France: The Legacy of French Theory*, ed. Lisa Appignanesi (London: Free Association, 1989).

38. Steven Shaviro, *The Cinematic Body* (Minneapolis: University of Minnesota Press, 1993), p. ix.

39. *L'Événement* no. 201 (8–14 September 1988). Incidentally, the list of forty-five "leading men" (*chefs de file*) includes one woman: Françoise Dolto, noted for her work in child psychoanalysis.

40. See Raymond Boudon, "The Freudian-Marxian-Structuralist (FMS) Move-

ment in France: Variations on a Theme by Sherry Turkle," *The Tocqueville Review* 2, 1 (Winter 1980): 5–23.

41. See, for instance, *The Political Unconscious: Narrative as a Socially Symbolic Act* (Ithaca: Cornell University Press, 1981), pp. 46–48, 121–129, and elsewhere.

42. See the work of Luc Ferry and Alain Renault, particularly *French Philosophy of the Sixties: An Essay on Antihumanism,* trans. Mary Schnackenberg Cattani (Amherst: University of Massachusetts Press, 1990).

43. See "The Work of Art in the Age of Mechanical Reproduction," in *Illuminations,* ed. Hannah Arendt (New York: Schocken, 1969), p. 222. Benjamin cites Riegl and Wickhoff as having "drawn conclusions" about the organization of perception in the fifth century A.D. on the basis of certain art works. This is hardly sufficient to warrant Benjamin's claim that "during long periods of history, the mode of human sense perception changes with humanity's entire mode of existence" (p. 222).

44. Jonathan Rée, "Marxist Modes," *Radical Philosophy Reader* (London: Verso, 1985), p. 338.

45. Graeme Turner, *Film as Social Practice,* 2d ed. (London: Routledge, 1993), pp. 67–93.

46. For a detailed discussion of how the Look was rethought, see Martin Jay, *Downcast Eyes: The Denigration of Vision in Twentieth-Century French Thought* (Berkeley: University of California Press, 1993), chapters 5–7. Chapter 8 surveys French film theorists' selective appropriation of Lacan.

47. See my "Historical Poetics of Cinema," in *The Cinematic Text: Methods and Approaches,* ed. R. Barton Palmer (New York: AMS, 1989), pp. 385–92.

48. One of the few criticisms of subject-position theory on this score was William Cadbury and Leland Poague, *Film Criticism: A Counter Theory* (Ames: Iowa State University Press, 1982).

49. Raymond Bellour and Guy Rosolato, "Dialogue: Remembering (this memory of) a film," in *Psychoanalysis and Cinema,* pp. 199, 212.

50. Perhaps Rosolato mildly rebukes Bellour for this strange leap when he responds: "It can also be pleasant to return to one's past" (ibid.). If Rosolato is right, it would sometimes be pleasant to experience flashbacks—in which case nothing informative has been said by either party.

51. "The Phenomenal Nonphenomenal: Private Space in *Film Noir,*" in *Shades of Noir,* ed. Joan Copjec (London: Verso, 1993), pp. 167–97. Citations from the article are henceforth given in parentheses.

52. Although the *modern* detective story is born with Poe, there are several ancient crime/solution puzzles. Apart from *Oedipus,* there are the tales of Bel and of Susanna in the Apocryphal Scriptures. See *The Omnibus of Crime,* ed. Dorothy L. Sayers (Garden City: Garden City Publishing, 1929), pp. 51–55.

53. An excellent criticism of this state of affairs is Paul R. Gross and Norman Levitt, *Higher Superstition: The Academic Left and Its Quarrels with Science* (Baltimore: Johns Hopkins University Press, 1994).

54. "Psychoanalysis" in Robert Stam, Robert Burgoyne, and Sandy Flitterman-Lewis, *New Vocabularies in Film Semiotics: Structuralism, Post-Structuralism, and Beyond* (New York: Routledge, 1992), p. 124. Subsequent page numbers in parentheses in the text refer to this article.

Flitterman-Lewis' wording seems derived from Laplanche and Pontalis, *The Language of Psychoanalysis,* trans. Donald Nicholson-Smith (London: Hogarth Press, 1973), but in place of their claim that "Metapsychology constructs an ensemble of conceptual models which are *more or less far-removed from* empirical reality" (p. 249;

italics mine), she asserts that it "*defies* empirical *verification*" (italics mine)—quite a different matter.

55. "Psycho-Analysis," Standard Edition of the Complete Psychological Works of Sigmund Freud, ed. and trans. Ernest Jones, James Strachey, et al. (London: Hogarth, 1953–74) vol. 20, (1925–26), p. 266.

56. Consider his definition: "Psycho-analysis is a medical procedure which aims at the cure of certain forms of nervous disease (the neuroses) by a psychological technique" ("The Claims of Psycho-Analysis to Scientific Interest," in *SE* vol. 13 [1913–14], p. 165). For a discussion of the scientific ambitions of Freud's metapsychology, see Patricia Kitcher, *Freud's Dream: A Complete Interdisciplinary Science of Mind* (Cambridge: MIT Press, 1992).

57. See *Making Meaning: Inference and Rhetoric in the Interpretation of Cinema* (Cambridge: Harvard University Press, 1989), pp. 97–104.

58. A book-length example is Janet Staiger, *Interpreting Films: Studies in the Historical Reception of American Cinema* (Princeton: Princeton University Press, 1992).

59. Tony Bennett and Janet Woollacott, *Bond and Beyond: The Political Career of a Popular Hero* (New York: Methuen, 1987), p. 153.

60. Miriam Hansen, *Babel and Babylon: Spectatorship in American Silent Film* (Cambridge: Harvard University Press, 1991), pp. 232–233.

61. *Making Meaning*, pp. 29–42, 201–4, 215–23, 252–54.

62. A useful study in this lineage is Vincent Descombes, *Modern French Philosophy*, trans. L. Scott-Fox and J. M. Harding (Cambridge: Cambridge University Press, 1980). See also Judith P. Butler, *Subjects of Desire: Hegelian Reflections in Twentieth-Century France* (New York: Columbia University Press, 1987); Michael S. Roth, *Knowing and History: Appropriations of Hegel in Twentieth-Century France* (Ithaca, N.Y.: Cornell University Press, 1988).

63. Many adherents of Grand Theory have confused *empirical* inquiry with *empiricist* inquiry. Empiricism names a philosophical tradition that places primary emphasis upon experience in explaining how humans acquire knowledge. Historically, empiricism has often embraced views that the mind is a passive receptacle and that concepts may be reduced to aggregates of sense impressions. No one in film studies espouses an empiricist position.

An *empirical* inquiry is one which seeks answers to its questions from evidence available outside the mind of the inquirer. Film history is empirical in just this way; but so too are all varieties of film criticism, which base their interpretations on evidence intersubjectively available within texts. And most film theory, from Münsterberg to Mitry, has been empirical. Only Grand Theory claims to be nonempirical. (As I've argued earlier in the text, however, its application in interpretation would seem to give it at least some empirical substance.)

Noël Carroll's accompanying essay explores this distinction in detail. Suffice it to say that the middle-level inquiry I am tracing here is at once theoretical and empirical, without being empiricist.

64. Influential examples of gay/lesbian research include Vito Russo, *The Celluloid Closet: Homosexuality in the Movies*, rev. ed. (New York: Harper, 1987) and Richard Dyer, *Now You See It* (New York: Routledge, 1990). On the rediscovery of women filmmakers, see Barbara Koenig Quart, *Women Directors: The Emergence of a New Cinema* (New York: Praeger, 1988); Thérèse Lamartine, *Elles: cinéastes ad lib 1895–1981* (Quebec: Remue-ménage, 1985); and Catherine Portuges, *Screen Memories: The Hungarian Cinema of Márta Mészáros* (Bloomington: Indiana University Press, 1993). G. William Jones's *Black Cinema Treasures Lost and Found* (Denton: University

of North Texas Press, 1991) signals a new era in archival research into African-American cinema. Of the many instances of postcolonial historical analysis, I mention only Randal Johnson, *The Film Industry in Brazil: Culture and the State* (Pittsburgh: University of Pittsburgh Press, 1987); Sumita S. Chakravarty, *National Identity in Indian Popular Cinema, 1947–1987* (Austin: University of Texas Press, 1993); Lizbeth Malmus and Roy Armes, *Arab and African Filmmaking* (London: Zed, 1991); Keyan Tomaselli, *The Cinema of Apartheid: Race and Class in South African Film* (New York: Smyrna/Lake View, 1988); and Nwachukwu Frank Ukadike, *Black African Cinema* (Berkeley: University of California Press, 1994).

65. See André Gardies and Pierre Hafner, *Regards sur le cinéma négro-africain* (Brussels: OCIC, 1987); Manthia Diawara, "Oral Literature and African Film: Narratology in *Wend Kuuni*," in *Questions of Third Cinema* (London: British Film Institute, 1989), ed. Jim Pines and Paul Willemen, pp. 199–212; *Tradition orale et nouveaux médies* (Brussels: OCIC, 1989); and Ukadike, *Black African Cinema*.

66. Examples are the works of Georges Sadoul, Jean Mitry, Lewis Jacobs, and Jay Leyda.

67. See Tino Balio, *United Artists: The Company Built by the Stars* (Madison: University of Wisconsin Press, 1976), *United Artists: The Company That Changed the Film Industry* (Madison: University of Wisconsin Press, 1987), and the work gathered in his anthology, *The American Film Industry*, 2d ed. (Madison: University of Wisconsin Press, 1985); Douglas Gomery, "The Coming of Sound to the American Cinema: A History of the Transition of an Industry," (University of Wisconsin–Madison, Ph.D. diss, 1975); Robert C. Allen, *Vaudeville and Film 1895–1915: A Study in Media Interaction* (New York: Arno Press, 1980); Janet Staiger, "The Hollywood Mode of Production: The Construction of Divided Labor in the Film Industry" (University of Wisconsin–Madison, Ph.D. dissertation, 1981); Kristin Thompson, *Exporting Entertainment: America in the World Film Market, 1907–1934* (London: British Film Institute, 1985); David Bordwell, Janet Staiger, and Kristin Thompson, *The Classical Hollywood Cinema: Film Style and Mode of Production to 1960* (New York: Columbia University Press, 1985).

68. See, for example, Richard Abel, *French Cinema: The First Wave, 1915–1929* (Princeton: Princeton University Press, 1984), and Colin Crisp, *The Classic French Cinema, 1930–1960* (Bloomington: Indiana University Press, 1993).

69. For a discussion of this tradition and citation of other work, see the chapter by Vance Kepley, Jr., in this volume.

70. Discussion of how this might proceed can be found in Robert C. Allen and Douglas Gomery, *Film History: Theory and Practice* (New York: Knopf, 1985), pp. 193–212.

71. I discuss this process in "The Power of a Research Tradition: Prospects for Progress in the Study of Film Style," *Film History* 6, 1 (Spring 1994): 59–79.

72. Jay Leyda's New York University seminars played a pivotal role in promoting fine-grained study of Griffith and his contemporaries. Noël Burch also pioneered work on early film and Japanese cinema, not only in his books (usually published long after he had written them) but also through his teaching in Paris, London, and New York. See Noël Burch, *To the Distant Observer: Form and Meaning in Japanese Cinema* (Berkeley: University of California Press, 1979) and *Life to Those Shadows*, trans. Ben Brewster (Berkeley: University of California Press, 1990).

73. Barry Salt, *Film Style and Technology: History and Analysis* (London: Starword, 1983); Joyce E. Jesionowski, *Thinking in Pictures: Dramatic Structure in D. W. Griffith's Biograph Films* (Berkeley: University of California Press, 1987); *Early Cinema:*

Space Frame Narrative, ed. Thomas Elsaesser (London: British Film Institute, 1990); Ben Brewster, "*Traffic in Souls:* An Experiment in Feature-Length Narrative Construction," *Cinema Journal* 31, 1 (Fall 1991): 37–56; and Bordwell, Staiger, and Thompson, *Classical Hollywood Cinema,* pp. 155–308, 341–64.

74. See Lea Jacobs, "Belasco, DeMille, and the Development of Lasky Lighting," *Film History* 5, 4 (1993); John Belton, *Wide-screen Cinema* (Cambridge: Harvard University Press, 1992).

75. See in particular the work done in the New York University Cinema Studies Department during the 1970s. Affiliated with this tendency is P. Adams Sitney's *Visionary Film: The American Avant-Garde, 1943–1978* (New York: Praeger, 1974).

76. *The Wages of Sin: Censorship and the Fallen Woman Film, 1928–1942* (Madison: University of Wisconsin Press, 1991).

77. See the special issues of *Millennium Film Journal* nos. 14/14 (Fall/Winter 1984–85) and of *Persistence of Vision* 5 (Spring 1987). See also Ian Jarvie, *Philosophy of Film: Epistemology, Ontology, Aesthetics* (New York: Routledge, 1988), and *Philosophy and Film,* ed. Cynthia Freeland and Thomas Wartenberg (New York: Routledge, 1995).

78. See, for example, Edward Branigan, *Point of View in Cinema* (New York: Mouton, 1984); Rick Altman, *The American Film Musical* (Bloomington: Indiana University Press, 1987).

79. See Seymour Chatman, *Story and Discourse: Narrative Structure in Fiction and Film* (Ithaca, N.Y.: Cornell University Press, 1978) and *Coming to Terms: The Rhetoric of Narrative in Fiction and Film* (Ithaca, N.Y.: Cornell University Press, 1990); George M. Wilson, *Narration in Light: Studies in Cinematic Point of View* (Baltimore: Johns Hopkins University Press, 1984); David Bordwell, *Narration in the Fiction Film* (Madison: University of Wisconsin Press, 1985); Sarah Kozloff, *Invisible Storytellers: Voice-Over Narration in American Fiction Film* (Berkeley: University of California Press, 1988); and Edward Branigan, *Narrative Comprehension and Film* (London: Routledge, 1992).

80. See, for example, Stephen Prince and Wayne Hensley, "The Kuleshov Effect: Recreating the Classic Experiment," *Cinema Journal* 31, 2 (Winter 1992): 59–75. I propose another way to think about spectatorship in "A Case for Cognitivism," *Iris* 9 (Spring 1989): 11–40 and "A Case for Cognitivism: Further Reflections," *Iris* 11 (Summer 1990): 107–12.

81. For instance, Mike Cormack's *Ideology and Cinematography in Hollywood, 1930–39* (New York: St. Martin's Press, 1994) utilizes no primary documentation for its historical claims and simply absorbs the research of Balio, Bordwell, Burch, Gomery, Maltby, Roddick, Salt, Thompson, et al. as a basis for subject-positioning readings of some well-known 1930s films.

2

Prospects for Film Theory:
A Personal Assessment

Noël Carroll

Introduction:
The Theory Is Dead, Long Live Theory

The rapid expansion of the film studies institution over the last two decades in the United States was undoubtedly abetted, in one way or another, by something called film theory, or, as its acolytes are apt to say, simply Theory— a classy continental number, centrally composed of elements of Louis Althusser, Jacques Lacan, and Roland Barthes, often with optional features derived, often incongruously, from Michel Foucault, Julia Kristeva, Pierre Bourdieu, Gilles Deleuze, and (*maybe* sometimes) Jacques Derrida, along with contributions from French cinéphiles like Christian Metz, Raymond Bellour, and Jean-Louis Baudry, although generally filtered, albeit with a difference, through exegetes like Stephen Heath, Kaja Silverman, and Teresa de Lauretis.

Universities regarded film studies programs as an economic boon, likely to spur demand and, in this context, Theory, so called, played an economic role in legitimating the formation of film programs. For what went by the name of Theory was surely abstruse enough to convince an uninformed administrator or a hesitant trustee that film studies was at least as complex intellectually as string theory, DNA, or hypotheses about massive parallel processing.

Whether it was necessary to enfranchise film studies in this way is an open question. Perhaps (as I tend to think) market forces alone would have sufficed to establish the institution. But, in any case, Theory appears to have played the ideological-institutional role of enfranchiser, even if the role was ultimately an epiphenomenal one. Furthermore, the expectation of gold in "them thar hills" also encouraged too many university presses to invest in film publications, especially when the arcane peregrinations of Theory facilitated their rationalization of their relaxation of their traditional role as academic gatekeepers. Hence film studies has been flooded with repetitive decoctions of the Theory in search of the same market in much the same way that consumers are confronted with so many marginally differentiated shampoos.

Interestingly, now that film studies seems ensconced in American universities—with TV studies and cultural studies queuing up behind it for legitimation—Theory looks to be on the wane. Certainly people like myself would like to imagine that this is a result of the recognition that the Theory has been soundly refuted, though even I would have to concede that more accurate explanations may be that Theory has outlived its academic utility or that it has merely run out of gas (that is, exhausted itself). But, in any case, however the demise of Theory came about, as it continues to petrify, it becomes appropriate to speculate about whether theorizing—in a small "t," not-a-proper-name sort of way—is possible. For even if Theory is dead, one wonders whether theorizing about film has a future.

Given these circumstances, it is the aim of this essay to explore the prospects for film theory. In order to approach this subject, I shall begin by sketching, in the longest part of this essay, what I take to be major obstacles to film theorizing at present, many of which are legacies of the Theory alluded to above. It is my conviction that as long as these obstacles continue to grip the imaginations of scholars, fruitful theorizing about film will be unlikely.

I will also attempt, in a more abbreviated way, to provide a minimal characterization of what I take to be the most useful framework that we might employ for film theorizing today. Lastly, I will look at the consequences of adopting that framework for assessing one of the leading debates (or, maybe, one of the *only* debates) among contemporary film theorists, namely: the rivalry between psychoanalytic film theory and cognitive theory (a tendency represented by some of the essays in this volume).

Impediments to Film Theorizing

1. Monolithic conceptions of film theory. The history of film theorizing, it seems to me, has been dominated by a conception of what a film theory should be in terms of the model of a unified body of ideas with certain core propositions from which conclusions about concrete cases follow in various ways, once certain empirical possibilities are considered. Metaphorically, we might call such a construal of film theory foundationalist. It is my contention that such monolithic conceptions of film theory stand in the way of productive theorizing about film, which theorizing might be best construed in terms of producing film theories rather than Film Theory.

Film theor*y*, as most frequently practiced heretofore, has been singular; a film theory was generally conceived to be a rather comprehensive instrument that was supposed to answer virtually every legitimate question you might have about film. This view naturally contrasts with a view of our arena of inquiry as plural, that is, a view that commends thinking in terms of film theor*ies* rather than in terms of film theor*y*. That is, rather than theorizing about every element of film style in light of a set of limited theoretical presuppositions— for example, about the purported commitment of the medium to a realism or about its inevitable ideological destiny to suture—one might proceed by constructing local theories—for example, of film suspense, of film metaphor, of camera movement, or narrative comprehension, and even of the rhetoric of ideology—without expecting that these small-scale theories can be collected and unified under an overarching set of presuppositions about either the nature or function of cinema.

Nor is there any reason to think that film theorizing must be restricted to the stylistic features of film. Let us call hypotheses about the operation of international markets on corporate decision making film theory, so long as the hypotheses involve general conjectures about patterns or regularities in the practices of filmmaking, which practices include distribution and its influences as well as cinematic construction and reception. That is, let anything count as film theorizing, so long as it involves the production of generalizations or general explanations or general taxonomies and concepts about film practice.

This view of film theorizing conflicts sharply with certain of the most traditional preconceptions of film theory. What is often called classical film theory not only conceptualizes the activity as Film Theory, but as *Film Theory*—that is, as committed to medium specificity in such a way that whatever counts as theorizing about film must be connected to features of the medium that are thought to be uniquely or essentially cinematic. Film theory must pertain to what is distinctly cinematic, otherwise it shall not count as film theory but as something else, like narrative theory.

Admittedly, narrow, essentialist views of film theory of this sort are infrequently voiced nowadays. However, where they remain influential, as they do in the work of the psychoanalytic film theorist Christian Metz and in the conception of photography of Roland Barthes and his cinematic followers, they are impediments to film theory and need to be dismantled dialectically.

Of course, the greatest problem with essentialist film theory is that it gives every indication of being false. But at the very least, another problem with essentialist film theory is that it blinkers the theoretical imagination by limiting what questions are the correct ones to ask about cinema. Yet, especially since cinematic essentialism seems philosophically dispensable, there appears to be scant reason to abide its restrictions.

Instead of thinking of film theory as a unified, single theory, it might be better to think of it as a field of activity, perhaps like sociological theory, where many different projects—theories of homelessness in America, of generic social cohesion, of class conflict in India, of the resurgence of religious fundamentalism worldwide—of different levels of generality and abstraction coexist without being subsumed under a single general theory. Similarly, film theorizing today should proceed at varying levels of generality and abstraction.

Even if some day, film theorizing might be organized into a general theory (which seems unlikely to me), nevertheless we are hardly in a position to frame such a theory now, since we know so little at this time. And, in any event, the only way that we shall come to know more is by developing small-scale theories about virtually every imaginable aspect of film.

Film theorizing, as I have argued elsewhere, should be piecemeal. But it should also be diversified. Insofar as theorists approach film from many different angles, from different levels of abstraction and generality, they will have to avail themselves of multidisciplinary frameworks. Some questions about film may send the researcher toward economics, while others require a look into perceptual psychology. In other instances, sociology, political science, anthropology, communications theory, linguistics, artificial intelligence, biology, or narrative theory may provide the initial research tools which the film theorist requires in order to begin to evolve theories of this or that aspect of film.

In opposition to the essentialist theorist who might disparage explorations in other disciplines as fatally alloyed, it is my claim that anxieties about theoretical purity are impediments to theoretical discovery. Film theorizing should be interdisciplinary. It should be pursued without the expectation of discovering a unified theory, cinematic or otherwise. That is, it should be catholic about the methodological frameworks it explores.

Perhaps at this historical juncture is seems strange to urge that film theory be multidisciplinary, since it might be asserted that the Theory—that assemblage of Althusser, Lacan, Barthes, et al.—is patently interdisciplinary, given that Althusser was a philosopher, Lacan a psychoanalyst, and Barthes a literary critic. And yet, I wonder about the interdisciplinary pretensions of Theory since Theory, as it is practiced in film departments—and neighboring literature departments—is really a body of canonical texts or authors, which body of authors serves rather like the paradigm of a *single discipline* in the making. It hardly encourages multidisciplinary exploration. It always endorses, when it comes to pictorial perception, for example, another look at the enigmatic sayings of Foucault on *Las Meninas,* rather than reading any recent experimental psychology on the topic of vision.

Indeed, in the mid-1970s, a leading French film Theorist was introduced to an audience which was reassured that, in addition to his expertise in cinema, the speaker was also a master of anthropology, philosophy, art history, semiotics, psychoanalysis, literary studies, linguistics, and so on; to which one wag replied: "Of course, in Paris, it's all the same thing anyway." Whether or not this remark did justice to Parisian intellectual life, at this point in time it provides a fair characterization of Theory (U.S. style) which, far from being multidisciplinary, is rather the approved reading list of assorted departments of textual analysis (both literary and cinematic).

Ironically, film studies in the United States was probably more interdisciplinary in the early seventies, before its apotheosis or, at least, "professionalization" under the auspices of Theory. But that period of experimentation with alternative frameworks—from anthropology and kinesics to phenomenology—was stamped out by the juggernaut of Theory.

It hardly pays to be too nostalgic about the theoretical excursions of the early seventies since, in almost every case, it was dilettantish rather than rigorous, a tendency unfortunately continued under the dispensation of Theory, since its practitioners are almost always getting their philosophy or anthropology from a second- or thirdhand source (rather than generating it themselves). Ideally, film theorists in the future will be genuinely interdisciplinary in the sense that they will have at their command the genuine expertise of a practitioner in more than one discipline, rather than being epigones of a school of thought, united by an approved reading list, with designs for cross-disciplinary imperialism.

Like classic essentialist theory, Theory is an obstacle to authentic theorizing, because it is presented as a unified or totalizing system. Under its aegis, the film theorist sets out to subsume every aspect of cinematic phenomena under the putative laws and categories of his or her minimally customized version of the reigning orthodoxy. Theorizing becomes the routine application of some larger, unified theory to questions of cinema, which procedure unsurprisingly churns out roughly the same answers, or remarkably similar answers, in every case. The net result, in short, is theoretical impoverishment.

The antidote to this impoverishment, I think, is to resist the temptation of totalizing film theory and to follow the lead of piecemeal theorizing wherever it takes us. We should countenance as film theory any line of inquiry dedicated to producing generalizations pertaining to, or general explanations of, filmic phenomena, or devoted to isolating, tracking, and/or accounting for any mechanisms, devices, patterns, and regularities in the field of cinema. As already remarked, this inquiry may transpire at many different levels of generality and abstraction and may take as its objects things as different as cutting practices and industrial contexts.

What makes something film theory is that it is a general answer to a general question that we have about some phenomenon which we think, pretheoretically, falls into the bailiwick of film. Such inquiry is theoretical because it is general, and it is film theory because it pertains to filmic practice. Furthermore, since we can ask so many different kinds of general questions about film, there is no common feature that all of our answers should be expected to share. Some theoretical questions about film—for example, about cinematic perception—may have answers that primarily advert to cinematic forms and structures, whereas other different answers to different questions might refer to economic forces. That is, some theories may be formal, while others may be social. Our collection of film theories may very well comprise a mixed bag. There simply is no reason to think that every film theory will have something to tell us about the same subject—such as the way in which each and every aspect of film figures in the oppression or emancipation of the film viewer.

2. The conflation of film theory with film interpretation. Perhaps the major impediment to film theory in the present moment is the confusion of film theory with film interpretation. Many film scholars imagine that they are producing film theory when they are actually merely contriving interpretations of individual films, albeit in arcane, "theoretically" derived jargon. Unquestionably, it seems to me, one reason we have reached this impasse is that film scholars generally have little, if any, background in the actual practices of theory building, since most of them have exclusively hermeneutical training, as opposed to education in theoretical disciplines such as the natural or social sciences, or philosophy. Consequently, most film scholars do not really understand the difference between theory and interpretation, an obvious liability if film theory is to prosper.

As has been pointed out by David Bordwell in *Making Meaning,* film theory is generally integrated into film studies as a template from which film scholars strike interpretations of individual films. Film theory supplies major premises from which interpretive conclusions can be deduced, once the film has been described (or misdescribed) in such a way as to yield pliable (a.k.a. equivocating) minor premises; or film theory provides the so-called semantic fields against which the exegete does something which looks very much like free association. Moreover, this expropriation of theory for the sake of interpretation is exacerbated by the typical condition of film education, which puts such a high premium on the construction of interpretations of individual films, since standardly film education is mired in the one class/one film format (a format reflected in a great many professional articles on film).

One could, of course, imagine the production of a theory of film interpretation. However, the interpretation of individual films is not theory, no matter how technical the language of the interpretation appears. For theory involves evolving categories and hypothesizing the existence of general patterns; but finding that those categories and hypotheses are instantiated in a particular case is not a matter of theory. It's the difference between discovering the existence of a viral syndrome and finding that Henry has it.

In addition, not all, but a great deal of theorizing involves causal reasoning, which is different from the interpretation of meaning. What is so strange about the spectacle of "film theory" over the last two decades is that so often film exegetes proceed by reading the Theory into a film, as if the presence of subject positioning—putatively a causal process—could be confirmed by hermeneutically alleging to find the allegory of the Imaginary retold in a selected film. Given enough latitude, you can probably allegorize anything to say whatever you wish, but that won't establish causal connections where there are none. Where film theory provides interpreters with allegories to read into whatever they wish, the prospects for causal research are bleak.

There are no grounds for thinking that film theory must have anything to do with film interpretation in every case. Indeed, in many cases, one would anticipate that the two activities would have to part company. Film theory speaks of the general case, whereas film interpretation deals with problematic or puzzling cases, or with the highly distinctive cases of cinematic masterworks. Film theory tracks the regularity and the norm, while film interpretation finds its natural calling in dealing with the deviation, with what violates the norm or with what exceeds it or what re-imagines it.

Perhaps, at times, film theory provides a background that enables a critic to locate what is interesting about some divergence from the general pattern or function of a device or a cinematic figure. Even allowing this possibility, two other thoughts should be kept in mind. First, that one doesn't require a theory in order to spot a divergence, since an intuitively constructed comparison class will turn the trick. Second, that not every theory can function in this way. Certain economic theories of industrial formation may be irrelevant to interpretation, due to their level of generality, while certain physiological theories of film perception may be equally irrelevant, because they are exceptionless. And, of course, it is also the case that the theory of some standard filmic device, like point-of-view editing, may remark upon some phenomena so mundane that it turns out to be never germane to interpretation.

Nor, in fact, would a general theory be a panacea for interpretation. For showing that a film is an instance of a general theory would imply that the film is, in certain respects, routine, that is, pretty much like everything else in the same theoretical domain, and, therefore, not really worthy of special interpretation.

Over the last two decades, what has been called Interpretation Inc. has proceeded, oblivious to the preceding objection, applying the Theory, or fragments of the Theory, like a philosopher's stone, transforming every film in sight into a glittering interpretation. But not only does this seem in tension conceptually with the idiographic (as opposed to the nomothetic) direction of interpretation; it also becomes deadly monotonous as every film comes out of the standard-issue sausage machine, looking and smelling the same.

Not only do contemporary film scholars pretend to find technique after technique and film after film that exemplify this or that general pattern—such as imaginary identification or subject positioning—film scholars also claim to find films that *express* the theories in question, that is, films, including B pictures, that share themes with such figures as Freud, Lévi-Strauss, and Lacan. Probably anything can be made to say anything else once interpretive protocols get as loose as they are in criticism departments nowadays, but the problem I wish to point to is not the obvious anachronism of so many of these interpretations, but to the fact that counterfeiting such interpretations does not constitute theory building. If indeed it could be plausibly shown that the film *Every Man For Himself and God Against All* independently discovered the Lacanian scenario of the child's entry into language, then it would be Herzog and not his exegete who would count as a theorist.

Moreover, where the purposes of interpretation drive theory choice, the prospects for film theory are slim. For the theories that are most serviceable for exegetes will be those whose central terms are maximally vague, ambiguous, or unconstrained in terms of criteria of application. For such theories can be applied to the widest number of cases, if only by equivocation and fanciful association. Interpretive productivity would seem to vary inversely with the precision of a theory. Theories with the greatest "weasel factor" are more attractive to scholars concerned primarily with producing interpretations, because such theories will be applicable almost everywhere and in more ways than one. They will be, as the saying goes, "productive." And yet, where clarity and precision are altogether ignored, theory might as well be skywriting.

Not only has theory been confused with interpretation in recent film scholarship; it also becomes conflated with film criticism, where Post-Structuralism gets identified with modernist, or, if you prefer, postmodernist film practice. Thus, Laura Mulvey discovers that classical filmmaking is nothing short of psychosexually regressive, while the difficulty of her own counter-cinema promises evolution to the Symbolic, as if avant-garde, modernist film practice went hand in hand with maturity. Indeed, far too often over the last two decades has so-called Theory been enlisted to serve in the partisan cause of various film movements.

It might be argued that the preceding characterization of the conflation of interpretation and theory fits the eighties better than it does the present. For today, it might be said, there is much less faith in the Theory than there was yesteryear. Fragments of the Theory remain in the vocabulary of film scholars; they talk of subject positioning, for instance. But this is done without commitment to the full Theory from which such fragmentary phrases derive. However, if this is true, it provides an even greater obstacle to future theorizing, since the persistence of archaic Theory-talk accentuates the illusion that people are doing theory. Thus, whereas in the past the prospects for theory were impeded by the conflation of interpretation with theory, now it seems that what can be said about Interpretation Inc. is that interpretation is being conflated with the illusion of theory.

3. Political correctness. As has been repeated endlessly in narratives of the cinema studies establishment, its Theory was perceived to have been erected on the barricades as part of the cultural upheavals of the late sixties and early seventies. May 1968 is the date fashionably bruited about, though this is more a matter of symbolical than historical significance, as far as the literal institutionalization of film studies is concerned. Nevertheless, it is true that the by-now middle-aged film establishment underwent its rite of passage through the New Left, and, though presently well over thirty, the survivors still trust themselves as keepers of the light.

Certainly, one would not want to demean what was humane and just in the political claims of the student movement of the Vietnam years, nor to deny that a great deal of that agenda was and still is worthy of endorsement. However, it is not clear that those ideals are served in any respectable way by allegiance to the Theory.

Proponents of the Theory let on that the Theory grew out of the student movement and out of a resistance to oppression everywhere. Consequently, from their point of view, criticism of the Theory virtually represents a clear and present danger to the very Revolution itself. Anyone who opposes the Theory, for whatever reason, is politically suspect—probably a ruling class, neoconservative, homophobic misogynist. Criticisms of the dubious psycho-analytic premises of the Theory are denounced as reactionary—in a political sense!—as if a belief in the equality of the races requires assent to Lacan and the rest of the pet paraphernalia of the Theory. Wrapping themselves in virtue, as others might wrap themselves in a flag, Theorists frequently resemble nothing so much as radical versions of those scoundrels whose last resort is said to be patriotism.

Though the issue of political correctness on American college campuses is generally ballyhooed by the right wing through horror stories about student suspensions and the theft of newspapers and artworks, it seems to me that the real threat of political correctness is far more subtle. Namely, it protects bad scholarship. Fear that one will be denounced as politically incorrect—as racist, sexist, classist, homophobic, etc.—intimidates generally liberal scholars in such a way that they refrain from speaking out honestly about the extremely poor quality of much of what passes for argument and research in the humanities today. Instead they complain in hushed tones among themselves. Academic cowardice promotes self-censorship both inside and outside film studies, restraining frank criticism of often shoddy thinking and slapdash scholarship on the part of many who fear being publicly labeled politically suspect, even in cases where the actual voting records and the actual political positions—on gay rights, the ERA, affirmative action, and so on—of many of those who hawk Theory and those who oppose it would be indistinguishable.

The Theory has been effectively insulated from sustained logical and empirical analysis by a cloak of political correctness. Speaking from personal experience, I can recall more than one occasion when, as a result of my criticism of the Theory, people told me that they were surprised by my conversion to neoconservatism, despite no discernible changes in my real-world political views (which amount to a version of democratic socialism).

Skepticism about the theoretical usefulness of concepts like the male gaze, or, to be more timely, about the glance, invites accusations of reactionary backlash. It is as if Lacanian psychoanalysis and civil rights advocacy (for persons of color, for women, for gays) were so indissolubly linked logically that one could not affirm one without the other. This is not only patently ridiculous; it is also an immensely self-serving idea for proponents of the Theory to encourage. And, it almost goes without saying, such an atmosphere is inimical to a context in which genuine theorizing might flourish, since theoretical discourse requires open channels of critical communication, not repression.

In film studies, rival theories to the Theory are rejected out of hand as politically pernicious. One very popular gambit, which I will discuss, is to argue that competing views are "formalist." These "arguments" are little more than ad hominem attacks. Furthermore, inasmuch as the very practice of theorizing requires maximally free and open debate, the veil of political correctness that envelope film studies compromises the very discursive structure that makes film theory possible.

Contemporary film Theorists, along with many of their colleagues in literature departments, are very confident of their ability to detect the ideological perspective of rival theories. Rather than debate the explicit, cognitive claims of competitors, they seek to unmask the putatively underlying politics of critical views of the Theory. In this, they appear to ape the Marx and Engels of *The German Ideology*. However, I wonder whether these exercises in "ideology critique" are really fundamentally sound.

A great many film theories come without political badges affixed to them. And in such cases, it is surely a mistake to think that the theory strictly entails any specific political view on concrete issues, such as gay civil rights, the thirty-five-hour work week, abortion, or ecology, or even broad political stances, such as Leninism. I have evolved theories of movie music and point-of-view editing, but they do not, in any sense that could be called logical, imply my political position about anything from gun control, to sexual harassment, to communal ownership of the means of production. For these theories, like so many others, underdetermine whatever political allegiances a given individual might believe in addition to believing them. Many film theories, including ones which their proponents (like Eisenstein) may think have explicit political implications, may in fact be compatible with an extremely wide range of political alignments, including even nonconverging and conflicting political commitments.

If with respect to a given specific film theory, an ideologue can tell a story about how it goes with reactionary politics, it is generally the case that, logically speaking, one can tell just as good a story about how it might go with emancipatory politics. For example, one might say that the New Criticism in post–World War II literary studies was reactionary because it bracketed political considerations, but, equally, the case might be made that it was democratic, since it freed the reader from the supposed tyranny of The Author. Moreover, this sort of egalitarianism, even if it is ultimately misplaced, is certainly as discernible in the writings of Monroe Beardsley as it is in those of Roland Barthes.

Insofar as aesthetic theories, such as film theories, generally underdetermine the political viewpoints with which they are compatible, there is generally no real point in diagnosing them for their political allegiances. Of course, in a concrete case, a film theorist may actually link a theory with a political agenda, and that linkage is certainly worth comment, especially in terms of whether the linkage really has the logical substance its proponents aver. For example, the claimed linkage may be exaggerated. Think of how many avant-garde pretensions to Marxism come to look strained in retrospect. However, the likelihood that many explicitly unallied theories actually entail political positions is too low to warrant the wholesale, unrestrained witch-hunt for unacknowledged ideological taintedness abroad in the humanities today.

I would not want to preclude the possibility that someone might hold a certain theory due to ideological bias. And such bias, where it can be shown to exist, deserves criticism. Nevertheless, one has to establish the bias *independently of the theory held*. For as we've seen already, a theory that makes no explicit political reference rarely wears any political affiliation on its sleeve. Furthermore, even when a given theorist has been shown to be politically biased, one still must ask whether the theory might be held by others for reasons that are unbiased.

Film Theorists, like their colleagues in literature departments, appear to accept something like a holistic account of theoretical commitments, by which I mean they believe that every aspect of a theorist's belief system has repercussions for every other aspect. It is something like the doctrine of internal relations applied to the belief systems of theorists. This is why when it was discovered that people like Paul de Man and Martin Heidegger had Nazi sympathies, the hermeneutical establishment in this country was thrown into apoplexy. For since it was presumed that theory entails politics and vice-versa, the personal Nazism of the theorists in question raised worries about the latent fascism of the theories.

But, if I am right, and the relation between theory and politics in most cases is logically indeterminate, then there was in reality little reason for the comic efforts at damage control that were staged in the name of deconstruction. One might have observed that, for example, Heidegger's Nazism was a personal inclination logically detachable from the more abstract formulations of existential phenomenology. Ironically enough, deconstructionists were unable to avail themselves of such sober detachment because their Hegelian proclivities predisposed them to a residue of unacknowledged holism.

Generally, literary theories and film theories underdetermine political commitments. Rarely does a theory follow in any strict sense from one's politics, or vice-versa. Given theories may be espoused by either the forces of light or the forces of darkness. If only for this reason, one should be chary of assessing film theories solely in terms of ideology-critique. Moreover, in order to establish that a theory is ideologically tainted, one needs to show that it is false *and* that one could only come to embrace the theory for politically unsavory reasons (involving some motive of political domination). But in order to show even this requires a discursive theoretical context free from and unconstrained by preemptory, ad hominem charges of political incorrectness.

4. *Charges of formalism.* This impediment is really a corollary of the problem of political correctness. For it seems a fair conjecture that charges of political incorrectness are most often leveled at rivals to the Theory in the language of

formalism. To call an alternative theory formalist is, in other words, a way of saying that the alternative theory is politically incorrect.

Like most bullying epithets, "formalism," as used in contemporary film studies, is rather ill-defined. In general, it seems counterposed to the "political." Sometimes, of course, it is also opposed to the "historical," but usually by persons who presume, strangely enough, that a historical approach is coeval with a politically sensitive one. Calling a theorist a formalist may signal that the theorist is concerned with form rather than content, with structures rather than their political consequences, or with cinematic forms, irrespective of the political content that is thought to be inherent in those forms.

In the current context of theoretical debate, charges of formalism are most frequently leveled at positions that are often labeled cognitivist, a label that fits some of the contributions found in this volume. Cognitivism itself is not a unified theory. Instead, it is a stance toward film research, one that advocates the exploration of hypotheses about film reception in terms of the cognitive and perceptual processes of spectators, rather than in terms of the unconscious processes and syndromes favored by the Theory.

Proponents of the Theory usually endorse psychoanalysis because they believe that ideology works through unconscious processes. Insofar as they are confident that they can link the interaction of cinematic structures and unconscious processes to ideology, they think that their program is not formalist. But inasmuch as cognitivists proceed as if they can analyze some forms of cinematic perception without connecting them with political consequences, cognitivists are said to be formalist. Indeed, it is generally assumed, though never demonstrated, that cognitivism cannot, in principle, deliver insight about the political consequences of cinematic design for audience reception.

But, in at least one respect, the charge of formalism against cognitivists is bogus. For there is no reason to think that putative connections between cinematic form and political consequences can only be forged by psychoanalysis, and not by cognitivism. The cognitivist need not be a formalist in the sense of denying—like some latter-day Clive Bell—that film has nothing to do with politics, or that cinematic structures never have political consequences. That would be absurd.

Film has political and ideological dimensions. Cognitivists have never rejected that fact, and they have even attempted to analyze such phenomena where it has seemed pertinent. For example, though I am frequently called a formalist, I have tried to provide theoretical frameworks for discussing the image of women in film and the relation of film, rhetoric, and ideology (see the selected bibliography for this volume), and in doing this I surely acknowledge that cinematic structures can have political consequences. David Bordwell, reputedly the epitome of arch-formalism, has examined the institutional bases of film technology and the political significance of Ozu's films.

Cognitivists can readily acknowledge that film has a political dimension, and they can and have studied it. Though, of course, insofar as they are cognitivists, they will attempt to discover the role that *cognitive* processes play in the dissemination of ideology. Nothing, in principle, implies that it is impossible for cognitivists to illuminate the relation between film and politics, and, in point of fact, some cognitivist research in this direction has already been attempted. Surely there can be nothing politically or theoretically suspicious about hypothesizing that ideology might engage cognitive processes. After all, if one studies the action of ideology on cognitive processes, one must acknowledge the relevance of politics. Moreover, why should anyone antecedently assume that hypotheses about cognitive processes in the formation of ideology are any less germane than psychoanalytic ones?

But this concession, of course, would indicate that cognitivism is a rival to the established Theory, a rival that proposes alternative ways of dealing with much of the same phenomena that interests proponents of the Theory. And if this is the case, shouldn't one refrain from prejudging which hypotheses are superior, until the debate has been fully joined?

Unfortunately, the frequent ad hominem charges that cognitivism is naught but formalism attempt to block meaningful debate before it begins. Proponents of the Theory muddy the waters by crudely insinuating that cognitivists cannot even play in the same political ballpark that the Theory does. Such allegations attempt to shout cognitivism off the playing field. In this regard, charges of formalism are an evasion and in that sense an impediment to genuine theoretical debate.

Film scholars, in my experience, seem so anxious about the issue of formalism because of their convictions that we find ourselves in a moment of political crisis, in which an understanding of the operation of ideology is paramount. In such circumstances, a concern with forms and structures strikes them as being as frivolous as Nero fiddling while Rome burned. But this obsession with crisis, again, should not, in principle, set them against cognitivism, since cognitive hypotheses about the operation of ideology in film and TV may be as useful as tools, or even more useful than those available from the Theory. Thus, if political understanding is really what they care about, rather than preempting the debate between cognitivism and the Theory, shouldn't film scholars want it to proceed?

There is, of course, one noteworthy difference between cognitivists and proponents of the Theory. Cognitivists, unlike proponents of the Theory, tend to believe that there are aspects of cinematic reception that can be studied independently of questions of political or ideological consequences. Thus, one will find cognitivists offering theories about cinematic perception or about narrative comprehension, without talking about the political or ideological consequences of these processes. Cognitivists like myself would even contend that, in certain relevant respects, some of these processes may be politically or ideologically neutral.

But this does not make me a formalist *tout court*, since I also agree that there may be—indeed, I think there *are*—other processes crucial to film research where the consideration of political and ideological consequences is pertinent. I think, for example, that one can theoretically isolate certain mechanisms that are responsible for the propagation of racism through film. Thus, though I think that theories about point-of-view editing might be framed, pace Daniel Dayan, without a discussion of some putatively invariant, ideological effect, I am not a formalist in the sense that I think it is never intelligible to examine the relation of film and ideology.

Proponents of the Theory are likely to respond to this as proof that cognitivists like me are formalists. For they believe that *every* level of cinematic reception is fraught with political and ideological repercussions. Yet this, it seems to me, must be an empirical conjecture. And as such, it seems highly dubious.

For example, if we are studying horror films, it strikes me as incontrovertible that filmmakers often play upon what psychologists call the "startle response," an innate human tendency to "jump" at loud noises and to recoil at fast movements. This tendency is, as they say, impenetrable to belief; that is, our beliefs won't change the response. It is hardwired and involuntary. Awareness of this response enables theorists like me to explain the presence of certain audiovisual patterns and effects in horror films, without reference to politics and ideology. Indeed, insofar as the startle response is impenetrable to belief, it could be said to be, in certain respects, beyond politics and ideology. Moreover, such examples indicate that there is a stratum of theoretical investigation at the level of cognitive architecture that can proceed while bracketing questions of ideology.

I would not, of course, deny that a film critic might want to analyze the use of the startle response in a given horror film in terms of the political agenda of the film in question. But as I argued earlier, this is a matter of film interpretation, not film theory. The fact that cognitivist theoretical insights at the level of generic structures might enable political interpretation in no way indicates that cognitive research cannot advance without bracketing political questions in certain cases.

It is my contention that certain questions that theorists of cinema address are, in relevant respects, nonpolitical, and that the answers theorists provide to them are also nonpolitical. Theories about the perception of cinematic movement and about the recognition of cinematic images are obvious candidates here. Theories in this domain may indeed concentrate on what might be thought of as forms and structures. But, again, this stance is not formalism *tout court,* since the cognitivist may, in addition, freely acknowledge that other cinematic phenomena, such as the reinforcement of sexual stereotypes, will involve considerations of both content and the mechanisms by which that content is conveyed.

But proponents of the Theory, on the other hand, presuppose that every aspect of cinema is implicated in ideology and that the cognitivist attempt to conceptualize some aspects of cinema as detachable from ideology is nothing but rank formalism. As I have already argued, this claim seems empirically insupportable. Nor is it conceivable that all cinematic phenomena are by definition political. Surely, the perception of cinematic movement, the recognition of the cinematic image, and the comprehension of narrative will have the same biological, psychological, and cognitive foundations in any humanly imaginable, nonrepressive, classless, egalitarian utopia that those perceptual and cognitive processes have in present-day Los Angeles. To stamp one's feet and to insist that every dimension of film must have an ideological dimension (by dint of cinematic ontology?) is simply dogmatic.

But perhaps the proponent of the Theory will defend her or his political perspective by saying that it is simply a *heuristic* hypothesis. In other words, it might be advocated that it is empirically productive to begin with the supposition that, when approaching any cinematic phenomena, it is most fruitful to think about it in terms of ideology. That is, in every case, first ask yourself how the phenomenon at hand contributes to ideology. This is always a revelatory question. This is a powerful research program, and it will yield compelling results.

Maybe.

And yet, if this is how the Theory is to be defended, I would argue that we have already seen its results and they are underwhelming. For the last two decades, under the pressure of this heuristic hypothesis, we have witnessed an array of hypotheses that stretch credulity. They have been either vacuous or strained to the breaking point by "explanations" that turn out to be little more than puns. This is not the place to enumerate, once again, the well-known flaws of the Theory, but only to point out that as a heuristic, the record shows that it has little to recommend it.

The underlying presupposition of the Theory, on the basis of which it dismisses its competitors as formalist, is that every aspect of cinematic reception is ideological. But if the preceding discussion is accurate, then this presupposition is unwarranted and the charges that have been issued on its account are overdrawn. This, of course, does not mean that no aspect of cinematic reception involves ideology. And, indeed, a theoretical position that embraced that assumption might, in fact, (depending on its details) be formalist, and, in any case, false, at least to my way of thinking. However, competitors to the Theory, like cognitivism, do not presuppose that questions about ideology are necessarily foreign to theoretical research, and cognitivists have attempted to model some cognitive mechanisms that might be important to understanding the operation of ideology in film.

Whether cognitivism provides the best inroad to studying the role of ideology in film remains to be seen. However, there may be one insight of the cognitivist approach that commends itself for future film theorizing. The cognitivist regards the phenomena to be explored as multidimensional. Some dimensions may invite ideological analysis, others may not. Theorizing must be adjusted appropriately. Some theoretical questions may be best answered in what might be called formal or structural terms, others may be best answered with an eye toward political consequences. Sometimes the theoretical answers to questions about one dimension of analysis may be segued with answers from another level of analysis; sometimes not. Future theorizing depends on openness to a variety of research projects of different levels of abstraction in the theoretical field.

On the other hand, to suppose, as the regnant Theory does, that all theorizing must be political is, as I have been proposing, a dogmatic obstacle to future theorizing. It is an inexcusable contraction of the field. Moreover, indiscriminate charges of formalism, as they are currently bandied about, are an instrument of that dogmatism; we can hope for little progress in film theorizing until there is a moratorium on such name-calling. To continue otherwise, at this point in time, is nothing less than an evasion of the intellectual responsibilities of film theorizing.

5. Biases against truth. Oddly enough, though the last two decades of film studies is generally heralded in terms of the importance of Theory, there is often a reluctance among film scholars to say that they believe that theoretical hypotheses (including, presumably, their own) are true. Indeed, often objections to the Theory are discounted on the grounds that critics like me hold onto the naïve, benighted belief that theories might be true or false, whereas your sophisticated, postmodernist film Theorist realizes such thinking is a merely residual Enlightenment fantasy.

I have actually attended a film conference where one of these sophisticated, postmodernist film Theorists announced that he and his confreres were skeptical about ideas of truth and falsity. He said that they doubt the idea of truth. But, I (probably naïvely) must confess that I couldn't make any sense of this paradoxical pronouncement, since it seemed to say that he and his friends believe that the idea of truth—or the proposition that "some statements are true"—is not true, or, perhaps, that it is false. But such judgments unquestionably presuppose some conception of truth in order to be intelligible.

Of course, if we jettison notions of truth and falsity, it is hard to imagine the way in which film theorizing will proceed. Perhaps it will be suggested that this is simply my own failure of imagination, since we might talk about film theories in terms of plausibility and implausibility, rather than in terms of truth and falsity. But then again, it is hard to get a handle on the concept of plausibility without a notion of truth, since to be plausible is to give the appearance of truth, or to be worthy of acceptance as true, or to be likely to be true.

On the other hand, maybe some notion of political efficacy is supposed to substitute for the role that truth and falsity play for the likes of me in evaluating theories. But how can one gauge what is politically efficacious—that is, truly politically efficacious—without some background notions of truth and falsity, or plausibility or implausibility? Indeed, what could political efficacy come to if it were determined altogether independently of what is or is not the case, or, at least, what is likely or unlikely to be the case? And, furthermore, who could care about a conception of political efficacy totally divorced from what is or might be the case?

Film scholars are not alone in abjuring truth. It is open season on truth throughout the humanities. But why, one wonders, are scholars across the humanities so cavalier about their commitment to the idea of truth? Especially where the scholars in question are politicized, one would predict that they should be concerned with the truth, since most frequently in the real-world political debates that they care about, they are more likely to have the truth than they are likely to have the ballots on their side.

But that is not the way it is. Throughout the humanities, those who cleave to standards of truth and falsity are regarded as at best a confused remnant and at worst the academic equivalent of racist skinheads. How did truth come to get such a bad name?

It seems to me to rest on a fallacious argument that has many variations in different arenas of humanistic discourse. I call it the refutation of absolute truth argument, or the argument from absolute truth, for short. Before sketching the general form of this argument, however, it is useful to consider some of its most familiar variations. The first one goes like this.

Consider the interpretation of a text, filmic or otherwise. Most texts (indeed, it is frequently said, *all* texts) have more than one legitimate interpretation. Therefore, it is surmised, there is no true interpretation of a text. Now clearly this argument is stupendously unconvincing. For a text may have more than one, true interpretation. It is true that *Animal Farm* is about totalitarianism *and* it is true that it is about Stalinism. Thus, it does not follow that if a text has more than one interpretation, that there are not true interpretations of the text. For, obviously, there may be more than one *true* interpretation of a text.

But why do people think that the no-true-interpretation is acceptable? Because they seem to believe that if an interpretation is true, then that means that it is exhaustive—that it says everything that there is to say about a text. In other words, they assume that truth is a matter of what we might more accurately call Absolute Truth, where the Absolute Truth about a text gives you everything that there is to know about it. If an interpretation is absolutely true, then there is nothing left over to add.

But there is generally something else to say; there is generally room for further interpretation. So, no interpretation is absolutely true, or, at least, the prospects for an absolutely true interpretation are very, very, very slight (pertaining perhaps to some minimal texts that are virtually completely and determinately explicit, if there are any such texts).

So far, so good. But the fatal error in the refutation of absolute truth argument is to move from a denial that there are *absolutely* true interpretations to a denial that there are *true* interpretations—that is, true interpretations in the garden variety sense of truth that applies to propositions like "George Washington was the first president of the United States."

Similarly, it is often argued with respect to narratives that no narrative can be true. Why? Because with respect to a given event or state of affairs, it can always be emplotted as an element in another story. But again, that the assassination of Lincoln can figure in the history of the Reconstruction *or* in the history of nineteenth-century acting does not show that both stories cannot be true. It only shows that neither history is absolutely true, or, to say it differently, it only shows that there are no Absolute Stories (perhaps of the sort to which Hegel aspired).

But the plausibility of the conjecture that there are no (or, perhaps, very, very few) Absolute Truths of the variety suggested above does not show that there are not true stories or true interpretations. Nor does the implausibility of there being any Absolute Truths—that is, completely exhaustive, comprehensive, final statements—about my furniture undermine the truth of the time-indexed proposition that "My computer is now on my red table."

What does this excursus into Absolute Truth have to do with the vaunted suspicion of truth amongst film scholars? Simply this: Just as film scholars suppose that there is no absolutely true film interpretation, they suppose that there is no absolutely true film theory—one that is completely comprehensive, that says everything there is to say about film from every perspective, and that is final, unrevisable in principle, and closed *sub specie aeternitatis*.

Well, that's (dare I say it?) true. But, even if this admission begins to make some sense of our colleagues' professed skepticism about truth, it certainly doesn't justify that skepticism. For there might be some limited theoretical conjecture—about the perceptual process of recognizing a cinematic image of Gregory Peck to be the image of a man—which is true, but which does not pretend to be an exhaustive analysis, theoretical or otherwise, of any given image from *Behold a Pale Horse*. That is, one may recant the dream that film theories are "true," in the sense of exhaustive, final-word, unrevisable, Absolute Truth, while still employing what high school teachers, perhaps not so jejunely, sometimes call the concept of "small-t" *truth*.

When one questions film scholars and their colleagues in literary criticism about their oxymoronic "doubt of the concept of truth," the argument from absolute truth is what I have generally been offered in return. But clearly the argument is directed at a straw man (straw person?).

Put schematically, it maintains that, for any imaginable topic, there is always something more that can be said about it than can be summarized in a single pronouncement, assertion, theory, story, interpretation, and so on; therefore, there is no true pronouncement, assertion, theory, story, interpretation, and so on. But this conclusion makes logical sense only if we take it to indicate that there is no *single*, true assertion, theory, story, or interpretation about the subject. And this is compatible with there being more than one true assertion, story, interpretation, theory, and so on. Thus, the argument poses no objection to the discourse of garden-variety truth and falsity when it comes to constructing and evaluating aesthetic theories.

A major ramification of this for film theory is that proponents of the Theory cannot resort to the argument from absolute truth in order to silence their critics. For in the pertinent context of debate, the argument is made of straw. It wrongly presupposes that critics of the Theory, like me, are possessed by some childish faith in Absolute Truth, the silliness of which can be quickly exorcized with a splash of postmodernism. But this putative refutation is painfully irrelevant. When I claim to evaluate tenets of the Theory in light of ordinary standards of truth and falsity, I have nothing so arcane as Absolute Truth in mind, and, in consequence, my objections, and objections like them, cannot be dismissed as Enlightenment extravangances.

Contemporary Theorists not only suspect truth for the roughly pop-philosophical reasons just rehearsed, but also because they believe that experience has taught them that horrible things have been done in the name of the truth. Racial discrimination and sexual oppression have been justified in virtue of theories that were said to be true. Claims about truth have been used to deny certain people opportunities on the grounds that it was supposedly *known* that the people in question were unsuited for education, for intellectual labor, or even civilized treatment. Thus, it is concluded, it always pays to distrust or to be wary of truth claims, since they may be as useful, if not more useful, a lever for social domination as a cudgel. Hence, skepticism about truth.

But, of course, before reaching this conclusion, one must consider whether there is *anything* that cannot ever be used in the service of social oppression. For it should be clear that we cannot refrain from every practice and every concept that might be manipulated or distorted to advance social oppression. Instead, one must be careful and vigilant, rather than ataractic in the ancient skeptical sense. It is one thing to greet truth claims with healthy distrust, as any scientist would, and another thing to deny the relevance of criteria of truth and falsity altogether. That is throwing the baby out with the bath water. Moreover, disregarding the baby in question is particularly reckless when one recalls that the most effective weapon against ideological rationalizations advanced in the name of truth is the possibility of revealing them to be false.

Perhaps one of the strangest results—at least from the viewpoint of emancipatory politics—of the inveterate skepticism of film scholars toward truth was the response of many members of the Society of Cinema Studies to the tape of the Rodney King beating. Insofar as many SCS members are skeptics about truth, they also appear to doubt the evidentiary value of film and video. Consequently, their theory parted company with their politics in the King case. Politically they wanted to be as outraged as everyone else, whereas theoretically they "had proven" antecedently that film and video could never convey truths, but only fictions.

In order to negotiate this embarrassment, some members of the SCS declared the doctrine of "strategic realism." This seems to be the notion that if it suits your politics, then you can talk with the vulgar and act as if film images and videotape can be evidentiary, even though you know that, theoretically, this is a pipe dream. However, strategic realism can hardly be a satisfactory solution. Not only does it strike members of the vulgar crowd, like myself, to be opportunistic and, indeed, a form of lying (one that is so transparent that it seems laughable); but strategic realism does not stave off the necessity for acknowledging standards of truth and falsity for long, since notions of truth and falsity will surely come into play in determining what does and does not suit one's political purposes in a given context.

As long as standards of truth and falsity are thought to be altogether eminently dispensable, Neanderthal throwbacks, film theory will flounder. It will be difficult to understand the way in which we should take theoretical "assertions," including those of the Theory, as well as how we are to assess them. At the same time, without notions of truth and falsity, along with derivative concepts, like plausibility and implausibility, it is unclear how we shall criticize theoretical hypotheses. But if we are unable to criticize theoretical hypotheses, there are no prospects for film theory.

A Framework for Film Theorizing

I have just indicated my conviction that criticism is integral to film theory. In this, I am not claiming film theory is distinctive, but that, like most other forms of theoretical inquiry, it proceeds dialectically. Theories are framed in specific historical contexts of research for the purpose of answering certain questions, and the relative strengths of theories are assayed by comparing the answers they afford to the answers proposed by alternative theories. This conception of theory evaluation is pragmatic because: (1) it compares actual, existing rival answers to the questions at hand (rather than every logically conceivable answer); and (2) because it focuses on solutions to contextually motivated theoretical problems (rather than searching for answers to any conceivable question one might have about cinema).

I suspect that if one were to scan the history of film theory, one would see that the dialectical element is generally present in one way or another in most film theories. Film theorists have always been involved in debates in which they advance the superiority of their findings over competing views. This is to be expected since dialectical criticism has been a basic route for theoretical inquiry at least since Plato. Defending one's own theory by demonstrating that it succeeds where alternative theories falter is a natural direction of argument, as well as of spirited conversation. Even proponents of the Theory begin by criticizing alternative approaches as a primary means for arguing for the advantages of their own hypotheses over others. Thus, in maintaining that the fundamental framework for film theory is dialectical, I am not saying anything very contentious. Few today, I suppose, will want to maintain explicitly that film theories typically derive from first principles or axioms.

However, although a conception of film theorizing as dialectical is unexceptionable, I suspect that the importance of this feature for the practice of film theory has been frequently underappreciated. For sustained, detailed, intertheoretical debate and criticism is rare in the history of film theory. There are, of course, exceptions. Christian Metz's writings are particularly noteworthy for their careful, extended consideration of previous research and its shortcomings; and the deft way in which V. F. Perkins (in *Film as Film*) introduces his own theory by first clarifying the dialectical context in which its intervention is to make a difference is exemplary.

Nevertheless, in the normal course of events in film theory, the dialectical moment is hasty. Nowadays this tendency is particularly pronounced in discussions of cognitivism, which view is swiftly dismissed by castigating buzzwords like "formalism" or maybe "idealism," uttered just before the author goes on to repeat at length, yet again, the received wisdom of Theory.

Speaking as a self-appointed reformer, I wish to emphasize the need for film theorizing to become more conscious of its dialectical responsibilities. Where film theory blurs into film criticism, there is the ever-present danger that theoretical premises will be taken as given—as effectively inoculated from criticism—and, once so assumed, then used to generate "interesting" interpretations. My concern is that more attention be focused on these premises, that they be subjected to intense theoretical criticism, and that alternative answers to the questions these theories address be developed and analyzed through dialectical comparison with each other.

In the spirit of such reform, many of the essays in this volume are critical, especially of the established Theory, and many introduce criticism of the flaws in extant theory as part of a process of dialectical argumentation by which new theories are advanced, constructed, and defended. Indeed, generally one of the most effective ways in which to argue in behalf of a theory and to defend it is to show that it does a better job answering the questions posed by competing views, or by showing that there is a better way to pose the questions that animate existing views. That is why criticism is so integral to film theory, as well as other areas of inquiry.

Theory building builds on previous histories of theorizing as well as upon data (which may be theory-laden). Present theories are formulated in the context of past theories. Apprised of the shortcomings in past theories, through processes of continued scrutiny and criticism, present theories try to find more satisfactory answers to the questions that drive theoretical activity. Sometimes advances involve incremental improvements within existing paradigms; sometimes new paradigms are required to accommodate the lacunae made evident by the anomalies that beset previous theorizing. Sometimes the driving theoretical questions need to be redefined; sometimes they need to be broken down into more manageable questions; sometimes these questions need to be recast radically. And all this requires a free and open discursive context, one in which criticism is not the exception, but the rule.

Methodologically, as I have already indicated, I believe that in the present context piecemeal theorizing is the way to go. In many cases, this means breaking down some of the presiding questions of the Theory into more manageable questions, for example, about the comprehension of point-of-view editing, instead of global questions about something vaguely called suture. As compelling answers are developed to small-scale, delimited questions, we may be in a position to think about whether these answers can be unified in a more comprehensive theoretical framework.

The considerations here on behalf of piecemeal theorizing are practical, not philosophical. For it is my hunch that we do not yet know enough to begin to evolve a unified theory, or even the questions that might lead to a unified theory. So, for the duration, let us concentrate on more manageable, small-scale theorizing. Perhaps one day we will be in a position frame a unified or comprehensive theory of film. I have no argument to show that this is not possible. But whether our theories are large-scale or piecemeal, the process of theorizing will always have a dialectical component.

By emphasizing the dialectical dimension of theorizing, one concedes that it is historical. For debates will be relative to the disputants involved and the situated questions that perplex them. Thus, film theorizing under the auspices of the dialectical model does not pretend to the discovery of Absolute Truth. The theoretical answers it advances are shaped in response to the existing questions it answers and refines and to the perspectives and theoretical interests that are inscribed in those questions. Moreover, insofar as a dialectical conception of film theorizing admits that theorizing evolves over time, the dialectical film theorist must be aware that his or her theories may be open to revision as the debate matures. A dialectical conception of the film theory is not a form of absolutism since it neither supposes total comprehensiveness nor unrevisability. Rather, it is pragmatic.

Nevertheless, in conceding the historicity and revisability of theories, I have not given up truth as a regulative ideal for film theorizing. For the fact that theorizing has a history does not compromise the possibility of discovering what is the case, since that history may involve, among other things, the successive elimination of error. Furthermore, the fact that we are constantly revising our theories in the light of continued criticism and new evidence does not preclude the possibility that our theories are getting closer and closer to the truth. In the physical sciences, we may refer to some of our theories as approximately true, acknowledging that they may be revised, augmented, and refined, but that they are on the right track. Moreover, there is no persuasive reason to concede that we cannot also craft film theories in the here and now that are approximately true.

The dialectical conception of film theory that I am advocating is consistent with trends in the postpositivist philosophy of science. It respects the Kuhnian, antipositivist emphasis on the importance of historical and social contexts for inquiry. It is also not positivist in that it conceives of the process of theoretical argumentation as situated as a debate between existing rivals, rather than as a debate between every conceivable theory, before a court of fully rational participants, endowed with full information.

On the other hand, I do not think that we are compelled, on the basis of Kuhn's insights, to become social constructivists, a tendency exemplified by the Edinburgh Strong Program and widely shared in the humanities. We may argue that the history in question may represent the process of a society (for example, the community of chemists) whose social practices have evolved to provide a better and better purchase on what is approximately true.

I am presuming that what can be claimed for science may be claimed eventually for film theory. This does not mean that I think that film theory is a science, or that it can be or should be transformed into one, though I do think that there may be certain questions of film theory—perhaps concerning perception—that may be pursued scientifically. Rather, I invoke discussions about scientific methodology in proselytizing for a dialectical conception of film theory, not because I believe film theory is a natural science, but only because the philosophy of science provides us with some of our best models for understanding theoretical inquiry.

Undoubtedly, some will dismiss my suggestions on the grounds that I am confusing film theory with natural science. Let me say now that this is a misinterpretation. What I am saying is: let us take advantage of the insights derived from reflection on the scientific enterprise in order to think about what the structure of our own practice might be. We should not attempt to slavishly imitate any of the natural sciences. We need to be alert to the special features of our own field of inquiry, and to modify our methods appropriately. And yet we may still derive some useful hints about the process of inquiry by listening to sophisticated discussions about science.

Even this moderate proposal is apt be met with revulsion by the film studies establishment, since they, like their cohorts in literary criticism, are as skeptical about science as they are about truth—perhaps not accidentally, since it is common to think of the scientific enterprise as truth-tracking. However, the arguments for suspecting science are as feckless as those for suspecting truth.

Sometimes science is decried because it is noted that certain scientific programs in the past, like eugenics, have served the forces of oppression. Right. But so has the law, humanism, poetry, music, and even putatively emancipatory politics. And anyway, the dubitable science in question, where we are not talking about its technological implementations, has, through dialectical criticism, been unmasked by the continued, self-correcting application of scientific practice. We need to be very careful about accepting scientific theories as incontrovertible, especially where they have political implications. But that sort of wariness is no rebuke to scientific thinking; it is a testament to it.

Nowadays, humanists, including film scholars, express misgivings about science because they claim that it parades its findings as if they were infallible. This is merely a variation on the argument from absolute truth, and it is no more conclusive than the other specimens of that gambit that we've seen so far. The argument begins by noting, as I have, that scientific theories are historically situated and revisable. Hence, again for reasons I have already produced, scientific theories cannot pretend to absolute truth. Therefore, they are arbitrary. In effect, we are presented with a disjunctive syllogism: either scientific theories are absolutely true or they are arbitrary. They are not absolutely true; so they are arbitrary. And if they are arbitrary, why should they or the methodologies that yield them be privileged?

But as is always the case with such arguments, the conclusion depends on canvassing all the viable alternatives. And in this instance, it is easy to see that there are overlooked options. One is what is called *fallibilism*, which I would contend provides a much better framework for comprehending scientific practice than the allegation that it aspires to infallibility.

The fallibilist agrees that he or she may have to revise his or her theories in light of future evidence or in response to the implications of later theoretical developments, because the fallibilist realizes that theories are at best well-justified and that a well-justified theory may turn out to be false. There is no claim to absolute truth here. But that does not entail that the theories in question are arbitrary. For we are not open to revising our theories in any which way, but only in virtue of the best available, transcultural standards of justification, that is, ones that have a reliable track record.

The fallibilist does not believe that we can revise all our theories and methods at once. He or she accepts the possibility that any subset thereof might be revised in the appropriate circumstances, and even that all our theories might be revised, but only ad seriatim. Theories and methods are revisable. They do not yield absolute truth. But they are not arbitrary either. For they are only revisable in accordance with practices that, though themselves incrementally revisable, have a reliable record for tracking the truth. The truth, here, where we do secure it, is approximate truth, in the garden variety sense of the term, not Absolute Truth. But if we can conceive of science in such a way that detaches it from pretensions to Absolute Truth, then taking note of its failure to deliver Absolute Truth should not dispose us to dismiss it as arbitrary.

Humanists in general and film scholars in particular reject science because they endorse a strong social constructivist conception of science. Science, on this view, is historical not simply in the sense that there is a history of scientific practice, but in the sense that that practice is embedded in a sociohistorical context, which it reflects. Under this view, the history of a scientific movement often makes the movement sound like an allegory of the social concerns of the period in question. And where this variant of social constructivism takes a Marxist turn, scientific discoveries are frequently characterized as answering to pressing economic forces.

But the social constructivist view scarcely fits the facts. If scientific theories were as historically and culturally relative as the social constructivist declares, how could one explain that scientists operating in different historical and cultural contexts can concur on the same theories? How can one account for convergence between Maoist and American physicists? Moreover, is it plausible to hypothesize that Newton's explanation of Kepler's celestial ellipses by means of the inverse square law answered the pressing economic needs of seventeenth-century merchants and seamen? They would have preferred better chronometers.

Social constructivists and their followers in film studies, and elsewhere, like to say that science *constitutes* reality, putatively in ways that facilitate prevailing cultural agendas. But such talk of constituting reality is barely intelligible. If science constitutes reality, then how are we to explain the fact that scientific theories are constantly confronted by contrary data and anomalies? That is, where did they come from, if the scientific theory constitutes reality?

In any case, social constructivism seems to totter on the brink of self-refutation. It claims to have *discovered* that all theories are culturally relative, but that discovery itself is a theory, one that appears to request transcultural assent. But why should we grant such immunity to social constructivism? That sounds really arbitrary!

I have spent so much time sparring with contemporary academic skepticism about science for two reasons: first, because in the current context of debate, any proposal, like mine, that a framework for aesthetic theorizing might profit from thinking about scientific theorizing is apt to elicit an intemperate rejoinder on the basis of one or more of the considerations I have just attempted to undercut; and second, because it is frequently alleged that cognitivism, a stance often defended in this volume, is an attempt to turn film theory into science, and, therefore, cognitivism can be "refuted" handily by the preceding skeptical arguments about the integrity of science. But I contend that these arguments refute nothing, except possibly social constructivism itself.

Many of these arguments begin, as I do, with an acknowledgment of the insights of postpositivist philosophy of science. However, where many humanists and film scholars often take those insights to imply the arbitrariness of science, I try to exploit them in favor of a view of science as a dialectical, incremental process for securing approximate truths through practices of, among other things, error elimination and criticism. Furthermore, this very broad conception of inquiry may be fruitful to our thinking about film theory. In order to test its usefulness and to descend from the preceding perhaps unduly rarefied stratosphere of abstraction, I shall apply this conception of the dialectical framework for film theory to a contemporary question, namely, the issue of cognitivism.

Cognitivism versus Psychoanalysis

Psychoanalysis, conjoined with Marxism and later blended with various other radical, political perspectives, has dominated film theorizing for two decades. In the eighties, an approach to film theorizing, labeled cognitivism, began to take shape as an alternative to psychoanalysis. Cognitivism is not a unified theory. Its name derives from its tendency to look for alternative answers to many of the questions addressed by or raised by psychoanalytic film theories, especially with respect to film reception, in terms of cognitive and rational processes rather than irrational or unconscious ones. This might involve explicit reference to cognitive and perceptual psychology or to Anglo-American–style linguistics rather than to psychoanalysis. Or the hypotheses might be more homemade.

Some so-called cognitivists may offer armchair speculations about audience reasoning, practical and otherwise, while others advert to established theories of cognitive processing or even experimentation. Some cognitivists try out conjectures employing suppositions about natural selection where others fear to tread.

Cognitivism is not a unified theory, not only because the theoretical domains cognitivists explore differ, but because cognitivist film theorists, like cognitive psychologists, may disagree about which proposals—of the competing cognitivist proposals—best suit the data. So, once cognitivists stop arguing with psychoanalysts, they will have to argue with each other. And this is why it is a mistake to imagine that cognitivism is a single, unified theory. It is a stance.

However, it is a stance that has increasingly come to define itself as an alternative to psychoanalysis in film studies. It advances its hypotheses, as diverse and as discordant as they may be, by claiming to characterize or to explain phenomena better than extant psychoanalytic theories. Cognitivists have increasingly come to conceptualize their project dialectically. Cognitivists take their task to be a matter of answering certain questions about film, especially about film reception and comprehension, most of which questions have already been asked or at least acknowledged by psychoanalytic film theorists. But cognitivists claim that they do a better job answering those questions than psychoanalytic film theorists have.

Some film scholars have responded to cognitivism with high dudgeon. I have already suggested a number of their reactions. However, as befits the pluralistic zeitgeist, others are insouciant. "What's the big deal?" they want to know. You can have cognitivism, if you want it; the others can have psychoanalysis. The more the merrier. Why not have them all? It's good to have lots of theories.

And, of course, anyone who believes that the dialectical conception of film theory is the most productive one should readily concur, because, it would appear, the more theories that are in play, the more opportunity there is for heightened theoretical refinement. Doesn't theoretical pluralism seem like it should go hand in glove with a dialectical conception of film theory?

Here it pays to distinguish between two versions of theoretical pluralism, one which suits the dialectical conception of film theory, and the other, which doesn't. One kind of theoretical pluralism might be called peaceful coexistence pluralism. Coexistence pluralism is very laid back. Everyone has his own theory; if you want to conjoin theories, well, that's a matter of personal taste. You can accept some cognitivist hypotheses, but if you also like some aspects of psychoanalysis (at this point, it is usually said, "I find it useful"), you can have that too.

On the other hand, there is also methodologically robust pluralism. On this view, it is good to have lots of theories around as well. But it is good to have these theories around so that they can be put in competition with each other. From the point of view of the robust methodological pluralist, it is good to have a number of theories in the field at the beginning of the day, but by the end of the day, one hopes that some will be eliminated through processes of criticism and comparison in light of certain questions and the relevant evidence. Some ostensibly competing theories may, upon examination and debate, turn out to be complementary or supplementary. But many are also likely to fall by the wayside.

Obviously, from my manner of describing these alternative pluralisms, I believe that the type of pluralism that is presupposed by a dialectical conception of film theory is robust methodological pluralism. It presumes that lots of theories are a methodologically good thing just because they provide grist for robust criticism. Undoubtedly, some readers will chide my competitive metaphors for being too agonistic or macho. But, on the one hand, we are talking about eliminating theories, not people; and, on the other hand, feminist theories are standardly advanced on the grounds that they provide better explanations than their patriarchal competitors. It is hard to resist the intuition that theory selection involves some competition.

Perhaps the coexistence pluralist will demand to know why we need to eliminate any theories at all. But the answer is simple: some theories are provisionally superior than others and they exclude a number of alternative theories. This is not to say that the alternatives cannot, so to speak, make a comeback. But that presupposes a forum where debate, rather than coexistence, is the norm. Theories compel assent, at least provisionally, by demonstrating that they provide certain explanatory advantages and solutions to certain anomalies lacking in their opposing number.

This view of theory should not surprise psychoanalytic film theorists. For they should recall the way in which Freud argues for his own theory of dreams. Prior to Freud, dream research regarded dreams as purely somatic phenomena, the reaction of a mental organ veritably sunk in the state of sleep in response to environmental stimuli which partially activate it. By examining the content of certain dreams, Freud showed that this theory was not comprehensive—it did not cover a great many facts presented by the data—and that it was unable to provide any functional-biological account of why we dream. (N.B.: Psychoanalytic critics who chastise cognitivists for dabbling in biological hypotheses should remember that Freud was not averse to speaking about biological functions.)

Freud's own theory not only supplied the wherewithal to account for the anomalies ignored by previous dream research but was also able to identify a candidate for the function of dream, namely, that it was the guardian of sleep. It has been the burden of subsequent researchers to see how well Freud's theory squares with the data and to develop alternative hypotheses to accommodate the anomalies in the data that erupt from the collision between the evidence and Freud's famous generalizations, such as the hypothesis of wish fulfillment.

Staging the debate between psychoanalytic film theory is too elaborate a task even for a longish essay like this. One reason for this is that, since cognitivism often proposes piecemeal theories, a thorough confrontation would require facing off each cognitivist theory—of narrative comprehension, of cinematic perception, of the horror film, of melodrama, of film music, and so on—with its psychoanalytic counterparts, where there are counterparts. Frequent examples of that sort of close engagement can be found throughout this volume. Nevertheless, it is still possible to offer some overarching comments about the rivalry between cognitivism and psychoanalysis in what remains of this chapter.

I have urged that we think of theories in terms of dialectical competition. However, due to certain conceptual features of psychoanalysis, the debate between cognitivism and psychoanalysis is peculiar in a way that said competition redounds to the advantage of cognitivism. What is special about psychoanalysis and what makes the debate between cognitivism and psychoanalysis somewhat different from most other theoretical debates is the fact that psychoanalysis is a theory whose object is the irrational. Or, to put the matter differently, the realm of psychoanalysis is the irrational, which domain has as its criterion of identification that it be phenomena that cannot be adequately accounted for in terms of rational, cognitive, or organic explanations. It is analytical to the very conception of psychoanalytic explanation that is appropriate field of activity is defined by what is not rationally, cognitively, or organically explicable.

Psychoanalysis, in other words, kicks in which there is an apparent breakdown in the normal functioning of our cognitive-perceptual processing, our capacities for rational calculation and decision making, our conative and emotional behavior, our motor capabilities, and so on, which breakdowns cannot be explained either organically or in virtue of the structural features of the processes in question.

If I cannot walk because I have lost my legs in a car accident, there is no call for psychoanalysis. But if I am biologically sound, and no rational motive can be supplied for my inaction, psychoanalysis is appropriate. If I am angry when I am mugged, ceteris paribus, that is a rational response, where psychoanalysis is out of place. But if I consistently explode whenever a teacher asks me a question, we think about psychoanalysis. Similarly, errors in adding long strings of large numbers can be readily explained by the way in which such input might overload the processing system. But if I consistently answer "three" to the question "how much is two plus two," then a visit to a therapist may be in order. In short, there is a conceptual constraint on psychoanalysis; it is restricted to dealing with phenomena that cannot be explained by other means.

Moreover, this has interesting consequences for the debate between cognitivist and psychoanalytic film theories. Namely, wherever a plausible cognitivist theory can be secured, the burden of proof is shifted to the psychoanalytic theorist. For a plausible cognitivist theory precludes the necessity for psychoanalysis. The mere plausibility of a cognitivist theory gives it a special advantage over psychoanalytic theories of the same phenomenon.

It is not generally the case that the mere plausibility of one scientific theory excludes a respectable, competing theory from the field. But insofar as psychoanalysis is defined as just what explains what otherwise has no *plausible* explanation, psychoanalytic explanation starts with a disadvantage where plausible cognitivist theories are available.

Contemporary film theorists, like Judith Mayne in her recent book *Cinema and Spectatorship,* tag cognitivist theorists with the complaint that they simply bracket the psychoanalytic approach, as if willfully. What such criticism fails to comprehend is that where we have a convincing cognitivist account, there is no point whatsoever in looking any further for a psychoanalytic account. It is not the case that psychoanalysis is being unfairly or inexplicably bracketed. It is being *retired,* unless and until good reasons can be advanced to suppose otherwise.

Psychoanalytic theories face a special burden of proof when confronting cognitivist theories. For a psychoanalytic theory to reenter the debate, it must be demonstrated that there is something about the data of which given cognitivist (or organic) explanations can give no adequate account, and which, as well, cannot be explained by some other cognitive theory, which remainder is susceptible to psychoanalytic theory *alone.* I have no argument to prove conclusively that no psychoanalytic theory will ever be able to cross this hurdle. But, at the same time, I think it is also fair to say that psychoanalytic film theorists behave as though they are unaware of this obstacle and, in any event, they have failed to meet it *even once* in their skirmishes with cognitivists.

Because of this special burden of proof, the possibility of pluralistic coexistence between cognitivism and psychoanalysis is never a foregone conclusion. Confronted by cognitivist hypotheses about the perception of the cinematic image, the psychoanalytic critic must show that there is something about the phenomena that is alien to cognitivist theorizing. That is why it is not enough for psychoanalytic theorists, like Richard Wollheim and Richard Allen, to merely tell a coherent, psychoanalytic story about pictorial perception; they must also establish that there is something about the data that cognitivists are unable to countenance before they, the psychoanalysts, postulate the operation of *unconscious* psychic mechanisms like projection. For if their cognitivist competitors can frame a coherent, comprehensive account of the data without resorting to unconscious mechanisms, postulating unconscious ones is a nonstarter.

Dialectical arguments are primarily matters of shifting the burden of proof between rival theories that are grappling with roughly the same questions. Quite frequently (most frequently?) it is difficult to find a completely decisive refutation of rival theories. That is one reason why we must fall back on the laborious processes of removing the burden of proof from ourselves and re-distributing it amongst our competitors. The preceding argument has not shown that psychoanalytic theories of film will never be admissible. At best, what it may show is that the burden of proof is now with the psychoanalysts. Perhaps they will rise to the occasion.

However, if I am correct in maintaining that psychoanalytic film theorists have not yet even recognized that they have this burden of proof, then that indicates that, at present, the ball belongs to the cognitivists. Psychoanalytic film theory may succeed in countering this argument dialectically, but unless it does, the continued elaboration of the psychoanalytic paradigm, conducted in isolation from cognitivist challenges, represents an evasion of film theory, not a contribution to it.

Furthermore, there is another general problem with psychoanalytic film theory that deserves mention. Putting aside the admittedly pressing question of whether psychoanalysis as a general theory is acceptable, something disputed by many psychologists, philosophers, and psychiatrists, it is nevertheless the case that we can say that psychoanalysis is an empirical discipline. It may not be generally concerned with testing, but it typically has an empirical basis, namely, the practice of therapy. Psychoanalysts from Freud (Sigmund and Anna), to D. W. Winnicott, Melanie Klein, Karen Horney, Heinz Kohut, Erik Erikson, and Otto Kernberg base their concepts and their postulation of psy-chic forces with their attending regularities, as well as their criticisms of other psychoanalytic theorists, on their therapeutic observations. Without a thera-peutic practice, psychoanalysts would have no grounds for introducing, ad-justing, modifying, refining, and even, at times, abandoning their concepts and theories.

However, when we turn to psychoanalytic film theorists, we note immedi-ately that most, if not all, of the leading theorists have no therapeutic practice. They modify previous psychoanalytic theories and they even introduce new concepts, concoct novel theories, and project patterns, but on what basis? One would think that such theory building should be keyed to some group of analysands—to their experiences and associations, and the analysis thereof. But psychoanalytic film theorists do not have therapeutic practices. They are confecting theories, but with no empirical constraints. How can they pretend to implement an empirically based inquiry like psychoanalysis without any data? Perhaps that question can be answered theoretically. But until it is, the rest of us, on legitimate *psychoanalytic* grounds, will want to know how contemporary psychoanalytic film theory is possible.

Concerns about empirical evidence are generally ridiculed by film theorists. For, as Judith Mayne recounts, empirical research is seen by proponents of the Theory as part and parcel of the philosophical position of empiricism. But such reservations about empirical research rest on little more than an equivocation. It is certainly the case that there are few philosophical positions as beleaguered as empiricism. However, it is equally true that there is no necessary connection between the philosophical doctrine of empiric *ism* and an empiri *cal* research program.

Obviously, gestalt psychologists advanced their theory on the basis of empirical evidence. But their theory of perception was forged in the teeth of an empiricist philosophy of perception. And one can certainly construct macroeconomic theories without any commitment to an empiricist theory of the mind and its related epistemological doctrine of phenomenalism. Chomsky relies on empirical data—elicited linguistic intuitions—but his arguments in favor of innateness are stridently unLockean. And so on. It is just a howler to respond to requests for empirical evidence on the grounds that since the philosophy of empiricism has been discredited, evidence is tacky or out of style. For even *if* empiricism were down for the count, empirical research would still be independently creditable.

I have just outlined two of the many challenges that cognitivism has evolved for psychoanalytic film theory. Inasmuch as film theory is a dialectical procedure, it now falls to psychoanalytic film theorists to show how they can negotiate the special burden of proof with which cognitivists confront them and to account for how psychoanalytic film theory is possible in the absence of the sort of empirical base that psychoanalytic theory, outside the environs of film and literature departments, requires. So far, psychoanalytic film theorists have evaded these charges. If they continue to evade them, then the prospects for intellectually exciting theorizing in film studies, as it is presently constituted, are meager.

Concluding Remarks

Throughout this chapter, and elsewhere, my criticisms of the prevailing Theory have been stern. I predict that this approach will be rebuked, especially by peaceful coexistence pluralists. They will want to know how I can hope to sway proponents of the Theory if my tone is so relentless.

But, I must admit that I have little or no expectation about changing the hearts and minds of advocates of the Theory. There are sound sociological reasons for believing that scholars who are already deeply invested in a paradigm are unlikely to surrender it. Careers, tenures, promotions, publications, and reputations have been and continue to be built by espousing the Theory. There is too much social investment already at stake in propounding the Theory to anticipate that many of its adherents will be moved, in a disinterested spirit, by rational argumentation. The Theory has too much institutional weight behind it to permit conversion. And, in any case, most academics remain locked in the paradigm they learned in graduate school. It is too late for most of them to change their spots.

So I do not write for defenders of the Theory. I have no illusions about the possibility of converting them; thus I make no concessions in portraying how dreadful their Theory is. There is no point in pulling one's punches. If anything, that might worsen the situation by implying that things in film studies are not as bad as they are.

But if I am not writing the Theorists, who is my intended audience? The uncommitted: those in film studies and those (historians, sociologists, psychologists, philosophers, and so on) in related disciplines that study film who are interested in evolving frameworks for comprehending cinema but who are doctrinally unaligned. Let them decide between the claims of psychoanalysis and the claims of cognitivism. Let them weight the different voices in the discussion. It is for this audience that I and other cognitivists have staged the debate.

Perhaps the most important sector of this uncommitted audience is made up of dedicated film students, both advanced undergraduates and graduate students. Neither their minds nor their careers are at present so set in stone that they are unable to respond to the claims of alternative voices. And, anyway, they are the ones who will inevitably reconstruct film studies or whatever, in the wake of technological innovation, the field becomes.

Of course, it may be that my pessimism about the adherents of the Theory is too extreme. Maybe some of them, along with the unaligned, will take a serious interest in the debate that cognitivists have initiated. But, in that case, the rigor with which I have propounded my arguments will serve their purposes, insofar as it will supply them with strong, clear objections to attempt to refute. For it will be more convenient for them to confront robust positions than it would be for them to confront ones that are politely hedged or that are overly qualified and conciliatory.

The prospects for film theory hinge on critical debate. In the best of circumstances, the participants of that discussion will include cognitivists, psychoanalysts, and unaligned scholars. In my view, over the last two decades, film studies has squandered what may turn out to have been a once-in-a-lifetime opportunity by effectively stifling debate between Theory and alternative paradigms. Whether film theory has a genuine future depends on its becoming truly dialectical.

PART TWO

FILM THEORY
AND AESTHETICS

The essays in this section explore the possibilities of sharply focused "piece-meal" theory. Unlike adherents to all-encompassing Grand Theory, the writers in this section start from particular problems and build their theories as they go. The topics are diverse, ranging from women's roles in horror films to the place of imagination in empathizing with characters. In the spirit of dialectical argument, the writers critically examine established positions before mounting their own. While some of the contributors adopt an explicit cognitivist stance, many do not. The essays are united by two assumptions: that theorizing should be driven by questions and problems, not by doctrines of Grand Theory; and that theorizing is most fruitful when its conclusions are tested against both logical criteria and empirical data.

The first three essays highlight methodological problems. Stephen Prince contrasts psychoanalytic film theory, which has usually not considered how its claims might be supported by empirical evidence, with recent research in visual communication, particularly that focusing on attention. David Bordwell argues that we can understand the concept of convention without recourse to extreme dichotomies between "nature" and "convention." He suggests that a moderate constructivism would acknowledge the importance of "contingent universals" in cinematic representation. James Peterson's essay argues that a cognitive model of spectatorial activity is the best candidate for explaining how competent spectators make sense of avant-garde films. Among his methodological suggestions is the proposal that, pace semiotics, a code-based model of cinematic communication needs supplementation by an inference-based one.

Of particular concern in recent film theory has been the issue of how spectators "identify with" characters or respond emotionally to cinematic displays. These matters are taken up from various angles in the next three essays. Murray Smith criticizes the Brechtian tradition of subject-position theory for a reductive dichotomy between reason and emotion. He proposes that the concept of identification be dissected into more manageable aspects and illustrates his case with an analysis of *The Accused*. In considering cinematic characterization, Paisley Livingston offers a discussion of how fictional truth operates in general and sketches an intentionalist perspective for considering these matters. Similarly, Alex Neill explores how features of the imagination may create the possibility of our empathizing with fictional characters. These features, he maintains, depend in turn upon beliefs.

The rest of the essays in this part concentrate on particular types of films or cinematic techniques. Cynthia A. Freeland examines various feminist approaches to horror films. After a critique of psychoanalytic approaches, she moves to a consideration of how other methods can generate critical interpretations of gender ideologies. A similar strategy is pursued by Flo Leibowitz in her study of melodrama. Here she counterposes psychoanalytic explanations of the emotional pleasures of the genre to more cognitive ones, emphasizing the conceptual judgments implicit in even the most apparently "irrational" emotions.

Jeff Smith provides the first of two essays on film music. He criticizes the dominant psychoanalytic model of "unheard melodies" and suggesting a more wide-ranging account of the ways in which viewers become consciously aware of Hollywood scores. Jerrold Levinson develops a conception of nondiegetic, or "external," music as part of the film's narrational dynamic. In the course of his analysis, he links his theory to conceptions of authorial agency in film narrative generally.

Documentary film is the subject of the contributions by Noël Carroll and Carl Plantinga. Carroll considers versions of postmodernist skepticism about the possibility that nonfiction film can convey objective information about the world. Apart from rebutting contentions about documentary, his analysis suggests that self-contradiction haunts postmodernist theory more generally. Plantinga's essay also targets postmodernist conceptions of documentary, with special attention to their neglect of the genuine recording that takes place in the nonfiction film. Plantinga instead proposes approaching documentary rhetoric from an instrumentalist angle, recognizing recorded images and sounds as only part of the evidence put forward by the film.

Illusory motion has long been presumed to constitute the sine qua non of cinema, but this premise is interrogated in the final essay of this part. Gregory Currie suggests provocatively that there is no illusion of movement in cinema and that cinematic motion is as literal and real as the color we see in the world. Currie's discussion scouts alternative conceptions of realism and criticizes influential notions of illusion circulating in recent semiotic and psychoanalytic film theory. In addition, his philosophical inquiry into the nature of movement provides a bridge to the psychological investigations of cinematic representation in Part Three.

3

Psychoanalytic Film Theory and the Problem of the Missing Spectator

Stephen Prince

As a field of inquiry, film studies is today composed of three distinct, though somewhat interdependent, areas of focus: history, criticism, and theory. Though there is some overlap, each area is characterized by a distinguishing set of conceptual and methodological issues. With a heavy reliance upon primary sources, film historical investigations demonstrate admirable scholarly rigor and are furnishing us with an increasingly detailed portrait of the medium's past. Colorful anecdotes, in which the earliest histories heavily trafficked, have been replaced with an intelligent understanding of the interconnections among social and technological factors as they have shaped the medium.

Film criticism has continued as it always has, and probably always will, to furnish the reader with interesting accounts of the meeting between critical minds and artists and their creations. The critic proceeds, and convinces, by virtue of the power of his or her rhetoric and command of the language and by skillfully referencing these against observable features of the films under study. The finished product can become a stimulating supplement to the films themselves, deepening the viewer's appreciation of them. Film criticism is among the most durable, popular, and, for the general public, visible products of our field.

Film history and criticism are doing just fine currently, but in the third area of focus—film theory—all is not well. Some serious problems exist, not just in terms of confusion over what "film theory" is and what it should do, but also in terms of how it should do it. Film theory is sometimes understood as providing sets of shared perspectives that facilitate scholarly dialogue; yet in the area of spectatorship, issues of evidentiary support often go unexamined. Let me be very clear. In what follows, I am not trying to conflate theory with supportive data nor to suggest that the former should be reducible to the latter. Positivism is not my goal. To remain theoretical, theory needs to place its evidentiary supports within a philosophical or aesthetic framework. I do not wish to slight or to underestimate the importance of such a framework. It is, after all, part of what makes theory theory. But our problem today in film studies is that theories of spectatorship fly well beyond the data and in ways that pay little or no attention to the evidence we do have about how people watch and interpret films and television.

Contemporary theories of spectatorship are distinguished by a preference for employing psychoanalysis as the primary modality for explaining film viewing. Indeed, a recent review of theories of spectatorship warns that the failure by cognitivists to take psychoanalysis seriously can only result in limited and imperfect accounts. Accepting psychoanalysis as a given, the author asserts, somewhat dogmatically, that the spectator's activity "needs to be read in relation to unconscious processes."[1] Contemporary theories of spectatorship are also characterized by a reluctance to engage empirical modes of investigation. I will be suggesting in this chapter, however, that questions about how people process, interpret, and respond to cinematic images and narratives are empirical questions, or, at the least, incorporate an empirical dimension, which can be investigated by observing the behavior of real viewers. Theory building can, and should, come from this. Research on real viewers will need to be placed within a theoretical framework, but any theory of spectatorship which fails to deal at some level with the empirical evidence on spectatorship should be suspected of being insufficiently grounded. One result of film studies' disdain for empirical methods has been the construction of theories that deal with "subjects" but not real viewers, with ideal spectators who exist in the theories but who have no flesh-and-blood counterparts. As Judith Mayne explains:

> One can understand the historical necessity for bracketing "real people" when the only available way to talk about such viewers was in the language of sociological or mass communications research—a language, that is, totally drenched in the assumptions of a white, male, heterosexual norm and a belief in conscious, rational responses presumably untainted by contradiction or unconscious desires.[2]

This kind of blanket and egregiously unfair dismissal of an entire tradition of research has tended to impede the ability of film studies to understand how viewers make sense of films, despite the contributions of several decades of psychoanalytic theory. The aim of this essay is to clarify the nature of that handicap and to suggest several ways in which it may be overcome. Rather than discussing all of the many grounds in which psychoanalytic theory is weak (for example, the issue of its being unfalsifiable), I'd like to briefly consider one problem that, in itself, should be cause for great skepticism about the utility of employing psychoanalytic categories to explain issues of spectatorship. Then I will illustrate this problem by using an essay of Freud's that is much quoted by film scholars, "A Child Is Being Beaten" (1919). Psychoanalytic film theorists have closely scrutinized several key essays by Freud, among them *Fragment of an Analysis of a Case of Hysteria* (1905), *Three Essays on Sexuality* (1905), "Instincts and their Vicissitudes" (1915), "The

Economic Problem in Masochism" (1924), "Fetishism" (1927), and "A Child Is Being Beaten." Although I will focus only on the latter essay and will use it as a kind of test case for evaluating the character of the theories that have been spun from it, much of what I will say is generalizable to the other essays and to their use in film theory. In general, I am interested to show the weak foundations on which some of the most elaborate current theories of spectatorship rest and to clarify the general problem of what I call the "missing spectator." Finally, I ask, what do scholars in empirically oriented disciplines, such as psychology and communications, know about the film and TV viewer that we in film studies do not?

The primary and to my mind insurmountable problem with basing general theories of spectatorship on psychoanalysis is that such theories must remain unsupported because psychoanalysis is a discipline without reliable data. I realize this statement may seem harsh or astonishing, so let me clarify it.

The criticisms that follow are not directed at the therapeutic context where an individual may come seeking relief from unpleasant feelings or behavior. In such a context, psychoanalysis may very well be valuable. It is, instead, the use of what passes as clinical data by film theory which is problematic and for several reasons. Published reports of analyses, whether by Freud, Lacan, or others, are typically unaccompanied by transcripts showing what the patient really said and how the analyst responded. Readers of published cases have no access to this information. In addition, psychoanalysis as a discipline lacks established standards for interpretation that can ensure inter-analyst reliability. Different analysts produce different interpretations. Furthermore, the published accounts of clinical cases present a grossly inadequate description of the therapeutic encounter between patient and therapist. The therapist will summarize and paraphrase the client's words, typically leaving out the rich nonverbal channels of communication that establish a context in which the patient's verbalizations have a unique meaning. In private notes and published summaries of the cases, the analyst will select only a subset of the range of behaviors and words on display during the session, and each analyst's standards of selection are uniquely his or her own. One cannot, therefore, work backward from the published descriptions to a comprehensive data set in order to check the analyst's interpretations. Most problematically, each clinical encounter is non-repeatable, is uniquely eccentric, and, as noted, features non-traceable disclosures.

All of these problems have been noted by Colby and Stoller in a discussion of why psychoanalysis should not be counted as a science. They point out that "Psychoanalytic evidence is hearsay, first when the patient reports his or her version of an experience and second when the analyst reports it to an audience."[3] They conclude that "Reports of clinical findings are mixtures of facts, fabulations, and fictives so intermingled that one cannot tell where one begins and the other leaves off."[4]

Despite the problem of finding reliable data within the psychoanalytic paradigm, contemporary film theory has proceeded as if Freud's and Lacan's case studies are trustworthy reports of authentic observations. Once again, let me stress that not everything we count as knowledge should be testable and that theory both incorporates and transcends the data sets from which it draws. The problem is that we cannot reference the psychoanalytic theories against available, unambiguous evidence. Let us look at how, in practice, the ambiguous data furnished by psychoanalysis are utilized by film theory.

As previously noted, one of Freud's most widely quoted essays by film theorists is "A Child Is Being Beaten: A Contribution to the Study of the Origin of Sexual Perversions." Here Freud discusses the beating fantasies he claims are reported by both male and female patients. Film theorists have recently used this essay to revise the rather monolithic and rigid accounts of identification typical of early psychoanalytic film theories. Early accounts tended to see the gaze of male characters on screen as an expression of male subjectivity and as a basis for the identification of male spectators. Counterposed to the active male gaze was the passive female object of the gaze.[5] Film scholars[6] have used Freud's essay to revise the bipolar terms of active male gazing and female passivity. In "A Child Is Being Beaten," Freud describes his patients' fantasies developmentally in terms of three distinct phases. Freud claims that his female patients report having fantasies in which, initially, a child of unspecified gender is being beaten by its father. In phase two, the patient reports "I am being beaten by my father," thus sexualizing the victim as female and, of course, as the patient herself. In phase three, an authority figure, such as a teacher, is beating a number of children, most frequently boys. In this third variation, the gender of the victim changes to male. Film theorists have interpreted phase three as representing a cross-gender identification figure for the fantasizing female patient. Indeed, throughout the fantasies, the gender of the fantasized characters is not stable. Instead, gender changes.

Psychoanalytically inclined film theorists have analogized these beating fantasies, in which the patient is an onlooker to the beating spectacle, to the cinema, since both—the patient's fantasies and the cinema—are thought to play off unresolved sexual and Oedipal conflicts. (Metz found the cinematic signifier to be susceptible to psychoanalysis to be "precisely Oedipal in type.")[7] The Freud essay has been accepted by film theorists as a reliable, if sometimes improperly inflected, clinical account and has been used to argue in favor of adopting a flexible conception of emotional identification in the cinema in which male and female viewers may identify with characters of either gender. D. N. Rodowick, for example, notes that "the essay is nonetheless about the difficulty of aligning masculine and feminine identifications with a 'final' sexed subjectivity."[8] Freud's essay has been the basis for understanding the spectator's identification with characters on screen in terms of oscillating, rather than fixed, allegiances which are capable of crossing gender boundaries.

In keeping with my earlier remarks about the problem of usable data in psychoanalytic accounts, let us look at this difficulty in the Freud essay and how it has failed to slow the launching of theoretical claims in film studies. Typically, in the sciences, measures of quantitative data are evaluated in terms of the issues of validity and reliability. Is the researcher really measuring the phenomenon in question or some other unsuspected phenomenon? Are the results consistent, assuming all conditions could be replicated? Freudian data, of course, are qualitative, but one still wishes to know whether the linkages between clinical data and the high-level theories (in the case of the essay on beating, theories of sadism and masochism) spun from them are warranted.

Unfortunately, several characteristics of the Freud essay help produce a weak foundation for theory, especially when trying to analogize Freud's discussions to the cinema. First is the extremely limited number of patients Freud used as the basis for his discussion—six patients, of whom four were female and two male. The bulk of the essay is confined to descriptions of the fantasies of the four female patients. His findings, therefore, are based on an extremely small sample, and, beyond the clinical diagnoses of obsessional neurosis or hysteria, he provides no particulars on the patients. One cannot even tell if the quotations Freud presents to summarize the content of the fantasies (for example, "My father is beating the child") are his own words paraphrasing his patients' reports or are actually the words of one of the patients. They seem to be paraphrases because of the peculiar manner in which he presents them and because they are meant to represent the common elements in the descriptions of all four patients. This succeeds in further mystifying the particulars of the patients since we do not even have their own words before us.

In light of this, I submit that it is extremely difficult for film theorists to evaluate the validity of Freud's claims in this essay and, especially, to generalize from this small sample in ways that permit the construction of grand theories of cinema spectatorship sui generis. But extremely intelligent film scholars have not been reluctant to generalize to a much larger population. Thus, in film theory we can read confident announcements that "there are three basic factors in common between the beating fantasies of men and women."[9]

More troubling even than the extremely small sample upon which Freud bases his macrotheories of sadomasochism is his own admission, clearly stated in the essay, that phase two—"I am being beaten by my father"—is fictive, is made up for the purposes of analysis. Freud writes:

> This second phase is the most important and the most momentous of all. But we may say of it in a certain sense that it has never had a real existence. It is never remembered, it has never succeeded in becoming conscious. It is a construction of analysis, but it is no less a necessity on that account.[10]

By Freud's own admission, data were apparently manufactured to justify the interpretation and theory built from them. Despite Freud's acknowledgment that some of the information he reports is fictive, film theorists have written about this essay as if it provides a secure basis from which to construct theories of cinema spectatorship. Kaja Silverman points out Freud's fabrication of phase two and emphasizes the audacity behind it but decides, nevertheless, that "I can find nothing to dispute in Freud's account of phase 2. . . ."[11]

Empirical Portraits of Spectatorship

As these examples indicate, theories of spectatorship have tended to go far beyond what the data can clearly show, a practice supported by film studies' tendency to view concerns about evidence as the hallmarks of an ideologically suspect empiricism. This tendency notwithstanding, a review of Freud's beating essay reveals problems of sampling, of fabrication of data, and of the introduction of a response set in his subjects. Psychoanalytic film theorists have remained untroubled by these issues. Unconstrained by empirical support, Freudian and Lacanian theories of spectatorship have resulted in constructions of spectators which differ remarkably from the rather detailed portraits of film and television viewers furnished in the disciplines of psychology and communication. In order to understand more fully the limited terms of our prevailing theoretical accounts of film spectators, we need now to consider this research and these portraits.

Some of the theoretical constructs and modes of research that figure in the following discussion may seem quite far removed from the purview of film studies, but to recognize that is also to glimpse the limits of narrow disciplinarity. Scholars conducting empirical work in psychology and communication now know a great deal about how people process and make sense of visual images. I submit that it is an embarrassment that film scholars have written so much about spectatorship at a level of almost total theoretical abstraction while other disciplines have done systematic work on real viewers.

What do scholars in other disciplines know about the film and television viewer that film scholars do not? What general shifts of conceptual emphasis might be productive for constructing better accounts of spectatorship and, more generally, of how cinema communicates? I will concentrate on two general areas where a great deal of empirical work has already been done and where, consequently, bodies of data exist that point toward some rather different operating principles in moving picture media than those that have been postulated by psychoanalysis. In recommending the kinds of shifts of orientation that I'll be outlining, I do not mean to imply that fantasy plays no role in the attractions viewers feel for the cinema. Rather, the emphasis upon fantasy derived from models of unconscious psychological processes has deflected a recognition of spectatorship as a phenomenon that can be, and has been, empirically investigated and about which valid and reliable evidence can be furnished.

Before describing and recommending two conceptual shifts that can make our research and theory more productive, I should point out that the move toward a more cognitive and empirical orientation can help close a gap in our understanding of film viewing which psychoanalysis has helped to produce. Psychoanalytic film theory fails to deal with the complex role that perceptual processes play in a viewer's understanding of visual media. Perception tends to get conflated with sexual energy as a "scopic" drive, a sexually based urge to view things voyeuristically. Metz claimed that "the practice of cinema is only possible through the perceptual passions: the desire to see (= scopic drive, scopophilia, voyeurism). . . ." [12] For Metz, visual perception was understood as a kind of sweeping searchlight mounted on top of the viewer's neck, and psychoanalytically inclined theories of perception have not gained much in sophistication since Metz's uninformed description. [13]

Aside from psychoanalytic film theory's failure to model a sophisticated perceptual process, the claims it does make ill fit the available evidence on how viewers watch film and television. The problem with the "scopic drive" is that it models viewing as a driven and reactive process during which the viewer's passion for looking is cathected by particular formal cues (for example, "fetishizing" close-ups). The scopic drive implies a unifocal fixation within the viewer maintained by a match of formal features and inner fantasy.

Observations of real spectators furnish a rather different portrait of viewing behavior. A great deal of research has studied the ways young children watch television. Preschool children in a room furnished with toys and containing other adults or children do not stare with steady fixation at the screen. Instead, the child will repeatedly glance away from the screen, averaging about 150 looks toward and away from the screen per hour. Furthermore, glances at the screen are quite brief, and most last no longer than 15 seconds. [14] Observations of adult television behavior reveal a similar pattern: looks at the screen are extremely brief and are punctuated by regular glances away from the screen, with non-looking pauses averaging as high as 22 seconds. The researchers conclude that "continuous episodes of visual attention as long as 60 seconds are relatively rare." [15]

These data, of course, are derived from television viewing behavior. The psychoanalytic film theorist could object that the conditions of film viewing, in relation to which the scopic drive is discussed, are crucially different—the film viewer sits before a huge screen in a theater free of the distractions that typically accompany television viewing. However, most people now watch their movies on television via the VCR, and the psychoanalytic theorist would still need to be able to explain how a sexually driven "perceptual passion" yields patterns of viewing behavior in which visual attention is intermittent, subject to continual breaks and interruptions, and is discontinuous. While the scopic drive might not rule out intermittent attention, scopic theory needs to deal with this phenomenon, which the drive-based model of vision as fetish has tended to downplay.

At the very least, theorists of the scopic drive should begin to specify those factors that might produce the onset and cessation of glances at the screen. Empirical research has already pointed toward a host of such factors, among which are specific formal features. Not surprisingly, cuts and on-screen movement tend to maintain visual attention, but so do auditory features, which are especially effective in stimulating glances back to the screen since a viewer can monitor audio changes while looking away from the screen, as signs that important changes are occurring in the show or film that bear attention.[16] Theories of the scopic drive say little about the role of auditory features as cues regulating a viewer's levels of visual attention because attentiveness, an active and conscious process, is not posed as a major variable by the theories.

Furthermore, empirical evidence suggests that visual attention to television is a function of age and may have a developmental basis in terms of cognitive growth and increasing sophistication of medium-specific skills,[17] rather than being something driven by a fixed current of libidinal energy. Empirical evidence, in other words, can deal with differences among spectators better than can psychoanalysis. Levels of attention and comprehension will vary among film and television viewers depending on such characteristics as age, degree of cognitive development, and amount of prior experience with the medium. The empirical research on factors affecting levels of attention and comprehension can give us a more nuanced portrait of spectatorship than does psychoanalysis, and this, in turn, can help us to construct theories that are sensitive to the differences, as well as the similarities, among viewers.

Rather than continuing to base theories on a concept of the scopically driven, fixated (or "positioned") viewer, I suggest that we begin to derive our theories and research from the constructs of "attention" and "attentiveness." This will enable us to make a key advance in the way we model viewing behavior. It will enable us to conceptualize, and study, viewing processes in terms of levels of information processing and emotional response.[18] Conceptualizing attention as a multilevel process and researching spectatorship from that angle, rather than in terms of a unifocal drive, can help bring our theories more in line with the available empirical evidence on film viewing.[19] This is an important step that film studies needs to take in order that our theories be consistent with well-established evidence about media viewing. The constructs of "attention" and "attentiveness" can be usefully employed to build flexible, multilevel models of how viewers of visual media process visual narratives.

An example can be instructive here. Communication researcher Frank Biocca has recently proposed a sophisticated model of semantic processing which bears a close relationship to some of the stipulations of contemporary film theory, yet it is inclined in a different, cognitively oriented direction.[20] Biocca's model rests upon the synthesis of a great deal of empirical research from the fields of psychology and communication, as well as input from film theory, and, by working at a high level of abstraction, it demonstrates how theory both incorporates and transcends the empirical data from which it draws.

Biocca points to the differences between the model viewer that filmmakers and other communicators have in mind during production and the actual, "instantiated" viewer who sees the program or film. He stresses, like reader-response theories, variability of response across viewers, but he comes at these issues from a cognitive context emphasizing multilevel semantic processing of the message in terms of seven "schematic frames," so called because they access the viewer's schemata or frameworks of interpretation. From the first seconds of programming, Biocca points out, viewers begin to construct models of the intended message and, during the course of the show or film, they are continuously revising these models in accordance with the shifting formal and semantic structures of the message. This interpretive work carried out by the viewer is complex and ongoing and is informed by data-driven processing of formal codes as well as by schema-driven inferences about meaning and values. Biocca suggests that viewers organize incoming information by assigning it to, and evaluating it within, seven overall frameworks. The spectator judges information with respect to its discursive topic, its membership in a "possible world," the actors or agents in a causal sequence, point of view understood in terms of both mode of address and position of sight, narrative structure, ideological organization, and the relation of all of these issues to the viewer's own self-identity.

> In the mind of the viewer, schematic frames organize information and inferences about places and social situations (possible worlds); people, causes, and agents (actants); topics (discursive frames); as well as inferences about ideologies and how the programming relates to the viewer (ideological and self-schematic frames).[21]

Biocca's account emphasizes the viewer's response as a series of interpretive moves, as information from the program or film is selected and assigned membership in one of a series of conceptual frameworks. As viewing continues, interpretations are revised and program information can be supplemented with new, incoming information or reassigned to another interpretational framework.[22] Biocca concludes by pointing to the relationship between a message's formal structure and the kinds of information processing it may cue.

> The way a television program or message introduces information and topics (strategy of semantic disclosures embedded in the semantic frames of the message) will influence while semantic frames are foregrounded by the viewer (which information is attended to and how it guides the viewers' inferences).[23]

We are a long way here from the unidimensional framework of psychoanalytic film theory. Psychoanalytic theory fails to grasp what is apparent in Biocca's model: when watching media presentations, the viewer simultaneously executes multiple levels of information processing and engages in a series of interpretive moves. Psychoanalytic theory tends to collapse the viewer's responses into a single dimension fed by primary process energy and the unresolved childhood traumas associated with it. Film theory needs to discard the kind of reactive and passive viewers who are built into theories of "suture" and "positioning" and, instead, place viewers within an altogether more rational, flexible, and multivalent context.

Film Viewing and
Perceptual Correspondence

By employing the constructs of "attention" and "attentiveness," film scholars can formulate investigable problems. Indeed, we ought to stipulate as a criteria of future theory building that postulated theories be able to generate researchable questions. Current psychoanalytic theories of spectatorship do not do this, in part because psychoanalytic critics often aim only to produce interpretations of particular movies and because many film scholars employing psychoanalytic theory seem interested in abstract and ideal, as opposed to actual, viewers.

Formulating researchable questions, however, may require taking a more pragmatic and less abstracted approach to theory construction and in our general thinking about film and how it references the world for viewers. In line with this recommendation, and to show an additional way in which it might be carried out, I propose a second area in which our thinking about film ought to be reoriented. Film studies has grossly underestimated, and underepresented, the important correspondences that exist between photographic images, the narratives constructed using them, and the spatial and visible world that may be photographed. We have preferred to analogize visual representation to linguistic signification instead of grasping the essential differences between film and language. We need to reemphasize and carefully study those points of correspondence between photographic or moving picture images and the real-world visual experience available to viewers. In short, we need to recover a recognition of cinematic images as iconic rather than as symbolic signs, depending on relations of similarity to, rather than difference from, what they represent.[24] Recognizing this will support our appreciation for the constructs of "attention" and "attentiveness." Understanding cinematic signs as iconic enables us to ask about those structural features, or points of similarity with the viewers' real-world experience, that facilitate attentiveness. (For example, children attend more closely to other children's voices on television than they do to adult male voices.)[25]

A wide range of evidence indicates that film spectatorship builds on correspondences between selected features of the cinematic display and a viewer's real-world visual and social experience. Interpretive frames (or schemas) derived from this experience may be used by viewers to make sense of the film narrative. I have already discussed a good deal of this research in an earlier article.[26] Briefly, experimental evidence indicates that naïve or first-time adult and child viewers have little difficulty identifying either simple, familiar pictured objects when presented as line drawings and photographs[27] or simple culturally familiar narratives when presented using continuity editing.[28] The reasons for this are likely found in the variety of ways in which photographic images are isomorphic with their corresponding real-world displays (for example, replication of edge and contour information and of monocular distance codes; in the case of motion pictures, of motion parallax; and in the case of continuity editing, the projective geometry of successive camera positions creating a screen geography whose coordinates we can readily analogize with our own visual experience). So powerful is this isomorphism that pictorial images have even been shown to elicit apparent recognition responses in a wide range of nonhuman subjects—primates, birds, fish, reptiles, even insects. These apparent recognition responses have been demonstrated across different classes of pictorial media—black-and-white and color photographs, high contrast photographs, film and videotape, even line drawings.[29]

In addition to the foregoing sources of iconic isomorphism, an additional area of correspondence between film images and their associated real-world referents includes the stock of socially defined interpersonal and behavioral signals that viewers routinely use as cues for evaluating on-screen characters. Psychoanalytic film theory has had almost nothing to say about the way spectators will use interpersonal cues and behavioral assumptions, derived from social experience, as a way of judging the personality and actions of characters on screen. These cues and assumptions may be iconic or noniconic. In either case, a large amount of empirical evidence indicates that viewers' assessments of media characters and of real peers are based on common perceptual criteria. Similar cognitive processes and socially derived assumptions about motive, intent, and proper role-based behavior are used when evaluating both media-based and real-life characters and individuals. Indeed, as Elizabeth Perse and Rebecca Rubin have pointed out, "'people' constitutes a construct domain that may be sufficiently permeable to include both interpersonal and [media] contexts."[30] Communication researcher Aimee Dorr has recognized that

> the people on television and their interactions present interpretive tasks which are common to all presentations of social life, whatever the medium. They include such tasks as understanding that another person has his or her own perspective, inferring the other's perspective, and judging the morality of another's actions.[31]

Dramatic evidence of how viewers use construct domains derived from real-life experience or beliefs emerged from a study of children's and adults' responses to a photographic narrative. A doctor is shown arguing with his secretary, encountering a traffic accident victim on his way home, and continuing on his way without helping the victim.[32] Second-grade children, in contrast to adult viewers and older kids, reported that the doctor had indeed helped the victim, even though they had not seen this in the narrative. They attributed behavior to the doctor based on a cultural stereotype of doctors as individuals who help other people. They attributed unseen behavior to the fictional character based on socially derived conceptions of what real-life doctors do.

Other empirical research has demonstrated that preschool and elementary school children will evaluate the behavior of fictional film characters based on analogizing that behavior with real-life concepts of individual motive and intent in ways the researchers point out are consistent with both social learning and cognitive-developmental theories of moral development.[33] Similar age-related trends have been found to underlie the evaluative constructs viewers may apply to the behavior of television characters and real-life individuals. Second-, fourth-, and sixth-grade school children have demonstrated a stock of evaluative constructs that become increasingly differentiated, abstract, and integrated with age and can apply these constructs to evaluate behavior on TV and in real life, suggesting that a common person-perception process underlies both spheres.[34]

Other age-related trends that have been demonstrated indicate that at different ages children shift from perceptual to conceptual categories for evaluating behavior. Preschool and elementary school children viewed one of four versions of a videotaped story in which an old woman's appearance was presented as either attractive or ugly and her behavior as either kind or cruel. Younger kids based their evaluation of the woman more on her appearance, older kids more on her behavior.[35] The researchers found that appearance stereotyping was demonstrated among all the age groups studied. Despite this, however, the older children still tended to weigh behavior more than the younger kids. This age-related shift from perceptually based responses (for example, the youngest kids who evaluated the woman character's behavior according to how she looked) to more cognitively based, morally inflected judgments of behavior points toward complex dimensions of spectatorship which psychoanalytic film theory has either ignored or been unable to explore. To the extent that the scopophilic drive is activated by visual imagery, psychoanalytic film theory tends to see all spectators as being positioned by perceptual stimuli and has remained silent about how viewers process that imagery by constructing rational analogies with their real-life experiences, values, and precepts.

Given that photographic images are visually isomorphic with the appearance of the photographable world, and given the usual standards of verisimilitude that prevail in narratives, it follows that viewers are behaving quite rationally in using interpersonal cues derived from personal experience to evaluate the behavior of characters on screen. In an important sense, viewers are not being "positioned" by films. Rather, they are positioning film events and characters according to socially derived, extra-filmic knowledge of appropriate and inappropriate real-world behavior. It should be noted that these evaluations are facilitated by iconic information about facial expression and gesture. This information, as Ray Birdwhistell has pointed out,[36] is systematically patterned within cultures and is situationally articulated as a communicational form in daily life. Motion picture viewers are expert decoders of the gestural and facial displays sanctioned in their culture and may even be sensitive to certain displays across cultures.[37] (In cases where facial and gestural cues might be unfamiliar, filmmakers can always build redundant information into the narrative and dramatic context of a scene to clarify for viewers the appropriate responses, thus ensuring the general comprehensibility of their product.) This reproduction by the cinema of culturally patterned streams of facial and gestural expression provides an important incentive to viewers to measure the content of the cinematic image against their horizon of extra-filmic life experience.

Psychoanalytic film theory has tended to ignore these dimensions of iconic and noniconic correspondence or has dealt with them in a negative fashion by postulating viewers who are duped by "transparency effects" or the "illusions" of realist, perspective-based imagery. It is clear, however, that these correspondences facilitate the viewer's easy comprehension of cinematic images and encourage an entirely rational process whereby the viewer maps aspects of the cinematic display onto dimensions of his or her real-life visual and social experience. Psychoanalytic film theory has had little to say about the complex ways viewers seek correspondences between their experience and what they see on screen—at least little to say that is truly researchable. Virtually all of the evidence cited in the foregoing discussion has come from the disciplines of psychology and communication. Researchers in the disciplines which have established traditions of empirical study, have looked carefully at how viewers watch film and television, and they have gone some way toward understanding that process. Film theorists, by contrast, with little tradition of work in (and little respect for) empirical procedures, have constructed spectators who exist in theory; they have taken almost no look at real viewers. We are now in the unenviable position of having constructed theories of spectatorship from which spectators are missing.

Spectators are absent from our accounts of spectatorship because psychoanalysis has failed to furnish valid or reliable data that could be used to construct or modify theory. Our field's dilemma in this area is not that it needs to engage in better "theorization" but that it needs to revise some of its basic methodological procedures. As a field that encompasses the domains of history, theory, and criticism, film studies sprawls over a large area. Not all of the questions it confronts are empirical ones, nor should they be approached using empirical methods. But some clearly are, and I submit that spectatorship is an area for empirical inquiry. Two excellent avenues for approaching questions of spectatorship empirically would involve application of the concepts of correspondence (both iconic and noniconic) and of attention and attentiveness. In this essay, we have seen how these concepts can produce fruitful investigations of spectatorship and, I hope, how nicely they fit as constructs with the evidence that is available on the ways that people watch visual media and infer meaning from visual displays. These concepts have already informed a great deal of research elsewhere, and there is no reason why film studies cannot further these lines of inquiry. Doing so, however, will involve a rethinking of what spectatorship is and a recognition that theory is more than a set of shared perspectives facilitating dialogue among adherents of the theory.

At a minimum, we should ask that our theories be capable of generating researchable questions and be responsive to the evidence our studies furnish. As this chapter has suggested, psychoanalytic film theory is flawed in both of these areas. Once again, it is important to emphasize that the approach outlined here does not entail minimizing the richness of our philosophical or conceptual frameworks. The results of our research always will need to be integrated within a broad explanatory framework, that is, will need to be accounted for theoretically. But our theories of spectatorship will also need to be referenceable in terms of the available evidence on spectators. Above all, we need to start our search for the missing spectator who has been lost to film theory for several decades now. It will be a difficult search since film studies has a long way to go. But if film scholars can undertake it, film studies will lay claim to what should always have been an essential area of distinguished accomplishment—a sophisticated portrait of what it means to watch a film.

NOTES

1. Judith Mayne, *Cinema and Spectatorship* (New York: Routledge, 1993), p. 59.

2. Ibid., p. 37.

3. Kenneth Mark Colby and Robert J. Stoller, *Cognitive Science and Psychoanalysis* (Hillsdale, N.J.: Lawrence Erlbaum, 1988), p. 3.

4. Ibid., p. 29.

5. See Laura Mulvey, "Visual Pleasure and Narrative Cinema," *Screen* 16, 3 (Autumn 1975): 6–18, and her reconsideration of this essay in *Visual and Other Pleasures* (Bloomington: Indiana University Press, 1989).

6. See D. N. Rodowick, *The Difficulty of Difference* (New York: Routledge, 1991); Mary Ann Doane, "The 'Woman's Film': Possession and Address," in *Re-Vision: Essays in Feminist Film Criticism,* eds. Mary Ann Doane, Patricia Mellencamp, and Linda Williams (Frederick, Md.: AFI/University Publications of America, 1984), pp. 67–80; and Miriam Hansen, "Pleasure, Ambivalence, Identification: Valentino and Female Spectatorship," *Cinema Journal* 25, 4 (1986): 6–32.

7. Christian Metz, *The Imaginary Signifier: Psychoanalysis and the Cinema,* trans. Celia Britton, et al. (Bloomington: Indiana University Press, 1982), p. 64.

8. Rodowick, *The Difficulty of Difference,* p. x.

9. Ibid., p. 71.

10. Sigmund Freud, "A Child Is Being Beaten: A Contribution to the Study of the Origin of Sexual Perversions," in Sigmund Freud, *Collected Papers,* 5 vols., trans. supervised by Joan Riviere (New York: Basic Books, 1959), 2:179–80.

11. Kaja Silverman, "Masochism and Male Subjectivity," in *Male Trouble,* ed. Constance Penley and Sharon Willis (Minneapolis: University of Minnesota Press, 1993), p. 50.

12. Metz, *The Imaginary Signifier,* p. 58.

13. Ibid., pp. 49–50.

14. Daniel R. Anderson and Elizabeth Pugzles Lorch, "Looking at Television: Action or Reaction?" in *Children's Understanding of Television: Research on Attention and Comprehension,* ed. Jennings Bryant and Daniel R. Anderson (New York: Academic Press, 1983), pp. 10–11.

15. Daniel R. Anderson and Diane E. Field, "Online and Offline Assessment of the Television Audience," in *Responding to the Screen: Reception and Reaction Processes,* ed. Jennings Bryant and Dolf Zillmann (Hillsdale, N.J.: Lawrence Erlbaum, 1991), p. 213.

16. Anderson and Lorch, "Looking at Television," p. 19.

17. Ibid., p. 12–13.

18. Cognitive approaches are frequently criticized for failing to deal with emotion, but emotion and cognition are not separate. Affective responses include cognitive dimensions which can stipulate how physiological arousal is labeled as particular emotions. Classic work here includes Stanley Schachter and J. Singer, "Cognitive, Social and Physiological Determinants of Emotional State," *Psychological Review* 69 (1962): 379–99, and Stanley Schachter, "The Interaction of Cognitive and Physiological Determinants of Emotional State," in *Advances in Experimental Social Psychology,* ed. Leonard Berkowitz (New York: Academic Press, 1964), 1:49–80. See also the essays in *Approaches to Emotion,* ed. Klaus R. Scherer and Paul Ekman, (Hillsdale, N.J.: Lawrence Erlbaum, 1984).

19. Edward Branigan discusses narrative comprehension in terms of multilevel information processing in *Narrative Comprehension and Film* (New York: Routledge, 1992).

20. Frank Biocca, "Viewers' Mental Models of Political Messages: Toward a Theory of the Semantic Processing of Television," in *Television and Political Advertising, vol. 1, Psychological Processes,* ed. Frank Biocca (Hillsdale, N.J.: Lawrence Erlbaum, 1991), pp. 27–89.

21. Ibid., p. 81.

22. Empirical evidence indicates the ways that increasingly elaborate viewing schemas can facilitate and enhance information pickup. See, for example, Jeanne M. Meadowcroft and Bryon Reeves, "Influence of Story Schema Development on Children's Attention to Television," *Communication Research* 16, 3 (June 1989): 352–74.

23. Ibid., p. 81.

24. For an additional discussion of this point, see my article "The Discourse of Pictures: Iconicity and Film Studies," *Film Quarterly* 47, 1 (Fall 1993): 16–28. See also Noël Carroll, "Toward a Theory of Point-of-View Editing: Communication, Emotion, and the Movies," *Poetics Today* 14, 1 (Spring 1993): 123–41.

25. L. F. Alwitt, D. R. Anderson, E. P. Lorch, and S. R. Levin, "Preschool Children's Visual Attention to Attributes of Television," *Human Communication Research* (1980) 7: 52–67.

26. Prince, "The Discourse of Pictures: Iconicity and Film Studies," *Film Quarterly* 47, 1 (Fall 1993): 16–28.

27. Julian Hochberg and Virginia Brooks, "Picture Perception as an Unlearned Ability: A Study of the Child's Performance," *American Journal of Psychology* 74, 4 (Dec. 1962): 624–28.

28. Robin Smith, Daniel R. Anderson, and Catherine Fischer, "Young Children's Comprehension of Montage," *Child Development* 56 (1985): 962–71; Renée Hobbs, Richard Frost, Arthur Davis, and John Stauffer, "How First-Time Viewers Comprehend Editing Conventions," *Journal of Communication* 38, 4 (1988): 50–60.

29. For a comprehensive review of this literature, see Patrick A. Cabe, "Picture Perception in Nonhuman Subjects," in *The Perception of Pictures*, 2 vols., ed. Margaret A. Hagen (New York: Academic Press, 1980), 2:305–43.

30. Elizabeth M. Perse and Rebecca B. Rubin, "Attribution in Social and Parasocial Relationships," *Communication Research* 16, 1 (February 1989): 73.

31. Aimee Dorr, "How Children Make Sense of Television," in *Reader in Public Opinion and Mass Communication*, ed. Morris Janowitz and Paul M. Hirsch (New York: Free Press, 1981), p. 374.

32. Paul Messaris and Larry Gross, "Interpretations of a Photographic Narrative by Viewers in Four Age Groups," *Studies in the Anthropology of Visual Communication* 4 (1977): 99–111.

33. Thomas J. Berndt and Emily G. Berndt, "Children's Use of Motives and Intentionality in Person Perception and Moral Judgement," *Child Development* 46 (1975): 904–12.

34. Austin S. Babrow, Barbara J. O'Keefe, David L. Swanson, Renee A. Meyers, and Mary A. Murphy, "Person Perception and Children's Impression of Television and Real Peers," *Communication Research* 15, 6 (December 1988): 680–98.

35. Cynthia Hoffner and Joanne Cantor, "Developmental Differences in Responses to a Television Character's Appearance and Behavior," *Developmental Psychology* 21, 6 (1985): 1065–74.

36. Ray L. Birdwhistell, *Kinesics and Context* (Philadelphia: University of Pennsylvania Press, 1970).

37. See Paul Ekman and Wallace V. Friesen, "Constants Across Culture in the Face and Emotion," *Journal of Personality and Social Psychology* 17, 2 (1971): 124–29, and Paul Ekman, "Expression and the Nature of Emotion" in *Approaches to Emotion*, ed. Klaus R. Scherer and Paul Ekman pp. 319–43.

Convention, Construction, and Cinematic Vision

David Bordwell

Cinema is partly pictorial representation, and we have come to expect, especially after the dissemination of Structuralist and Post-Structuralist theories, that the most enlightening accounts of pictorial representation will involve a theoretical account of conventions. Yet the humanities have not yet solved the problem of how to understand conventions; indeed, I am not convinced that we know precisely what a convention is.[1]

In this chapter I aim to clarify the operations of visual conventions in cinema, but I have broader goals as well. I shall suggest that we can make progress toward understanding artistic convention by rejecting some tenets of Structuralist and Post-Structuralist doctrine—notably the equation of "convention" with "arbitrariness." I go on to sketch a criticism of the radical "constructivist" position that is often associated with such doctrines. The chapter also point toward the relevance of cross-cultural regularities for understanding even the most local and idiosyncratic conventions.

I

The problem of convention in filmic representations can be strikingly posed by considering one film technique. What is called "shot/reverse-shot" editing prototypically involves displaying two figures in face-to-face interaction. The camera shows each one alternately, with either the other character absent or only partly visible. The filmmaker cuts from one shot to another, following the flow of the conversation and facial response (Figs. 4.1–4.2).

The shot/reverse-shot device deserves to be called a stylistic invention. It was not determined by the technology of the cinema, and I can find no plausible parallels in contemporary representational systems, such as comic strips, paintings, or lantern slides. It was not utilized as a stylistic device in the first fifteen years or so of filmmaking; that period was dominated by the so-called tableau style, which showed the entire scene in a single shot. In the early 1910s, some fiction films used the shot/reverse-shot device occasionally, while by the end of the teens it was common in American features. Fairly soon

Fig. 4.1. *Metropolis* (Fritz Lang, 1927).   Fig. 4.2. *Metropolis* (Fritz Lang, 1927).

after this, it was adopted around the world. It continues to be one of the most commonly used techniques in film and television.

What makes the shot/reverse shot comprehensible? Theorists have offered two fairly distinct answers to this question. The first, and older, view is that the device offers a kind of equivalent for ordinary vision. An important early discussion is offered by the Soviet filmmaker Vsevolod Pudovkin.

Editing, Pudovkin says, aims to guide the spectator's attention to important elements of a scene. "The lens of the camera replaces the eye of the observer, and the changes of angle of the camera—directed now on one person, now on another . . .—must be subject to the same conditions as those of the eyes of the observer."[2] This is rather vaguely put, but the idea that editing simulates the change of glance of an observer makes shot/reverse shot a kind of heightening of our ordinary perception of an event involving participants. More recently, Barry Salt has compared such editing to "what a spectator before the scene would see, standing there and casting his glance from this point to that point within it."[3]

For these theorists, then, filmmakers discovered in the shot/reverse shot a correlate to spontaneous perceptual activity. Call this the "naturalist" position.

The naturalist position answers several questions. What enabled shot/reverse shot to be discovered? Presumably, filmmakers seeking to engage audiences hit upon it by trial and error, perhaps guided by their own perceptual intuitions. Why was it so rapidly taken up? Because it achieved the requisite purposes of presenting an intelligible structure of information to the spectator. Why has shot/reverse shot been so enduring and pervasive? Because, as an obvious correlate to perceptual experience outside the movie house, it does not require viewers to have special training in order to understand it.

Yet there are problems with this account. Most notably, the device is more *un*faithful to perceptual experience than it ought to be. The best equivalent to a viewer moving her or his glance from one character to another would seem to be obtained by simply swiveling ("panning") the camera from speaker to speaker. But this is a very rare stylistic option in mainstream cinema. The instantaneous transfer of attention given by the cut would seem to be a conventional substitute for this swiveling of the imaginary spectator's attention—a substitute that has no exact correlate in ordinary perceptual experience.

The shot/reverse-shot device is also unfaithful to ordinary vision because it changes the camera position so as to favor ¾ views. A profiled shot/reverse shot (such as that in Figs. 4.3–4.4) would provide a closer equivalent to "what a spectator before the scene would see" than does the angled, over-the-shoulder views presented by the majority practice. When we watch a face-to-face interaction, we are not perceptually capable of shifting our angle of view as drastically as is normal in shot/reverse-shot cutting.

Fig. 4.3. *Class Relations* (Jean-Marie Straub and Danièle Huillet, 1983).   Fig. 4.4. *Class Relations* (Jean-Marie Straub and Danièle Huillet, 1983).

Such difficulties were noticed in Pudovkin's day. He therefore added a proviso: the camera allowed the director to create not an actual observer but an "ideal," omnipresent one. Similarly, as Karel Reisz and Gavin Miller point out, the change of angle within shot/reverse-shot cutting has "no analogous experience in real life."[4] The director aims at creating "a ubiquitous observer, giving the audience at each moment of the action the best possible viewpoint. He selects the images which he considers most telling, irrespective of the fact that no single individual could view a scene in this way in real life."[5] This is justified as artistic selection.

But this deviation from the natural-equivalent premise opens the door to quite a different theoretical position. Once shot/reverse-shot cuts are admitted to be dependent upon purely "artistic" considerations, we can ask if they are not simply conventions. Any artistic device as widely used as shot/reverse shot, if not significantly motivated by perceptual equivalences, is likely to be seen as a stylistic convention.

This view, it is fair to say, dominates film studies today. From this perspective, shot/reverse-shot cutting is an arbitrary device, having no privileged affinities with natural perception. But what is a convention, on this view?

Minimally, I suppose, most contemporary scholars would say that shot/reverse shot is a convention because it is a piece of artifice, and because it must be learned. Most theorists are content to leave the matter there, but neither point really blocks the naturalist position. The naturalist position does not have to claim that shot/reverse-shot editing is not artificial in some sense. After all, it is an invention; it was not present at the birth of cinema, and people decided to use it. Nor does the naturalist position have to deny the role of learning. Once we have learned to perceive the world, the naturalist might argue, we can learn to grasp artistic devices that provide equivalents to the world. Accordingly, our ability to grasp those devices ought to ride upon the appropriate sorts of perceptual skills.

To this a contemporary theorist might reply that the typical convention is arbitrary. Here, arbitrariness must mean something like this: In principle, an indefinitely large number of other representations would serve as well; the one chosen is simply assigned that task by the rules of the *langue* or code in force. A dog might as easily have been called a *chien* or a *hund*.

There are some problems with extending to non-linguistic phenomena a conception of arbitrariness derived from the lexical items in a language. Consider the turn signals on a car. To an observer on Sirius, the fact that I flash the right signal when I intend to turn right might appear arbitrary. Other options are logically possible: people could signal a right turn by activating the *left* signal. But in fact such mechanisms are designed to fit to our propensities to signal rightward movement by something that itself stands in a rightward relation to our body. Our nonverbal symbol systems, like our technical gadgets, are engineered to our fixed dispositions, including innate ones, and the choice among all possible options is not indifferent.[6]

A similar case can be made about the shot/reverse-shot technique. If the director seeks to represent two people looking at each other, it is less arbitrary to show them looking *at* each other than to show them, say, looking *away* from each other or at the moon. A visual "code" which showed figures looking at each other in order to signify that they are *not* looking at each other would be bizarre in the extreme. We would, I think, be inclined to call *that* alternative code "arbitrary," but not the normal case, which reflects naturalistic assumptions about the image's representation of the state of affairs. For creatures like us, the two options are not equiprobable.

Nevertheless, the naturalist's position on shot/reverse shot remains problematic because of the undeniably "unrealistic" qualities present in orthodox uses of the device. And something theoretically stronger is probably required to allay the conventionalist's worries. At this point I want to suggest a middle way between the two positions, one which captures the intuition that such visual devices are constructed and significantly artificial while also preserving the idea that they are not utterly arbitrary.

2

In contrasting the two views of shot/reverse shot, I followed precedent in distinguishing something called "nature" from something called "convention." The first step in forging a more comprehensive theory, I believe, is to discard these notions and offer some more flexible concepts in their place.

The term "nature" comes to us fraught with connotations. To most film theorists, it suggests either biologically innate capacities or universal laws operating in the physical world generally. It also suggests the realm of necessity, that which cannot be changed by human will or skill. Such conceptions of "the natural" have been frequently attacked by Structuralist and Post-Structuralist theorists, who insist that all signification is constructed, conventional, and culture-bound.

Still, only dogmatists would deny that representation, especially visual representation, relies at least partly on the perceiver's psychophysical capacities. It seems very unlikely that our abilities to recognize humans and objects in images owes *nothing* to our biological heritage. Our understanding of images could hardly be unconnected to our capacities to move through a three-dimensional environment and to recognize conspecifics. The individual's development of language, according to the most powerful theories now available, is as much a biological capacity as the inclination to grow arms rather than wings.[7] Certain relevant abilities may not even be species-specific: pigeons and monkeys respond to photographs as if recognizing the sorts of things represented.[8]

Nonetheless, I propose that we can make some progress if we bypass the nature/culture couplet for the moment and concentrate upon some "contingent universals" of human life. They are contingent because they did not, for any metaphysical reasons, have to be the way they are; and they are universal insofar as we can find them to be widely present in human societies. They consist of practices and propensities which arise in and through human activities. The core assumption here is that given certain uniformities in the environment across cultures, humans have in their social activities faced comparable tasks in surviving and creating their ways of life. Neither wholly "natural" nor wholly "cultural," these sorts of contingent universals are good candidates for being at least partly responsible for the "naturalness" of artistic conventions.

Paradigm cases of contingent universals would seem to be practical skills such as the ability to use language for communication, to divide labor tasks, to distinguish between living and nonliving things, and so on. I have stated these rather generally; it is an empirical question as to whether there are not much more specific contingent universals, such as recognizing focal colors or taking turns during conversation.[9]

I have stressed contingent universals as involving behavior, but it seems likely that they constitute a conceptual frame of reference as well. The anthropologist Robin Horton calls such a framework "primary theory," and characterizes it as follows:

> Primary theory gives the world a foreground filled with middle-sized (say between a hundred times as large and a hundred times as small as human beings), enduring, solid objects. These objects are interrelated, indeed, interdefined, in terms of a 'push-pull' conception of causality, in which spatial and temporary contiguity are seen as crucial to the transmission of change. They are related spatially in terms of five dichotomies: 'left'/'right'; 'above'/'below'; 'in-front-of'/'behind'; 'inside'/'outside'; 'contiguous'/'separate'. And temporally in terms of one trichotomy: 'before'/'at the same time'/'after'. Finally, primary theory makes two major distinctions amongst its objects: first, that between human beings and other objects; and second, among human beings, that between self and others.[10]

Horton suggests that while different communities may emphasize some aspects of primary theory and leave others comparatively undeveloped, as a conceptual framework it does not vary significantly from culture to culture.

Note that no decisive claim need be made that contingent universals, whether practices or "primary theory," are either biologically prewired or culturally acquired. In a trivial sense, the capacity to undertake any action must precede that action, so there must be some "natural" capacities. At the same time, it is unlikely that there is a genetic program for knowing how to hammer or weave, so certain factors of circumstance and culture play an irreducible role as well. It seems reasonable for students of visual culture to assume that, say, the ability to discriminate colors or the skill at working material with tools is a contingent universal of human activity, and leave the detailed story of the growth of that activity to research within the appropriate disciplines.

This perspective casts the concept of "convention" in a fresh light. "Arbitrariness" as a measure of conventionality stems, I think, from a misapplication of Saussure's claims about the arbitrariness of the linguistic sign.[11] There is another way to conceive of conventions: as norm-bound practices that coordinate social activities and direct action in order to achieve goals.[12]

If we think of convention in terms of practical action, "arbitrariness" is not a very fruitful way of characterizing it. In one important sense, an action counts as arbitrary if the same goal could have been achieved by an alternative means, with no additional costs or difficulties. If I want a bag of potato chips and I am equidistant between two stores selling such tasty snack treats, all other things being equal the choice is arbitrary. But most artistic conventions are not arbitrary in this sense. First, for reasons already mentioned, some choices are weighted because human proclivities favor certain options. It is nonarbitrary that the right rear turn signal on an automobile announces that the driver intends to turn right, not left. Moreover, many artistic conventions are more appropriate to certain ends than others. If I am a film director and I want spectators to notice an actor's expression, my choice of a close framing is not arbitrary, since that is an option more favorable to achieving my purpose than, say, selecting an extreme long shot.[13] I conclude that we want an account of convention that accommodates two demands: the "engineering" ought to fit human predispositions, and the means ought to be weighted in relation to ends.

A final piece of brickwork needs to be laid in place. One of the attractions of the concept of culturally conventional "codes" is the premise that works transmit or produce meanings. Meanings are cultural; where there is meaning, so goes the reasoning, there must be codes. Instead, though, we may think of works as producing *effects,* of which meanings are certain types. If we take the artist's goal to be that of eliciting discriminable effects, we can consider a wider range of theoretical possibilities. Now we can conceive of conventions as part of the artist's means for producing effects of many sorts. And these effects take their place in a fabric of human action; they are consequences of practical action on the part of artists, and grasping the conventions is bound up with larger activities pursued by perceivers.

Our middle way between sheer naturalism and radical conventionalism, then, is signposted by the notions of contingent universals, conventions as norm-governed patterns of behavior, and artistic goals conceived as effects. The map I propose involves a scale of visual effects, with distinct regions but loose boundaries between them. Here I am picking up on E. H. Gombrich's hint that we could consider "representational method" as ranked on "a continuum between skills which come naturally to us and skills which may be next to impossible for anyone to acquire."[14]

1. At one end lie visual effects which are dependent upon cross-cultural, even universal factors. Roughly, these would seem to be of two types.

First there are what we can call "sensory triggers." These are cues which automatically stimulate spectators. In the pictorial arts, contrasts of tonality and texture would seem good candidates. Gombrich's interest in visual illusions has led him to insist particularly on the importance of such triggers. He will frequently draw analogies to the behavior studied by ethologists, such as the ability of a rigged scrap to draw attack from the stickleback fish. But Gombrich also suggests that such triggering mechanisms need not be in the service of illusion; they can also stimulate a search for meaning, creating perceptual anticipations which run ahead of the evidence. One of Gombrich's great accomplishments is to have discovered that sensory triggers play a much larger role in the visual arts than most theorists had recognized.

All nonlinguistic arts exploit such sensory triggers: scale and volume in sculpture, rhythm and loudness in music, and so on. They are among the best candidates we have for "wired-in" responses. In cinema we do not have to look far for such triggers. Apparent motion, the basis of cinematic movement, is an obvious one. We still do not know exactly how apparent motion works; it may involve a cluster of specific mechanisms, possibly including motion-detecting cells in the visual system.[15] Apparent motion is a prime instance of a contingent universal: we did not evolve in order to be able to watch movies, but the inventors of cinema were able to exploit a feature of the design of the human optical system to create a pictorial display which is immediately accessible to all sighted humans. Other sensory triggers available in cinema are the use of extreme contrasts of visual tonality; the startle response evoked by sudden intrusions into the frame; and, if Gombrich is right, the use of lighting to create texture and volume within the shot.

Apart from sensory triggers, there are visual effects which draw upon contingently universal factors. These rely on regularities of experience that are reasonable candidates for being cross-cultural. Recognizing and reacting to these activities almost certainly requires some learning, but their ease of recognition among adult members of all cultures make them function as contingent universals, instances of Horton's "primary theory."

As in our case of face-to-face interaction in shot/reverse shot, these contingent universals are so firmly fixed that we can scarcely imagine what arbitrary alternatives would be. For example, we are so used to thinking about the variability of the representation of pictorial space across different periods and places that we often forget that these variations stand out against the background of a remarkable constancy in the portrayal of human beings. If visual representation were truly arbitrary, then we ought to find humans portrayed with four eyes or five legs as frequently as with two of each. Yet in art across the world, the human body is represented in broadly comparable terms: the right number of limbs, the anatomically correct placement of head and feet and hands, approximately similar canons of proportion, and so on. Indeed, deities and monsters are marked as such at least partly by violations of such norms. Just as we can recognize other members of our species in ordinary life, so too can we recognize the human being in art of very distant or ancient societies. Surely cinema draws upon this cross-cultural ability to recognize our conspecifics without any special training.

Returning to our example of shot/reverse-shot cutting, I suggest that face-to-face personal interaction is a solid candidate for a cross-cultural universal. This is probably why a visual code is unlikely to represent shared glances by divergent glances, as noted above. It is also perhaps why the situation portrayed in shot/reverse shot is instantly recognizable across cultures and time periods.

2. Moving along the continuum, we can turn our attention to visual effects which depend on culturally localized skills but which can be learned easily. "Easily" here translates into "quickly, on the basis of our comparatively limited exposure, and/or without special training or expert guidance." These are norm-bound practices which can be picked up largely through participating in a culture's life as a whole.

For instance, line drawings seem not to be culturally universal, and so they rely on skills specific to certain cultures. Yet we have no reason to doubt that someone can learn the conventions of line drawing very easily—certainly much more easily than learning a first or second language.

Sometimes such conventions are acquired in the course of normal human development within the culture. There is considerable evidence that in our culture children at least learn to understand line drawings of objects in tandem with learning to distinguish (name, indicate, use) such objects in the world.[16] For an adult learner, such norms require only the most minimal exposure and the most nontechnical, ostensive training. Often, these norms can be guessed from context, as the speed lines in comic strips are.

Cinema is full of such easily learned visual effects. Arguably, most transitions, such as dissolves or fades; most acting styles; and most stylistic innovations, such as crosscutting or complex camera movements, instantiate such skills. Moreover, once the viewer has mastered narrative structure to a useful degree, she or he has a sufficiently strong sense of context in which to "place" particular cinematic devices. Once the viewer has the working concept "scene," for instance, she or he can hazard a guess that the darkening and lightening of the screen serve to mark one scene off from another. If cinema does have "codes," they are mostly codes of this very easily acquired sort—which makes them significantly different from the codes governing language-based sign systems.

3. At the other end of the continuum are those visual effects which depend on culturally specific skills requiring more learning. Acquiring them is time-consuming and requires wide exposure to exemplars and/or special training and/or expert guidance. In these respects there is perhaps a genuine analogy to language—not to speech comprehension and production, but to reading and writing.

In the arts generally, modernism is marked by such comparatively recondite conventions. Cubist painting, the novels of Joyce, the poetry of Pound or the Acmeists, serial or minimalist music—all demand that the perceiver cultivate highly specific skills. Such skills need not be wholly of form or style, since understanding the depicted material itself could require training. Sacred iconography would be a key instance. In Quentin Metsys's *Mocking of Christ* (1466), one might recognize a man standing on a balcony, hands bound and wearing a crown of thorns, without knowing the tradition whereby the situation and objects identify him as Christ before his persecutors.

In film, there may be relatively few visual effects which depend upon such specialized skills. The avant-garde cinema is a plausible place to look for such effects, and it seems likely that the films of Stan Brakhage or Yvonne Rainer require an audience to be conversant with Abstract Expressionism or contemporary Post-Structuralist theory. More mainstream art cinema of the 1960s may have cultivated certain comparable devices, such as plays with narrative time or shifts between black-and-white and color.

The spectrum I have outlined, from sensory triggers to comparatively recondite "expert-system" effects, is intended as no more than an initial shot at an account of visual effects. Many of my examples are speculative and are open to empirical disconfirmation. But the general aim is to produce a frame of reference for theoretical reflection and concrete analysis. Such a continuum lets us avoid the difficulties of the naturalist/conventionalist couplet. In order to achieve certain effects, artists may tap biological propensities and contingent universals; in order to achieve other effects, artists may invoke more localized and recondite skills.

Does all this ascribe too little a role to culture? I think not. For one thing, as Gombrich has often pointed out, the tasks and interests which shape the ways in which visual effects are manipulated proceed from culture. If conventions are relations of means and ends, the social purposes of a representation necessarily govern how the activity is conducted, how the first region of effects is formed into more complex ones. Moreover, the centrality of artistic schemata—those inherited patterns and formulas through which the artist achieves effects in the medium—assure that culture plays a central role. "Only where there is a way is there also a will," Gombrich notes. "The individual can enrich the ways and means that his culture offers him; he can hardly wish for something that he has never known is possible." [17]

3

One advantage of tracing out this gamut of factors is that it allows us to see that the most intuitively obvious phenomena of visual representation seldom fall neatly on one point of the continuum. It is unlikely that a single image, or a design system like linear perspective, or even a technical device like shot/ reverse shot editing, will constitute a pure instance of any sort of effect along this spectrum. [18] As critics and historians we inherit a language of practical craft, and this has other ends in view than the distinctions that produce the continuum I have sketched.

More likely, a garden-variety representational device will present a bundle of effects of different sorts. Any given image may call upon sensory triggers (such as color contrast to indicate contours), contingent universals such as identification of the human figure, easily learned effects such as outline drawing, and more complex skills, such as that of identifying allegorical figures.

It seems plausible to go further and hypothesize that the cues lying closer to the "sensory trigger" end of the scale will specify and constrain those cues which are more culturally specific and more difficult to pick up. That is, part of what we mean by understanding something "because of its context" is that in the representational package we are offered, the more contingently universal cues lead us to make sense of more esoteric cues in particular ways. This would obviously facilitate learning: not only do we need little exposure to certain effects, but in each image, the universal factors reinforce our hypotheses about the proper reaction we should have to the more culturally specific ones.

I suggest that shot/reverse shot is best considered along these lines—as a composite phenomenon, drawing on features from various regions of the continuum. I cannot itemize all the relevant cues here, but let me make a start.

In its prototypical form, shot/reverse shot is predicated on a two-person, face-to-face encounter. This phenomenon would seem to be a good candidate for a contingent universal of social intercourse—something that would be intelligible across cultures and periods. This consideration is so rudimentary that neither the naturalist nor the conventionalist position or shot/reverse shot deems it necessary to weigh it, but in my argument it forms a kind of cross-cultural bridgehead. For instance, Figs. 4.5–4.6 from *Yaaba* may present facial or gestural cues specific to rural life in Burkina Faso. Nonetheless, the cutting and camera positions present a face-to-face encounter between the young protagonist and his elder, and they do so through a prototypical shot/reverse-shot construction.

Fig. 4.5. *Yaaba* (Idrissa Ouedraogo, 1989).　　Fig. 4.6. *Yaaba* (Idrissa Ouedraogo, 1989).

The pattern may capture other contingent universals at work as well. Conversational turn-taking, with its interchanging role of speaker and listener, might furnish an approximate structure for the alternation of images we get in shot/reverse-shot. Indeed, it would seem likely that this alternating editing grows out of an effort to capture the turn-taking phenomenon in cinematic form. Another important cue, at least in the prototypical instance, is the glance of the persons represented on the screen. Noël Carroll has suggested that the informational saliency of eye movements in primates gives filmmakers a powerful opportunity to engage audiences cross-culturally.[19] In the terms I have proposed, the direction of the glance would function as a sensory trigger, informing us of the object of the person's attention. It stands as another cross-cultural regularity of human activity that can elicit effects in beholders.

Out of such basic materials—the face-to-face encounter, the marked look, the turn-taking structure of conversation—the cinematic shot/reverse shot elaborates a more complex construction. The immediately intelligible aspects of shot/reverse shot anchor what we might consider to be more culturally specific sorts of effects. Because it is universally intelligible to people from a very young age, the dyadic face-to-face encounter offers a constant which can contextually guide inferences of somewhat more specialized sorts.

Consider the propensity we already noted for shot/reverse-shot images to be ¾ views. There is some experimental evidence that for human faces in pictures, the ¾ view may be more easily recognized than other orientations.[20] Whereas the straight-on and profile views of police mug shots are aimed at recording measurable facial data and easing recognition of the real face, the ¾ view has generally been found to be strongest when pictures are to be compared with other pictures. Since the viewer does not have to pick the actor out of a lineup, the ¾ view in shot/reverse shot serves the purpose of maximizing rapid recognition (at least in cultures that have pictures). The fact that profiled shot/reverse shot seems to be rare in the world's filmmaking practice suggests that filmmakers have exploited a widespread, easily learned norm of representation.

As for the instantaneous change of view which is said to create the "ubiquitous" or "ideal" observer: this would seem to be a special case of the immediate leap in time or space caused by any cut, of any sort. And once spectators, presumably from a very young age, have acquired the skill of taking a cut to signal such a shift in orientation, the other cues present in shot/reverse shot may suffice to motivate the distinct changes of angle.[21]

There are doubtless other cues that are ingredient to the shot/reverse-shot device, such as the more localized norm that the figures will be observed from the same side of an imaginary "center line."[22] Nevertheless, these remarks indicate the directions in which my account would move. Against the naturalists, I suggest that we do not have to take the shot/reverse-shot technique as straightforwardly conforming to ordinary perception. It is not necessary to posit the device as creating an invisible observer; it is at least as likely that the shot/reverse shot presents a patterned display organized to highlight certain information. Hence its avoidance of a panning movement to simulate the glance and the physical implausibility of its canonical angles. The shot/reverse shot can best be considered as a bundle of norms, some less "stylized" than others.

Against the conventionalists, I suggest that this bundle of norms draws upon contingent universals of human culture as well as pervasive, easily learned practices of filmmaking. And it seems likely that the former *constrain* and *specify* the latter: if the viewer knew nothing of face-to-face conversations, eyelines, or turn-taking, it would be impossible to grasp the purpose of the camera positions and editing. In a metaphorical sense, the prototype of shot/reverse shot is *constructed* out of such contingent universals: it is a refined elaboration of them, a piece of artifice serving cultural and aesthetic purposes.

The multiplicity of those purposes can best be grasped, I think, if we turn to a final issue. Gombrich has argued that the history of style in the visual arts is usefully understood as a process of schema and revision. The artist takes an available pattern and recasts it in the light of the capacities of the medium, the purposes she or he has in view, and the available means of achieving particular effects on the beholder. Art has a history, Gombrich suggests, because all these factors can change over time.[23]

From this standpoint, the shot/reverse-shot device can be seen as a schema within the history of film style. Once invented and found to achieve the desired effects, it became a formula for rendering the dramatic scenes that make up most narrative films. It proved enormously flexible. The shot/reverse shot could be adjusted to include several characters (Figs. 4.7–4.10). It could

Fig. 4.7. *Suvorov* (Vsevelod Pudovkin, 1941).   Fig. 4.8. *Suvorov* (Vsevelod Pudovkin, 1941).

Fig. 4.9. *The Land* (Youssef Chahine, 1969).   Fig. 4.10. *The Land* (Youssef Chahine, 1969).

show characters sitting side by side or perched at different heights (Figs. 4.11–4.12). It could present characters with their backs to each other. It could display only portions of characters' bodies (Figs. 4.13–4.14). The cam-

Fig. 4.11. *Prunella*
(Maurice Tourneur, 1918).

Fig. 4.12. *Prunella*
(Maurice Tourneur, 1918).

Fig. 4.13. *Gossette* (Germaine Dulac, 1923).

Fig. 4.14. *Gossette* (Germaine Dulac, 1923).

era could be placed at various distances and angles as well. For example, we may have shot/reverse shot with individuals or groups looking at the camera—that is, at the other participant(s) in the exchange (Figs. 4.15–4.18).

Fig. 4.15. *Toni* (Jean Renoir, 1934).

Fig. 4.16. *Toni* (Jean Renoir, 1934).

Fig. 4.17. *School Daze* (Spike Lee, 1988).

Fig. 4.18. *School Daze* (Spike Lee, 1988).

The shot/reverse-shot schema has proved capable of fulfilling more self-consciously expressive purposes. In *The Cloak,* Grigori Kozintsev and Leonid Trauberg alter angle and distance so drastically as to make the Important Personage loom very large and to make the supplicating Akaky Akakevich seem tiny (Figs. 4.19–4.20). John Woo stresses the affinities of cop and killer by making the graphic design of the shots very similar (Figs. 4.21–4.22). In order to convey the idea that two separated lovers are thinking of each other,

Fig. 4.19. *The Cloak* (Grigori Kozintsev and Leonid Trauber, 1927).

Fig. 4.20. *The Cloak* (Grigori Kozintsev and Leonid Trauber, 1927).

Fig. 4.21. *The Killer* (John Woo, 1989).

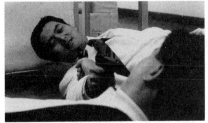

Fig. 4.22. *The Killer* (John Woo, 1989).

René Clair joins them in a shot/reverse-shot (Figs. 4.23–4.24). More disturbing is the famous shot/reverse-shot series in *Nosferatu*, when Dracula's attack on Jonathan Harker is halted by Nina's beseeching gesture in distant Bremen (Figs. 4.25–4.26). Once the shot/reverse-shot formula has been ab-

Fig. 4.23. *À Nous la liberté*
(Rene Clair, 1932).

Fig. 4.24. *À Nous la liberté*
(Rene Clair, 1932).

Fig. 4.25. *Nosferatu* (F. W. Murnau, 1922).

Fig. 4.26. *Nosferatu* (F. W. Murnau, 1922).

sorbed, "modernist" approaches can push it to elliptical limits: the opening of *Muriel* revises the scheme by making the shots abnormally fragmentary and brief, many less than half a second long (Figs. 4.27–4.30). One can take this passage as recasting the sort of intercutting of body parts employed in *Gossette* (Figs. 4.13–4.14).

Such sequences require that audiences know standard shot/reverse shot well enough to recognize the play between continuity cues and idiosyncratic factors working against the canonical effect. Even in the highly experimental cases, though, certain pervasive constants remain visible. Without the default assumption of proximate space, and without the cues of angle, distance, orientation, and cutting provided by the schema, such passages would be unin-

Fig. 4.27. *Muriel* (Alain Resnais, 1963). The medium shot of Hélène's client is 17 frames long (.7 seconds).

Fig. 4.28. The next shot, showing the client's coat button, is 12 frames long (.5 seconds).

Fig. 4.29. The next shot, of her hat, lasts only 11 frames (.45 seconds).

Fig. 4.30. The "reverse shot" of Hélène's hands is also 11 frames long.

telligible. This is not, one more time, to say that shot/reverse shot is some-how mimicking ordinary perception. But neither is it to say that the schema which is here revised is wholly artificial, completely arbitrary; for it requires some contingent universals as its bridgehead, and it presupposes some (easily learned) norms.

4

If any slogan wins immediate acceptance in contemporary theory in the hu-manities, it is that a given phenomenon is "culturally constructed." The term gathers its force partly from implicit contrast to alternative positions. The phe-nomenon is *constructed,* and thus in some sense artificial; it is the result of human praxis, not natural process. The phenomenon is *cultural,* and so nei-ther natural nor "individual"; it is broadly social, not narrowly psychic. So far, what I have been sketching out here is consistent with these general implica-tions of the phrase.

What I have been trying to say is not, however, compatible with another implication. Sometimes the phrase "culturally constructed" is used to suggest that the phenomenon is not universal or even widespread; it is assumed to be specific to a particular culture. Yet even if cultural models exercise a local va-lidity, it does not follow that all of them are unique to a single society or period. It is perfectly possible for a phenomenon to be culturally constructed and at the same time to be very widespread, or even universal, among human societies.

Too often advocates of radical cultural constructivism have supposed that humans in groups dispersed across time and space never face recurring con-ditions or problems and that they never develop similar or even identical so-lutions to these conditions. It is a cardinal error to assume that cross-cultural convergences indicate only a shared "biological" or natural propensity, and that all else must be a matter of divergence and variability, somehow traceable to the vagaries of cultural differences.

Not only perceptual equipment but also the disposition to see the world as a three-dimensional space in which free-standing objects exist independent of the observer; not only language "in general" but pronouns and proper names, lies and narratives, grammatical redundancy and the greater frequency of short words for familiar objects; not only toolmaking but the fashioning of pounders and containers; not only spontaneous smiling but also expressions of skepticism and anger, as well as a fear of snakes and loud noises—all these and many more activities are current candidates for being "cultural univer-sals." Apparently all cultures distinguish between natural and nonnatural ob-jects, between living and nonliving things, between plants and animals.[24] All societies have created fibers for tying, lacing, and weaving.[25] (To paraphrase Marjorie Garber: "No culture without string.")

The value of recalling such anthropological data is, I hope, to help us get beyond the equation of "cross-cultural" (or even "cross-subcultural") with "natural" or "biologically determined." Not even the most hubristic socio-biologist would postulate a genetic basis for proper names, containers, and twine. If we assume that culture has changed across history, we should not be surprised that regularities of the physical environment and of interpersonal relations, to which humans are attuned by species-specific propensities, have called forth from social collectivities many similar and even universal practices. If sociality requires communication, widely shared rules for face-to-face inter-actions and conversational turn-taking will assist the process in any circum-stance in which humans meet.

We ought not, therefore, to balk when the metaphor of construction leads us to recognize that social practices may be "built out" of biological propen-sities or contingent universals. I have argued elsewhere that a "constructivist" theory of social convention and mental activity requires some conception of materials out of which a representation is fashioned.[26] These materials need not be "raw," nor even "material" in the strict sense (since "constructivism" is a metaphor to start with).

Theoretically, the most comprehensive and powerful explanations of con-ventions in any art would seem to be those which show them to be functional transformations of other representations or practices, some of which may be biological predispositions or contingent universals. Methodologically, the best strategy would seem to be constantly on the alert for the cross-cultural factors which would be part of any representational process. Sometimes, these may go without saying; at other times, examining these may shed light on how familiar formulas achieve their distinctive power.

Something like this position, I think, has the best of both naturalism and conventionalism. This view also points toward ways of understanding how conventions may develop in specific social circumstances. Perhaps most tell-ingly, a "moderate constructivism" along these lines points toward an under-standing of the cross-cultural powers of visual art.

NOTES

This essay has benefited from comments made by audience members in various venues: the University of Wisconsin–Milwaukee Center for Twentieth Century Studies in 1991; the 1992 Convention of the American Society for Aesthetics; the 1993 Society for Cinema Studies convention; and the Annenberg School of Communication in 1994. I also thank Ben Brewster, Noël Carroll, Lea Jacobs, and Kristin Thompson for their criticisms. Kristin also provided several of the illustrations.

1. We have, however, made progress. This paper has benefited particularly from points made in the essays collected in *Rules and Conventions: Literature, Philosophy, Social Theory,* ed. Mette Hjort (Baltimore: Johns Hopkins University Press, 1992).

2. V. I. Pudovkin, *Film Technique* (1926; reprint, New York: Evergreen, 1970), p. 70.

3. Barry Salt, *Film Style and Technology: History and Analysis* (London: Starword, 1983), p. 164.

4. Karel Reisz and Gavin Millar, *The Technique of Film Editing*, 2d ed. (London: Focal Press, 1968), p. 215.

5. Ibid.

6. Someone might object that a more sophisticated semiology of cinema would classify turn signals as Peircean "indexical" signs rather than arbitrary symbols à la Saussure. After all, to signal a turn is rather like pointing to the direction in which I wish to go. To analyze this objection fully would take us afield, but let me quickly record my doubts.

First, I regard the appropriation of the Peircean triad of index/icon/symbol as suspect because this is only one of the several "trichotomies" which Peirce sets forth. He proposes three "trichotomies" of signs in his manuscript "Nomenclature and Divisions of Triadic Relations, as far as they are determined [c. 1903]." Three years later he proposed *ten* trichotomies, accounting for sixty-six types of signs! (See *Collected Papers of Charles Sanders Peirce*, vol. 2, *Elements of Logic*, ed. Charles Hartsthorne and Paul Weiss [Cambridge: Harvard University Press, 1932], pp. 134–73.) To my knowledge, no film theorists have confronted the dizzying array of sign relations set out within Peirce's overall system, even though this would seem a prerequisite for any serious assessment of his theory's usefulness for film study.

Furthermore, we should be chary of appropriating one piece of a conceptual system; taking that piece out of its context can easily lead to misunderstanding or inconsistency. For example, the Peircean trichotomy of symbols comports ill with the hodgepodge semiotics practiced by most film theorists. Peirce remarks that the Symbol actually denotes "a conventional sign, *or one depending upon habit (acquired or inborn)*" (*Elements*, p. 167; italics mine). This claim poses problems for those film semioticians who think of the Peircean Symbol as wholly conventional or arbitrary. ("The third category of sign, the symbol, corresponds to Saussure's arbitrary sign. . . . [The symbol] is conventional"; Peter Wollen, *Signs and Meaning in the Cinema* [Bloomington: Indiana University Press, 1972], p. 123.)

Moreover, by one of Peirce's definitions, an index "refer[s] to an Object . . . by virtue of being really affected by that object" (*Elements*, p. 143). Among his examples are weathervanes and photographs. But my turn signal does not refer to the "Object" right turn by being affected by that Object, the way that the wind affects the weathervane or the pattern of ambient light reflected from an object affects the chemically sensitized emulsion of a strip of film.

Finally, let me just register a skepticism about the clarity and precision of the positions taken in Peirce's writings. Film theorists (and semioticians in general) write with breezy confidence about his conception of signs, as if his texts (largely unpublished) were consistent, rigorously argued, and (above all) clear. You will not find in the film literature a recognition of the puzzles arising from a passage like this: "A rap on the door is an index. Anything which focuses the attention is an index. Anything which startles us is an index, in so far as it marks the junction between two portions of experience" (ibid., p. 161).

7. For an entertaining popular introduction to this line of argument, see Steven Pinker, *The Language Instinct: How the Mind Creates Language* (New York: William Morrow, 1994).

8. Some examples are discussed by Arthur Danto in "Description and the Phe-

nomenology of Perception," in *Visual Theory: Painting and Interpretation,* ed. Norman Bryson, Michael Ann Holly, and Keith Moxey (New York: HarperCollins, 1991), pp. 209–11.

9. For an exciting exploration of the empirical possibilities, see Donald E. Brown, *Human Universals* (Philadelphia: Temple University Press, 1991).

10. Robin Horton, "Tradition and Modernity Revisited," in *Rationality and Relativism,* ed. Martin Hollis and Steven Lukes (Cambridge: MIT Press, 1982), p. 228.

11. See Roy Harris, *Reading Saussure* (La Salle, Ill.: Open Court, 1987), pp. 64–69.

12. This sense is close to that posited by David Lewis in *Convention: A Philosophical Study* (Cambridge, Mass.: 1969). See also Paisley Livingston, *Literature and Rationality: Ideas of Agency in Theory and Fiction* (Cambridge: Cambridge University Press, 1991), chapters 1 and 2.

13. The idea that conventions are designed for utility in action echoes Noël Carroll's argument that many "arbitrary conventions" are in fact cultural *inventions* aimed at achieving specific goals. See his *Mystifying Movies: Fads and Fallacies in Contemporary Film Theory* (New York: Columbia University Press, 1988), pp. 142–44.

14. E. H. Gombrich, "Image and Code: Scope and Limits of Conventionalism in Pictorial Representation," in *The Image and the Eye* (Oxford: Phaidon, 1982), p. 283.

15. See Julian Hochberg, "Representation of Motion and Space in Video and Cinematic Displays," chapter 22 of *Handbook of Perception and Human Performance,* vol. 1, *Sensory Processes and Perception,* ed. Kenneth R. Boff, Lloyd Kaufman, and James P. Thomas (New York: Wiley, 1986), pp. 31–40.

16. See Julian Hochberg, "The Representation of Things and People," in *Art, Perception, and Reality,* ed. E. H. Gombrich et al. (Baltimore: Johns Hopkins University Press, 1972), pp. 67–73.

17. E. H. Gombrich, *Art and Illusion: A Study in the Psychology of Pictorial Representation* (Princeton: Princeton University Press, 1961), p. 86.

18. One theorist has proposed that "artificial perspective" as usually understood is just such a package of devices. John Hyman suggests that the distinct techniques of overlapping, foreshortening, and perspective diminution find "harmonious integration into a unified system" known as artificial perspective. See Hyman, "Perspective," in *A Companion to Aesthetics,* ed. David Cooper (Oxford: Blackwell, 1992), pp. 324–27.

19. Noël Carroll, "Toward a Theory of Point-of-View Editing: Communication: Emotion, and the Movies," *Poetics Today* 14, 1 (Spring 1993): 127–31.

20. See Vicki Bruce, Tim Valentine, and Alan Baddeley, "The Basis of the 3/4 View Advantage in Face Recognition," *Applied Cognitive Psychology* 1 (1987): 109–10; Robert H. Logie, Alan D. Baddeley, and Muriel M. Woodhead, "Face Recognition, Pose, and Ecological Validity," *Applied Cognitive Psychology* 1 (1987): 53–69.

21. Empirical research on these problems suggests that the conventions of shot change and eyeline-matching are quickly grasped at a young age and by members of widely different cultures. For a lucid discussion see Paul Messaris, *Visual Literacy: Image, Mind, and Reality* (Boulder, Colo.: Westview, 1994), pp. 74–86.

22. For a discussion of this principle, see David Bordwell and Kristin Thompson, *Film Art: An Introduction,* 4th ed. (New York: McGraw-Hill, 1993), pp. 262–75.

23. Gombrich, *Art and Illusion,* pp. 146–91.

24. See Scott Atran, *Cognitive Foundations of Natural History: Towards an Anthropology of Science* (Cambridge: Cambridge University Press, 1990).

25. Brown, *Human Universals,* p. 135.

26. "A Case for Cognitivism," *Iris* no. 9 (Spring 1989): 11–40.

5

Is a Cognitive Approach to the Avant-garde Cinema Perverse?

James Peterson

Let me begin with an assumption: that a cognitive perspective is a useful means of explaining *some* aspects of the viewer's response to *some* kinds of cinema. For example, I take it that it is relatively uncontroversial that research on canonical story formats has something to say about spectators' engagement with Hollywood-style films, which are often cut close to the pattern of the canonical story.[1] The skeptic might object that such a cognitive perspective doesn't address the most interesting or important issues raised by Hollywood-style films, but I don't hear many saying that a cognitive approach isn't at all appropriate to the Hollywood cinema.

Still, such is not the case with respect to the avant-garde cinema. Even some who accept cognitive approaches to commercial narrative films resist the idea that a cognitive perspective might help theorize the viewer's response to the avant-garde. Put in its plainest form, the complaint is that cognitive theory's conception of the viewer as conscious and rational is poorly matched to the unruly and sometimes irrational avant-garde. The Hollywood cinema cuts with the grain of perception and cognition, playing into the spectator's perceptual and cognitive inclinations and habits.[2] But the avant-garde cuts against this grain, challenging and resisting those same inclinations and habits. Commercial narrative films implicitly address the kind of rational viewer posited by cognitive theory, but the avant-garde cinema seems to call for some other kind of viewing, and a cognitive explanation of this kind of viewing would be perverse.

At the risk of defusing whatever suspense the title of my essay may have generated, let me say that I don't think a cognitive theory of the avant-garde cinema is perverse at all. In fact, the cognitive aspects of avant-garde film viewing were of particular interest to critics during the heyday of Structural film in the late 1960s and 1970s. Many of the avant-garde films of that period, notably work by Hollis Frampton, Peter Kubelka, and Michael Snow, were thought to explore the nature of consciousness by openly calling forth particular cognitive processes from the viewer.[3] And in the writing of Annette Michelson and P. Adams Sitney, one finds attempts to draw extended analogies between human consciousness and the avant-garde cinema.[4] As Sitney put it in his survey of the avant-garde film, "the often unacknowledged aspiration of the American avant-garde film has been the cinematic reproduction of the human mind."[5]

Certainly Structural films lay bare the cognitive aspects of the viewer's response with particular clarity, but it would be a mistake to think that a cognitive approach would be relevant only to Structural film. Cognitive processes are central to the viewer's experience of all avant-garde films. It would also underestimate the explanatory power of cognitive theory to limit our inquiry to drawing analogies between human cognition and the avant-garde cinema. My objective here is, in a sense, the reverse of Sitney's: I want to show not how the avant-garde cinema reproduces the mind, but how the mind comprehends the avant-garde cinema. The crux of my argument is that we might usefully consider avant-garde film viewing to be a kind of problem solving, which cognitive theories can help explain. Resistance to such a cognitive approach to the avant-garde cinema is rooted in misconceptions about both the nature of the avant-garde film experience and about cognitive theory.

An example of a kind of problem solving in the avant-garde cinema can be seen in J. J. Murphy's film *Print Generation* (1973–74). The film begins rather mysteriously, as dots of light dance around the screen. Gradually it becomes apparent that these lights form repeating patterns, and that with each cycle they seem to grow clearer. At some point along the way, the viewer realizes that these patterns are actually a series of shots of recognizable objects and scenes, although what these objects and scenes are isn't yet clear (Fig. 5.1). The images are just fragments of the filmmaker's home movies, yet *Print Generation* becomes an oddly compelling guessing game, as viewers struggle to identify each of the film's sixty images. At the halfway point, the images are presented in their maximal clarity, and all the little perceptual puzzles are solved (Fig. 5.2). (Though only for the moment, as the viewer must then solve the puzzles in reverse. The viewer tries to remember each image for as long as possible, but ultimately they all decay into the same indecipherable patterns that began the film.)

Fig. 5.1   Fig. 5.2

Print Generation is a particularly vivid example of how visual perception is guided by problem-solving principles, but we shouldn't think of it as unique. In fact, one main strain of cognitive work on perception suggests that *all* perception may be properly seen as a kind of problem solving. For example, Irwin Rock's *The Logic of Perception* argues that thought-like, cognitive processes underlie virtually all visual perception, though most often we're not consciously aware of it. Rock's conclusion, based on many ingenious experiments, is that visual perception is a series of thought-like steps through which the perceptual system "explains" the array of light and color before it as a comprehensible scene.[6]

Print Generation is a useful example, because the process of perceptual problem solving, which is usually rapid and unconscious, is here slowed and brought to our conscious awareness. But I cite this example with some hesitation: it might leave the impression that a cognitive approach to the avant-garde is fatally limited to basic perceptual issues, and that the most important questions about the avant-garde cinema are beyond its scope. There is more to cognitive theory than cognitive psychology and perception. I hope to show that a cognitive approach—based largely on cognitive theories of language and reasoning—offers a useful means of exploring a range of issues that are of central concern to our understanding of the avant-garde cinema.

A Refinement of the Problem-solving Model

Let me refine the notion that avant-garde film viewing must usefully be thought of as a kind of problem solving. We can move beyond issues of basic perception by considering a common feature of avant-garde film viewing—one that usually passes without comment: viewers initially have difficulty comprehending avant-garde films, but they learn to make sense of them. Students who take my course in the avant-garde cinema are at first completely confused by the films I show; by the end of the term, they can speak intelligently about the films they see. And this transformation isn't limited to naïve and immature students. Scott MacDonald writes of his initial bafflement vis-à-vis the avant-garde cinema when he was a college teacher of film and literature.[7] What is the difference between the new, uncomprehending viewer and the experienced viewer? Since even literate and sophisticated adults undergo this transformation, I take it that it is not a fundamental change in the machinery that is often purported to explain film spectatorship, such as a change in the structure of the unconscious, or the viewer's situation within language, or the interpellation into ideology.

A more plausible explanation is, I think, that viewers acquire knowledge. Specifically, experienced viewers have acquired both *procedural* knowledge, what we might call knowing *how*, and *declarative* knowledge, what we might call knowing *that*.[8] The avant-garde film viewer's procedural knowledge consists of tips, guidelines, rules of thumb—what theorists of problem solving would more formally call heuristics. Viewers use these to match the images and sounds of a film to meaningful patterns. For example, one such heuristic might be "look for bits of narrative, but be prepared for digressions in which graphic patterns in the images become more prominent than the activities of the characters." A more basic heuristic is "pay most attention to the elements over which the filmmaker has most control." Or, more basic yet, "try to relate the images and sounds of a given film to the distinctive concerns of the filmmaker." Acquiring this procedural knowledge involves not merely learning these heuristics, but *over*learning them, so that viewers can use them more or less automatically, while directing most of their attention to the details of the film at hand.

Declarative knowledge dovetails with this procedural knowledge. Consider Stan Brakhage's *Thigh Line Lyre Triangular,* a film about the birth of Brakhage's third child. In the roughest terms, the film is a documentary about a childbirth, but a dense layer of scratches and paint on the surface of the film all but prevents us from seeing the birth itself (Fig. 5.3). To follow our simple heuristic that tells us to try to relate the images of *Thigh Line Lyre Triangular* to the concerns of the filmmaker, it would be helpful to know that Brakhage believes that the naïve vision of the infant is a worthy model for the artist, who ought to escape conventional ways of seeing. To a novice viewer, the film is incomprehensible. But a viewer with the procedural knowledge that he or she

Fig. 5.3

should relate the film to the concerns of the filmmaker, and some declarative knowledge about Brakhage's interest in childhood, can solve at least one of the puzzles posed by the film: why are these images of the film's ostensible subject so intentionally obliterated? *Thigh Line Lyre Triangular* makes sense to experienced viewers because they understand that its "degraded" images are meant to evoke both the subjective experience of the newborn, and the kind of artistic vision Brakhage was trying to recapture for himself.

I realize that the acquisition of the knowledge necessary to understand avant-garde films could be explained in the more familiar vocabulary of semiotics. What I've referred to as declarative knowledge could be laid out as a system of codes, such as the semic, cultural, and symbolic codes of Roland Barthes' *S/Z*.[9] But the translation of the avant-garde film viewer's procedural knowledge into a system of codes isn't quite so straightforward.

Productive semiotic analyses (say, Christian Metz's *Grande Syntagmatique* and Roland Barthes' work on narrative) tend to address highly conventional, rule-affirming art, such as the Hollywood film or realist fiction. Semioticians' affinity for conventional art is not merely the idiosyncratic preferences of these critics; it is, to a significant degree, built into semiotic theory itself. According to semiotic theory, the prototype for all signification is language—in fact, a particular view of language in which the link between the signifier and the signified is thought to be arbitrary and conventional. Thus, according to semiotic theory, the central—if not the sole—engine of meaning is the code, a social convention that arbitrarily pairs some physical manifestation (the signifier) with a concept (the signified). For semioticians, even in pictorial representation the apparent nonarbitrary component is thought to play a subsidiary role, with the main meaning still derived from conventional codes.[10]

There are many linguists, philosophers, and film theorists who would energetically reject this whole line of theory, and challenge the idea that the code is the engine of meaning.[11] But I'll leave that argument to the side, and concentrate on a problem semiotic theory has with the novelty of avant-garde art. In so far as the meaning of a "text" is derived through conventional codes, signification is comprehensible only to the extent that its "readers" have already learned those codes. Semiotics is most at home, then, in what the semioticians like to call the realm of the "always already" said. Of course, if you are examining highly conventional art, such as the Hollywood cinema, this might not be an immediate problem. Even if we were to concede that semiotics had soundly theorized highly conventional forms of representation, it would still have a problem with more innovative, experimental forms. The avant-garde cinema puts a high premium on novelty, and viewers can't always count on interpreting a novel element of a film by using a code they already know.

Instead of a *code-based* model of communication, such as semiotics, an *inference-based* model might better explain our response to the kind of novelty we find in the avant-garde cinema.[12] A code model maintains that communication is possible because messages are encoded and decoded according to a system of conventions shared by the users of the code. Examples of such useful codes abound: Morse code, traffic lights, and, probably, significant parts of natural language. An inferential model suggests that communication can take place *without codes* when, rather than encoding a message, the "speaker" provides evidence that allows the "listener" to infer the speaker's intended meaning.

An example might make this distinction between coded and inferential communication clearer. Imagine that you are visiting Lyndon Johnson in his hospital room after his gall bladder surgery. You ask him how he is feeling. A good code-based response would be if he said "I feel great." You and he share the code (English), and you decode his meaning from his words. Imagine now an inference-based response to your question: instead of saying anything, he hikes up his hospital gown to reveal an enormous, coarsely stitched incision. Again, you get the idea, although rather than decoding his meaning from his words, you infer it from the evidence presented. And this evidence is not just that Lyndon Johnson has a big incision, but that he showed it to you when you asked how he was doing. Note that there needn't be any previously agreed upon, shared convention for you to understand President Johnson's response.

The inferential model doesn't preclude the operation of coded communication. Codes may well be at work in every linguistic communication.[13] But the inferential model suggests that the code model can never fully account for the full meaning of the utterance. The code model may be able to explain how we get from the physical manifestation of a sentence—the sounds in the air or the words on the page—to the linguistically encoded meaning of that sentence. But any given sentence might mean a potentially infinite number of things, depending on the context in which it is uttered. Imagine that Lyndon Johnson said "I feel great" *while* he was lifting his hospital gown. In that context, we would have to infer that the sentence was meant ironically, and that its full meaning would be more aptly paraphrased as "I feel rotten, and that's a stupid question." Thus, the inferential model considers decoding the linguistic meaning of the sentence only the first step in comprehension. That encoded meaning is just one piece of the evidence from which we must infer the full meaning of the utterance.

To see how this kind of communicative inference might work in the context of the avant-garde cinema, let us consider Ernie Gehr's *Eureka* (1979). Gehr made his film from a turn-of-the-century film shot from the front of a trolley as it traversed San Francisco's Market Street. Gehr has step-printed the original so that the original 3 ½-minute film is now 30 minutes long. In optically printing the film, Gehr has also increased the contrast of the images and accentuated subtle variations in exposure among the frames. The final product is apparently simple: an old film, in slow motion and slightly flickering. *Eureka* is *not* a film that obviously calls for a cognitive analysis. It doesn't demand a great deal of problem-solving effort in order to understand its overall structure.

But the film's simplicity is part of the problem it poses for the viewer. The film is highly unified, and it is, in fact, quite easy to establish its internal structure. *Eureka* poses a problem for the avant-garde viewer because it is does not explicitly represent concerns of the community that views it. If this film were shown at the San Francisco Historical Society, its relevance would be apparent, because the film is a record of places and objects that would be of interest to the historical society. Even the film's extension through loop printing would be understandable: the filmmaker has slowed down the film so that the members of the historical society might be better able to examine the clothing and behavior of the passersby, the details of the architecture, and the operation of the vehicles.

Of course most people who view *Eureka* do so somewhere other than the San Francisco Historical Society, and the details of life in turn-of-the-century San Francisco are of only incidental interest to them. On the night of its premiere, for instance, on January 13, 1979, at the Collective for Living Cinema in New York City, how did viewers manage to figure out how *Eureka* was relevant to the concerns of their community? It is worth noting here that *Eureka* appeared in the closing days of the dominance of Structural film. Before long, this kind of minimal filmmaking would seem passé to avant-garde film viewers. But in 1979, avant-garde film viewers would have been ready to solve the problem posed by *Eureka* by applying a few strategies that had been in use for such films for more than a decade.

Structural film, in part, the product of the avant-garde cinema's intimate association with the world of the contemporary visual arts in the 1960s and 1970s.[14] In fact, we can think of Structural film as the avant-garde's minimal strain of filmmaking, equivalent to minimalism in painting and sculpture. And viewers who are familiar with the concerns of the visual arts during this period can make sense of minimal films like *Eureka* with strategies similar to those viewers use to make sense of minimal art. Our analysis of the viewers' response to *Eureka*'s premiere doesn't have to be entirely speculative: we have a published account of the event by a prominent film critic. Jim Hoberman's account nicely demonstrates two art-world strategies in common use throughout the 1970s.[15]

The first, derived from the influential aesthetics of composer John Cage, is what we might call the "art process" strategy. According to this strategy as applied to film, the viewer attends to the projected images only provisionally; the viewer uses these images to reconstruct the steps the filmmaker took to produce them, and these procedures are the point of the film. Thus, *Eureka*'s internal structure is exceedingly simple, and we shift our attention to Gehr's intervention: the optical printing. We interpret Gehr's willingness to leave the original film substantially intact as a gesture that demonstrates his willingness to accept chance and coincidence in his work. And this openness to the aleatory stands in sharp contrast to other, overly controlled and contrived acts of film creation. From this perspective, it is precisely his willingness *not* to interfere with the original footage that is his most important gesture. In this way, Gehr's presentation of apparently irrelevant footage is ultimately made relevant to the concerns of the avant-garde film community.

Hoberman's second strategy draws on the art criticism of Clement Greenberg. Greenberg conceived of modernism as a kind of self-analysis, in which every artistic medium is pared down to its essence. Painting is pigment on a flat surface; by definition it must be this, and according to Greenberg, modern painting should be *only* this. As applied to the avant-garde cinema, this strategy suggests that viewers look at films as reflexive analyses of features of the medium, such as *Wavelength*'s celebrated analysis of the zoom lens, or Gehr's own *History*'s analysis of film grain. In *Eureka* (which was originally titled *Geography*), Hoberman finds an analysis of how the flatness of the screen undercuts the apparent depth in the image:

> . . . the viewer becomes acutely conscious of every scratch, scar or defect on the original emulsion. But as the materiality of the film is pushed smack up to the foreground, the eye is drawn deep into the frame, not only by the camera's head-long movement, but also by the classic example of these parallel trolley-tracks converging towards infinity. Thus, *Geography* precipitates a dizzying and majestic play between the exaggerated flatness of the image and the rigorous perspective it represents.[16]

Hoberman argues that although its imagery is largely irrelevant, Gehr's film explores fundamental features of the film medium. It is, therefore, relevant to the modernist project, and to the avant-garde film community that saw itself as participating in that project.

Some Objections to a Cognitive Approach

I have so far been arguing for a couple of modest propositions: that avant-garde film viewing involves a measure of conscious activity, and that theories of perceptual problem solving and communicative inference offer a useful vocabulary for discussing such activities. Still, it might be objected that these activities represent only a small part of the viewer's response to the avant-garde film, and that the cognitive perspective has troubling blindnesses that outweigh these minor insights. Let me consider here what I think are three common objections along these lines.

1. Avant-garde films call for something other than rational comprehension. Cognitive film theory generally concerns itself with the spectator's rational processes, as opposed to the unconscious response to cinema. And in the context of narrative cinema, cognitive film theory has primarily addressed the viewer's basic comprehension, as opposed to the interpretation of hidden meanings. David Bordwell's *Narration in the Fiction Film*, for example, concerns itself with how viewers of various modes of narrative cinema reconstruct the web of causal relationships among the agents in the story. But this concern with rational comprehension might be problematic vis-à-vis the avant-garde cinema. It is sometimes suggested that the appeal of the avant-garde cinema is that it encourages, even demands, responses that are irrational, idiosyncratic, or otherwise unanalyzable. And it might be questioned whether the viewer's response to the avant-garde cinema has a component analogous to basic comprehension in the narrative cinema. The expression of these concerns takes several forms.

A considerable number of avant-garde films might be thought to defy rational comprehension because they are abstract, in the sense that they have minimal representational content, like instrumental music. Films that are abstract in this sense include the work of Oscar Fishinger, Viking Eggeling, and much of the work of Len Lye and Harry Smith, among many others. As the musical titles of films such as *Rhythmus 21* (Richter, 1921) and *Symphonie Diagonale* (Eggeling, c. 1925) suggest, these films cannot be interpreted with methods appropriate to narrative film. Similarly, the basic comprehension of these films, whatever that might turn out to be, is certainly not like the reconstruction of the causal relationships that is central to the basic comprehension of narrative art.

But even if we grant that these films call for something very different from the comprehension of narrative art, this does not commit us to the idea that there is no basic comprehension involved. If, following the precedent of studies of discourse processing, we define comprehension as the discovery of structures that establish coherence among the film's elements, then comprehension of some sort happens with these films, too.[17] And this comprehension might still call for a kind of problem solving along the lines suggested by cognitive theories of perception and language. Fred Lerdahl and Ray Jackendoff's study of musical cognition, *A Generative Theory of Tonal Music,* and E. H. Gombrich's study of decorative art, *The Sense of Order,* suggest one such line of attack.[18] These studies aim to show how even the comprehension of abstract art can be explained as a search for solutions in the form of structures that match the details of the artwork. A compatible approach has been applied to abstract avant-garde films by Gregory Taylor in his analysis of Sidney Peterson's *The Lead Shoes.*[19]

Even if there are fruitful cognitive approaches to some forms of abstract art (and even if they might occasionally be applied to the avant-garde cinema) it might still be objected that the avant-garde cinema is so idiosyncratic and irrational that any generalizations about the viewing experience are hard to make. A few years ago, for example, Fred Camper wrote that the avant-garde cinema was "fundamentally anarchic" and that the

> avant-garde film addresses each viewer as a unique individual, speaks to him in isolation from the crowd, invites him to perceive the film according to his own particular experience and perception, to see it differently from the way the viewer seated next to him would.[20]

I'm sympathetic to this argument because it captures something important about the avant-garde: its films support a broader range of experiences than do almost any other mode or film practice. Still, Camper's statement is surely exaggerated.

At the level of basic comprehension, where viewers discover the most apparent structures in the film, viewers' experiences of avant-garde films are remarkably consistent. There is no denying that *Thigh Line Lyre Triangular* is about the birth of a baby, that one prominent feature of *Wavelength* is the irregular and gradual narrowing of the field of view, or that *Tribulation 99* is a documentary-style fiction about an alien invasion. Certainly these observations are not all that is interesting and important in these three films. But in a good many avant-garde films, this level of basic comprehension can be quite complex. In *Zorn's Lemma* or *Print Generation,* for example, puzzling out the basic structures and the images is the main pleasure of the film. In *Meshes of the Afternoon,* struggling to establish the border between dream and waking reality on the basis of cinematic cues and real-world knowledge is an absolutely central part of the viewer's experience—even though those borders are ultimately indeterminate. Any analytical framework that *didn't* account for this level of these films would have serious shortcomings.

But even as we move up from the level of basic comprehension toward the level of interpretation, from the discovery of the most apparent structures to those that are less evident, we still find systematic consistencies in response. Judging by published criticism, the avant-garde cinema evinces a finite range of interpretive patterns and styles. This needn't suggest that critics of the avant-garde cinema lack imagination. A more plausible reason for this consistency is that critics, like viewers, are problem solvers: they have to find ways to make the films of the avant-garde coherent and relevant to the communal concerns of the institution of the avant-garde cinema.[21] The responses in published criticism may not perfectly reflect the responses of "regular" viewers. But the line between critics and viewers is much harder to draw in the avant-garde cinema than it is in most modes of narrative cinema. The avant-garde expects viewers to be familiar with current issues and ideas, and takes steps to promulgate these issues and ideas to them. Journal essays, university courses, program notes and the filmmaker's pre- and post-screening presentations all ensure that a common fund of specialized knowledge circulates among the avant-garde's critics and its normal viewers alike. So, while it is fair to say that the avant-garde film supports a much broader range of experiences than most kinds of cinema, the avant-garde's own discourse suggests strong regularities in the range of experiences supported by the avant-garde cinema, and these regularities can be explained in cognitive terms.

Of course, a few avant-garde films seem to frustrate any attempts to interpret them according to approved patterns of interpretation. Some films are interesting precisely *because* they challenge rational expectations and try to outflank every effort to recuperate them into some sort of meaning. One classic example of this sort is *Un Chien Andalou,* at least according to Luis Buñuel's view of the film. According to Buñuel, he and Salvador Dali constructed the film as a series of purely irrational juxtapositions—any sequences that seemed to make rational sense were discarded.[22] Assuming for the moment that the film actually is such an exercise in total irrationality, the film nevertheless implicitly addresses the *rational* viewer. A genuinely surrealist sensibility (which, according to André Breton, would completely dissolve the distinction between the rational and the irrational) would find the irrational at work everywhere, and making a film like *Un Chien Andalou* for such a viewer would be unnecessary. The point of Dali and Buñuel's effort is to force rational viewers to confront the irrational, and the response of such viewers is predictable, at least to a significant degree.

I expect that irrational provocation is a central characteristic of only a small group of films, since avant-garde film criticism is tailored to make some sort of sense of practically every film that gets made and circulated. We might otherwise have to consider the work of Peter Gidal to be such a radical challenge to coherence. After all, Gidal's notion of the Structural/materialist film rejected not only Hollywood-style comprehensibility, but just about every sort of coherence imaginable. But the refusal of coherence in Gidal's work was itself comprehensible as a form of ideological critique, according to the materialist anti-illusionism that was a prevalent strain of avant-garde film criticism of the 1970s.

The work of Stan Brakhage offers a more instructive example of this type, however. Brakhage argues that the Hollywood cinema, and in fact, the whole tradition of perspectival representation, had so radically constrained seeing, that members of Western cultures "see" only a pathetically small range of the visual phenomena available to them. Thus, Brakhage's cinema aims to represent some of these hitherto unseen phenomena, such as phosphenes, closed-eye vision, and hypnagogic images. From one perspective, then, Brakhage's work aspires to be a direct, precognitive cinema, one that transcends the cognitive operations I've been arguing are central to the viewer's response to the avant-garde cinema. But the precognitive directness of Brakhage's cinema is mediated in two ways. First Brakhage could not "directly" photograph the internal visual phenomena that so interested him. Rather, he had to find some representational equivalent of these phenomena, such as scratching and painting directly on the film. Brakhage's viewers are not treated to an unmediated view of Brakhage's vision, but to a series of representations of his vision, representations that are comprehended only through significant cognitive effort. Second, Brakhage tried to attain for himself the kind of precognitive vision of the child, and he hoped to provide the means through which viewers might glimpse this vision. In this sense, we might think of Brakhage's films as the avatars of a revolution in seeing. But most of Brakhage's viewers are the as-yet-unconverted; his films are representations of pre-linguistic vision for post-linguistic viewers. And the fact that Brakhage felt it necessary to publish volumes of explication of his own work can only support the idea that the cinema of the irrational, or in this case the pre-rational, is pitched to the rational viewer.

2. Cognitive theory unrealistically assumes a super-rational viewer, and posits a single, idealized response. At bottom, I think this objection derives from the connotations of the term "cognitive." For some it suggests a super-rational, computer-like viewer who takes in cues from the film and unproblematically spits out the correct interpretation. This objection is leveled at cognitive film theories of all sorts, but it has special pertinence to the avant-garde, since its films are justifiably thought to resist fixed interpretations. Any theory of the avant-garde that suggests that its viewers can unproblematically produce the proper interpretation of its films would certainly be wrong, but a cognitive approach implies no such thing. A cognitive approach does not commit one to the view that each film has only one "right" experience, or that the experience always involves active engagement.

As I've already suggested with examples from perception and linguistics, the cognitive approach suggests that a good many mental processes might be understood as problem-solving procedures. When we turn to cognitive studies of problem solving itself, we see that conscious human problem solving rarely follows the rigorous principles of formal logic. Indeed, by the standards of formal logic, even philosophy professors reason poorly on abstract problems that are removed from familiar domains of knowledge. In the decade and a half since the groundbreaking work in human reasoning by Philip Johnson-Laird, Amos Tversky, and Daniel Kahneman, there is less interest in abstract, formal logic, and increasing interest in what we might call "embodied" reasoning.[23] A significantly different view of rationality emerges from this exploration of embodied reason.

One basic principle of practical problem solving is that it does not require algorithms, the kind of step-by-step procedures that drive computers. More often, practical problem solving depends on what problem-solving theorists call *heuristics,* "rules of thumb" that guide the search for workable solutions. These heuristics are particularly important to the kind of "ill-formed" problems one encounters in social situations. In such ill-formed problems, what counts as a "solution" is rarely clear-cut, and decisions must be made on the basis of incomplete and ambiguous information.[24] I think it's obvious that avant-garde film viewing is closer to this kind of social judgment than it is to the solving of well-formed abstract problems. How to make sense of the avant-garde film is an ill-formed problem with no clear-cut solution, and viewers must make sense of these films with limited knowledge and in a limited time. And the goals of individual viewers can vary greatly.

Theories of practical problem solving don't give us ready-made theories of avant-garde film viewing. One of the main tenets of this line of research is that reasoning and problem solving are not cut to a single universal pattern, but are context-bound. Nevertheless, problem-solving theory suggests three broad approaches that we might adapt to avant-garde film viewing.[25] *Maximizing* strategies are generally appropriate for well-formed problems for which there are clear-cut solutions. A jigsaw puzzle, for example, isn't considered solved until every piece is put in place. The maximizing strategy aims to produce the best possible solution regardless of cost. On the other hand, *satisficing* strategies minimize problem-solving effort and aim to produce only "good enough" solutions. Theorists suggest that satisficing strategies are common approaches to some real-world problems, which tend to be ill-formed, and which often must be solved quickly and with incomplete information. *Optimizing* strategies produce better solutions than satisficing strategies, but at the cost of somewhat greater problem-solving effort. The optimizer weighs the cost of additional effort against the benefit of the improved solution, and, unlike the maximizer, at a certain point decides that the extra effort no longer pays enough.

The avant-garde cinema probably has viewers of each type, but most viewers and critics of the avant-garde are optimizers who are not satisfied with making minimal sense of a film. The supposition in the avant-garde seems to be that one should get as much out of these films as one can, and that one should be sensitive to a wider range of effects in the avant-garde than in other modes of filmmaking. Through experience, avant-garde film viewers develop heuristics that help them identify the most significant elements of films. By reading about films and filmmakers, optimizing viewers collect information that will help them establish greater coherence among the elements of the film, and between the film and its social context. I believe it is fair to say that all viewers do this, though each may do so in his or her own way. And to suggest that all these viewers are rational does not imply that they are identical.

3. Cognitive theory is essentialist, and therefore is insensitive to historical and cultural context. This assertion is based on ignorance of the full range of cognitive literature. Rather than advocating an ahistorical, transcultural mind, cognitive theory seeks to theorize the mechanisms that account for cultural differences.[26] This literature, it seems to me, is eminently more sensitive to cultural difference than much contemporary discourse on the cinema.

Nevertheless, cognitive theory maintains that there are innate features of the human mind. This runs counter to a common presumption in much contemporary film theory, as in cultural studies generally, which generally holds to an extreme conventionalism: there is nothing about the mind that could not be different if the social formation were different in the right way. The weight of the evidence is on the cognitive side—our perceptual and cognitive capacities are constrained in some ways by our biological material. But this isn't really the sticky point, because no cognitivist thinks these innate features *directly* determine aspects of human experience. Human subjectivity is a complex interaction between physiology, the physical environment, and culturally determined choices. And, on the other hand, no one objects to appealing to innate capacities to explain some low-level perceptual elements of film viewing. For example, no one objects when the notion of flicker-fusion (a transcultural cognitive mechanism) is mobilized to explain the perception of flicker films.[27] Disagreement arises when a transcultural cognitive mechanism (either innate or produced by a universal human experience) is used to explain some high-level aspect of cinema. If you argue that transcultural capacities help explain something like pictorial representation or narrative structure, you can expect some resistance, to say the least.

Consider here Noël Carroll's argument that the international appeal and success of Hollywood-style films owes something to the way their structure suits transcultural cognitive habits and abilities.[28] For two reasons we are justifiably suspicious of claims that the facts of our social lives are determined by our natural inclinations and abilities. First, it is not at all clear which of our inclinations and abilities are biologically given, and which develop as a result of our acculturation, though surely we benefit (and suffer) from significant contributions of both types. And second, such claims tend to legitimate the status quo, because the preponderance of examples seems to support the notion that things are the way they are because that is the natural way.[29]

This issue is of interest to us here because partisans of the avant-garde often take a radically conventionalist position and argue that alternative film forms would appeal to larger audiences, if only those audiences had not been indoctrinated by the ideology and formal devices of the mass media. Brakhage has stated this position with particular eloquence and force, but it is implicit in much of the avant-garde's rhetoric. In contrast, Carroll challenges the conventionalist position by appealing to transcultural cognitive habits and abilities. He apparently suggests that Hollywood-style filmmaking is "naturally" popular worldwide; thus he seems to justify the ideological and aesthetic domination of the world by a Western representational agenda. He also sounds the death-knell for the avant-garde, because, lacking Hollywood's natural appeal, the avant-garde's revolutionary aspirations will certainly come to nought. If Carroll is right, the avant-garde cinema's prospects as the avatar of a revolution in film form are severely limited.

The conventionalist's evidence marshalled against Carroll's argument concerns the Hollywood-style films' "subject matter, the distribution networks which deliver them to theaters all over the world, and the advertising campaigns which fill those theaters."[30] Surely these are important factors contributing to the popularity of the Hollywood cinema, which Carroll doesn't deny. But he poses a different, and more fundamental, question: Would another kind of film be as universally comprehensible and popular if it had the same subject matter, distribution, and advertising? If Stan Brakhage had a distribution deal with a major studio, would viewers the world over be watching *Dog Star Man* instead of *Star Wars?* Would children have been weeping over *Sirius Remembered* instead of *Old Yeller?* It seems to me as foolish to ignore transcultural cognitive habits and abilities as it would be to suggest that they determine every detail of our social lives. And it seems obvious to me that the prospects of the avant-garde cinema are, in fact, severely limited. They always have been; and filmmakers have counted on a small, well-educated audience willing to pick up the necessary heuristics and to acquire extensive knowledge of art history, film history, and the lives of the filmmakers. Without such an audience, a mode of filmmaking that frustrates our cognitive habits and abilities would never have developed.

A Sample Cognitive Analysis

Many of the examples I have cited so far pose rather pointed, clear-cut problems for viewers. In this regard, *Print Generation* represents an extreme: not only are its perceptual puzzles very evident, one can't help being drawn into them. And although it presents a set of more open-ended problems, *Thigh Line Lyre Triangular* will prompt just about anyone to engage its central question, why all the paint and scratches have been put over the images of the birth. But what about avant-garde films that don't pose such pointed questions, films that don't seem to call so clearly for the problem-solving approach I've been advocating? To demonstrate how the cognitive problem-solving approach would work with such a film, let's briefly consider Bruce Baillie's *Quixote* (1964–65).

Quixote is an example of what Sitney called the "lyrical" film; it generates its effects through evocative images and their associations, rather than through a dramatic storyline or an intricately patterned overall structure. This 30-minute film contains imagery drawn from a wide variety of sources. We see animals, businessmen at lunch, American Indians, a circus, a basketball game, Civil Rights marches, and footage from the Vietnam War. Some of the footage Baillie shot himself, some is drawn from old documentaries, TV shows, movies, and the news. Most is in black and white; some is color. The problem the film poses for the viewer is, quite simply, how to make sense of this dense montage of images and sounds.

This problem has two components. First, at the overall level, the viewer must figure out how all this material is organized and, taken all together in the form Baillie has arranged it, what it all means. Second, at the level of the individual details, the viewer might ask of any particular image or sound, why this element is in the film at all, and why in this particular spot? For the sake of our analysis, we can treat these levels separately, though viewers have to work through them both at the same time.

Before we turn to the analysis of these two levels of the viewer's problem solving, I should point out that Baillie's work provides some important examples of films that might be thought to transcend cognitive analysis because their appeal lies primarily in their images of great formal beauty. His *Castro Street,* for example, is a poetic documentary about an industrial area in San Francisco. But the film's interest lies not in what it tells us about Castro Street, which is practically nothing, but in the beautiful images Baillie has created, using the Castro Street landscape as raw material. I've already suggested how a cognitive approach might be appropriate for abstract films without representational content. But in Baillie's work, particularly *Quixote,* the situation is a bit different: abstract images and images of formal appeal work *within* other kinds of structures, and those other structures are more prominent. Since those other structures are more prominent, we might be tempted to simply ignore the impact of any images that didn't fit into them. But the prevalence of such playful imagery in many avant-garde films that are not totally abstract suggests a useful heuristic: viewers of *Quixote,* and of the avant-garde cinema generally, should be prepared for images that are included, repeated or emphasized, not for their role in the structure and meaning of the film, but for their beauty. In *Quixote,* Baillie is particularly drawn to beautifully lit scenes, and unusual framings and camera angles. For example, in an early section of the film, Baillie includes a shot of a billboard for Barry Goldwater's presidential campaign (Fig. 5.4). In terms of the overall theme of the film, this shot would suffice, but Baillie reiterates the image of the billboard from unusual and dramatic camera angles (Fig. 5.5). Throughout the film, there are many images whose elegance and beauty outstrip their contribution to the film's structure and meaning, and this elegance and beauty provides one kind of solution to the problem posed by the film's material.

Fig. 5.4

Fig. 5.5

At the overall level, much of the film's imagery is topically related to the westward expansion of the United States and its sphere of influence. The film begins with an image of a grizzled old man in a beat-up cowboy hat, and the notion that this anachronistic character is a pioneer of some sort is reiterated a bit later by an image of a covered wagon pulled by mules. Still later, we will see short scenes of Western landscapes, American Indians, buffalo, and a horse and rider. This set of images is less prominent toward the end of the film, where images of the Civil Rights struggle and the Vietnam War are more prominent. It would be stretching a point to call this film a narrative, but these images obliquely suggest a story about manifest destiny, beginning with the settling of the West and the oppression of the American Indian, and ending with the war in Asia and the oppression of the Vietnamese. The idea of this narrative framework is reinforced by the repeated leftward—that is to say, the westward—movement of the hero figures that appear throughout the film, such as the pioneer in the covered wagon (Fig. 5.6) and a flying spaceman from a science-fiction program (Fig. 5.7).

Fig. 5.6   Fig. 5.7

The example of *Quixote*'s narrative helps illustrate how comprehension and interpretation are intertwined in the avant-garde cinema. The viewer's comprehension of *Quixote*'s narrative framework as a story about manifest destiny entails understanding something like an overall theme—a theme that is nowhere explicitly stated in Baillie's film. In other modes of filmmaking, such an appraisal of an implicit theme would be considered interpretation, an operation generally thought to be separate from the comprehension of the basic storyline. *Little Big Man,* for example, might be thought to have the same general theme as *Quixote.* But viewers of *Little Big Man* could certainly make sense of the actions of its characters without thinking about manifest destiny or drawing analogies between the oppression of American Indians to the Vietnam War. In *Quixote,* on the other hand, it is impossible to separate interpretation from basic comprehension: without an appraisal of the film's implicit theme, the viewer will not link the images of the West and the images of Vietnam, and the structural coherence of the film would be impossible to grasp.

Quixote's implicit theme and narrative framework would remain a hollow and uninteresting shell, were they not enriched by a system of contrasts, analogies, and ironies at the local level. Throughout the first two-thirds of the film, Baillie juxtaposes aspects of white culture to Indian culture in a wide variety of ways, and viewers can make sense of many images as elaborations of the contrast between white and Indian. One generally gets the sense that Baillie's view of Indian culture is sympathetic, and that his view of white culture is critical. But the filmmaker's sympathies are communicated in indirect and often ambivalent ways that make the viewer's task of relating the film's details to its overall structure and meaning more difficult. For example, Baillie juxtaposes images of a circus (Fig. 5.8) with images of an Indian powwow (Fig. 5.9). Both images are in color, and the colorful, decorative qualities of the costumes suggest rather strong formal parallels between the two social rituals rather than the stark opposition that the film's overall theme might suggest.

Fig. 5.8   Fig. 5.9

Even when Baillie creates conceptual contrasts that reinforce the film's central theme, these contrasts are often linked rather obliquely to the contrast between white and Indian culture. In one section we see Indians in a somewhat down-at-the-heels restaurant (Fig. 5.10), and white businessmen at a banquet (Fig. 5.11). The businessmen's accommodations are certainly more

Fig. 5.10   Fig. 5.11

comfortable than those of the Indians, but the real bite of the segment comes from a more complex analogy. The Indians are compared to silent and stationary buffalo, shown in shots matching the lighting and framing of the shots of the Indians themselves (Fig. 5.12). The businessmen, on the other hand, are juxtaposed to squealing pigs being led to slaughter, shown in shots that match the lighting, contrast, and, to a degree, the composition of the shots of the banquet (Fig. 5.13). An example of a set of images that fit the overall

Fig. 5.12   Fig. 5.13

theme even more obliquely comes near the middle of the film. Baillie cuts from a close-up of chains being placed on a tire (Fig. 5.14) to a shot of a bird in flight (Fig. 5.15). It's easy enough to figure out that the chains/bird juxtaposition suggests the opposition between enslavement and freedom (though it's harder to pick out in the film than in my carefully selected frame enlargements). But the links of the bird to Indian culture and the tire chains to white culture is never made explicit. Both whites and Indians are compared to animals in the film; but viewers will probably associate the tire chains and the heavy machinery in that segment with typically white exploitation of the land.

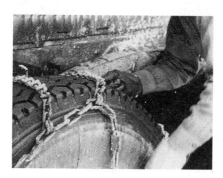

Fig. 5.14   Fig. 5.15

Near the end of the film, the biting contrast between white and Indian culture is less apparent, and viewers are likely to see the film's final images and their juxtaposition as an ironic commentary on the Vietnam War. Images of the war—its battles, wounded soldiers, aircraft, and graveyards—are superimposed over images of American cities and images culled from American popular films. And very near the end of the film, Baillie cuts from a shot of African-Americans at a Civil Rights demonstration to a similarly framed shot of North Vietnamese soldiers, rather overtly suggesting an analogy between the struggle of the Vietnamese against the United States and the Civil Rights movement. The analogy to the ongoing struggle of the Native American is not explicit in this part of the film, but for viewers who can draw that analogy, the film has a deep coherence beneath its apparently chaotic surface.

I realize that I have only scratched that surface in my discussion of this rich, evocative film. But my aim has not been to interpret every detail of *Quixote*. Instead, I have tried to show in broad terms how viewers might go about identifying and solving the set of problems posed by the film.

My aim in this essay has been to show that a cognitive approach to the avant-garde cinema is not perverse, and that some potential objections to it are unfounded. Along the way, I have tried to put into relief the differences between an inference-based cognitive theory of film meaning and a code-based theory, such as semiotics. I hope that I have also demonstrated that cognitive film theory is not, as one writer has suggested, an audacious and haughty challenge to all of contemporary film studies.[31] A cognitive approach is instead an invitation to consider a provocative literature and a rich and varied body of theory and data relevant to the central issues of film scholarship.

NOTES

1. See, for example, David Bordwell, *Narration in the Fiction Film* (Madison: University of Wisconsin Press, 1985), and Edward Branigan, *Narrative Comprehension and Film* (New York: Routledge, 1992).

2. Noël Carroll, *Mystifying Movies: Fads and Fallacies in Contemporary Film Theory* (New York: Columbia University Press, 1988), and David Bordwell, "Cognition and Comprehension: Viewing and Forgetting in *Mildred Pierce*," *Journal of Dramatic Theory and Criticism* 6, 2 (Spring 1992): 183–98.

3. See Bill Simon, "Reading *Zorn's Lemma*," *Millennium Film Journal* 1 (Spring/Summer 1978): 38–49 and Elena Pinto Simon, "The Films of Peter Kubelka," *Artforum* 10, 8 (April 1972): 33–39.

4. P. Adams Sitney, *Visionary Film: The American Avant-Garde, 1943–1978*, 2d ed. (New York: Oxford University Press, 1979). Of Annette Michelson's work, see especially "Toward Snow," *Artforum* 9, 10 (June 1971): 30–37.

5. Sitney, *Visionary Film*, p. 370.

6. Irwin Rock, *The Logic of Perception* (Cambridge: MIT Press, 1983).

7. Scott MacDonald, "Acquired Tastes," *Facets Video Catalog* (Chicago: Facets Multimedia, 1989), pp. 6–8.

8. For discussions of the distinction between declarative and procedural knowledge, see Gilbert Ryle, *The Concept of Mind* (New York: Hutchinson's University Library, 1949) and John R. Anderson, *Language, Memory, and Thought* (Hillsdale, N.J.: Lawrence Erlbaum, 1976).

9. Roland Barthes, *S/Z*, trans. Richard Miller (New York: Hill and Wang, 1974).

10. For a strongly conventionalist account of the photographic image, see Roland Barthes, "The Rhetoric of the Image" in *Image/Music/Text,* trans. Stephen Heath (New York: Hill and Wang, 1977): 32–51.

11. For a linguistic and philosophical critique of code-based theories of communication see the collection of essays in *Radical Pragmatics,* ed. Paul Cole (New York: Academic Press, 1981); for a critique of the code-based tradition in film theory, see Carroll, *Mystifying Movies.*

12. For a thorough account of an inference-based model of linguistic communication, as well as another critique of code-based models, see Dan Sperber and Dierdre Wilson, *Relevance: Communication and Cognition* (Cambridge: Harvard University Press, 1986).

13. Though exactly what dimensions of language are properly thought of as codes is far from clear. Proponents of the radical pragmatic view would argue that much of what once was thought to be code-based is actually inferential.

14. For useful overviews of the relationship between Structural film and the world of the American visual arts of this period, see James Hoberman, "After Avant-garde Film," in *Art after Modernism: Rethinking Representation,* ed. Brian Wallis (New York: New Museum of Contemporary Art, 1984): 59–73, Noël Carroll, "Film," in *The Postmodern Moment,* ed. Stanley Trachtenberg (Westport, Conn.: Greenwood Press, 1985): 101–33 and James Peterson, *Dreams of Chaos, Visions of Order: Understanding the American Avant-garde Cinema* (Detroit: Wayne State University Press, 1994), especially chapter 5.

15. James Hoberman, "Ernie Gehr's *Geography*," *Millennium Film Journal* 3 (Winter/Spring 1979): 113–14.

16. Hoberman, "Ernie Gehr's *Geography*," p. 114.

17. Teun A. van Dijk and Walter Kintsch, *Strategies of Discourse Comprehension* (New York: Academic Press, 1983). Of course, how much and what kind of coherence the viewer will need to establish will vary depending on the viewer's goals, knowledge, talent and on other circumstances. But these distinctions are not central to our purposes here. For a more thorough discussion of comprehension in the avant-garde cinema, see Peterson, *Dreams of Chaos, Visions of Order,* especially chapter 2.

18. Fred Lerdahl and Ray Jackendoff, *A Generative Theory of Tonal Music* (Cambridge: MIT Press, 1983). E. H. Gombrich, *The Sense of Order: A Study in the Psychology of Decorative Art* (Ithaca, N.Y.: Cornell University Press, 1979).

19. Gregory Taylor, "Beyond Interpretation: *The Lead Shoes* as an Abstract Film," *Millennium Film Journal* no. 25 (Summer 1991): 78–99.

20. Fred Camper, "The End of Avant-Garde Film," *Millennium Film Journal* no. 16/17/18 (Fall/Winter 1986): 100.

21. For a thorough treatment of the notion that film interpretation is a problem-solving activity that requires critics to address the concerns of film-viewing communities, see David Bordwell, *Making Meaning: Inference and Rhetoric in the Interpretation of Cinema* (Cambridge: Harvard University Press, 1989).

22. Luis Buñuel, *My Last Sigh* (New York: Knopf, 1983).

23. Daniel Kahneman, Paul Slovic, and Amos Tversky, eds., *Judgment under Uncertainty: Heuristics and Biases* (New York: Cambridge University Press, 1982), P. N.

Johnson-Laird, *Mental Models: Towards a Cognitive Science of Language, Inference, and Consciousness* (Cambridge: Harvard University Press, 1983); Mark Johnson, *The Body in the Mind* (Chicago: University of Chicago Press, 1987).

24. Howard Margolis, *Patterns, Thinking, and Cognition: A Theory of Judgment* (Chicago: University of Chicago Press, 1987).

25. Jan D. Sinnott, "A Model for Solution of Ill-Structured Problems: Implications for Everyday and Abstract Problem Solving," in *Everyday Problem Solving: Theory and Applications*, ed. Jan D. Sinnott (New York: Praeger, 1989): 72–99.

26. See especially Eleanor Rosch and Barbara B. Lloyd, eds., *Cognition and Categorization* (Hillsdale, N.J.: Lawrence Erlbaum, 1978), and George Lakoff, *Women, Fire, and Dangerous Things: What Categories Reveal about the Mind* (Chicago: University of Chicago Press, 1987).

27. Stuart Liebman, "Apparent Motion and Film Structure: Paul Sharits's *Shutter Interface*," *Millennium Film Journal* 1, 2 (Spring/Summer 1978): 101–9.

28. Carroll, *Mystifying Movies.*

29. The political nature of these arguments should be apparent. Demonstrating that what we once thought was the product of nature is really the product of culture has been a favorite trope of academic humanists for several decades. This is usually thought to be a politically progressive gesture, but such arguments can cut both ways. Suggesting that women are naturally weaker at mathematical and spatial reasoning is widely regarded as reprehensibly sexist. But suggesting that some members of our society are homosexual by nature rather than by choice can be thought to be progressive, because it tends to lift the moral stigma associated with homosexuality. In both cases the "natural" state is legitimated, though only in one case does the legitimation of the natural strike us as reactionary; in the other it may seem quite progressive.

30. Jennifer Hammett, "Essentializing Movies: Perceiving Cognitive Film Theory," *Wide Angle* 14, 1 (January 1992): 92.

31. Dudley Andrew, "Cognitivism: Quests and Questionings," *Iris* no. 9 (1989): 1–10.

6

The Logic and Legacy
of Brechtianism

Murray Smith

In spite of Bertolt Brecht's own ambivalence toward the cinema, his ideas have exerted a wide and enduring influence on both its practitioners and theorists. In stressing the centrality of emotion, mobilized around and through characters, to the ideological and political functioning of narratives, Brecht produced one of the most tenacious arguments within twentieth-century aesthetic theory. For Brecht, "Aristotelian" or "dramatic" narrative form produces a powerful illusion of reality, a central feature of which is an overwhelming *Einfühlung* ("in-feeling," empathy or identification) with the protagonist, an empathy which obfuscates a broader and more critical perspective on the social conflicts upon which narratives depend. Brecht associates this effect with Aristotelian catharsis—roughly, the "purging" of emotional states through the experience of them in the form of tragic drama, the "spiritual cleansing of the spectator."[1] "Dramatic" narrative thus tends to accommodate spectators to the social ills that it represents, rather than encouraging them to address such problems outside of the aesthetic domain.

Against this, Brecht developed in his practice what he termed "epic" theater, which attempted to supplant empathy with a more critical, "estranged" or "distanciated" response (*Verfremdung*). Such a response, Brecht argued, would lead spectators to tackle the real-world social problems represented by narratives, in the belief that such problems could be transformed and solved. It is this strand of argument that I call "Brechtianism." It can be traced through the work of Roland Barthes and Louis Althusser, and within film studies, a variety of authors more or less closely associated with *Screen* in the 1970s: Ben Brewster, Stephen Heath, Colin MacCabe, Martin Walsh, and Paul Willeman.[2] In this essay I examine Brecht's arguments concerning the conditions necessary for both "empathic" and "distanciated" responses to narrative artworks, and the consequences of these responses in the aesthetic domain and in everyday life. I trace the itinerary of certain Brechtian ideas as they have been developed by the Post-Structural positions of certain of the authors named above. The legacy of these ideas, I will argue, is an oversimplified account of the role and nature of emotional responses to fiction, and in particular of the political and ideological consequences of emotional responses to conventional narrative cinema.

This simplicity can be gauged by the dualistic oppositions which are offered as a basis for understanding emotional responses to representations. Brecht presents a table of oppositions to contrast the features of "dramatic" theater with those of "epic" theater, including the contrasts between "feeling" and "reason," "suggestion" and "argument," placing the spectator "in the thick of" the represented experience and placing the spectator "outside" it.[3] In spite of a qualifying footnote which states that the table represents "shifts of accent" rather than "absolute antitheses," the dualism of the table reemerges in the writings of later ciné-Brechtians, as in the opposition between "identification" and "estrangement" posited by Peter Wollen as one of seven contrasts which distinguish Godardian "counter cinema" from Hollywood cinema.[4] Similarly, Martin Walsh describes the Brechtian aesthetic position through a series of oppositions with the "illusionism" of mainstream narrative cinema, where "illusionism" is defined as "a mode of artistic experience that has as its most central characteristics: a desire to (psychologically) penetrate individual experience; its primary appeal is to the emotions rather than the intellect, desiring the audience's empathetic involvement with the events presented before them."[5] "Illusionism" as described here may be a straw man, serving more as a justification of alternative representational practices (Straub, Godard) than as a description of mainstream narrative cinema; but the more sophisticated theoretical machinery of Post-Structuralism, I will argue, fails to produce a more robust framework.[6]

Brecht's Spectator

For Brecht, dramatic "illusion" and the attendant effect of empathy are accomplished by certain forms of narrative as realized by particular strategies of staging and performance. Brecht regarded linear narrative form—a continuous chain of cause and effect organized around a central protagonist—as a fundamental condition of *Einfühlung:* "strong emotional participation . . . needs a single inevitable chain of events."[7] This is often, though not exclusively, linked with the norms of staging and performance of "naturalist" theater: an emphasis on mimetic detail in setting and costuming, a performance style which replaced the formulaic repertoire of gestures of much nineteenth-century theater with a less obviously conventionalized style of acting, and the exclusion of overt commentary in the form of character asides, prologue, or chorus. Although empathy is the more fundamental effect for Brecht, it often results in the equally deleterious catharsis, glossed by Stephen Heath as the "spiritual absolution of the spectator as this can be seen most notably in tragedy which gleans from a consideration of human suffering a harvest of essence—this is 'how it is,' the Reality of Man's Condition."[8]

Many questions could be raised about the adequacy and precision of Brecht's terminology. The concepts of linear narrative and "empathy," I will argue, fail to capture the complexity of both conventional narrative form and the nature of spectatorial response to such form. Later in this essay, I will suggest that any attempt to grasp with precision the sort of phenomena that the terms "empathy" and "identification" point toward needs to begin with a more refined model of narrative form. I want to begin, however, by considering Brecht's depiction of the spectator rather than his conception of narrative form. Brecht's argument in this regard seems to rest upon two key premises. These can be stated as follows:

> *Premise 1:* Emotional response of the empathic type requires that the spectator mistake the representation for reality.

> *Premise 2:* Having an emotional response of the empathic type deadens our rational and critical faculties.

Neither of these premises is unique to Brecht; in fact, both are common in everyday and theoretical discussions of narrative. Premise 1 differs little from our everyday conception of "identification," while premise 2 restates another commonplace with very ancient roots in Western culture, concerning the purportedly antagonistic relationship between reason and emotion. The influence of Brecht's critical writings may be due in part to the fact he was drawing on long-standing assumptions in Western culture but combining and politicizing them in an original manner.

Both premises are, however, extremely vulnerable. That Brecht believed the theater capable of deluding the spectator in the way described by the first premise is evident when he complains that "[t]oo much heightening of the illusion in the setting, together with a "magnetic" way of acting . . . gives the spectator the illusion of being present at a fleeting, accidental, 'real' event. . . ."[9] The most damning observation concerning this first premise is that spectators simply do not behave as if they mistook represented actions for real ones—for if they did, they would in many instances flee or intervene, rather than weep and laugh. But this premise has been subjected to close examination elsewhere in film theory in recent years, so I will not dwell upon it.[10] Rather, I want to examine the second premise, the idea that undergoing empathy deadens our rational faculties. We have already encountered this assumption in the table of oppositions referred to above. Under scrutiny, however, it hardly fares any better than the first premise.

The first problem with this premise is the assumption that emotion and reason can be regarded as dichotomous, or even antinomous. By contrast, the dominant view of emotions in contemporary cognitive science and philosophy of mind is that different emotions can be distinguished by the distinct *cognitive evaluations* which lie behind them. Fear, for example, involves a judgment—a cognition—that someone or something threatens me; joy involves a judgment that something extremely beneficial for me or those I care about has occurred. Neither fear nor joy can be reduced to cognitions, insofar as their existence is palpably somatic, but they cannot be defined without this cognitive element. Moreover, emotions play what Ronald de Sousa calls a *strategic* role in our behavior, by directing our attention and thinking toward particular aspects of situations, and deflecting them from other aspects. Fear makes us attend to what is potentially threatening in a situation; joy, by contrast, predisposes us to a positive interpretation of events that we encounter. "For a variable but always limited time," de Sousa writes, "an emotion limits the range of information that the organism will take into account, the inferences actually drawn from a potential infinity, and the set of live options among which it will choose."[11]

The point here is that emotion is integrated with perception, attention, and cognition, not implacably opposed to any of them.[12] There may be affective states other than those I have discussed which may be more difficult to account for along cognitive lines—states like dread, melancholia, various phobias—but these states, which might subvert rationality in the way suggested by the traditional Western view of emotion, cannot be regarded as a paradigm for all emotions. The burden of proof falls on the Brechtian to show that emotion and reason are, in general, antinomous rather than integrated.

Moreover, even the more "irrational" responses take on a different role in an aesthetic context, precisely because we are not subject to an illusion whereby we actually confuse a representation for its referent, as Brecht often implies. (For this reason, Kendall Walton has argued that we should not refer to emotions in the context of aesthetic response, but rather to "quasi-emotions." A real emotion, Walton argues, requires a belief in the reality of the event that the emotion is a response to, not merely a "make-belief" in the reality of the event, as elicited by a fictional representation.[13]) Victor Erlich's description of the force of the word "blood" in an aesthetic ("poetic") context makes the point well:

> The ordinary word, transferred into poetry, is not cleansed of its emotional coloring or the multiple associations which have clustered around it in the course of its history. . . . The distinguishing characteristic of poetic language lies not in the fact that it is "trans-emotional," but in that its emotional load, along with its acoustic texture and grammatical form, becomes an object of esthetic contemplation rather than a catalyst of fear, hatred, or enthusiasm; something to be "perceived" and "experienced," as part of a symbolic structure rather than acted upon.[14]

Erlich is, of course, invoking the Russian Formalist notion of *ostranenie* (defamiliarization), and insisting that it does not amount (as some of Viktor Shklovsky's writings suggest) to a rejection of reference to the social, cognitive, or affective dimensions of existence, in the name of an abstraction whose sole interest is perceptual ("trans-emotional"). The argument here is that the engagement of emotion in the context of aesthetic representation is, *by definition*, defamiliarized. (The force of defamiliarization is, of course, variable, but that is another question.) Another way of putting this is to say that all artistic representations depend upon a measure of what Brecht would call "distanciation" merely to function as aesthetic objects.[15] The divide that Brecht sought to make between the "empathic" and the "distanciating" work cannot, therefore, be made, at least not in the terms he appeals to. The Post-Structural appropriation of Brecht, I will argue, succeeds no better in forging a new set of concepts free of these difficulties.

Brecht and Post-Structuralism

Along with the various references to Brecht in the early work of Roland Barthes, a key text in the effort to recruit Brecht to the (Post-)Structuralist cause is Althusser's early essay "The 'Piccolo Teatro': Bertolazzi and Brecht" (1962), which develops what is essentially an early version of Althusser's theory of ideological "interpellation." Not only does the essay itself represent an attempt to adapt Brechtian notions to Structuralist theory, the essay was translated into English by Ben Brewster, who himself examined the legacy of Brechtian ideas in relation to cinema in the pages of *Screen* and elsewhere.

In the "Bertolazzi and Brecht" essay, Althusser transforms the Brechtian model of spectatorship in the direction of the very sweeping theory characteristic of Althusser's later work ("Ideology and Ideological State Apparatuses," [1970]).[16] He claims that before a spectator identifies psychologically with any individual character, his or her very attendance in the theater is an occasion for a cultural and ideological *recognition*—a term meant to imply a spontaneous, unreflective mode of existence, a lack of self-knowledge. Althusser implies that this recognition is unconscious: ". . . what, concretely, is this uncriticized ideology if not simply the "familiar," "well-known," transparent myths in which a society or an age can recognise itself (but not know itself), the mirror it looks into for self-recognition, precisely the mirror it must break if it is to know itself?"[17] The mirror metaphor here anticipates, of course, Althusser's later explicit use of Lacanian theory, reinforcing the sense that "recognition" is an unconscious process.[18] As spectators, we are "already ourselves in the play itself, from the beginning . . . the play itself *is* the spectator's consciousness—for the essential reason that the spectator has no other consciousness than the content which unites him to the play in advance. . . ."[19] Clearly, recognition is the theoretical ancestor of "interpellation."

The concept that Althusser struggles with here is that of "consciousness." If we can reduce Brecht's dramaturgy to a single ambition, it is surely to produce a "true" (fuller, more complete) consciousness in the spectator. However, one of the very premises of Structuralism, in its reaction against phenomenology, is the denial that subjects (spectators) can *ever* have a consciousness of the structures that determine their existence.[20] What is interesting in Althusser's essay is the difficulty he has in marrying the Brechtian ambition (which he wishes to maintain) with this tenet of Structuralism. On the one hand, the concept of "recognition" is highly deterministic, suggesting that the spectator is trapped in a hermetically sealed bubble of ideology: "we are first united by an institution—the performance, but more deeply, by the same myths, the same themes, that govern us without our consent, by the same spontaneously lived ideology."[21] On the other hand, some of Althusser's descriptions suggest that spectators can achieve some form of true consciousness (consciousness of the real conditions of class society), which is "visible to the spectator in the mode of a perception which is not given, but has to be discerned, conquered and drawn from the shadow which initially envelops it, and yet produced it."[22]

This conflict between the legacy of Brecht and the imperatives of Structuralism is most apparent toward the end of the essay, where Althusser deals with Brechtian theory most directly. Althusser argues that one of the models of "spectatorial consciousness" which we have to reject is that of the self-conscious spectator:

> It accepts that the spectator should not identify with the "hero": he is to be kept at a distance. But is he not then outside the play judging, adding up the score and drawing the conclusions? Mother Courage is presented to you. It is for her to act. It is for you to judge. On the stage the image of blindness—in the stalls, the image of lucidity, led to consciousness by two hours of unconsciousness.[23]

Althusser calls this a "classical model" of spectatorial consciousness, implying that it is an aspect of the dramatic tradition that Brecht was reacting against. If anything, however, it is a quintessentially Brechtian model—a caricature to be sure, but an apt one.

In later essays, Althusser resolves the struggle between the possibility of consciousness and the incarceration of the spectator in an eternally benighted "in-structuredness" by introducing Lacanian concepts. Brecht's objective, endorsed and described by Althusser as an attempt to move the spectator into consciousness, to produce a "new spectator, an actor who starts where the performance ends, who only starts so as to complete it, in life,"[24] becomes impossible to theorize in this later framework. Yet such resolution remains all but impossible in the Bertolazzi essay. Althusser's final suggestion is that the essay he has just written in fact represents the play itself continuing *its* work through him. In the familiar Structuralist dictum, language speaks us, we do not speak language:

> I look back, and I am suddenly and irresistibly assailed by *the* question: are not these few pages, in their maladroit and groping way, simply that unfamiliar play *El Nost Milan*, performed on a June evening, *pursuing in me* its incomplete

meaning, searching in me, despite myself, now that all the actors and sets have been cleared away, for the *advent* of its silent discourse?[25]

This is an attempt to deflect the objection that the subject "Althusser" has a true consciousness of the working of a play and its relations to ideology and the real conditions of existence, and has made this consciousness available to the reader. And yet Althusser cannot evade the active construction: "I look back. . . ." The essay presents the bizarre spectacle of a theorist actively and consciously theorizing that he cannot theorize his own activity and consciousness.[26] Althusser is haunted by pronouns, emblems of the ghost of agency in the purportedly impersonal Structuralist system.

The itinerary of Brechtian ideas can be traced through Althusser to a number of essays published by *Screen* in the mid-1970s, including Colin Mac-Cabe's "Realism and the Cinema: Notes on some Brechtian Theses" and Stephen Heath's "Lessons from Brecht."[27] The two essays form an important bridge between Brecht, Althusser, and the psychoanalytic semiotics that was to dominate *Screen* and film theory in general for a decade or more. Mac-Cabe's essay reconceives Brecht's "Aristotelian" theater in terms of what he calls the "classic realist text." This form is characterized by the way in which the various "discourses" (roughly, the interests and values of the various characters) within the narrative are controlled and unified by a "metalanguage" ("the camera," or what we *see* in the film), which establishes a dominant discourse. The metalanguage establishes a univocal judgment within the text, but it does this "transparently," that is, as if it were merely representing the events of the narrative objectively, entirely without value judgments.

MacCabe's essay has been influential and widely commented on.[28] Equally influential has been the work of Stephen Heath, although his essay on Brecht has been little discussed. Along with references to Brecht, Benjamin, and Freud, Heath's essay includes an extended and approving quotation from Althusser's "Bertolazzi and Brecht" essay. Interestingly, Heath does not appeal to Lacan's notion of the "mirror stage" in order to theorize the relationship between "dominant" cinema and ideology, although it is implicit in his frequent references to "interpellation" and in the praise of the Althusserian model of ideology, the process of "recognition-miscognition." Instead, taking his cue from Barthes,[29] Heath drafts Freud's account of *fetishism* in an attempt to provide a more sophisticated understanding of "empathy" and "distanciation" than a simple opposition between the two terms.

Commodity fetishism for Marx is defined as the concealment of relations between producers (humans) behind those of products (things); for Freud's case study, fetishism involves the male "disavowal" of the female's lack of a penis, by the substitution of the nose for the "absent" penis, out of fear for his own potential castration. Heath fuses the two notions, and maps the resulting concept onto mainstream or "dominant" cinema (explicitly regarded as parallel with Brecht's "Aristotelian" theater) on the grounds that such cinema represses the labor underlying cinema and provides us only with ideology, that is, "the imaginary relation of men to their real conditions of existence." According to this analysis, the usual characterization of empathy—the psychological state elicited by dominant cinema—is inverted. Rather than being a state of intimacy and involvement, empathy is cast as a state of "separation"—separation from a consciousness of the real conditions of one's existence. "Representation" (the totality of the conventions of dominant cinema and Aristotelian theater) is identified with this separation, and opposed to "production," which works to confound the "structure of fetishism" by revealing the contradictions the latter attempts to mask (in the original scenario, the "contradiction" between male and female subjects; in "representation," contradictions between the interests and desires of the narrative agents).[30] Here we see the yoking of Brecht's suspicion of linear narrative to the dynamic of *repression* as posited by psychoanalysis. The outcome, however, of this injection of psychoanalytic theory, is simply another dualism: "representation—production" instead of "empathy—estrangement."[31]

Following Althusser in his essay on Brecht, Heath emphasizes the task of "production," of constructing (in theatrical and cinematic practice) and theorizing the critical spectator delineated by Brecht. In doing so he encounters, like Althusser, the difficulty of accounting for critical consciousness within the terms that he has chosen to theorize subjectivity, ideology, and dominant cinema. Heath is clear on this point:

> What is required is a way of thinking that is subtle enough—dialectical enough—to grasp that the individual is always the subject of ideology but that he is always more than simply that figure of representation. . . . [T]he need is for a work in and on representation, for, that is, the introduction of distance, a work within representation that produces an understanding of its formations and of the construction of the subject in the positions assigned by those formations.[32]

But what is the status of the "understanding"? What would a critical spectator-subject be, if the very coherence of the subject is dependent on ideological interpellations? If the "structure of fetishism" can explain the empathic spectator, what psychoanalytic concept will illuminate the critical spectator? There is a conspicuous absence here. The reason is that the states opposed to the "festishistic" in psychoanalysis (at least, as it has been taken up by film theory), far from being self-reflective, are pre-social states (like *l'hommelette* in Lacanian theory), and are utterly inappropriate analogies for the description of the critical, Brechtian spectator. Effectively, Heath paints himself into a corner by adopting psychoanalytic theory as a way of explicating the state of empathy, while the theory offers no complement for the state of distanciation. The only possibility here would seem to be the figure of the supine patient on the analyst's couch, dependent on the latter's skill in unearthing the real motivations of the analysand. It is a potentially flattering image of the critic, but not one that Heath explicitly appeals to as a way of modeling the critical spectator within psychoanalytic theory.

The conception of narrative and narrative comprehension that Heath draws out of Brecht is crucial in understanding the impasse that the theory reaches. "What better way to avoid contradiction than narrative?" Heath asks. Conventional narrative, he goes on to argue, resolves the social contradictions embodied by the conflicts between narrative agents by always directing our attention to "what happens next," the resolution of each conflict rather than the moment of conflict itself. The process is sealed by the traditional climax in which the fundamental conflict of the narrative is brought to a resolution. Against this, Brecht posits a "subjunctive"[33] form of narrative, in which the different possible outcomes of each moment of conflict are stressed rather than a single ("inevitable") outcome: what "might have been" rather than simply "what happens next." As a way of opening up alternative aesthetic possibilities, this analysis has some value. The problems arise when this is taken as a precise and exhaustive description of "classic" narrative form, and when it is assumed that the form can be mapped directly onto the nature of its comprehension by the spectator.

The argument that narrative eradicates certain possibilities in the course of its development rests upon a conception of the spectator as one who cannot think beyond the boundaries determined by the narrative and its development. This assumption is clear in Brecht's remarks on linear narrative form, in which he states that "this way of subordinating everything to a single idea, this passion for propelling the spectator along a single track where he can look neither right nor left, up nor down, is something that the new school of play-writing must reject."[34] The argument may be challenged by appeal to the dynamic concept of the spectator developed in recent narratology, in which the spectator is conceptualized as an active being, filling the gaps left by the narrative and forming expectations about the development of the narrative.[35] If we grant that an expectation may be fulfilled *or frustrated,* then we must admit that the spectator is not merely passively ingesting the turns taken by the narrative. In the film theatre cries of dissent may go up when a narrative development does not conform to a strongly held expectation or desire of the audience. Now it is certainly true that once a narrative has taken a certain turn, it usually adheres to it, but if a spectator has formed an expectation of an alternative event occurring, we should not assume that this alternative is repressed in the spectator's mind. It may be suppressed—made latent, put "off-line"—but it is surely not wholly inaccessible to consciousness. The resolution of narrative conflicts in the narrative cannot be assumed to directly "erase" the social contradictions that the conflicts evoke in the minds of spectators.

The problem is this: if traditional "indicative" narrative form exerts this kind of power over the spectator, and if only a revolutionary "productive" textual form can produce a critical spectator, then the critical spectator is as much an "effect" of the text as the naïve spectator. Such a conception is at odds with the kind of critical spectator Brecht wished to create: how critical is the spectator who can only be constructed as critical by an estranging text? If the assumption is that critical spectators are as textually determined as naïve spectators, then it makes a mockery of the distinction itself. There is, in other words, something intrinsically self-defeating in the idea of "producing" a critical spectator. The project is self-defeating because the means by which the result is arrived at negates the difference between it and its supposed opposite, the naïve or credulous spectator.[36] The estranging text becomes simply a miniature "ideological apparatus," eliciting a different set of ideological answers, but still through a process of "interpellation." At root, the problem arises from the strongly deterministic nature of the Post-Structural paradigm as a whole. In its desire to scupper any notion of "free" and autonomous agency, it removes any possibility of the kind of critical spectator Brecht had in mind, which depends on the spectator acquiring a measure of consciousness and agency.

In these essays, Althusser and Heath expand upon Brecht's critique of naturalist aesthetics and "bourgeois humanism" more generally. Raymond Williams has argued that the initial impulse of naturalism was to relocate power and agency at the level of human activity (thereby displacing agency from the domain of the supernatural): "The driving force of the great naturalist drama was not the reproduction of rooms or dress or conversation on the stage. It was a passion for truth, in strictly human and contemporary terms."[37] Such an emphasis on the simply "human," for Brecht, ironically amounted to a denial of the possibility of change in human society: the human environment becomes as rigid and unchangeable as Fate itself. In filtering this aspect of Brecht through the structural model, however, the notions of consciousness and agency, on which the possibility of change must depend, are lost in the theory itself. And the underlying implications of such a theory can only be nihilistic.

Brechtianism and Narrative Theory

My comments have focused so far on assumptions made about the spectator in relation to cognition, emotion, and consciousness (of representations as representations, and of the place of ideology in representations). In this last section, I want to examine the way in which the Brechtian conception of the spectator is tied in with assumptions about narrative form which are equally problematic. The two sets of assumptions are mutually reinforcing—that is, the conception of spectatorship centered on the notion of *Einfühlung* obscures important narratological distinctions, while the model of linear narrative reinforces an overly homogenous notion of response. Jonathan Kaplan's *The Accused* (1988) provides a useful focus for this discussion. The film has been subject to criticism posed in overtly Brechtian terms concerning the compromises it makes in the representation of political and feminist story material. As such, the film is a good test case for the Brechtian argument that the representational conventions of mainstream narrative cinema, and the concomitant effect of *Einfühlung,* foster moral and political prevarication.[38] Moreover, in examining *The Accused* and criticism of the film from a Brechtian perspective, I can set out some alternative answers to the questions bequeathed to us by the Brechtian tradition.

Based on a true story, the film concerns the gang rape of Sarah Tobias (Jodie Foster). The plot begins in the immediate aftermath of the rape, with a young man reporting the rape from a call box outside the bar in which the rape occurs. The first phase of the film concerns the awkward relationship between Sarah, a working-class woman, and the middle-class assistant D.A. who represents her, Katheryn Murphy (Kelly McGillis). Murphy attempts to build a case against the men, but she encounters problems with reluctant witnesses, unwilling to testify against the rapists, and the constraints of the law itself. Murphy compromises with the lawyers representing the rapists, who are charged with and convicted of "reckless endangerment" rather than rape.

Outraged at the implications of this redefinition of the crime, Tobias confronts Murphy. Murphy responds by building a case for the crime of "criminal solicitation" against the men who goaded and cheered on the direct agents of the rape. This will enable the events themselves to be publicly redefined as rape, and will allow Tobias to tell her story on the stand. Moreover, the case will go further than a strictly defined rape case by demonstrating the complicity of those who give active approval to—or even those who fail to intervene in—the act of rape. Murphy wins the case, but only on the basis of the testimony of Kenneth Joyce (Bernie Coulson), who had witnessed the gang rape in its entirety before making the phone call we see at the film's opening. Tobias's testimony, though revealed to be true through Joyce's flashback, is undermined by the defense attorney's questioning.

In specifically Brechtian terms, Mallorie Cook has argued that the film uses Joyce as an "identification figure" who supplants Tobias, and with whom we are plunged into an empathic and cathartic relationship.[39] Like Joyce, we watch the rape, and perhaps enjoy it as a spectacle, just as those who are charged with criminal solicitation do; but our guilt is expiated through our empathy with Joyce, affirming a sense that we are neither the direct or indirect agents of rape, like the other men in the bar. If we come to the film out of a liberal sense of responsibility, the film seems to confirm that this is enough: it reaffirms, through Joyce, our sense of moral worthiness. In this affirmation and self-congratulation—Althusser's recognition—we re-enter the world outside the cinema complacent, with anything but a sense that the world itself needs changing.

There can be no doubt that the film displays many of the features of Hollywood films that tackle oppression from an avowedly radical perspective; the film steers a tricky course among "social concern, feminism and exploitation."[40] But the Brechtian approach is still too crude. I have already discussed the problems with the notion of illusion as literal deceit; any sense of empathy with Sarah Tobias or Kenneth Joyce, therefore, should not be thought of in terms of a total absorption within the characters. Moreover, the mutually supporting notions of "empathy" and linear narrative ("a single, inevitable chain of events") obscure two distinct narrational processes. The first of these, which I shall call *alignment*, concerns the way a film gives us access to the actions, thoughts, and feelings of characters. The second, *allegiance*, concerns the way a film attempts to marshall our sympathies for or against the various characters in the world of the fiction. Now clearly these two phenomena interact, but they are not reducible to a singular "identification" or "empathy": a fiction film can align us with an unsympathetic character. In other words, while in classical cinema our sympathy is most often elicited for those characters with whom we are aligned, it is possible to have alignment without allegiance. In the rape scene in *The Accused*, for example, point-of-view (POV) shots are used that perceptually align us with the rapists, but this does not magically effect an empathy with them. Once we begin to distinguish these two aspects of narrative form, rather than subsuming them under a homogenous "empathy," the complexities of the film can be discerned.[41]

The structure of alignment throughout the film is more complex than the Brechtian critique of the film suggests. At different points in the film, the action follows Tobias, Joyce, Murphy, the investigating lieutenant, Tobias's friend Sally (another waitress at the bar), even the barman. The result is that the film gives us access to the thoughts and feelings of a range of characters, interleaving the attitudinal perspectives and interests of all the participants. Thus, while the film possesses a linear narrative in that it is based upon a continuous chain of cause and effect organized around a protagonist—all the events are related to Tobias—this does not result in the empathic "tunnel vision" evoked by Brecht. Leaving aside the other questions we have raised about the idea of empathy as literal "loss of self" in a character, it is surely a basic requirement of such a state that the narrative aligns us more or less exclusively with the empathic target, and this the film avoids.

Cook nevertheless argues that, at a crucial moment in the film, the "spectator's perspective is . . . incorporated into that, and only that, of Kenneth Joyce."[42] Just prior to the scene in which Joyce testifies in court, he comes to Murphy's office to warn her that he will not, after all, testify. At one point, Joyce and Tobias are left alone in Murphy's office, and an exchange takes place between them represented through a standard shot/reverse-shot structure. The framings of Tobias are slightly closer than those of Joyce, so that in the shots of Tobias we see her alone, while in the reverse shots of Joyce, we see Joyce "over" Tobias's shoulder framed in the foreground. For Cook, this asymmetry in shot scale demands that the spectator view "Sarah as though through the eyes of Kenneth Joyce."[43] Now if Cook's claim is that the shots of Tobias represent Joyce's optical viewpoint, she is simply wrong, since Foster clearly looks off right rather than directly into the camera. A more metaphorical interpretation of seeing "through the eyes of" Joyce fails as well, however.

If anything, the effect of the asymmetry in the framings is to give more emphasis to Tobias's thoughts and feelings than to Joyce's—until the very end of the conversation, when the framings of Joyce become closer as his resolve not to testify begins to weaken.

The pattern of multiple alignment in the film as a whole is mirrored in the structure of the rape scene itself. Much has been made of the fact that the rape is narrated by Joyce: that is, we witness the rape as a flashback when he is on the witness stand. Tobias's experience is only legitimized by the "good" male presence of Joyce. For Cook, this seals the "transformation" of "identification" from Tobias to Joyce initiated by the scene in Murphy's office. While the visual representation of the rape is initiated as a flashback by Joyce's testimony, and while the scene certainly stresses Joyce's experience by cutting to shots of him both in the bar and on the witness stand, the representation of the rape is much more multilayered than this might suggest. The narration of the film shuttles our optical perspective through virtually all of those present: Joyce, Tobias, the rapists, Sally, those goading and cheering. We see shots of all of these characters, showing us how they relate to the event (ranging from intense pleasure and excitement to horror), and shots representing their optical viewpoints.

Thus, while the narration of the rape is framed and given immediate motivation by Joyce's recounting of the event in court, its internal structure is not limited to Joyce in terms of what he could have witnessed. In this, the film conforms to a classical convention whereby a flashback frequently moves well beyond the range of knowledge of the motivating character; flashbacks in Hollywood films are rarely strictly or thoroughly subjective. Far from our perspective being "incorporated into that, and only that, of Kenneth Joyce," the sequence represents the optical and attitudinal perspectives of all the parties present at the rape. It stresses Joyce's reactions to the event, but not by aligning the spectator exclusively with him, or by creating an undifferentiated empathy with him.

The claim that the film works towards an overpowering empathy with Joyce misrepresents not only the structure of alignment in the film, but also its pattern of allegiance. For the Brechtian interpretation of the film, the figure of Cliff "Scorpion" Albrecht (Leo Rossi) is central. Scorpion is one of the three men tried for inciting the rape. During the rape, he acts as a grotesque master of ceremonies, clapping and cheering and directing other men to engage in the rape itself. Earlier in the film, after Murphy has compromised on the original charge and the three rapists have been imprisoned for "reckless endangerment," Scorpion encounters Tobias in a record store and taunts her cruelly. Scorpion is thus set up as a figure of almost metaphysical evil. Alongside Scorpion, Joyce looks suitably angelic, and it is this Manichaean opposition which, the Brechtian argues, issues in the comforting empathy with the good man, the one who is revolted by rape and ultimately acts in spite of masculine peer pressure not to "betray" his fellows.

What this description leaves out is the range of other men implicated in the rape, who are depicted as neither monstrous nor angelic but rather as, well, regular guys. One of rapists is a "good-looking" college boy; one of them is taunted by Scorpion for sexual inadequacy. The other onlookers, though not characterized in detail, are depicted as unremarkable, blue-collar men. Moreover, the middle-class men in the film—the lawyers—are generally represented as cynical and unsympathetic. And the treatment of the rape as a spectacle of pleasurable violence by the blue-collar men in the bar is echoed by Murphy's male colleagues' attendance at an ice hockey game (the violence of which unsettles Murphy). The film posits a continuity of masculinity across the different men which implicates the ordinary men in the act of rape, rather than exempting them from it.

Our responses to Murphy and Tobias are equally mixed and complex. Tobias is sympathetic from the beginning. The film underscores the sympathy elicited by the character's experience by casting Foster in the role, and by first dwelling on the physical effects of the rape, and then showing how Tobias is effectively violated a second time by an impersonal, cynical, and corrupt legal system. Tobias lives in a trailer, works as a waitress, smokes dope, and gets drunk. Much of her self-esteem is vested in her sexual attractiveness, which she enjoys displaying. She is, in other words, a sitting duck for a legal system shot through with patriarchal prejudice. Murphy, while sympathetic to Tobias, is initially a vehicle for these prejudices, accepting the compromise on Tobias's behalf as the best a working-class, "sluttish" woman can get. Confronted by Tobias in the midst of a dinner party, Murphy is shamed into an awareness of how the legal compromise effectively negates Tobias a second time. As Murphy pursues the criminal solicitation charges, however, Tobias is revealed to have lied to her concerning some details of the events leading up to the rape. By the time the rape itself is depicted, then, both Tobias and Murphy have been shown to be imperfect, though unambiguously victims (in different ways and to different degrees) of a deeply prejudiced society. Thus, the film does not rely on a Manichaean structure of allegiance juxtaposing figures of absolute evil with characters of pure goodness.

The Brechtian riposte to this would presumably be: yes, but the emotional rhetoric of the film is such that we are ultimately swept up into an empathic relationship with Joyce, who, with Tobias and Murphy, is represented as part of a triumphant, morally virtuous trio at the end of the film. In terms of MacCabe's adaptation of the Brechtian argument, the film ultimately establishes a dominant "discourse" or perspective, a perspective with which we become wholly identified and which provides a spurious sense of faith in both the goodness of gender relations in our society, and the ability of the legal system ultimately to protect against gender (and class) oppression. Or, in Heath's terms, the film erases every contradiction between the interests and attitudes of the various agents involved, in order to "fix" us in the "position" of the patriarchal subject, flushed with confidence in the goodness of his society and legal system.[44]

Analyzed in terms of alignment and allegiance, however, the film precipi-

tates no structure of unqualified empathy with any one figure. Although Tobias's experience is the dramatic hub of the film, we are aligned exclusively
neither with her nor with any other figure, including Joyce. Moreover, those
segments of the film in which we are aligned with Joyce do not result in an
automatic loss of allegiance with (sympathy for) Tobias, precisely because allegiance is not reducible to alignment. Finally, those sequences that not only
align us with Joyce but generate sympathy for him do not erase our allegiance
with Tobias, because sympathy is not defined by a total identification with, or
loss of self in, a character. Watching Joyce agonize over "betraying" his rapist
friend does not obliterate the fundamental sympathy for Tobias that the film
has established.

In addition to collapsing the distinction between alignment and allegiance,
and thereby overlooking the intricacies revealed by the analysis of the two
levels of structure, the Brechtian view of the film ignores two further factors.
First, the film finishes not with the happy trio elated at the moment of victory,
but with a title providing statistics on rape and gang rape in the United States,
informing us that a rape is committed every six minutes and that one in four
involves more than one assailant. Cook argues that the "euphoric" conclusion
undermines the force of these statistics.[45] But surely the statistics are as likely
to undermine the euphoric tone of the ending, insofar as they *follow* the dramatic conclusion, and suggest that rape in general, and gang rape specifically,
is far more widespread than we realize. What we might be tempted to regard
as a sensational and exceptional story is revealed to be commonplace. It is not
clear to me that the title is a final gesture which propels us back into the
workaday world filled with confidence and complacency concerning justice
between the sexes. And, as I have argued, there is much in the body of the
film itself that accords with this less-than-affirmative final title.

Even without the final title, the Brechtian analysis would remain reductive.
While there can be no doubting the rhetorical weight carried by the outcome
of a story, narratives do not rely on a repression that eradicates either earlier
phases of the narrative or alternative possibilities that they do not instantiate.
The definition of masculinity through physical violence, and the way in which
the law fails to address this, do not become inaccessible to consciousness, as
implications of the film, because the narrative represents a case in which a
woman gains some measure of redress. One can imagine other, less affirmative, outcomes; and the film may be as much an aid as a hindrance in this
process. The Brechtian analysis of the film founders on the same objections I
have directed against the premises of the Brechtian argument: engaging with
any representation, even a "dramatic" or "classic realist" one, necessarily involves a degree of "distanciation," insofar as it does not involve deceit; a
strong emotional response to a character never results in identification or empathy conceived as "self-oblivion;"[46] and emotional responses do not necessarily cloud the spectator's critical reasoning and thereby "consume his capacity to act."[47]

My purpose here is not to suggest that *The Accused* is either politically radical or formally innovative. It is precisely its "ordinary" qualities that interest me, for my argument is that even a film such as this, which articulates a political issue within the confines of what Brecht termed "dramatic" narrative form, and what later Brechtians termed "classic realism" (MacCabe) or simply "representation" (Heath), offers a potential complexity of experience which such analyses deny. We should not be too surprised by this. It is in the nature of Hollywood product, even today, to address as large an audience as possible. This often involves compromises and hedging, but it also depends upon a product rich enough to incorporate the perspectives of different social groups with different attitudes and interests. The ultimate legacy of Brechtianism is that the cluster of assumptions and answers analyzed in this essay produce a set of evaluative criteria by which the ordinary movie is automatically judged negatively, a formula which is simply inadequate to the complexity of the institution we know as Hollywood and the movies it produces.

NOTES

1. Bertolt Brecht in *Brecht on Theatre,* trans. and ed. John Willett (London: Methuen, 1964), p. 87.

2. For example, Colin MacCabe, "Realism and the Cinema: Notes on Some Brechtian Theses," *Screen* 15, 2 (Summer 1974); Paul Willeman, "Distanciation and Douglas Sirk," *Screen* 12, 2 (1971), and "Towards an Analysis of the Sirkian System," *Screen* 13, 4 (1972–73); Ben Brewster, "The Fundamental Reproach (Brecht)," *CinéTracts* 1, 2 (Summer 1977). Two issues of *Screen* were devoted to Brecht: 15, 2 (Summer 1974) and 16, 2 (Winter 1975–76). Reference is made to other key text below.

3. Brecht, *Brecht on Theatre,* p. 37.

4. Peter Wollen, "Godard and Counter Cinema: *Vent d'Est,*" *Readings and Writings* (London: Verso, 1982), p. 80.

5. Martin Walsh, *The Brechtian Aspect of Radical Cinema* (London: British Film Institute, 1981), p. 11; see also p. 71.

6. Not all of these ideas do justice to the complexity and dynamism of the work of Brecht himself, which developed considerably over his career. Still, such ideas are unquestionably rooted in his writings. For example, Brecht frequently *did* characterize emotion as wholly anathema to critical thought, and this view of emotion has become central to Brechtianism; his qualifications of this view are not often registered within that discourse. I make no claim to an exhaustive account of Brecht here; the aim is to explicate and examine critically those aspects of Brechtian thought which have proven most influential.

7. Brecht, *Brecht on Theatre,* p. 45. Brecht's assumptions concerning the effects of continuous narrative are also revealed by the claims he makes for his alternative strategy—a narrative that develops by "curves" and "leaps," and in so doing prevents the blinkered perspective on the action fostered by empathy with a single protagonist.

8. Stephen Heath, "Lessons from Brecht," *Screen* 15, 2 (Summer 1974): 109.

9. Brecht, *Brecht on Theatre,* p. 219. Brecht also uses the metaphors of "hypnosis," "intoxication," and "seance" in discussing dramatic "illusion": ibid., p. 38.

10. See James R. Hamilton, "'Illusion' and the Distrust of Theater," *Journal of*

Aesthetics and Art Criticism; and Noël Carroll, *Mystifying Movies: Fads and Fallacies in Contemporary Film Theory* (New York: Columbia University Press, 1988), pp. 90–106.

11. Ronald de Sousa, *The Rationality of Emotion* (Cambridge: MIT Press, 1990), p. 195.

12. I pursue this argument in greater detail, in part through an analysis of Jean-Pierre Melville's *Le Doulos* (1962), in my essay "Cognition, Emotion, and Cinematic Narrative," *Post-Script* 13, 1 (Fall 1993), and in *Engaging Characters: Fiction, Emotion, and the Cinema* (Oxford: Clarendon Press, 1995).

13. Walton's argument raises a number of issues which I do not have the space to discuss here. I do not mean to endorse his argument that an emotion requires belief in the object of the emotion, merely to set up a dramatic contrast with the Brechtian tenet that "Aristotelian" fictions actually deceive us with respect to their status as representations. Walton shares with Brecht the idea that belief in the reality of the event prompting the response is a necessary condition of real emotional response; but where Brecht assumes that spectators respond with real emotions and must therefore at the time of the response believe in the reality of the event, Walton assumes that spectators are not so deceived and so therefore cannot be said to experience an emotion proper. See Kendall Walton, "Fearing Fictions," *Journal of Philosophy* 75, 1 (January 1978).

14. Victor Erlich, *Russian Formalism: History—Doctrine* (New Haven: Yale University Press), p. 210.

15. On the conceptual and biographical links between Shklovsky's notion of *ostranenie* (defamiliarization) and Brecht's notion of *Verfremdung* (distanciation, alienation, estrangement), see John Willett's editorial remarks on the essay "Alienation Effects in Chinese Acting," in *Brecht on Theatre,* p. 99; Stanley Mitchell, "From Shklovsky to Brecht: Some Preliminary Remarks Towards a History of the Politicisation of Russian Formalism," and Ben Brewster, "From Shklovsky to Brecht: A Reply," both in *Screen* 15, 2 (Summer 1974).

16. In Louis Althusser, *Lenin and Philosophy and Other Essays,* trans. Ben Brewster (New York: Monthly Review Press, 1971).

17. Louis Althusser, "The 'Piccolo Teatro': Bertolazzi and Brecht," in *For Marx,* trans. Ben Brewster (London: Allen Lane, 1969), p. 144.

18. This is explicitly stated in "Marxism and Humanism," in *For Marx.*

19. Althusser, *For Marx,* p. 150.

20. Or at least, an important strain of structuralism, which would include Althusser. See J. G. Merquior, *From Prague to Paris: A Critique of Structuralist and Poststructuralist Thought* (London: Verso, 1986), pp. 1–6; and Claude Lévi-Strauss, *The Savage Mind* (Chicago: University of Chicago Press, 1966), p. 252.

21. Althusser, *For Marx,* p. 150. Ideology is still described in this essay as "false consciousness," although in later essays Althusser breaks away from the realism implicit in the wording—that is, the implication that there could be "true consciousness."

22. Ibid., p. 146; cf. p. 142.

23. Ibid., p. 148.

24. Ibid., p. 151.

25. Ibid.: "pursuing in me" my emphasis.

26. Merquior, pp. 205–9, comments on the absence of concern with causality and change in Althusser and structuralism in general.

A further index of the incompatibility of Brecht and Post-Structuralism may be found in the work of Jean-Louis Baudry. Baudry argues that the "work" of film production is repressed, in order to guarantee the purported transcendence of the spectator-subject. If this "work" were to be revealed (for example, through the visible presence of the camera in the image) the spectator would lose her sense of control or "mastery" over the film, and would realize that the film controls (or even "produces") her, rather than vice versa: "Both specular tranquillity and the assurance of one's own identity collapse simultaneously with the revealing of the mechanism, that is of the inscription of the film work" (Jean-Louis Baudry, "Ideological Effects of the Basic Cinematographic Apparatus," trans. Alan Williams, *Film Quarterly* 28, 2 (Winter 1974–75): 46.) On the face of it, this claim conforms with the Marxist critique of commodity fetishism, in which the tie between labor and product is severed, and bears a striking resemblance to Brecht's critique of naturalism, in which the artwork is regarded as concealing its status as a product of labor. But there is a crucial difference. For Brecht, revealing this work can result in a more critical spectator; for Baudry, the spectator's identity "collapses." Of course, it is far from clear what the nature of this collapse is; but it seems very distant from Brecht's confident, cigar-smoking, rational spectator.

27. Both in *Screen* 15, 2 (Summer 1974).

28. For critical views, see David Bordwell, *Narration in the Fiction Film* (Madison: University of Wisconsin Press, 1985), pp. 18–20; and George M. Wilson, *Narration in Light: Studies in Cinematic Point of View* (Baltimore: Johns Hopkins University Press, 1986), chapter 10.

29. Roland Barthes, "Diderot, Brecht, Eisenstein," in *Image/Music/Text*, trans. Stephen Heath (London: Fontana, 1977).

30. Heath, "Lessons from Brecht," p. 106.

31. Heath argues that he is precisely not setting up "a simple opposition" (p. 111). Heath is here describing the internal structure of "distanciation," arguing that it involves an oscillation between "separation" and "identification," not a complete exclusion of the latter. What I am arguing, however, is that this still depends on a dualistic opposition between "production" so defined, and "representation," defined as unalloyed "identification."

32. Heath, "Lessons from Brecht," pp. 114 and 119.

33. The term is used by Raymond Williams in "Brecht and Beyond," *Politics and Letters* (London: Verso, 1981).

34. Brecht, *Brecht on Theatre*, p. 44. Like Heath, though in rather vaguer terms, Peter Wollen echoes the Brechtian conception of narrative when he writes that Godard avoids "narrative transitivity" in order "to disrupt the emotional spell of the narrative and thus force the spectator, by interrupting the narrative flow, to reconcentrate and refocus his attention" (Wollen, p. 81).

35. See, for example, Bordwell, *Narration in the Fiction Film*.

36. On these matters, see Jon Elster, *Sour Grapes: Studies in the Subversion of Rationality* (Cambridge: Cambridge University Press, 1983), part 2.

37. Raymond Williams, *Drama from Ibsen to Brecht* (Harmondsworth, England: Penguin, 1973), p. 384; cf. p. 391.

38. Mallorie Cook, "Criticism or Complicity? The Question of the Treatment of Rape and the Rape Victim in Jonathan Kaplan's *The Accused,*" *CineAction* 24/25 (1991): 80–85. Cook bases her analysis of the film on the Brechtian-influenced articles by Wollen and MacCabe cited above, as well as referring to Brecht himself.

39. Ibid., p. 85.

40. Pam Cook, review of *The Accused, Monthly Film Bulletin* 2, 1 (May 1992): 35.

41. The concepts of alignment and allegiance are discussed at greater length in Smith, *Engaging Characters*.

42. Mallorie Cook, "Criticism," p. 84.

43. Ibid.

44. '[R]epresentation is exactly a fixing of positions.' Heath, "Lessons from Brecht," p. 104.

45. Mallorie Cook, "Criticism," p. 85.

46. Mallorie Cook, drawing on Martin Esslin's exposition of Brecht, describes identification as "self-oblivion," in ibid.

47. Williams, *Drama from Ibsen to Brecht,* p. 317.

Characterization and Fictional Truth in the Cinema

Paisley Livingston

People who make fiction films typically devote a great deal of effort to the invention and portrayal of characters. Making sense of these characters is, in turn, a central part of most filmgoers' experiences. An adequate model of critical expertise would explain how competent spectators arrive at appropriate understandings and evaluations of characters in films. No such model, however, is available in the literature of film theory, which in recent times has largely been dominated by psychoanalytic condemnations of the moviegoer's guilty pleasures.[1]

In this chapter I attempt to clarify some basic issues relevant to cinematic characterization. I begin with the problem of providing a general definition of characterization and then turn to the question of the specific features of the cinematic variety. It turns out that in trying to deal with cinematic characterization we quickly come up against a number of difficult and more general problems, including the notorious question of truth in fiction. I do not propose detailed solutions to all of these problems in what follows, but I do attempt to identify them and discuss some of the relations between them. One theme that emerges at several key points in my discussion is that working with intentionalist principles is the most promising way of approaching some of the problems that arise with regard to fictional characterization. Elucidating and defending these intentionalist principles is one of my main goals.

What Is Characterization?

Most generally, characterization can be said to be a matter of someone's describing, depicting, or representing something. In aesthetics, however, a more restricted usage of the term is required.[2] Here the something being represented must be an agent or agents, as in the phrase "Orson Welles's characterization of Charles Foster Kane in the film *Citizen Kane* is rather simplistic." "Agent," which is essential to this more restricted usage, can be defined broadly as referring to any entity capable of performing an intentional action. And intentional action can, in turn, be identified as behavior produced and oriented by the agent's intention, that is, by a mental attitude that represents the state of affairs the behavior is meant to realize. (There are, of course, alternative definitions of action, and many of my claims about characterization are compatible with at least some of them. This is not a paper on the fundamental problems of action theory, so I shall take for granted the assumption that we are warranted in drawing a distinction between intentional action and unintentional behavior.[3])

According to my proposed definition, there is an instance of characterization just in case some agent intentionally represents some agent or agents. The intended target of a characterization can be some particular individual (for example, Jean-Jacques Rousseau) or a type of agent (for example, Rousseauesque intellectuals). Represented agents, or characters, need not be actual. Shakespeare and his colleagues characterized an imaginary Prince of Denmark, and literary critics continue to publish detailed characterizations of the ever-elusive Hamlet. But for there to be an actual event or episode of characterization, some actual agent or agents must perform the right sort of representational action, intentionally producing a representation of some agent or type of agent with the intention of thereby representing that agent or agent type.

Two kinds of agency, then, contribute to characterization. The first is a matter of the doings of actual agents. The second is depicted or represented agency, which need not resemble the first kind in many respects.

To state that characterization must involve a representation of at least one agent is hardly a severe restriction on our use of the term in aesthetics, for in fictional narratives, such items as balloons, automobiles, mansions, oceans, and teakettles can function as characters, provided they are depicted as engaging in some sort of purposeful activity in the story. According to this usage, then, some cinematic works, such as Stan Brakhage's *Mothlight* (1963), literally have no characters. But such works are not meant to tell stories, so the absence of characters is hardly surprising, and we hardly feel a need to employ the concept of characterization in talking about them.

The means agents can use in order to perform the action of characterization are quite varied, and include such items as gestures, verbal utterances, printed documents, audiovisual recordings, hand-drawn inscriptions, and so on. The term "characterization" is often used to refer to these means exclusively, as when someone says that some film *is* an unfair characterization. But I think the latter usage is best understood as shorthand, for unless some agent has done something with the right sort of intention, there can be no action of characterizing anyone, and hence no characters.

My central claim, then, is that an intentional action of representation is necessary for characterization, and I provide additional arguments in favor of this intentionalist thesis below. One may ask, however, whether the proposed conditions are sufficient. Does any and every intentionally produced description or depiction that is meant to be about some actual or imagined agent, or type of agent, count as a characterization? What about someone's saying, "Paolo is in the kitchen eating" in response to a trivial question? Isn't this too thin to count as a characterization of Paolo? After all, the point of the utterance is not to characterize Paolo, but merely to relate his whereabouts and activity. As it stands, my definition includes such cases.

A theorist who wants to develop a more narrow notion of characterization than mine could place restrictions on the kinds of ends a representation must serve if it is to count as a characterization. For example, it might be proposed that characterizations are all and only those descriptions or depictions directly aiming at relating the essential personality features of some agent. So a banal report that Paolo is in the kitchen would be ruled out. Such a stipulation, however, has the disadvantage of yoking the theory of characterization to what social psychologists call the fundamental attribution error, roughly, the idea that agents have personality structures that explain most, if not all, of their actions.[4] In my view we are better off working with a broader conception, namely, one that allows that the intentional attribution of any properties to an agent suffices to make a representation count as a characterization—but not necessarily a good or nontrivial one. I do not think we want a definition of "characterization" to be yoked to any particular theory about the "character" or personality structure characteristic of individual agents. All kinds of strange, metamorphic agents appear in fiction, and no one *personality* theory applies to all of them. The price to be paid is to allow that even trivial descriptions involving agents can be characterizations, unless, that is, we find another way to set a limit to which descriptions should count as characterizations. My proposal has the modest advantage, at least, of squaring with prevalent talk about "flat" and "superficial" characterizations.

Characterization, I claim, should be understood as a species of intentional action. I shall argue that the comprehension of key aspects of literary and cinematic characters requires the recognition of features of the intentional action that produced them. For some this is a banal claim, but for others it is highly controversial. How can this intentional thesis be justified? It may be useful to begin by illustrating the thesis with an example. Let's assume that Lord Byron meant to characterize Jean-Jacques Rousseau when he wrote the following lines in *Childe Harold's Pilgrimage*: " . . . he knew / How to make madness beautiful, and cast / O'er erring deeds and thoughts, a heavenly hue / Of words. . . ."[5] (There is, in fact, ample internal and external evidence supporting such an interpretation.) Assume also—if only for the sake of the argument—that these phrases can now be read as an apt description of Michel Foucault. My claim is that it does not follow that Byron's poem characterizes Foucault, for the poet had no such intention. Rousseau is a character in the poem, but Foucault is not.

Part of the rationale behind an intentionalist definition of characterization can be clarified with reference to the distinction between lying and sincere assertion. We are often interested in knowing whether a statement is accurate or inaccurate; but we are also often interested in whether it is sincere or insincere. People who are sincere but misleading should get credit for sincerity—but not reliability—and it would be unfortunate if we had no concept with which to distinguish such cases from those where someone purposefully attempts to mislead someone else. We often care about the difference between cases where someone does someone good or harm intentionally and cases where someone's action or inaction inadvertently leads to beneficial or harmful consequences. Similarly, intentional slander is one kind of offense. It should be distinguished from cases where speakers do not aim to describe some particular person but unwittingly say things that turn out to be applicable to some individual or individuals. It is my view that the concept of characterization should mesh with such salient and deeply entrenched intentionalist features of our communicative framework.

It is sometimes objected to this, however, that notions in aesthetics need not be compatible with our everyday pragmatic assumptions. This objection is dubious, not only because we should not isolate characterization from norms pertaining to communication and interaction, but also because there are specifically aesthetic reasons for relying on intentionalist criteria. For example, we often take a special interest in skillful (as opposed to unintended and accidental) artistic performances, characterization included, which is why words such as "original," "derivative," "hackneyed," and "studied," figure on lists of aesthetic properties.[6] One may prize some passages from Byron's text because they can be read as being applicable to Foucault, but it does not follow that Byron should be credited or blamed for having produced a characterization of the twentieth-century theorist.

Another potential objection to an intentionalist definition of characterization has an ethical (or political) basis: when making judgments of strict liability, it may be argued, we do not care whether the harmful or offending consequences were intended. Someone could harmfully characterize someone else without having had any such intention, and it would be a mistake to accept a theory that stipulates that no such harmful act of characterization could occur. In response, I would acknowledge the relevance of judgments of strict liability to depictions and representations, which are sometimes harmful and beneficial in ways unforeseen by their makers. But to identify and evaluate such actions we need not recognize them as characterizations. As I have already noted, we remain interested in the difference between intentional and unintentional (for example, accidental or neglectful) cases of representational wrongdoing (for example, slander). An adequate ethics of representation cannot be based entirely on intentionalist principles, but nor can it dispense with the latter.

A few additional remarks on this hotly contested topic may be useful to prevent misunderstandings. In a valuable essay on the ethics of basing fictional stories on actual individuals, Felicia Ackerman makes a number of useful points.[7] Her basic setup is a situation where some author, A, writes a fictional story and bases at least one of the story's characters on some actual individual, S (the source of the character). Under what conditions, Ackerman asks, is such an action culpable? In response, Ackerman delineates some ways in which the author's storytelling activity may cause harm to S. Readers (or spectators) who recognize that the fictional character has been based on S may learn secrets about S or may acquire false beliefs or suspicions about S; this may in turn produce unwanted consequences for S, for example, should these persons treat S differently as a result of these new beliefs. If the author presents a negative evaluation of the character, such judgments may be carried over in the readers' evaluations of S. Even if no one recognizes S in the fictional character, S may be harmed by the action if he or she feels betrayed or exploited by the author's action. And even if the story is never publically published or screened, the very fact of the author's planning to use S as a source may rightly constitute such a betrayal in S's mind. (We note in passing that a poignant illustration of the latter point is provided in Ingmar Bergman's *Såsom i en spegel* [*Through a Glass Darkly,* 1961], when Karin is devastated to learn that her father has been recording her mental illness as material for his next novel.)

Basing a character on an actual person, then, can be harmful to that person in a variety of ways. The author's culpability in such cases, however, depends on a number of factors. Whether the resemblance between S and the character was intentional and was meant by the author to be noticed are two key factors. Ackerman proposes that authors are morally obligated not to write "what seems likely to induce false and damaging beliefs about an actual person."[8] Ackerman also deems that S's informed and voluntary consent is also relevant, but cannot alone suffice to relieve the author from blame in all cases. Nor can claims about the importance or value of the ensuing work of fiction serve reasonably to offset any harm caused to the source. Not only would it have to be shown that the work would have greatly suffered in the absence of the resemblance between the character and S, but it would also have to be shown that the work's aesthetic (or other) value genuinely offsets the harm to S.

Ackerman's analysis is focused uniquely on cases where a fictional character may be recognized as resembling and having been based intentionally on some one, actual individual. She does not take on the more general issue of the ethics of depictions involving recognizable groups or types of agents, but no *single* actual individual. The two kinds of cases, however, seem analogous, and the same moral principles may apply to both, once the harm done to the individual S is replaced by harm done to at least one actual member of the group or type represented in the fiction. Thus, even though Veit Harlan's anti-Semitic *Jud Süss* (*Jew Süss,* 1940) was not a *film à clef,* the director and his coworkers are culpable for intentionally creating a damaging representation of members of an actual group. Cases of unintentional wrongdoing of this sort are harder to legislate, however, for here we face a difficult decision in which we must weigh a number of different factors, including the gravity of the harm done and the extent to which the relevant agent(s) could reasonably have been expected to foresee that harm would be done. A lot of theoretical work remains to be done on this topic, and some prevalent critical judgments seem underwritten by overly simple notions. An intentionalist approach to characterization provides the right background for these difficult deliberations.

Fictional and Nonfictional Characterizations

Characterization takes place in many contexts and can be oriented toward a wide variety of ends, only some of which are primarily aesthetic or artistic. Employers characterize their employees in letters of recommendation (which were once commonly known as "characters"). The authors of items in the personal column of *The New York Review of Books* characterize themselves as well as the kind of companions they hope to attract. Sometimes characterizations are intended to carry conviction, but not always. We often have good reason to apply a distinction between fictional and nonfictional characterizations whereby the latter, but not the former, are a matter of genuine assertions. For example, Bergman's *Det sjunde inseglet* (*The Seventh Seal,* 1957) is fiction: the Swedish director did not make his film with the intention of convincing us that in the Middle Ages death actually walked around in human form playing chess and speaking Swedish. Erroll Morris, on the other hand, expects us to believe there really is a Stephen Hawking and that *A Brief History of Time* (1993) gives us insight into this actual person's life and work. There are interesting borderline cases as well, such as the status of Henri Laborit in Alain Resnais's hybrid work, *Mon Oncle d'Amérique* (*My Uncle from America,* 1980). Nor is it clear (to me at least) whether Oliver Stone and his coworkers were guided by a consistent fiction-making intention in producing *JFK* (1991). But such problem cases do not invalidate the distinction.

I hasten to acknowledge that no one pragmatic account of fiction is currently the object of a consensus amongst the experts. Even so, I think it safe to assume that the fiction/nonfiction distinction can usefully be described in terms of a type of illocutionary force, which is determined, like all other types of illocutionary acts, by the kind of communicative or expressive intention that informs the speaker's or producer's behavior. With regard to fiction, I follow Kendall Walton, Greg Currie, and others who think that the type of intention governing fictional utterances can be described in terms of an attitude of imagining or "make believe" that belongs to our commonsense psychology.[9] I disagree with various details in Walton's and Currie's different accounts, but shall postpone a discussion of these matters. Some of the problems will come up below when the issue of fictional truth comes to the fore. Roughly, the idea we are after is that a work is fictional just in case it is the product of the right sort of fictive intent: that is, its author(s) must have a communicative intention that some target audience adopt the attitude of imagining toward the work's propositions.

Characterization and Cinematic Depiction

Given the general definition of characterization proposed above, the key difference between fictional characterization per se and fictional characterization in the cinema resides in the respective means employed by the characterizer(s). Much of what is special and puzzling about characterization in the cinema derives, then, from the photographic, or more precisely, audiovisual depiction of actors' performances. Remarks by Theodor Adorno, Maurice Merleau-Ponty, and Stanley Cavell can serve to underscore this point, for these three philosophers tried to describe the special qualities of cinematic representations of human beings. Let's begin with Adorno:

> Even when dialogue is used in a novel, the spoken word is not directly spoken, but is rather distanced by the act of narration, or even by the typography. It is thereby abstracted from the bodily presence of living persons [*der Leibhaftigkeit lebendiger Personen*]. Thus, no matter how minutely they are described, fictional characters in novels never resemble empirical persons. In fact, the very precision of their presentation may be what removes them even further from empirical reality, so that they become aesthetically autonomous. In film such distance is abolished: as long as a film is realistic [*verhält sich realistisch*], the semblance of immediacy [*der Schein von Unmittelbarkeit*] cannot be avoided.[10]

Although I am not sure I understand Adorno's statement about the novel's aesthetic autonomy, it strikes me that he raises important issues in speaking of cinema's semblance of immediacy, and in contrasting verbal characterization to a living being's *bodily presence* (the German *Leibhaftigkeit* is difficult to render in English; *Leib* is the body, and *haftigkeit* stresses its very identity, immediacy, and self-same presence; " *der leibhaftige Geiz*," for example, can be translated as "greed incarnate" or "in person"). Yet Adorno's comments remain somewhat puzzling. If cinematic immediacy is an illusion or mere appearance—a *Schein*, as he puts it—how can it "abolish" the distance between the actual living body and a characterization in a movie? It seems that something about cinematic characterization has led Adorno to overstate his point.

I turn now to a passage in which Merleau-Ponty seems to be grappling with a similar problem:

> This is why human expressivity can be so striking in the cinema: the cinema does not give us people's thoughts, as the novel has long done; instead, it gives us their behavior, their special way of being in the world, their manner of dealing with things and with each other. It makes this special way of being in the world visible in those gestures, looks, and expressions which clearly serve to define the people we know.[11]

Merleau-Ponty appears to have believed that the cinematic medium can offer direct perceptual access to character, a mode of access that closely resembles that of actual intersubjective understanding. But is this literally the case? Merleau-Ponty does not discuss any of the differences between the conditions of everyday intersubjective understanding and the process of making sense of a movie's fictional characters. Two-way, face-to-face conversation, for example, is an aspect of everyday intersubjective understanding that has no equivalent in our relation to cinematic characters. When we interpret cinematic characters, we often think about ways in which they have been designed to serve the filmmaker's expressive aims; such a mode of interpretation is wholly absent in our understanding of actual persons. Merleau-Ponty's remarks are best read as an expression of his stylistic preference for an idealized form of naturalist cinema, and not as a sound generalization about cinematic characterization.

Consider now Cavell's discussion of the special nature of cinematic depictions of people:

> It is an incontestable fact that in a motion picture no live human being is up there. But a human *something* is, and something unlike anything else we know. We can stick to our plain description of that human something as "in our presence while we are not in his" (present *at* him, because looking at him, but not present *to* him) and still account for the difference between his live presence and his photographed presence to us. We need to consider what is present or, rather, since the topic is the human being, *who* is present.[12]

Cavell's reference to a rather singular "human something" is evocative, but hardly provides us with a satisfactory analysis or even a "plain description" of the phenomenon. Presumably Cavell would not have us say that we are present at anything we happen to look at, in actuality or in a depiction. Is the astronomer present at the moon, and is someone who views Poussin's painting present at the rape of the Sabine women? Cavell's strange idea of *presence at* requires explanation and can hardly provide a ready clarification of the puzzles of the cinematic experience.

My three citations may give the impression that some very intelligent philosophers may have gone on holiday when they decided to write about the cinema, but I think there is a genuine intuition motivating these passages. There is indeed something powerful about the cinema's depictions of people, something having to do, as all three philosophers suggest, with the special role played by perception. Filmmakers often can, if they so choose, employ the cinematic apparatus in such a way as to provide the spectator with sounds and images that depict the physical appearances of a performer in a manner that no verbal narration could ever achieve. It is one thing to read in Proust that Charles Swann's nose had become "enormous, tumefied, crimson [énorme, tuméfié, cramois]."[13] It is rather different when we watch Volker Schlöndorff's cinematic adaptation of Proust entitled *Eine Liebe von Swann* (1984), for then our notion of the specific features of Swann's face is based in part on the experience of perceiving a motion picture image that depicts Jeremy Irons in makeup. My point is not that cinematic characterizations are necessarily better or more realistic as a result of the special features of the medium; my point, simply, is that perception plays a different role in our reception of film than it does in our reception of prose fiction. If you doubt this, consider how the special capacities of the cinematic medium are used by Federico Fellini to provide an especially poignant moment in his film *Intervista*, where Marcello Mastroianni, Anita Ekberg, and Fellini gather in 1987 for a screening of Fellini's 1960 film, *La dolce vita*. Over twenty-seven years later, we can see images of the aging performers playing themselves as they nostalgically watch images of their own youthful performances. Only in the cinema could the devastating physical contrast between the faces of youth and the tearful, nostalgic faces of old age be made so vivid.

This having been said, we are still a long way from an adequate analysis of the specific nature of cinematic depictions and of the fictional characterizations they make possible. Saying what visual depictions of any sort are, and how they work, is a rather difficult task, and there are, in the literature, a number of intelligent rival conceptions. I cannot presume to have solved this problem, and will limit myself here to saying that I am at least temporarily inclined to think, along with Christopher Peacocke, that the cinema's audiovisual depictions cannot be adequately explained in terms of make-believe, nor exclusively in terms of convention-governed symbolic or semiotic systems.[14] Instead, a successful analysis of cinematic depiction would have to describe how a film can enable the moviegoer to have an experience of perceptual similarities between the cinema's sounds and images, and what they depict. When we recognize that a cinematic image depicts a red balloon we do so in part because the depiction is experienced in our visual field as being similar to a red balloon in shape and color. Many of us have had the experience of instantly recognizing in the street some famous person whose looks were previously known to us only through the mediation of audiovisual depictions. Such acts of recognition are not the result of the application of some grammar or code of cinema to the world of everyday experience. Instead, the act of recognition is possible because of experienced perceptual similarities, the psychophysical basis of which remains to be described.

Although it is important to emphasize the role of perception in the functioning of cinematic depictions, it is also crucial to recognize that a film spectator's uptake of an audiovisual text is oriented by various nonperceptual beliefs, including beliefs about the relevant activities of those who produced the images. For example, as I follow the story of Robert Eroica Dupea in Bob Rafelson's *Five Easy Pieces* (1970), I believe that I am seeing images that have been made by filming Jack Nicholson. This is, I think, the basis for Cavell's talk of the viewer's "presence at" the performer, for as spectators we believe that some particular person had to be present before the camera for these images to have been made, which is not the case with regard to Poussin and the Sabine women.

Such beliefs about what Adorno calls the "immediacy" of cinematic representations of the body are not always justified, however. Filmmakers play a lot of tricks on the audience. Viewers regularly fail to notice that shots of stand-ins or "body doubles" have been spliced in alongside shots of a star. The shots of the double are meant to depict the same character that shots of the star depict; they are also meant to be mistaken for photographic images of the famous performer, even though they were not produced by actually making images of that performer's body. Only under certain conditions, then, is the spectator really justified in believing that the images provide a reliable depiction of a specific actor. I shall not attempt here to provide a general theoretical account of these conditions. The potentially relevant factors are rather diverse; they can include, for example, such items as the filmmaker's motives and the absence of unusual interventions and wayward causal processes during the various stages of a film's processing, editing, reproduction, and distribution. Spectators must also have good reason to assume that they are not looking at images generated ex nihilo by a computer or some process of animation—a condition that will become increasingly difficult to satisfy as the relevant technologies develop.

Characterization and Fictional Truth

A successful explanation of cinematic depiction per se has yet to be provided. But even if we had one, it would not by itself yield an account of characterization in fiction films. George Wilson has usefully underscored this point by distinguishing between *photographic* and *dramatic representation* in the cinema.[15] Wilson suggests that an individual shot can provide a *photographic representation* of an actress and of actions she has actually performed before the camera. At the same time, however, her performance is a *dramatic representation* of a fictional character since her filmed behavior represents the same or similar actions of that character.

Having drawn a distinction between dramatic and photographic representations, Wilson cogently objects to notorious attempts to seize upon either of the two types of representation in an effort to define the "essence" or "specificity" of the cinematic medium. He goes on to claim that the interaction between the two types of representation is such that it is "impossible, in analyzing a film, to unfuse the interaction, to treat them as discernibly separate and distinct," and Wilson adds that it is a mistake to treat the interaction as "a phenomenon to be analytically unwoven."[16] This strikes me as being overstated. Wilson's sound point, I think, is that there is no simple way to draw the line between a film's *narrative* (by which he means the story, or the content of the fiction), and the *narration* that portrays that story. The elements of dramatic and photographic representation do not fall neatly on either side of that distinction, Wilson claims, and the idea that these two levels of representation can be readily discerned tends to contribute to the mistaken idea that narrative and narration may be easily distinguished from each other.

Wilson provides examples to illustrate these difficulties. In King Vidor's adaptation of *War and Peace* (1956), Henry Fonda plays the part of Pierre. Although some of the actor's behavior can be identified as a dramatic representation of the character's behavior, other elements of Fonda's photographed appearance and behavior cannot. It would be wrong to infer from the actor's distinctive accent, for example, that the character Pierre has an American accent in the story. Many of Fonda's other features and actions should, however, be attributed to Pierre.

This example may not be as straightforward as Wilson suggests. On at least one understanding of what it means to be an expert spectator, the viewer should in fact recognize that the difference between Fonda's accent and that of the other performers is a flaw in this film. Wilson might agree, and would perhaps respond by saying that the critic should still be able to decide that this flaw is not part of the film's story. In any case, other examples are easily provided to demonstrate that the issue Wilson has raised is indeed central to cinematic characterization. Some highly prevalent cinematic devices depend on the viewer's willingness and ability to apply a distinction between explicitly depicted aspects of performances that do and do not count as parts of the story. When one performer portrays a character in his childhood and another actor represents the same character in later life, the spectator is supposed to be tolerant about physical differences that appear to contradict the character's physical continuity. For example, no fewer than five persons portray a character named Aron in Liv Ullmann's *Sofie* (1992), but the striking physical metamorphoses this character appears to undergo while growing up are simply not supposed to count as part of what happens in the story.[17] A more bizarre example is provided by Luis Buñuel's *Cet obscur objet du désir* (*That Obscure Object of Desire*, 1976). In this film's story, an elderly man narrates his fascination with a young woman, who is portrayed in flashback sequences by two strikingly different actresses. The explicitly incompatible physical traits of two performers, then, are somehow meant to contribute to those of a single character. The inverse possibility, that is, one performer's traits generating those of two (or more) characters, has been exploited in many works, such as Curtis Bernhardt's *A Stolen Life* (1946), Paul Henreid's *Dead Ringer* (1964), and David Cronenberg's *Dead Ringers* (1988). In each of these films, a well-known performer portrays twins. Another odd case is Bernardo Bertolucci's *Il conformista* (*The Conformist*, 1971), in which Dominique Sanda appears as three different individuals, figuring as a prostitute, as Professor Quadri's wife, and as the consort of a fascist official. The Clerici character, who encounters all three, comments that they resemble each other, but the spectator may well wonder why he cannot see that there is more than a "resemblance" here. Is it true in the story that the women are identical triplets?

These examples suffice to show that the traits of a fictional character in a film are not comprised of all and only those behaviors and appearances some one agent is explicitly depicted as having in that film. In Wilson's terms, this means that what an actor's behavior represents *dramatically* is not logically equivalent to what is represented *photographically*. Instead, the logic of these matters is more complicated. The fact that an agent is explicitly depicted in a film as having some property, *p*, does not entail that the fictional character that agent portrays has that property in the film's story. It follows that viewers must make inferences about which explicitly depicted properties and states of affairs are part of the story and which are not. What is more, some, but not all, of a character's properties are explicitly depicted in the film; thus, viewers must make inferences about other, undepicted properties the character has in the story.

In spite of these complexities, spectators somehow converge with regard to judgments about at least some of the inferences that may and may not reasonably be drawn about fictional agents and situations. How is this convergence to be explained? This question is common to fictional characterization in various media, for it is ultimately a matter of providing a principled way of determining what some philosophers have called "truth in fiction." Wilson has expressed some skepticism about finding a solution, and it is true that theorists of film and literature have yet to provide an adequate account of how people distinguish between what is and is not part of the story related by a fictional narration.[18] But we should not let the difficulty of the topic prevent us from trying to explore new proposals. In what follows I shall delineate a broad, intentionalist principle underwriting spectators' expertise in making inferences about implicit story content.

First some background. In David Lewis's influential account, statements about what is true in a fiction, such as "Sherlock Holmes shook hands with Gladstone," are analyzed as abbreviations of longer sentences beginning with an operator, "In the fiction f . . ."[19] A prefixed sentence to the effect that in a particular fiction, Sherlock Holmes shook hands with Gladstone, does not entail the non-prefixed sentence that the actual Gladstone had his hand shaken by Holmes, but it does entail a prefixed sentence to that effect. Nothing follows from mixtures of prefixed and unprefixed sentences. Thus in a first, provisional analysis, Lewis proposes that the propositions true in a given fiction are all and only those explicitly stated in the text in question plus any other propositions entailed by them. Lewis does not dwell on the matter, but he assumes that propositions explicitly stated in a text are those produced when the text is interpreted standardly in the appropriate language. We have just seen that with regard to the cinema, the latter clause would have to be altered suitably. The text's explicitly depicted fictional truths could, for example, be analyzed as what the recorded sounds and images depict when perceived standardly; but as I have already noted, cashing this out is no small matter, and viewers have to think about which perceived properties are and are not part of the story.

In any case, Lewis notes that his first analysis is inadequate because additional premises are required to arrive at some crucial conclusions about what is the case in a fictional story. For example, our background knowledge of the broad outlines of the geography of London is relevant to the Sherlock Holmes stories and makes possible important inferences about what is the case in them. In light of this problem, Lewis goes on to propose two different analyses of truth in fiction, both of which are meant to provide readers with a broader base for making inferences about the implicit content of a story. In both cases, statements about truth in fiction are treated as counterfactuals. The prefixed, fictional premises are taken as suppositions contrary to fact, and in reasoning about them, we are to rely on unprefixed premises as well, departing from actuality only as far as we must to reach some possible world or worlds where the counterfactual supposition comes out true. Suppose, for example, that Holmes lived on Baker Street. Given that in the actual London, Baker Street is closer to Paddington Station than to Waterloo Station, it would follow that in the fiction Holmes lived nearer to Paddington. Similarly, mundane factual premises allow us to infer that Holmes never visited the moons of Saturn, even though no such statement can be found in the relevant texts. Kendall Walton has dubbed this approach "The Reality Principle," as it is at bottom a matter of assuming that what happens in fictional stories is as close as possible to what we know the real world to be.

The other analysis that Lewis proposes is motivated by the fact that the implicit premises required for reasoning competently about fictions do not all derive from the competent reader's storehouse of knowledge—or even beliefs—about what is the case in the actual world. Lewis proposes, then, that truth in fiction be taken as the joint product of the text's explicit content and a background of beliefs overtly believed in the community in which the fiction originates. So if a supernatural belief figures in the network of reciprocally held consensual beliefs in the storyteller's community, a reader who does not share that belief should nonetheless adopt it as a premise in reasoning about what goes on in a fiction having that origin. Walton has dubbed this the "Mutual Belief Principle."

Lewis tells us that he decided to abstain from trying to determine which of these two proposals is more conducive to appreciation and critical insight, which was just as well, since neither of them will do the job. The reality principle does not underwrite a competent manner of determining the content of a fiction because it warrants too many inappropriate inferences and fails to yield other, crucial ones. For example, in various films starring Humphrey Bogart and Lauren Bacall, the characters are depicted as frequently smoking cigarettes; but it is inappropriate to infer, on the basis of our current medical knowledge, that the characters in these old movies were imprudently increasing their chances of getting cancer. Or suppose—but only for the sake of the argument—that it is a fact that people's morbid fear of sharks has castration anxiety as its root cause. We would not, as a result, be warranted to decide that any of the characters in Steven Spielberg's *Jaws* (1975) are driven by a fear of castration. More generally, readers who import all of their beliefs about the actual world into the stories they read will populate the latter with scads of irrelevant and inappropriate facts and characters.

The Mutual Belief Principle is also inadequate, for it too warrants inappropriate inferences while failing to support other ones that any moderately skillful reader should be able to come up with. Modern consumers of fantastic fictions and horror films sometimes need to deploy incredible ideas about supernatural processes when making connections between explicitly depicted events. Suppose, for example, that early on in a fiction film viewers see a close-up of a dog's eyes followed by a shot of a man falling to his death from a balcony. In some contexts, this sequence should be interpreted as implying a causal relation between the two events: the dog is not a passive witness, but a malevolent character with the evil eye, who has killed the man by directing its powerful gaze at him. The evil eye belief is part of many communities' mutual belief systems, but not that of the Hollywood filmmakers and their audiences, so it is clearly not the Mutual Belief Principle that warrants such an inference. And sometimes the premises needed to make inferences about story content are not part of any community's system of mutual beliefs.

In response to the limitations of Lewis's two analyses, Gregory Currie has stressed the need for an alternative. Currie's basic move is to suggest that truth in fiction should be analyzed along the lines of a person's system of beliefs as opposed to truth in a set of possible worlds. One advantage of this suggestion, Currie usefully notes, is that belief sets are not closed under deduction, can be globally inconsistent, and are "negation incomplete." What is true in a fiction, then, is what the teller of the story believes. Currie calls this teller the fictional author, defining this entity as "that fictional character constructed within our make believe whom we take to be telling us the story as known fact."[20]

Currie's proposal, however, does not really solve the problem. He suggests that in order to find out which beliefs are pertinent in determining fictional truth, we should refer to the beliefs of a construct known as the fictional author. But how do we know what beliefs to attribute to the fictional author? Using the text as a guide, we are supposed to build a model of the particular belief system of the fictional author. We must assume that this fictional author believes as fact what is true in the fiction. Yet saying how people figure out what is true in the fiction was our problem to begin with. As far as the reader's methods are concerned, Currie tells us that the way to find out what the fictional author's beliefs are is to start with what was mutually believed in the real author's community and only deviate from these beliefs when something explicit in the text contradicts them. Currie himself goes on to call this a "simple strategy" and admits that it is inadequate because writers can and have created fictional authors whose beliefs are only implicitly at variance with those of the real author's community. Yet Currie admits that he has no rules to substitute for the simple strategy, and simply adds that there will be "considerable agreement in practice about how such inferences as this ought to proceed." [21] But the goal of the analysis was to develop a principled account of such agreement.

Where else, then, may we turn in search of principles that effectively guide readers in judging what happens in a story? The reader's ideas about the *genre* to which a narrative belongs is one place to look, and many students of literature are quick to embrace this option. The idea is that once we are convinced that the work we are reading is, for example, a gothic novel, we recognize that we should set aside aspects of our actual worldview and work with the kinds of ideas, such as supernatural notions of causality, that we associate with this type of fiction. I do not doubt that the ability to make apt generic decisions is an important part of our literary and cinematic expertise. But we have to say how a reader makes such decisions, and it is dubious to assume that the text's intrinsic features suffice. The viewer's or reader's decision about a work's genre often depends on notions about the author's intentions, just as in everyday communication decisions about irony, joking, and the like require reference to the speaker's likely aims and intentions. And surely story content plays a role in generic decisions, which means we cannot provide a noncircular analysis of the former in terms of the latter. What is more, generic concepts cannot explain the reader's ability to make judgments about what is happening in nonstandard and hybrid narratives. We would also need to know how generic expectations and norms get established in the first place. So I think the recourse to generic concepts fails as a fundamental analysis, while being in a sense partly compatible with an intentionalist approach.

A more promising alternative is the idea that the appropriate choice of background beliefs is underwritten by a complex intentionalist principle. Competent readers and spectators do not make inferences about the implicit truths in a story by obeying the Reality Principle or by activating entire belief systems of bygone or alien communities. Instead, they do so by paying attention to the text's features and by reasoning about the aims and attitudes of the actual storyteller. Yet this intentionalist principle must be one that does not succumb to various familiar objections against intentionalism.

The intentionalist principle I want to propose does not rest on the mistaken idea that fictional truths are necessarily determined by the author's beliefs about reality. Storytelling is not always a matter of the storyteller sincerely expressing his or her convictions, so many of an author's beliefs, including beliefs about literature or cinema, do not determine story content and thus are not appropriate premises for inferences about fictional truth. Even so, in writing a story or making a film, an author has attitudes about the story he or she aims to tell, as well as attitudes concerning how readers or viewers should make sense of the text. An author may be fairly open-minded or even confused about what happens in the story, but to invent and tell a story at all one must make some hard and fast decisions about what is and is not the case in the story. So what we are after is not the belief set of a fictional author who tells a story as known fact; rather, we are interested in what the actual author decided was to be the case in the story he or she was inventing and trying to communicate. At least some of these authorial decisions about story truths inform the author's intentional activity in conceiving and making a text. We can call those intentions that actually initiate and guide the author's fiction-making activities the author's effective intentions. Effective, proximal intentions may be contrasted to future-directed intentions that may later be reconsidered and retained, revised, or abandoned; although I am convinced that the latter are an important part of the overall creative process, I think we should set them aside when we reason about a work's fictional truths.[22] I also think it important to identify a category of suitable *communicative* intentions involved in storytelling, and will rely on such a notion below.

Note, before we go on, that an author's effective intention to endow his or her text with some property, p, does not necessarily mean that the resulting text actually has that property, for the simple reason that even effective intentions, that is, the ones we act on, can misfire. For example, while directing a star's performance, a filmmaker may want her gestures to express a certain complex emotional attitude, but the intended effect may not in fact be realized in the final footage. Nor does the fact that a stretch of film depicts a character as having some property entail that the director intended to realize such a state of affairs. For example, a filmmaker who effectively works with the intention of keeping the cinematic apparatus from appearing in the frame can inadvertently produce and use a shot in which a microphone protrudes down into the scene from the top of the frame. Seeing that the microphone is actually depicted in the shot, we cannot infer that the author intended to have the character be shown standing under a microphone.

These points are overlooked in those versions of intentionalism in which textual meaning and the author's intended meanings are held to be logically equivalent.[23] The latter assumption leads to a well-known objection taking the form of a dilemma: textual meaning cannot be logically equivalent to intended meaning because appeals to intentions in interpreting a text are either unnecessary or insufficient. If the artist successfully realized her intentions, then the ensuing text will mean what the artist meant it to mean, in which case claims about intentions are unnecessary. But if the artist did not successfully realize her intention, then evidence about the latter can hardly tell us what the text really means, so claims about intentions are insufficient.

The type of intentionalism I want to defend does not include the contested thesis concerning the logical equivalence of textual and intended meaning. I agree that evidence about an author's unrealized plans and unsuccessful intendings can be irrelevant to some interpretive claims about a work's meanings. Intentions alone, then, are not sufficient. I do want to argue that they are in a sense necessary, however, so I attack the other horn of the dilemma. To do so, I contend that successful artistic intentions need not result in the *explicit* presentation of fictional truths in a text in order for these intentions to be crucial to some, but not all, interpretive decisions about story content. Part of a story's content is implicit as far as textual evidence is concerned, so the latter is insufficient to determine the story's content, which means it is possible that authorial decisions and intentions are necessary to some successful interpretive decisions taking story content as their focus. I do *not* claim, however, that reference to intentions is necessary to all valuable or acceptable interpretive claims.

The intentionalist principle I want to defend specifies that truth in the story is jointly determined by the relevant authorial attitudes and the text's features. We ought to think of story content as being partly constituted by authorial choices and by the communicative, storytelling intentions that effectively motivate the making of a text. With regard to the issue of which premises are to be used in making inferences about *implicit* story content, the intentionalist principle specifies that readers and viewers should adopt those premises the author has reasonably decided upon in conceiving and communicating the story. Some of these intended premises are directly manifested in what is explicitly depicted in the text, but others are not. If an author's decision about the story's implicit content is incompatible with the resulting text's actual features, it is the latter, not the former, that the interpreter should normally accept. If, in the case of the accidentally intruding microphone evoked above, viewers are right in deciding that it is not fictionally true that there is a microphone hovering above the *character's* head, such a decision is not justified by an intentionalist principle alone, but also because viewers correct the mistake in light of its incompatibility with other, explicit textual evidence (more on this below).

Very generally, then, I propose the following breakdown with regard to story content or fictional truth. Some fictional truths are explicitly depicted in the text (provided that the text's features are perceived and interpreted standardly). Complex inferential work is required with regard to such truths, for viewers must be able to decide that some explicitly depicted states of affairs are not indicative of fictional truths (for example, the microphone that accidentally intrudes above the performer's, but not the character's, head). Amongst the explicitly depicted states of affairs that *are* indicative of fictional truths, some are intended by the author(s), others not. A director who films a character standing out of doors may not have intended to have a fly buzz past the character's head during the shot, but unless there is good reason to deem this detail to be incompatible with the rest of the story, we may count it as fictionally true that a fly buzzed past the character's head. As I have argued above, other fictional truths are not explicitly depicted in the text. Some of these are entailed by propositions warranted by explicit depictions. Others are based on the author's effective, communicative storytelling intentions.

As a first objection to this proposal, one may well ask whether authors have any attitudes with regard to premises that they are not going to depict or state explicitly in the text. I think authors do, in fact, settle on such premises and that such choices can make a difference to the story. Here's why. Having decided on some of the story's fictional truths, an author tries to produce a text that will enable members of some target audience to make believe at least some of those fictional truths. These fictional truths include a subset comprised of those truths that are meant to be implicit—implicit, that is, with regard to the text's features. With the goal of actually provoking the desired response in some target audience, authors may settle on general principles or beliefs that the members of the target audience should employ as they figure out what happens in the story. Settling on such background principles is no idle matter, for thinking about implicit content accompanies and informs various other decisions and intentions involved in producing the text. Authorial decisions about background premises, then, are linked to preferences concerning ways in which the target audience should make sense of the text; these decisions and preferences in turn motivate and inform an author's effective intentions in producing the text. An author can intend to make a text that is logically compatible with more than one story premise, while simultaneously having a decisive attitude concerning which premises determine the story's content and should be communicated to, and adopted by the audience. More generally, the point to be grasped here is that authors cannot make everything explicit and sometimes have good reasons for wanting to proceed by means of insinuations and hints, leaving crucial inferential work to the spectator.

Let's apply the intentionalist principle to the simple example of the film in which a shot of a dog's eyes is followed by a shot of a man falling from a balcony. At least four interpretive options are relevant here, for the viewer can decide that (1) in the story it is true that the dog's evil eye killed the man; (2) in the story the man's fall was accidental; (3) the story is ambiguous on this point, which can be taken to mean that the storyteller did not intend to make a work with regard to which a principled choice between interpretations would be possible, even though it is supposed to be true in the story that there is a fact of the matter in this regard; and (4) the story is indeterminate on this point, that is, there is not supposed to be a fact of the matter, not even an unrevealed fact, in this regard. Let's assume as well that none of these interpretations is directly contradicted by anything else explicitly presented in the audiovisual text, or by any of the inferences based on explicit textual evidence. This could mean, for example, that the viewer is not provided with overwhelming evidence of the dog's supernatural powers later on in the film, just as there is no conclusive discovery to the effect that supernaturalism is just a matter of false belief.

The intentionalist principle implies that knowledge of authorial intentions with regard to a story can warrant a decision between our interpretive alternatives. Suppose, for example, that we have conclusive external evidence that the filmmaker effectively intended to produce a work in which supernatural processes are part of the story. Interviews, letters, and the filmmaker's previous work and personality all support this idea. We know, for example, that in preparation for the making of the film, the filmmaker read a number of anthropological studies of evil eye beliefs; he also read, and was influenced by Théophile Gautier's nineteenth-century fantastic tale, "Jettatura."[24] The author has expressed admiration for the fantastic genre as well as a desire to make a new film in this vein. At some point, then, the author decides that it will be true in the story that a dog stares at a man on a balcony, so he forms and successfully acts on the intention to make shots that explicitly depict the dog and the man; the filmmaker goes on to include these shots in the film. The author also determines that a supernatural premise should govern our reasoning about the connection between these explicitly depicted events. The intentionalist principle tells us that these authorial attitudes are indeed decisive with regard to the story. Applied to the shots of the dog and the man's fall, the basic evil eye belief to the effect that looks can have direct causal influences on physical objects yields the conclusion that the dog's gaze made the man fall. Note that this inference can and should go through even though (a) the evil eye belief is false; (b) the spectator knows that it is false; (c) the filmmaker does not actually believe in the evil eye; and (d) evil eye causation is not a part of the author's community's web of mutual beliefs.

Consider now a case where all of the evidence reliably points to the conclusion that the author was settled on a highly idiosyncratic story truth that is logically compatible with the textual evidence but somehow irrelevant or inappropriate. For example, the author genuinely decided that the dog in his story was a Martian in disguise whose every behavior and appearance would be that of a demonic, supernatural creature. The author, then, fully intended this to be an implicit story truth. This case seems to challenge our intentionalist analysis because we do not want our knowledge of the author's bizarre intention to warrant the absurd conclusion that it is fictionally true that the dog is a Martian. To make the challenge even stronger, we may add that none of the propositions entailed by the text's features and/or by other authorial intentions directly contradicts the Martian hypothesis. How, then, can we rule the latter out?

The answer resides, I think, in a needed constraint on those authorial intentions that readers should rely upon in interpreting fictional truth. The problem with the Martian case is that the viewer could only hit upon the target hypothesis by the wildest stroke of luck, for the author has done nothing to make this hypothesis the least bit accessible to the text's viewers. It is compatible with, but totally unsupported by, the textual and other evidence. Imagining a story is one thing, but engaging in a reasonable attempt to tell or convey it is another. Our analysis of story content is meant to focus on the communicative variety of fiction-making, as opposed to private fantasy or solitary make-believe. In other words, the intentions we want viewers to rely upon when they think about story content are the authors' effective, *communicative* intentions, not idle musings or solitary imaginings. The communicative intentions an author actually acts on are not just a matter of intending that something be fictionally true in the story, for they also involve the author actually trying to convey this fictional truth to some audience in some appropriate manner, such as publically screening an audiovisual text, which, in the context, has some chance of being interpreted in the intended manner. As a minimal constraint on decisions about which of the storyteller's intentions are relevant to story content, then, we may specify that the author's effective intention must be a suitable sort of communicative intention. We require the author to have good and sufficient reason to believe that the intended story propositions he has settled on actually have some chance of being grasped, on the basis of available evidence, by some target audience. This clause is not meant to impose a strong belief constraint on all possible authorial intendings, but only on those worthy of being relied upon in determining fictional truth. Competent spectators are ideally attuned to authorial intentions satisfying this constraint, and are not led astray by those that do not.

What about contradictory fictional truths? Authors can successfully communicate a story in which some proposition and its negation are both true. Authors also inadvertently tell stories in which there are inconsistencies. Although we speak of an incoherent story with regard to the latter cases, we tend to think of them as mistakes in the work and we strive to eliminate the story's inconsistencies. It is not true, we think, that in the fiction the microphone was and was not present in the room, or that the purse was and was not on the table, and so on. But intentional inconsistencies have a different status. In such cases, we have to acknowledge that the storyteller wants the story to contain an inconsistency. It does not follow that the author intends for every other arbitrarily chosen proposition to follow from an intended inconsistency, so viewers should not hold all such consequences to be fictionally true.[25]

Here, then, is a sketch of an analysis of fictional truth according to the form of intentionalism I have been defending:

A proposition is fictionally true in a work's story just in case it satisfies either one of the following conditions (1) or (2), while also satisfying (3):

(1) the proposition is directly warranted by something the text depicts or is entailed by other propositions so warranted;

(2) the proposition is consistent with all propositions satisfying condition (1), and either the work's author had a reasonable and effective communicative intention that the proposition be imagined by members of the work's audience (that is, the author has good and sufficient reason to believe that the proposition can be imagined, on the basis of available evidence, by members of the target audience); or the proposition is entailed by other propositions so intended.

(3) Unintended contradictions are not fictionally true in the work's story, and intended ones are only true if they also satisfy condition (1). Warranted contradictions do not entail all other propositions.

In the pages that remain, I shall briefly respond to some additional objections that have been raised against intentionalist approaches.

Some Unsuccessful Refutations of Intentionalism

Epistemological objections are widespread. The wild things of current literary theory often object to intentionalist principles on the grounds that we can never know for sure what an author actually believed or intended. I am happy to concede this point, as long as "knowing for sure" is understood in some suitably severe sense. I respond to this objection by asking whether the doubts being marshalled are in any way specific to the case of authorial attitudes. Are the anti-intentionalists equally skeptical about psychological knowledge in general? Are they just as skeptical about the possibility of knowing readers' attitudes? Foucault, for example, lays it down in "What Is an Author?" that it is impossible to know an author's mind, but he then makes any number of sweeping assertions about what goes on in other readers' minds when they interpret texts, and no justification of this asymmetry is provided.[26] If it is possible to know something about other readers' constructive operations, why would authors' storytelling aims constitute a special and insurmountable problem?

Obviously we cannot always know everything we want to know about authors' states of mind.[27] Sometimes the documents simply are not available, and other times we encounter intractable interpretive problems in reading those documents that are available. These difficulties are not, however, good grounds for abandoning the intentionalist principle. In many cases readers and viewers do in fact have fairly reliable and specific information about an author's attitudes. On other occasions, readers work with a highly schematic conception of an unknown author's likely aims and interests. Readers then can tentatively fill in or project the author's intentions by supplying what they take to be a historical and context-relevant variety of background belief. Often the reader simply works with those beliefs any author can be expected to deem relevant to the comprehension of a story. In short, our conjectures about authorial attitudes are fallible and contingent, but nonetheless important. Anti-intentionalists who want an infallible discovery procedure, or absolute certainty about authorial intent, are, I think, simply asking for the wrong things.

Another common objection has it that cases of multiple authorship and collectively produced works (which are, after all, highly prevalent in the cinema) cannot be accommodated by intentionalist principles.[28] It is a mistake, however, to claim that groups of people can never engage in collective actions guided by shared intentions.[29] What is more, the fact that (some of) a work's features may have been shaped by the intentional activities of more than one agent, or may even have been intended by no one, does not entail that references to these activities (and to the attitudes that informed them) are always irrelevant to interpretive claims. Another mistake is to assume that accepting moderate intentionalist principles entails adherence to a great man theory of history and/or an aesthetics of solitary genius. Embracing a sweeping form of anti-intentionalism is not a good way to take one's distance from such bad ideas about history and art.

I turn now to a different kind of objection to an intentionalist account of story content. I have in mind some passages in *Mimesis as Make-Believe* where Walton appears to argue that moral truths in fiction constitute a special category with regard to which the Mutual Belief Principle, as well as even the most attenuated form of intentionalism, must be overridden. Here is how Walton puts it:

> If, in a story from a fascist society in which it is firmly and mutually believed that mixing of the races is evil and its repression a moral necessity, it is fictional that people of different races strike up a friendship and are punished by the authorities for doing so, must we set aside our own contrary moral convictions even for the limited purposes of understanding and appreciating the story? Must we allow the story to imply that fictionally the friendship is immoral and its oppression justified?[30]

Walton's response is negative. Instead, when we read such a story we should shift to the Reality Principle and decide that it is false in the story that the friendship is immoral and its oppression justified. Now, I think this is simply wrong as an account of principles underlying readers' and viewers' competence in understanding stories. Walton's principle, we should note, makes it effectively impossible for anyone to tell a story that readers deem immoral, for his principle states that the only moral truths in fiction are those fully embraced by the reader. This is highly counterintuitive. Fascists in fact made films in which fascist values inform what happens in the story, an important example being Harlan's *Jud Süss,* a historical fiction in which the Germans of eighteenth-century Stuttgart are rescued from chaos when they finally rise up and put a supernaturally evil Jew to death. Georges Sadoul, for example, characterizes this film as "criminal."[31] To be in a position to articulate a moral condemnation of filmmaking of this sort, we must first be able to recognize the offensive attitudes that were meant to be implicitly true in the fiction. An intentionalist account of truth in fiction makes this possible, for it stipulates that readers should try to recognize what moral, and more generally, evaluative truths storytellers effectively wanted the target audience to work with. Recognizing these values does not entail condoning them, which is why spectators are sometimes outraged and offended by what they think is implicitly going on in fictional stories. Walton, on the other hand, seems to think that in order to make believe that some proposition is the case in some fiction, a reader or viewer must experience a complete emotional and imaginative acceptance of that belief. Not only is this dubious, but one wonders why moral or evaluative truths would constitute a special case. Why wouldn't some non-evaluative fictional truths be too hard to swallow? The key problem with Walton's argument, finally, is his linking of the viewer's emotional acceptance and appreciation with the *recognition* of a story proposition or assumption. Understanding story meaning, I think, is just one part of the interpretive process, and although it certainly has implications for other interpretive issues, it rarely settles them.

Conclusion

The intentionalist definition of characterization presented in the first section of this paper has the advantage of meshing nicely with our intentionalist proposal regarding the more general issue of story content. Our grasp of characters' actions, traits, and relations—which are, after all, the nuts and bolts of stories—depends in part on our fallible comprehension of the actions and attitudes of the storytellers. In other words, our understanding of actual agency is crucial to our understanding of fictional agency.

In conclusion, I should like to underscore the fact that competence at inferring story content, or fictional truth, is only one part of critical expertise, even with regard to characterization, which is again only part of the picture. So even if the intentionalist principle does help to account for the determination of story content, it still does not provide an adequate overall theory of critical appreciation and insight. The moral of my story, then, is that we are still a long way from having built a comprehensive model of the reader's or viewer's competence.

NOTES

My thanks to Greg Currie, Andrew Burday, and David Davies for helpful discussions of these issues. Al Mele, Noël Carroll, and David Bordwell made useful comments on a draft of this paper. My research was funded by the Social Science and Humanities Research Council of Canada.

1. For criticisms of the trend in question, see David Bordwell, *Making Meaning: Inference and Rhetoric in the Interpretation of Cinema* (Cambridge: Harvard University Press, 1989), Noël Carroll, *Mystifying Movies: Fads and Fallacies in Contemporary Film Theory* (New York: Columbia University Press, 1988), and "The Image of Women in Film: In Defense of a Paradigm," *Journal of Aesthetics and Art Criticism* 48, 4 (1990): 349–60; Gregory Currie, "The Long Goodbye: The Imaginary Language of Film," *British Journal of Aesthetics* 33 (1993): 207–19; and my "Film and the New Psychology," *Poetics* 21 (1992): 93–116.

2. My understanding of literary characterization has been greatly enhanced by discussions with Uri Margolin (who may disagree with many of my claims). Margolin's important essays on the topic include "Characterization in Narrative: Some Theoretical Prolegomena," *Neophilologus* 67 (1983): 1–14, "The Doer and the Deed: Action as a Basis for Characterization in Narrative," *Poetics Today* 7 (1986): 205–25, "Introducing and Sustaining Characters in Literary Narrative: A Set of Conditions," *Style* 21 (1987): 107–24, "Structuralist Approaches to Character in Narrative: The State of the Art," *Semiotica* 75 (1989): 1–24, and "The What, the When, and the How of Being a Character in Literary Narrative," *Style* 24 (1990): 453–68. Other valuable studies are Baruch Hochman, *Character in Literature* (Ithaca, N.Y.: Cornell University Press, 1985), and James Phelan, *Reading People, Reading Plots: Character, Progression, and the Interpretation of Narrative* (Chicago: University of Chicago Press, 1989). For an alternative, and in my view, hopelessly muddled approach, see Hélène Cixous, "The Character of 'Character,'" *New Literary History* 5 (1975): 383–402.

3. For background, see Alfred R. Mele, *Irrationality: An Essay on Akrasia, Self-Deception, and Self-Control* (New York: Oxford University Press, 1987), *Springs of Action: Understanding Intentional Behavior* (New York: Oxford University Press, 1992), and *Autonomous Agents* (New York: Oxford University Press, 1995). I survey some literatures and topics related to agency and rationality in the first two chapters of *Literature and Rationality: Ideas of Agency in Theory and Fiction* (Cambridge: Cambridge University Press, 1991).

4. For background, see Adrian Furnham, "Commonsense Theories of Personality," in *Everyday Understanding: Social and Scientific Implications*, ed. Gün R. Semin and Kenneth J. Gergen (London: Sage, 1990), pp. 176–203; Richard J. Gerrig and David W. Allbritton, "The Construction of Literary Character: A View from Cognitive Psychology," *Style* 24 (1990): 380–91; and Daniel T. Gilbert, "Thinking Lightly about Others: Automatic Components of the Social Inference Process," in *Unintended Thought*, ed. James S. Uleman and John A. Bargh (New York: Guilford, 1989), pp. 189–211.

5. Lord Byron, *The Complete Poetical Works*, ed. Jerome McGann (Oxford: Oxford University Press, 1980), 2:105.

6. For background on aesthetic properties, see Göran Hermerén, *The Nature of Aesthetic Qualities* (Lund, Sweden: Lund University Press, 1988), and Francis Sparshott, *The Theory of the Arts* (Princeton: Princeton University Press, 1982).

7. Felicia Ackerman, "Imaginary Gardens and Real Toads: On the Ethics of Basing Fiction on Actual People," in *Philosophy and the Arts: Midwest Studies in Philosophy*, ed. Peter A. French, Theodore E. Uehling, Jr., and Howard K. Wettstein (Notre Dame, Ind.: Notre Dame University Press, 1991), pp. 142–51.

8. "Imaginary Gardens and Real Toads," p. 149.

9. Gregory Currie, *The Nature of Fiction* (Cambridge: Cambridge University Press, 1990); Kendall L. Walton, *Mimesis as Make-Believe: On the Foundations of the Representational Arts* (Cambridge: Harvard University Press, 1990). These authors do not agree on various points and may have revised some of their views, but I cannot deal with such matters here.

10. Theodor W. Adorno, "Filmtransparente," in *Ohne Leitbild* (Frankfurt: Suhrkamp, 1967), p. 80.

11. Maurice Merleau-Ponty, "Le cinéma et la nouvelle psychologie," in *Sens et non-sens* (Paris: Nagel, 1966), p. 104.

12. Stanley Cavell, *The World Viewed: Reflections on the Ontology of Film* (Cambridge: Harvard University Press, 1971), pp. 26–27.

13. Marcel Proust, *A la recherche du temps perdu* (Paris: Gallimard, 1954), 2:690.

14. Christopher Peacocke, "Depiction," *Philosophical Review* 96 (1987): 383–410. For useful corrections involving photographic depictions and some puzzles, see G. N. Kemp, "Pictures and Depictions: A Consideration of Peacocke's Views," *British Journal of Aesthetics* 30 (1990): 332–41. For background, see also Gary Malinas, "A Semantics for Pictures," *Canadian Journal of Philosophy* 21 (1991): 275–98, and Noël Carroll, "The Power of Movies," *Daedalus* 114, 4 (1985): 79–104.

15. George M. Wilson, *Narration in Light: Studies in Cinematic Point of View* (Baltimore: Johns Hopkins University Press, 1986), p. 139.

16. Ibid., p. 140.

17. Kristin Thompson points out that even when the performers do look like they are representing different stages of some one person's life, the spectator typically notes this unusual fact, perhaps because so many filmmakers rely upon (and in fact strain) the viewer's tolerance of physical differences. An exceptional twist worth mentioning is provided by Daniel Vigne's *Le Retour de Martin Guerre* (*The Return of Martin Guerre*, 1982), where the real Martin Guerre, young and old, is portrayed by two actors having rather different looks. The fact that Gerard Depardieu bears no physical resemblance to the performer who portrays the young Martin Guerre could alert some viewers to the fact that the former is an imposter, which would in turn spoil the desired uncertainty and suspense. Yet the habit of tolerance about a lack of physical resemblance may lead some viewers to fail to draw the inference that the Depardieu figure is not in fact Martin Guerre since he bears no resemblance to the person who initially bears that name in the film. After all, the same spectator has seen countless films in which extraordinary metamorphoses of maturation are meant to go unnoticed.

18. See, for example, Wilson's trenchant critique of Walton's proposals in "Comments on Mimesis as Make-Believe," *Philosophy and Phenomenological Research* 51 (1991): 395–400. More recently, Wilson criticizes Edward Said's failure to provide principled constraints on acceptable interpretations in "Edward Said on Contrapuntal Reading," *Philosophy and Literature* 18 (1994): 265–73.

19. David Lewis, "Truth in Fiction," in *Philosophical Papers* (Oxford: Oxford University Press, 1983), 1:261–80.

20. *Nature of Fiction*, p. 76.

21. Ibid., p. 80.

22. For background on intentions and intentionalism in aesthetics, see Paisley Livingston and Alfred R. Mele, "Intention and Literature," *Stanford French Review* 16 (1992): 173–96; and Alfred R. Mele and Paisley Livingston, "Intentions and Interpretations," *MLN* 107 (1992): 931–49. A valuable recent discussion of the topic is Noël Carroll, "Art, Intention, and Conversation," in *Intention and Interpretation,* ed. Gary Iseminger (Philadelphia: Temple University Press, 1992), pp. 97–131.

23. See, for example, Peter D. Juhl, *Interpretation: An Essay in the Philosophy of Literary Criticism* (Princeton: Princeton University Press, 1980).

24. Théophile Gautier, "Jettatura," in *Romans et contes* (Paris, 1863). For background and an insightful reading of the story, see Tobin Siebers, *The Mirror of Medusa* (Berkeley: University of California Press, 1983).

25. For more on inconsistency in fictions, see Currie's useful remarks in *Nature of Fiction*, pp. 68–70, 87–89.

26. Foucault writes, for example, that an author's subjective attributes are only "the projection, in more or less psychological terms, of the operations that we force texts to undergo, the connections that we make, the traits that we establish as pertinent, the continuities that we recognize, or the exclusions that we practice" ("What is an Au-

thor?" in *Textual Strategies: Perspectives in Post-Structuralist Criticism,* ed. Josué V. Harari [Ithaca, N.Y.: Cornell University Press, 1979], p. 150). Valuable criticisms of Foucault's historical theses in this highly overrated essay are presented by Roger Chartier, *L'ordre des livres* (Aix-en-Provence: Alinea, 1992).

27. I refer throughout to real, not implied, postulated, or fictional authors. Although I cannot rehearse the arguments here, I assume that there are no good grounds for abandoning the former notion in favor of any of the latter. See Gérard Genette, *Narrative Discourse Revisited* (Ithaca, N.Y.: Cornell University Press, 1988), and Robert Stecker, "Apparent, Implied, and Postulated Authors," *Philosophy and Literature* 11 (1987): 258–71, and "Hypothetical Intentions and Implied Authors" (forthcoming). An intentionalist account of fictional truth based on idealized authors and readers is presented by Alex Byrne in his "Truth in Fiction: The Story Continued," *Australasian Journal of Philosophy* 71 (1993): 24–35. Byrne's version of the story is contested by David Davies in "Inviting Authors and Declining Readers: A Response to Byrne" (forthcoming).

28. Some interesting examples of multiple authorship are presented by Jack Stillinger, *Multiple Authorship and the Myth of Solitary Genius* (New York: Oxford University Press, 1991).

29. On shared intention, see Michael Bratman, "Shared Intention," *Ethics* 104 (1993): 97–113. Bratman's analysis is a promising alternative to various proposals made by John Searle, Margaret Gilbert, and Raimo Tuomela. See Searle's "Collective Intentions and Actions," in *Intentions in Communication,* ed. Philip Cohen, Jerry Morgan, and Martha Pollack (Cambridge: MIT Press, 1990), pp. 401–18; Tuomela's "We Will Do It: An Analysis of Group-Intentions," *Philosophy and Phenomenological Research* 51 (1991): 249–77, and "What Are Goals and Joint Goals?" *Theory and Decision* 28 (1990): 1–20; and Gilbert's *On Social Facts* (New York: Routledge, 1988), especially chapter 7.

30. *Mimesis as Make-Believe,* p. 155.

31. Georges Sadoul, "Le Cinéma," in *Histoire des spectacles,* ed. Guy Dumur (Paris: Gallimard, 1965), 1694.

8

Empathy and (Film) Fiction

Alex Neill

I

Ancient questions as to how and why it is that we can respond emotionally to characters and events which we know to be fictional, and whether it is rational to do so, have in recent years resurfaced and been at the heart of a debate as lively as any in contemporary aesthetics, a debate which continues to fill the pages of philosophical journals but which has so far resulted in little agreement even about the nature of the problems involved, let alone their solutions.[1] Part of the reason for this lack of resolution, I believe, is that our emotional responses to what we know to be fictional have typically been treated as monolithic; for example, since the very beginnings of the debate, the pity and the fear that works of fiction may evoke from us have been lumped together. But our emotional responses—whether to fictional or to actual persons and events—are not all of a kind. For example, we can distinguish (at least roughly) between emotional responses in which the focus of concern is *oneself* (as, for example, in fear for oneself), and those in which the focus of concern is *another*. And among "other-focused" emotional responses, we may distinguish between *sympathetic* responses (such as those in which I fear *for* you), and *empathetic* responses (for I may also feel fear *with* you). By looking closely at the variety of our emotional responses, and at the variety of the emotional responses that fiction can evoke in us, I suggest, we stand a better chance of understanding those responses, the roles they play in our understanding and valuing of fiction, and their significance with respect to broader concerns in the philosophy of emotion and mind, than we do by treating them as if they constituted a homogeneous class.

With this broad strategy in mind, I wish to focus on empathy, with particular reference to the possibility of empathetic responses to fiction films. One (oversimple) way of getting at the difference between sympathetic and empathetic responses is as follows: with sympathetic response, in feeling *for* another, one's response need not reflect what the other is feeling, nor indeed does it depend on whether the other is feeling anything at all. Your happiness may make me happy for you, but it may also irritate me; and I may feel pity or fear for you irrespective of what *you* happen to be feeling. In contrast, in responding empathetically to another I come to *share* his feelings, to feel *with* him; if he is in an emotional state, to empathize with him is to experience the emotion(s) that he experiences.

It is interesting that empathy and empathetic responses have received short shrift in the contemporary debate on the nature and rationality of our emotional responses to fiction. In part, this is doubtless due to the tendency noted above to treat our emotional responses to fiction as homogeneous. But it has also been suggested that empathetic response simply does not play a significant role in our emotional engagement with fictional works in various genres. Richard Wollheim, for example, suggests that "the empathic audience does not provide the model for the understanding of the drama, and . . . any theory of the drama that puts him in the forefront is to that degree wrong." [2] Dolf Zillman notes that "It is a widely held belief that those exposed to drama featuring sympathetic, liked protagonists tend to 'identify' with those protagonists and to '*vicariously experience*' whatever those protagonists experience. In fact, this view is commonly treated as a secure and unquestionable key element of our understanding of the enlightenment that drama provides." [3] However, Zillman argues, this view—the view that empathetic responses are central to our experience of fiction—is far from "secure" and "unquestionable." He invites us to consider the responses to suspense films of children, who "tend to talk to their heroes, shouting out warnings of the dangers their heroes face (dangers about which the heroes, because of the very nature of suspense, are ignorant)" (142). If the child's response were empathetic, surely it should reflect or "be controlled by the hero's expression of calmness and self-confidence." But in fact the response is far from expressive of calm or confidence. Zillman argues that the hypothesis that our responses to suspense fictions are empathetic responses "thus not only fails to explain distress in response to most scenes of entrapment and peril" (where the hero/ine is calm and self-possessed), but also falsely predicts "an absence of distress unless (or until) the hero is seen in fear and agony" (142). At least with regard to suspense fictions, he concludes, our responses are better understood in terms of "feeling for" (in my terms, sympathy) than they are in terms of "feeling with" (in my terms, empathy). [4]

A similar point has been made by Noël Carroll, in the course of his argument to the effect that the notion of "character-identification" is unhelpful in attempting to understand our emotional engagement with the protagonists of fiction. [5] As we shall see, Carroll does leave room for an account of the place of empathy in our engagement with fiction. Indeed, he argues that in horror fictions the responses of the characters to monsters serve as "cues" for the responses of the audience, and that "our emotional responses as audience members are supposed to parallel those of characters in important respects" (18). However, Carroll's argument against "character-identification" is based in large part on his claim that "in a great many cases, the emotional state of the audience does not replicate the state of the characters": for example,

"When the heroine is splashing about with abandon as, unbeknownst to her, a killer shark is zooming in for the kill, we feel concern for her. But that is not what she is feeling. She's feeling delighted" (90). Again, "if we feel pity at Oedipus' recognition that he has killed his father and bedded his mother, that is not what Oedipus is feeling. He is feeling guilt, remorse, and self-recrimination. And, needless to say, we are feeling none of these" (91). If empathy is construed as "feeling with," as the mirroring of a protagonist's emotional state by the audience, as I have construed it above, then Carroll's remarks suggest that empathetic responses do not play a large part in our emotional engagement with fiction.

2

Nonetheless, there are a number of factors which suggest that the possibility that empathetic response plays an important part in our engagement with works of fiction may merit further consideration. First, the idea that our emotional engagement with fiction, and in particular film fiction, is somehow rooted in something like "identification" with and empathetic response to the characters of fiction is, as Zillman notes, very widely held. For what it is worth, my own experience is that practically *all* those not "professionally" concerned with these issues with whom I have discussed them have made some sort of appeal to identification and empathy in explaining our emotional engagement with movies. Carroll is surely right to note that it is often unclear just what is meant by "identification" in discussion of our engagement with fiction, and that some of the meanings that are commonly attached to the notion render it at best of little explanatory value, at worst incoherent. However, the commonness of the claim that our affective responses to a work of fiction are somehow the result of identifying with its characters, and the equally common linking of "identification" with empathetic response, suggests that we should be very cautious before giving up the idea that empathetic responses may play an important role in our emotional engagement with fiction. In brief, a good many people claim that at the heart of their affective engagement with fiction is empathetic engagement. Such people may of course simply be confused about the meaning of "identification," or of "empathy," or indeed about the nature of their own responses. However, before drawing any conclusion of the latter sort, we ought to look closely at just what might be involved in responding empathetically to fiction.

The common tendency to talk of empathetic response and identification in the same breath suggests a further and related reason that such an investigation may be valuable. For the notion of identification has also attracted a good deal of attention from professional film theorists. In film theory, not surprisingly, reflection on identification has typically involved appeal to psychoanalysis. Anne Friedberg, for example, writes of identification as "that which conceals and defers the recognition of dissimilitude. *If fetishism is a relation incurred by the anxiety of sexual difference, identification is a relation incurred by the anxiety of pure difference.* . . . The process of identification is one of denying the difference between self and other. It is a drive that engages the pleasures of sameness. If the subject is constituted in a series of identifications which force similarity, identification is one long structural repetition of this denial of difference, a construction of identity based on sameness."[6] On this sort of analysis, identification is a pathological process, a process of "denial" incurred by "anxiety." And to the extent that empathetic responses depend on or involve identification, this sort of analysis suggests that our empathetic responses to others, be they fictional characters or actual persons, are at heart pathological responses, symptomatic of self-deception. Is this in fact the case? If so, and if the claims made by many people about the centrality of identification and empathy to our engagement with fiction are accurate, then we should be faced with a new version of one of the most ancient criticisms of storytelling: Plato's charge that poetry "waters the passions," to the detriment of reason. That possibility surely gives us good cause to take another look at the nature of empathetic engagement with fiction.

And this is not the only motivation that we have for doing so. The notion that empathetic engagement with others plays a central role in understanding and explanation has had and is gaining increasing support in contexts beyond that of discussion of our engagement with fiction. The idea that historical and social scientific explanation involves *verstehen,* that it depends on "seeing things from another's point of view," which I shall argue later is central to empathetic response, has a distinguished and influential history.[7] In moral philosophy and psychology, from the "moral sentiment" theories of Adam Smith and David Hume to recent and broadly speaking feminist work on "the ethics of care," our capacity for empathetic response has often been mooted as the source of morality.[8] And more recently, a growing number of philosophers and psychologists have been arguing that empathy is crucial to our "everyday" ability to understand, explain and predict the behavior of those around us: that our "folk psychological" attribution of mental states to others depends on empathetic understanding.[9] In short, there is an increasing acceptance, in a number of theoretical circles, of the importance of empathy in understanding and explanation. Of course, this does not in itself mean that empathy plays a large role in our engagement with and understanding of *fiction.* However, if empathy does play a crucial role in our understanding of history, of society, and of others, wouldn't it be at least somewhat *odd* to find that it is marginal or of little importance in our understanding of fiction? In sum, then, given the historical and growing emphasis on the role of empathetic thought and response in attempts by human beings to engage with, understand, and explain their worlds, it is surely worth our while to reflect further on the possible roles that empathy might play in our attempts to engage with, understand, and explain the worlds of works of fiction.

Finally, one of the arguments that is sometimes offered concerning the *value* that we attach to fiction suggests that empathetic responses have more than a marginal place in our affective engagement with fiction. It is often held that the value of fiction lies largely in what it can contribute to the education of emotion. For example, in the *Poetics,* Aristotle holds that the pleasure that we take in mimetic works is a pleasure that comes from learning. The source of the pleasure that we take in *tragedy,* he holds, lies in the arousal and subsequent *catharsis* of pity and fear. Thus Aristotle links "tragic pleasure" to both learning and to emotional response; which suggests that the *value* of tragedy lies (at least partly) in what it can contribute to our emotional education.[10] Similar positions about the value of art can be found in various versions of the expression theory of art. And George Eliot, describing herself as an "aesthetic" rather than a "doctrinal" teacher, linked the value of fiction with our affective engagement with it when she said that her aim was to arouse the "nobler emotions" in her readers, in order that they should be better able to experience pity and sympathy in their everyday lives.[11]

But just what contribution can fiction make to our emotional education? Part of the answer to this question, as Eliot hints, surely lies in the fact that fiction can make available to us new emotional experience. Now in many cases we can learn about the character of our emotions through reflection on the sympathetic responses which fiction may evoke from us; for example, reflection on the peculiarly ambivalent mixture of admiration and pity that the eponymous hero of Werner Herzog's *Fitzcarraldo* evokes from us may be a source of insight into the nature of both admiration and pity. In contrast to this sort of case, however, it seems reasonable to say that if we learn about any emotion through watching Nicholas Roeg's *Don't Look Now,* for example, it is grief. And yet we don't grieve *for* John and Laura Baxter (Donald Sutherland and Julie Christie). If what we learn about grief through watching the movie is based on the experience of emotion, then, it will be based on empathetic response: on grieving *with* them. Similarly, Abel Ferrara's *Bad Lieutenant* is in part a movie about loneliness; but loneliness is not something that we feel *for* others. Again, then, to the extent that what we learn about loneliness from the movie is based on emotional experience, our learning must be based on empathetic experience.

Indeed, and leaving fiction aside for a moment, one of the most important ways in which we can gain new emotional experience is through empathetic response. It is true that our sympathetic responses to others may be new to us; we may find ourselves surprised that we feel as we do, and we may be surprised at what we find ourselves feeling about. However, in feeling *with* another, empathetically rather than sympathetically, we may find ourselves feeling in ways that are not only new to us, but in ways that are in a sense *foreign* to us. In responding sympathetically to others, we may respond in ways that we did not know were "in us." But in responding empathetically, as I shall argue, we may respond in ways that are not in *us* at all: in ways that mirror the feelings and responses of others whose outlooks and experiences may be very different from our own. Hence empathetic engagement with others may play an important part in the education of emotion. If fiction makes available to us possibilities for empathetic as well as sympathetic emotional engagement, then, that will go a long way toward justifying (as well as explaining) the claim that the value of fiction has a good deal to do with its contribution to education of emotion.

3

The considerations that I have outlined here suggest that our thinking about the ways in which we understand and value works of fiction may be illuminated by further exploration of the ways in which empathy might enter into our engagement with works of fiction. Thus far, I have said very little in particular about empathy and *film* fiction. In part, this is because I believe that the issues here are of quite general significance: I believe that further exploration of empathetic response may illuminate our engagement with fiction in all its forms. However, this is not to say that I regard the differences between the media of fiction as unimportant. Later, I shall have more to say about film fiction, in particular, and empathetic response. At this point, however, a couple of (necessarily brief) examples taken from fiction film may be useful in illustrating the ways in which empathetic response may be connected with understanding and valuing a work of fiction.

First, consider a well-known scene from Robert Wise's *The Haunting*. In the middle of the night, Eleanor (Julie Harris) and Theodora (Claire Bloom) are woken by a knocking or pounding sound coming from the corridor outside. For what seems an eternity, the sound continues, fading and rising (and as it fades other noises—a child's running footsteps, the sound of something being dragged across the floor, animal grunting—can be heard coming from the corridor) until it is deafeningly loud, and apparently directly outside the bedroom door. Finally, and suddenly, it stops, to be replaced by the sound of a woman's or girl's laughter. This is truly a terrifying scene; indeed, perhaps one of the most terrifying scenes in fiction film. (And all the more remarkable for its simplicity; apart from the sound effects, which are perfectly done and might justifiably be described as "special," the terror here depends on no technical wizardry.) And yet what sort of terror is it that the scene evokes in us? In watching it, we are not terrified for ourselves; we are under no illusion that *we* are in danger. We know that whatever it is that is outside that bedroom door "exists" only in the world of the film (if indeed it "exists" even there). Later, after the film is over, reflection may make us nervous—perhaps even terrified—about the ghosts who just might be outside *our* bedroom doors. But as we watch the scene, it is not for ourselves that we are terrified. It may be suggested that as we watch we are terrified *for* the two women in the film;

that is, that our terror is sympathetic. And perhaps part of our terror here *is* sympathetic. But what this misses is the extent to which *our* terror is based on *their* terror; if *they* were not so terrified, neither should *we* be. In Carroll's terms, their responses (which we are shown in close-up shots of their faces) are the "cues" for our responses. But of course this does not mean that our responses are merely a matter of mimicry. Rather, and I shall have more to say about this later, we respond as we do because in this scene we see the situation that the two women are in *from their point of view*. We find it terrifying because *they* find it terrifying. In short, our terror here is at least largely empathetic terror; and without acknowledgment of the role of empathy in our experience of the scene, I suggest, our terror would hardly be intelligible.

Empathy also plays a critical role in our response to and understanding of Roeg's *Don't Look Now*. The film begins with the death by drowning of the Baxters' daughter, and it is this event, or rather its effects, which drive the film. The opening moments of the film, culminating in the child's death, are extremely powerful, and demand an emotional response from us. But what *sort* of response is demanded here? Well, given what happens to them, one might of course pity the Baxters. But such a response would, I suggest, be inadequate. And it would be so not simply for the reasons that pity is so often an inadequate response to the suffering of others, but rather, or also, because a different sort of response is necessary in order fully to *understand* the rest of the film. When they get to Venice, the Baxters meet two elderly English women, sisters, one of whom is blind and claims to have psychic powers. Indeed, she claims that she has "seen" the Baxters' daughter with them in Venice, and that the little girl is attempting to warn them to leave the city. Laura takes this very seriously. She is comforted by the thought that their child is somehow still with them; she pleads with John to meet and talk to the women; and she pleads with the women to try to "contact" the girl. More to the point for my purposes here, it is clear that we, the audience, are meant to take Laura seriously in all this. If we do not do so, if we regard her merely as pathetically (and perhaps understandably) deluded, as we will if our governing or controlling response to her is one of pity, the rest of the movie will be lost to us; we simply will not understand the significance of the events that follow. The point here is that (at some level, anyway) Laura is *right* to take the psychic business seriously; and if we fail to do so, Roeg's extraordinarily powerful film turns into a second-rate suspense thriller. For example, consider John's lengthy search for Laura after he glimpses her riding on the funeral gondola with the two elderly women. If the psychic elements in the plot are regarded as mere charlatanry on the part of the English women, something that a confused and pathetic Laura has merely been taken in by, John's search for Laura itself becomes pathetic, a bizarre matter of illusion or mistaken identity. But of course it is not; and to understand that—and indeed the rest of the film— we, like Laura, have to take the psychic possibilities seriously. And that, at least for those of us who are not given to taking such things seriously, depends on our being prepared to see the events from her point of view, on our taking her perspective as our own; in short, on our responding empathetically. And as a result of seeing things from her perspective, we do not pity her, but come to feel something of her horror at the loss of her child. In short, I suggest, our controlling response to both John and Laura is not one of pity or sympathy, but rather one of shared horror at the events that have transformed their lives. And only by sharing their horror can we fully understand and be gripped by the events that follow.

4

Thus far, then, I have offered a number of reasons for thinking that there is good reason to take another look at the place of empathy in our engagement with fiction. The insistence of so many people that at least some of their responses to fiction are empathetic; the growing emphasis in other areas of philosophy and psychology on the role of empathy in understanding; the possible relationships between empathetic responses and the value that we attach to fiction—all these suggest that the subject merits further discussion. However, thus far I have said very little about what empathetic responses actually involve, beyond characterizing them as a matter of feeling with another, or sharing her feelings. It's time to say more. And first, it is important to notice that not all cases of shared response are cases of empathy. For example, if you and I both get letters informing us that we have not been short-listed for a lucrative and prestigious research fellowship, we may both feel disappointment, anger, a sense of futility, and so on. However, the fact that we share these feelings does not in itself make this an instance of empathy. For my feelings to be empathetic, the fact that I feel as I do must be related to the fact that you feel as you do; loosely speaking, empathy involves my feeling as I do *because* you feel as you do. Clearly, this "because" needs elaboration; just what sort of relationship must obtain between the psychological states of two people in order for the response of one to the other to be properly characterized in terms of empathy?

In a recent philosophical investigation of empathy, Susan Feagin argues that in empathetic responses the connection between my mental state and yours is made by way of *belief*. Empathy, she suggests, is a cognitive state; it is essentially a matter of my holding second-order beliefs about your beliefs. In empathizing with another, she argues: "a belief that something may happen to *him* affects me emotionally as if I were him. . . . The beliefs involved in empathetic emotions will thus be slightly different from the beliefs involved in the emotions with which I empathize: if I am empathically afraid for (and with) my nephew that he will flunk out of school, it is because I believe that *he* believes that he is in danger . . . , or because I believe that *he* believes that if he doesn't pass the test he will flunk out . . . and I believe that he desires not to flunk out. . . ."[12] "Empathetic emotions," Feagin argues, "always involve higher order beliefs than those involved in the emotion with which one empathizes: beliefs about someone else's beliefs."

Feagin's claim that empathy is founded on belief gives rise to a set of familiar-sounding problems with respect to the possibility of our empathizing with what we know to be fictional characters. For, Feagin says, fictional characters, inasmuch as they do not exist, do not *have* beliefs or feelings for us to form second-order beliefs about. Thus: "whether we are empathizing with the emotions of a real person depends on what our second order beliefs are. But whether we are empathizing with a fictional character does *not* depend on what our second order beliefs are. This is because there aren't any *first* order beliefs (or desires, or other psychological states) for them to be about, since neither fictional characters, nor their psychological states, exist. The existence of the empathy [with a fictional character] therefore does *not* depend on whether we 'feel' the way the [character] feels, and for the right reasons" (493). However, Feagin thinks that we can nonetheless respond empathetically to fictional characters, and her suggestion is that in doing so, *imagination* rather than belief comes into play. On her view, in such cases "we don't form second order beliefs about an individual's first order beliefs, but rather *imagine* what these beliefs, desires, etc., might be" (494). On the one hand, then, empathizing with an actual person "involves the formation of second order beliefs about that person's beliefs"; in such cases empathy is "dependent on (or explained by) our beliefs about what is involved in the beliefs (desires, etc.) of the person with whom we empathize" (496). In contrast, empathizing with a fictional character depends on our *imagining* what her beliefs, desires, and so on, might be.

Feagin's account contains some valuable suggestions, which I hope to bring out and develop in what follows. However, her suggestion that in our empathetic responses to fiction imagination functions as an *alternative* to belief results in a distorted conception of empathy. We can begin to see this by noticing that forming second-order beliefs about another's beliefs is certainly not sufficient for empathy. On the one hand, my beliefs about what you believe may leave me utterly unmoved. On the other hand, such beliefs may move me to a sympathetic response; my belief that you believe that your roses have suffered terminal damage from greenfly, for example, may move me to pity (or, for that matter, to scorn or to glee): to feel something *for* or *about* you rather than *with* you.

What the account in terms of belief fails to capture is the sense in which empathizing with another is at least partly a matter of *understanding how things are with her*. (Empathy differs from sympathy in this regard; sympathizing with another doesn't depend on my getting her mental state, or for that matter anything else about her, right. If I don't, my sympathy may well be misplaced, but it will none the less be sympathy. In contrast, if I am wrong about the mental state and/or situation of another, I won't be able to empathize with them at all. I shall return to this matter later.) And whatever this understanding of how things are with another amounts to, it is not simply a matter of holding (true) second-order beliefs about another's beliefs. We might more happily say that to empathize with another's depression (for example) involves having a sense of the *tone* of her beliefs, thoughts, desires and so on; or that it is partly a matter of coming to know *what it is like* to have certain beliefs, desires, hopes, and doubts.

5

These somewhat vague intuitions are explored and given substance by Milan Kundera in his novel *The Unbearable Lightness of Being*.[13] Kundera's central theme (or at any rate one of them) is compassion; he writes: "there is nothing heavier than compassion. Not even one's own pain weighs so heavy as the pain one feels with someone, for someone, a pain intensified by the imagination and prolonged by a hundred echoes" (31). Despite the conjunction of "with" and "for" here, Kundera's "compassion" is what I have been referring to as "empathy." He notes that while Latin-derived languages form the word "compassion" by combining the prefix "with" (*com-*) and the root "suffering" (*passio*), in other languages the word is translated by a noun formed of the prefix "with" combined with a word for "feeling." (Thus, he tells us, the Czech *soucit*, Polish *współczucie*, German *Mitgefühl*, Swedish *medkänsla*.) Compassion is in this sense "co-feeling," or "feeling-with"; to have compassion is "not only to be able to live with the other's misfortune but also to feel with him any emotion—joy, anxiety, happiness, pain. This kind of compassion . . . therefore signifies the maximal capacity of affective imagination, the art of emotional telepathy" (20).

Kundera's discourse on compassion, which is woven into his fictional narrative, illuminates not only the possible scope of his readers' relationships to the characters, but also the relationships between the characters themselves. Early in the novel, Tomas's lover Tereza reveals to him that she has been through his desk and discovered love-letters written to him by his mistress, Sabina. Kundera writes: "Anyone who has failed to benefit from the Devil's gift of compassion (co-feeling) will condemn Tereza coldly for her deed, because privacy is sacred and drawers containing intimate correspondence are not to be opened. But because compassion was Tomas's fate (or curse), he felt that he himself had knelt before the open desk-drawer, unable to tear his eyes from Sabina's letter. He understood Tereza, and not only was he incapable of being angry with her, he loved her all the more" (21). Instead of throwing Tereza out, Tomas feels her pain: "he seized her hand and kissed the tips of her fingers, because at that moment he himself felt the pain under her fingernails as surely as if the nerves of her hand led straight to his own brain." Kundera's extraordinarily powerful depiction of the relationship between Tomas and Tereza demonstrates the futility of any attempt to give an account of empathy solely in terms of belief; it is not simply Tomas's *beliefs* about Tereza's psychological state that enable him to understand her and share her pain. Empathizing with another, Kundera suggests, is above all an *imaginative* activity; it involves "the maximal capacity of affective imagination."

But appeals to imagination are all too often a signal that explanation has come to an end. Just what *sort* of imaginative activity is involved in empathy? Some remarks by Noël Carroll are suggestive with regard to this matter. Carroll argues that part of what underlies and makes possible our response to fictional characters is our "assimilation" of their situations. In part, he suggests, "this involves having a sense of the character's internal understanding of the situation; that is, having a sense of how the character assesses the situation." In other words, "I must have a conception of how the protagonist sees the situation; and I must have access to what makes her assessment intelligible." Carroll describes this as a matter of understanding a character's situation "internally" (95). Now in the case of horror, he suggests, this understanding is easily come by: since we and the protagonists of horror fictions "share the same culture, we can readily discern the features of the situation that make it horrifying to the protagonist"; given the similarities between the protagonists and us, "we easily catch on to why the character finds the monster unnatural" (96).

I believe that Carroll is right to mark the centrality of "internal" understanding in our engagement with fiction. And he is right that in (at least many) cases of horror fiction this understanding is not difficult to come by: we know how the protagonist feels when she is faced by a monster because we know how we would feel if we were faced by that monster. But in other cases, achieving "internal understanding" of a character's situation may demand rather more from us. Consider the case of Laura Baxter in *Don't Look Now:* we certainly "share the same culture" with her, but understanding her response to the claims made by the psychic woman requires more than merely reflecting on how we would feel when faced with such claims. If we are skeptical by nature, for example, or if we have never lost a child, our response is likely to be an extremely unreliable indicator of what her response is. In this sort of case, I suggest, achieving "internal understanding" of another, be she a fictional character or an actual person, requires that I imagine the world, or the situation that she is in, *from her point of view.* She becomes the "protagonist" of an imaginative project, a project in which I represent to myself her thoughts, beliefs, desires, feelings, and so on *as though they were my own.*[14]

To return to Kundera's novel: after Tereza returns to Prague leaving Tomas in Zurich, he at first feels "a beautiful melancholy." After a few days, his mood changes completely: "Tereza forced her way into his thoughts: he imagined her sitting there writing her farewell letter; he felt her hands trembling; he saw her lugging her heavy suitcase in one hand and leading Karenin on his leash with the other; he pictured her unlocking their Prague flat, and suffered the utter abandonment breathing her in the face as she opened the door" (30–31). Tomas's mood changes not because he comes to hold new *beliefs* about Tereza's beliefs, but because he comes to *imagine* her situation from her point of view rather than from his own. In doing so, he comes to see their world as Tereza must see it, to see how things are with and for *her.* And in doing so, his mood changes not to one of sympathy—he is not moved to *pity* Tereza— but rather to *match* hers; Tomas not only imagines but actually *suffers* her feeling of "utter abandonment." Kundera describes Tomas as "sick with compassion"; and an extreme example of the phenomenon that he describes so powerfully here is what is sometimes known as "sympathetic" or "phantom" pregnancy, where a man becomes so imaginatively involved in a woman's experience of pregnancy that he comes to experience some of the symptoms of pregnancy himself. As I have characterized the difference between sympathy and empathy, it would be more accurate to describe cases of this sort as "empathetic pregnancy," for what marks them out is the specificity of what the man involved feels: *he* feels what the *woman* feels; he feels *with* her rather than *for* her. In representing to himself in imagination the physical and psychological state of a pregnant woman, that is, a man may himself come *actually* to feel what the woman is *imagined* as feeling. This sort of case serves to remind us how natural, indeed instinctive, is the sort of imaginative activity that lies at the heart of empathy. In many, perhaps most, cases, we do not have to set out to *try* to empathize with another; often, though not always, this sort of imaginative activity is something that happens *to* us, that we are passive to, rather than something that we actively have to *pursue.*

6

If empathy is essentially an imaginative activity, then, is there anything to be made of Feagin's proposal that empathizing with another "involves the formation of second order beliefs about that person's beliefs" (96)? I have argued that no account which attempts to construe empathy *solely* in terms of belief and judgment can possibly do justice to the concept; however, this is not to say that belief plays *no* role in empathizing with another. For one thing, holding beliefs of the sort that Feagin is concerned with is a *precondition* of empathy. I have suggested that the imaginative activity that is characteristic of empathy involves taking another's perspective on things, imaginatively representing to oneself the thoughts, beliefs, desires, and so on of another as though they were one's own. In order to do this, however, one has to know, or at least have some beliefs about, what the other's thoughts, beliefs, and desires *are*.[15] The less substantial the knowledge I have about another, the more difficult it will be to imagine things from his point of view; thus most of us will find it difficult to imagine the world from the point of view of a Hannibal Lecter, for example, and easiest to imagine in this way a state of affairs in which the protagonist is an imagined version of oneself. Furthermore, one's beliefs about another also act as a set of *constraints* on the imaginative activity that lies at the heart of empathizing with her. Consider the scenes in *Don't Look Now* where John Baxter catches glimpses of the small figure in the red mackintosh and hood. If I am imagining the events depicted from John's point of view, I cannot see the small figure "neutrally"; given what I know about John, I cannot help but see the figure as he does, as an unhappy child, a reminder (and perhaps more than that) of his daughter. The directions that a person's imaginings (in this sense), and so her empathizing, may take are *bound* by what she knows or believes about the protagonist of her imaginative project.

Recognition of the role played in empathy by one's knowledge of and beliefs about another allows us to see some of the ways in which an attempt to empathize with another may fail. First, it may be that the knowledge that I have about another is so slight that the kind of imaginative project that I have argued is central to empathy cannot get off the ground; if I know nothing about another's psychological state, I will be unable to represent it to myself as though it were my own, and empathizing with him will be impossible. Alternatively, I may fail to empathize with another if the beliefs that I have about him are largely false. In this case, some of the beliefs, desires, and so on that I represent to myself as though they were my own will not be *his* beliefs and desires, and so I will not come to see things as he sees them, nor—except perhaps by accident[16]—to feel as he feels. The more accurate my beliefs about another are, the more likely I am to be able to succeed in empathizing with him. Again, I may be unable to empathize with another if, although I have all the right beliefs about her mental state, for some reason I cannot represent that state to myself as though it were my own. In order for me to be able to imagine a state of affairs from the point of view of another, she must be to a certain extent *like myself;* and in some cases the beliefs, desires, and so on of another may be so alien to me that I will be unable to represent them to myself as though they were my own. As we have seen, empathy is essentially an imaginative activity, and failure to empathize with another may be essentially a (more or less understandable) failure of imagination.

The role of knowledge and belief in empathizing with others also goes a good way toward explaining the common tendency to regard film fiction as a medium which encourages—perhaps demands—empathetic response more than literary fiction does. As I said earlier, of the people with whom I have discussed these issues, almost all make some sort of appeal to identification and/or empathy in characterizing their responses to movies; far fewer do so in characterizing their engagement with literary fiction. And this tendency is mirrored in theoretical writing about our engagement with fiction, where discussion of character identification and audience identification is much more common in writing about film than it is in writing about literary fiction. Why is it that empathy is commonly regarded as more important in our experience of film fiction than it is in our experience of literary fiction? The answer, I suggest, lies partly in the fact that in literary fiction, we are very often informed in great detail about the situation a character is in, and told precisely what her thoughts, desires, and so on are. This can mean that attempts to empathize with literary fictional characters have a great chance of success; as we have seen, the greater our knowledge of another's psychological state and situation, the more likely we are to succeed in empathizing with her. However, the detailed knowledge that we so often have about the psychological states of literary fictional characters may also be an *impediment* to empathizing with them. We may be told so much about such characters that we do not *need* to empathize with them in order to understand them. Our motive for empathizing with others, I suggest (and it may not be a conscious motive) is the desire to understand how things are with them. And, given sufficient information about another, we simply may not need to empathize with her in order to understand her.

Of course, this is not to say that we can never, or need never, empathize with literary fictional characters. But the considerations noted above suggest that when we do so, our empathy may well have a different character from our empathy with actual persons. The difference I have in mind here is not the difference that Feagin marks out, namely, the difference between empathizing on the basis of belief and empathizing on the basis of imagination. The difference is rather that in empathizing with actual persons, even persons very close to us, we rarely have the detailed knowledge of their psychological states and situations that we so often have about literary fictional characters. Empathy with actual persons is thus likely to be, and to feel like, a precarious business. But it may be the only way we have of understanding a fellow human being. And the same is true with regard to the characters of film fiction. We typically know much less about such characters than we do about literary fictional characters; empathy with them is thus likely to be more precarious than is empathy with literary fictional characters. But, as is the case with regard to actual persons, empathizing with a film fictional character may be the only way that we have of understanding her.

So in engaging with the characters of film fiction we are in a position much closer to the position we are in when we engage with actual persons than we are when we read about the characters of literary fiction. Of course, there is the obvious fact that in the former cases, sight and hearing play a critical role in our engagement as they do not in the latter case. But in addition to this, in the former cases empathy may be crucial to understanding in a way that it is often not in the latter case. And it is partly this, I suggest, that gives film fiction its value: it gives us practice, so to speak, in a mode of engagement and response that is often crucial in our attempts to engage with and understand our fellow human beings.

7

However, all this presupposes that empathetic response to fictional characters is possible in the first place. And it may be argued that on the account of empathy I have outlined here, any suggestion that certain of our affective or emotional responses to fictional characters may be empathetic responses is highly problematic. Indeed, it would seem that the problem we should be faced with in making this suggestion is just the problem with which, as I noted earlier, Feagin is largely concerned. For I have argued that although empathy cannot be construed *solely* in terms of belief or judgment, the imaginative activity which lies at the heart of empathetic response both presupposes and is constrained by one's knowledge of and beliefs about the other's psychological states. But as Feagin notes, neither fictional characters nor their psychological states exist. And if fictional characters do not *have* psychological states, how can we form beliefs about their beliefs, desires, hopes, and fears? Again, if fictional characters do not have feelings, what sense can be given to any suggestion that certain of our affective responses to fictional characters involve coming to *share* their feelings?

As we saw earlier, Feagin attempts to meet these difficulties by appealing to imagination; while empathizing with actual people involves forming second-order beliefs about their beliefs, she suggests, in empathizing with fictional characters we rather imagine what the beliefs, desires, and so on might be (494). It is clear, however, that the conception of imagination that Feagin has in mind here is not the conception I have sketched above. For while I have argued that the imaginative activity characteristic of empathy *involves* belief, for Feagin the very point of appealing to imagination here is as an *alternative* to belief. If Feagin is right, then, empathizing with a fictional character will be very different from empathizing with an actual person, both in her own terms and as I have characterized the latter. More importantly, however, as it stands it is far from clear that Feagin's account of what it is to empathize with a fictional character is in fact an account of *empathy* at all. As we have seen, an attempt to empathize with another may *fail*. And I have argued above that failure to empathize is to be explained by reference to the knowledge or beliefs that the imaginer has about the psychological states of the person with whom he is attempting to empathize, from whose point of view he is imagining things. In Feagin's view, however, we do not *have* knowledge of or beliefs about the psychological states of a fictional character, since fictional characters—and hence their psychological states—do not exist. The question thus arises, What constrains or binds the imaginative activity that, on Feagin's account, constitutes empathizing with a fictional character, if that activity is not constrained by belief? Feagin is silent on this point, but some answer is needed. For if the imaginative project characteristic of empathizing with a fictional character is *un*constrained, there will be nothing by which to determine the success of such a project; there will be no way, that is, of deciding whether or not empathy has been achieved. Since empathy is based on a kind of imaginative activity that may fail, unconstrained imaginative activity cannot constitute empathy.

If empathy with fictional characters is to be explained in terms of imagination, then, we need some explanation of what constrains or binds imagination in this context. And in effect, I suggest, the explanation that is needed here will be provided by a successful account of the language of fiction. For a major criterion of adequacy that any such account must satisfy is that it be able to explicate the sense in which it is true, or at any rate "true," that (for example) the Baxters in Roeg's *Don't Look Now* had a pretty miserable time of things; and so that it be able to explain the sense in which we can *believe* that they had a miserable time. Following Kendall Walton, for example, it might be argued that it is fictional or "make-believe" that the Baxters existed, and fictionally or make-believedly the case that they had certain beliefs, desires, hopes, feelings, and so on; in which case, we can have *beliefs* about what is fictionally or make-believedly the case with respect to the Baxters and their psychological states.[17] I won't attempt to adjudicate here between the complex variety of accounts of the language and logic of fiction that have been offered to date; however, something *like* this must, I think, be right. And our beliefs about what is fictionally or make-believedly the case can, I suggest, ground and constrain the kind of imaginative project that I have argued is characteristic of empathizing with another. That is, beliefs of this sort can ground and constrain our imagining a situation or state of affairs from the point of view of a fictional character.[18]

A further difficulty that may be thought to arise with regard to the possibility of our responding empathetically to fiction is suggested by Richard Wollheim. As we saw earlier, Wollheim suggests that any account of our affective responses to fiction that puts empathetic responses to the fore must in that respect be wrong. For, Wollheim suggests, "the empathic member of the audience selects who it is whose deeds and inner states he will centrally imagine. [For example,] Watching *King Lear* he rewrites the text of Shakespeare so that it can be acted from the point of view of Gloucester."[19] The implication is that "rewriting" in this sense is an inappropriate way to engage with the text, and hence that inasmuch as empathy involves "rewriting," it is an inappropriate way of responding to the characters. In response to this suggestion, it might be argued that Wollheim's remarks have more than a whiff of aestheticism about them; a play—or a film—may be more enjoyable and more rewarding when "rewritten" in this sense. So why *not* "rewrite" it? But secondly, and more importantly, "rewriting" a work may not be necessary in order to respond empathetically to one or more of its characters. Certainly one does not have to "rewrite" *The Haunting* to see the events in the scene discussed earlier from the perspective of Eleanor and Theodora. And one does not distort Roeg's film by seeing the events from the point of view of Laura or John Baxter; indeed, I have argued that we may need to empathize with them, to see things from their point of view, if we are to understand the film. Nor does one have to "rewrite" or distort Shakespeare's text in order to imagine the world of *King Lear* from Gloucester's point of view; arguably *not* to respond in this way is to miss one of the central experiences that the play has to offer. Indeed, it might plausibly be argued that allowing the audience to see and to understand his or her fictional world from a variety of perspectives and characters' points of view—making a variety of empathetic responses to his or her work possible—is one criterion, among others, of a writer's or director's success.

8

I have argued, then, that in order to give anything like an adequate account of empathy we must recognize that empathy is *essentially* an imaginative matter, and that the imaginative activity characteristic of empathy both presupposes and is constrained by belief. Not only does empathizing with actual persons involve imagination as well as belief, but empathizing with fictional characters involves belief as well as imagination. So Feagin misconstrues the case when she claims that "unlike real life empathy, the art emotion of empathy [that is, empathy with fictional characters] is not dependent on (or explained by) our beliefs about what is involved in the beliefs (desires, etc.) of the person with whom we empathize" (496). It needs to be emphasized here that empathizing with a fictional character is not, pace Feagin, radically different from empathizing with an actual person. In empathizing with another, whether she be actual or fictional, one imagines the situation she is in from her point of view; one imaginatively represents to oneself her beliefs, desires, hopes, fears, and so on as though they were one's own. And in both cases, one may come *actually* to feel what the other in question, be she actual or fictional, is *imagined* as feeling. Imagination occupies center stage here not because it is needed specifically in order to explain certain of our affective responses to fictional characters, but rather because it is constitutive of empathy per se.

But given that we *can* empathize with fictional characters, *why* do we do so? The answer to this question, I believe, will be more or less the same as the answer to the question as to why we empathize with actual persons; the fact that we sometimes do one is no more and no less mysterious than the fact that we sometimes do the other. However, I am not at all confident about my ability to answer these questions adequately. For in large part, I think, they ask why it is that we *care* about each other and about fictions at all; and an adequate answer to that question is beyond me. However, we can say *something* about why it is that we sometimes respond empathetically to others. For in empathizing with others, we come to know how things are with them, by seeing the world from their point of view, as they see it, and feeling as they feel. In short, we come to understand them better; so that we are better placed to understand why they have reacted and behaved as they have done, and to predict how they will react and behave in the future.[20] And inasmuch as empathy contributes to our understanding of others, it has great practical value to us. Given that when we engage with fiction we want to understand its characters and events, then, and that empathizing with others (be they fictional or actual) contributes to our understanding of them, it is hardly surprising that in responding to works of fiction we sometimes respond empathetically to their characters. But the value of empathy does not lie solely in what it can contribute to our understanding of others and their worlds of experience. Empathizing with others also makes available to us possibilities for our *own* emotional education and development. In coming to see things as others see them and to feel as they do we gain a broader perspective on the world, an increased awareness and understanding of the possible modes of response to the world. In short, through responding empathetically to others we may come to see *our* world and *our* possibilities anew. That is valuable. And, as I suggested earlier, part of the value of fiction, and in particular film fiction, lies in the fact that by encouraging and sometimes demanding empathetic responses from us, it makes such broadening of perspective available to us.

Where then does this leave us with regard to the role of identification in our engagement with fiction? Earlier, I noted that on certain psychoanalytically inspired accounts, identification is construed as a pathological process, symptomatic of one or another form of anxiety and self-deception. And if empathetic responses are based on identification, as common parlance suggests, then on such accounts empathetic responses must themselves be regarded as pathological, as rooted in anxiety and self-deception. I do not believe that this is the case: one of the guiding thoughts in this essay has been that our empathetic responses to fiction can be invaluable in understanding and learning from works of fiction; so far from being symptomatic of self-deception, such responses may be the means to increased understanding of ourselves and of others. If this is accurate, then perhaps common parlance is misleading: perhaps empathetic responses to others do *not* depend on identification with them. On the other hand, perhaps empathetic responses *are* based on identification, and identification is not the pathological process that some theorists suggest that it is. I do not believe that it is worth trying to settle this issue. The fact is that the term "identification" can refer to so many different sorts of processes that as things stand it is simply not very helpful in attempts to get clear about our emotional engagement with fiction: as D. W.

Harding writes, "We sacrifice little more with the term 'identification' than a bogus technicality."[21] I suggest that we need to reverse the approach so often taken in discussions of these matters: rather than beginning with a psychoanalytically inspired account of identification and then going on to consider its implications with regard to our experience of fiction, we need to *begin* with our experience of fiction. And in doing so, I believe, we will find ourselves needing and developing a wide variety of descriptive and explanatory resources more fine-grained than is the notion of identification. The concept of empathy, I suggest, is one such resource.

NOTES

Thanks to David Bordwell, Curtis Brown, Noël Carroll, and Marianne Neill for helpful suggestions.

1. The first philosopher to address these questions, so far as I know, was the sophist Gorgias. See Jonathan Barnes, *The Presocratic Philosophers*, vol. 2, *Empedocles to Democritus* (London: Routledge, 1979), pp. 161–64. For a list of most of the important recent contributions to this debate, see the bibliography in B. H. Boruah's *Fiction and Emotion* (Oxford: Clarendon Press, 1988).

2. Richard Wollheim, "Imagination and Identification," in *On Art and the Mind* (Cambridge: Harvard University Press, 1973), p. 68.

3. Dolf Zillman, "Anatomy of Suspense," in *The Entertainment Functions of Television*, ed. Percy H. Tannenbaum (Hillsdale, N.J.: Lawrence Erlsbaum, 1980), p. 141. Emphasis added.

4. Zillman himself uses "empathy" to cover "feeling for" as well as "feeling with."

5. Noël Carroll, *The Philosophy of Horror, or Paradoxes of the Heart* (New York: Routledge, 1990), pp. 88–96.

6. Anne Friedberg, "A Denial of Difference: Theories of Cinematic Identification," in *Psychoanalysis and Cinema*, ed. E. Ann Kaplan (New York: Routledge, 1990), p. 40.

7. For example, it is central in the work of Vico and Dilthey.

8. For examples, see Adam Smith's *The Theory of Moral Sentiments* (Oxford: Clarendon Press, 1976), David Hume's *A Treatise of Human Nature* (Oxford: Clarendon Press, 1978), and Carol Gilligan's *In a Different Voice* (Cambridge: Harvard University Press, 1982).

9. See Robert Gordon's much discussed paper "Folk Psychology as Simulation," *Mind and Language* 1 (1986): 158–71, and chapter 7 of his *The Structure of Emotions* (Cambridge: Cambridge University Press, 1987). *Mind and Language* 7, 1–2 (1992) is a special issue devoted to discussion of "simulation theory," which holds that empathetic understanding is central to our everyday, pretheoretical understanding of others. I am indebted here to Alvin Goldman's extremely helpful survey of some of the main issues involved, in his presidential address to the Pacific Division of the APA: "Empathy, Mind, and Morals," *Proceedings and Addresses of the American Philosophical Association* 66 (November 1992): 17–41.

10. Needless to say, just what Aristotle means by *catharsis* in the *Poetics* has been a subject of intense debate for centuries. The scholar who has done most to connect *catharsis* to learning, or "intellectual clarification," about the emotions is Leon Golden. See his *Aristotle on Tragic and Comic Mimesis* (Atlanta: Scholars, 1992). See also

Martha Nussbaum, *The Fragility of Goodness* (Cambridge: Cambridge University Press, 1986).

11. Quoted by Peter Jones in his *Philosophy and the Novel* (Oxford: Clarendon Press, 1975), p. 66.

12. Susan L. Feagin, "Imagining Emotions and Appreciating Fiction," *Canadian Journal of Philosophy* 18 (1988): 485–500. The quotation is from pp. 489–90.

13. Milan Kundera, *The Unbearable Lightness of Being*, trans. Michael Henry Heim (New York: Harper and Row, 1984).

14. Here I am drawing on Alvin Goldman's "Empathy, Mind, and Morals," in *Proceedings and Addresses*, and especially on Richard Wollheim's discussions of empathy. See his "Imagination and Identification," in *On Art and the Mind*, and chapter 3 ("Iconicity, Imagination and Desire") of his *The Thread of Life* (Cambridge: Cambridge University Press, 1984). Wollheim makes a distinction between "central" and "acentral" imagining that in some respects parallels Carroll's distinction between "internal" and "external" understanding.

15. Thus Wollheim suggests that one of the restrictions on whom I can centrally imagine is that it must be "someone for whom I have, or have the capacity to form, a repertoire of substance" (*The Thread of Life*, p. 74). The "repertoire" that one has for a person with whom one empathizes consists of the beliefs that one has about his beliefs, desires, hopes, fears, and so on.

16. I have in mind here cases analogous to Gettier-type cases of true justified belief that is nonetheless not knowledge. See Edmund L. Gettier, "Is Justified True Belief Knowledge?" *Analysis* 23 (1965): 121–23.

17. See Kendall L. Walton, *Mimesis as Make-Believe* (Cambridge: Harvard University Press, 1990).

18. I discuss this and related issues concerning emotion, belief, and fiction in more detail in my "Fiction and the Emotions," *American Philosophical Quarterly* 30 (January 1993): 1–13.

19. Wollheim, "Imagination and Identification," p. 68.

20. Again, see Goldman's "Empathy, Mind, and Morals."

21. D. W. Harding, "Psychological Processes in the Reading of Fiction," in *Aesthetics in the Modern World*, ed. Harold Osborne (New York: Weybright and Talley, 1968), p. 309. See also Carroll's *The Philosophy of Horror*, pp. 88–96.

9

Feminist Frameworks
for Horror Films

Cynthia A. Freeland

The horizon for feminists studying horror films appears bleak. Since *Psycho*'s infamous shower scene, the big screen has treated us to Freddie's long razor-nails emerging between Nancy's legs in the bathtub (*A Nightmare on Elm Street I*), De Palma's exhibitionist heroine being power-drilled into the floor (*Body Double*), and Leatherface hanging women from meat hooks (*The Texas Chain Saw Massacre*). Even in a film with a strong heroine like *Alien,* any feminist point is qualified by the monstrousness of the alien mother, the objectification of Sigourney Weaver in her underwear, and her character Ripley's forced assumption of a maternal role.

Despite all this, there has been some feminist work on horror, and I believe there is room for more. In the first part of this paper I shall survey and criticize currently dominant psychodynamic feminist approaches to horror. In the second part, I propose an alternative framework for constructing feminist interpretations of horror films by critically interrogating their gender ideologies. My proposal focuses less on the psychology of viewers than on the nature of films as artifacts with particular structures and functions. In the third part I illustrate my recommended framework by sketching readings of *Jurassic Park* (Spielberg 1993), *The Fly* (Cronenberg 1986), and *Repulsion* (Polanski 1965).

Part I: Psychoanalytic Feminist Approaches to Horror

Most current feminist studies of horror films are psychodynamic. That is, though they may consider films as artifacts, recognizing such aspects as plot, narrative, or point of view, their chief emphasis is on viewers' motives and interests in watching horror films, and on the psychological effects such films have. Typically this sort of feminist film theory relies upon a psychoanalytic framework in which women are described as castrated or as representing threats evoking male castration anxiety. These theories also standardly presume some connection between gazing, violent aggression, and masculinity, and they suggest that there are particularly "male" motivations for making, watching, and enjoying horror films.

Feminist psychodynamic approaches to film in general were launched by Laura Mulvey's influential essay "Visual Pleasure and Narrative Cinema" (1975).[1] Mulvey's model presupposes a Lacanian psychoanalytic perspective and draws upon key Lacanian conceptions of castration anxiety and visual fetishism, and the association of the "Law of the Father" or patriarchy with such traditional film features as narrative order. Mulvey argued that narrative forms characteristic of mainstream Hollywood cinema differentially use women and serve men. There is a dual analogy between the woman and the screen (the object of the look), and between the man and the viewer (the possessor of the look). A tension arises in the viewer between libido and ego needs, and this tension is resolved by a process of identification, whereby the [male] viewer identifies with the [male] protagonist in the film. Thus possessing the film character of the woman by proxy, the viewer can proceed to focus energy on achieving a satisfactory narrative resolution.

Mulvey's view has come in for a number of persuasive criticisms by other feminist film theorists, and she has even revised it herself.[2] Nevertheless, it will be instructive to begin by extrapolating from her basic model so as to generate a simple feminist, psychoanalytic account of horror, as follows: The tension between the viewer's desire to look and the ongoing narrative of a film is especially acute in the horror film. Typically in horror, the woman or visual object is also the chief victim sacrificed to the narrative desire to know about the monster. Horror flirts directly with the threat of castration underlying the fetish or visual appearance of the woman, and this means that looking (visual pleasure) is even more immediately at odds with narrative in horror films than in other mainstream Hollywood movies. The woman's flesh, the reality behind the surface appearance, *is* made visible, and horror shows the "wound" that we are revolted to look upon. To make up for this horror, this account continues, the viewer must turn attention to the narrative thrust of the investigator, typically a male, who will complete the story for us.

For example, in *Psycho,* we, like Janet Leigh, see the vague blurred and threatening shape of the attacker behind the shower curtain. But after this central murder scene, the audience and camera look into the blind eye of the victim. Since the woman herself can no longer see, and her beautiful body no longer be looked upon, we viewers are forced to proceed beyond her vision. And once our identification with the woman/victim has been disrupted, it shifts to the male investigators who will solve the crime and identify the murderer, and ultimately to the male psychiatrist who, in the film's words, "has all the answers."

A modified version of the simple Mulveyan schema I have just sketched is offered by Linda Williams, who scrutinizes one of the more vulnerable aspects of Mulvey's theory, her straitjacketed association between males and the pleasures of looking or spectatorship.[3] Williams points out that often in horror, contrary to mainstream cinema, women do possess "the gaze." That is, they are typically the first to get to see, inquire about, and know the monster. Similarly, although monsters may threaten the bodies of women in horror, even so, the fates of women and monsters are often linked. Both may somehow seem to stand outside the patriarchal order. (Think of vampire stories, for example, where a fascinating foreign Dracula seduces women away from their husbands and fathers, undermining the patriarchal institutions of law, marriage, motherhood, medicine, and religion.) Despite these observations about the shortcomings of a Mulveyan account, Williams's account remains consistent in its outlines with the sort of Mulveyan view I have just sketched. Williams argues that women who possess the gaze in horror, and who become aligned with monsters, are typically shown themselves to represent threats to patriarchy and hence to require punishment. In the end Williams seems to accept the basic idea that horror films reinforce conceptions of the active (sadistic) male viewer and the passive (suffering) female object. Women are punished for their appropriation of "the gaze," and a sort of masculine narrative order (what Lacan would call the Law of the Father) is restored.

More recently, feminist film theorists have turned to the work of one of Lacan's successors, the French feminist psychoanalyst Julia Kristeva. Kristeva's book *Powers of Horror: An Essay on Abjection*[4] focuses on literature and not film, but her views have been adapted to the study of visual horror by Barbara Creed, in a 1986 *Screen* article about *Alien,* and in her more recent book *The Monstrous-Feminine: Film, Feminism, Psychoanalysis.*[5] Kristeva locates the sources and origins of horror not in castration anxiety, but in the preoedipal stage of the infant's ambivalence toward the mother as it struggles to create boundaries and forge its own ego identity. The mother is "horrific" in the sense of being all-engulfing, primitive, and impure or defiled by bodily fluids—particularly breast milk and flowing menstrual blood. Kristeva uses the term "abjection" to designate the psychic condition inspired by this image of the horrific mother. For Kristeva, horror is fundamentally about boundaries—about the threat of transgressing them, and about the need to do so. Hence she emphasizes the duality of our attraction/repulsion to the horrific.

In applying this theory to *Alien,* Creed stresses the film's repeated birth scenarios and numerous versions of the engulfing, threatening, voracious, horrific Alien mother, "a toothed vagina, the monstrous-feminine as the cannibalistic mother." Creed also offers an explanation of why, in the final scenes of *Alien* (notoriously), Sigourney Weaver undresses before the camera, strolls around in her thin undershirt, and eventually returns to her sleeping pod with the small orange cat she has rescued: "Ripley's body is pleasurable and reassuring to look at. She signifies the 'acceptable' form and shape of woman."

Creed departs in certain important respects from the simplistic Mulveyan model I sketched. She emphasizes, contra the Mulveyan-Lacanian position, that horror importantly concerns not just women as victims—women who are attacked because they present a horrific vision of a castrated body—but also monstrous women who threaten to castrate men. "Virtually all horror texts represent the monstrous-feminine in relation to Kristeva's notion of maternal authority and the mapping of the self's clean and proper body."[6] More specifically, Creed thinks that horror texts all serve to illustrate "the work of abjection."[7] They do so in three basic ways. First, horror depicts images of abjection, such as corpses and bodily wastes; second, horror is concerned with borders, with things that threaten the stability of the symbolic order; and third, horror constructs the maternal figure as abject.

Let me pause now for some assessment. As I have noted, both the Mulvey-Lacanian and Creed-Kristevan frameworks for feminist film theory build upon a psychoanalytic foundation. Despite all the details of their different pictures, each view construes the familiar tensions of horror in terms of an opposition between "female" and "male" aspects, where these are understood or defined within the terms of depth psychology. There is, in other words, a tension between spectacle or the horrific feminine (associated with the castrated woman, preoedipal mother, or castrating woman), and plot or narrative resolution (associated with the patriarchal order that the child achieves after resolving the Oedipal complex). In broader ways that go beyond psychoanalysis, in all these theories (Mulvey's, Creed's, and Williams's) the focus is also psychodynamic—that is, there is some presumed general or universal psychological theory that grounds their analysis. To back up speculations of this sort Creed, for example, begins her book by appealing to both universal cultural practices and classical mythology. Psychodynamic feminist theorists speculate about why "we" are interested in horror and more basically about why certain things are horrifying. These kinds of question are seen to require an answer within a psychological theory, which remains the chief concern even when the theorist speaks about how to "interpret" such films or about what various aspects of these films "represent." The "deep" explanations offered are (putative) psychological explanations. For instance, here is Creed on *The Exorcist:*

> Regan's carnivalesque display of her body reminds us quite clearly of the immense appeal of the abject. Horror emerges from the fact that woman has broken with her proper feminine role—she has "made a spectacle of herself"—put her unsocialized body on display. And to make matters worse, she has done all of this before the shocked eyes of two male clerics.[8]

The theoretical approaches of feminist film analysts like Creed, Mulvey, and Williams are significantly constrained by their psychodynamic framing, and more particularly (and significantly) by the theoretical apparatus of psychoanalysis. I here present six objections to such approaches.

First, psychoanalysis is itself a very problematic enterprise that is far from achieving anything like general acceptance as a psychological theory. Feminists adapting the views of Lacan or Kristeva do so either in ignorance of or indifference to forceful philosophical critiques of psychoanalysis offered by Crews, Grünbaum, Deleuze and Guattari, and others.[9] Attempts to defend psychoanalysis by reconceiving it as hermeneutic explanation are also problematic, because they loosen the theory from its crucial underpinnings in causal hypothesizing, leaving key theses, about, say, abject preoedipal mothers, castration anxiety, and so on, as, at best, hermeneutical aids to reading film "texts." Such hermeneutical aids should be taken seriously only insofar as they produce valid readings. But typically in film studies, psychoanalytic interpretations are advanced a priori, rather than in an open-minded spirit of testing how well they actually work. Though a Kristevan reading may seem illuminating for *Alien*, with its many birth scenarios and theme of monstrous mothering, why should we believe in advance that it will work equally for all kinds of examples of horror? The notion of abjection expands in Creed's theory so as to be almost vacuous, because we are to understand in advance that all the varieties of horrific monstrousness we can think of really just are "illustrations" of the "work" of abjection. This includes an astonishing variety, ranging from *Alien*'s monstrous mother to the disintegrating cannibalistic zombies in *Night of the Living Dead*, or from Seth Brundle's hideously gooey and amoral fly to the *Texas Chain Saw Massacre*'s cannibalistic family. In what sense is a psychological theory of abjection "explanatory" when it becomes so broad? And in any case, why can't it be the case that there are unique, distinctive, sui generis human fears of a variety of things? Keep in mind that abjection in a Kristevan framework always refers at bottom to the necessity of separation from the primal mother. Why must all other fears somehow equal or be reduced to fear of the primal mother?

Second, even supposing one were to grant that psychoanalysis is a worthy psychological theory, this is not an argument for the particular psychoanalytic views of Lacan or Kristeva. There are many alternatives; so why settle on these? Lacan makes problematic and philosophically disputable metaphysical assertions about the self, the nature of desire, and so on.[10] Kristeva makes equally problematic quasi-empirical claims about, say, the infant's acquisition of language. Her views are quite controversial even within feminism; she has been criticized for, variously, essentialist theorizing, promoting anarchy, idealizing maternity, or adopting views that are fascistic, apolitical, or ahistorical.[11] Luce Irigaray offers both scathing critiques of Lacan and intriguing alternatives to some of Kristeva's most basic claims.[12]

Clearly, within psychoanalysis, we can identify many alternatives to Lacanian or Kristevan frameworks that might also be fruitful for film studies. Stanley Cavell, for example, borrows from traditional Freudian psychoanalysis to offer quite subtle and complex accounts of viewers' desires and interests in relation to both male and female actors' embodiments of film characters' roles.[13] He seems to provide a promising framework for the analysis of certain types of films, such as melodrama or the genre he calls the "comedy of remarriage." Alternatively, for all we know, Jungian or Reichian psychoanalytic theories might be intriguing psychological theories to put to the test in film studies. Jungians, with their theory of universal unconscious archetypal structures, might pay more attention to cross-cultural considerations in films, or to films' links with various kinds of fairy tales and myths. Reichians have the virtue of emphasizing concrete external sociomaterial factors in identity formation and repression. Perhaps Horney's notion of womb envy or Klein's of the bad mother would enable us to offer better interpretations of certain films, like *Frankenstein* or *The Brood*.

Third, moving away from the particular restrictions of psychoanalysis, I find that psychodynamic theories often tend to be weak as film readings because they are too reductive. They tend to utilize a one-dimensional system of symbolic interpretation. For example, even when a Kristevan interpretation seems illuminating for certain aspects of a film, as for example it does when Creed uses it to comment on horrific aspects of the climactic birth scene in *The Brood,* her focus on this aspect of the film alone seems to lead her to neglect many other important features of the film.[14] In my view this film offers a critique of several concrete contemporary social problems: the evils of charismatic psychotherapists, and the ways in which child abuse gets perpetuated from one generation to the next. It is limiting to translate a social critique into a depth-psychological thesis about how we all (allegedly) have deep ambivalences about our abjected mothers. Even more of a problem is the fact that Creed's framework locates the film's chief source of horror in the freakish mother (Samantha Eggar), setting aside the film's apparent depiction of the megalomaniac psychiatrist, Dr. Hal Raglan (Oliver Reed), as its central villain. Creed's account thereby becomes insensitive to historical allusions the film makes (and that Cronenberg quite typically makes) to the tradition of mad scientist horror films. She also misrepresents the structure of the film's plot, which depicts an appropriate punishment that Dr. Raglan suffers for his hubris—as he is destroyed by the monstrous children he has so freakishly "fathered."

Fourth, psychodynamic film theories that depend upon very basic distinctions between males and females—whether as viewers, objects of the gaze, or pursuers of distinct sorts of pleasures—rely upon certain notions of gender that are themselves problematic and under question by feminists. Many feminist and other critics have pointed out that assertions about fears of castration, or about the masculinity of logic and language, may be radically culture- and era-bound. To make very broad generalizations about "male" or "female" viewers blocks the recognition of significant individual differences among viewers that surely affect how they experience films. These include significant differences of social class, sexual orientation, age, race, and so on. For example, given that racial identity seems an important factor in some horror movies, such as *Night of the Living Dead* and its sequel *Dawn of the Dead*, it seems unreasonable to presume that white and black female viewers will experience the film, its "gazes" and its "visual objects" in just the same ways.

These films seem explicitly to pair white females and black males as sharing a certain "victim" status.[15]

Even the most basic assumption of psychodynamic feminist film theorists, that it is conceptually useful and appropriate to distinguish between male and female viewers, and even between heterosexual and homosexual men or women, have been placed under attack in recent theoretical work in queer and performance theory by writers like Judith Butler and Eve Sedgwick. A focused awareness of issues in queer theory could lead, for example, to intriguing re-visions of a movie like *The Silence of the Lambs*. I have in mind not the obvious problems with the film's homophobic depiction of the "Buffalo Bill" character, but critical textures that may be added to readings of the film when we focus on its strange pairing of Jodie Foster, who was at the time of the film's release controversially "outed" by ActUp, with the villainous yet charming "Hannibal Lecter" character whose fussy mannerisms allow him to be read as "an old queen."[16]

Fifth, another difficulty with a psychodynamic, especially a psychoanalytic, framework for feminist film studies is that this view has mysteriously acquired a predominance within feminist film theory that is completely disproportionate to its status within contemporary feminist theorizing in general. British, American, and French feminists differ from one another and among themselves, not to mention from Third World anticolonialist feminists, and major books in both popular and academic feminism in the United States have adopted widely divergent theoretical bases—but these are typically not psychoanalytic. Instead, they range from a rather vague and standard liberalism grounded in the tradition of John Stuart Mill, to more radical forms of Marxist socialism; and from Foucauldian emphases on disciplinary techniques of knowledge and bodily control to new, visionary feminist work on ecosystems and the possibly liberating role of technology. Surely these diverse and flourishing forms of feminist theory also have something to offer to film studies. Many of them focus, for example, on subjectivity and desire, on visual objectification and equality, or on technologies of representation in ways that would seem readily adaptable to film studies.

Sixth and last, I doubt that whatever insights are produced by psychodynamic readings of horror films require a grounding in some particular psychogenetic theory that allegedly explains viewers' interests and responses in general filmic narratives and representations. As I have noted, psychoanalytic feminists construct genderized accounts of the tensions in horror between key features of spectacle and plot. But it is entirely possible to construct a theory of horror that emphasizes these same tensions without genderizing them. As far back as the ancient world, Aristotle's account of tragedy in the *Poetics* recognized a tension between the aesthetic effects evoked by tragedy and its narrative structures.[17] Noël Carroll's *The Philosophy of Horror* follows Aristotle and similarly pays central attention to the dichotomy horror typically depends upon between the cognitive pleasures of following out the narrative and the emotional pain of art-horror associated with monsters and spectacles.[18] If an account like Carroll's grasps these same tensions and offers reasonable explanations of them without alluding to either gender or depth psychology, it is hard to see why as feminists thinking about horror we need to resort to such theorizing. To my own mind, if there is any particular merit in the sort of comment that Creed makes about *The Exorcist* in the passage I quoted above, we can make this judgment by looking at the movie, without any special devotion to or even knowledge of the intricate theoretical grounding (and jargon) of Kristevan psychoanalysis.

Some of the general problems I have just enumerated will likely arise for other psychodynamic feminist approaches to horror, even ones that do not begin from a strictly psychoanalytic framework, such as Carol Clover's "gender rezoning" proposal in her recent book *Men, Women, and Chain Saws: Gender in the Modern Horror Film*.[19] Clover's approach does have much to recommend it: she discusses subgenres of horror rather than trying to create a wholly uniform theory; she attempts to locate horror films within their sociocultural context; and she recognizes and indeed focuses on some of the elusiveness of gender categories. Her theory is much less subject, then, to my fourth objection listed above.[20]

Yet even so, Clover's account is problematic because, in the place of psychoanalysis, she assumes the validity of an alternative theory of gender and of our psychological conceptualizations of it—Thomas Laqueur's "one sex" model. According to Laqueur, sex is primitively conceived as involving one norm, masculinity, of which femininity is a defective version. Clover thinks this model is somehow operative both in the construction and in the experience of works in the horror genre. There are several distinct questions to raise here. First, one might ask on what basis we should be persuaded to adopt this particular theory of gender. Laqueur is a historian of science whose views are by no means universally accepted, and so relying on his theory is a rather strange and arbitrary choice. It seems doubtful to me that any book of film theory can argue convincingly for the truth of a particular psychological theory of gender. Next, we might ask Clover to argue for the applicability of this theory of gender to the horror genre. She does make a stab at this, but only vaguely, by asserting that horror originated in the time of the rather primitive science that Laqueur is analyzing. This claim itself needs more detailed defense. Does it even hold of the early works *Frankenstein* and *Dracula* for instance? I doubt it. Finally, even granted that her historical claim about the psychological theories prevalent during the creation of early works of horror were correct, Clover ought to recognize that such a theory is hardly predominant any longer. Accordingly, it would seem reasonable for us to expect more recent forms of horror to reflect the current state of public knowledge and scientific theorizing about sex. My doubts about all the gaps in Clover's exposition lead me to question her particular observations about individual films. Again, where I find such observations insightful, I am inclined to think that their value stems more from how acutely they "read" film texts than from how accurately they reflect the real human psychology of actual viewers.

Part 2: A Proposed Feminist Framework for Reading Horror Films

In Part 1 I described various approaches to horror within contemporary feminist film studies and identified problems in these approaches, some involving specific psychoanalytic tenets, others, more general problems about psychodynamic approaches. But the feminist theorists I have examined are limited by more than their problematic universalizing views about human psychosexual development. They also lack a deep and well-grounded historical awareness of horror's roots and varieties. Clover's book does focus on a range of horror plots and on their social and cultural contexts, but only on horror films of the past two decades. Horror has a much longer, more complex history. It originated from the gothic novel, a fact in itself important for feminists to note because of the unusual prevalence of women as both writers and readers in this genre.[21] Much good feminist work has been done in recent years concerning gothic romance and the origins of horror in works like those of Mary Shelley.[22] Ideally, feminist readings of horror films would benefit from awareness of this research and of related work in cultural studies that examines the history of horror in relation to specific sociocultural contexts.[23]

Further, feminist psychodynamic accounts do not seem sensitive to the dazzling diversity of horror's subgenres: gothic, mad scientist, alien invader, slasher-psycho, rape revenge, B-movie, cult film, science fiction, monster, possession film, zombie, comedy, Japanese horror (Godzilla), and so on—even music video horror (Michael Jackson's *Thriller*)! In light of all this genre diversity, I doubt there can be any one "feminist theory of horror." Reflecting on the astounding variety of styles, nuances, and tones within this genre would also lead me to doubt any particular theory that associates gender with the kind of looking, or monstrousness, or victimization that is typical of horror, or with some "work" of abjection that horror films necessarily "illustrate." Films within a single subgenre like the vampire film may present male monsters as distinctive as the emaciated Kinski Nosferatu, the campy Bela Lugosi, the languid Frank Langella, the sinister Christopher Lee, and the macabre ball-goers of Polanski. A quite horrific and gory movie can also be wildly funny (*Texas Chain Saw Massacre II, An American Werewolf in London*). Horror films can be very eerie and subtly creepy (*The Dead Zone*), or they can revel in over-the-top, hair-raising, outrageous effects (*Evil Dead II*). They can be depth-psychological "family romances" (*Repulsion*) or virtual cartoons (*Predator 2*). They can be historical costume dramas (Herzog's *Nosferatu*, Coppola's *Bram Stoker's Dracula*) or technophilic futuristic visions (*Alien*). They can be vividly realistic (*Jurassic Park*) or ridiculously fake (*Godzilla*).

They can be incredibly original (*Scanners, Brain Dead*), mindlessly imitative (*Silent Madness, Orca*), or a little of both (*Body Double*).

I assume, then, that a promising feminist approach to cinematic horror should be historically aware and also broad and open enough to work for all of these varieties of horror. In light of these observations, as well as the list of six criticisms I made in Part 1, the task of building a "feminist theory of horror" may seem monumental. And in fact, this is not exactly what I aim at here. My proposal is perhaps best understood not as a "theory" of horror, but as an attempt to begin making good on some of the deficiencies and positive requirements I have outlined. I suggest a strategy or framework for constructing feminist readings of horror films. My strategy would emphasize the structure of horror films and place special weight on their gender ideologies, in a sense I shall explain further below.

First, it is useful to distinguish various roles that feminism can play in film studies. For convenience I shall label these roles, somewhat pretentiously, the "extra-filmic" and "intra-filmic." By the "extra-filmic" role, I mean to refer to feminist investigations, in a sociological, anthropological, or historical vein, into actual concrete issues concerning the historical context, production, and reception of horror films. In this role, feminist critics would ask questions, for example, about women's motives and experiences in producing, writing, directing, editing, and acting in horror films. Alternatively, they might explore reception theory, looking at actual examples of how various kinds of periodicals and audiences, such as feminist and lesbian audiences, review and read horror films—perhaps in unusually creative and nonstandard ways.[24] Another type of extra-filmic exploration would be that of the cultural historian who aims to locate specific periods or varieties of horror movies within the sort of historical and social context that I find absent in most current feminist theorizing. In this role, feminist critics could examine the links between horror films and related works of literature.

Though I consider all the types of extra-filmic exploration that I have just mentioned very important, my own focus, stemming in part from my own perspective in philosophy—a notoriously nonempirical discipline—will instead be on what I call the intra-filmic questions about horror. My proposal for producing feminist readings or interpretations of horror films is that we should focus on their representational contents and on the nature of their representational practices, so as to scrutinize how the films represent gender, sexuality, and power relations between the sexes. I suggest that feminist readings of a horror film proceed by looking at various crucial sorts of film elements. Some of these elements concern the representation of women and monsters within films. Others explore how the film is structured and how it works. Within my recommended framework, we must shift attention away from the psychodynamics of viewing movies, and onto the nature of films as artifacts that may be studied by examining both their construction and their role in culture. To study their construction we look at such standard features as plot, characters, and point of view. To study their role in culture—that is, to inquire about this as feminists—we examine their gender ideology. This is my chief goal in producing feminist readings of horror films.

Let me offer some clarifying comments here about my proposal. The label "ideology" I borrow from Marxist theory, supposing that an ideology is a distorted representation of existing relations of power and domination. In the particular project I am interested in, obviously, these would be relations of patriarchy or male domination (together with any relevant associated relations of class or race dominance). Feminist ideology critique is a deep interpretive reading that criticizes or analyzes a film's presentation of certain naturalized messages about gender—messages that the film takes for granted and expects its audience to agree with and accept. These will typically be messages that perpetuate the subordination and exploitation of women; they present gender hierarchy or genderized roles and relations that are somehow portrayed as normal in the discourse of the film.[25] Or, occasionally and more interestingly, an analysis of the film's ideology might show that the film itself is raising questions about "normal" relations of gender dominance.

It might be thought that the strategy I favor resembles a somewhat old-fashioned feminist approach to film studies, the "images of women" approach.[26] On this approach, one would analyze a genre of horror like the slasher film, say, by observing how images of women are presented in these films. Thus, typically, young women are shown either as tomboys or as teen-aged sex fiends who somehow deserve their dismemberment at the hands of a Jason or Michael Myers. I do recommend that to explore a film's gender ideology, we ask various questions that would also be asked on this approach, such as, How does the film depict/represent women—as agents, patients, knowers, sufferers? or, What role do women play vis-à-vis men in the film? However, I take feminist ideology critique to go beyond this rather simple set of questions in two main ways.

First, I want to emphasize films as complex functioning artifacts composed of a wide variety of elements, including more than simply the representation of characters. Obviously, films also include technical and formal filmic features such as editing, visual point of view, lighting, sound, and costuming, as well as features shared with literary works such as plots, dialogue, audience point of view, and narrative structure. Feminist ideology critique will explore any or all of these features that seem relevant to understanding a film's presentation of gender ideology. This may include focusing on what Noël Carroll has called rhetorical strategies, such as the elicitation of audience presumptions in completing gaps in the story.[27] So on my approach we would ask questions like these: How do the film's structures of narrative, point of view, and plot construction operate in effecting a depiction of gender roles and relations? Does the film offer a "heroic modernist" narrative of mastery, centered upon a male character, offering up either a clear resolution or a noble tragedy? Or, is there a nonstandard narrative centered upon female characters, offering, perhaps, a more open-ended and ambiguous conclusion? Does the film reference historical or genre precedents—say, a particular earlier vampire film, or the mad scientist genre in general—and if so, how does it comment upon, replicate, parody, or revise the gender thematics of its predecessors? What are the film's implicit rhetorical presuppositions about natural gender roles and relations? Does the film present possibilities of questioning or challenging these presumptions?

Second, I do mean something by calling feminist ideological critique of horror a "deep" interpretive reading. An interesting and creative feminist reading of a film may look "below" its surface representations of male or female characters to consider gaps, presumptions, and even what is "repressed," by which I mean simply blocked, omitted, or avoided, in these representations. My strategy accords with advice laid out by the French feminist Luce Irigaray in her discussions of how to construct disruptive feminist readings of the discourse of the male western philosophical tradition: "The issue is not one of elaborating a new theory of which woman would be the subject or the object, but of jamming the theoretical machinery itself, of suspending its pretension to the production of a truth and of a meaning that are excessively univocal."[28] Referencing Irigaray may seem inconsistent on my part, given that she operates within the Lacanian psychoanalytic tradition. However, Irigaray has in fact written some of the strongest feminist critiques I have read of the most basic assumptions of Freudian and Lacanian psychoanalytic theory. Further, I do not believe that a use of her recommended strategies of reading—for philosophy, literature, or film—must rely on any specific psychosexual assumptions. That is, as strategies of *reading* they work much like deconstructive textual strategies that are logically separable from those psychological assumptions. A brief example may help show this.

Irigaray has written critically about Plato's and Aristotle's treatment of form and matter in their metaphysics. She shows how they regard form as more valuable because they associate it with masculinity and order. Now, it could well be said that Irigaray proceeds by offering some sort of depth psychological reading of how these philosophers treat matter: Plato, as the "womb," Cave, or receptacle; Aristotle as the "envelope" or penis sheath. This sort of reading could be regarded as an analysis of their motives or of the ongoing appeal of Greek philosophical frameworks to subsequent, mostly male philosophers. However, it strikes me that Irigaray's critique functions equally as a deconstructive reading that enables one to question some of the most basic assumptions of the discourse she is examining, in this case, ancient metaphysics. One can find actual passages in which these philosophers associated form with masculinity. So, Irigaray's "deep" reading conforms with my conception of ideology critique, in that she questions the most basic ways in which an apparently neutral and objective field, metaphysics, conceals and contains hierarchized gender notions. One need not accept any psychoanalytic tenets to use this style of reading so as to query the particular discourse at issue, asking in this case, not only why form was associated with masculinity and considered by the ancient Greeks as more valuable than matter, but also what an alternative metaphysical schema would look like.[29]

Similarly, to try to transfer the point of this last paragraph to film studies, Carol Clover, in her examination of the depiction of the feminine in slasher films, has provided something like an Irigarayan "deep reading" that criticizes an existing form of discourse. She points out first, the obvious, that these films typically show young women as somehow bad—too sexy and alluring—before they are attacked by a male. Beyond this, she offers a "deeper" reading by arguing that slashers also reinforce cultural messages about the virtues of masculinity by presenting a villain who is defectively masculine—often someone pudgy, awkward, shy, or seemingly impotent—and a heroine (the "Final Girl") who is more masculine than feminine. I would call this a "deep" reading because it shows that the apparently male villains are actually bad because they are culturally coded as feminine. Where I part ways with Clover is that I reject her assumptions about the need for grounding this sort of reading in the truth of a given psychosexual model (Laqueur's), or about the processes through which slasher audience's psychological investment (and hence pleasure) in these movies alleged reflects certain standard, universal, gender-associated psychological interests.

My recommended approach is continuous with previous approaches to artworks in the Western aesthetic tradition, ranging from Aristotle's account of tragedy in the *Poetics* and Kant's *Critique of Judgment* to more contemporary works like Kendall Walton's *Mimesis as Make-Believe*. Philosophers have typically supposed that it is appropriate in aesthetic theory to discuss aspects of the psychology of our response to artworks, but they have done so without presuming any particularly detailed theory of the psyche. They emphasize that paintings, tragedies, or even landscape gardens are a particular kind of phenomenon, intentionally created and structured to produce a certain kind of effect—catharsis, aesthetic distance, the free play of the imagination, and so on. It is enough for purposes of philosophical aesthetics to employ commonsense, everyday notions of human psychology, to assume that we are capable of being frightened, excited, horrified, and so on, by artistic representations, and then proceed to try to analyze how this occurs.

Adopting my proposed framework means simply that a feminist critic will construct a reading that focuses on gender representation within a film, beginning with a list of specific questions that can vary as appropriate—according to the film's own period, style, and tone. Distinct feminist readings of the same horror film could easily be constructed. It is indeed always possible that a film may not have much to say that is particularly exciting or illuminating on the subject of gender. Also, and importantly, a feminist reading need not be a "complete" reading of the movie that purports to attend to all its many elements.

I believe that my proposal to use a basic set of questions about gender ideology as a broad strategy for feminist film readings helps overcome some of the defects of current feminist film theorizing I enumerated in Part 1, and I want to explain more here how I see it as an improvement. Recall that my first two objections concerned the problematic assumptions of a particular psychoanalytic theory or of psychoanalysis generally. Obviously, my proposed strategy does not encounter these problems. It does not adopt any particular psychodynamic theory or theory of sexual or gender difference. My third objection queried currently dominant presumptions about gender dichotomies between, for example, the aggressive masculine gaze and the passive female spectacular body. I avoid these sorts of assumptions about gender precisely by foregrounding as my first question the issue of *how* a film depicts gender. My fourth objection was a challenge to the theoretical reductivism of dominant feminist film criticism; on this point, I would hope that my strategy opens out to connected issues concerning race, class, and so on.

My fifth objection concerned the narrowness of psychodynamic feminism in comparison to other important forms of feminist theorizing. One could use the map I propose in combination with many types of feminism. For example, to diagnose the gender ideology of a film, one could adopt the viewpoint of a Marxist or liberal feminist; in either case I would suppose one could be critical, though of different aspects of the film, and to different ends. Similarly, a feminist theorist steeped in Foucault or Donna Haraway might ask about some of my questions by looking at very different features of a film— at, for instance, how it portrays disciplines of the female body, or how it depicts women in relation to technology.

My sixth objection stated that one might equally well achieve the insights of feminist psychoanalytic film theory without its propping in a psychodynamic theory. I think that some of the questions I have listed above actually do this, that is, would work to take the place of others posed on the more problematic basis of, for instance, depth psychoanalysis. Questions about "the gaze," the sadistic male viewer, the masculine narrative order, and so forth, are replaced here by questions about whether the film presents women as primarily suffering and tortured physical beings, or whether they are also shown to be alert, curious, intelligent, capable of independent investigation, and so on, and also by questions about whether the women characters help move the narrative along, or are simply targets of the horrific spectacle. I would hope that a careful consideration of these questions would avert reductivism and allow flexibility in recognizing that horror movies often have very complex, mixed representations of women.

Part 3: Illustrations

It is time to illustrate how I would use my own recommended strategy to generate critical feminist readings of horror films and their gender ideologies.

I will first discuss *Jurassic Park* and *The Fly*, films I choose specifically because, on the surface at least, they seem to present positive images of strong, intelligent, and active women. This makes them especially interesting to read for underlying ideologies. Next I shall compare these films to *Repulsion*, a film that on the surface seems problematic because it features a horrific female slasher/murderer, but which I find to present a surprisingly radical questioning of existing gender ideology.

I begin with *Jurassic Park*. First, how does the film represent women? Superficially at least, it displays a contemporary, 1990s feminist vision of women and girls. The female paleobotanist Dr. Ellie Sattler (Laura Dern) is presumably well-educated and authoritative in her own field; she shows enthusiasm and expertise in classifying the ancient plants in the park. She is courageous and physically active, and she makes cracks about the other characters' sexism. And the young girl is said to be a computer hacker.

Nevertheless, we can hardly call the movie an unmitigated feminist achievement. The paleobotanist's own scientific expertise is never treated as especially deep or relevant. It is rather the male scientist Dr. Alan Grant (Sam Neill) who espouses a controversial theory (about dinosaurs' close relation to birds) that will get tested and confirmed in the park. Ellie is shown enthusiastically identifying plant species in the park but, importantly, the plants themselves are not intrinsically interesting here but function only as fodder for the dinosaurs. Thus, even in her scientific role, the woman could be said to be chiefly concerned with nourishment and caregiving. Amazingly, she has never heard of chaos theory, and the male mathematician Ian Malcolm (Jeff Goldblum) explains it to her in the context of a teasing sex scene that treats her like a silly teenage bimbo. This sort of depiction is further enforced by the fact that she is blonde, pretty, slender, and at least ten years younger than her male scientist colleague and lover. Further, through most of the film she, unlike any of the male characters, consistently wears little shorts that show off her long coltish legs.

Similarly, the young girl (Ariana Richards) spends most of the film in abject fear of the T-rex. She is even afraid of the large gentle brontosaurus, who sneezes all over her and makes her look ridiculous. The fact that she is a computer hacker is introduced rather casually and coincidentally toward the end of the film and does not seem especially well integrated into her character. When she manages to get into the computer system, her task is the relatively minor one of figuring out how to get a door to close properly.

Next, how is monstrousness in the film related to femininity? All the monsters (dinosaurs) in the movie are female, but initially it seems that not much is made of this—nothing particularly horrific about primal mothers on the scale of *Alien*, at least. It is not easy to read the feminity of the monsters here, since it is not uniform, but seems to permit a great range of difference: some varieties are huge and voracious; others (the raptors) are smaller, clever, and vicious; yet others are large, gentle, cow-like beings vulnerable to indigestion or colds. I would suggest that the film presents a standard array of culturally coded, negative messages about females through its depiction of these various dinosaurs. Some dinosaurs, like some women, are fat, sweet, and gentle; and others are thin, vicious, and scheming. (There can be, in other words, no sweet, smart dinosaurs!) One could go further in noting that from the perspective of the male scientists who create and study the park, all female dinosaurs have a mysterious sexuality that is "other": their peculiar threat lies in their frog-derived ability to convert their sex so as to be able to reproduce independently. Thus on a deep reading, the female dinosaurs represent a culturally coded threat centering upon a kind of uncontrolled, rampant female sexuality, as well as awesome reproductive abilities.

Another question to ask about in assessing a film's gender ideology concerns who moves the narrative along, who its chief agents are; here, clearly in *Jurassic Park* it is not the woman or girl. There are no women involved in the creation or operation of the park itself. The key human agents of the movie who initiate the chain of events presenting the movie's central problem—the park mogul, the shark lawyer, and the computer wizard—are all men. Men are thus shown in the film as running the show in all the relevant senses: setting up the problematic situations, making them worse, and then resolving them. True, girls can be hackers and scientists, but this seems peripheral to their chief roles, since during most of the action sequences of the movie they are relegated to functions of nurturing the ill or taking care of men. Ellie is not at the center of the key scenes that depict the children's being threatened, then escaping, the tyrannosaurus. Instead, the male scientist/father figure does this, while she is confined mainly to nursing, first the sick triceratops, then the wounded mathematician. Her sudden interest in the sick triceratops seems poorly explained by her alleged scientific expertise in the plants it eats, but it furthers a general depiction of her as caring and nurturing. She has, literally, the ideal human mother's ability to deal with mounds of shit!

On the whole, then, the gender ideology of *Jurassic Park* seems to be to confirm that women, even when they are brave and scientific, must remain pretty, flirtatious, and nurturing. From the very start the film represents it as a central aim in Ellie's life to convince her lover to have children. Thus in the film's trajectory, Grant fulfills his chief aim, demonstrating his scientific hypothesis about dinosaurs, while she fulfills hers in parallel, as one of the film's closing scenes shows her smiling happily (in a view we share) at Alan, now appropriately fatherly, sleeping with the two children he has saved cuddled in his arms. The film's ending thus depicts a resolution that produces a happy, relieved, and idealized nuclear family. It includes none of the foreigners who are lowly park laborers, no computer nerds, no greedy lawyers, and no black members—just the white surrogate parents and grandfather whose regret signifies that he is to be exonerated for his mistakes in the otherwise "innocent" desire to entertain people. Even more significantly, the very last scene of the film is a vision of flying birds—pelicans who, seen in silhouette over the water, resemble pterodactyls. Thus the film concludes with a subtle message that reinforces the "heroic" male scientist's creative vision and theoretical achievement in hypothesizing correctly about the bird-like nature of dinosaurs.

I move now to my second example, David Cronenberg's remake of *The Fly*. In this film, the heroine, Veronica Quaife (Geena Davis), is represented as an ambitious, intelligent, pragmatic, and successful career woman, a science writer. She is also charming, funny, beautiful, and sexually forward—either a fantasy woman who falls straight into bed with men, or the confident new woman assertive about her own sexual desires. True, she could be said to behave in unprofessional ways (having first slept with one of her college professors, who is now her editor, and later with the subject of her current research article)—but so do the men in the movie. More problematic is the fact that she only seems to exist in the film in relations of subordination to men. As a science writer her position is more lowly than that of the creative scientists whose genius she will simply record and report on to the world. Similarly as a writer, she is subordinate to her editor at the science magazine.

These relations of subordination parallel Veronica's position in the film's plot and narrative structure. She exists in the movie primarily in a dependent relationship to the male scientist Dr. Seth Brundle (Jeff Goldblum). The film is a variant on the mad scientist genre, and Brundle is the mad scientist at the center of its narrative trajectory. If this film reaches greater tragic heights than many other mad scientist movies, that may be because it fulfills some of Aristotle's criteria for a tragic plot: the hero is a great man, sympathetic, deserving of our pity, who engages in action that involves some sort of fatal mistake and hubris bringing about his downfall.[30] This film is a narrative about *the man's* activities, his heroism, and tragic downfall. Veronica functions in it as an aspect of his tragedy and loss, and also as a modern variant on the ancient Greek chorus guiding our responses of pity and fear (or in this case, horror). The film often puts viewers into her viewpoint, forcing us to observe from closer up, so to speak, the hideous transformations that occur as the fly takes him over.[31]

The particular horrific threat of this movie is an invasion by the other species of *both* the male and female body. It does take a specific turn against women when the scientist seeks his own rescue by demanding to use, and corrupt, her reproductive abilities (showcased in a disgusting nightmare she has of giving birth to a giant maggot). Yet ultimately it is he and not she who suffers; he is punished for his scientific hubris, as she fights for survival (with some male assistance, but nevertheless she is very courageous) and resists his final appeals to sacrifice herself for him. It is difficult to force a reading of the monstrousness here as a feminization of his body; what makes more sense is to see these transformations as metaphors for aging or for ravaging illnesses like cancer or AIDS.

The Fly's narrative has a very traditional, male-centered and male-driven form: the male scientist exceeds his role and must pay for it. The male acts, the woman feels. She occupies a traditional role in the sense that her emotions and perceptions are clues to guide us, the film viewer, to regard the man, despite his hubris, with love, pity, and sympathy. In *The Fly* as in *Jurassic Park,* the mad scientist who creates the crux of the story is a man, and the woman has to deal with the man's problem; love and empathy are the key female traits. There is no real challenge to this gendered division of labor or to the idea that stories are primarily about men, only secondarily about the women who love them. Consider, for example, the fact that Veronica's own tragedy in this movie is in itself a subordinate tragedy brought about by Brundle's mistake, and one centered in the realm of her body and her emotional life: the loss of a lover, together with a forced abortion. The movie makes absolutely nothing of the fact that she loses out on what could easily be the biggest scientific scoop of her journalistic career! (Indeed, wouldn't the savvy and competitive woman journalist she seemed to be at the start immediately begin writing up the whole thing, complete with video illustrations?) In other words, just as in *Jurassic Park,* beneath the surface depiction of an independent career woman in *The Fly* lies the ideological message that women are primarily creatures of their emotions who exist first and foremost in their love relations to men and potential offspring.

These are two examples of films I have chosen because they seem to offer positive depictions of independent women characters which I believe are undermined by deeper ideological messages. Further, they are interesting to examine in contrast with typical feminist psychoanalytic views because their depictions of the horrific monsters are not the typical ones of castrating woman or primal mother. Instead I would locate the most problematic aspects in their gender ideology at the level of their narrative, which is in each case predominantly a narrative focused on male energies, activities, triumphs, or tragedies.

Now let me shift and describe a very different example of a horror movie with a quite different logic, *Repulsion.* Again I want to argue that surface appearances can be deceiving. On the surface this is a horror story in which a very beautiful and sexy woman, Carol Ledoux (Catherine Deneuve) becomes a mad slasher and villain who attacks and destroys men. One might initially suppose then that this is a sort of film noir anticipating the recent genre of *Fatal Attraction*-style villainess females. Carol seems to be depicted as the alluring yet shy and inhibited femme fatale whose repressed sexuality must unleash itself ultimately in horrific acts of violence against the men she desires. This view of her as repressed and even voyeuristic might seem to be confirmed by various aspects of the plot and the filmic depiction of her; she dresses demurely, speaks in a low voice, hides behind her hair, constantly peers out the windows of her flat, listens in on her sister's sexual moans and cries, inspects and throws away the shaving glass used by her sister's lover, and so on.

However, I think that this surface reading does not capture much that is going on in this film. Many of the point-of-view shots in the movie identify the audience members with leering men, from her erstwhile boyfriend to the construction workers who jeer and whistle at Carol as she walks past them on the sidewalk. On the other hand the film also switches to adopt the young woman's own viewpoint as she is chased and visually assaulted by these men. In doing so, it shows her to be a victim who merits our sympathy and empathy. Thus the feeling of the scene where she overhears her sister's lovemaking is less one of voyeurism than one of tormented embarrassment and the desire to escape. Clearly she feels threatened by her sister's involvement with the man and by her departure with him for vacation. Once she is alone in the flat, Carol becomes increasingly psychotic and delusional. As she goes mad, the audience shares her heightened perceptions, nightmares, and hallucinations. Polanski shocks and frightens us in parallel with her by showing faces that suddenly materialize in mirrors, hands that reach out from rubbery walls, or menacing shadows creeping from above on the bedroom ceiling, accompanied by weird and threatening grunting noises. Given this increasingly deranged system of perceptions, we can actually be persuaded that Carol's reaction as she reacts and kills men who enter her apartment is a reasonable one. This is particularly true when she repulses the advances of her lecherous landlord, who has offered to accept something other than money for his rental payments.

This means that what is really horrific in this movie is not the female killer (as it is, say, in *Basic Instinct* or *Fatal Attraction*); it is instead lechery, male attitudes of lust toward such a beautiful woman. The film highlights Carol's victimization by men and strongly hints that her psychosis and sexual repression stem from a history of child sexual abuse. She cannot escape the pursuit of men who wolf-whistle at her on the street, press her for dates, or attack her in her own apartment. Her sister's lover has carelessly scattered his personal hygiene items all around in the bathroom. She is even trapped in her job as a manicurist in the industry of making women beautiful so as to please men. By repeated shots linking Carol to the naked, stripped rabbit that rots uncooked on an empty plate in her flat, she is represented as childlike, vulnerable, and psychically decaying.

The overall narrative structure of *Repulsion* reflects a logic of disruption and fragmentation rather than resolution; of suffering and reacting, rather than action. The story could not be said to be a tragedy in the classic sense, even one like that of *The Fly*. That is, *Repulsion* does not offer a narrative of a deed and its consequences, or a heroine whose action is somehow flawed, precipitating her tragic downfall. Instead this is a sort of antinarrative that presents an inability to act, a continual waiting, passivity, and suffering. Even Carol's final acts of killing the two men seem to be reactions rather than genuinely intended deeds. Surely Carol does not "deserve" her suffering, nor is she an evil *Fatal Attraction*-style femme fatale. To be sure, this film is not visionary in the sense of offering up an alternative model of gender roles. Nevertheless, it certainly does call existing roles and attitudes into question in a particularly interesting way, by implicating the audience in watching this woman—who is indeed very beautiful—by following her as she walks down the street, by extreme close-ups of her face and appearance—so much so that she begins to seem to want to hide from the camera itself behind her long pale hair.

In *The Fly* too the heroine's story revolves around her emotional suffering, but as I interpreted that film's gender ideology, it represented such suffering as appropriate for a woman character whose fate is basically subordinated to that of the male hero. Her suffering functions as a cue for us in the audience, guiding us to react "appropriately" to Brundle with sympathy and pity. By contrast, in my view *Repulsion* presents a certain gender ideology in such a way as to raise a number of serious questions about it. It constructs a surprisingly critical representation of male sexual desire and the accompanying objectification of women, and it even links this kind of visual objectification to acts of violence and sexual abuse like incest. Moreover, and finally, it suggests that when women fight back against such violence and abuse, their actions may be reasonable and warranted. But it does *not* suggest, as do many movies in the recent "rape revenge" genre, that women who fight back against such abuse will achieve psychological satisfaction or be backed by a powerful judicial system.[32] It would be a less good movie, in my mind, if it did so—more problematically ideological—because it would misrepresent and gloss over existing power and dominance relations within patriarchy.

Conclusion

In closing, I would like to make one cautionary point about my recommended framework for producing readings of horror films that focus on their gender ideologies. One reason I distinguish my recommended feminist ideological critique from an ordinary Marxist sort is that I want to resist a certain sort of Marxist line that places great power within the hands of the productive apparatuses of Hollywood, and correspondingly little power in the hands of audience members, treated generically as members of one social class. I believe that audience members have the power to create individual, often subversive readings of films. To speak of a film's ideology suggests that some powerful agent is distorting a message for sinister purposes of domination and control. This is misleading, I think, both because the nature of the agency in question in filmic representation is actually very diffuse, and also because it makes viewers into powerless Pavlovian dogs. Horror movie viewers are in fact often highly sophisticated and critical; horror movie screenings, in my experience, may be much more participatory than other forms of films. If the dominance relations distorted by ideology in my approach are those of patriarchy, I believe that individual viewers, in particular female viewers, may either see through such relations or reread intended ones in subversive ways. This means that even when a film presents a problematic image of women, the audience reaction may subvert or undercut it. For example, the audience may react so as to bring out the potential dark humor of a scene. Let me offer an example here. Douglas Kellner and Michael Ryan, in their book *Camera Politica,* adopted a more standardly Marxist view of film ideology than my own. Ryan and Kellner discuss, among other topics, sexist ideologies of horror films in the early 1980s, which they interpret as expressing male backlash against feminist advances of the time.[33] They are highly critical, for instance, of the bondage scenes in *Cat People;* their discussion seems to assume that the filmmakers had an agenda that would determine audience responses by buying into their assumed agreement, that is, a shared resistance to new feminist values. Yet when I saw the film in a crowded theater in New York at the time of its release, the audience hooted derisively at just these scenes. That is, they seemed to see through this maneuver of the filmmakers so as to resist the film's surface ideology. Horror films seem often to solicit just such cynical, subversive audience responses.

In this paper I have presented not so much a feminist *theory* of horror films as a framework that I hope will prove useful for producing readings of horror films. I would like to emphasize that in my view, for any given film, a number of feminist readings might be possible. Feminist film readings interpret how films function as artifacts, and to do this they may successfully explore such diverse aspects of a film as its plot, editing, sound track, point of view, dialogue, character representations, use of rhetoric, or narrative structures. But film artifacts function within a context, and the context is constantly changing. I do not contend, for example, that the sort of reading of *Repulsion* I have offered here would have been possible or even appropriate in 1965 when the movie was released. We may see this film differently in retrospect, for example, against the contemporary background of *Fatal Attraction* and *Basic Instinct,* as well as by comparison with the recently emerging genre of the rape revenge movie. Further, there is much greater social awareness in 1995 than in 1965 of problems of incest and child sexual abuse, and these might significantly affect how a feminist of today sees certain slight allusions in the film.

My quick sketch here of film readings of *Jurassic Park, The Fly,* and *Repulsion,* is only that, a sketch. I have mainly intended to suggest how such critical feminist readings can be engaged in, and prove potentially fruitful, without psychodynamic underpinnings. Again, I emphasize films as functioning complex artistic artifacts, and I emphasize audience's critical readings rather than purportedly universal or totalizing psychological responses. My readings ask a set of central questions about films' representations of gender roles and relations, the horrific monster, and the type of resolution presented. I believe that my proposal offers a more flexible, potentially illuminating framework than psychodynamic approaches for constructing creative feminist readings of horror films.[34]

NOTES

1. Laura Mulvey, "Visual Pleasure and Narrative Cinema," originally published in *Screen* 16 (1975); reprinted in Mulvey, *Visual and Other Pleasures* (Bloomington: Indiana University Press, 1990); my page references are to the reprinted version in *Issues in Feminist Film Criticism,* ed. Patricia Erens (Bloomington: Indiana University Press, 1990), pp. 28–40.

2. Feminist critics have argued against Mulvey on various grounds, particularly that she ignores the social and historical conditions of gendered subjects and oversimplifies the role of the viewer/director/camera (so that, for example, a subtler view may be necessary to account for the ambivalence of certain film directors like Hitchcock). See, for example, Mary Ann Doane, "Film and the Masquerade, Theorizing the Female Spectator," in *Issues in Feminist Film Criticism,* pp. 41–57; Jane Gaines, "Women and Representation: Can We Enjoy Alternative Pleasure?" also in *Issues in Feminist Film Criticism,* pp. 75–92; Marian Keane, "A Closer Look at Scophilia: Mulvey, Hitchcock, and Vertigo," in *The Hitchcock Reader,* ed. Marshall Dentelbaum and Leland Poague (Ames: Iowa State University Press, 1986), pp. 231–248; and Naomi Scheman, "Missing Mothers/Desiring Daughters: Framing the Sight of Women," *Critical Inquiry* 15 (Autumn 1988): 62–89. Mulvey's revisions of her view may be found in "Afterthoughts on Visual Pleasure and Narrative Cinema," in *Visual and Other Pleasures.* But for limitations that seem to persist in this volume, see my critical review of *Visual and Other Pleasures* in the *APA Newsletter on Feminism and Philosophy* 89, 2 (Winter 1990): 52–55.

3. Linda Williams, "When the Woman Looks," in *Re-Vision: Essays in Feminist Film Criticism,* ed. Mary Ann Doane, Patricia Mellencamp, and Linda Williams (American Film Institute, 1984), pp. 83–99, and "Film Bodies: Gender, Genre, and Excess," *Film Quarterly* 44 (Summer 1991): 2–13.

4. Julia Kristeva, *Powers of Horror: An Essay on Abjection,* tran. Leon Roudiez (New York: Columbia University Press, 1982).

5. Barbara Creed, "Horror and the Monstrous-Feminine: An Imaginary Abjection," *Screen* 27, 1 (1986): 45–70, and *The Monstrous-Feminine: Film, Feminism, Psychoanalysis* (London: Routledge, 1993).

6. Creed, *The Monstrous-Feminine,* p. 13.

7. Ibid., p. 10.

8. Ibid., p. 42.

9. See Frederick Crews, "The Unknown Freud," *The New York Review of Books* 11, 19 (November 18, 1993): 55–66; Adolf Grünbaum, *The Philosophical Foundations of Psychoanalysis* (Berkeley: University of California Press, 1984): Gilles Deleuze and Félix Guattari, *Anti-Oedipus,* trans. by Robert Hurley et al. (New York: Viking, 1977).

10. See my "Woman, Revealed or Reveiled? An Approach to Lacan via the *Blithedale Romance* of Nathaniel Hawthorne," *Hypatia, a Journal for Feminist Philosophy* (Fall 1986): 49–70.

11. See Kelly Oliver, *Reading Kristeva: Unraveling the Double-Bind* (Bloomington: Indiana University Press, 1993), introduction, "Oscillation Strategies," and chapter 1, "The Prodigal Child."

12. See ibid., chapter 7, for discussion of Irigaray's differences with Kristeva.

13. Stanley Cavell, *Pursuits of Happiness: The Hollywood Comedy of Remarriage* (Cambridge: Harvard University Press, 1981); for feminist departures that build upon Cavell's work, see Naomi Scheman, "Missing Mothers/Desiring Daughters: Framing the Sight of Women," *Critical Inquiry* 15 (Autumn 1988): 62–89.

14. Creed, *The Monstrous-Feminine*, pp. 43–58.

15. For a particularly acute critique of feminist film theory's neglect of race issues, see Jane Gaines, "White Privilege and Looking Relations: Race and Gender in Feminist Film Theory," in ed. *Issues in Feminist Film Criticism*, pp. 197–214.

16. This observation was made by Douglas Crimp in a lecture he delivered at the University of Houston in the fall of 1991.

17. Of course, certain of Aristotle's sexist assumptions may have had an impact on his evaluational schema for tragedies; for more on this, see my "Plot Imitates Action: Aesthetic Evaluation and Moral Realism in Aristotle's *Poetics*," in *Essays on Aristotle's Poetics*, ed. Amelie Rorty (Princeton: Princeton University Press, 1992), esp. pp. 126–28.

18. Noël Carroll, *The Philosophy of Horror: Paradoxes of the Heart* (New York: Routledge, 1990).

19. Carol J. Clover, *Men, Women, and Chain Saws: Gender in the Modern Horror Film* (Princeton: Princeton University Press, 1992). See also my review in *Afterimage* (March 1993).

20. Despite her attention to "rezoning" of gender distinctions and to social factors in horror film plots, Clover still seems at times to fall prey to reductive generalizations or rather simplistic dichotomies and associations between viewer characteristics and stereotyped gender notions. By her own admission, she is mainly interested in why the predominantly male viewers of horror subject themselves to being "hurt" (= "feminized") by the genre. Her fourth chapter, "The Eye of Horror," examines the role of eyes, watching, and gazing in horror films like *Peeping Tom* (1960). On the one hand, Clover argues that this film depicts what she calls the "assaultive gaze" of the camera, which is "figured as masculine" ("A hard look and a hard penis mean the same thing"); but on the other hand, it also critiques that gaze and showcases the "reactive gaze," "figured as feminine, of the spectator" (p. 181).

21. Eugenia de la Motte, *Perils of the Night: A Feminist Study of Nineteenth-Century Gothic* (New York: Oxford University Press, 1990)

22. See Anne K. Mellor, *Mary Shelley: Her Life, Her Fiction, Her Monsters* (New York: Methuen, 1988); and Susan Gilbert and Susan Gubar, *The Madwoman in the Attic*) (New Haven: Yale University Press, 1979), especially chapter 7, pp. 213–47.

23. See James Twitchell, *Dreadful Pleasures: An Anatomy of Modern Horror* (Oxford: Oxford University Press, 1985), and Andrew Tudor, *Monsters and Mad Scientists: A Cultural History of the Horror Movie* (London: Basil Blackwell, 1989).

24. As a parallel, see "Illicit Pleasures: Feminist Spectators and *Personal Best*," by Elizabeth Ellsworth, in *Issues in Feminist Film Criticism*, pp. 183–96.

25. For another example of an ideological examination of horror films that takes a different approach from mine, see Tania Modleski's "The Terror of Pleasure: The Contemporary Horror Film and Postmodern Theory," in *Studies in Entertainment: Critical Approaches to Mass Culture*, Tania Modleski, ed. (Bloomington: University of Indiana Press, 1986), pp. 155–66. Modleski advances a complicated set of reasons for rejecting the ways in which certain postmodern theorists have championed some horror films for allegedly deconstructing the self, revealing the primacy of spectacle, and so on. She sees these films as attacking the feminine through their attacks on represen-

tatives of the family or consumer culture; examples she discusses are *Halloween* and *Dawn of the Dead*).

26. For discussion of this approach, see Noël Carroll, "The Image of Women in Film: A Defense of a Paradigm," *The Journal of Aesthetics and Art Criticism* 48, 4 (Fall 1990): 349–60.

27. Noël Carroll has discussed a somewhat different notion of the ideological effects of cinema. The particular conception Carroll criticizes, the "Althusserian Model," rather narrowly alleges that films' contents and formal structures function to present a certain distorted picture of the viewing subject. Carroll offers persuasive objections to this approach and considers an alternative rhetorical analysis that draws upon Aristotle's, to show how "rhetorical strategies may be implemented in narrative film" (p. 223). Noël Carroll, "Film, Rhetoric, and Ideology," in *Explanation and Value in the Arts*, ed. Salim Kemal and Ivan Gaskell (Cambridge: Cambridge University Press, 1973), pp. 215–37.

28. Luce Irigaray, "The Power of Discourse," in Irigaray, *This Sex Which Is Not One*, tran. Catherine Porter (Ithaca, N.Y.: Cornell University Press, 1985), p. 78.

29. For more thoughts about the usefulness of Irigaray's approach for a non-psychoanalytic feminist analytic philosophical reading of historical texts, see my "Nourishing Speculation: A Feminist Reading of Aristotelian Science," in *Engendering Origins: Critical Feminist Essays on Plato and Aristotle*, ed. Bat-Ami Bar On (Albany, N.Y.: SUNY Press, 1994), pp. 145–87, and "Reading Irigaray Reading Aristotle," in *Re-Reading the Canon: Feminist Essays on Aristotle*, ed. Cynthia Freeland (Pennsylvania University Press: forthcoming), pp. 126–42. Kelly Oliver offers a somewhat similar approach, which she also calls ideology critique in drawing upon both Irigaray and Kristeva's theories, in her article "The Politics of Interpretation: The Case of Bergman's *Persona*," in *Philosophy and Film*, ed. Cynthia A. Freeland and Thomas E. Wartenberg (New York: Routledge, 1995), pp. 233–48. However, I believe that Oliver shows much more sympathy to psychoanalytic accounts of, say, "the maternal" than I do.

30. For some thoughts about the sexism implicit in Aristotle's basic articulation of the nature of tragic plot, see my "Plot Imitates Action: Aesthetic Evaluation and Moral Realism in the *Poetics*," in *Essays on Aristotle's Poetics*, ed. Amelie Rorty (Princeton: Princeton University Press, 1992), pp. 111–32.

31. David Bordwell has suggested that a "reading against the grain" approach might take this film to be a subversive exposé of the mad scientist's "hypermasculinity" ("Nerd becomes barroom thug and rapacious seducer"). While this is an intriguing line of interpretation, I do not think it can work, mainly because of the film's continued sympathy for Brundle. Here again, as I suggest, the fact that Veronica's love and pity persist despite his ugly behavior and transformation is meant to be our guide as to how to react. I think my interpretation of the movie as a high-end horror mad scientist tragedy is more in accord with the plot and its ultimate conclusion when the creature mutely asks to be put out of its misery.

32. On the rape revenge genre, see Carol J. Clover, *Men, Women, and Chain Saws*, chapter 3, "Getting Even," pp. 114–65.

33. Michael Ryan and Douglas Kellner, *Camera Politica: The Politics and Ideology of Contemporary Hollywood Film* (Bloomington: Indiana University Press, 1988), pp. 136–67.

34. For a more extended illustration, see my discussion of *Henry: Portrait of a Serial Killer* in "Realist Horror," in *Philosophy and Film* (New York: Routledge, 1995).

10

Apt Feelings,
or Why "Women's Films"
Aren't Trivial

Flo Leibowitz

It is common for philosophers of art to be interested in the elevating powers of tragedy, but it is equally common to scorn melodrama. Melodrama is typically considered to be bad art and hence of little interest. This is no wonder, since melodrama as a narrative form is typically associated with contrivance, drastic reversals and disasters, and narrow escapes, and, perhaps as a corollary, the emotional responses to melodrama have been dismissed as trivially based. John Morreall, a philosopher, has stated an objection of this kind to the character of the emotions of melodrama. Describing a common objection to sentimentality, he writes:

> Melodramas of the 19th century and their film counterparts in the twentieth, for example, often had as their primary effect getting the audience to feel pity by presenting a one-dimensional innocent character being abused by a villain. What is objectionable here is not the evocation of pity—after all, tragedy does that—but the unsubtlety of the vocation and the shallowness of the emotion. When I find myself crying at just the intended moment in a sentimental film, I feel ashamed that I have let the director manipulate me in so obvious a way. . . . But the director found an easy "pity-releaser," say a completely innocent person being mistreated by a completely evil one, presented it in an unambiguous way, and here I am crying right on cue. The director has simply pushed my pity button. Unlike the pity evoked by great tragedy, the pity evoked by melodrama is emotion that is not coupled with any larger emotions, or with insight into the character or with any new perspective on the human condition. It is quick, easy, thoughtless emotion.[1]

The genre called the women's film is a species of melodrama which, I shall argue, presents a counterexample to Morreall's remarks.[2] Morreall's comments weren't made about these films in particular. But if they are applied to women's films, they would constitute a caricature and this caricature is common enough, so it is worth discussing at some length why the caricature really is a caricature, and proposing an alternative account of these films. That is what this chapter is about.

I

Women's films detail the lives of women in crisis, and in these films, sorrow and anxious concern for a woman protagonist is evoked as a means of calling the audience's attention to her motivations and priorities. Films of this kind evoke a family of emotions related to pity, but these emotions are not trivial. For the audience's "pity," when reanalyzed, is not felt thoughtlessly, and, while these films are meant to be exciting, the excitement is a means, rather than an end in itself. The sorrow and the concern evoked depend on understanding the protagonist in the context of a life history which it is the business of the film to relate and illuminate.

Women's films address the assumptions, conflicts, and ambiguities, which audiences attach to (or are believed to attach to) abstract goods such as love, happiness, autonomy, and material success, and the emotions these films evoke are produced by the representation of these values in the film. This is not to say that all these films amount to philosophical reflections. Generally, they don't, and they typically depend less on revolutionary assumptions than on familiar ones. But their dramatic premises make use of the value-ladenness, and in this respect, the open-ended definition, of concepts with which people tend to be personally invested. In this way, these films address matters of substance.

Women's films are sometimes referred to dismissively as "weepies" and "tearjerkers." These are in fact descriptive expressions, and it's regrettable that they have become derogatory sneers. In fact, women's films typically contain a climactic tearjerking scene. These are the scenes that can move audiences to tears, and they are scenes which have made many women's films famous: for example, Stella Dallas (Barbara Stanwyck) watching her daughter's wedding while standing outside in the rain, Amber (Linda Darnell) giving up her son in *Forever Amber,* Terry (Deborah Kerr) hiding her crippled legs from Nicky (Cary Grant) in *An Affair to Remember.*

The canonical response to these scenes is also a paradoxical one, which suggests further that these films are more complex than they at first appear to be. The paradox is this: these scenes can bring audiences to tears, yet these scenes contribute materially to the enjoyment of the films they're part of. How is it possible for both of these claims to be true? Part of the answer is that these scenes bring audiences to tears because they are sad scenes. Another part of the answer is deeper. Audiences don't watch these films for these scenes alone, nor do they watch in spite of them. Rather, the sad events are part of the characteristic form of these films, and it is the form of these films that engages and pleases audiences, and which evokes emotions.

These scenes are sad scenes because they represent a loss or near loss. But that is not all they do. In addition, in these scenes the audience's attention is drawn to the meaning or the value of what it is lost or nearly lost. This intensifies the sadness, with an added understanding. Walter's (John Boles) dying phone call in the 1932 version of *Back Street* is a particularly striking example of the sources of sadness in these kinds of scenes. The telephone represents the separation which had shaped his relationship with Jean. So this scene isn't just about Walter dying, it replays once more the sad feature of their relationship. This makes the scene sad in a deeper way.[3] Similarly, the wedding scene in *Stella Dallas* is not simply a device to make us feel for Stella herself: it also aims to move the audience with the idea of sacrificing for one's children, or with the more disturbing notion that social mobility is something which the members of the audience may never experience themselves. The empty office at the end of *Soldier in the Rain*, a film which the philosopher Marcia Eaton has described,[4] represents the death and absence of Maxwell (Jackie Gleason). The sadness of this scene is not only sadness for his buddy, Eustis (Steve McQueen), it is also sadness at the meaning of bereavement. The scene serves as a reminder of the space, so to speak, which one person may take up in another's life.

Scenes of near loss work the same way, by representing the value of what was almost lost. In *All That Heaven Allows,* Cary's love for Ron gives her the courage to take her life in what is presented as a more rewarding, though less materially comfortable, direction, and so the near-rupture of their relationship is cause for alarm. *An Affair to Remember* represents Terry's life as serious in purpose but dutiful, and Nick's as glamorous but empty. That's why the audience awaits continuation of their romance. Later, Nick and Terry are reunited, but the reunion may be fleeting. The audience hopes it isn't fleeting, but Terry's pride conflicts with her desire for him, and so it isn't clear how matters will resolve themselves. When she does come forth with the whole story, the audience is relieved, but the relief gives way to something more complicated. The reestablishment of their mutual affection and honesty calls attention to these attributes, and thereby calls attention to what exactly it is that was almost gone for good.

The importance of loss in women's films helps explain the role of outlandish coincidences and accidents in many of them. This is something which is important to explain, since these narrative contrivances may, on the face of it, seem out of place in the women's films, which typically adopted classical forms of film narration where an internal coherence of the film's events could be assumed.[5] The combination of coincidence and internal coherence may sound like a prescription for bad art, but it isn't one. Narrative contrivance in these films serves a purpose: it sets up the scenes of loss and near loss (and, in turn, the response to these crises) which are so important to these films. In *An Affair to Remember,* the intended meeting is thwarted by an auto accident. This, of course, is when the movie really gets started as a melodrama, since it is as result of the accident that the conflict between pride and fidelity arises. In *All That Heaven Allows,* Ron's (Rock Hudson) accident (this time, a fall) forces the timeout which both parties need to recognize what each has so far failed to accept or understand in the other. There is a particularly improbable set of coincidences in *Magnificent Obsession,* a film in which Bob Merrick (Rock Hudson) twice causes major misfortunes to Helen Phillips (Jane Wyman): first, he makes her a widow, then he makes her blind. And she falls in love with him anyway. But even this contrivance can't be dismissed as bad writing, since, taken on its own terms, the story assumes a world in which altruism makes good on the damaging consequences of egoism, and in which the altruism in the world somehow compensates for the egoism in it.

Typically, the scene of loss elicits not only sorrow, but also admiration. Many tearjerking scenes evoke sorrow and admiration at the same time, and part of the enjoyment of women's films is in the experience of these mixed emotions. Consider again the final scenes from *Stella Dallas* and *Forever Amber,* and the scenes in *Dark Victory* in which Judith (Bette Davis) realizes that she is going blind and keeps this a secret from her husband. In each instance, the audience feels both sorrow and admiration for the protagonist and, indeed, the feeling of sorrow enhances the admiration. And in each instance, the protagonist is represented as doing what she has to do—hence our admiration. However, the protagonist presumably wishes that she did not have to do it—hence, also, the sorrow. Thus, Stella presumably would prefer to be inside (but for her daughter's future); Judith would like to fill her husband in (but for her husband's future); and Amber would prefer to raise her own son (but for his future).[6]

The scene of loss is placed within the whole film so as to invite, indeed, to promote, the mixed emotions. Both emotions have to do with the same situation or prospect, but they have to do with the different elements of it. Consider *An Affair to Remember.* The tearjerking scene isn't Terry's implied accident, it's Nicky's surprise return. You pity Terry the possible loss (once again) of Nicky, but you admire her refusal to beg him to take her back. Here, the pity and the admiration respond to the idea of a willful, as opposed to unintended, rupture of the relationship. Likewise, Cary's loss in *All That Heaven Allows* isn't Ron's accident, rather it is the loss of her grown children, for whose sake she had earlier given Ron up. You pity her the loss of Ron, you admire her loyalty to her family. Cary's realization of her mistake changes things. Now you admire her reevaluation and the commitment to personal authenticity it is represented as depending upon, but you pity her the loss of social standing and reputation. In *Stella Dallas,* the mixed emotions respond to different aspects of her daughter's marriage—sorrow at the rupture the marriage represents, joy at the mobility it represents, and admiration for Stella's willingness to accept this mixed blessing. The contrivances of women's films play a role in setting up the mixed emotions, since they set up the scenes of loss by which the mixed emotions are evoked: If Stella could change her style, then her daughter's new life might not have meant a rupture with her; if Ron hadn't been injured in an accident (or, Terry, or Helen Phillips's husband), then there might have been no reexamination and no meaningful romance.

2

Some women's films endorse self-sacrifice, for example, *Stella Dallas, Jezebel, Magnificent Obsession*. Some others appear to punish its abandonment (*Mildred Pierce*). However, this type of film is complemented by a group which presents alternatives to self-sacrifice. Stanley Cavell calls these "melodramas of the unknown woman."[7] A well-known melodrama of this kind is *Now Voyager* in which the once-silenced Charlotte (Bette Davis) reclaims her autonomy and her erotic desires from her family. It's something of an ambiguous case, however, since she doesn't simply reject marriage and motherhood; rather, she redefines them. *All That Heaven Allows* is less ambivalent: Cary decides that her duties to herself outweigh her duties to her neighbors and children, which, the film suggests, she has more than discharged.[8]

The recent film *The Piano* is a melodrama of the unknown woman for contemporary audiences. There are numerous allusions in *The Piano* to *Now, Voyager:* the protagonist who is silent because of a romance that turned out badly, a younger daughter (or, in *Now, Voyager*, daughter figure) who behaves like her mother must once have, a sea voyage to a new life (in *The Piano*, there are two of these). There is even an allusion to a scene of Charlotte's uncertainty about her deeper nature: the scene in which Charlotte observes her reflection in a window, hoping to discover the kind of person she really is. In *The Piano*, Ada's (Holly Hunter) near drowning is a similar stop-time scene. The difference is that where Charlotte is contemplative, Ada simply acts. However, *The Piano* is less about self-knowledge than about self-possession, and the mystery in it is not about what it is that Ada really wants (which isn't a mystery), it's about how she manages to get it. In *Now, Voyager*, sexual connectedness was represented as tactile, with the lighting and smoking of cigarettes. In *The Piano*, as well, sexual connectedness is represented as a tactile experience, rather than a verbal or even a visual one—Ada doesn't speak and George doesn't read, and in both films, longing and its frustration is represented by studied looking.

The Piano contrasts the manifestations of power and of moral and material desires in different characters. By the standard of the film, Ada is a match for George Baines (Harvey Keitel) because she is a match in these respects. The contrast between George Baines and Ada's husband (Sam Neill) is a contrast in attitudes toward power and possession. One desires domination and ownership. The other desires intimacy and autonomy, which are sometimes in conflict. In this way, the film is a melodrama in the additional, older sense of personifying a contrast between evil (the husband) and good (George Baines). Accordingly, the film is not told from either of their points of view. The scene of loss in *The Piano* is the scene where the husband chops off Ada's fingertip with his ax. Here, the film reverts to gothic horror in form, but in content, it is still very much a story about power. The scene comes across not so much as a sad turn, but rather as a horrifying calamity. This is because of the more extensive (and not wholly bodily) loss that is represented by it. Ada's fingertip connects her to the piano and to George and to the people for whom she signs or writes her intentions down. So, the threat here isn't only to deprive her of George, but to deprive her of her agency—powers of expression—altogether.[9] Once again, there are mixed emotions, once again they are pity and admiration, and once again a narrative contrivance makes them possible. Were Ada not withholding speech, her fingers would not represent her connectedness and her power. It is the threatened loss of them that you pity and her regaining them that you admire.

3

In this essay, I have been assuming that a commercial fiction film is a representation of a generic situation, visually realized so as inventively to produce generic effects. These effects are understood here in terms of emotions. In regard to these effects, I have been assuming further that films of different genres (action films, women's films, horror films) provide characteristic and distinguishable pleasures of imagination and that these pleasures are linked to different characteristic emotions or families of emotions, and that the emotions are linked in complex ways to the form of the film.[10] In this framework, therefore, particular emotions or combinations of emotions explain the pleasures of particular genres. Moreover, the desires and aversions which particular emotions include are individuated, that is, sorted into particular desires, and it is this particularity that gives emotions and their components the power to explain the pleasures they explain. Accordingly, the pleasures of women's films depend on feelings of pity and admiration, which depend in turn upon there being included in the film a strategically located scene of loss. The meaning of this loss contributes to the emotional effect of the scene.[11]

By contrast, the analyses of women's films produced within the current paradigms in film studies locate the pleasures of these films in womanly desires. Since the satisfactions of cinema in this tradition are thought to be gendered as male, explaining women's films depends on explaining their feminization of Desire and its satisfaction, along with accounting for how the visual and narrative strategies in the film contribute to this transformation. In this theoretical tradition, the study of women's films becomes the study of the pleasures of the female imagination in contrast to and in conflict with the pleasures of the male imagination, and of the expression of this difference in the films.

These two explanations of the pleasures of women's films explain those pleasures differently, and perhaps not equally well. What follows are some selected, but I think, representative differences between the cognitive explanation that I've offered and the psychoanalytic explanation. In *The Desire to Desire: The Woman's Film of the 1940s*,[12] Mary Ann Doane describes love stories in terms of a desire for the condition of desiring itself. She thus proposes a response which is unconnected to the meaning of what is represented in the film. Further, love stories are said to lack "a meaning effect,"[13] except for love stories using a famous historical event or period as a setting. This suggests that love stories lack meaning insofar as they are about personal rather than historical matters: "The ordinary love story, rather than activating history as mise-en-scène, as space, inscribes it as individual subjectivity closed in on itself."[14] This rescues the familiar appellation of costume drama from the level of a mere sneer, but at the price of trivializing the issues which love stories as love stories raise.

Doane comments further that:

> Symptomatic of this apparent over-reliance on unbounded affect is the exaggerated role of music in the love story. Music is the register of the sign which bears the greatest burden in this type of text—its function is no less than that of representing that which is unrepresentable: the ineffable. Desire, emotion—the very content of the love story—are not accessible to a visual discourse but demand the supplementary expenditure of a musical score. Music takes up where the image leaves off—what is excess in relation to the image is equivalent to what is in excess of the rational.[15]

She appears to be saying here that love stories contain an emotional salience which cannot be represented visually exactly because of its connection to emotion. But this is unwarranted. Films evoke emotion by means of their narratives, and they also express emotion through their visual form. As Doane asserts, music and pictures are different means of expression, but the differences surely depend on more complex relationships than an association of pictures and rationality, and music and irrationality.[16] The role of the music in a film must be explained in some other way.

Doane also writes that:

> The love story, more than other subgroups of the women's film, solicits an identification with the two major actants in the drama. The process is reminiscent of Freud's description of hysterical identification, and in fact, the notion of love as a kind of barely controlled hysteria is widespread.[17]

But there is something wrong with this account, too. First, love is not represented as barely controlled hysteria in the love stories discussed. It is represented there as a strong emotion and as a motivator of actions, and (on a cognitive theory of emotion, at any rate) strong emotions are not intrinsically irrational. Secondly, Doane is assuming that there is some conceptual oddity about love stories, which is that the woman spectator identifies with the romantic couple and therefore must divide herself in a way that doesn't make sense. But this paradox is a false one, because the spectator does not identify with the couple in the sense of imaginarily merging with the couple, and this is the sense which Doane is addressing. You can be invested in the outcome of a fictional relationship without having to imagine being all parties in it, just as you can do in real life.

On a cognitive model of film, identifying with film characters is a cognitive skill, just as identifying with real people is, and the paralleling of the audience's emotions and the emotions of film characters is the result. This is worth observing, because there have been many intellectual traditions which regard the exercise of the imagination with suspicion, and many more in which the imaginations of women are so regarded. The hysteria model of the love story ultimately invites more imagination bashing, and one great merit of a cognitive approach to film is the contribution it can make to showing that blanket suspicions of this kind are unfounded.[18]

A paradox of women's films is that they represent suffering and audiences enjoy these films in some sense for the depiction of suffering rather than despite it. This widely noticed feature of women's films, a feature which melodrama shares with tragedy, may explain the assimilation to masochism by Doane and others of the pleasures of these films. But this assimilation lacks deeper justification. For one thing, the sacrifices for which women's films are known are not presented as occasions for unmitigated misery, but as producing mixed blessings, and the silver lining is the protagonist's rationale (or, if you prefer, her rationalization) for the sacrifice. Second, the protagonist is typically represented as acutely aware of the mixed-ness of these blessings, and the audience, following the protagonist, is aware of it, too.[19]

Doane has argued that a desexualizing intention is sometimes present in women's films. She observes that, in Freud's writings, the masochistic fantasies of his women patients were not sexual fantasies, as they were for his men patients; rather, they were fantasies of escape from sexual demands. Hence, the comparison of the audiences for women's films, which are also fantasies of escape, to masochists.[20] But the link still isn't justified. It isn't only on account of her daughter that Stella Dallas's taste is a cause for alarm; it's on her own account as well. Stella's daughter is not just her daughter; she is the only intimate connection she has in sight, and Stella knows it. Had Stella a second husband or the prospect of one, the final scene might have come across as less tragic. But according to the film, there is no such prospect, and this is a part of its sadness.

A cognitive model of film can treat women's pictures as serious film, or at any rate, as serious as any other genre of popular film. This is no mean result, since the Western, another genre of popular film which was once dismissed as pulp fiction on celluloid, has been elevated to a kind of folkloric form by the institution of film studies. Further, a cognitive model doesn't have to explain the pleasures of imagination as if they were a kind of sickness. This model accounts for the pleasure of the fanciful representation of personal crises in terms of a kind of pleasure in discovery, namely, a discovery of the meanings of certain families of value-laden concepts.

There is nothing inherently female or feminine about women's films on the model presented in this paper, and that may be looked upon as a weakness by some. But it isn't one, because there is a limit to the degree these films are gendered. Both men and women can feel sad when rotten things happen to nice people, which is what happens in these films, and in that respect the term "women's film" is a misnomer. Certainly the point of view of a film is in the film. But I have assumed that gender isn't an intrinsic part of point of view, and that the gendering of imaginative pleasures is not intrinsic to imagination.

NOTES

1. John Morreall, "Cuteness," *The British Journal of Aesthetics* 31, 1 (January 1991): 46.

2. Collections of scholarship on these films include *Imitations of Life: a Reader on Film and Television Melodrama*, ed. Marcia Landy (Detroit: Wayne State University Press, 1991), and *Home is Where the Heart Is: Studies in Melodrama and the Woman's Film*, ed. Christine Gledhill (London: British Film Institute, 1987).

3. The social barriers between men and women and between people of different classes appears to be an additional theme of the film. But I am not emphasizing it here.

4. Marcia Eaton, "A Strange Kind of Sadness," *Journal of Aesthetics and Art Criticism* 41 (1982): 51–63.

5. On coherence in classical film narration, see, for example, David Bordwell, Janet Staiger, and Kristin Thompson, *The Classical Hollywood Cinema: Film Style and Mode of Production to 1960* (New York: Columbia University Press, 1985).

6. It's interesting that all three women are represented as acting from duty and against inclination. American populism, like Kantian moral theory, evidently demands that a degree of difficulty be attached to a moral decision for it to be praiseworthy.

7. Cavell discusses *Now, Voyager* as a melodrama of the unknown woman and as a "systematic negation" of comedies of remarriage in "Ugly Duckling, Funny Butterfly: Bette Davis and *Now, Voyager*," *Critical Inquiry* 16 (Winter 1990): 213–47. For previous discussions of this genre, see also Stanley Cavell, "Naughty Orators," in *Languages of the Unsayable: the Play of Negativity in Literature and Literary Theory*, ed. Sanford Budick and Wolfgang Iser (New York: Columbia University Press, 1989), pp. 340–77; "Psychoanalysis and Cinema: The Melodrama of the Unknown Woman," in *The Trial(s) of Psychoanalysis*, ed. Françoise Meltzer (Chicago: University of Chicago Press, 1988), pp. 227–58; An earlier discussion by Cavell of *Now, Voyager* is "Two Cheers for Romance," in *Passionate Attachments: Thinking About Love*, ed. Willard Gaylin and Ethel Person (Glencoe, Ill.: Free Press, 1980), pp. 85–100. George M. Wilson discusses *A Letter from an Unknown Woman* in *Narration in Light: Studies in Cinematic Point of View* (Baltimore: Johns Hopkins University Press, 1986).

8. It's interesting that *Now, Voyager* also contains a scene of loss featuring mixed emotions, the scene where Charlotte, who is apparently going to marry Elliott, contrives to meet up with Jerry at the Boston train station. You pity Charlotte the apparent loss of her romantic idealism—in marrying Elliott, she'd be marrying a man she loves less than she'd like to—but you admire Charlotte's comprehending that this is exactly what marrying him will mean.

9. The figure of the piano as Ada's voice calls to mind the seventeenth-century

theory of music which compared the expression of emotion in music to its expression in human speech. This antiquarian, though suggestive, analogy is discussed in Peter Kivy's study of emotion in music, *Sound Sentiment: An Essay on the Musical Emotions* (Philadelphia: Temple University Press, 1989).

10. For another example of this approach to film genre, see Noël Carroll, *The Philosophy of Horror; or Paradoxes of the Heart* (New York: Routledge, 1990).

11. In the present paper, as in Noël Carroll's book, an emotion is assumed to be a recognition, though an emotion need not be an insight in the laudatory sense. An emotion in this sense is a response to the very idea of something. Thus, an emotion such as anxious concern may have visceral effects, but these effects are not primarily what anxious concern is. Aristotle and David Hume are two figures who have treated emotion in this way, and this general approach to emotion is sometimes referred to as a cognitive model of emotion. Some recent works in which philosophers have discussed emotion in cognitive terms include William Lyons, *Emotion* (Cambridge: Cambridge University Press, 1980); Ronald de Sousa, *The Rationality of Emotion* (Cambridge: MIT Press, 1987); Patricia Greenspan, "Mixed Feelings: Ambivalence and the Logic of Emotions" in *Explaining Emotion*, ed. Amelie Rorty (Berkeley: University of California Press, 1980); and Cheshire Calhoun, "Cognitive Emotions?" in *What Is an Emotion?* ed. Cheshire Calhoun and Robert Solomon (New York: Oxford University Press, 1984).

Like most generalizations, this general grouping of cognitive models glosses over considerable differences. But the generalization has a point here, in separating one general approach to emotion from a second one. This second approach conceives of emotion as an awareness of bodily agitations, and is also represented in the history of philosophy, for example, in Descartes and William James.

12. Mary Ann Doane, *The Desire to Desire: The Woman's Film of the 1940s* (Bloomington: Indian University Press, 1987).

13. *Ibid.,* p. 96.

14. *Ibid.*

15. *Ibid.,* p. 97.

16. If a musical score can echo the emotions evoked by a song lyric, couldn't a musical score echo the emotions evoked by a film narrative? For a general cognitive theory of emotional expressiveness in music, see Peter Kivy, *Sound Sentiment.*

17. Doane, *Desire,* p. 117.

18. In the previous chapter, Doane writes: "But theories of scopophilia, the imaginary relation of spectator to film, and the mirror phase all suggest that aggressivity is an inevitable component of the imaginary relation in the cinema. In the Western and detective film, aggressivity or violence is internalized as narrative content. In maternal melodrama, the violence is displaced onto affect—producing tearjerkers. Its sentimentality is, in some respects, quite sadistic" (ibid., p. 95).

This connection of imagination, strong emotion, and violence is presented as a suggestive connection only and so it does not do to dwell on it. Still, the passage calls to mind the historical denigration of imagination, and in this respect it is striking that it is presented as an implication of a contemporary theory.

19. William Rothman sees Stella's happiness in the last scene partly in terms of a freedom from attachments, "even the attachments of a viewer." The interpretation of Stella's happiness given in the present paper is a rather more conventional one. (William Rothman, *The "I" of the Camera: Essays in Film Criticism, History, and Aesthetics* [Cambridge: Cambridge University Press, 1988, p. 95]).

20. Doane discusses women's film and masochism in *Desire* and in "'The Woman's Film': Possession and Address," in *Re Vision: Essays in Feminist Film Criticism,* ed. Mary Ann Doane, Patricia Mellencamp, and Linda Williams (Frederick, Md.: University Publications of America, 1984), pp. 78–80.

11

Unheard Melodies?
A Critique of Psychoanalytic
Theories of Film Music

Jeff Smith

The critical concept of "unheard melodies" has exercised considerable power in recent years among film music scholars. According to this line of argument, film music somehow escapes or eludes the film spectator's perceptual awareness during the viewing experience. Because of the primacy of visual elements and narrative and because of certain psychic processes in the spectator, film music is subordinated to the film's diegesis in a manner which renders it inaudible. Though film music serves important narrational and structural functions, it performs these functions "unheard" by the spectator, who is too immersed in the film's fiction to attend to the interplay of image and sound, music and narrative.

Yet one wonders if such claims to inaudibility are not overstated. Certainly, as composer Maurice Jaubert notes, people do not go to the cinema to listen to music.[1] However, Hollywood marketing practices have traditionally placed great importance on filmgoers' awareness of film music in the sale of sheet music and soundtrack albums. It seems illogical to suggest that film spectators pay great attention to film music when it is playing on their stereo but ignore it once they are in the theater seated before the flickering images on the screen. Far from being "inaudible," film music has frequently been both noticeable and memorable, often because of the various demands placed upon it to function in ancillary markets.

The consideration of film music within its economic context raises a number of significant theoretical questions regarding the notion of film music's "inaudibility." Because of its extratextual autonomy, popular film music leads us to ask whether there are moment in a film in which its music shifts toward the forefront of a viewer's perception. Moreover, because it offers prima facie evidence against notions of spectatorial absorption, we might also ask the extent to which the various narrational functions of film music depend upon the viewer's awareness of it.

I wish to address these questions by problematizing the conventional wisdom of film music's subservient relation to the image. I will argue that though this may serve as a general way of thinking about film music, it is a simplistic and reductive description of how music actually functions in a film, one that is incapable of addressing the variability of both its narrative functions and our responses to it. The first part of the essay will discuss how the notion of inaudibility informs the fundamental precepts of current film music theory. Much of this recent work has incorporated various aspects of psychoanalytic and suture theory in film, and I will review what I take to be the most powerful claims articulated within this theoretical framework.[2] In the second section, I will offer a critique of these models by analyzing the central paradox upon which they are founded, the notion that a good score is one you do not hear. Lastly, I will also offer a provisional alternative to these models in a brief analysis of Franz Waxman's music for *Love in the Afternoon* (1957).

Film Music and Contemporary Theory

Though the notion of inaudibility has taken on renewed strength in the wake of Post-Structuralist film theory, it is important to remember that the concept has a long tradition in film music studies, one embraced by both theorists and practitioners alike. As early as 1936, Kurt London posed this apparently elemental question about the relation between film music and its auditor. London asked:

> But then how did one hear film music? Did one hear it all? Music heard in the concert-hall differs fundamentally from music heard in films, because absolute music is apprehended *consciously*, film music *unconsciously*. In the course of the musical illustration of a film familiar or characteristic bars of music may have struck the filmgoer once or twice, but otherwise he could hardly have told you, especially in an instance of well-made music, what he had really heard. Only at points where the music diverged from the picture, whether in its quality of meaning, was his concentration on the picture disturbed. Thus we reach the conclusion that good film music remains "unnoticed."[3]

Early film music theorists were not alone in their interest in this problem; many composers echoed their sentiments. In a 1949 *New York Times* article, Aaron Copland wrote: "No discussion of movie music ever gets very far without having to face this problem: Should one hear a movie score?"[4] RKO composer Roy Webb adds that "unless you want them to be aware of it for a particular reason, . . . you can hurt a picture a great deal by making audiences conscious of the music."[5]

Though many reasons are given for the composer's concern about the audience's awareness of the music, the most common is that the music will somehow distract the audience from the narrative and the visual action. Such wariness is evident in composer Miklos Rozsa's warning, "If the music is too complicated, too technical, the public, whose attention is to a far greater ex-

tent directed towards the visual image, will never get its message."[6] Moreover, as Max Steiner noted, the music must not only have an emotional directness, but also must maintain a certain median level of quality in order to
be appropriate for the film. According to Steiner, "The danger is that the
music can be so bad, or so good, that it distracts and takes away from the
action."[7]

Because they feared confounding and distracting film spectators, classical
Hollywood composers operated according to a set of implicit aesthetic guidelines through which they fashioned scores which can be fairly described as
self-effacing, subtle, and unobtrusive. As numerous film music scholars point
out, classical Hollywood composers developed a number of scoring practices
designed to assure both film music's appropriateness and unobtrusiveness.
Among these were the practice of sneaking (beginning a cue at a low volume
underneath dialogue); the use of instrumental colors that would complement
rather than clash with the actor's speaking voice; the careful timing of sequences; and the development of click tracks (sequences of audible, metro-
nomic clicks used to synchronize music and image), which furthered the possibility that music might be meticulously fashioned to fit on-screen actions.

Additionally, during the classical Hollywood era these scores served a remarkably stable set of narrative functions. As early as 1949, Aaron Copland
suggested five general areas in which film music served the screen: 1) it established a convincing atmosphere of time and place; 2) it underlined the unspoken feelings or psychological states of characters; 3) it served as a kind of neutral background filler to the action; 4) it gave a sense of continuity to the
editing; 5) it accentuated the theatrical build-up of a scene and rounded it off
with a feeling of finality.[8]

Most current theories of film music are derived from each of these ideas.
However, in developing a model of film music's inaudibility, contemporary
scholars make a critical move that separates them from their classicist predecessors. For Hollywood composers and early film music theorists, the notion
of unobtrusiveness was only an implicit aesthetic criterion governing the production of film music, a kind of pragmatic guideline employed to create dramatically effective scores. In contrast, recent theorists like Claudia Gorbman
and Caryl Flinn extend the principle of unobtrusiveness to film reception and
spectatorship. They argue that because composers intended film music to be
elusive and unnoticeable, it was rendered transparent, invisible, and inaudible
to movie audiences. In this respect, these models bear important links to the
various suture and enunciation theories that predominated in the field
throughout the seventies and eighties, and it is in this context that this work
is best understood.

Historically, suture and enunciation theories grew out of a burgeoning interest in linguistics, semiotics, and psychoanalysis as they might be applied to
cinema. Theorists such as Raymond Bellour, Christian Metz, Jean-Pierre
Oudart, Colin MacCabe, Daniel Dayan, and Stephen Heath all suggested

ways in which stylistic elements were constituted as a kind of cinematic discourse, and further explored the various ways in which this discourse engaged the psychic processes of the spectator. Though the theories often diverged in the specifics, what unified this work was an overarching interest in how the classical realist film effaced all marks of its cinematic construction and established a subject position which bound the spectator into the fiction. By masking the operation of cinematic narration, this "suturing" was believed to produce a text which was both seamless and transparent in terms of its discursive structures.[9]

In this context, the claim for film music's inaudibility is primarily a consequence of its function as narration. Parallel to the way in which camera movement, framing, and other stylistic devices are said to be rendered invisible by the dual processes of suture and narrativization, film music is supposed to be made inaudible by these seemingly elemental facets of filmic signification. Interestingly, the importance of Stephen Heath's concept of narrativization to contemporary film music theory is echoed in Flinn's claim that it is "finally *narrative* that requires music's fullest servitude."[10]

However, rather than simply rest on the conclusion that film music is inaudible, psychoanalytic critics argue that this very property assigns film music a privileged position within a suture model. Because of its tendencies toward both inaudibility and abstraction, film music is thought to be especially well suited to the process of binding the spectator into the world of the fiction. Though individual theorists will emphasize different aspects of music's greater play of signification, they collectively maintain that music stakes a special claim on the spectator's psyche by returning the subject to a preoedipal, prelinguistic state, and restaging the primordial childhood experience of maternal loss. Film music skulks guerrilla-like in the perceptual background, attacking the subject's resistance to being absorbed in the diegesis and warding off potential censorship by the subject's preconscious.

Within a psychoanalytic framework, the reason film music is able to do this is because of its direct access to the spectator's psyche. According to the oft-cited theories of Guy Rosalato and Didier Anzieu, sound plays an important role in the constitution of the subject. The infant experiences auditory space as a kind of "sonorous envelope," which is made up of the sounds of the child's body and environment. Rosalato suggests that the pleasure of listening to music inheres in its invocation of the subject's auditory imaginary in conjunction with a preoedipal language of sounds associated with the primordial sonorous envelope. Rosalato even goes further to argue that Western musical harmony, the movement away from and return to a tonal center, replays the subject's nostalgia for the maternal body.[11]

In applying this idea to cinema, critics argue that the pervasiveness of background music in sound film is inherent in its evocation of the psychic traces of the subject's bodily fusion with the mother. Film music fosters the regression of the subject during the viewing experience, and helps to create what Jean-

Louis Baudry calls the "subject-effect" of cinema.[12] Music's special relation to the spectator's psychic experience is exploited in classical cinema to abet the process of suture by both fusing the subject to the screen, which Baudry argues is analogous to the mother's breast, and encouraging the spectator's narcissistic identification of his or her own perceptions with that of the film.

In explicating the reasons for this pervasiveness, Gorbman argues that film music serves two overarching functions in the sound film, one being semiotic and the other being psychological. In either case, film music, like other kinds of utilitarian music, "lulls the spectator into being an *untroublesome* (less critical, less wary) *viewing subject.*"[13] In doing so, film music must fend off two potential displeasures which threaten the spectator's filmic experience. The first is the threat of uncertain signification, what Roland Barthes has called "the terror of uncertain signs."[14] In defusing this threat, film music uses its cultural codes and connotations to anchor the image in meaning. Like a photographic caption, music harnesses the elusive visual signifier, and assures us of a safely channeled signified.[15]

Second, film music also fends off displeasure by diverting the spectator's potential awareness of the technological basis of cinematic discourse. Like the primordial sonorous envelope, music's bath of affect is thought to smooth over gaps and roughnesses, cover spatial and temporal discontinuities, and mask the recognition of the frame through its own sonic and harmonic continuity.[16] By veiling the lacks and deficiencies of other discursive structures, film music, according to Gorbman, lubricates the various cogs and pistons of the cinematic pleasure machine, and thereby eases the spectator's absorption into the diegesis.[17] In this respect, film music does not so much displace the importance of narrative in engaging the process of suture, but rather makes narrative a more efficient means of implementing the identification upon which the text's positioning of the subject depends.

Significantly, any psychoanalytic theory of film music will depend quite heavily on the concept of inaudibility. According to Gorbman, "Were the subject to be aware (fully conscious) of its presence as part of the film's discourse, the game would all be over. Just as the subject who resists being hypnotized might find the hypnotist's soothing language silly or excessive, the detached film spectator will notice the oversweet violin music in a romantic scene. Like the good hypnotic subject, on the other hand, the cinematic subject receptive to the film's fantasy will tend not to notice the manipulations of the background score."[18]

Caryl Flinn also cites Rosalato, Anzieu, and Barthes in her account of film music's appeal to spectators. In contrast to her colleagues, however, Flinn is less concerned with how these theories relate to cinema's construction of a subject-effect than she is with how they connect with various facets of Romantic ideology. Flinn asserts that the link between music and the maternal is expressed in the child's primordial fantasy of wholeness, an illusion that is ruptured upon the subject's move from the Imaginary to the Symbolic and the child's entry into language. In Julia Kristeva's view, music, as a kind of preoedipal, poetic language, returns the subject to this point of origin, and responds to the traces of the subject's Imaginary feeling of fusion with the mother, with its attendant associations of nostalgia and plenitude.[19]

For Flinn, this same concern for nostalgia and plenitude is evident in classical Hollywood film music and the Romantic ideology which supported it. Romanticism's drive toward the unity and totality of the artwork was itself a kind of expression of the idea of lost plenitude. Classical film music thus taps into this primordial experience and confers upon the film text a feeling of completeness or unity that the cinematic apparatus cannot maintain without it. Moreover, because of the widespread cultural associations music has with notions of nostalgia and utopia, music in film activates the spectator's nostalgia for a lost and idealized world outside the structures of capitalism, which one might argue is itself the social mirror of the childhood drive for unity and plenitude. As Flinn tries to show through textual analysis, films noirs and melodramas offer particularly clear examples of film music's relation to nostalgia because of their obsessive investment in lost objects and anterior moments.

Throughout *Strains of Utopia*, however, Flinn's relationship to psychoanalytic theory is far more distanced than that of other critics.[20] Flinn's book is not so much a theory of film music as it is an analysis of how a particular ideology of music functions within Romantic, Marxist, and psychoanalytic discourses. Yet the notion of film music's inaudibility is no less important here; according to Flinn, although film music's abstraction constituted a threat to the classical Hollywood cinema's production of meaning, this threat was diffused by placing this music entirely in the context of a visual narrative.[21]

As I noted in my introduction, however, there are a number of reasons for questioning film music theories based on notions of inaudibility. For one thing, the concept itself was often questioned by the same Hollywood composers whom suture theorists believe to be its chief proponents. Max Steiner, for example, responded to the suggestion that a good score is unheard by asking, "What good is it if you don't notice it?"[22] Miklos Rozsa was even more direct in his criticism of the idea. Said Rozsa, "I don't know who originated the idea that good film music is the kind that isn't heard, but I disagree entirely with this silly theory. Music should be heard, even if it is heard subconsciously. . . ."[23]

Though these composers state their objections baldly, a much more subtle criticism lurks within their statements. They hint at the fundamental paradox of classical film scoring: though composers intended their music to be unobtrusive or "unheard," they also realized that it must nevertheless be "heard" in some sense in order to serve any narrational function. Indeed, if film music is to play any part in the text's construction of meaning through its cuing functions, it could not act only on the unconscious, but would need to be perceived and cognized by film spectators. Put this way, the question becomes not one of whether or not spectators actually hear film music, but rather a question of the level at which such perception takes place.

By itself this claim does not really weaken a psychoanalytic account of film music. For one thing, some theorists disclose an awareness of this paradox. Gorbman, for example, continually sets the term "inaudibility" in quotes to acknowledge the obvious fact that "of course, film music can always be heard."[24] Moreover, as both Flinn and Gorbman's models indicate, there is no reason why film music in theory cannot both serve narrational functions and contribute to the film's creation of a subject-effect. Rather, what the issue of spectatorial perception suggests is that the relation between the score's unobtrusiveness and its narrational functions is far more complex than that presented in either model.

The major question elided in psychoanalytic models is that of how the spectator moves from an unconscious to a conscious apprehension of film music's effects as a part of the film's narration. For example, how does one know that Max Steiner's "Tara" cue in *Gone with the Wind* refers to Scarlett O'Hara's ancestral home if the music is perceived entirely at an unconscious level? Likewise, how does a spectator know that "As Time Goes By" in *Casablanca* refers to Rick and Ilsa's past love affair if that melody remains "unheard" throughout the film? In each case, important elements of the story, characters, and settings would be missed if the spectator were always unaware of the music.

Though these counterexamples are particularly notable because of the familiarity of these scores, they are neither isolated nor exceptional. As Kathryn Kalinak points out, there are usually a number of instances in a classical film in which music is privileged over other elements of the soundtrack, and becomes more noticeable by virtue of this priority. Using Erich Korngold's *Captain Blood* as a case study, Kalinak argues that credit sequences, montages, and moments of spectacle are typical examples of this phenomenon. Generally the sound mixing of these moments also makes them more noticeable: naturalistic sound disappears, the volume of the music is boosted, and music becomes the only sonority on the soundtrack.[25]

To these we might also add the cases, too numerous to list, in which music is used by the classical Hollywood composer to convey some bit of information that is not evident in the visual track. Mark Evans offers an example of this in Alex North's score for *A Streetcar Named Desire;* whenever Blanche recalls her husband's suicide, a dance tune called "Varsouviana" arises to signify this process of memory. Here cues of performance, camerawork, and mise-en-scène are used to show Blanche thinking, but it is North's music which conveys the substance of her thoughts.[26]

In all of these examples, music is foregrounded in order to further the spectator's sense of structural unity or narrative coherence. The range and frequency of such moments in classical cinema suggest that filmgoers are quite commonly made aware of film music as a part of the cinematic experience, and that these moments are so highly codified and conventionalized that they neither disrupt nor weaken the cinematic illusion, but rather encourage narrative comprehension.

Consequently, a psychoanalytic model would seem to require some mechanism through which the unconscious apprehension of film music yields the cognitive awareness of how music cues setting, mood, or character. Still, the very possibility that the spectator might be aware of the film's music itself problematizes the whole process of suture. If Gorbman, for example, is right in claiming that "noticeable" music reminds the viewer of cinema's materiality and thereby weakens the subject-effect, we must then conclude that the spectator is constantly slipping in and out of the very subject position that the text has constructed for him, incessantly moving between identification and cognition, pleasure and unpleasure, belief and disbelief, rapture and distance. However we might describe such a shifting of psychic registers, it would not seem either easy or unproblematic.

In addition, this slippage would seem further exacerbated by the intermittent nature of film music. Because psychoanalysis asserts that music bears a special relationship to psychic mechanisms and thus is a particularly important component of the suture process, one might well ask what happens to the spectator in sequences or entire films where music is not present. Long stretches of a film like *A Marked Woman* (1937) or *Lifeboat* (1944) do not include any music whatsoever, diegetic or nondiegetic. *Out of Africa* (1985) contains only 35 minutes of music in its nearly 2½-hour running time. In the latter case, we might well ask what happens to us during the two hours where music is absent. If music is indeed a "hypnotic voice" aiding the spectator's passage into subjectivity, are the seams of the text and the machinery of the apparatus made more apparent when the hypnotist is gone? Or put another way, if music is so spellbinding, why don't all mainstream films use it all of the time?

The intermittence of film music similarly problematizes the metaphor of music as enacting a series of lost phantasmatic representations in the subject. Psychoanalytic critics are attracted to the metaphor of the "sonorous envelope" because it depicts music's drive toward unity, completeness, and plenitude in its positioning of the subject. However, the intermittent nature of film music suggests that it is at best partial and fragmentary, a slatted playpen rather than a womb, a topical lotion rather than an enveloping bath. Though Jerry Goldsmith's music for *Patton* might well function nostalgically within the context of the film's narrative, it strains credibility that plenitude could arise from a score that is present in only 30 minutes of a 3-hour film. Viewed this way, film music could be at best an aesthetic sealant applied only when gaps threaten to break through the text's smooth surface, and not a cure-all for the inherent deficiencies of editing or framing.

Though the question of intermittence is usually not addressed by psychoanalytic theorists, their failure to consider it leads them into a familiar trap in contemporary theory: frequently theorists give a sweeping causal account of some cinematic device or effect, but do not think through the consequences generated by their hypotheses. Contemporary film theorists are often so concerned with detailing the particular psychological effects of some device that they forget about what must happen when the device is absent. In this instance, the premises of suture theory dictate that music's absence unequivocally weakens the text's production of a coherent subject position. Where music is not present to cover the gaps associated with editing, framing, and the silences of the soundtrack, there is a concomitant threat to both cinematic identification and cinematic pleasure. Without music's special connection to the unconscious, cinematic articulation is once again endangered by the threats of uncertain signification and the spectator's recognition of film's materiality. Moreover, the absence of music should make the censors of our preconscious more wary, and heighten our sense of disbelief in the cinematic illusion. Here again the absence of film music would seem to produce a spectator that is constantly wavering between belief and disbelief, pleasure and unpleasure.

So far my objections hinge on the special relationship between music and subjectivity which usually subtends psychoanalytic theories of film music. Speaking hypothetically, one could overcome these objections by denying film music this unique link to the spectator's psyche. In other words, a theorist might contend that the suture effect is overdetermined in classical cinema, and that the absence of one device, such as music, does not negate either the suture process or the creation of a coherent subject position. According to this line of argument, music is not needed at all times during the film, but rather only at moments when the text's gaps, fissures, and discontinuities are especially menacing or threatening.

Still, if one were to adopt this position, the suture theorist would nonetheless be faced with the problem of how one sets apart those moments in a film when music is present from those moments when it is not. In a given film, are there scenes where the discontinuities are obviously more threatening—and thus in need of suture—than other scenes where there is no music? What are some examples? Can we draw any general correlations between patterns of editing and framing that seem to require music versus those that do not? Is it really plausible to believe that such intermittent music appears at just those places where particularly menacing fissures gape and at no others?

In considering these questions, experience and common sense tell us that we do not and cannot draw distinctions between scenes where film music is present and scenes where film music is absent. We view a film in its entirety in roughly the same way. We watch those sequences without music as attentively as those with music. Our suspension of disbelief is as strong in those segments unaccompanied by music as those with it. The cinematic apparatus is no more visible in those scenes lacking music as those where it is present. In summary, a theorist might mitigate some criticisms by arguing that music is the same as other suturing devices, but this places the suture model in the untenable position of claiming that film music has no special relation with the spectator's psychology. And without that relation, one is inevitably led back to the problem of why film music is necessary in the first place.

Moreover, by calling film music "unheard," suture theories advance a model of spectatorship in which the viewer is a kind of passive receptacle of musical affect, a repository of subject effects which he can neither understand nor consciously perceive. The source of this monolithic conception rests ultimately on a false assumption regarding differing modes of musical apprehension. Too often suture models of film music presume a drastic opposition: either the listener consciously attends to all the complexities and details of musical structure, or the listener completely ignores all aspects of music as a component in the film. Given these two alternatives, the only person who could get anything from a film score would be someone who was musically educated and familiar with Western classical musical codes. This is undoubtedly one way to approach a score, as many textual analyses of film music demonstrate, but I would argue that film music and music more generally is apprehended through a variety of different listening modes and competencies.

As philosopher of music Peter Kivy points out, listeners often bring a variety of different strategies to the interpretation of music, and these strategies lie along a continuum of increasingly complex musical cognition. Borrowing four characters from E. M. Forster's *Howards End* to illustrate this point, Kivy argues that these strategies range from a kind of gross, almost physiological response, the toe tapping of untutored listeners, to the close attentive apprehension of musical form and structure. In between these extremes, however, lie two other interpretive strategies of untutored musical listeners: the free association which takes music to be representational, and the understanding of music in terms of emotional expressivity.[27] Though we might not posit these as ideal listening strategies, they are nevertheless very common ones, and they are complex enough to require a general grasp of musical expression from the tempo, modality, orchestral color, and dynamic levels of a given piece. More important, I would argue that most film music is apprehended using these middle levels of musical cognition. To return to the examples mentioned earlier, our recognition of the "Tara" theme or "As Time Goes By" theme actually depends on a rather broad understanding of these themes' function as a form of internal musical representation. Similarly, our gross recognition of stylistic parameters and cultural connotations allows us to attribute a particular emotional cast to the music's accompaniment of a scene.

It is important to remember, however, that in none of these different interpretive strategies is our understanding mindless or unconscious. According to cognitive music theorists Fred Lerdahl and Ray Jackendoff, even the most basic of these strategies, the identification of a pulse or beat, involves a complex set of mental operations that include establishing a kind of metric hierarchy, breaking a phrase into smaller and smaller chunks or groups, and identifying the middle level of that hierarchy that provides the basis for a piece's metric organization. Suture theories often overlook these more mundane aspects of musical perception by claiming that "hearing" music necessitates comprehending complex musical structures and leitmotivic organization.

Given all of these theoretical difficulties, one might well heed Noël Carroll's suggestion that psychoanalytic models of film narration only be sought when rationalist and cognitive explanations either break down or are exhausted. Put this way, contemporary film music theory's neglect of cognitive explanations is extremely troubling. A cognitive account of film music would not only more directly address the issue of the spectator's awareness of film music, but would also address the spectator's mental activities in utilizing cues that musically convey setting, character, and point of view. Indeed, a growing body of literature on musical cognition shows that this would be a fruitful area for further research into the phenomenology of film music.[28]

Undoubtedly, however, such cognitive account would still have to grapple with issues of musical representation and expressivity. As such, we might profitably proceed along the lines sketched out in Noël Carroll's theory of "modifying music."[29] Though this section of *Mystifying Movies* is brief, it offers a cogent examination of how music and image reciprocally function to create meaning. Music, which acts roughly like a linguistic modifier, helps to clarify the particular mood, character, or emotive significance of a scene or visual action. The visuals, narrative, dialogue, and sound effects, on the other hand, imbue the music track with a referentiality that it inherently lacks. What Carroll describes here is not so different from Gorbman's *ancrage* function. However, where Gorbman sees this phenomenon as a means of warding off psychic disturbance, Carroll sees it as an aspect of musical cognition, a means of enabling spectators to gauge the emotional qualities of a scene.

Further research into an alternative model of film music could proceed along a similar path. Carroll's concept of modifying music might be correlated both with various musical codes and stylistic parameters, on the one hand, and with Kivy's different interpretive strategies on the other. Additionally, an account of musical cognition could also be employed to address film music's other functions, its various means of representation, and its ability to provide a sense of structural unity.

Toward an Alternative Model of Film Music

To get a sense of what such an account might look like, I will briefly analyze Franz Waxman's score for *Love in the Afternoon*, a Billy Wilder comedy starring Audrey Hepburn, Gary Cooper, and Maurice Chevalier. Though the score adapts six different popular melodies, one theme, the 1932 classic "Fascination," is especially prominent in terms of the music's structure and function. Through its repetition and its explicit identification of "Fascination,"

Love in the Afternoon is at once typical in its adherence to classical Hollywood scoring practices and unusual in the degree to which it makes apparent the spectator's cognition of film music's narrative functions.

As befits a Lubitsch-style romantic comedy, *Love in the Afternoon* has a rather complexly plotted narrative involving jealous husbands, deceptive lovers, and a charming but cynical detective. The detective, Claude Chavasse, is hired by a man (known only as "Mr. X") to investigate his wife's trysts with an American playboy named Frank Flannagan. Claude reports that the couple have been discreetly meeting for a week in Flannagan's hotel suite, accompanied by a Gypsy band and an army of servants. Upon learning of the affair, Mr. X loads his gun and threatens to shoot Flannagan that night just after the Gypsies complete their performance. Ariane, Claude's daughter, overhears their conversation while eavesdropping, and decides to warn Flannagan of the impending assault. Later that night Ariane sneaks into the suite and takes the place of Mrs. X as Flannagan's "lover." A drunken Mr. X bursts into the suite, but is embarrassed to find that Flannagan's date is not his wife after all.

Intrigued by his mysterious savior, Flannagan asks Ariane to return the next afternoon. She does, but refuses to give any personal information about herself, including her name, and pays lip service to Flannagan's philosophy that no emotional involvement means no pain and no tears when they must inevitably separate. However, when Flannagan's interest seems to wane, Ariane feigns a profligate sexual history using information gleaned from her father's files.

Though he doubts her stories, Flannagan becomes obsessed with learning the truth about his mysterious lover. Flannagan hires Claude to investigate Ariane's stories but can give him very little information about her identity. Flannagan knows only a few sketchy details about her past relationships and that her name begins with the letter "A." Claude ultimately realizes his daughter's involvement with Flannagan, and asks him to end their relationship before Ariane becomes too emotionally involved. However, instead of breaking it off, Ariane and Flannagan are united in a romantic closing scene at the Paris train station. From Claude's voice-over, we learn that they become husband and wife, thus closing the case file of Mr. and Mrs. Frank Flannagan.

To be sure, the importance of "Fascination" to this story is signaled in some measure both by its appearance during the credits and through the careful motivation of the theme within the diegesis. The characters are continually humming, whistling, and playing "Fascination," and these diegetic cues often play a crucial role in advancing the film's narrative. Claude's meeting with Mr. X early in the film offers a good example of this diegetic function and the way in which it firmly establishes the identity of the tune. Describing a typical rendezvous between Flannagan and Mrs. X, Claude notes that, among other things, the Gypsy band plays a program of music that includes some Liszt, some Lehar, and always concludes with "Fascination" at five minutes before ten. Claude asks Mr. X if he knows the tune, but the latter only groans in response. Mistaking the groan for singing, Claude remarks, "That's not the way it goes," and proceeds to hum "Fascination" for both Mr. X and the audience.

While waiting to warn Flannagan, Ariane overhears the band playing "Fascination" outside the door of his suite. At this point, the spectator has been clearly cued to both recognize the song and to understand the events which will be initiated by the song's conclusion. By delaying the shooting and restricting our knowledge, the narration momentarily uses the theme to create suspense and to allow Ariane the opportunity to somehow prevent the attack. Ironically, the music does not achieve suspense by adopting a menacing or threatening character, but rather by playing against these emotions. In Carroll's terms, the neutrality of the music actually reinforces the emotional hue of the film by underscoring the scene's comically suspenseful tone. The music cues us that Mr. X is not a real threat, but rather merely a stock character—the cuckolded husband—of romantic comedy.

When Ariane warns Flannagan of Mr. X's presence outside the suite, however, the function of "Fascination" suddenly changes again. From this point on, the theme will denote the evolving relationship between Ariane and Flannagan, and the film's music will help to chart their movement from attraction to romantic obsession to love.[30] Having been made aware of the song's title, the audience recognizes it as an astute comment upon the mental states and feelings of the central characters. Thus throughout the remainder of the film, the tune will consistently serve as a handy reminder of Frank and Ariane's increasing "fascination" for one another.

The importance of this new function becomes apparent in the sequence which follows. Ariane's boyfriend, Michel, who had taken her to the Ritz, hears her singing "Fascination" and remarks, "Will you stop humming that idiotic tune? It lacks any musical merit whatsoever." Even when Ariane does stop humming, however, the song continues to haunt her imagination. As Ariane dreamily picks up her cello and enters her apartment, the theme is played nondiegetically by the vibes and violins. The narrative import of the moment is clear; the tune pervades Ariane's thoughts because it is associationally linked to her encounter with Flannagan in the hotel. From this and other contextual cues, the spectator infers that "Fascination" refers to her new infatuation. Ariane does not hum because she likes this "idiotic tune"; she hums because the song reminds her of Flannagan.

Subsequent appearances of the theme support this initial linkage. For example, a little later Ariane writes a letter to Flannagan breaking her afternoon appointment with him. By the time she finishes the letter, however, Ariane has changed her mind. She burns the letter, and the film dissolves to an exterior shot showing her entering the Ritz. The reason for Ariane's change of heart is supplied by "Fascination," which plays nondiegetically to cover the transition between the two scenes. Though Ariane is aware of Flannagan's philandering reputation, her attraction to him, which is signified by the musical theme, overwhelms her initial objections and motivates her to meet him anyway. The linkage between "Fascination" and Ariane's mental processes is reinforced later when her father finds Flannagan's carnation in their icebox. The theme plays once again on the soundtrack as a reminder of the pair's relationship. In this instance, the tune is an objective correlative of the flower in that both are affectively and associatively linked to Flannagan.

I should note, however, that "Fascination" is not exclusively linked to Ariane's desires and emotions. In the second half of the film, the theme will consistently refer to Flannagan's growing obsession with Ariane's claims to sexual promiscuity. For example, when Ariane arrives in an ermine coat borrowed from one of her father's clients, Flannagan questions her about it. Ariane claims the coat was a gift from a rich, generous friend, and then proceeds to describe her previous "romances" with a duke and an Alpine guide. As Ariane and Flannagan dance to "Fascination," he insists that she take off the ermine, a gesture which signifies his growing anxiety about her sexual past.

Later, in one of the film's most outrageous sight gags, the Gypsy band will accompany Flannagan on a trip to a steam bath. Flannagan, who got drunk the previous night while listening to a dictaphone message enumerating Ariane's previous lovers, is now unable to get the "thin girl" out of his mind. The band's performance of "Fascination" inside the steam bath both serves as a none too subtle reminder of this obsession, and initiates Flannagan's coincidental meeting with Mr. X. Recognizing the tune, Mr. X remembers Flannagan and recommends hiring Claude as a way of satisfying his curiosity.

Finally, when Flannagan, rather ironically, hires Claude to investigate his own daughter, both Claude and Ariane are heard humming "Fascination." This in turn sets up the prospect that either Flannagan or Claude will come to realize the true identity of the mysterious woman possessing Flannagan's thoughts. This hypothesis is confirmed when Claude finally puts the pieces of the puzzle together—the familiar details of the woman's past affairs, the initial "A," Ariane's constant humming of "Fascination"—and comes to realize that Ariane is Flannagan's mystery woman and Flannagan is the reason for Ariane's odd behavior.

Interestingly, Claude's moment of recognition fittingly hints at the spectator's own response to the film's music. Like Claude, viewers use "Fascination" to make inferences about character motivation, to read characters' emotional states, and to draw connections and make hypotheses about past and future events of the story.[31] I should note, however, that the music does not function in isolation in providing these narrational cues. Much as Claude draws his conclusion from a number of clues strewn throughout the film— "Fascination," the carnation, the missing ermine, Ariane's curiosity about his files—the viewer makes inferences from a number of narrative and stylistic cues, one of which is music. This does not invalidate the importance or audibility of "Fascination" in advancing the story, but simply acknowledges the music's place within a larger system of classical narration, a system which, as David Bordwell notes, encourages a relatively high degree of redundancy in its presentation of story information.[32]

Thus, just as it is absurd to suggest that Claude has not heard "Fascination" in the course of the film, it is similarly absurd to suggest that spectators do not "hear" the film's score. By explicitly identifying "Fascination," the film, in effect, teaches us to recognize both the melody and its textual functions. We might agree with Michel that the theme is an idiotic tune, but we must also recognize how our awareness of it contributes to our overall comprehension and interpretation of narrative information.

One might object that *Love in the Afternoon* is too easy an example to illustrate my hypothesis. Generally speaking, films do not diegetically motivate their music to this extent, nor do they typically identify individual musical themes. While I will grant that *Love* is a particularly favorable case for my argument, its difference is one of degree rather than kind.

Casablanca, for example, makes comparable use of "As Time Goes By" to aid in the viewer's understanding of Rick and Ilsa's past affair and their renewed passion for one another. Though the tune notably does not appear during the credit sequence, it is introduced and identified by Ilsa about a half hour into the film.[33] Ilsa asks Sam to play "As Time Goes By," but Sam pretends to be unable to remember it. Like Claude in *Love,* Ilsa then hums a few bars in order to stimulate Sam's memory. Sam responds by playing the song for Ilsa, but is interrupted by Rick's angry admonition to stop. When Rick and Ilsa's eyes meet, however, the tune is picked up nondiegetically in Max Steiner's underscore, and subsequently linked to Rick and Ilsa's brief reminiscence of their last meeting in Paris. From this point on, the theme dominates *Casablanca* in countless variations played both diegetically and nondiegetically. As in *Love,* the song is used to chart the development of the couple's relationship, and its explicit identification similarly serves as apt comment on the memories and emotional states of its two central characters.

In one way or another, films are frequently "educating" viewers about their music, both within the text and outside of it. Film music's presence in radio and record markets often encourages us to pay particular attention to it during our viewing experience. A credit sequence customarily features one or more of the film's significant musical themes. More important, because it typically offers little or no important narrative information, we are especially attuned to the way in which a credit sequence establishes these themes and gives us an overview of the tonality, timbre, dynamics, and mood of the music which follows. Moreover, even when a viewer fails to recognize a particular theme or leitmotif, the immediacy of the music's modality, tempo, timbre, and dynamics often encourages spectators to make hypotheses and draw inferences about a scene's structural features and expressive qualities.

The mental activities I have just described are the kinds often elided in psychoanalytic accounts of film music. To their credit, theorists like Gorbman and Flinn have done much to stimulate recent research, to provide sophisticated frames of reference for their inquiry, and to push film music theory in provocative new directions. Yet while much can be gleaned from their work, their reliance on psychoanalysis ultimately makes their account of film music problematic. In *Unheard Melodies,* Gorbman poses the following question: "One could imagine a narrative cinema that did not deploy music, but would it be as successful on all fronts?"[34] Clearly the answer is that this cinema would not be as successful. However, this has far less to do with any relationship between music and psychoanalysis than it does with music's remarkable economy as a signifying structure, and its traditional functions as a form of representation and emotional expression.

NOTES

1. Maurice Jaubert, "Music on the Screen," in *Footnotes to the Film,* ed. Charles Davy (New York: Oxford University Press, 1937), p. 111. I should note here that Jaubert's comment is germane only to American and European cinematic traditions. In other countries, such as India, music is commonly thought to be one of the chief attractions of filmgoing.

2. Though notions of "inaudibility" are commonly found in much recent film music theory, I will be focusing my attention on the two most important theorists of the past ten years: Claudia Gorbman and Caryl Flinn. For relevant examples of Gorbman's work, see *Unheard Melodies: Narrative Film Music* (Bloomington: Indiana University Press, 1987); and "Narrative Film Music," *Yale French Studies* 60 (1980): 183–203. For examples of Flinn's work, see *Strains of Utopia: Gender, Nostalgia, and Hollywood Film Music* (Princeton: Princeton University Press, 1992); "The Most Romantic Art of All: Music in the Classical Hollywood Cinema," *Cinema Journal* 29, 4 (Summer 1990): 35–50; and "The 'Problem' of Femininity in Theories of Film Music," *Screen* 27, 6 (November–December 1986): 56–72.

3. Kurt London, *Film Music* (London: Faber & Faber, 1937), p. 37.

4. Aaron Copland, "Tip to Moviegoers: Take off Those Ear-Muffs," *New York Times,* November 6, 1949, section 6, p. 28.

5. Quoted in Randall Larson, *Musique Fantastique: A Survey of Film Music in the Fantastic Cinema* (Metuchen, N.J.: Scarecrow Press, 1985), pp. 47–48.

6. Miklos Rozsa, *Double Life* (New York: Wynwood Press, 1982), p. 203.

7. Quoted in Tony Thomas, *Film Score: The Art and Craft of Movie Music* (Burbank: Riverwood Press, 1991), p. 72.

8. Copland, "Tip to Moviegoers," p. 28.

9. In a recent review of *Strains of Utopia* and Kathryn Kalinak's *Settling the Score,* James Buhler and David Neumayer do an excellent job of placing the work of Gorbman and Flinn within the context of this Post-Structuralist/postmodern critical theory. See "Film Studies/Film Music," *Journal of the American Musicological Society* 47, 2 (Summer 1994): 364–85.

10. Flinn, "The Most Romantic Art of All," p. 38.

11. Gorbman, *Unheard Melodies,* pp. 61–63.

12. See Jean-Louis Baudry, "The Apparatus," *Camera Obscura* 1 (December 1976): 104–26.

13. Gorbman, *Unheard Melodies*, p. 58. The italics in this quote are Gorbman's.

14. See Roland Barthes, "Rhetoric of the Image," in *Image/Music/Text*, trans. Stephen Heath (New York: Hill and Wang, 1977), pp. 32–51.

15. Gorbman, *Unheard Melodies*, p. 58.

16. Ibid., p. 59.

17. Ibid., p. 69.

18. Ibid., p. 64.

19. See Flinn, *Strains of Utopia*, pp. 51–69.

20. To Flinn's credit, she does not unproblematically accept the premises of psychoanalytic, Marxist, or Romantic theories of music. Rather, she subjects them to rather rigorous analysis in order to illustrate how the broad circulation of these ideas came to inform the compositional practices of classical Hollywood film music and the critical practices of contemporary theorists. As an examination of these various ideological contexts, *Strains of Utopia* is an impressive dissection of how music is commonly thought to function within our culture. As a description of film music itself, however, Flinn's account simply does not address how film scores actually function. In focusing so exclusively on how these theoretical utopias were inscribed within film music, Flinn ultimately oversimplifies the complexity of the classical score and misdescribes spectators' responses to it. Ironically, Flinn's actual film analyses are the book's weakest component, and thus her work as a whole offers a much better discussion of music in culture than it does of music in cinema.

21. In explaining this process of containment, Flinn says, "To compare: whereas Hollywood classicism downplays the role of music, late nineteenth-century romanticism openly celebrates it. Yet both maintain that because of its abstract nature, music mounts a challenge to conventional representation, epistemology, and narrative. With its investment in the ineffable and its suspicion of language, romanticism championed this notion, while Hollywood seemed to allow these challenges and disruptions only to dismantle and contain them. This censure, of course, was achieved by the demand that film texts absorb their scores. . . ." See *Strains of Utopia*, pp. 39–40.

22. Quoted in Thomas, p. 72.

23. Ibid., p. 27.

24. Gorbman, *Unheard Melodies*, p. 76.

25. Kathryn Kalinak, *Settling the Score: Music and the Classical Hollywood Film* (Madison: University of Wisconsin Press, 1992), pp. 97–99.

26. Mark Evans, *Soundtrack: The Music of the Movies* (New York: Hopkinson and Blake, 1975), p. 225. I should note here that such moments typically involve either relating the thoughts of a character or suggesting the off-screen presence of a character. In fact, Fred Karlin used the latter idea as a totalizing strategy in his score for *The Stalking Moon*. In order to suggest the constant presence of the film's unseen antagonist, Karlin used a soft, sustained string and woodwind chord whenever "there was a sense that the Indian might be lurking just out of eyesight, just over the next hill. . . ." According to Karlin, the unseen Indian's centrality to the drama had to be suggested through the music, and thus the whole idea of the score "involved coloring the entire film with his presence." See Fred Karlin and Rayburn Wright, *On the Track: A Guide to Contemporary Film Scoring* (New York: Schirmer Books, 1990), pp. 86–87.

27. See Peter Kivy, *Music Alone: Philosophical Reflections on the Purely Musical Experience* (Ithaca, N.Y.: Cornell University Press, 1990).

28. See, for example, Stephen McAdams, "Music: A Science of the Mind," *Contemporary Music Review* 2 (1987): 1–61; J. Sloboda, *The Cognitive Psychology of Music* (Oxford: Clarendon Press, 1985); Fred Lerdahl and Ray Jackendoff, *A Generative*

Theory of Tonal Music (Cambridge: MIT Press, 1983); and Ray Jackendoff, *Consciousness and the Computational Mind* (Cambridge: MIT Press/Bradford Books, 1987).

29. See Noël Carroll, *Mystifying Movies: Fads and Fallacies in Contemporary Film Theory* (New York: Columbia University Press, 1988), pp. 213–25.

30. In fact, the song's lyrics aid our comprehension of this progression by reiterating the emotional character of Ariane and Flannagan's relationship. The title itself nicely captures the casual nature of Frank and Ariane's association. Ariane describes herself as an "aperitif" for Frank, and the kisses, passing glances, and touch of a hand depicted in Dick Manning's lyrics perfectly reflect the frivolity and delicacy connoted by her characterization. Moreover, the song's closing line, which describes how "fascination" changes to love, neatly summarizes the development of the film's central plot line.

It is important to note, however, that at no time during the film are these lyrics actually sung. This raises an especially vexing question regarding the ways in which a song's lyrics shape an auditor's interpretation of a film. This question is too complex to be sorted out in this essay, but I will offer some commentary pertinent to the subject at hand. Though the lyrics are not actually sung in the film, it is reasonable to assume that audiences would likely have some familiarity with them. "Fascination" was originally written in 1932 and had become a standard in the literature of popular music in the twenty-five years leading up to *Love in the Afternoon.* Moreover, the filmmakers' use of "Fascination" is entirely in keeping with industry practice during the fifties and succeeding decades. By exploiting film music in sheet music, record, and radio markets, filmmakers assumed that audiences would often have some awareness of a film's score before they even entered a theater. Though one can only speculate about the extent to which this awareness constrains or shapes a spectator's interpretation, it seems reasonable to assume that it did have some effect.

31. For a more general account of the cognitive activities of viewers, see David Bordwell, *Narration in the Fiction Film* (Madison: University of Wisconsin Press, 1985), especially pp. 29–47.

32. Ibid., p. 161.

33. Though music is heard almost continuously throughout the film's first thirty minutes, the bulk of it is diegetic music performed by Sam and the orchestra in Rick's club. The tunes played during these scenes include such classics as "Baby Face" and "It Had to Be You." In this respect, Sam's orchestra serves a function very similar to the Gypsy band in *Love in the Afternoon.* Not only do they motivate the film's central theme, but they flesh out the score with a number of popular melodies of the time.

34. Gorbman, *Unheard Melodies,* p. 69.

12

Film Music and
Narrative Agency

Jerrold Levinson

I

In this essay I address certain issues about paradigmatic film music, that is, the music that is often heard in the course of a fiction film but that does not originate in or issue from the fictional world revealed on screen. What most interests me is the question that confronts every filmgoer at some level, and to which he or she must, explicitly or implicitly, accord an answer, of who or what is responsible for such music. That is to say, to what agency is film music assigned by a comprehending viewer, and what is this music understood to be doing, in relation either to the film's internal narrative, the viewer's experience of that narrative, or the film as an aesthetic whole? Furthermore, by what principle does a viewer assign, however tacitly, responsibility for the music he or she hears?

It will turn out that different answers to this question of agency are in order from one film to another, and even from one cue to another within a given film. The upshot is a basic division within the realm of film music, one I have not seen marked elsewhere, but which is probably more fundamental than others regularly noted.

2

I begin with some preliminaries. First, the music I am concerned with is usually designated *nondiegetic* film music, that is, music whose source is not the story (or *diegesis*) being conveyed by the film's sequence of images. It is sometimes also designated *soundtrack* as opposed to *source* music, and sometimes as *extrinsic,* as opposed to *intrinsic,* music.[1] Second, the films I am concerned with are all *narrative fiction* films, both of the "classical" (or "Hollywood") sort, and the "modernist" (or "art film") sort, though not any of the more extreme examples of the latter, in which the bounds of fictionality or narrative coherence are stretched to their limits.[2] Third, I will consider film music here only as an integral component of a complete film, and not as a genre of music which, in the form of suites or soundtracks, might be enjoyed and evaluated on its own.

Certain kinds of answers to our opening queries can be put aside immediately as not to the point. For instance, the source of nondiegetic film music might in one sense be said to be the composer who composes it, or the producer who commissions it, or the sound editor who integrates it into the finished film, but this does not address the question of where, in relation to the fictional world projected, the music is situated or positioned in comprehending the film. Similarly, the function of nondiegetic film music might be said to be, somewhat vaguely, the aesthetic enhancement of the film, or more specifically, the emotional manipulation of the film viewer, or more crassly, the augmentation of the film's marketability and secondary profits, but none of these answers addresses the question of how such music is understood to function in relation to the central narrative of sight and sound, and thus to contribute ultimately to a film's meaning.

It should be noted straight off that there are two basic sorts of musical score regularly encountered in the domain of the sound film: the first, more traditional sort consists of music composed specifically for the film in question, and generally tailored by the composer to the rough cut, scene by scene; the second sort consists of preexistent music chosen by the filmmaker, often in conjunction with a musical consultant, and applied or affixed to scenes or parts thereof. Call the former sort a *composed* score, and the latter an *appropriated* score.

We can make at least two observations about these two types of score. First, with appropriated scores the issue of specific imported associations, deriving from the original context of composition or performance or distribution, rather than just general associations carried by musical style or conventions, is likely to arise. Second, with appropriated as opposed to composed scores, there will, ironically, generally be more attention drawn to the music, both because it is often recognized as appropriated and located by the viewer in cultural space, and because the impression it gives of chosenness, on the part of the implied filmmaker, is greater. To these two observations I add a third, more contentious one, that later discussion will support: music composed *for* a film (for example, the soundtracks of *Vertigo* or *The Heiress* or *On the Waterfront* or *La Strada*), is more likely to be purely narrative in function than preexisting music appropriated *by* a filmmaker (for example, the soundtracks of *A Clockwork Orange* or *Barry Lyndon* or *Love and Death* or *Death in Venice*).

3

There are some theoretical claims prevalent in the recent literature on film with which I will be disagreeing, and it is best I signal what they are at the outset. One is that nondiegetic film music is standardly "inaudible," that is, is not, and is not meant to be, consciously heard, attended to, or noticed.[3] This seems to be clearly false, or at any rate, false for a wide range of films in which soundtrack music calls attention to itself unmistakenly, or requires the viewer to attend to it explicitly if he or she is not to miss something of narrative importance. The "inaudibility" claim seems most true for what is called *underscoring,* music at a low volume that serves as a sort of aural cushion for dialogue that remains the main order of business, or for melodically and rhythmically unmarked music helping to effect transitions between scenes of notably different character. Even here, when the music hovers in the penumbra of consciousness, it is rarely very far from being consciously focused, as is perhaps reflected in the fact of being immediately noticed if stopped. If nondiegetic film music were generally unheard, or not consciously noted by the viewer, then there would not be much of an interpretive issue for the viewer of how to construe such music in relation to the rest of what is going on in the film. But, with respect to many films, there manifestly *is* an issue of some significance. Finally, even if it were the case that casual viewing of films with significant music tracks often goes on without a viewer's explicit awareness of that music, it hardly follows that an aesthetically justified or optimal viewing of such films remains similarly oblivious.

Another idea with some currency is the disavowal of what might be called narration proper—the conveying of a story by an intelligent agent—as actually characterizing the standard fiction film. One variant of this has it that such films are not really narrated by anyone or anything within the film world, but instead narrate themselves. A second variant insists that such films are constituted as narratives only by the viewer, and contain no narration apart from that. A third variant maintains that such films are not only constituted as narratives by viewers, but are in fact narrated by viewers to themselves as well, in the course of viewing.[4]

I reject the first sort of disavowal on grounds of incoherence; if narration means anything, it is the conveying or imparting of a story by means that are distinct both from the story being conveyed and from that which is doing the conveying; if the film, or its processes, are the means of narration, then it, or they, cannot also be conceived to be the agent or source of narration. I reject the second and third sorts of disavowal because they seem based on conflating the viewer's actual task of comprehending a film's story and significance by actively reconstructing or piecing together the narrative on offer, with the viewer's literal creation of that narrative, which would thus not exist apart from the viewer. But this is unnecessarily fanciful; our responsibility as filmgoers is to grasp what the narrative is, so as to further reflect on what it might signify, rather than to create that narrative for ourselves. Furthermore, were we really to create the narrative for ourselves, its significance would not, at any rate, be that of the film we were putatively attempting to understand.

So I am going to assume, following Seymour Chatman,[5] that if there is narration of events in a fiction film, if a comprehensible story comprising them is being conveyed to us, then there is an agency or intelligence we are entitled, and in fact need, to imagine is responsible for doing this narrating—to wit, a narrator, though not necessarily an ordinary human being.

There are, of course, alternatives to this assumption. As noted above, there are those who propose that films or filmic processes are themselves the performers or executants of narration, there not being of necessity any narrator within the film's world on the same plane as the events being displayed. But in addition to the fundamental incoherence remarked above, this proposal, to the extent it can be made out, is simply less interpretively useful than that of a narrator, however minimally characterized, for every successful narration. My response to yet another alternative, that in many cases of filmic narration, we imagine we are presented directly with the events of the story, without imagining there is any agent presenting them to us,[6] is much the same: the postulate of narrative agency in cinema does a better job of accounting for how we, admittedly largely implicitly, make sense of films as conveyors of stories.

For those who yet balk at this postulate, I would offer this. What I want to say about assigning nondiegetic music to narrative agents as opposed to implied filmmakers can, I believe, be translated so as to require instead only the assumption of narrative processes or mere appearances of being narrated. So even if one does not regard the positing of internal narrators or presenters in film as inevitable, the issue will still remain whether soundtrack music is to be thought of as an element in the narrative process or as an appearance of narrative presentation, as opposed to an element, standing outside both the story and its narration, in the construction of the film by a filmmaker. It is that issue I hope to illuminate.

4

I will now review Chatman's brief for both cinematic narrators and cinematic implied authors (that is, implied filmmakers).[7] Chatman begins with an appeal to ordinary language, one hard to gainsay:

> It stands to reason that if shown stories are to be considered narratives, they must be "narrated" . . . I would argue that every narrative is by definition narrated— that is, narratively presented—and that narration . . . entails an agent even when the agent bears no signs of human personality (p. 115).

If narrative films are then necessarily narrated by a narrator, what kind of narrator is this? Not, of course, the essentially linguistic narrator of a standard literary fiction:

> Film often has nothing like a narrative voice, no tell-er. Even the cinematic voice-over narrator is usually at the service of a larger narrative agent, the cinematic show-er. But that shower can reasonably be called a presenter . . . (p. 113). Films,

in my view, are always presented—mostly and often exclusively shown, but sometimes partially told—by a narrator or narrators. The overall agent that does the showing I would call the cinematic narrator . . . The cinematic narrator is not be identified with the voice-over narrator . . . (pp. 133–34).[8]

Chatman also proposes that a cinematic narrator, operating mainly through the affording of sights and sounds, is closely analogous to the mute presenter of dialogue in a purely dialogic short story.

So though in a film a teller, whose standard format is that of the voice-over, is usually absent or secondary, a *shower*—or better, because the term covers more comfortably aural information, a *presenter*—can be taken to be invariably in place, and the primary agent of narration. The presenter in a film presents, or gives perceptual access to, the story's sights and sounds; the presenter in a film is thus, in part, a sort of *perceptual enabler.*[9] Such perceptual enabling is what we must implicitly posit to explain how it is we are, even imaginarily, perceiving what we are perceiving of the story, in the manner and order in which we are perceiving it. The notion of a presenter, whose main charge is the providing of perceptual access on the fictional world, is simply the best default assumption available for how we make sense of narrative fiction film.[10]

While I thus accept Chatman's postulate of narrative agency wherever there is narration, I do not endorse certain of his claims about the separation of narrators from the story worlds they are narratively presenting. Chatman says, for instance, that "the [literary] narrator, by definition, does not *see* things in the story world; only characters can do that, because only they occupy that world" (p. 120), and that "the narrator cannot impinge on story space but must stay within the bounds of discourse space" (p. 123). It is, however, incoherent to postulate a narrator who offers us a window on or reportage concerning the doings of a set of individuals the narrator takes and presents as real, and yet insist the narrator is on a different plane, fictionally speaking, from those individuals, and in principle incapable of perceptual awareness of them. Chatman is confusing a narrator's *fictional level,* which must standardly be the same as that of the other characters whose doings he/she/it is purporting to convey,[11] and the narrator's *degree of story involvement,* which is variable, at often rather small, and at the limit, nil.[12]

A narrator and the events narrated by the narrator must be on the same fictional plane, otherwise cognitive relations posited between narrator and events would not make sense. The cinematic narrator's logical status vis-à-vis the film world is to be distinguished from the narrator's degree of involvement—causal, emotional, experiential—in the story, that is, what literary theorists mark as the narrator's being either homodiegetic or heterodiegetic. Being heterodiegetic, or an "outsider" to the events being related, does not remove a filmic narrator ontologically from the characters he/she/it serves to offer us perceptual access to. Chatman fails to see that the narrator must perforce share the fictional plane of the characters, since they are apparently real and reportable to that narrator, and this is true whether the narrator is homodiegetic, that is, involved in the story events, or heterodiegetic, that is, uninvolved in them, standing to those events in merely a witnessing and transmitting capacity.

I turn now to the notion of implied author in film. The need for this concept is clear from the fact that films, like novels

> present phenomena that cannot otherwise be accounted for, such as the discrepancies between what the cinematic narrator presents and what the film as a whole implies . . . unreliable narration presents the clearest but not the only case for the implied author [in film] (pp. 130–31).

> . . . in cinema as in literature, the implied author is the agent intrinsic to the story whose responsibility is the overall design—including the decision to communicate it through one or more narrators. Cinematic narrators are transmitting agents of narratives, not their creators (p. 132).

> In short, for films as for novels, we would do well to distinguish between a *presenter* of the story, the narrator (who is a component of the discourse), and the *inventor* of both the story and the discourse (including the narrator): that is, the implied author . . . (p. 133).

So in film we must generally distinguish between, on the one hand, the narrator or presenter of the story and, on the other hand, the ostensible inventor of (all of) the narrator, the story narrated, the narrative structure, and the cinematic entirety in which these are embodied—to wit, the implied filmmaker. The implied filmmaker is the agent who appears to have invented, arranged, and integrated the various narrative agents and aspects of narration involved in the film, as well as everything else required to constitute the film as a complete object of appreciation. The implied filmmaker, in short, is the picture we construct of the film's maker—beliefs, aims, attitudes, values, and personality—on the basis of the film construed in its full context of creation.

A film's narrator presents the events of the film's world from within it, whereas the implied author of a film, if he or she can be said to present anything other than the film itself, presents the world of the film, at one doxastic remove, from a position external to it. For the implied filmmaker, as for the viewer, but in contrast to a film's narrator, the film's world is a fictional one, acknowledged as fictional throughout. The implied filmmaker can't be in the position of directly affording us—as with a silent gesture of "behold!"—the vision and audition of something that is only fictional with respect to himself, namely, the characters and their circumstances; that remains the prerogative of the film's narrator or presenter, who is, in a fundamental sense, and pace Chatman, "one of them."

5

Before proceeding to my main concerns, I will address the worries about the general postulate of a filmic narrator formulated by George Wilson in his penetrating study, *Narration in Light*.[13] These worries are the most substantial and explicit of which I am aware, so if they can be allayed, the ground for such a postulate will be that much clearer.

A reason Wilson offers initially for being wary of a standing postulate of a cinematic narrator is that such is often conceived as an agent who is necessarily *observing* events, the image track being thus identified as the visual experience of that fictional observer. But this, as Wilson quickly notes, is unnecessary. The essential function of such a narrator is to *show* us what is to be seen—or more broadly, to present to us what is to be seen and heard—in other words, to enable perception, albeit fictional perception, of those events. The agent that shows, or permits us to see, need not be thought of as seeing as well. This is apparent in Wilson's own useful sketch of what a cinematic narrator would have to be: "a fictional or fictionalized being, presupposed in any viewing of the film narrative, who continuously provides to the audience, from within the general framework of the fiction, the successive views that open onto the action of the film."[14]

The alternative, then, is to conceive the cinematic narrator as a kind of perceptual pilot through the film world, rather than as an observer of it whom we opportunistically inhabit. "Considered in this fashion, the narrator is a fictional figure who, at each moment of the film, asserts the existence of certain fictional states of affairs by showing them to the audience demonstratively; that is, by ostending them within and by means of the boundaries of the screen. It is certainly part of our experience in film viewing that we feel, usually subliminally, a constant guidance and outside direction of our perception toward the range of predetermined fictional facts which we are meant to see."[15]

Having so well formulated this alternative, what problem does Wilson find with it? Just this: that the entity described is analogous not to the narrator of a novel, but rather to its implied author. His reason for this reluctant conclusion seems to be that although ". . . the exact style and manner of this guidance—the fine-grained articulation of the processes of showing—manifests traits of sensibility, intelligence, and character. . . ," these traits are ones we will naturally take to define the persona of the *filmmaker* as expressed through the film, or equivalently, the personality of the *film's implied author,* thus leaving no room for a filmic narrator as such.

This seems to me too quick. First, Wilson gives no reason why such traits should not be assigned, in some cases, to a filmic narrator, and in others, to the implied filmmaker. Second, Wilson fails to consider that the assignment of traits to the implied filmmaker might very well interpretively depend on the assignment of traits, the same or different ones, to such a narrator, much as our image of the implied author of a novel is necessarily based, in large part, on our image of the narrator and how the narrator is managed or positioned by the author.

But third, and most important, Wilson overlooks the fact that the implied filmmaker just cannot occupy the role of perceptual guide to the film's occurrences, and so, a fortiori, his particular mode of doing that cannot be what cues us to some of his traits. And that is because the implied filmmaker cannot logically be the presenter—the ostender—of events that are fictional with respect to him. That is to say, if we imagine anyone giving us access to those events, it cannot coherently be the filmmaker, in any guise. To be sure, the filmmaker can present representations of those events, that is, the shots or images the totality of which constitute the film, but he cannot offer us the vision and audition of those events themselves.[16] If he be allowed a surrogate, however, a narrating agent presupposed by the process of narration, and fictionally on the same level as its subject matter, then this difficulty disappears.

A fourth and related reason why the filmmaker cannot do duty for the film's narrator in this connection is this. Often we want not only to attribute traits of character, sensibility, or intellect to some agent connected with the film, but more specifically, attitudes or views concerning the story that is unfolding. But the filmmaker is not in the right cognitive position for this; that is to say, he or she will not actually have attitudes or views toward the fictional personages or occurrences involved in the story, knowing they are merely fictional.[17]

I suspect that Wilson is unable to find a place for, and thus underestimates the rationale for, the cinematic narrator, because he subtly conflates the devices or powers at the service of a director as crafter of a representation, and those in the command of an imagined perceptual guide to the world such a representation makes fictional[18]; but these are different, and the ways they function to control our experience as viewers differ too. The filmic narrator allows us to perceive first this person, then that, at such and such an apparent range, and for so long, clearly or not so clearly, and so on, all of which manner of showing may give us a certain impression of the shower's attitudes or motivations; the filmmaker chooses or stages the profilmic events that are to be filmed, decides on the camera distances and movements required for a shot, determines the lighting and length of shots, orders those shots in a certain fashion, and so on, thus ultimately composing a narrative of a particular sort, with a particular sort of implied narrator, all of which manner of making may give us a certain impression of the maker's personality or outlook. But the view we form of the narrating agency or intelligence, from the way it carries out its main charge as perceptual facilitator, need not coincide with the view we form of the human maker of the film, from the way he or she fulfills the demands of filmmaking.[19]

Curiously, Wilson allows that we can indeed imagine a film where we would have "grounds for a distinction between a voyeuristic filmic narrator and a satirizing implied film maker. In such a case, there would be enough of a personification of the manner in which the action is shown and enough of a contrast between the personification and what is implied about the filmmaker's views of this to motivate the identification of [the former] as a narrator."[20]

But to my mind, the very possibility of this kind of divergence is predicated on and presupposes the logical distinctness of the roles of filmic narrator and implied filmmaker, even if in most films, unlike the one Wilson conjures up, the personal traits ascribable to the occupants of the two roles tend to coincide.[21]

As we have seen, Wilson questions whether every standard film narration must be understood to entail an implicit narrator distinct from the filmmaker. He maintains that in films governed by the classical paradigm of transparency, which covers almost all narrative film, we simply see the fictional events for ourselves, defeasibly taking the facts about them to be what we see them to be. But to my mind this sidesteps the question of *how it is* we are seeing what we are seeing, however reliable or unreliable it turns out to be. If this question, however, is not simply set aside, then the only satisfying answer to it is that we are being *shown* such and such, by some agent, in some perhaps unspecifiable manner. That is to say, the posit, however unvoiced, of an agency that is offering us sights and sights—an agency with certain powers, motivations, and limitations—seems inescapable if we are to justify our taking anything to be fictional in the film world, on the basis of the moving images that are the only thing we are literally confronted with. It is not enough to just say that, with fiction film, the film's world is made visible to us, perhaps adding that there is a convention to that effect. Reason—albeit reason operating in service of the imaginative understanding of fiction—demands an answer to how it is that a world is being made visible to us, and that demand, it appears, is only satisfied by the assumption of an agency responsible for that.

One might still seek to avoid this conclusion by adopting the following stance: it is, indeed, *as if* we are being shown such and such, from a given perspective, by an agent within the film's world, with certain powers to make views of that world available to us, but we need not assume that there *is* such an agent. Here, though, we arrive at a distinction virtually without a difference. If it seems to us, at some level, as if we are being shown such and such, are we not in effect imagining that we are being shown such and such, and thus, finally, that there is, on the imaginative plane, something doing the showing? So I would claim.

6

That nondiegetic music standardly serves to advance a film's narrative is something on which theorists of film appear to agree:

> Narrative is not constructed by visual means alone. By this I mean that music works as part of the process that transmits narrative information to the spectator. . . .[22]

> Voice-over is just one of many elements, including musical scoring, sound effects, editing, lighting, and so on, through which the cinematic text is narrated.[23]

The moment we recognize to what degree film music shapes our perception of a narrative, we can no longer consider it incidental. . . .[24]

Another point widely agreed upon is that even if the primary purpose of nondiegetic film music is the advancing of the narrative, there may very well be others. Here is a typical admonition concerning film music's multiplicity of ends:

> There is not *one and only one* function that music can perform in relation to movies. Aaron Copland suggested five broad functions: creating atmosphere, underlining the psychological states of characters, providing background filler, building a sense of continuity, sustaining tension and then rounding it off with a sense of closure. These do not seem to be necessarily exclusive categories, nor do they exhaust the range of functions that music can perform in movies.[25]

Not surprisingly, I am happy to join this double consensus: film music often serves narrative in some way, but there is a range of other functions that such music sometimes performs. What I am concerned to demonstrate, however, goes beyond those two pieces of received wisdom. It is that the most fundamental division in the realm of film music concerns the viewer's assignment of responsibility for such music, that is, the agency the viewer posits, usually implicitly, as responsible for the music being heard. It will turn out that there is a rough coincidence between film music to which we intuitively accord narrative significance and film music for which we implicitly hold an internal cinematic narrator accountable, and between film music to which we do not accord narrative significance and film music that we implicitly assign directly to the implied filmmaker.

When, though, can film music be said to have narrative significance? When does nondiegetic music function narratively? In order to answer this question we must have a plausible criterion of narrativity or of actions within the purview of a narrator. In trying to arrive at one, it will be helpful to have before us a survey of the various functions that critics or theorists have observed film music to perform.

These functions include: (1) the indicating or revealing of something about a character's psychological condition, including emotional states, personality traits, or specific cognitions, as when the music informs you that the heroine is happy, or that the hero has just realized who the murderer was; (2) the modifying or qualifying of some psychological attribution to a character independently grounded by other elements of the film, as when the music tells you that a character's grief over a loss is intense; (3) the underlining or corroborating of some psychological attribution to a character independently grounded by other elements of the film, as when music emphasizes something about a situation on screen which is already fully evident; (4) the signifying of some fact or state of affairs in the film world other than the psychological condition of some character, for example, that a certain evil deed has occurred, off-screen; (5) the foreshadowing of a dramatic development in a situation being depicted on screen; (6) the projecting of a story-appropriate mood, attributable to a scene as a whole; (7) the imparting to the viewer of a sense that the happenings in the film are more important than those of ordinary life—the emotions magnified, the stakes higher, the significances deeper; (8) the suggesting to the viewer of how the presenter of the story regards or feels about some aspect of the story, for example, sympathetically; (9) the suggesting to the viewer of how he or she is to regard or feel about some aspect of the story, for example, compassionately; (10) the imparting of certain formal properties, such as coherence, cogency, continuity, closure, to the film or parts thereof; (11) the direct inducing in viewers of tension, fear, wariness, relaxation, cheerfulness, or other similar cognitive or affective state; (12) the lulling or mesmerizing of the viewer, so as to facilitate emotional involvement in the fictional world to which the viewer would otherwise prove resistant; (13) the distracting of the viewer's attention from the technical features of the film as a constructed artifact, concern with which would prevent immersion in the filmic narrative; (14) the expressing by the filmmaker of an attitude toward, or view on, the fictional story or aspect thereof; (15) the embellishing or enriching of the film as an object of appreciation.

Without deciding, for each of these functions, which are properly considered narrative and which not, it would appear that some of them unequivocally are and some unequivocally are not. What I will do at this point is explore a number of suggestions as to what the criterion of narrativity might be in regard to nondiegetic film music, assessing them against the background of this array of observed functions, some of which, at any rate, would have to come out counting as narrative, some clearly not, and some having a status that might only be settled, clarifyingly, once a given suggestion is adopted.

One possible criterion is this: (C1) does the music seem to issue from, be in service of, the agency one imagines to be bringing one the sights and sounds of the film's world? If so, then it can be reckoned part of the narration proper, and assignable to the cinematic narrator. Perhaps an equivalent formulation would be: (C2) does the intelligence one thinks of as bringing one the music seem to be the same as that charged with conveying the story—as opposed to that charged with constructing the film? If so, then the music can be reckoned part of the narration, and assigned to the cinematic narrator.[26]

Though I think these criteria point in the right direction, there is an evident problem with them, insofar as we hope to look to them for guidance, especially in difficult cases. And that is that they are uncomfortably close to what they purport to analyze or elucidate, namely, whether a use of nondiegetic music is narrative or not. So if we are unsure whether a given cue is functioning narratively, we are likely to be almost equally unsure whether it feels as if it derives from the film's narrative agent. Thus, it would seem desirable to have some other mark, could we discover one, whose conceptual distinctness from the idea of narrative functioning was greater than that of C1 or C2.

Such a mark might be that of *making a difference* in the narrative. Instead of appealing directly to an intuition of a connection of the music to a film's internal narrator, we can appeal instead to the notion of *making fictional,* or generating fictional truths, in a film. A criterion of nondiegetic music having a narrative function, and thus being attributable to a narrative agent, could be thus: (C3) the music makes something fictionally true—true in the story being conveyed—that would not otherwise be true, or not to the same degree or with the same definiteness. A counterfactual form of the suggestion is perhaps more transparent: (C4) would deleting the music in a scene change its represented content (that is, what is fictional in it), or only how the scene affects viewers? If the former, then the music is an aspect of narration; if the latter, then not.

We must briefly discuss what it means to make something fictional in a work of fiction such as a narrative film. Something is fictional in a film, according to a well-developed recent account, if it is *to be imagined to be the case* by viewers concerned to experience the film properly.[27] What thus makes something—a proposition about the film's world—something that is to be imagined in the course of viewing is, in short, perceivable features of the film, a public object, taken as a prop for guided imaginings.

When we make believe in accord both with the features of artistic props and the usually tacitly grasped principles for imagining that are in effect in a given art form, we are engaged in tracing out imaginary worlds, ones in which things are *make-believedly,* or *fictionally,* so. The fictional world of a representational art work, unlike that of a daydream or fantasy, is as it is because features of the associated prop—text, canvas, film—properly construed, are the way they are; not all is up to the imaginer. Props, through their existence and nature, generate fictional truths independently of what individual perceivers might choose to imagine.

What does it mean for a proposition to be fictional, or true in a fictional world, in respect of a given work of art? Simply that there is a *prescription to imagine* it, a prescription encoded in the particulars of the artifact that serves as a prop for making believe, and whose force derives from underlying conventions of construing works of the sort in question. Being fictional thus has an ineliminable normative dimension: it is what *is to be* imagined in a given context, rather than merely what *may* be imagined.

For example, in *Citizen Kane,* Orson Welles's image on-screen being that of a large man makes it fictional that Charles Foster Kane is a large man; the opening shots—a series of lap dissolves—having a certain visual content makes it fictional that at the beginning of the story one is shown Kane's estate, Xanadu, from a distance and shrouded in mist, and then at progressively closer range; Ray Collins's voice saying certain things on the soundtrack in the scene at Susan Alexander's apartment makes it fictional that Collins's character, Jim Gettys, has threatened Kane; the way the shot of Kane expiring is sequenced in relation to others which are understood as a flashback to Kane's childhood, makes it fictional that Kane's dying word, "rosebud," refers to his beloved old sled, and so on. Of course, much of this generation will be indirect, dependent on various conventions of the medium in effect and on other things taken provisionally as fictional, and accordingly, much of our knowledge of such fictional truths will be inferential. And sometimes, what is made fictional by a film's narration is orthogonal to, or even the opposite of, what first appears to be the case, that is, what it initially seems we are to imagine is the case; unreliable, uninformed, or unforthcoming narrators, though not as common in film as in literature, are still a significant possibility.

Applying this suggestion to the issue of narrativity in film music, then, the question becomes, of a given cue, whether it generates, contributes to generating, or at a minimum, more firmly grounds, a fictional truth in the scene which it accompanies. Thus, film music that, when interpreted in light of prevailing conventions of the medium and the surrounding narrative context, indicated that a character was afraid or was remembering a past incident, or that a man had been executed or an agreement reached, or that a situation was fraught with danger or else full of hope, where these things would not be established, or not so definitely, without the music, would clearly count as narrative.[28]

We should note that nondiegetic music may, indeed, generate fictional truths even if only attended to with half a mind, or not consciously remarked at all while present. It will do this by causing a viewer to, say, perceive a scene as fraught with danger, even if the viewer is not aware of what is making her have that perception. Nevertheless, if such an imaginative perception is reliably produced in attuned viewers, and not undermined by subsequent aspects of the narration, then it may well be fictional that the scene is fraught with danger, even though the rest of the narrative indicators are insufficient to establish that and the viewer never realizes that it is the background music that in fact makes it so.

7

It is time to look at a range of illustrative examples of film music. I begin with examples whose narrative functioning is obvious, and which conform, expectedly, to the making-fictional criterion proposed above. I then explore another range of examples, ones that exhibit a different sort of narrativity, and show how, on a more encompassing construal of the making-fictional criterion, these can be accommodated as well. Eventually, though, I turn to films containing nondiegetic music that is not, by that criterion or any other, reasonably construed as narrative. The music in such films instead serves other sorts of artistic function, ones attributable directly, I will argue, to implied filmmakers.

One of the least ambiguous narrative uses of soundtrack music in recent film occurs in Steven Spielberg's 1975 blockbuster, *Jaws*. I have in mind the "shark" motto devised by the composer, John Williams. This consists of an ostinato alternation of low staccato notes at the interval of a second—a kind of aural sawing. The motto has an unarguable informational mission, namely, to signal the presence of the shark. It is true that there is another, visual, indicator of the shark's presence when unseen, namely, shots from an offshore point of view, at the water line or slightly below it. But that indicator is not invariant in meaning, since it is sometimes employed when there is no shark about. The musical "shark" motto is the only reliable signifier of the shark, and so has an ineliminable fact-conveying function. Correspondingly, it is clear that it is the presence of that motto on the soundtrack at a given point that makes it fictional that the shark, though as yet unseen, is in the vicinity of what is shown.

David Raksin's ground-breaking score for Otto Preminger's *Laura* provides some further instances of straightforward narrative use of film music. The "Laura" theme, first encountered diegetically on a record player in the apartment of the ostensibly murdered heroine, pervades critic Waldo's (Clifton Webb) represented recollections of the early days of his relationship with Laura (Gene Tierney), and signifies unmistakeably his joy and delight in her companionship. Subsequently we are treated to apprehensive versions of the "Laura" theme as detective McPherson (Dana Andrews), alone in Laura's apartment, studies the portrait of Laura over the fireplace; this cue then climaxes unsettlingly, revealing or underlining McPherson's frustration with his investigation at this point. The most striking cue, one much noted in the film music literature,[29] is a weird version of the theme which is produced by playing it on a piano but only recording the overtones of each note struck. This is heard as McPherson views Laura's portrait on a second occasion, before drinking too much and falling asleep, and it suggests the ghostly influence Laura is beginning to exert over this poor detective's mind. In each of the foregoing cases, the music is plausibly viewed as making, or contributing to making, something fictional in the story: that Waldo delighted in Laura inordinately, that McPherson is (earlier) almost terminally frustrated with Laura's case, that McPherson is (later) succumbing to bewitchment by Laura's spirit.

Another film rich in narrative pointing of a theoretically unproblematic sort is Martin Scorsese's *Taxi Driver*. Regarding a scene in which Travis (Robert De Niro), the film's semipsychotic protagonist, is induced to move his cab away from the Manhattan workplace of a girl he is infatuated with and back into the grime and disorder of the city, one writer affirms that "the music . . . here reveals that Travis's thoughts are not with the street but with Betsy." And of the bluesy, sensual saxophone tune itself, which stands for Betsy (Cybill Shepherd) in Travis's mind, the same writer has this to say: "Travis's vision of idealized womanhood, the music implies, is strongly erotic."[30] Thus, Bernard Herrmann's music does not serve merely to inform us about Travis's mental life, or to second redundantly what other elements of the film establish about his mentality, but rather enters into making it *fic-*

tional in the film that Travis's mental life is a certain way at a certain time. Commenting on the blade-game fight scene in Nicholas Ray's *Rebel without a Cause,* Noël Carroll offers the following: "The uneasy, unstable quality of the music [by Leonard Rosenman] serves to characterize the psychological turmoil—the play of repression and explosive release—with which the scene, and the movie, is concerned."[31] If Carroll is right, the music of this scene, which intuitively seems an aspect of its narration, serves to underwrite as desired a fictional truth about the specific, highly volatile, character of the turmoil afflicting the young protagonists. Another instructive example from *Rebel without a Cause* occurs later in the film, and consists of a montage of two-way phone calls among various adults concerned with the whereabouts of three main youngsters. This montage is covered by tense nondiegetic music, displacing the dialogue that would ordinarily be heard, the music thus signifying that the conversations, whatever their specific contents, are anxious ones.

The opening of Elia Kazan's *On the Waterfront* affords another illuminating example. An establishing shot of city docks, ocean liner in the distance, gives way to a street scene in which longshoreman Terry (Marlon Brando) becomes the focus of attention. Leonard Bernstein's jazz-inflected score at this point involves a persistent drum tattoo overlaid with saxophone insinuations. Terry, in the darkening street, yells up to friend Joey's window, persuading him to go to the roof to recover one of his pet pigeons, where unbeknownst to Joey, two men are waiting for him. After Terry releases the pigeon he's been holding, and promises to join Joey in a moment, the score becomes loud, aggressive, and insistent, its rhythms more syncopated. The music telegraphs us that something bad is in store, that the men glimpsed on the roof are trouble; the music can be said to prefigure Joey's fall, pushed off the roof by thugs of the corrupt union boss, though without defining precisely what is about to happen. The cue is clearly narrative, and just as clearly, makes it fictional that Joey is in danger, even before he leaves the window for his fatal visit to the roof.

Later on, after the boss tells right-hand man Charley (Rod Steiger) to straighten out his brother Terry or else, Charley leaves union headquarters to do something, we know not what. Bernstein's music at this point is very dramatic and tense: a series of rising notes in the brass, leading to a rhythmic explosion, the whole heard twice. The cue arguably conveys Charley's complex state of mind, as he faces the necessity of keeping his errant brother, who is threatening to do the right thing, in line: a mixture of anger, shame, and angst. If it does not single-handedly make it fictional that that is Charley's state of mind, the cue contributes ineliminably to making it so. A dissolve leads directly to the famous conversation between the brothers in the rear of a taxi.

Consider, lastly, the final sequence in Fellini's *La Strada.* Five years ago, Zampano the strongman (Anthony Quinn) has abandoned his assistant, the childlike Gelsomina (Giuletta Masina), after she became too withdrawn and depressed to work. He now discovers, by accident, her fate. That evening he does his act perfunctorily, gets drunk, starts brawling, then goes down to the beach, which reminds us of where he first acquired Gelsomina from her impoverished family. He walks into the water, returns to the beach, looks up at the sky apprehensively, then starts to bawl and grasp at the sand, on which he has flung himself in despair. At this point the "La Strada" theme on the soundtrack removes all doubt as to what it is Zampano is bemoaning—namely, the loss of Gelsomina and her innocent love.

8

Clearly, making something fictional in a film is a *sufficient* condition of musical narrativity. Is it, however, a necessary one? Though providing the basic fictional truths of a story may be the central activity of a narrator, there are others that are almost equally paradigmatic of narration. One is the evincing of attitudes or feelings on the narrator's part toward the story presented, in virtue of how the story is presented; another is the inviting of the viewer to adopt certain attitudes or feelings toward the story presented. In other words, in addition to giving access, in a particular manner, to the fictional states of affairs that constitute a story, a narrator generally manifests attitudes regarding the states of affairs to which access is afforded, and thereby suggests to the narratee attitudes to be adopted. In literature, for example, the narrator standardly tells us what happened, after his or her fashion, reveals, knowingly or unknowingly, his or her view of these happenings, and also suggests, explicitly or implicitly, how we should view what we are told happened.[32]

Now it seems plain that such narrational effects are often achieved by appropriate nondiegetic music: the music tells you how the presenter of the story regards the events being presented, or else how he would like you to regard them. But on the surface, this does not appear to be a matter of establishing, nuancing, or even confirming a fictional state of affairs in the story. So in light of that, can making fictional be sustained as the effective mark of musical narrativity?

I believe so. We need to make a distinction between what is fictional *in a film's story* and what is fictional *in the world of a film*. The latter is a broader notion than the former. What is fictional in the film's world comprises, in addition to the facts of the story, the facts of its narration by the special, often almost effaced, fictional agent known as the narrator. All that is still within the sphere of the fictional, of propositions to be imagined by a viewer in comprehending the film. The film's story consists of what is fictional about the characters who figure in the action; the film's world includes, as well, what is fictional about the narrator, in relation to either the story narrated or the implied audience of that narration.[33]

Returning to film music, a plausible construal of some nondiegetic cue will often have the implication, not that it makes something fictional in the story, but that it makes it fictional either that the cinematic narrator has a certain attitude or feeling toward some event being presented, or that the narrator encourages viewers to have such an attitude or feeling toward it. In either case, musical narrativity will still correlate with music's making something fictional, only here it is a making fictional in the film's world, as opposed to a making fictional in the embedded story. Some examples will serve to clarify this more encompassing interpretation of musical narration in terms of making-fictional.

Music functions narratively, by any intuitive assessment, in Hitchcock's *Shadow of a Doubt,* particularly at junctures when a scrap of Lehar's "Merry Widow" waltz intrudes itself, suggesting the "Merry Widow Murders" that are central to the plot. Several characters are heard singing or humming the tune in the course of the film, these occurrences being of course diegetic, but the tune is heard, in an altered form, as early as Dmitri Tiomkin's title music, which accompanies a stylized shot of waltzing couples. Two notable nondiegetic occurrences after that are these. First, a few bars of the waltz theme in the cue that accompanies the family's greeting of Uncle Charlie (Joseph Cotten) at the train station, as they walk off to their car to take him home: a tracking shot of the group, heading toward the camera, is eventually reframed so that only Uncle Charlie is in view, and that is when the scrap of tune is heard. Second, a more prominent statement of the theme when Uncle Charlie gives young Charlie (Teresa Wright) an emerald ring, and she notices it is already engraved inside with an unknown someone's initials. In both cases, the music arguably serves to communicate something to the viewer about Charlie's identity, connecting him in some as yet unexplained way to the waltzing image presented at the beginning.

But does the music make, or even contribute to making, something true in the film's story as such, something that would not otherwise be the case? It is not clear that it does. To consider just the most obvious candidates, neither cue makes it true—even viewed in retrospect, when a connection to Lehar's tune is understood to import as well a connection to the "Merry Widow" murders—that Uncle Charlie is the murderer, nor does the second make it true, say, that young Charlie suspects that he is. The reason is that those fictional truths are firmly established, and independently, by other elements in the film.[34]

What, then, might they be doing? I suggest that the first cue makes it fictional that the narrator is obliquely hinting to viewers with regard to Uncle Charlie's identity, and the second makes it fictional that the narrator is, even more directly, connecting Uncle Charlie to something sinister in his past, though at that point viewers have no notion of what it might be. The second cue may, in addition, function as the narrator's proposing of a deep psychic link between Uncle Charlie and young Charlie, one that her subsequent moral corner-cutting, in dealing with an uncle she then knows to be an un-hinged killer, partially bears out.[35] In any event, the status of these cues as narrative can be recovered in the guise of what is made fictional, not in the story as such, but in the narrator's attitudes or actions with respect to viewers.

But what of the curious musical image of waltzing couples first encountered in the title sequence, which recurs nondiegetically and unchangingly at three crucial points in the story? In each case the image is superimposed over the action already on view, which continues underneath. The first occurrence is after the interaction between Uncle Charlie and young Charlie over the emerald ring, as young Charlie goes off to clear the supper dishes, leaving only Uncle Charlie on screen. The second occurrence is at night in the town library, when young Charlie, after reading the newspaper account of the "Merry Widow" murders, gets up, almost reeling, as the camera tracks upward and away from her. The third and last is just as Uncle Charlie falls to his death beneath the wheels of a hurtling locomotive.

The first and second of these might be interpreted as the narrator's display of the mental contents of the character then in frame, in the one case signifying Uncle Charlie's meditation on his hidden identity, in the other, his niece's realization of that identity. But in addition to being implausible because not reflecting the very different emotional tones with which uncle and niece would have contemplated this identity, this sort of interpretation seems unavailable for the last occurrence, where ascription to the terrified and soon-to-be-obliterated Uncle Charlie of a contemplative thought about his past strains credulity to the breaking point.

This suggests that the recurrent waltzing image should be construed as a form of narrator's commentary: it is employed by the cinematic storyteller at crucial moments to underline in an intentionally jarring manner—because achieved through the elegance and innocence of a waltz—Uncle Charlie's horrific identity. Thus, what is made fictional by these musical cues is *not* that Uncle Charlie is the murderer, but that the *narrator* is adverting to that fact, almost sardonically, both before and after it is narratively established.

Rebel without a Cause provides another example whose analysis helps us to see our way here. The opening scene unfolds at a police station, where three juveniles whose lives will soon importantly intersect find themselves separately in trouble. At one point Jim Stark (James Dean), who has been talking with a sympathetic counselor, bangs and kicks a desk in frustration, at the counselor's explicit invitation. As his outburst concludes, dissonant music surges up briefly on the soundtrack. This undoubtedly adds tension to the scene, but does it contribute to defining the fictional world in any way? That Jim is wildly and angrily frustrated is fully established by what the perceptual enabler of the film has allowed us to see and hear of his outburst. What, then, is the music, which certainly seems to have narrative force, doing there in narrative terms?

Perhaps this: it serves to get across the phenomenology of Jim's feelings, giving viewers access to the quality of his outburst from the inside, supplementing the access afforded from the outside by the ordinary perceptual data of the scene. Suppose that is so. Then on the one hand, this could be construed as a subtle sort of making-fictional in the story, namely, making it fictional that the quality of feeling in Jim's outburst was precisely such and such—the quality the musical cue in question is expressive of. On the other hand, this could equally well be construed as a making-fictional concerning not Jim, whose emotional condition is perhaps overdetermined by other indicators in the scene, but instead the narrator's stance toward the audience. That is, perhaps the cue's cash value is that the narrator is inviting viewers to share in rather than merely observe what Jim was feeling, and as a consequence, encouraging viewers to adopt a sympathetic attitude to him. The cue's narrativity, in other words, may be a matter of its definition of the fictional world of the film, comprising both narrator and story narrated, rather than that of the story per se.

Consider now the common use of background music to create atmosphere in a scene, but without attributing mental states to any character therein. Is there anything that can thus be said to be made fictional in the film world? In cases where an appropriate atmosphere is created, that is, one that seems consonant with the way the story is otherwise told, what is made fictional might be that the narrator wants the viewer to assume a particular mood or frame of mind as certain events are presented for perception. In cases, though, where the atmosphere created does not gibe with the style or tone of narration already established, then even indirect fictional generation of that sort may be absent. The musical creation of mood may then have to be understood not as a narrative action, but rather one of aiming to immediately affect the viewer in a way that has no fictional upshot. Where nondiegetic music adds atmosphere to a scene without plausibly making anything fictional in the film's world, simply producing a mood in viewers, it seems that responsibility for it, as for other nonnarrative, purely compositional elements of a film, must rest directly with the implied filmmaker.

Exploring the interpretive option just broached—of assigning musical cues to the implied filmmaker rather than the film's narrative agent—will be the focus of the remainder of this essay. But before turning to that I conclude this section with a brief look at narrative uses of nondiegetic music in Hitchcock's *Vertigo*. *Vertigo* boasts perhaps the greatest of classical film scores, and its greatness as a film is due, in no small measure, to that score and its masterful integration into the film in almost every respect.

The intrinsic interest and sophistication of Bernard Herrmann's score has been much discussed, but what is most striking about it in the context of the film is how significant a burden it bears for limning the mental states and traits of characters, by comparison with most other films. *Vertigo* abounds in occasions where not only are viewers fictionally *informed* about the inner lives of the characters through soundtrack music, but the music is what in large part *makes* it fictional that their inner lives are to be so characterized.

When Scottie (James Stewart) first sees Madeleine/Judy (Kim Novak) at the rear of a restaurant in San Francisco, the music serves significantly to characterize her for us and for him: " . . . if the camera movement toward Madeleine lets us experience the physical nature of Scottie's immediate attraction to her, it is the music that most fully conveys the sensual mystery of the woman."[36] This scene is instructive in other ways as well. Madeleine gets up to leave, comes toward Scottie, pauses momentarily, and is very noticeably framed and lit in profile—shown, in effect, to best advantage. But who is doing that? The cinematic narrator, in order to indicate something about Madeleine and the overwhelming psychic effect she has on Scottie on first encounter. The filmmaker, Hitchcock, cannot do that—though he can do certain parallel things to Kim Novak and the set in order to bring about, on a fictional plane, the narrative result. The cinematic narrator is the one who, fictionally, showcases Madeleine, for our benefit as trackers of the story, and then underscores this showcasing through the musical resources under its control, for example, by crescendoing at the point of held close-up.[37]

After the crisis of the first part of the film, Scottie spends some time in a sanitorium, sunk deep in depression and aimless longing. Soon after his release, we are given a high pan over the front of Madeleine's apartment building, as the "love" motif—a four-note Tristan-like descending figure—is sounded romantically by French horns. This foreshadows Scottie's appearance in frame at the end of the camera movement, with Madeleine obviously in mind: he approaches a blonde woman in front of the building, about to get into what was Madeleine's car, only to discover that it isn't her. The exact content of his hope and then disappointment is supplied by the musical cue.

Scottie's vertigo first occurs in the film's opening scene, while he is hanging from a rain gutter, high above the city, having slipped in the course of pursuing a fleeing felon. This is importantly recalled in the plot's pivotal event, occurring halfway through the film, which takes place at the Mission of San Juan Battista, from whose tower the real Madeleine, unwanted wife of Gavin Elster, will appear to have leapt to her death. As Madeleine rushes into the church, and Scottie begins to follow, Herrmann's music foretells the recurrence of Scottie's vertigo: " . . . milder variants of the clash of tonalities which were heard in the [opening] rooftop sequence hint at the probable effect climbing the tower will have upon Scottie. . . . "[38] The musical cue, it seems, generates the fictional truth, at the point it sounds, that Scottie is *going* to experience vertigo when he climbs, though he is not experiencing it *now*. In other words, that Scottie's vertigo is coming becomes something that is to be imagined by viewers at that point in the film. Alternatively, perhaps the truth is generated that *Scottie* knows it is coming, or is concerned that it might.[39] In the film's final scene, also set in this tower, the tremolo trills which are prominent during this, Scottie's second ascent, suddenly cease, suggesting he has at that point overcome his vertigo and will be able to complete his trip to the top.

At the start of the "letter" scene, the moto perpetuo string figures prominent in the opening rooftop scene recur, in an overwrought vein, accompanying Judy's detailed recollection of the tower incident and her role in the deception perpetrated there. This underscores sonically how emotively charged the incident remains for her, and helps us understand why she is ultimately unable to carry through the writing of the letter of confession. In the famous "nightmare" sequence, the habanera music associated with Carlotta—a dead woman with a tragic past with whom Madeleine appears to identify—becomes more discordant, almost parodic, through the addition of stereotypical castanets and tambourine, conveying unmistakeably the intensity of Scottie's oppression by Carlotta/Madeleine. But more specific psychological pointings yet have been laid at the door of the scoring in this film, with some plausibility. According to one writer, the rather banal music that accompanies a walk taken by Scottie and Judy in the park adjacent to the Palace of Fine Arts, soon after he meets her and senses a kinship with the lost Madeleine, "suggests Scottie's feeling of dissatisfaction with this working-class version of the elegant, sophisticated woman of his memory."[40]

I have tried to show, through the varied examples in this section, the viability of a "making-fictional" criterion of narrativity for nondiegetic film music. There is, I submit, an intuitive match between the concepts: any nondiegetic music we would regard as narrative in status is music that can be seen as contributing to making something fictional in the world of the film—and vice versa.

9

Narration, though, however broadly construed and however subtly carried off, is not always the basic charge of nondiegetic film music, and serving a narrative function not always the best explanation of its presence. I want now to consider films where nondiegetic music is featured that appears *not* to be of a narrative sort—where thus, in my terms, the music does not make anything fictional in the world of the film and is not reasonably assignable to the film's internal narrator. Instead, the music seems best understood as directly at the service of the implied filmmaker. I begin with some films that are in different ways intermediate or borderline in regard to the contrast I want eventually to draw.

In Fellini's semiautobiographical *8 ½*, Guido (Marcello Mastroianni), a famous but floundering director, has gone to a fashionable spa to try to recover his mental equanimity and decide on a direction for his new film. We find him in a spacious bathroom, as Wagner's "Ride of the Valkyries" begins on the soundtrack. There is a cut to masses of people taking the waters at the spa, walking in rows and carrying parasols, among whom Guido eventually takes his place and receives his allotted glass. We see a conductor conducting, though with no orchestra in sight, and later see that he is leading a small salon group—one that could not be the source of the music we hear in the form we hear it. That cue ends and Rossini's overture to *The Barber of Seville* immediately starts up, but with a robustness, once again, that surpasses the resources of the musicians visually established as present. The effect of both cues, it seems, is one of gentle mockery of the behavior and attitudes of the spa's clientele.

The musical soundtrack during this sequence is what one might call *quasi-diegetic*. That is to say, the music can be thought to be audible in the world of the story, because it is fictionally grounded in an observable source, and even confirmed later as something heard by a character (as by Guido's subsequent whistling of snatches of the Rossini)—but not in the precise form heard by the viewer, in respect of volume, instrumentation, or performance quality. The same quasi-diegetic status attaches to the music in the final scene, the press conference-cum-party—designed to launch Guido's supposed film—at the extravagantly erected "Spaceship" site. We hear Rota's excited music, which begins with a variant on Khatchaturian's "Saber Dance," and eventually brings in almost all the other motives heard earlier in the film, as Guido is mobbed by impatient questioners and alternately shielded or prodded by his handlers, all captured in swooping, restless camera movement. Once again, we are shown a small band set up on a platform, and can even observe at one point the synchronization of the soundtrack with the rhythm, visually apparent, of the band's drummer, but there is still a discrepancy between what we can hear of Rota's marvelous score and our sense of what sort of sound the band visually in evidence could have produced.

So, does such quasi-diegetic music serve a narrative function? To the extent the music is considered nondiegetic, its function seems to be, in the first scene, satirical commentary, and in the second, mood enhancement, both arguably from a point of view internal to the film. So despite their peculiar status, these cues, insofar as they are nondiegetic, are plausibly ascribable to the cinematic narrator. They make things fictional: in the first instance, that the narrator views the spa goings-on satirically, and in the second, that the narrator wants to induce a certain mood in viewers with regard to the final episode. The soundtrack music's equivocal status as diegesis thus does not seem to yield anything correspondingly intermediate as regards narrative assignability.

Another example of intermediate status occurs in the "rogue auto" scene in Hitchcock's *North by Northwest,* in which the villain Vandamm's (James Mason) henchmen attempt to do in the hero, Thornhill (Cary Grant), by forcing him to drive down a dangerous cliff road while completely inebriated. I would claim that the music of this scene not only generates tension and underlines the driver's state of drunkenness, but at the same time signals, through its jokey style and lighthearted character, the absence of any real danger for Thornhill. Is this then a communication from the cinematic narrator, or from the implied filmmaker? That is to say, is it fictional that Thornhill is not truly in peril, or at least that the narrator knows he is not? Or is it rather that Hitchcock is telling us, on the sly, that he does not intend to do away with his main character at this point? It is hard to say which, but in a film whose borderline self-conscious (or modernist) character has often been re-marked, this is perhaps not surprising.[41]

Most of the music in Peter Weir's *Witness*, composed by Maurice Jarre, functions in the by now familiar mood-setting, character-delineating, atti-tude-evincing, or thought-specifying way, and is unproblematically categoriz-able as narrative. It begins with floating, gently pulsating synthesized chords, as images of Amish farmers looking up out of fields and buggies traveling down roads occupy the screen.[42] What is conveyed is a sense of harmony and awe, a sense of the homogeneous spirituality of the world inhabited by the Amish, especially as compared with the vulgar and violent world of "English-ers" (the Amish term for their secular neighbors). During a sequence in which an Amish boy in Philadelphia's 30th St. Station gazes high above him at an erotic statue of two mythic figures in some sort of embrace, the pulsating music, in voice-like chords, comes back, suggesting his bewilderment and wonder at the statue and what it depicts. A variation of this gently pulsing music is prominent during detective John Book's (Harrison Ford) night of healing with Rachel (Kelly McGillis), a beautiful Amish widow, at whose farmstead he has ended up with a gunshot wound. The music serves to sug-gest the growing intimacy and spiritual bond between them. After the violent climax, in which Book manages to dispose of his corrupt pursuers—with the help of some Amish corn, providentially stored in a silo—the pulsing music underscores the long, silent glances of farewell between the two protagonists, reaffirming the essential goodness of their interaction, which stops poignantly short of actual love-making. In all the foregoing, the music is naturally con-strued either as establishing something about the characters or else as evincing the attitudes of the cinematic narrator toward them—attitudes we are clearly invited to share.

However, there is the virtuoso "Barn Raising" scene, located roughly in the center of the film, to consider. This provides the occasion of the film's main musical cue: an extended piece, lasting about four minutes, on the order of the Pachelbel's *Canon* (that is to say, variations on a ground bass). The image track shows us wagons laden with supplies, coming together, people on foot congregating, getting ready to work, and then, in stages, the raising of the barn, beginning with walls assembled at an earlier time, and finishing with the whole superstructure in place. The music, by means of its unity, solid flow, and arching sureness of direction, admirably symbolizes the strength of the Amish and the spirit of life-affirming communitarianism exemplified in the activity of cooperatively building a newlywed couple the barn they will need to sustain themselves.

What, then, gives any pause in regarding this cue as wholly narrative? Only this: the meter and rhythms of the music in this scene are largely and significantly, though not slavishly or mechanically, synchronized with the actions visually depicted. The pace and pattern of the visual editing seems to respond, not so much to any internal narrative demand, but rather, to the steady progression of the music. The cue is not so much designed to flesh out the scene as the scene seems designed to illustrate the cue. All told, this suggests assignment of the cue's music to the implied filmmaker, as opposed to the internal narrator, since the artful synchronization noted is most naturally taken as an aspect of the aesthetic construction of *the film* as the conjunction of an image track and a sound track, rather than an aspect of how the narrator is presenting, through resources available to him, *the story*. It seems plausible to regard the music of "Barn Raising" as attributable, at least in part, directly to the implied filmmaker.

The main cue in Hugh Hudson's *Chariots of Fire* occurs near the beginning of the film, accompanying a scene of athletes in training: two dozen or so men running along the ocean in gym whites, represented as the fifty-year-old memory of one of the runners. Vangelis's synthesized music, a tune of simple nobility over a throbbing bass with snare-drum-like accents, is heard throughout, as the credits roll. The cue lasts a few minutes, and the scene ends visually with the group of men cutting inland and returning to the grounds of a building in Kent, where they have gone to train in preparation for the 1928 Olympics.

Now this cue may contribute in part to narration—understood as making-fictional—by making more precise the state of the runners as exhilaration, as opposed to mere determinedness, or by evincing a narratorial attitude, for example, one of confident control, or by indicating a mood the narrator would like to impose on the viewer, for example, one of heroism. But there still seems to be a certain "surplus value," as it were, to the cue. Those narrative ends do not appear to exhaust the functioning of the cue; its scale and expressiveness seem more than is called for with respect to those ends, imparting to the activity of jogging on the beach an almost godly aspect, without it becoming fictional in the story that such activity really has such status, or even that the narrator believes that it does. Instead, it seems tempting to regard it as attributable, at least in part, to the implied filmmaker directly: it appears to testify to the almost religious regard in which he holds the athletic efforts of those young Britishers of yesteryear. The emotive "surplus value" of this cue, as far as plausible narrative functioning is concerned, is what points, it seems, to the implied filmmaker as a locus of attribution.

10

Having uncovered some cases of film music with equivocal or partial narrative status, we are now ready to contemplate cases of substantially, perhaps wholly, nonnarrative film music. My claim is that such music, which I characterize as *additive* (or *juxtapositional*) film music, is attributable directly to the implied maker of the film. Such music alters, often powerfully, the artistic content or effect of the complete film, but it does not do so by nuancing narration, that is, by making or helping to make things fictional in the film's world.

As a first example, consider Robert Bresson's *Mouchette*. There is only one significant musical cue in the film, a segment of Monteverdi's Magnificat. It is heard very near the opening, during which the titles are projected, and again at the end, when Mouchette, an abused country girl of thirteen or so, commits suicide by rolling in a sheet into a pond and drowning. Lindley Hanlon gives a sensitive reading of the music in this film that supports, I think, a large nonnarrative understanding of it, an understanding that connects it rather more closely with the filmmaker than with the film's internal storyteller:

> From *Mouchette* on, Bresson uses music only at the beginning or the end of a film unless the source of the music can emanate from the space and situation of the film narrative. . . . It is a more subtle, less intrusive means on Bresson's part of authorial commentary on the action of the film. . . . Recurring after Mouchette's death, the Monteverdi music seems to function as Bresson's requiem for the girl, who has wrapped herself in a shroudlike vestments. . . . The words of the "Magnificat" affirm the possibility of another life after death and sanctify Mouchette's decision to escape from the despair of her own life.[43]

The music here is most plausibly assigned to the implied filmmaker—as affirming the general possibility of grace as exemplified in the tale of Mouchette[44]—rather than to the film's relatively effaced internal presenter, especially as it seems to frame the fictional narrative from without, like a pair of musical bookends, as opposed to shaping it from within.

Terrence Malick's singular film *Badlands* provides an outstanding example of an appropriated score, consisting mainly of extracts from Carl Orff's "Musica Poetica" and Erik Satie's "Trois Morceaux en Forme de Poire." This score also serves as one of my key examples of nondiegetic film music that is not, in the main, usefully construed as narrative.

Badlands, based loosely on Charles Starkweather's 1958 shooting spree in the Midwest, contains a partially unreliable narration, since two components of it, the image track and the voice-over narration by one of the main characters, Holly (Sissy Spacek), are at odds with one another (in some respects, only at certain points, and in other respects, throughout). Here, as is customary, the visual representation is taken to be the more truthful, "on the convention that seeing is believing,"[45] and so when what is shown wars with what is told, we are inclined to credit the former.

Orff's and Satie's music, I maintain, is characteristically employed in *Badlands* in a mode of distanced and reflective juxtaposition to the story narrated, by an intelligence standing just outside that narration. It is not, in general, attributable to the film's narrating agent, but only to the implied filmmaker. To make this point I examine at length one particular cue.

Fairly early on, we are shown Kit (Martin Sheen), the film's other main character, working cattle in a feedlot, after having been fired from his job as a garbage collector. On the soundtrack is a striking, far from inaudible, portion of Orff's score, consisting of sharply rhythmic xylophone or marimba music, built on an exotic scale, having no obvious connection with, or fittingness to, gritty scenes of cows being force-fed and almost expiring in the heat. That is to say, there is nothing in the character of the states of affairs depicted that the music could plausibly be thought to second, nor anything indeterminate about those states of affairs that the music might plausibly be thought to specify.

Could it be narrative in the sense of expressing the cinematic narrator's view of the situation depicted? This seems unlikely, if only because it is rather unclear what sort of attitude could be signaled by such music in relation to the events shown. In addition, the cinematic narrator, who often visually corrects or gainsays Holly's romantic and simplistic notions of what has transpired in her time with Kit, comes across as an agency too sober and straightforward, almost nonhuman in its detachedness—consider the odd montages of nature shots that occur occasionally during the film, giving the impression of an iguana-eye's point of view—to be credited with a sentiment as quirky and mischievous as that expressed by this musical cue.

Might the music be narrative in virtue of acting to characterize Holly's recollective impression of Kit's job at the feedlot? Such a hypothesis is multiply problematic. First, we haven't been given any reason to think the nondiegetic music is in the service of the voice-over narrator, but at most, the cinematic narrator operating from the point of view of or on behalf of some character; that is to say, there must be rather special indications, not here present, before we will think of nondiegetic music as a resource belonging to, rather than applied in elucidation of, a character in the story. Second, since there is reason not to regard the image track as an accurate version of Holly's memories—it regularly outstrips, and occasionally contradicts, her verbal narration of what happened—the ground for thinking of the soundtrack music as signifying Holly's impression of those sights seems lacking.[46] There is little reason to think, in particular, that she ever visited Kit at the feedlot or witnessed the kinds of scenes we see on screen. Third, whatever attitude we found such music to connote, it seems not to be one we would ascribe to hazy-minded Holly while the thought of Kit at the feedlot was before her mind.

This leaves as the only interpretively live possibility the assignment of the music to the implied filmmaker who, from a point outside both the story and its narration, has apparently added this music as a kind of counterpoint to the fictional drama. To what end? It is hard to say, especially without an interpretation of the film as a whole, but possibly one of aesthetic embellishment, or derangement of the viewer's moral compass, or refraction of the story's content in a distorting mirror, or external meditation on the film's happenings.

Now the music of Orff and Satie is characterized in general by an intentional simplicity, a primitiveness of musical materials, and a studied directness of effect, and that employed in this film is no exception. Thus perhaps the function of this music in the film—on a global plane, rather than scene-by-scene—could be said to be reflection of the basic childlikeness and obliviousness to social reality of the two principals, and especially that of Holly, the verbal narrator. I think that is so, but for the reasons given above this music, and that aspect of the film's content, is best laid at the door of the implied filmmaker, rather than any agent internal to the narrative.

My next examples come from Woody Allen's *Love and Death,* whose appropriated score is derived entirely from the suites to *Lt. Kije* and *Alexander Nevsky* by Prokofiev. The sleigh-like music from *Lt. Kije* starts up after Natasha (Diane Keaton) announces her engagement to a herring merchant, and extends through her riding off in a carriage and subsequent shots of Russian troops in training, marshalled to protect Russia against Napoleon. This music has a satirical effect, more properly attributed to Allen as *auteur,* than to Boris, Allen's character, as narrator, or even the cinematic narrator conceived as encompassing Boris's verbal narration. A farcical battle scene between Russian and French troops, shortly thereafter, is accompanied by the grim and heavy music for the "Battle on the Ice" from *Alexander Nevsky;* the mismatch is palpable, and the implied equation of the two battles laughable. Both the satirical intent inherent in this juxtaposition, and the frame of cultural reference with which it operates, seem to put it beyond ascription to either Boris or the cinematic narrator.

The last example I discuss of a film much of whose musical soundtrack is best seen as additive or juxtapositional, rather than narrative, is Stanley Kubrick's *A Clockwork Orange.* The opening credit—the words "A Clockwork Orange" on a garish orange field—is followed by a close-up of Alex (Malcolm McDowell) and his pals (droogs) in a bar that dispenses drugged milk (moloko) that disposes its consumers toward acts of "ultraviolence." Soon Alex's voice-over is heard, which establishes what we will soon see as Alex's recollections of his recent past. Walter Carlos's synthesized music here is a slow-moving, quasi-Handelian progression, with a hint of Dies Irae. It functions narratively in setting an appropriate mood, in suggesting something of the effect of moloko drinking, and in perhaps foreshadowing some of the grim doings the narrator, acting on Alex's behalf, has in store to present to us, in due course. But the appropriated music employed in the film, notably that of Rossini and Beethoven, functions rather differently.

Rossini's *La Gazza Ladra* Overture begins on the soundtrack as an old man is being beaten by Alex and his droogs, continues over a cut to another gang of youths assaulting a naked girl on a stage, leading to a fight between the two gangs, and covers the escape of Alex and his droogs from the scene by car, fading out only as they approach a house in the country whose occupants they are going to terrorize.

There is no obvious narrative appropriateness to the music: it seems neither to convey information about the events shown, nor to suggest the narrator's perspective on those events, nor to suggest an attitude that viewers should plausibly adopt toward them. I take it the first and third points will be granted without dissent; the second, though, might be supported further, as follows. If the claim of narrative function is to be sustained on that ground, it seems we would have to posit either a perversely inhuman cinematic narrator, whose lighthearted view of the proceedings is reflected in the music, or else a psychologically more normal one who merely signals to us, through the music, Alex's perversely comic perspective on the violence he is perpetrating on others. The first possibility strikes me as unmotivated, while the second, though more promising, faces the problem that it casts Alex's reactions as on perhaps too high a level of sophistication.

Thus we arrive, once again, at the assignment of this music directly to the implied filmmaker as interpretively the most reasonable option. As such, how does it function? Pasted on to the scenes of violence presented by the film's internal narrator, it invites us, at least initially, to see them as a joke, thus making us complicit in the mindless pleasure of Alex and his pals in inflicting pain, in the expectation, presumably, of getting us to be even more horrified when we realize what we've been duped into. Kubrick, and not the cinematic narrator, is addressing us directly through this odd and unsettling juxtaposition of music and story.

A similar scene takes place in Alex's room at home, with two girls he has picked up in a record shop. It is filmed in extremely fast motion, to the accompaniment of Rossini's *William Tell* Overture. Here both the fast-motion filming and the superimposed frenetic music seem to reflect the activity of the implied filmmaker, as opposed to that of the film's perceptual enabler or internal commentator.

A related, though distinct, use of music occurs in a scene also set in Alex's room, to which he has repaired after the first night's round of ultraviolence. He deposits things in his booty drawer, checks on his pet python, and puts the scherzo of Beethoven's *Ninth Symphony* on his sound system. The music, here diegetic, is synched to a montage of close-ups of statue parts, as Alex imagines acts of sex and violence, recounted in voice-over. But this intrastory perversion of Beethoven by the protagonist echoes and parallels the implied filmmaker's superficially warped overlaying of Alex's recollections of occasions of torture and fornication with Rossini's diverting scores.[47]

Near the very end of the film, Alex is being questioned by a few intellectuals, including the writer he crippled earlier in the film, about behavioral conditioning via background music. It is not too much to suggest that this scene obliquely raises within the film the issue of film music's legitimacy and role, and of its possible subversive effects, for example, the undermining of autonomy or the blunting of rationality. This self-consciousness in the film about what we may call nonaesthetic or incidental uses of music reinforces the assignment of additive, as opposed to narrative, status to the Rossini overtures appropriated by Kubrick for *A Clockwork Orange.*[48]

II

Though in many cases where nondiegetic film music is more reasonably assigned to the implied filmmaker rather than the film's narrative agent, we find that such music is being used ironically or satirically, for example, as with *Love and Death* and *A Clockwork Orange,* it is important to remember that that is not the only possibility. The examples of *Mouchette* and *Badlands,* and in a partial vein, *Witness* and *Chariots of Fire,* illustrate as much.[49] And we may also observe, at this point, that nondiegetic music is not the only music in a film responsibility for which may redound, without intermediary, to the implied filmmaker, and which may be read by us as a direct reflection of authorial stance or personality. Jane Campion's recent film *The Piano* offers a case of film music commissioned and composed for diegetic insertion in a film— Michael Nyman's music for mute protagonist Ada's pianism—rather than nondiegetic accompaniment. The music's characterization of its fictional originator—Ada—is a function that can only be assigned, it seems, to the implied filmmaker, as the agent who has chosen the characters, their actions, and their traits, in constructing and arranging the elements of the filmic object as she has.[50]

How does the distinction we have been exploring, of film music as additive versus film music as narrative, relate to another standard classification, namely that of film music as commentative? The answer is: not simply. The equation of narrative and commentative will not do, for two reasons. First, some music of clearly narrative function is not reasonably thought of as commentative, unless all information-conveying counts as commentary. Second, some additive music seems to supply a commentary, if oblique, on matters with which a film is concerned. In light of this, we might distinguish between *externally* commentative music, assignable to the implied filmmaker, and *internally* commentative music, assignable to the cinematic narrator.

Still, it is important to stress that musical commentary on the events of a fictional story as such, or the characters figuring in those events, remains a possibility only for the cinematic narrator internal to the fiction. Additive music, assignable to an implied filmmaker, might generate, as noted, a kind of commentary as well, but it could not be on the fictional events themselves, from a perspective internal to the fictional world, but at most on the representation of those events or on the significance of events of that type. The implied filmmaker of a fiction film is not on the same plane as the events of the film's world—which are for him, as for us, fictional—and so his direct commentary on those events is not a coherent option. For instance, if the Magnificat cue at the end of *Mouchette* expresses Bresson's attitude of consolation toward

Mouchette's suicide, this has to be understood not as an attitude literally directed on the suicide of Mouchette—an event in which Bresson presumably does not believe—but instead as an attitude bound up with the film's representation of that event, or directed toward events of the sort represented by the film.

A standard function of nondiegetic film music, we have observed, is to reveal, confirm, or make precise a character's feelings or attitudes toward something or other in the story.[51] Such a function makes most sense in connection with a narrator, rather than an implied filmmaker, since it presupposes an agent on the same plane, fictionally, as the characters, whose existence the narrator believes in, and whose lives the narrator selectively presents to us. The deliverances of narrative film music seem to come from one who shares a world with the characters, rather than one who has invented them, and everything else in the fictional world, from whole cloth.

On the other hand, another standard function of nondiegetic film music is to bind the incidents of a film together in a common ambience. The thematic, instrumental, and stylistic continuities typical of film scores help to create a consistency of tone or feeling across the span of a film, especially where the events presented are not very tightly connected in a dramatic sense. Thus this, rather than any narrative task, seems to be the main function of Rota's score for Fellini's *Amarcord*. When nondiegetic film music has this function, it is more naturally ascribed to an implied filmmaker than to an internal cinematic narrator. Nondiegetic film music bridging scenes of different character, say, or smoothing over large lapses of time, is of this sort. Such music, like the presentational, voice-over, and mind-over narrators in a film, is understood primarily as constructed or arranged by the implied filmmaker in putting together the aesthetic object which is the total film, rather than as something used or employed by the cinematic narrator in its different narrative capacities.

Returning to the five functions of film music recognized by Copland, I would suggest that only two—underlining characters' psychological states and sustaining and releasing tension—are clearly assignable to the cinematic narrator. The others—ensuring continuity, providing background filler, and creating atmosphere—can with equal, or more, justice be thought of as activities of the implied filmmaker, in that they seem aimed directly at the viewer as an aesthetic subject, at causing his or her experience to be a certain way, rather than at defining or delineating the film's fictional world.[52] If we consider, similarly, the list of functions drawn up by Gorbman in her study of the operation of classical film music,[53] I would suggest that two—the signifying of emotion, and the referential and connotative cuing of narrative—are assignable to the cinematic narrator, while the remaining two—the provision of continuity and the achievement of unity—make most sense as the charge of the implied filmmaker.

What of my own list of fifteen functions of film music, drawn up earlier (section VI)? By present lights, I think they sort out as follows: functions (1),

(2), (3), (4), (5), (6), (7), (8), and (9) are arguably narrative, in that they involve making something fictional in the film, and so music functioning in such ways is assignable to the cinematic narrator. Functions (10), (11), (12), (13), (14), and (15) are arguably nonnarrative, and are often achieved through music of additive status, assignable only to the implied filmmaker. There is not, however, a perfect correspondence between the division of functions as either narrative or nonnarrative, and the categorization of cues as either narrative or additive, because a cue can have significant functions of both sorts. What is true is roughly this: if a cue has significant narrative function, whether or not it functions in addition nonnarratively, then it is a narrative cue, whereas if a cue has no significant narrative function, then it is an additive cue.

The question I have been exploring in the latter part of this essay can be put as follows: when is nondiegetic film music primarily a compositional element in a film, at the command of the implied filmmaker, and when is it instead, or in addition, an instrument we imagine as at the service of the cinematic narrator, generating truths in the world of the film, either about the story as such or about the act of its narration? But perhaps the same question poses itself, on close examination, for a number of other filmic elements viewed initially just as compositional, for example, lighting or camera angle. When is the dim or filtered quality of light in a scene—as in *Vertigo*, when Judy reemerges into Scottie's presence as Madeleine—merely a directorial choice and when a manifestation, as well, of narrative activity on the part of the film's internal presenter, showing things in a light they would not otherwise appear in? When is an off-kilter view of a man running across a square— as in *The Third Man*—just a matter of the director's tilt of the camera in relation to the actor being filmed, and when is it to be regarded as well as connoting an intervention of the cinematic narrator, as showing us the character from an oblique perspective, with whatever that suggests about either the character or the narrator's view of him? The issues addressed here concerning the interpretation of nondiegetic film music resonate, I suspect, across the whole spectrum of meaning-making elements in film.

NOTES

I thank the editors, David Bordwell and Noël Carroll, for helpful comments on the style and substance of this essay. Needless to say, they do not agree with everything in it.

1. For more on these categories, see David Bordwell and Kristin Thompson, *Film Art: An Introduction*, 4th ed. (New York: McGraw-Hill, 1993), pp. 295–303.

2. For example, Snow's *Wavelength* or Resnais's *L'Annee Derniere à Marienbad*.

3. This is a central thesis in Claudia Gorbman's *Unheard Melodies: Narrative Film Music* (Bloomington: Indiana University Press, 1987), and is echoed by other recent psychoanalytically oriented writers on film.

4. Though he argues vigorously against the third form of disavowal in his attack on *enonciation* theorists, there remains something of the first and second in the constructivism about film meaning defended by David Bordwell; see his *Narration in the Fiction Film* (Madison: University of Wisconsin Press, 1985) and *Making Meaning* (Cambridge: Harvard University Press, 1989). For a critique of this aspect of Bordwell's otherwise salutory approach to film, see Berys Gaut, "Making Sense of Films: Neoformalism and Its Limits," *Forum for Modern Language Studies* (forthcoming). Bordwell's rejection of narrative agents in film as such is also criticized by Seymour Chatman, *Coming to Terms* (Ithaca, N.Y.: Cornell University Press, 1990), chapter 8.

5. See his *Coming to Terms*, especially chapters 5, 7, and 8. Another writer who seems to accept the necessity of positing narrative agency in narrative film, though he verges on abstracting this to the point of abandonment, is Edward Branigan, *Point of View in the Cinema* (Berlin: Mouton, 1984).

6. A position taken, for example, by Gregory Currie, in "Visual Fictions," *Philosophy Quarterly* 41 (April 1991): 129–43. I respond to Currie in "Seeing, Imaginarily, at the Movies," *Philosophy Quarterly* 43 (January 1993): 70–78.

7. All references that follow are to *Coming to Terms*.

8. This formulation of Chatman's is actually somewhat off the mark: it's not the *film* that is presented by the narrator, but various perceptual *contents*, various *sights and sounds*, that is, what one is enabled to see and hear, courtesy of the presumed powers of such a narrator. The film as such is rather presented by the *filmmaker* or, interpretively, the *implied filmmaker.*

9. This is not to deny that it is sometimes be in the purview of the cinematic narrator to present the mental contents of some character, for example, memories, fantasies, dreams, visualizations. But two points about this should be noted. One, it may be unclear in such cases whether it is the cinematic narrator, acting on the character's behalf, who shows the character's mentation, or rather the character, acting as his own narrator, who is doing so. Two, the possibility of this sort of presenting requires a background of presentings of perceptual reality at a more basic story level.

10. Problems of terminology loom here which a preemptive strike of clarification might dispel. Of the three ideas, *cinematic narrator, filmic presenter,* and *perceptual enabler,* the first is perhaps the broadest and the third the narrowest. Certainly there are actions of the cinematic narrator which go beyond those of perceptual enabling or filmic presenting, most notably in this context, narrative pointing through nondiegetic music. Whether there is a distinction worth making between filmic presenter and perceptual enabler is less clear; if so, the former would include the latter but comprise in addition resources such as character voice-overs or mind-overs, affording access to the fictional world in a wider-than-perceptual vein.

11. Except when the narrator's relationship to the story being presented is clearly signaled, in the novel or film, as one of relating a fiction as such, for example, as through a disclaimer like "this is only a story, it never happened." But this is quite rare in fiction film; it is even rare in literary fiction, Thackeray's *Vanity Fair* standing as a classic example, and John Fowles's *French Lieutenant's Woman* as a recent, though more ambiguous, one. Kendall Walton, in *Mimesis as Make-Believe* (Cambridge: Harvard University Press, 1990), marks this distinction as one between *reporting narrators* and *storytelling narrators* (pp. 368–72). The overwhelming majority of narrators in narrative fiction are reporting narrators, and as Walton points out, in such cases narrator and events narrated necessarily belong to the same world.

12. As in the event of a wholly "effaced" and "omniscient" third-person narrator, the norm for cinematic fictions.

13. See *Narration in Light* (Baltimore: Johns Hopkins University Press, 1986), chapter 7. See also my review of it in *Journal of Aesthetics and Art Criticism* 47 (Summer 1989): 290–92.

14. Wilson, *Narration in Light*, p. 132.

15. Ibid., pp. 133–34.

16. Of course he can and does offer us the vision and audition of various events which took place during the filming, namely, the enacting of various roles by various actors—but that is another matter.

17. Compare Walton, *Mimesis as Make-Believe*, p. 366.

18. Nor are supporters of the notion of a narrator internal to film immune to this confusion. Consider the formulation of Nick Browne, quoted by both Branigan and Chatman: "the authority which can be taken to rationalize the presentation of shots" [*The Rhetoric of Filmic Narration* (Ann Arbor: UMI Research Press, 1984), p. 1]. But since *shots* are constructional elements of films as made objects, that authority can only be the implied filmmaker; the authority, or agency, that Browne is really after is that which appears to rationalize the presentation of *views*, or sights and sounds.

19. There are other sources of Wilson's reluctance to embrace filmic narrators on a standing basis. He suggests at one point that a filmic narrator distinct from the implied filmmaker would, by analogy to literature, have to be "a *character* that the text *depicts* directly or indirectly" (*Narration in Light*, p. 136). But this is only half right; the narrator is indeed a kind of fictional character, but not one that need be depicted, as I understand that term. If purely dialogic short stories, or purely epistolary novels, have narrators, then such narrators are not depicted, either directly or indirectly. So the fact that cinematic narrators are standardly not depicted, that is, nothing in films shows or announces them as such, is not a principled impediment to acknowledging them.

20. Ibid., pp. 136–37.

21. My discussion so far may give the impression that I regard the role of the implied presenter of a narrative film as confined to that of providing views on events understood as fully constituted independently of the shower's activity. But while I think that that is indeed the dominant role of a film's presenter, it need not be the exclusive one. The cinematic narrator might in part be thought of as a fashioner or shaper of events that are only *then* presented, more straightforwardly, in certain ways (for example, in certain lights, or in a certain order). This fashioning or shaping of fictional events thought of as existing, on a more basic level, prior to narrative attention, can be seen as a more subtle way of presenting events taken to belong to the underlying event structure with which narration is concerned. If so, then the narrative structuring of films is a two-stage affair, and that which is effected through camerawork and editing is subsequent to that understood to be achieved in the staging of action and the manipulation of setting. (For more on this dimension of cinematic narration, and the rationale of its recognition, see Bordwell, *Narration in the Fiction Film*).

22. Kathryn Kalinak, *Settling the Score: Music and Classical Hollywood Film* (Madison: University of Wisconsin Press, 1992), p. 30.

23. Sarah Kozloff, *Invisible Storytellers: Voice-Over in American Fiction Film* (Berkeley: University of California Press, 1988), pp. 43–44.

24. Gorbman, *Unheard Melodies*, p. 11.

25. Noël Carroll, *Mystifying Movies* (New York: Columbia University Press, 1988), p. 216.

26. Note that this would apply even when such music is unforegrounded: if it appears to respond to the demands of storytelling, broadly understood, then it can be construed as something like musical musing, *sotto voce*, on the cinematic narrator's part.

27. See Walton, *Mimesis as Make-Believe.* For an entrée into this important work, see my critical notice, "Making Believe," *Dialogue* 32 (1993): 359–74.

28. "Film music . . . often contributes subtly but effectively to the generation of fictional truths—helping to establish, for example, that fictionally a character is nervous or cocky or ecstatic . . ." (*Mimesis as Make-Believe,* p. 172).

29. See Kalinak's informative discussion in *Settling the Score,* p. 178.

30. Graham Bruce, *Bernard Herrmann: Film Music and Narrative* (Ann Arbor, Mich.: UMI Research Press, 1985), p. 68.

31. *Mystifying Movies,* p. 217.

32. In some literary fictions, for example, Hemingway's *The Killers* or Robbe-Grillet's *La jalousie,* this latter function may seem to have lapsed. But I would argue that even in such fictions there are attitudes the narrator implicitly invites the reader to adopt, precisely in virtue of so pointedly eschewing normal commentary.

33. Of course, when a narrator in a film is also a character in the action, as with a homodiegetic voice-over narrator, then certain facts about such a narrator are also facts of the story.

34. For example, that Uncle Charlie is the murderer is underwritten by his unexplained money in the opening hotel room scene, by his evident concern to keep an item in the daily newspaper unread, by his unreasonable aversion to being photographed, by his maniacal utterance at the dinner table about fat, wheezing, useless widows, by the already-inscribed ring itself, and so on. That young Charlie suspects him does not become true until she is informed about the manhunt by one of the two detectives who have been trailing Uncle Charlie—though of course there have been signs, intended for and readable by the viewer, well before that.

35. Their psychic kinship is adumbrated earlier in the film, in the parallelism of our first views of them both, reclining on beds with their hands behind their heads, in the worried, almost cynical remarks about family values that young Charlie makes when we first hear her speak, and in the coincidence of young Charlie deciding to send her uncle a telegram just hours after he has, unbeknownst to her, sent one in her direction.

36. Bruce, *Bernard Herrmann,* p. 143.

37. This scene illustrates nicely a narrative possibility mentioned above (see note 22), whereby a cinematic narrator might be thought of as presenting story events, conceived of as already existing fictionally at a basic level, *in a certain way,* through a partial shaping of the event being viewed.

38. Bruce, *Bernard Herrmann,* p. 173.

39. Even more conservatively, perhaps the only fictional truth generated is that the *narrator* is reminding us of the possibility of Scottie's imminent vertigo, without it yet being fictional either that it is imminent, or that Scottie believes it is.

40. Bruce, *Bernard Herrmann,* p. 163.

41. See Wilson's discussion in *Narration in Light,* chapter 4.

42. The particular look of these images owes to Weir's trademark use of idealizing telephoto shots.

43. "Sound in Bresson's *Mouchette,*" in *Film Sound,* ed. Elisabeth Weis and John Belton (New York: Columbia University Press, 1985), pp. 329–30.

44. In identifying this theme as that of grace I of course rely on a knowledge of Bresson's oeuvre as a whole, and of the artist implicit in that oeuvre.

45. Chatman, *Coming to Terms,* p. 136.

46. The sequences that make it clearest the image track is not to be thought of as a reliable representation of Holly's occurrent memories are one in which we see Kit shoot a football and then hear Holly, a minute later, recount this event, and another in which we see Kit, trying to outrun his police pursuers, suddenly stop his car, get out,

shoot its left front tire flat, and then blatantly await capture, while Holly alludes to the incident, never observed by her, in a mode of speculation rather than reportage: "Many times I've wondered about why Kit didn't get away. He said he had a flat, but from the way he kept coming back to that, I doubt it."

47. A contrasting, rather more cynical, view of the mode of film scoring of which *A Clockwork Orange* was perhaps the pioneer is provided in this recent commentary: "Faced with the task of differentiating their scenes of brutality and mayhem from all the other scenes of brutality and mayhem, film makers are using music to distance the viewer from violence—or to comment ironically on it. As the images get more explicit, the accompanying tunes seem to be getting more frothy. Everything from Bach to hook-laden pop-rock songs provides background for images of fist fights, shootings, stabbings and torture" (Kenneth Chanko, "It's Got A Nice Beat, You Can Torture To It," *New York Times,* Feb. 20, 1994).

48. The scene may in fact be what Wilson calls a "rhetorical figure of narrative instruction," something offered by the filmmaker to the viewer as a key to interpreting the film's narration generally. See *Narration in Light,* pp. 49–50.

49. Another intriguing case is Slava Tsukerman's *Liquid Sky* (1983), whose soundtrack employs an overmodulated synthesized harpsichord version of eighteenth century composer Marin Marais's hypnotically repetitive "Sonnerie de Ste. Genevieve du Mont." It is unclear to me (on the basis of a single viewing, ten years ago) whether that music belongs in the satirical or the nonsatirical subcategory of additive film music.

50. One critic has remarked on the music for this film as follows: "Both the orchestral and solo keyboard music suggest a modern minimalist gloss of Chopin and Liszt but spun off plain, abrupt folk tunes . . . the pianism suggests someone doggedly trying to speak through the keyboard. . . . As distinctive as it is, the music is strangely cramped and emotionally arid . . . the solo piano passages sound too much like elementary practice exercises to soar into the stratosphere" (Stephen Holden, *New York Times,* Jan. 30, 1994).

51. A function highlighted by Noël Carroll in *Mystifying Movies,* pp. 216–23; Carroll labels film music of this familiar type "modifying music."

52. Though in regard to the last of these, creating atmosphere, it was suggested earlier how, in many cases, this can be understood as having narrative status, if the atmosphere involved is one the film's narrative agent can be plausibly thought of projecting.

53. *Unheard Melodies,* p. 73.

13

Nonfiction Film and
Postmodernist Skepticism

Noël Carroll

I

Perhaps no area of film theory invokes philosophy so quickly as does the discussion of nonfiction film. For inasmuch as a great many nonfiction films are meant to convey information about the world, film theorists are almost immediately disposed to reach for their favorite epistemological convictions in order to assess, and—nearly as often—to dispute the knowledge claims of nonfiction films.[1]

Among film theorists in times gone by, it was a popular sport to charge that insofar as nonfiction films unavoidably require selectivity—that is, cameras inevitably frame and focus; and editors must exclude and, just as importantly, *include*—then the pretensions of nonfiction filmmakers to deliver objective information about the world and to advance justifiable claims thereof are decisively vitiated.[2] For selectivity guarantees bias; and since motion picture technology is inherently and necessarily selective, it is necessarily biased. Bias, so to speak, is built into the apparatus itself. Therefore, any claims to objective knowledge on behalf of a documentary filmmaker are foreclosed a priori.

This argument contains two notions worth scotching: first, that there is something about nonfiction film, due to its inherent nature, that renders it, in contradistinction to other things (such as sociological treatises), uniquely incapable of objectivity; and second, that selectivity guarantees bias. Of course, the preceding argument connects these premises by means of a convenient essentialism: the film medium is by its very nature selective; therefore, it is by its very nature biased (incapable of objectivity).

But clearly, selectivity, even if it is an inevitable feature of film, is not a unique feature of film. Every mode of inquiry and its attendant channels of publicity—from physics through history to journalism—is selective. So nothing special is discovered by revealing the selectivity of the motion picture apparatus. Moreover, insofar as we do not regard physics or history as exiled from objectivity just because they select, then there should be no impulse to suspect the nonfiction film's credentials, on a priori grounds, merely because it is selective. We can't have chemistry or economics without selectivity. Indeed, it is their selectivity that makes them possible. Why should we expect things to stand differently with nonfiction films?

Needless to say, some film theorists may regard this response as too precipitous. They may argue that selectivity in any area of inquiry is suspicious. Thus, if I defend the possibility of objectivity in the nonfiction film by appealing to analogous practices of selectivity in physics, then, it might be argued, all that has been shown is that physics, along with any other mode of inquiry I choose for analogy, will also require reassessment. For selectivity implies bias and bias precludes objectivity.

Yet surely it is a mistake to presume that selectivity entails bias. It may in some cases be what makes bias possible; it may in some contexts even invite bias. But it does not *guarantee* bias. Furthermore, most (perhaps all) known practices of inquiry are alert to the possibility of bias. They possess established protocols of inquiry that, among other things, are designed to deter the operation of bias; and, moreover, if bias is detected as playing a role in the production of a certain body of research, then the burden of proof—that the findings are not thereby distorted—falls upon the researcher in question.

Modes of inquiry and their associated avenues of communication are governed by protocols that have been established in order to secure the objectivity of conclusions in the relevant area of discourse. Many of these protocols are concerned with filtering out or diminishing the epistemically baleful effects of bias. These protocols may not succeed in rooting out bias in every case; they do not make the operation of bias impossible. But there is no reason to suppose that they do not work some of the time or even much of the time.

That is, if selectivity makes bias possible or even invites bias, it is also possible to be aware of this and to design provisions against the influence of bias—both at the level of the individual researcher and at the level of the community of inquiry at large. Self-awareness can encourage self-regulation. Scientists, historians, journalists, and even nonfiction filmmakers can bring standards of objectivity to bear upon other inquirers in order to determine whether or not bias has distorted the claims they advance. And that we may criticize others for biases and correct them indicates that we can do the same in our own case.

Thus, selectivity can occur without bias; selectivity is compatible with objectivity; and there is no a priori argument from selectivity that shows that nonfiction filmmakers and physicists have no purchase on objectivity. For, among other things, the protocols of objectivity within an established community of discourse and inquiry provide a degree of insurance against bias which, though it may fail on occasion, is not predestined to fail always.

Undoubtedly, it would be misleading to talk as if there were simply one set of protocols or standards for nonfiction filmmakers. Nonfiction filmmakers abide by different, though not nonconverging, standards of objectivity relative to the type of inquiry in which they are engaged. For example, *Killer Whale,* directed by Jeff Foott and written by Malcolm Penny for the Time

Warner series *Predators*, abides by the protocols of a certain type of popular-science writing, whereas *Truth or Dare* seems committed to respecting little more than the protocols of honest, eye-witness reporting—namely, that what is portrayed happened and, perhaps, that it be a fair sample of what happened.

Not all nonfiction films succeed in meeting the relevant standards of objectivity, just as not all scientific research is above reproach. However, there is no reason to suspect that all nonfiction film fails in this regard, just as a parallel judgment about physics would be unwarranted. Indeed, the very fact that we can say that some nonfiction film fails to measure up to the relevant standards of objectivity suggests, if there is to be a meaningful contrast here, that some succeed, or, at least, could succeed. So, once again, the argument from selectivity appears philosophically harmless, since determining bias in a particular film is always an empirical matter and not the foregone conclusion of a piece of conceptual analysis.

Maybe as a result of its virtually transparent defects, the selectivity argument, as rehearsed above, is rarely mounted by film theorists nowadays. However, the obsolescence of the selectivity argument, at least in its simplest forms, does not signal any abatement in the skepticism with which film theorists regard the prospects for objectivity in the nonfiction film. For it appears that the selectivity argument has left the field only to be replaced by new arguments, derived from postmodernist dogma and preached with Post-Structuralist energy, which once again challenge the epistemic probity of non-fiction films on what are alleged to be generic, theoretical grounds. In the remainder of this essay, I will examine some of the leading postmodernist arguments of the moment concerning the nonfiction film for the purpose of refuting what I take to be overly facile skepticism about the possibility of making motion pictures that are genuinely in the service of knowledge.[3]

2

In the introduction to his anthology, *Theorizing Documentary*—a state-of-the-art compendium of received thinking about the documentary film—editor Michael Renov maintains that:

> In every case, elements of style, structure, and expositional strategy draw upon preexistent constructs, or schemas, to establish meanings and effects for audiences. What I am arguing is that documentary shares the status of all discursive forms with regard to its tropic or figurative character and that it employs many of the methods and devices of its fictional counterpart.[4]

and that

> . . . all discursive forms—documentary included—are, if not fictional, at least *fictive*, this by virtue of their tropic character (their recourse to tropes or rhetorical figures). As Hayden White has so brilliantly described, "every mimesis can be

shown to be distorted and can serve, therefore, as an occasion for yet another description of the same phenomenon." This is because "all discourse *constitutes* the objects which it pretends only to describe realistically and to analyze objectively."[5]

Both these quotations evince Renov's intention to deconstruct the distinction between nonfiction and fiction. Certainly, there is a strategic motive behind this; scholars specializing in the documentary film appear to feel their subject has always been eclipsed by the attention lavished on the far more popular fiction film. By claiming a parity with fiction, I suppose theorists like Renov hope to claim a larger piece of the pie, if not for themselves, then for their clients. Documentary filmmakers and documentary film theorists alike embrace an adversarial relationship to the larger institution of fictional film. Perhaps this deconstructive ploy expresses the desire to fight the fiction film by joining it (though in a way, I believe, that puts the integrity of the nonfiction film in jeopardy).

But, aside from the politics of the academic film world, a further point in deconstructing the distinction between nonfiction and fiction is to endorse "skepticism toward the traditional claims made for documentary's powers to see and to know. . . ."[6] The thinking seems to be this: If there is no principled difference between nonfiction film and fiction film, then the claims of the nonfiction film to either objectivity or to truth are no better than those of a fiction. The aforesaid documentary *Killer Whale* is in the same epistemic boat (or, to suit the case, *out* of the same epistemic boat) as the fictional movie *Free Willy*.

One reason that Renov introduces to call into the question the distinction between nonfiction films and fiction films is that many of the devices that are used in nonfiction films—like flashbacks and crosscutting—are central narrative devices in fiction films. And, furthermore, techniques associated with nonfiction films, like jittery, handheld camera movements, can be appropriated by fiction filmmakers for heightened affect. This is all true. But it does not support the conclusion that Renov draws. For the distinction between nonfiction and fiction was never really based on differences in formal technique in the first place; so one cannot deconstruct the distinction by citing shared techniques in the second place.

This, of course, should have already been apparent to film theorists on the basis of literature. No one can tell by reading a passage whether it is nonfiction or fiction, for the simple reason that a writer of fiction can adopt any strategy associated with nonfiction writing for aesthetic effect, just as nonfiction writers can always try to approximate fictional techniques for their own purposes. Likewise, the distinction between nonfiction film and fiction film cannot be grounded in differences of formal technique, because, when it comes to technique, fiction and nonfiction filmmakers can and do imitate each other, just as fiction and nonfiction writers can and do. The distinction between nonfiction and fiction, therefore, does not collapse with the recognition of stylistic correlations, since the distinction never rested upon such formal or technical differentiae in the first place.

Standardly, when one attends a film, one does not have to guess—on the basis of how it looks and sounds—whether it is fiction or nonfiction. Nor does one typically guess whether a written narrative is a novel or a memoir. The film and the writing come labeled, or, as I say, *indexed,* one way or another, ahead of time.[7] When a film like *Killer Whale* is indexed as a nonfiction film that tells us something about its commitments, specifically that it is committed to certain standards of scientific accuracy and attendant protocols of objectivity. We, in turn, base our evaluations of such a film, to a large extent, on its achievement with respect to these standards and protocols in virtue of the film's commitment to a specific form of nonfiction exposition.

It is not a defect to present a killer whale who understands that petroleum is flammable in a science fiction film like *Orca,* but it would be problematic in a documentary such as *Killer Whale.* For in virtue of the kind of nonfiction that *Killer Whale* is, as signaled by the way in which it is indexed and circulated, *Killer Whale* must abide by certain canons of accuracy that a film like *Orca,* which is indexed and circulated as science fiction, need not respect. The distinction between nonfiction and fiction is a distinction between the commitments of the texts, not between the surface structures of the texts. Therefore, Renov's attempt to deconstruct the distinction between nonfiction and fiction on the basis of shared technique misses the point altogether.

But, of course, Renov's case for the allegedly fictive status of nonfiction film—the truth about nonfiction, as he puts it—is putatively based upon something deeper than shared narrative techniques between fictions and nonfictions. Following the postmodernist historiographer Hayden White,[8] Renov maintains that nonfiction film (like history à la White) is tropological and, therefore, fictive. What does this mean and why would anyone believe it?

According to Hayden White, historical writing is tropological. By this, he means to claim that historical writing, inasmuch as it is narrative, relies on certain recurring plot structures (such as Romance, Tragedy, Comedy, and Satire) which, in turn, are associated with certain rhetorical tropes or figures (such as metaphor, metonymy, synecdoche, and irony).[9] Historians use these narrative structures to organize the states of affairs and events that comprise their accounts into intelligible wholes, that is, into tidy packages comprehensible to readers.

However, although narrative structures organize the historian's accounts of sequences of states and affairs and events, the relations posited by said narratives have no basis in historical reality. Narratives, for example, have closure. But this is a feature of stories, not of the world. Likewise, one historian may narrate a series of events as a tragedy while another narrates the same series as a comedy, just as Shakespeare's recounting of those happenings in Denmark is tragic and Stoppard's hilarious. But in all these cases, comedy and tragedy are fictional; they belong solely to the order of telling, not being.

The states of affairs and events the historian alludes to do have a basis in historical reality, and the historian's claims about those states of affairs and events can be literally true or false. But the narratives in which those states of affairs and events figure are inventions, constructions, indeed, *fictions.* A romantic plot structure, qua representation, does not correspond to anything that has or will exist; subtract the events emplotted by the structure, and what remains—the plot—has no reference to reality.

The narrative structure in the historical recounting is not true or false; it is fictional. It is imposed on events by the historian and, as Renov's quotation indicates, it is thought to distort, presumably necessarily. Thus no historical narrative can pretend to accuracy or objectivity because in virtue of its possession of a narrative structure, it is both fictive and distortive. It merely *pretends* to refer objectively to the event-structures that plot structures appear to depict, because those event-structures are in fact the fabrications of narration—that is, "all discourse *constitutes* the objects which it pretends only to describe realistically and analyze objectively." Or, to put it differently, that which plot-structures seem to portray has no independent historical existence outside of narrative discourse.

Renov imports White's claims about historical writing to the case of the nonfiction film. By hypothesis, this is warranted by the fact that nonfiction films are often historical and even more often narrative, though it might also pay to note that frequently nonfiction films are neither historical nor narrative, just as historical writing itself is not always narrative. But, despite these flagrant problems, Renov somehow thinks that the matchings between White's subject and his own are significant enough to allow extrapolation of White's supposed findings about history to nonfiction film. Consequently, nonfiction films are said to be fictive in virtue of their tropological or narrative structures, which, it is thought, implies that they necessarily distort.

Moreover, the claims of nonfiction films to make objective reference to event-structures in the world must fail, for those event-structures belong to (indeed, are constituted by and in) discourse, and are not, therefore, ontologically independent from the order of telling. The nonfiction filmmaker is caught in a doxastic cocoon, precluding objectivity in any strong sense of the term. And this problem, added to the fictive and distortive nature of nonfiction narration, undermines any faith that one might entertain in the possibility that a documentary could deliver objective knowledge to audiences.

One of White's favorite slogans, derived from the late Louis Mink, is that lives are led, and stories are told.[10] By this, White means that narrative structure is an artifact of our talking about the past—an artifact of retrospection; it is not, in other words, an actual feature of past events, awaiting discovery. It is something we construct or invent and then impose on the past. Our life is not really a comedy until we reconsider it and construct it that way. This is putatively borne out by the fact that the same events can be satisfactorily reconfigured in different narratives with different structures. That is, one might, the idea goes, reconfigure one's life as either a romance or a farce.

Renov wants to mobilize a comparable slogan, especially in terms of the ethnographic film. He writes: "the very act of plucking and recontextualizing profilmic elements is a kind of violence, particularly when cultural specificity is at issue as it is with ethnographic texts. There the question of the adequacy of a representational system as a stand-in for lived experience arises most forcefully." [11] That is, once again, the nonfiction film does not represent the world objectively, but proffers a surrogate superaddition in place of something called "lived experience."

Though at present it is quite common to extend White's theory of history to other precincts of the humanities in exactly the manner Renov does, it is far from settled whether White's views have much to recommend them. The crux of White's position is that the narrative element or, if you will, the plot structure in historical accounts is a fictional imposition on a series of events which renders the telling of those events intelligible, but which has no basis in reality. Stories end; but reality just keeps moving on. Historians configure events as romances or comedies; the different plot structures are optional, for the plot structures refer to nothing.

But this doesn't seem plausible. A major ingredient in the stories that historians tell involves causal relationships. If causation is the cement of the universe, it is also the cement of narration. This is not to say, as some might, [12] that a historical narrative is fundamentally only a chain of causation. Nevertheless, causation is an important element in virtually all narrative structures. Moreover, there is no reason to think that the causal relationships that are hypothesized to obtain in a certain course of events are fictional. For though causation is an ingredient of narrative structure, it also possesses historical reality. Ex hypothesi, the causal relationships that integrate the details of a historical narrative correspond to actual causal relationships in the relevant courses of events. [13]

To consider an example pertinent to the discussion of nonfiction film, recall the episode on gliders from the TV documentary series *Wings of the Luftwaffe*. That installment ends by referring to the wide-bodied jet transports of contemporary warfare in such a way that the viewer comes to appreciate that the transport gliders developed by the Germans to storm England and those developed, partly in imitation of the Germans, by the Allies for the invasion of Europe on D-Day were, in fact, steps in the evolution of the giant jet aircraft that the United States relies upon for the rapid deployment of its troops today.

Now, if we suppose that the makers of *Wings of the Luftwaffe* are correct in identifying the significance of German glider research as a forerunner of, as well as a contribution to, the evolution of contemporary military aircraft, then the relation between the glider research and the present is hardly occult or fictional. German glider research and development, if the account in the film is true, was a causal element in the evolution of modern military transport aircraft. Putatively, this is a real causal relation in an actual course of events.

For example, the documentary asserts that the German gliders which were developed to deliver armor to the front line in the East bear a relation to our own contemporary rapid deployment cargo planes. This relation is neither fictional nor fictive. It is that of a contributory causal condition to an effect. Moreover, if the account presented in *Wings of the Luftwaffe* is accurate—and there is no reason to suppose that it *can't* be—then it would make no sense to refer to the narrative structure under discussion as an imposition. Rather the narrative structure, in this case, tracks actual relations between states of affairs and actions in real courses of events. Insofar as relations between causes and effects—and, for that matter, between reasons and actions—are part of the fabric of courses of events, narrative structures may be said to illuminate those courses of events rather than to impose upon them.

For the same reason, it is as incorrect to suppose that narrative is always a distortion as it is to suppose that it is a fiction. For a given narrative may in fact *discover* actual patterns of relations between causes and effects, reasonings and actions, influences and evolutions in real courses of events. Historical constructivists like White and Renov may believe that closure is simply an artifact of storytelling and that the narrative that leads to it is a purely fictional invention. However, World War I did end in 1918, and the Allied victory was a function of the entry of the United States into the conflict. The first person to realize that made a discovery, and the story that recounts those events tracks an actual course of events through its very sinews to its terminus.

So far I have argued that historical narratives and, by extension, nonfiction films (or, at least, those nonfiction films that are narratives) need not, in virtue of their narrative (or "tropological") structure be thought to be necessarily fictive, nor need they be thought of as impositions upon or distortions of historically occurring sequences of events. I think that this is obvious once one reflects upon the fact that basic elements of narrative structure—such as causation, influence, and rational action—correspond to actual elements of courses of events.

When Hayden White thinks of narrative structures, he has in mind generic structures, such as the romance, which supposedly correlate with certain tropes.[14] But perhaps this is just the wrong level of generality (or vagueness) to think about the structures of historical narration. Focusing at this level of abstraction results in overlooking and then fallaciously denying the straightforward way in which narrative structure is keyed—nondistortively—to the structure of courses of events.

Insofar as White and Renov are defending a universal claim about the nature of all nonfiction narration, it is enough for me to establish that there are some cases of nonfiction narration, like my example for *Wings of the Luftwaffe*, that defy their generalization. Of course, I do not wish to deny that *some* narratives may distort history and may impose preconceived ideas upon it. But that is something that must be determined on a case-by-case basis. There is no a priori argument for narrative distortion. However, needless to say, this is compatible with admitting that sometimes specific nonfiction narratives do distort.

According to White and Renov, historical narration and nonfiction film *constitute* their objects, pretending that these objects have some independent existence about which historians and nonfiction filmmakers imagine they hypothesize objectively. If *constitute* here means something like "bring into existence," then it is surely false that the makers of *Wings of the Luftwaffe* brought into existence the German air force, the Allied air force, contemporary jumbo jets, or the influence of the development of wide-bodied transport gliders on our own wide-bodied transport jets. All these things have an ontological status that is independent of the discourse of *Wings of the Luftwaffe*.

On the other hand, if *constitute* means something less dramatic—such as "find adequate conceptualizations for their objects"—then it is not clear that we need to accuse historians and nonfiction filmmakers of pretense. For even if the makers of *Wings of the Luftwaffe* had proposed a novel, unprecedented conceptualization of the relationship between gliders and jet transports, that conceptualization was in the service of a discovery of a causal relation that obtained, whether or not anyone ever recognized it.

Lastly, Renov seems to believe that we should be skeptical about the epistemic status of nonfiction films because there is some question about the adequacy of representational systems to "stand-in for lived experience." Now I suppose that, in some sense, we all agree with part of Renov's anxiety here; most of the time, we prefer to be with our lover rather than with a picture of our lover. We may even say things like "A photograph is a poor substitute for a loved one." But what in the world does this have to do with the knowledge claims of documentary filmmakers?

When I watch *Gates of Heaven,* I am not looking for a close personal encounter with the owners of some pet graveyards in California. Though I may be interested in observing them and in hearing what they have to say, I prefer a detached to a live experience of them. Nor do I screen *Not a Love Story* in order to simulate a visit to a strip show. I watch it in order to attend to an argument. That is, I do not typically expect a representation, especially a nonfiction film, to stand in for (to replace?) a lived experience. Nonfiction films serve many purposes, but I'm not convinced that they are supposed to serve that one very often, if ever. Thus, it is strange to hear Renov advance the failure [15] of nonfiction film to stand in for lived experience as a basis for questioning its adequacy in terms of, among other things, serving as a disseminator of knowledge claims. After all, we don't cite the incapacity of chain saws to stitch trousers as a reason to question their usefulness in clearing forests.

Renov's argument, in other words, is a red herring.

3

Representing Reality by Bill Nichols eschews those facile deconstructions of the boundary between fiction and nonfiction that conclude that nonfiction film is just like any other kind of fiction.[16] Rather, he argues, nonfiction film is fiction, but it is not exactly like other forms of fiction film. For in his view, nonfiction films are not merely narrative (and, à la White, fictional), but they are argumentative as well; so they are fictional, though they are not exactly like narrative fictions. However, whether this putative distinction will do the work that Nichols assigns to it—since some nonfiction films are exclusively narrative, while some fictional narratives are argumentative[17]—is less of interest to us than is Nichols's epistemological contention that objectivity is impossible in the documentary.

Nichols writes:

> . . . they [documentaries] share with fiction those very qualities that thoroughly compromise any rigorous objectivity, if they don't make it impossible. *This impossibility* is also evident in the more standardized and enforced objectivity of journalism.
>
> Objectivity has been under no less siege than realism and for many of the same reasons. It, too, is a way of representing the world that denies its own processes of construction and their own formative effect. Any given standard for objectivity will have embedded political assumptions.[18]

Undoubtedly, this quotation is initially perplexing, because many readers, if not most, will wonder what *political* assumptions underlie documentaries like *City of Coral* (which was produced for the *Nova* series by Peace River Films in 1983). But Nichols believes that

> In documentary, these assumptions might also include belief in the self-evident nature of facts, in rhetorical persuasion as a necessary and appropriate part of representation and in the capacity of the documentary text to affect its audience through its implicit or explicit claim of "This is so, isn't it?"[19]

So, summarizing Nichols thus far, objectivity in the documentary is impossible because documentaries deny their own processes of construction (and their formative effects), and/or they make political assumptions, including these: that facts are self-evident, that rhetoric is an appropriate part of representation, and that documentaries have the capacity to move audience members to accept what they've been shown as true. Do all documentaries fall afoul of these accusations and, indeed, do all these accusations really amount to challenges to objectivity? My answer to both these questions is "no." In order to see why, let us take up Nichols's accusations one at a time.

A typical documentary film like *City of Coral* does not, for the most part, call attention to its own process of construction. I say "for the most part," in order to accommodate the fact that it does have a credit sequence at the end of which, of course, is something that Nichols will have to explain away if he wants to make the charge that such films attempt to *deny* their own process of construction. For if they were serious in that attempt, why would they publicize those credits?[20]

Nevertheless, I suppose that one would have to concede to Nichols the premise that most nonfiction films spend little or almost no time revealing the process of their construction to their viewers. But the question that arises as to whether *not calling attention to* such construction processes amount to *denying* the existence of those processes? In not exhibiting something about oneself, one is not thereby automatically denying that feature of oneself. In many conversations, I do not call attention to my Irish-Catholic heritage, but that does not entail that I have denied that feature of myself.

Denial, so to say, is its own speech act. In denying something, one generally has to do something. It doesn't simply happen that I deny my heritage if I ask someone to pass me the pepper without telling them I'm Irish. Similarly, *City of Coral,* like so many documentaries and informational films, does not deny anything about its process of construction (and certainly does not deny that it was constructed) by not mentioning it.

Of course, the deeper question is: why should it matter, in terms of the issue of objectivity, whether a nonfiction film acknowledges or denies the process of its own construction? Why does Nichols make such heavy weather over it? Surely, everyone who sees a nonfiction film knows that it was, as Nichols put it, "constructed." It is nice to see *The Making of Brief History of Time* after seeing *Brief History of Time,* but I would have known that the latter was constructed even if I hadn't seen the former. Why does Nichols place such emphasis on reflexivity and what does this emphasis on reflexivity have to do with objectivity?

Nichols's concern with reflexivity can be explained, I think, by the fact that film scholars are primarily interested in one kind of documentary film, a kind which, by the way, is probably less statistically significant than documentary motion pictures or informational films like *City of Coral.* That type of nonfiction film is what might be called the art-documentary, examples of which include: *The Thin Blue Line, Tongues Untied, Roger and Me, Sherman's March,* and earlier films such as *Man with a Movie Camera, Le sang des bêtes, Las hurdes,* and *Chronique d'un été.*

These films, admittedly in often extremely different ways, display a concern with the themes of reflexivity and authorial subjectivity with which we are already familiar from modernist and postmodernist art. And in that context, calling attention reflexively to the nature of film, to filmic devices, to film history, to filmic rhetoric, to film stereotypes, to the construction, as it happens, of the film at hand, to the filmmaker himself or herself, and so on, are all artistically significant gestures.[21] What Nichols has done in requiring reflexivity for objectivity is to mistake a benchmark of what is interesting from the perspective of modernist aesthetics (and its derivatives) for a requirement for objectivity.

But this is clearly wrong. The fact that I have not confided in you whether I wrote this article sequentially or wrote the sections out of order, or whether I prepared the first draft with a quill or a word processor has no bearing whatsoever on whether this article is objective. Undoubtedly, this article is not a modernist masterpiece. But that does not compromise its objectivity.

Nichols further alleges that objectivity is impossible in the documentary because such films have political assumptions. On the face of it, given our ordinary understanding of what constitutes a political assumption, this seems false. One would be hard put to identify any garden-variety political assumptions in *City of Coral,* and I suspect that this is probably true of a great many typical informational films such as those concerned with how to go about trout fishing or canning fruit or break dancing or transmission repair.

Of course, we quickly see that Nichols has some rather expansive views of what counts as a political assumption. For him, political assumptions include: the belief that facts are self-evident; that rhetorical persuasion is appropriate; and that documentary films claim of whatever they represent that "This is so, isn't it?" with the presumption that this will affect audiences. But is it true that documentaries that do not possess garden-variety political assumptions are likely to be guilty of these more recherché commitments?

If some nonfiction can be innocent of Nichols's allegations about political assumptions at the same time they do not *deny* their processes of construction, then Nichols's argument for the generalization about the impossibility of objectivity in the documentary will be undermined. Let us use *City of Coral* as a test case here, since we have already established that it is not in the state of Nicholsesque denial.

The film does not appear to be predicated on persuading us of anything, unless it be that the coral reef off St. Croix is interesting and the film, therefore, seems to make no assumptions about rhetoric.[22] Does the film assume that the facts are self-evident? Not really, since it is constantly preoccupied with explaining everything that we are seeing—that is, with enabling us to understand the nonobvious significance of whatever is in front of the camera, such as the adaptive relevance of various features of the flora and fauna. Indeed, if one had to identify an underlying presupposition of *City of Coral,* it might be that next to nothing about coral reefs is self-evident.

But maybe we are looking for the conviction of self-evident facts in the wrong place. Does the film assume that it is its own explanations, once offered, that are self-evident? I don't think so. In explaining the extremely thin girth of a gray angelfish, the narrator says that it *might* enable the fish to confuse predators by turning quickly and, thereby, virtually disappearing. And of the dorsal fin on the lancer dragonete, the narrator admits that it is mysterious, and he hazards three different hypotheses: that it might be used to frighten predators, to confuse predators, or to provide predators with a false target. That some of the narrator's hypotheses are tentative indicates that there is no presumption of self-evidence here.

It is true that the narrator speaks as though the film is committed to there being facts. We are told that pelican chicks grow down within a month after birth and that coral is part animal and part vegetable and leaves mineral deposits. But there is no indication that the filmmakers believe that these are self-evident facts, and if Nichols thinks that a belief in a fact is equivalent to a belief in a self-evident fact, then he is just confused.

But, in any case, one wonders why, even if the makers of *City of Coral* believe that there are some self-evident facts, that should count as a political assumption. Let me conjecture that the motivation revolves around the following error. Often it is argued that ideology proceeds by treating politically charged falsehoods as if they were self-evident truths. The belief that gay persons are unsuited for military service might be an example here. And, as a result of examples like this, one might become suspicious of claims of self-evident truths, especially concerning political matters.

However, it would be a mistake to infer from the fact that some claims of self-evident truth are politically motivated falsehoods that all claims that this or that is self-evident are politically suspicious. For, on the one hand, not every alleged self-evident fact concerns politics. On the other hand, not every alleged self-evident fact concerning politics need be an ideologically motivated falsehood. It may be prudent to inspect every alleged self-evident fact concerning politics scrupulously; but there is no reason to presume that none will pass inspection.

Of course, if Nichols thinks that the belief in facts is a political assumption, because there are no facts, then it is difficult to see how such a position would avoid self-refutation, since the claim that a belief in facts is a political assumption is presumably a fact.

Moreover, that politically pernicious propositions have sometimes been advanced as facts may warrant caution about factual claims, especially in political contexts, but it is no reason to deny that there are facts. For it is by means of facts that one unmasks politically oppressive falsehoods.

Nichols may, as a matter of philosophical conviction, believe that there are no self-evident facts. But even if there are no self-evident facts, it would not follow that those who assumed there are such facts are guilty of a political assumption. And if it is argued that it is a political assumption because the rhetoric of self-evidence is often employed for political purposes, that fails to show that claims about self-evidence are *always* a matter of political presumption. Even if it were false to say that it is self-evident that I am at least a thinking something, it is not a political presumption.

Not only is it the case that some documentary films do not assume that there are self-evident facts, but even supposing all nonfiction films did assume there were some self-evident facts, it would not necessarily be a political assumption. Consequently, insofar as Nichols worries that objectivity is impossible in nonfiction films due to their political assumptions about self-evident facts, he should worry no longer.

Nichols is also suspicious of the claims of nonfiction films to objectivity because such films, explicitly or implicitly, claim that what they show corresponds to the way things are and that this can influence audiences. This is somewhat baffling. For generally when people speak—save cases like irony and quotation—we take them to be making avowals about how they think matters stand. This is what makes lying possible.

If I say to you, "Here's an apple," I suppose you could say that that comes with an implicit claim that "This is so," along with my expectation that my assertion may affect listeners. But if such a claim is built into assertions in general, I find it hard to understand how that is particularly political, and, therefore, how it could possibly preclude objectivity. Consequently, on these grounds, if all the assertions in *City of Coral* are indeed accompanied with the "This is so" claim and the expectation of influence, I find that to be no barrier to regarding the film to be objective.

Nichols has an additional argument, not discussed so far, aiming to demonstrate that no nonfiction film can be objective. Basically he maintains that there is no viable notion of objectivity available to apply to nonfiction film. Nichols comes to this conclusion by examining and criticizing what he introduces as the three leading characterizations of objectivity that are relevant to the discussion of documentary film: (1) that the objective view is a third-person view; (2) that the objective view is one that allows each audience member to come to her own conclusion; and (3) that the objective view is disinterested.

Nichols contends that the identification of the objective view with the third-person view is not viable for nonfiction film because films that do not employ explicit first-person point-of-view devices may nevertheless be subjective. Moreover, I would hasten to add that grammatical personhood—and cinematic personhood, if there is such a thing—is not a test of objectivity, since a perfectly objective argument can be mounted in any grammatical person; if Eratosthenes had said "Given the evidence I have submitted about differences in shadow lengths, I hypothesize that the Earth is curved," that statement would nevertheless be objective, even though it is not in the third person.

Nichols rejects the notion that documentary films might be objective in the sense that they might present information in a way that leaves it up to the viewer to reach her conclusions on her own. Nichols's grounds here are his unshakable belief that rhetoric is necessarily inexpungible from any documentary. Nichols offers very little argument for this astounding surmise, save that Feyerabend and Kuhn say that rhetoric plays a role in securing scientific conversions.[23]

That rhetoric might have a role in conversions, is, of course, unsurprising, but how does that show that rhetoric is in operation in a film like Warhol's *Empire*, which is surely a documentary—indeed, perhaps the longest *actualité* in film history?[24] That is, some, if not, in fact, many nonfiction films are not in the business of persuasion, let alone conversion; so what grounds are there to suspect that they practice subliminal rhetoric?

However, even if Nichols is wrong in his reasons for rejecting the supposition that objectivity in the documentary amounts to inviting spectatorial freedom of choice, this position is surely irrelevant, on other grounds, to the question of whether a film is objective. A theorem whose steps are fully explicit and justified has a conclusion that is, from a logical point of view, not open to diverse opinions on the part of the readers, but it is nonetheless objective despite that. Similarly, many of Stephen Hawking's arguments in the film *Brief History of Time* are presented objectively, though they are not set out in a way that encourages the spectator to form alternative, differing hypotheses.

Structuring a film in a way that engages the spectators to think for themselves may be a virtue where one is committed to that form of liberalism which maintains that it is more important to develop a citizenry that autonomously arrives at its own opinions than it is for those opinions to be right. But this brand of political liberalism should not be mistaken for objectivity in the epistemic sense. For even if it is considered to be an important moral ideal, it is not a test for objectivity. It is an ethical standard, not an epistemic one.

The last notion of objectivity that Nichols rejects is that the objective view is disinterested. Nichols dismisses this on the grounds that disinterestedness is impossible. He claims that this

> definition—the absence of perceived bias—presupposes some englobing framework that can subsume personal bias and self-interest. This framework is, for individual filmmakers, the interpretive community of filmmakers that share a style, conventions, and a perspective, and—for journalists and reporters, along with anthropologists, sociologists, ethnographers, and other members of the scientific community—it is those institutional structures that regulate and control the shape of news and interpretation (networks, publishers, universities, and professional societies).
>
> What objectivity masks in this case is the specific point of view of institutional authority itself. Not only is there an inevitable concern with legitimation and self-perpetuation, other more historic and issue-specific forms of self-interest and partiality may also prevail, often in the all-the-more-powerful form of unacknowledged predispositions and assumptions rather than stated interests.[25]

This is a strange argument against the notion of objectivity as disinterestedness. For one supposes that whoever uses disinterestedness as a test for objectivity would contend that views arrived at through considerations of institutional concerns with self-perpetuation, institutional legitimation, and other forms of self-interest are exactly the views whose objective status would be challenged and criticized under the disinterestedness conception of objectivity. That is, if claims to objective knowledge are found to be interested in the ways Nichols sketches, then according to the concept of objectivity under examination, the claims are open to dispute. Nichols's examples do not seem to be counterinstances to the view that objectivity is disinterested; rather the examples seem to constitute paradigmatic cases in which the conception would be used to show that the claims in question are not objective.

Moreover, oddly enough, Nichols seems to be in agreement with this; he appears to question the preceding claims to objectivity because he does not think that these examples are truly disinterested. But that view coincides precisely with the conception of objectivity as disinterestedness. Indeed, is Nichols himself using anything but that conception of objectivity to call into doubt the objectivity of examples of institutional bias? Yet, then, how can Nichols be challenging the conception of objectivity as disinterestedness by means of these examples, if these examples become compelling as breaches of objectivity just when one adopts the disinterestedness conception of objectivity? That is, Nichols appears to be undertaking the self-contradictory task of refuting the viability of a standard of objectivity as disinterestedness by employing that very standard in his own putative refutation of it. After all, he appears to deprecate institutional claims to objectivity on the grounds that the institutions are not genuinely disinterested.

Clearly, Nichols thinks that every institutional practice adopted by scientists, historians, journalists, nonfiction filmmakers, and so on, for the purpose of facilitating objective inquiry will *inevitably* fail to insure objectivity because every one of them will be interested.[26] Nichols appears to think that the presuppositions of institutions like physics amount to interests. But it is hard to see why the view that nothing travels faster than the speed of light should count as an interest.

Nichols has not really provided us with any argument to show that this conclusion concerning the inevitability of institutional interestedness is conceptually necessary. So his conclusion must be an empirical finding. But if it is an empirical finding, and no empirically discoverable mechanism has been introduced to show why institutional self-interest is built into the nature of things,[27] then the very most that Nichols could claim to command as evidence is that so far, in all known cases, there is no example of appropriately disinterested knowledge.

In response, the proponent of the disinterestedness view of objectivity will simply say that even if Nichols is right (which is unlikely), then the best Nichols can claim is that thus far we have no examples of objective knowledge. The concept of objectivity as disinterestedness is not overthrown. It is just uninstantiated. And if more claims to objectivity come before us, and they are as Nichols describes them, then we will merely deny their objectivity.

Furthermore, the proponent of the disinterestedness conception of objectivity will also want to ask Nichols about the status of his own generalization. Does the generalization about institutional self-interest apply to Nichols's own theory? That is, according to his own theory, Nichols himself should turn out to be an agent in the service of the self-perpetuation of the cinema studies institution. But if that is true, then we should certainly deny that Nichols's theory makes any viable claims to objective knowledge. Again, Nichols's attack on the disinterestedness conception of objectivity, unless qualified in appropriate ways, is curiously self-refuting.

Perhaps there is some way in which Nichols can, in a principled way, segregate his own generalizations from the charges he levels at the generalizations of other inquirers, thereby dodging charges of self-refutation. But that may not be so easy, and, in any case, the burden of proof here is with Nichols. Moreover, I believe that he, in particular, will find this a hard row to hoe just because he appears unbudgeably committed to the view that everything is politically partisan.

In addition, if one could show that the kind of methodological paranoia that Nichols practices is nothing but a strategy adopted by humanities departments to legitimatize themselves in their competition with the sciences, natural and social, then we would have almost as much reason to suspect Nichols's findings as we would to suspect them if they were shown to be solely the result of a bribe. I am not saying that Nichols might not be able to clear himself of such a charge. My point is only that however we adjudicate a case like this— whether for or against—notions of disinterestedness will come into play.

Undoubtedly, the concept of disinterestedness will have to be refined further than it has been so far. It will also have to be supplemented by other concepts before we have a fully adequate concept of objectivity. But, nevertheless, I do not think that Nichols has shown that the disinterestedness conception of objectivity is irrelevant to the discussion of inquiry in general or to nonfiction film in particular.

Nichols takes claims of objectivity to be forms of disguise. For the individual, "it helps defend him or her against mistakes and criticism."[28] For institutions, objectivity provides the camouflage behind which practices of inquiry self-interestedly perpetuate themselves. What is so bizarre about Nichols's indictments is that he reacts to the potential problems he discerns by condemning the notion of objectivity, rather than by regarding the infractions in question as abuses. Moreover, if one is concerned to criticize these abuses, as Nichols appears to be, then it is inadvisable to jettison the concept of objectivity. For the activities at issue seem only definable as abuses when one cleaves to standards of objectivity.

Against the disinterestedness standard of objectivity, Nichols inveighs as follows:

> The impression of disinterestedness is a powerful reassurance and a seductive ploy. What objectivity itself cannot tell us is the purpose it is meant to serve since this would undercut its own effectiveness (lest that purpose be one that adopts the shroud of objectivity itself as a final purpose: the pursuit of truth, the quest for knowledge, the performance of service for the community good).[29]

Close attention to this passage indicates that Nichols had no argument, but only an attitude. He asserts that all invocations of objectivity have ulterior motives. He challenges believers in objectivity to state their purposes. But if they respond, easily enough, by saying that the purposes of their protocols of inquiry are the pursuit of truth or the quest for knowledge, then Nichols scoffs, and dismisses these remarks as "shrouds." But no argument is given to show why one cannot embark upon an inquiry with the primary purpose and interest in obtaining knowledge—an interest, by the way, which is compatible with the disinterestedness relevant to the objectivity. Nichols certainly thinks that this view is contemptible; but perhaps this is one of his own unexamined predispositions. Does it belie an interest?

4

As indicated in the opening section of this essay, attacks on the objectivity of the nonfiction film by an earlier generation of film theorists proceeded as though this defect was a specific limitation of nonfiction film, due to the nature of the motion picture medium. Selectivity was of special interest to them, since this seems to be something that was built into the very cinematic apparatus itself.

Moreover, given this particular line of attack, it is quite easy to see how to deflect it. One has only to point to the fact that the feature in question is shared with some other forms of inquiry or information communication—like history, journalism, or science—where there are no doubts about the possibility of objectivity. Therefore, for example, if selectivity poses no problem for the prospects of objectivity in history and science, then there is no principled cause for alarm with respect to nonfiction film. Surely, we can all agree that objectivity might be difficult to secure; but it is still a possibility for nonfiction film if it is also a possibility for science or history.

This defense of objectivity in the nonfiction film is predicated upon confronting what might be called local skepticism about the documentary, that is, skepticism about the possibility of objectivity in nonfiction films, construed essentially, that raises no questions about the possibility of objectivity in other disciplines of inquiry and/or communication. But, as we have seen in the cases of both Renov and Nichols, the postmodernist attack on nonfiction film is not based on local skepticism about the documentary. In Renov's case, skepticism about the documentary comes in tandem with skepticism about history, whereas Nichols seems skeptical of just about any institution of inquiry and communication.[30] This postmodernist tendency toward suspicion of the nonfiction film on the grounds of global skepticism about the prospects for knowledge and rationality in general has been most blatantly advertised by Brian Winston.[31]

Noting the preceding strategy for defending the nonfiction film against attacks motivated by what I have just called local skepticism, Winston claims that the strategy is "easily attacked" when the opponent of objectivity in the nonfiction film opts for general skepticism, which Winston enthusiastically insinuates is irresistible under the postmodernist dispensation. Winston does not provide us with much by way of argument for his general skepticism, but, perhaps in the spirit of postmodernist pastiche, he lays on a series of quotations reassuring us that general skepticism is a foregone conclusion. One of the more over-the-top of these comes from Lorraine Nencel and Peter Pels and it goes like this: "It is no longer possible to salvage Western rationality or its totalizing potential from the clutches of context by ahistorical claims to a superior theoretical and methodological armament." [32] Whatever is meant by this is pretty obscure; nevertheless, Winston gleefully admonishes us that such postmodern skepticism applies even to the hard sciences. [33]

Winston's position seems to be that claims of objectivity in behalf of the nonfiction film cannot be sustained in the face of global postmodernist skepticism. For postmodern skepticism denies the possibility of objective standards of rationality in general; rather (or because) rationality is historically and contextually specific.

And yet, however schematic this argument is, it is still an argument. Reasons are being advanced to substantiate what is supposed to be a fact. And furthermore, the text gives every indication that Winston thinks that these reasons, which he believes to be rooted in facts, are in principle ascertainable by anyone and that they should be compelling in principle to anyone.

For instance, Winston offers these reasons dialectically in the course of a debate with people like myself who are more conservatively minded epistemologically than he and his colleagues are. I think that he expects us to recognize the logical force of mobilizing global postmodernist skepticism against local defenses of documentary objectivity, while recognizing the way in which the claims of history and context mitigate against faith in objective standards of rationality.

That is, Winston does not say that his argument is only an argument for fellow postmodernists or that it is an argument whose validity only takes hold in contexts of debate against local defenses of documentary objectivity. He does not say his reasons are good only for postmodernists and not for old fuddy-duddies like me. He expects his reasons to be generally convincing. But why? Mustn't he be presuming that there are some objective standards of rationality and that his reasons can be compelling in principle for anyone, including people with rival theories, in light of those objective standards?

Winston points out that local defenses of the objectivity of nonfiction film are outflanked by global postmodernist skepticism. Isn't that a logical point? Doesn't Winston write as though it should be conceded by friend and foe alike? But then Winston must presume that there are objective standards of rationality. And like Nichols's, Winston's position against the possibility of rational standards of objectivity teeters on the brink of incoherence, insofar as his argument *also* seems to presuppose objective standards of rationality.

Like other postmodernists, Winston enters the arena of public discussion and debate not only with other postmodernists but with unaligned readers and opponents like myself. In order for that conversation to proceed in a way that is intelligible, the participants must be able to recognize reasons when they see them—whether or not they welcome them—and be able to feel the force of good reasons when they are advanced, by whomever advances them.

Postmodernists cite facts, make arguments, and provide reasons. The conversation moves intelligibly. Epistemic conservatives like myself realize when postmodernists raise issues that require logical damage control, while postmodernists sometimes acknowledge some of the logical difficulties of their own position. However, none of this would be possible unless underlying the debate was the presupposition of objective standards of rationality. That is, objective standards of rationality are a precondition of the debate—a precondition of the possibility that the participants be able to recognize reasons and to find them compelling in certain instances and ill-founded in others.

But if objective standards of rationality are a precondition of the debate in which Winston and I find ourselves, then Winston's position is certainly paradoxical. For if he were right, the very conditions which made that possible could not obtain. But they must obtain, if his argument is to succeed. So if Winston were right, he would have to be wrong. That is, it is self-refuting to claim in the context of a debate like ours that there are no objective standards of rationality and yet proceed as if reasons could be recognized and be logically compelling.[34]

Winston is logically correct to point out that various defenses against local skepticism about documentary objectivity are useless against arguments based on global postmodernist skepticism. However, neither Winston nor any other contemporary film theorist with whom I am familiar has insulated global postmodernist skepticism from the sort of predictable charges of incoherence that I have leveled at Winston. Unless and until postmodernist film theorists address this problem, their position is effectively a nonstarter. For at this point in the dialectic, given the choice between believing that some nonfiction films can be objective and the alternative that there are no standards of objectivity in any aspect of human life whatsoever, it seems far more reasonable to me to think that nonfiction films can be objective. Hell, I even think I've seen some of them.

5

I began by taking note of the fact that scholars of the nonfiction film are prone to resort to philosophy quite frequently. For inasmuch as nonfiction films often (though not always) involve knowledge claims, questions of epistemology may seem relevant. Unfortunately, the philosophy that attracts nonfiction film scholars is either shallow or is superficially understood.

Too often the philosophy in question is uncritically accepted as a major premise in debunking arguments. Thus Winston supposes that something called Western rationality has been soundly refuted on the basis of some fashionable, postmodernist fiat. But Winston fails to explore the possibility that this very pronouncement may be incoherent.

Surely it is ironical that debunkers like Winston buy into so much philosophy, embracing it as authoritative, without even thinking minimally about what might be wrong with it. Why are debunkers nowadays so often fervent believers when it comes to facile, postmodernist dicta? Skepticism, it appears, stops at home.

Theorists like Winston give one the impression that what are no more than presumptions are actually (as Nichols might put it) self-evident. They introduce these presumptions as givens, at least for everyone in the know. In effect, they substitute fashion reports for arguments. So-called Western rationality is as defunct as bell-bottom trousers because someone in the intellectual fashion industry says so.

But claims by such pundits about the state of the art of philosophy in terms of a consensus concerning, for example, conceptual relativism are vastly exaggerated, especially from a statistical point of view. The issues that Winston considers settled, in virtue of his authorities, are still very much in play in the arena of philosophy. One—particularly a debunker—should not blithely endorse pronouncements about what is philosophically established. Film theorists like Winston should become philosophers themselves and scrutinize claims about the refutation of rationality with the same debunking energy that they mobilize to challenge the knowledge claims of certain nonfiction films.

Perhaps in this regard, the flaws in contemporary nonfiction film theory show us something about one of the major problems in contemporary film theory in general. For there is a striking tendency for film theorists to repeat the errors of nonfiction film theorists insofar as they derive their preferred philosophical premises from second-hand sources. They do not evolve these premises themselves, but get them from authority figures, whom they paraphrase or have paraphrased for them by second and third-generation authority figures. Film academics typically do not subject these premises to criticism, but treat them as infallible axioms to be used deductively in film criticism and theory.

There is only one remedy for this sort of intellectual stagnation. Namely: film theorists, especially nonfiction film theorists, must become philosophers themselves, or, at least, learn to think philosophically about their deepest presuppositions. Film theorists need to become interdisciplinary—not in the sense that they simply quote authorities from other fields—but in the sense that they become capable of thinking for themselves in terms of issues addressed by those other fields that are germane to film studies. Nonfiction film theorists need to learn to think philosophically—as well as historically, sociologically, and so on—if the field is to develop beyond its present state of arrogant sloganeering.

NOTES

1. Not all nonfiction films are in the business of making knowledge claims, which is why I limit my observation only to "a great many nonfiction films." That is also why nonfiction films cannot be characterized in terms of a commitment to providing objective information about the world. For further discussion, see Noël Carroll, "Reply to Carol Brownson and Jack Wolf," in *Philosophic Exchange: A Journal of SUNY College at Brockport* 14 (Winter 1983); and Carl Plantinga, "The Mirror Framed: A Case for Expression in the Documentary," in *Wide Angle* 13, 2 (Summer 1991): 40–53.

2. For further elaboration and documentation of the selectivity argument, see Noël Carroll, "From Real to Reel: Entangled in Nonfiction Film," in *Philosophic Exchange* 14 (Winter 1983).

3. I am indebted to Carl Plantinga for the idea that there is an emerging *postmodernist* approach to the nonfiction film. See Carl Plantinga, "Motion Pictures and the Rhetoric of Nonfiction Film: Two Approaches," in this volume.

4. Michael Renov, "Introduction: The Truth about Non-Fiction," in *Theorizing Documentary,* ed. Michael Renov (New York: Routledge, 1993), p. 3.

5. Ibid., p. 7.

6. Ibid. In this quotation, Renov is speaking specifically about Trinh T. Minh-ha's skepticism with respect to the traditional documentary, but since he maintains that the same kind of skepticism echoes throughout his anthology (pp. 7–8), I take this to be a fair statement of Renov's attitude as well. Furthermore, in context, it is nearly impossible to read Renov's summation of Trinh T. Minh-ha's view as anything but an approving paraphrase of a position that he shares.

7. For a discussion of indexing, see Noël Carroll, "From Real to Reel," pp. 24–26.

8. For an elaboration and sustained criticism of Hayden White's philosophy of history, see Noël Carroll, "Interpretation, History and Narrative," *The Monist* 73, 2 (April 1990).

9. See Hayden White, *Tropics of Discourse: Essays in Cultural Criticism* (Baltimore: Johns Hopkins University Press, 1978), and Hayden White, *The Content of Form* (Baltimore: Johns Hopkins University Press, 1987).

10. White, *Tropics of Discourse,* pp. 90 and 111.

11. Renov, *Theorizing Documentary,* p. 7.

12. See Morton White, *Foundations of Historical Knowledge* (New York: Harper Collins, 1965), chapter 6; and Peter Munz, *The Shapes of Time* (Middletown, Conn.: Wesleyan University Press, 1977), p. 25.

13. There are at present certain debates in the philosophy of history about the status of historical causes. Are they only causally necessary conditions? Are they question-relative? And so on. Nevertheless, the existence of these debates does not compromise the preceding argument. For my argument only depends on the existence of processes of historical causation, however they are ultimately analysed. The debates about the status of these causes does not call into question the reality of processes of historical causation, nor does it show that historians cannot track them. It addresses the issue of how we are to characterize them precisely. Moreover, the proposals available in this area of debate are all compatible with the claims that I make about the reality of causal conditions in the relevant courses of events.

14. There are numerous other problems with White's account of narrative structuration and its relation to the theory of tropes. For example, White's master narratives are so vaguely defined that he seems to be able to be find them everywhere, whereas their relevance to historiography may be much less than he claims. For further criticism of White, see my essay, "Interpretation, History, and Narrative."

15. Can a nonfiction film be said to fail to stand in for lived experience if that is not its aim?

16. See Bill Nichols, *Representing Reality* (Bloomington: Indiana University Press, 1991), pp. 107–9.

17. Also, the distinction Nichols advances wouldn't differentiate documentary from historical accounts since they often mix narrative and argument as well. Thus, if you count history as fiction, for the reasons Hayden White advances, then documentary film would presumably be fiction in the same way history is. I am not, of course, endorsing White's view but simply pointing out that if you are drawn to it in the way that Nichols, like Renov, is, then it is not clear that one can agree, as a matter of logic, with Nichols that documentary is "a fiction (un)like any other."

18. Nichols, *Representing Reality*, p. 195 (emphasis added).

19. Ibid.

20. Also, most documentaries do not comment upon their formative effect on audiences for the obvious reason that before the film is screened the filmmakers don't really know what the formative effect of the film will be. Furthermore, the claim that Nichols makes about the *denial* by documentary filmmakers of the formative effects of their films on audiences can also be refuted by parallel arguments of the form that are used above to refute the claim that documentary filmmakers *deny* the processes of construction of their films.

21. In an interesting remark on contemporary documentary *art*-filmmakers, Paul Arthur calls attention to the way they fetishize their own failure, especially against backdrops of utopian epistemic expectations. Perhaps we might conjecture that documentary film theorists imitate their beloved nonfiction artists by incessantly replaying the drama of their failures with respect to utopian standards of objectivity, thereby ignoring the fact that lots of ordinary nonfiction, informational films are perfectly objective in straightforward ways all the time. For Paul Arthur's observation, see his "Jargons of Authenticity (Three American Moments)," in *Theorizing Documentary*, pp. 126–31.

22. This, of course, is not meant to suggest that there are not some information films that engage in persuasion. Carl Sagan's "The Shores of the Cosmic Ocean" for the TV series *Cosmos* is bent on coaxing viewers to sympathize with the view that there is life on other planets. However, this concedes nothing to Nichols's argument. For since he has advanced a generalization, the onus on us is to produce at least one counterexample. Of course, I think that there are far more nonfiction films than one which escape *all* of Nichols's defects vis-à-vis objectivity; but one is all that the counterargument really requires. Moreover, I should add that I am not convinced that the belief that rhetoric can be appropriate is necessarily an offense to objectivity. Rhetorical structures—such as rhetorical questions—often have a perfectly acceptable role to play in objective discourse.

23. Note that there is a presumption in Nichols's argument that rhetoric is always out of place and a defect with respect to objectivity. But unless one includes such defectiveness in one's definition of rhetoric, this is not immediately apparent. Is the presence of an enthymeme—which Aristotle claimed is the most effective rhetorical device—enough to compromise the objective standing of a sample of discourse?

24. Though it may prove to be a useful heuristic for film scholars like Nichols to

always look for the possible operation of rhetoric in a nonfiction film, this serviceable heuristic should not be confused with a theoretical discovery. For even if the heuristic often works, one must also be prepared to find cases where it doesn't.

25. Nichols, *Representing Reality*, p. 197.

26. This raises the question of how we should regard whatever Nichols proposes to us as facts in support of his arguments. For shouldn't Nichols's own candidates for status of the facts, which are certainly implicated in institutional epistemic protocols, be assessed to fall short of objectivity, according to Nichols's own arguments? But if they fall short of standards of objectivity, then why should *we* believe them?

27. Perhaps Nichols feels he has suggested an argument like this: all institutional practices of inquiry have unacknowledged predispositions and assumptions which may involve even more powerful self-interests than the stated ones; therefore, all institutional practices are interested in a way that precludes objectivity. The problem here is that even if it is true that every practice of inquiry possesses some unacknowledged or unexamined assumption or predisposition, one must still demonstrate that these unacknowledged or unexamined assumptions or predispositions are institutionally interested in a way that compromises objectivity. That the assumptions are unacknowledged or unexamined does not pose a problem in and of itself; the problem only arises when what is unacknowledged is interested. And whether that can be shown, as far as I can see, depends on looking at one case at a time.

28. Nichols, *Representing Reality*, p. 195.

29. Ibid., p. 198.

30. Nevertheless, Nichols is altogether carefree about his own allegations of fact— which are material to his arguments—even though he is obviously the representative of a well-known institution.

31. See Brian Winston, "The Documentary Film as Scientific Inscription," in *Theorizing Documentary*, especially pp. 53–55.

32. Quoted in ibid., p. 54.

33. Ibid.

34. Perhaps it will be argued that I have misinterpreted Winston. Instead of regarding him as a postmodernist skeptic, as I do, it might be said that we should read him as only reporting that postmodernist skepticism is the unstoppable intellectual movement of the moment, though it is a movement about which Winston, himself, is agnostic. However, if Winston takes what he has said to be a historical *fact* with which, in principle, *anyone* who reflected upon the evidence should assent, then Winston himself believes in objective standards of rationality and he should not be agnostic, save on pain of self-refutation.

14

Moving Pictures and
the Rhetoric of Nonfiction:
Two Approaches

Carl Plantinga

History provides many examples of suspicion of visual images, but none so celebrated as that of Plato. In the famous "Plato's Cave" analogy, unsuspecting cave dwellers see only the ephemeral shadows cast by a reality outside the cave. From their vantage point, to which they are shackled, they see only the cave walls, and not outside. Having never left the cave, and having no experience of that larger, extra-cavern universe, the cave dwellers naïvely experience shadows on the wall as actuality, appearances as the real thing, these mere semblances as the "really real." Could this be our condition in today's world of media images? Have the misleading images on the cave wall been replaced by the relentless flickering lights of television and movie screens? And if this is so, what of nonfiction films and videos and their claim to reveal aspects of the actual world, and to give us knowledge about a wider reality, at least in part through photographic images?

Current postmodernist theorists, chief among them Jean Baudrillard, revise Plato radically. They accept his claims about images as deceptive appearances that reveal nothing and produce no knowledge. But they take an enormous and fateful step beyond Plato, by denying the existence of any actuality or reality that may be revealed. Postmodernist epistemologists, and neopragmatists such as Stanley Fish and Richard Rorty, reject Enlightenment notions of truth, reality, objectivity, and so on, arguing that there exist no protocols that enable us to distinguish between appearance and reality, truth and lies, rhetoric and information.[1] Baudrillard's thought is an inverted Platonism, which by rejecting "the real," attempts to dissolve all distinctions between appearances and reality. For Baudrillard, we are mired in postmodern "hyperreality," where truth is simply the latest media consensus. Images, photographic and otherwise, have become a major component of this hyperreality, a means not of informing and revealing—for they refer to nothing beyond themselves—but of participating in the creation of the manufactured consensus which passes as truth and knowledge in the postmodern world. Note the sizable gap between what might be called a "critical realist" position and that of the postmodernist. While the critical realist finds means to distinguish appearance from reality *in some cases,* the postmodernist denies such a distinction, *in any case.*

In film studies, Post-Structuralism, sometimes allied with postmodernism, has produced similar suspicions of nonfiction films, and in particular, of their use of photographic images. Though I believe Post-Structuralist/postmodernist accounts of the image (and of epistemology generally) fail both as philosophy and as a ground for political analysis and action,[2] I cannot make that argument here. Instead, let me contrast such accounts with what I call an instrumentalist approach—"instrumentalist" because it assumes that both images and nonfiction films in general have no universal ideological effect, but are relatively neutral tools that can be used for a multitude of diverse purposes. Ideological effect may be determined in relation to specific contexts and uses, but not a priori.

What I hope to show is that the Post-Structuralist, from the lofty perspective of abstract Theory, views the nonfiction landscape only from afar. The alternative I propose—the instrumentalist approach—is better able to account for the complexity and specificity of nonfiction films and their uses of photographic images.

The Nature of Nonfiction Film

Many Post-Structuralists[3] poison the well from the outset by characterizing nonfiction film in a misleading way. They define the type according to a particular use of motion picture or video photography—the recording of profilmic scenes—which along with other film techniques "ensures," or better, "pretends to," a privileged relationship with actuality. This privileged relationship is alternately described as an assumed transparency, an unmediated recording, or a misleading claim to unfiltered truth. In other words, nonfiction films are inherently duplicitous because they pretend to be something they are not—unmediated records. For example, Michael Renov writes that nonfiction film "has most often been motivated by the wish to exploit the camera's revelatory powers, an impulse only rarely coupled with an acknowledgment of the processes through which the real is transfigured."[4] This assumes that when a film does not explicitly acknowledge its constructedness, it then poses as a transparent, unmediated record. Another theorist notes that claims to "heightened epistemic authority" anchor the nonfiction film, and that various strategies of authentication, in bolstering these claims, signify the "spontaneous, the anticonventional, the refusal of [the] mediating process."[5]

Such claims, stemming from a familiar hermeneutics of suspicion, tend to cast nonfiction films in a single role, that of deceptive representations. The Post-Structuralist story features nonfiction films posing as transparent imitations or objective recordings, but which in their true natures are the rhetorical products of filmmakers through which the covert workings of Ideology are instilled in the unsuspecting spectator. This suspicion of the normal workings of discourse hearkens back to 1970s cinesemiotic theory, a theoretical stance which conceives of discourses as decoys, tricks, lures, and legerdemain. The nonfiction film, one theorist writes,

> attempts to legitimize its discourse by means of a claim to a privileged relationship to the real. It imitates historiographical discourse as that which is supposed to have knowledge and allows its desire to be propped on certain epistemological and ontological yearnings. These yearnings, in turn, serve to position the spectator as an omnipotent and omniscient observer, able to traverse the gap between signifier and signified by means of various codes of authenticity and veracity. These codes, in turn, act to guarantee a position of unity and mastery, a suturing over of a lost plenitude and coherence.[6]

This quotation succinctly embodies a Post-Structuralist approach to nonfiction film. Notice how such "apparatus theory" empowers the critic and theorist as one who "sees through" the duplicity of representation, while the critic implicitly characterizes the filmmaker as one who naïvely constructs psychological and ideological traps for the viewer (the film "positions" the viewer). Also notice how Post-Structuralist theory, in its appeal to a universalist psychoanalysis, is unable to deal with difference, and assumes a uniform ideological and psychological effect (at least in relation to all realist texts) for every spectator, regardless of class, gender, ethnicity, education, or viewing context. Notice that the spectator is construed as a simpleton and a dupe, one who is unable to see beyond the motion picture photography and the continuity editing—"strategies of authenticity"—to the rhetorical project of a nonfiction film.[7]

Only the Post-Structuralist theorist emerges unscathed from Post-Structuralist theory. Post-Structuralists suspect that all claims of knowledge, or of filmmakers' attempts to illuminate or influence an audience, stem from Western colonialism, or patriarchy, or some other attempt to master the Other. If, as Michel Foucault claims, all attempts to disseminate knowledge are merely strategic moves in the struggle to attain (or more usually, to maintain) power, then the nonfiction film becomes a part of this questionable enterprise. Then the Post-Structuralist can posit an ideological machination in the very function of nonfiction film itself, rather than in particular *uses* of nonfiction films.

But Post-Structuralist theory has little relevance to specific instances of filmmakers using films as *instruments* of social action. Former Chinese Red Guard Xiaokang Su makes a documentary attempting to show the truth about Tiananmen Square, and the Chinese government reacts by confiscating all available video copies and crushing them with a bulldozer. Robert Epstein and Jeffrey Friedman make an Academy Award-winning documentary, *Common Threads: Stories from the Quilt*, that reaches millions on Home Box Office, expressing the pain and suffering caused by AIDS and presenting a powerful case for the common humanity of all of the victims, regardless of sexual orientation, gender, or race. Barbara Kopple, in *Harlan County, U.S.A.* and *American Dream,* insightfully explores elements of the American labor movement. Edward R. Murrow, in a move requiring significant personal courage, takes on powerful red-baiting Senator Joseph R. McCarthy in *See It Now*'s famous "Report on Senator McCarthy." In all of these cases, the filmmakers use their films as instruments of action, by which they inform, persuade, and perhaps initiate change. Contrast this with postmodernist/Post-Structuralist rhetoric, which values films freed from the "tyranny of meaning" and "work that reflects back on itself [and] offers itself infinitely as nothing else but work . . . *and* void."[8] It is difficult to imagine a more sterile and self-defeating political project.

It is clear that we must surpass such dogma to make sense of nonfiction films and their functions. Nonfiction films are a subspecies of nonfiction discourse in general—a broad grouping comprising films, essays, biographies, news reports, recounting the day's events to one's spouse, and so on. If we think of the documentary film as a specific instance of nonfiction discourse, it becomes clearer how to construe the documentary as an instrument of action rather than a passive record of the profilmic event. Nonfiction discourse asserts, or is taken by the spectator or listener to assert, that the states of affairs it presents occur or occurred in the actual world.[9] In the case of certain nonfiction films, this is quite clear. For example, *Vietnam: A Television History, CBS Reports'* "Harvest of Shame," and the *Why We Fight* series all make assertions about their subjects as they are thought to have occurred in fact in the actual world. On the other hand, a fiction may suggest thematic truths, but it presents particular states of affairs not to assert their occurrence, but to create a narrative fiction—a fictional world.[10] Thus we do not take *The Wizard of Oz, Star Wars,* or *Double Indemnity* to assert that the states of affairs they present actually occur; we do take "Harvest of Shame" and *Vietnam: A Television History* to make such assertions.

These are prototypical examples of nonfiction and fiction films. Of course, in the case of some films, it may be difficult to make out the distinction so clearly. However, my claim is not that the distinction between fiction and nonfiction is always clear; in fact, it is not, and some films mix fiction and nonfiction in intriguing ways (for example, *JFK* and *Medium Cool*). My claim is that the prototypical functions of fiction and nonfiction discourse provide a useful means of distinguishing between prototypical examples of fiction and nonfiction films.[11]

Noël Carroll introduced the notion of *indexing* to explain differences between fiction and nonfiction films.[12] According to Carroll, we typically view a film while knowing that it has been indexed, either as fiction or nonfiction. The particular indexing of a film mobilizes expectations and activities on the part of the viewer. A film indexed as nonfiction leads the spectator to expect a discourse that make assertions or implications about actuality. In addition, the spectator will take a different attitude toward those states of affairs presented, since they are taken to represent the actual, and not a fictional, world.

Indexing is a process initially begun by the filmmaker, but to function normally, it must be "taken up" by the discursive community. That is, if George Lucas had indexed *Star Wars* as nonfiction, I doubt whether the viewing public would have received it as a nonfiction film simply because Lucas introduced it as such. Similarly, recent feature documentaries—*Roger and Me* and *The Thin Blue Line,* for example—have been labeled "fiction" by various critics, despite their presentation as accounts of actual phenomena. Indexing is as much a social construction—dependent on what the discursive community will allow—as it is a designation of the filmmaker.[13]

It is important to note that though the nonfiction film asserts or implies that its states of affairs actually occur, it is through this broad function that it performs a variety of other actions—informing, questioning, challenging, revealing, and so on. Also important is that on this conception of the nonfiction film, the genre is defined not primarily as a deceptive photographic imitation or recording, as in Post-Structuralist theories, but as an instrument of action through which filmmakers perform a variety of functions. One of these functions may be to provide a photographic record of an event or scene. However, that is not the primary function of many documentaries. Many films present images used instead to expressively contribute to the rhetorical aim of the film, in addition to or in lieu of its use as a record or imitation of the actual scene.[14] On this view, the primary distinction between fiction and nonfiction films lies in the realm of discursive function and social contract, not in the use of moving photographic images as recordings or imitations.

This instrumentalist description of documentary has important implications for the way we look at documentary films, and for what we consider important to know about them. First, the Post-Structuralist sees the documentary as primarily an imitative photographic recording (or perhaps, a pretense of recording) that slips ideology and rhetoric through the back door via "strategies of authentication." The instrumentalist, on the other hand, sees that the photographic recording of a subject is but one among many functions of the nonfiction film, and not definitive of nonfiction film at the deepest level. The instrumentalist characterization of nonfiction film as asserting or implying (and not primarily imitating) enables us to see that the nonfiction film can be openly expressive, manipulative, and rhetorical, and nonetheless fulfill the functions of nonfiction discourse.

In addition, Post-Structuralists posit the rhetoric of documentary in its "strategies of authentication," the means by which it presents itself as imitation while it actually "transfigures the real." The instrumentalist, alternatively, does not assume that the documentary hides its rhetorical purposes, or that spectators necessarily mistake what they see for the truth; the instrumentalist examines rhetoric not as a necessary deception (though it may be deceptive), but as the age-old use of discourse for persuasion. Thus "strategies of authentication" become nothing more than implications and assertions about reality, coupled with attempts to persuade the spectator of their truth. Classical rhetoric, translated and updated to apply to visual discourse, is still the means to gauge the persuasive effects of nonfiction films; the Post-Structuralist insistence on rhetoric as necessarily deceptive only confuses issues.

Icons in Nonfiction Films

After claiming nonfiction film to be falsely posing as transparent actuality, the Post-Structuralist's next move is to remind us that such unmediated rendering of the real is impossible. Michael Renov notes the inadequacy of reflection theories of art which hold that mimesis "means producing simulacra which are the *equivalent* of their historical counterparts" (emphasis added). When we attempt to "fix" the profilmic event on tape or celluloid, "the results are indeed *mediated,* the result of multiple interventions that necessarily *come between* the cinematic sign (what we see on the screen) and its referent (what existed in the world)."[15]

Renov is partly right here. Of course, the moving photograph of a scene is not the *equivalent* of that scene, if we take "equivalent" in a strong sense. It is difficult to imagine what it would mean to believe that a film representation is *equivalent* to the scene represented. Would that belief entail that spectators rush from the movie theater when seeing the approaching locomotive in Lumiere's *Arrivée d'un train en gare?* Or, more likely, would it entail that spectators mistake the represented scene to be an unproblematic rendering of the "whole truth"?

The Post-Structuralist mistake here is to suppose that a realist theory of representation, or a spectator who recognizes homologies between representation and reality, is obliged to take such magnificently naïve views about the relationship between film and the world. Renov's argument, like too many in contemporary film theory, is a "straw man" argument, portraying its opposition by caricature. It attributes something outlandish—the attempt to be equivalent—to the nonfiction film and to realism, and then goes on to show that the outlandish view is a false and indeed pernicious attempt to put something over on us.

A documentary may assert or imply truths about a subject, and may reveal and/or record aspects of the profilmic scene, without being *equivalent to* or *identical with* that scene, and certainly without attempting to pass itself off as equivalent. For most viewers, I would venture, this is such a basic assumption that it need not come to consciousness to function as an element of our horizon of beliefs. Post-Structuralism has reified the "Deceived Spectator" into a model for all spectators.[16]

The contradiction the Post-Structuralist sees is between recording and objectivity on the one hand, and expression and subjectivity on the other. If the camera photographically records the pro-filmic scene, how can it be said to express a perspective or point of view?[17] Conversely, if a documentary has a point of view, how can it be said to photographically record or imitate the pro-filmic scene? Brian Winston finds this supposed contradiction to be quite troubling, especially in relation to Frederick Wiseman's explanations of his filmmaking strategies. On the one hand, Winston notes, Wiseman sees documentary as a means of discovery and the transmission of information. Wiseman describes this filmmaking as "using film and film technology to have a look at what's going on in the world."[18] With regard to *Titicut Follies,* about a mental institution (Bridgewater) in Massachusetts, Wiseman's expressed motivations were to teach, and in this case to show prosecutors the kind of institution to which they were sending people.

On the other hand, Winston notes, Wiseman rejects the idea that his films are objective. For Winston, this creates a "profound contradiction": "Either this invasion of Bridgewater is justified as a means of obtaining evidence or his project becomes 'mere opinion' and falls by the light of his own announced intention." Winston apparently assumes that only objective films could give information or serve a teaching function; if Wiseman denies that his films are objective, how can he simultaneously claim them as teaching tools? The contradiction, Winston thinks, is between "a Direct Cinema intention to acquire evidence . . . and so vehement a dismissal of the mimetic power of the camera. . . ."[19]

In response to Winston, note first that he slides between "objectivity" and "the mimetic power of the camera," assuming that the one necessarily implies the other. They do not; the camera may have mimetic possibilities and nonetheless be used to create subjective representations. Wiseman does not deny the mimetic power of the camera; when he says that his films are subjective, this says nothing about the ability of the camera to provide visual information about the pro-filmic scene. The fact that a shot is taken from a particular spatial station point in no way contradicts the informative possibilities of photography. In addition, filmmakers such as Wiseman and the Maysles brothers see the subjectivity of their films mainly in editing, and not in the photography itself.[20] Winston may question their positive assessment of the informative capabilities of photography, but it is not true that Wiseman denies its mimetic potential.

More important, to construe Wiseman's claims as contradictory, Winston must implicitly assume a positivist epistemology that equates knowledge with objectivity and science. Winston finds it contradictory to argue that a film can simultaneously both teach and be subjective, as though the imparting of knowledge comes only through objective or scientific discourse. Only a rank positivist believes this. For the rest of us, there simply is no contradiction between Wiseman's claims that his films are both subjective *and* have something to show us. Winston needs to explain why we cannot both recognize the subjective elements of nonfiction filmmaking, *and* admit that nonfiction films can be illuminating and informative.[21]

Moreover, Post-Structuralists often maintain that photography was invented and developed to serve particular ideological functions. For example, Jean-Louis Baudry claims that in response to Galileo and the end of geocentrism, artists produced *perspectiva artificialis*, a new mode of representation ensuring "the setting up of the 'subject' [that is, the self] as the active center and origin of meaning" and in its illusory nature hiding its constructedness. Photography supposedly fulfills similar ideological and psychological functions, creating a "hallucinatory reality," laying out "the space of an ideal vision," and assuring "the necessity of transcendence."[22] Though Baudry's claims are either vague or quite frankly fantastic, suppose, for the sake of argument, we grant his contention that photography was invented to serve a singular ideological purpose. Even so, this says little about the purposes of photography *now*, 150 years later, in a very different world, where photography is used by many different people for widely varied purposes. Is it really defensible to claim that all photography shares a unitary ideological effect? My assumption is that ideological and psychological effect depend on context as much as on origins; in fact, origins may have little to do with how we use photography today. To claim a uniform, seamless, decontextualized ideological effect for any apparatus is simplistic, ahistorical, and wrong.

Most of the debate about the nature of motion photography has centered on its use as an index, a sign that stands in a relationship of physical causality to its referent (as I discuss below) and which, therefore, might be thought to constitute visual evidence. However, the moving photograph is also an icon—related to its referent via resemblance—and its iconicity is at least as important in determining its communicative functions and possibilities.[23] One needs only to consider specific moving photographs to contradict the broad claims made by poststructuralism/postmodernism about images. The Rodney King video, for example, (a) has a referent, and (b) yields visual information about the referent. The referent in this case is the beating of Rodney King, an actual historical event that occurred, and occurred in a certain way, independent of the video of the event or what you or I say about it.[24] In addition, it is relatively uncontroversial that the video gives us visual information about the event it recorded. Of course, this information is not complete, and some aspects of it are ambiguous and subject to contrary interpretations; the verdict of the Simi Valley jury in the criminal trial of the police indicates that much. Yet my claim is that the video gives us *some* visual information, not perfect, or incontrovertible, or complete, or apodictic, but still *some* information. For example, it does show a black man being beaten by a group of white policemen. Much of the information given by the video is uncontroversial; the uniforms worn by the men imply that they are police; some stood by as others beat King; the beating occurred at night, and so on. We learned from the trial that some of the most important information *for a criminal prosecution* was not shown by the video, such as criminal intent, the actions of the police and King before and after the video footage, whether King's attempts to rise are motivated by self-defense or aggression, and so on. We can simultaneously recognize the function of the photographic image as icon, *and* its problematic nature in rendering visual information.

One could say that a photograph is an icon because it resembles the scene of which it is a photograph. More precisely, the photograph *may* provide visual information similar to that obtainable by an observer looking at the actual scene from the standpoint of the camera.[25] As J. J. Gibson notes, photography *records a sample of ambient light,* and the picture surface, under specified conditions, is treated in such a way that it contains the same kind of information as would come from the natural environment.[26] In the case of video, the visual information is projected onto the surface of the video screen; in the motion picture, the visual information is recorded on strips of film and projected onto a surface. In either case, this process accounts for our ability to receive accurate visual information about an extra-filmic referent from photographs.

Obviously, the photograph yields *visual* (as opposed to aural or tactile) information, showing us outlines, depth cues, the relative sizes of objects, and in general, how something looks.[27] The moving photograph also provides *moving* visual information. In the case of animals and humans, moving photographs render information about behavior, including gestures, body movement, facial expression, and interaction with the environment. If I want to learn how a lion stalks its prey, I can read a description of its behavior. Better yet, though, I can watch a photographic recording of the actual behavior.

As Gibson notes, both the quality and quantity of visual information available in the photograph will be inferior to the visual data available at the actual scene. A picture can never preserve all of the information available to an observer; it can only preserve *selected* and *degraded* information. In addition, though the photograph *can* impart visual information, this is not a necessary function of photography. Those interested in promoting photography as an art, for example, are often defensive about our seeing photographs as mere likenesses or imitations. If photography is mere imitation or recording, what room is there for art and expression? My point is that photographs *can* function as icons, not that they *necessarily do.* Those favoring expressive uses of photographs need not deny their special relation to the visual world nor the mechanical nature of the camera. For as an instrumentalist theory shows, just as we use the camera to record the look of a scene, we also may use it for more expressive purposes through a variety of manipulations.

The fact that many photographs are icons has important implications for nonfiction film. For one, it implies that understanding films requires a meld of interpretive schemas, some specifically filmic and others extending to our means of understanding the visual world around us. While we may refer to stylistic and structural conventions to make sense of a difficult film, we also make reference to schemas that extend beyond peculiarly filmic conventions, about gestures, fashion, body movement, and other cultural signs. This is true because the photograph shows us the gesture, the clothing, the movement, giving us some of the same visual information we might have seen were we present at the pro-filmic scene. Though we make reference to film conventions to make sense of nonfiction films, we also use many of the schemas required for perception and understanding in everyday life.

The Index and Documentary

If images functioned only as icons, they would lack their powerful rhetorical force. What gives images a sense of reliability, and what inspires epithets such as "pictures don't lie," is the fact that images are in part produced mechanically by a camera and, to an extent, can escape the intentionality of the camera operator.[28] Photographs are a powerful means of communication because they are often both icons *and* indices. Again, the Rodney King video provides an excellent example. We know little about the man who actually made that video, George Holliday. Frankly, we care little about his views on race relations, or what he thinks about the police and police brutality. The important factor here is that Holliday pointed and switched on his video camera, and that after that point the camera produced a veridical, mechanically produced representation of some of the events of that evening. To consider the moving photograph as a mechanically produced sign is to see it as what Charles Sanders Peirce calls an *index*, a sign related to its referent by causality.

In nonfiction film, the fact that the photograph is used as an index implies that the photographic image, unlike a painting, functions as a type of visual evidence that the profilmic scene looked a certain way, or that the profilmic event occurred in a certain way.[29] At this site—of the supposed evidential force of moving photographs in nonfiction films—the Post-Structuralist finds inherent dangers and snares. In the case of *icons*, remember, the Post-Structuralist thinks the spectator will mistake a photographic representation to be "equivalent to" the profilmic scene; photographs are thought to cause the illusion of presence, the chimera of plenitude, or at the most extreme, a narcissistic setting oneself up as the center and origin of all meaning. Still more, this *indexical* force that photography carries is thought to encourage gullibility and naïveté in the spectator, who is characterized as ready to believe that since photographs "cannot lie," anything that a documentary claims or implies must therefore be true.

Brian Winston, for example, argues that claims about the scientific nature of photography have conditioned spectators to think that "seeing is believing, and the photographic camera never lies." In fact, Winston claims, the discourse about science and evidence has become so pervasive that disclaimers by filmmakers themselves, admitting their subjectivity, their rhetorical uses of photographs, and so on, are "contradicted by the overwhelmingly powerful cultural context of science." As Winston goes on, "The centrality of this scientific connection to documentary is the most potent (and sole) legitimation for its evidentiary pretensions. Thus, documentarists cannot readily avoid the scientific and evidential because those contexts are 'built-in' to the cinematographic apparatus." [30]

There is nothing to be done; on Winston's prognosis, the spectator, cowed by the supposed scientific legitimacy of documentary photography, will necessarily mistake documentary photographs for incontrovertible evidence that the film is unproblematically true and real. Like most Post-Structuralist claims about the ideological effects of various filmic phenomena, this effect is thought to be *built into the apparatus itself,* apparently a permanent characteristic, irrevocably and universally appended to the cinema via its historical origins, making the nonfiction film suspect from the start.

In considering these claims, we should distinguish two distinct but related issues. One has to do with the spectator, and the other with whether and how photographs function as evidence in nonfiction films. When one examines the use of photographs in nonfiction films, one must recognize that they *do* often function as a form of rhetorical evidence, along with various manifestations of structure, style, and "artistic proof." However, photographs in documentaries operate only as a weak sort of evidence, often no more compelling than that available in a written description of an event, for example. In criminal proceedings in U.S. federal courts, photographs or videotapes of any kind must ordinarily satisfy many rather stringent conditions before they can be admitted as evidence. For our purposes, one of these conditions stands out as most important—the photographs or videos used must be shown to be "true and accurate representations." Those who would submit photographs as evidence (1) must show that the photograph has not been retouched, enhanced, subject to digital image processing, or tampered with in any way that alters the veridical record it provides; (2) must present the photographic evidence in tandem with a "testimonial sponsor," normally the person who operated the camera, but in some cases extending to a witness who can testify that the film or videotape provides an accurate representation of the event it records; (3) must provide details to illustrate contextual factors that may be important, such as the date, time, and persons present at the time the film or photograph was present, the location, what film stock and lens were used, the type of camera, shutter speed, f-stop, and information about processing. The point isn't that using photographs under such strict conditions is without problems, or reaches some ideal of science; the point is rather that photographs as they are used in nonfiction films rarely if ever meet *even these* requirements for evidence.

The Post-Structuralist might deduce from this that nonfiction films are therefore never evidence of anything. However, this would be a hasty conclusion, because within the context of our everyday lives, and in the discourses in which we engage, we rarely *require* evidence that meets the standards of the federal courts. In nonfiction film, and in other discourse, we turn to many factors other than photography to gauge the reliability of information. These are complex, but include (at least) coherence of argument, internal consistency, consistency of the claims with what we presume to know, and, finally, the reliability of the source of the claims.[31] Even when we are satisfied that a discourse more or less "tells the truth," it would be another matter to measure the evidence it presents against the requirements of science or the criminal courts. We may agree with the Post-Structuralist that the nonfiction photograph does not automatically constitute scientific evidence. Nonetheless, it may provide a wealth of visual information, and in some circumstances, may function as "rhetorical" evidence that the pro-filmic event occurred, or the scene looked, a certain way. The mistake is to assume that in the absence of this scientific or legal evidence, the photographic image has no evidentiary value whatsoever.

This still leaves the second, and very important issue—the spectator. The Post-Structuralist postulates a spectator who naïvely believes everything seen. As Winston implies, the universal belief of spectators in the scientific nature of the photograph extends to a gullibility about truth claims in nonfiction films generally, such that no amount of explanation by filmmakers, and presumably education by film and media teachers, can override the bias of science built into the apparatus. Of course, this universalizes the spectator, effecting a rhetoric that draws no distinctions between gender, race, level of education, class, and so on. Post-Structuralist notions of the spectator *cannot* recognize differences between spectators, because as we have seen, they build the ideological effect of the cinema *into the apparatus itself*, proclaiming it a kind of universal effects machine that works on everyone the same way.

The instrumentalist, conversely, not only recognizes a diversity of uses of nonfiction film, but also a diversity of spectators and a heterogeneity of responses. Doubtless there exists a core of similar responses to some elements of films, at least within a given community of discourse, and especially at the level of comprehension (as opposed to interpretation or emotional response). However, we need theories of spectatorship that can account for sociological differences between spectators at some level, for those differences in response clearly exist. Elsewhere I have argued that cognitive psychology, and especially cognitive theories of affect, can better account for differences between spectators than can psychoanalysis, the favored psychology of Post-Structuralism.[32] Cognitive theories of affect, for example, have distinguished between universal and culture-bound determinants of psychological phenomena. Whether it be facial expressions or emotional response, many are a complex mixture of the universally human and the culturally specific.

Ironically (for Post-Structuralists are mostly educators), Post-Structuralism implicitly downplays the role of education, since again, the apparatus is thought to have a built-in effect independent of level of education (the apparatus "positions" or "constructs" the spectator). The instrumentalist approach claims that no film has a necessary ideological or psychological effect apart from specific contexts and spectators. Since those contexts and spectators are so difficult to know, to make any generalizations about spectator response we often need to assume a homogeneity among viewers, at least at basic levels of comprehension. This is sometimes necessary and justifiable, but should be tempered by an acknowledgment that a theory of spectatorship is always subject to revision and nuancing in relation to context. In addition, the instrumentalist wishes to promote the benefits of education. Nonfiction films do not deceive *all* spectators; they may be misleading to *some* spectators, because some may mistake their representations to be "equivalent" to the real (whatever that means). However, this isn't a deception of nonfiction discourse, built into the apparatus, but a confusion among some viewers who do not understand the normative functions of visual discourse. The proper remedy isn't to castigate nonfiction filmmakers or realist films, as though they are attempting to deceive the public *as a group*. A more likely strategy is to promote media education, to enable more people to understand the rhetoric of the visual media. That, it seems to me, is one of the primary tasks of the scholar and teacher of nonfiction film.

Images in Context

The Post-Structuralist wrongly sees the recording function of nonfiction film and its rhetoric as antithetical or contradictory. I've argued that recording and expression exist side by side in nonfiction films, and often within the same image or sound. This is no contradiction, because, for example, while an image may record the look of the profilmic scene in some respects, it can simultaneously imply something about the scene via its textual placement, its camera angle, camera distance, choice of lens, or a host of other devices. It is shortsighted to deny completely the informative potential of the nonfiction film and to concentrate on its putative deceptions. The instrumentalist recognizes the complexities and ambiguities of nonfiction discourse, and its potential to inform, persuade, *and* deceive.

It is not necessary to deny iconicity while recognizing its limitations. The instrumentalist affirms the potential of moving photographs to provide visual information about a scene or event, while simultaneously acknowledging weaknesses of the image as a vehicle for conceptual knowledge or analysis. (Photographic images are therefore often accompanied by linguistic messages which help to determine the meaning of images within their context.)[33]

Neither need we deny indexicality to make clear the problematic nature of photographs as visual evidence. While the instrumentalist affirms the potential of photographs to function as evidence, she or he also notes that images as used in nonfiction films provide only an "artistic proof," and not the sort of evidence required in criminal law (which in itself may be problematic). While there are different levels of evidence, and while any assessment of the moving photograph must acknowledge the influence of the camera and other factors, to completely rule out the photograph's function as index only obscures matters.

Images and also sounds (which likewise have an iconic and indexical function) serve as building blocks in the complex textual system that every nonfiction film develops, by which the narration selects, orders, and emphasizes information. The narration presents images and sounds in conjunction with each other, or in a sequence with other images and sounds. They take on meaning only within the structure and purpose of the text as a whole, within its story, argument, or exposition. Images are mute in themselves, and their meaning emerges only in relation to the style and technique by which they are presented as part of a purposive discourse. A rhetoric of the nonfiction film must systematically examine structure, style, and the "artistic proof" (ethical, emotional, demonstrative) of classical persuasion.

The Post-Structuralist approach is both politically disabling and philosophically indefensible. It is misleading to characterize the nonfiction film as inherently deceptive due to its combination of moving pictures and rhetoric. Contrary to what some believe, Post-Structuralist theory has not at last opened our eyes to rhetorical manipulation and the possibility of deception in discourse; these topics have been in circulation at least since the ancient Greeks (consider, for example, Plato's characterization of the sophist in his dialogue, *Sophist*). But Post-Structuralism has made it more difficult to see the benefits of nonfiction filmmaking, and to rediscover the legitimate use of moving photographs as both icons and indices of the profilmic scene.[34]

Any rhetoric that denies the legitimacy and importance of informative and evidential uses of motion pictures, and finds only deceptions and manipulations, presents a one-sided, indeed, paranoid picture of the nonfiction film and its cultural and psychological effects. Film studies must move beyond Post-Structuralism to a less defensive, more nuanced study of nonfiction film and video discourse, one that can account for icons, indices, and their complex uses as elements of nonfiction films. Film studies must discard sterile theory that finds legitimacy only in a reflexive inward turn. It is both politically enabling, and accurate, to picture nonfiction films and videos as instruments with diverse purposes and effects, through which agents act in the world.

NOTES

1. See *Jean Baudrillard: Selected Writings*, ed. Mark Poster (Cambridge: Polity Press, 1988); Richard Rorty, *Consequences of Pragmatism* (Minneapolis: University of Minnesota Press, 1982); and *Philosophy and the Mirror of Nature* (Princeton: Princeton University Press, 1980); and Stanley Fish, *Is There a Text in This Class?* (Cambridge: Harvard University Press, 1980).

2. On these issues, see Christopher Norris, *What's Wrong With Postmodernism: Critical Theory and the Ends of Philosophy* (Baltimore: Johns Hopkins University Press, 1990), especially chapter 4, "Lost in the Funhouse: Baudrillard and the Politics of Postmodernism," pp. 164–93. Also see Richard Allen, "Critical Theory and the Paradox of Modernist Discourse," *Screen* 28 (Spring 1987): 69–85.

3. In this essay I use the term "Post-Structuralist" in a relatively broad fashion, to refer to a whole range of related and sometimes consistent beliefs about films and their use of images.

4. Michael Renov, "Toward a Poetics of Documentary," in *Theorizing Documentary*, ed. Michael Renov (New York: Routledge, 1992), p. 25.

5. Paul Arthur, "Jargons of Authenticity (Three American Moments)," ibid., pp. 108–9.

6. Susan Scheibler, "Constantly Performing the Documentary: The Seductive Promise of *Lightning Over Water*," ibid., p. 136.

7. No doubt some spectators fit this description. Yet in this age of media irony and reflexivity (for example, David Letterman, Beavis and Butthead), it is difficult to believe there are many. At any rate, the best cure for such spectators isn't for us to rail against realist representation, but to promote education about the rhetoric of the media.

8. Trinh T. Minh-ha, "The Totalizing Quest of Meaning," in *Theorizing Documentary*, p. 105. Although the political value of postmodernist and Post-Structuralist documentaries is often exaggerated (their audience is an educated, usually leftist elite—the "already converted," so to speak), the works of Trinh T. Minh-ha and Chris Marker, for example, are nonetheless remarkable for their aesthetic or formal qualities. Moreover, critics rarely see these films as "void" or without meaning; we usually find them to investigate representation or explore the documentary form itself. Reflexive films hardly escape "the tyranny of meaning"; they simply displace it onto another level.

9. The category of the "actual world" is one rejected by many Post-Structuralists and postmodernists. However, such a rejection has significant consequences. If the Post-Structuralist says there exists no actual world, then she or he can say nothing about that world or its contents. If there exists no actual world, and no evidence from which to evaluate assertions, then the postmodernist has no ground to contradict my claims: on his own view, there *are* no grounds on which to appeal.

In my view, the actual world consists (at least) of physical events and their relationships, matter, and entities such as stars, trees, persons, and social problems. My claim here is simply that nonfiction films make assertions and implications about elements of the actual world such as the ones listed. I do not assume that nonfiction films necessarily assert or imply *truths;* they assert and imply *truth claims.* A defining characteristic of nonfiction discourse is that it makes *direct* assertions about the actual world, not that it makes *true* assertions. A documentary that makes assertions about the actual world is no less a documentary if some (or all) of the assertions are false.

10. The distinction is more complicated than I have represented it here. For more developed accounts of the fiction/nonfiction distinction as it relates to cinema, see Noël Carroll, "From Real to Reel: Entangled in the Nonfiction Film," *Philosophic Exchange* 14 (1983): 5–45; Carl Plantinga, "Defining Documentary: Fiction, Nonfiction, and Projected Worlds," *Persistence of Vision*, 5 (Spring 1987): 44–54.

11. These thoughts about categories and distinctions stem from "prototype theory," most usefully described in George Lakoff, *Women, Fire, and Dangerous Things: What Categories Reveal about the Mind* (Chicago: University of Chicago Press, 1987).

12. "From Real to Reel: Entangled in the Nonfiction Film."

13. Some films may be ambiguously indexed, or perhaps not indexed at all. For example, Oliver Stone's *JFK* is not clearly documentary, docudrama, or fiction, and I'm not sure that Stone was clear about how to view his own film. On the one hand, he claimed that his strategy was to present a countermyth to the Warren Commission Report's assertion that Lee Harvey Oswald acted alone in assassinating John Kennedy. But if *JFK* is designed as myth, and not an account of what actually occurred, why did Stone hire researchers to carefully document many of the claims made in the film? The spectator has no way of knowing what in the film has been "carefully researched," and what is pure speculation on the part of Stone and his crew. This ambiguity of reception, it seems to me, is a function of ambiguous or contradictory indexing on the part of Oliver Stone.

14. See my "The Mirror Framed: A Case for Expression in the Documentary," *Wide Angle* 13, 2 (Summer 1991): 40–53.

15. "Towards a Poetics of Documentary," in *Theorizing Documentary*, p. 26.

16. Stephen Prince notes that Post-Structuralist film theory tends to posit a false dichotomy between arbitrariness and identity for signs. Either a sign is arbitrarily related to what it represents, or the relationship is described as one "of identity and transparence, with the latter condition being construed negatively in terms of illusion and error." One who accepts such a simplistic dichotomy would see signs either as wholly arbitrary or identical to their referents. See Prince's "The Discourse of Pictures: Iconicity and Film Studies," *Film Quarterly* 47, 1 (Fall 1993): 17–18. Such a dichotomy rules out any defensible manifestation of signs as icons or indices, because it implicitly (and falsely) assumes that iconic and indexical signs must bear a relation of identity and transparence with their referent. However, resemblance (iconicity) and causality (indexicality) are hardly coextensive with identity and transparence.

17. Post-Structuralists and postmodernists sometimes deny that the camera can successfully record the look of the pro-filmic scene or give veridical information about the pro-filmic event. In fact, some might deny the very existence of such a thing as the "pro-filmic scene," since all, on this view, is "always-already" discourse. As I will argue, such claims fall in the face of specific examples where it is necessary to distinguish between an actual scene and a photograph or video of the scene. One may deny such a distinction in theory, but looking at specific examples makes that denial somewhat perverse and capricious.

18. Wiseman quoted in Winston, "The Documentary Film as Scientific Inscription," in *Theorizing Documentary*, p. 48.

19. Winston, *Theorizing Documentary*, p. 49. Winston claims that Wiseman uses such allegedly contradictory rhetoric to escape from legal difficulties the film initiated, by in effect hiding behind a smoke screen of sophisticated and opaque rhetoric; he assumes that Wiseman tried to escape legal difficulties by overwhelming the judge and jury with academic double-talk.

20. As Albert Maysles says, "I'm interested in fictional technique as it relates to factual material . . . [I]n a sense, editing is fiction, really, because you're putting it together, you're taking things out of place." See "Albert and David Maysles," in *Documentary Explorations: 15 Interviews with Film-Makers* ed. Roy G. Levin (Garden City, N.Y.: Doubleday, 1971), p. 276. In my opinion, Maysles mistakes subjectivity for fiction (implying that only objective representations can be nonfictional). Still, his point that editing incorporates a subjective element into his films remains the same.

21. It is especially odd—even self-contradictory—that Winston makes these positivist assumptions within an essay that shows such a healthy skepticism of both objectivity and science.

22. "Ideological Effects of the Basic Cinematographic Apparatus," in *Film Theory and Criticism*, 4th ed., ed. Gerald Mast, Marshall Cohen, and Leo Braudy (New York: Oxford University Press, 1992), pp. 302, 304–5.

23. For a thorough discussion of iconicity and images, see Stephen Prince, "The Discourse of Pictures: Iconicity and Film Studies." "Icon," "index," and "symbol" are Charles Sanders Peirce's terms to describe his tripartite division of signs according to their relationship with their referents. The icon and index are defined in this essay. The symbol, according to Peirce, has an arbitrary or purely conventional relationship with its referent, as the word "cat" has with an actual cat. As I use these terms, the photographic sign is not fixed and unitary, but may function as icon, index, and symbol simultaneously, and may function differently depending on context.

Some will call my position here "Bazinian," but I wish to dissociate myself from the realism of André Bazin. The many differences between Bazin's thought and my own are too complicated to investigate here. For an examination and critique of Bazin on cinematic representation, see Noël Carroll, *Philosophical Problems of Classical Film Theory* (Princeton: Princeton University Press, 1988), pp. 94–171.

24. The beating had an independent ontological existence consisting of a series of physical events. Our access to that event is a question of epistemology, and is separate from the question of whether or not it actually occurred in a certain way.

25. I say "*may* provide" because this is not a necessary function of the photograph. Photographs may also be used to deceive the spectator or to mask visual information that may otherwise have been available. The use of high-contrast film stock or distorting lenses, for example, can mask or distort rather than inform. The fact that their use is unusual shows that a typical use of photography is to record and reveal.

26. See Gibson's *The Ecological Approach to Visual Perception* (Boston: Houghton Mifflin, 1979). Also see Edward S. Reed, *James J. Gibson and the Psychology of Perception* (New Haven: Yale University Press, 1988), pp. 239–59. David Blinder makes use of Gibson's theory in his "In Defense of Pictorial Mimesis," *Journal of Aesthetics and Art Criticism* 45, 1 (Fall 1986): 19–27.

27. Sounds may also function as icons and indices. Here again, film theorists have tended to emphasize the mediations of sound recording and deny its iconic and indexical possibilities. As in the case of images, preserving a recording function for sounds is thought to encourage illusionism, or the mistaking of an "absence" for a "presence."

28. Among writers on film, this point was first raised by André Bazin, in his "The Ontology of the Photographic Image," in *What Is Cinema?* vol. 1, trans. and ed. Hugh Gray (Berkeley: University of California Press, 1967), pp. 9–16. Charles Sanders Peirce earlier wrote about photographs as indexical signs, related to their referent in part via the causality of a physical process. Again, an essential point is that photographs do not *necessarily* escape the intentions of the photographer, and when they do, it is often only in some respects. For example, Holliday may have intended to videotape the police as they beat Rodney King. However, our use of the video to provide evidence depends little on his intentions, once the video is produced. The video becomes a veridical recording produced in part by a physical, mechanical process.

Noël Carroll rightly points out that cinematic images are not "automatically objective" simply because they are produced by a camera machine, as Bazin seems to imply. See *Philosophical Problems of Classical Film Theory*, pp. 152–57. My argument is not that moving pictures are "automatically objective," but that they can, under certain conditions, function as indexical signs, in part due to their being produced by a mechanical device. Though this is a subject too complex to investigate here, the two claims are widely divergent.

29. How and whether the moving image functions as an index in the *fiction* film is a complex issue that limited space makes impossible to deal with here.

30. Winston, *Theorizing Documentary,* pp. 40–41.

31. For these reasons, those who claim that digital imaging techniques signal the "end of the photographic era" exaggerate their effects. Within the bounds of discourse, savvy spectators have never relied solely on the image as evidence for a text's claims, as though only the photographic image could possibly serve as rhetorical evidence. If this were so, how could nonphotographic discourse ever present evidence?

32. See my "Affect, Cognition, and the Power of Moves," *Post Script* 13, 1 (Fall 1993): 10–29.

33. See Roland Barthes, "The Rhetoric of the Image" and "The Photographic Message," both in *Image/Music/Text,* ed. and trans. Stephen Heath (New York: Hill and Wang, 1977), pp. 15–51.

34. Among film scholars, Peter Wollen first emphasized the importance of images as icons and indices in *Signs and Meaning in the Cinema* (Bloomington: Indiana University Press, 1976).

15

Film, Reality, and Illusion

Gregory Currie

Introduction

It has been said that film is both a realistic and an illusionistic medium; indeed, these claims have often been treated as if they were indistinguishable. I wish to distinguish them, for I hold that film is a realistic medium—in a certain sense—and I deny that it is an illusionistic medium. I shall elaborate and defend a version of realism about cinema, and I shall identify two versions of illusionism, both of which I shall reject. In recent years these issues have most often been discussed within the framework of Marxist, psychoanalytic, or semiotic principles. I shall draw instead on recent Anglo-American philosophy of mind and language, within which there has been considerable debate about the nature and viability of realism. Since my concern is with cinema, I want to discuss a specifically representational form of realism that sheds light on the nature of film—and incidentally on other "pictorial" modes of representation. In line, I imagine, with most of the contributors to this volume, I do not aim at a systematic theory of cinema—not here, anyway. What I intend to do instead is to show how ways of thinking from within the broadly analytical tradition of philosophy can help us get a better grip on the issues of realism and illusion as they relate to film. I begin, in good analytic style, with some distinctions. I hope to end with something more speculative and challenging. I shall argue that we see movement on the cinema screen in the same sense that we see colors when we look at ordinary objects in the world under normal conditions. That is, we literally see movement on the screen, just as we literally see color. Colors are real, and so is cinematic motion. There is therefore no "illusion" of movement, and it is literally true that films are moving pictures.

Transparency, Realism, and Illusionism

Let us start by distinguishing three doctrines about cinema, all of which have been called "realism." They are, however, quite distinct, and to underline their distinctness I shall call only one of them "realism."

There is first the claim that film, because of its use of the photographic method, reproduces rather than merely represents the real world; this view is associated most notably with André Bazin.[1] Following Kendall Walton,[2] I shall call this the doctrine of *Transparency;* film is transparent in that we see "through" it to the real world, as we see through a window or a lens. Next is the idea that the experience of film watching approximates the normal experience of perceiving the real world. We might call this *Perceptual Realism,* since it says that film is, or can be, realistic in its recreation of the experience of the real world. This doctrine has been asserted, again by Bazin, in connection with long-take, deep-focus style. But, as I shall argue, this kind of realism is a matter of degree, and long-take style is merely more realistic in this sense than is, say, montage style. Perceptual Realism, as a thesis about cinema, is the thesis that film is, in general, more realistic than certain other modes of representation. Finally, there is the claim that film is realistic in its capacity to engender in the viewer an illusion of the reality and presentness of fictional characters and events portrayed. Let us call this view, which seems to be held by studio publicity writers as well as by the sternest Marxist critics of the Hollywood film, *Illusionism.*

Much of the history of film and film theory is reconstructible as a debate about the relations between these three doctrines. Some theorists—I am thinking of the early montagists and, more recently, the friends of Godard— have argued that Transparency requires us to play down the perceptual realism which film makes possible; film achieves the status of art (or subversion) when it employs mechanisms that go beyond the mere reproduction of reality. Others, like Bazin, say that film's dependence on Transparency *requires* the filmmaker to exploit to the full the possibilities for perceptual realism inherent in film; film presents the real world, so it should do so in a way which approximates as closely as possible to our experience of the real world. Some theorists have agreed—at least they can be read as agreeing—that Perceptual Realism makes for Illusionism. They agree, in other words, that the closer the experience of film watching approximates to the experience of seeing the real world, the more effectively film engenders in the viewer the illusion that he or she is actually watching the real world.[3] The disagreement between these theorists has concerned the question whether this is a desirable goal. Other theorists have taken a more radical view, and have argued that the very notion of realism in film is suspect or even incoherent.

If my absurdly brief account of the history of film theory is close to being right, the discipline has been to a large extent predicated on the assumption of a close connection between these three doctrines. I, on the other hand, take these doctrines to be independent, both logically and causally. Adopting any one of them, we are free to adopt or reject the others. I reject Illusionism, I accept Perceptual Realism, and I am neutral, for present purposes, about Transparency, which I shall ignore hereafter, having had my say on it elsewhere.[4] I want to defend Perceptual Realism, which has been under attack for a while now from those who reject the notion of likeness or resemblance between images and the things they are images of, and who stress instead the artifice, the conventionality, the "codedness" as they put it, of cinema. But I wish to avoid a misunderstanding about what I am claiming here. My defense of Perceptual Realism is a metaphysical and not an aesthetic defense. I am not advocating that filmmakers adopt styles which, like long-take, deep-focus style, attempt to exploit the possibilities for perceptual realism in film. I am arguing that Perceptual Realism is a coherent thesis, and that it is possible to achieve a considerable degree of this kind of realism in film. Whether you think that is a worthwhile project is another matter.

About Illusionism I want to say two things. First, I wish to argue that it is a mistaken doctrine. Second, I want to hazard a guess at why this doctrine, which strikes me as completely implausible, should have such a tenacious grip on the minds of many who concern themselves with film. My hypothesis is that its strength derives in part (and certainly only in part) from its being conflated with another doctrine which is even more widely believed and which has a certain plausibility. This is the thesis that the basic mechanism of film creates an illusion of *movement*. Sorting out these two doctrines will lead us to make a distinction between cognitive and perceptual illusions.

Perceptual Realism

Let us say that a mode of representation is realistic when, or to the degree that, we employ the same capacities in recognizing its representational content as we employ in recognizing the (kind of) objects it represents. A good-quality, well-focused, middle-distance photograph of a horse is realistic in this sense: you employ your visual capacity to recognize horses so as to determine that this is, indeed, a photograph of a horse. Roughly speaking, you can recognize a photograph, a cinematic image, or other kind of picture of a horse if and only if you can recognize a horse.[5] By contrast, a linguistic description of a horse is not realistic in the sense just specified, for the capacity visually to recognize horses is neither sufficient nor necessary to enable you to recognize the description as a description of a horse; recognizing the description requires a knowledge of the conventions of language. (There probably are *other* senses in which a description can be said to be realistic.)

Realism of the kind I am concerned with here is a matter of degree. Suppose we have a representation, R, of an object, A, and R represents A as having properties F and G. R might represent F realistically, and G in some other way. That is, R may be such that you are able to recognize R as representing the Fness of A in virtue of your capacity visually to recognize the Fness of an A when you see one, but you recognize R as representing the Gness of A in virtue of your knowledge of some convention of language, or perhaps in virtue of your knowledge of someone's intention. In that case, when we say that this representation, or mode of representation, is realistic and that one is not we probably mean that this one is *more* realistic than that one. It will be important to bear this in mind in what follows.

It is in this sense of realism—the sense which I have given to the phrase "Perceptual Realism"—that film is a realistic medium, and deep-focus, long-take style is an especially realistic style within that medium. We recognize that people, houses, mountains, and cars are represented on screen by exercising the capacities we have to recognize those objects, and not by learning a set of conventions that associate cinematic representations of these objects with the objects themselves. (There is, in other words, nothing comparable in cinema to learning the vocabulary of a language).[6] And when objects and events are represented on screen within a single shot, we come to know what spatial and temporal relations the film represents as holding between those objects and events by using our ordinary capacities to judge the spatial and temporal relations between objects and events themselves. We judge the spatial relations between objects represented in the same shot by seeing that they are spatially related thus and so; we judge the temporal properties of and relations between events represented within the take by noting that this event took (roughly) so long to observe, while that one was experienced as occurring later than the other one. That is exactly how we judge the spatial and temporal properties of things and events as we perceive them in the real world. In that way, long-take, deep-focus style extends the possibilities for the perceptual realism of film. (Length of take and depth of focus are independent of one another and do not always go together, as David Bordwell pointed out to me. But if I am right about their capacity to enhance perceptual realism in film, the combination of these two features constitutes something like a stylistic "natural kind".)

In montage style, on the other hand, where there is quick cutting between very distinct spatial (and sometimes temporal) perspectives, the spatial and temporal properties and relations depicted have, with greater frequency, to be judged by means of inference from the overall dramatic structure of the film. As my earlier remarks were intended to suggest, this is a matter of degree; long-take, deep-focus style is *more* realistic than montage style, and montage style can itself be said to be more realistic than some other modes of representation: more realistic certainly than linguistic description. Unqualified claims that long-take, deep-focus style is realistic should be taken as implicitly relativized to the class of artistic styles with which it is most naturally compared, namely other cinematic styles, just as the claim that elephants are large will be understood as relativized to the class of mammals.

It is often remarked that deep-focus style is unrealistic in that it presents us with an image in which objects are simultaneously in sharp focus when they are at considerably different distances from the camera, whereas objects at comparable distances from the eye could not be seen in focus together.[7] But this does not seriously detract from the perceptual realism of deep focus. Deep focus, particularly when used in conjunction with a wide screen, enables us to concentrate our attention on one object, and then to shift our attention at will to another object, just as we are able to do when perceiving the real world. Since we are usually not very conscious of refocusing our eyes, the similarities between viewing deep-focus style and perceiving the real world are more striking than the differences. With montage style on the other hand, we are severely limited by shot length and depth of field in our capacity to shift our attention from one object to another at will—though as I have said, this feature is not entirely absent in montage style.

Explicating the idea of perceptual realism in this way helps us avoid an error that has dogged theorizing about the cinema: that realism in film can be attacked on metaphysical grounds because it postulates an observer-independent world—an idea which is then further associated by some theorists with a politically conservative agenda of submission to prevailing conditions. But Perceptual Realism as I have explicated it here appeals to no such postulate of an observer-independent world (though one might argue that such a postulate is both philosophically respectable and politically neutral). The claim of Perceptual Realism is not the claim that cinema presents objects and events isomorphic to those that exist in an observer-independent world, but the claim that, in crucial respects, the experience of film watching is similar to the ordinary perceptual experience of the world, irrespective of whether and to what extent that world is itself independent of our experience of it.

When I say "the experience of film watching is similar to the ordinary perceptual experience of the world," I mean that *our* experience of film watching is similar to *our* ordinary perceptual experience of the world. There might be creatures as intelligent and perceptually discriminating as we are but who experience the world in ways rather different from us. They might not be able to deploy their natural recognitional capacities in order to grasp what is depicted in film, and in our other pictorial forms of representation. Richard Dawkins raises the possibility that bats might have visual experiences qualitatively similar to our own, but caused by their very different perceptual systems, which depend on bouncing sound waves off solid objects.[8] I understand this is not likely to be true of bats,[9] but we can imagine batlike creatures complex enough for this to be a plausible story. They wouldn't have much success detecting the spatial properties of objects as they are represented on a flat screen, and film would be a medium with little appeal for them. So there is a definite relativity about my conception of realism; what is realistic for us might not be realistic for other creatures. My concept of realism is what people these days are calling a response-dependent concept; it is a concept applicable to things in virtue of the responses to it of a certain class of intelligent agents, namely ourselves.[10] It is like the concept *being funny* or *being red*. Things are funny if people respond to them in certain ways (it's not easy to say exactly what ways); things are red if they look red to normal humans in normal conditions. So it is with Perceptual Realism.

Some people will find this relativistic concept of realism jarring, perhaps oxymoronic. Among them are those who, as I mentioned earlier, object to realism because they think realism presupposes some sort of absolutist conception of the world and all its aspects. They think that realism postulates a world describable without reference to any subjective point of view. But this is a mistake. Colors are real, relational properties of things: properties they have in virtue of our responses to them. Response-dependence is going to come up again, when we discuss the supposed illusion of movement in film. For the record, let us have a tolerably precise characterization of Perceptual Realism:

> A representation R is realistic in its representation of feature F for creatures of kind C if and only if
> (i) R represents something as having F;
> (ii) Cs have a certain perceptual capacity P to recognize instances of F;
> (iii) Cs recognize that R represents something as having F by deploying capacity P.

This characterization of realism has important consequences when applied to film. One is that there is a sense in which film is both a spatial and a temporal medium. Film represents space by means of space, and time by means of time. It is spatial (temporal) properties of the cinematic representation that we observe and rely on in order to figure out what spatial (temporal) properties of the fictional characters and events are portrayed. It is correctly said that painting and still photography are capable of representing the temporal. They may do so in a variety of ways: by encouraging the viewer to make an inference from what is explicitly depicted to what came before and what will come after; by juxtaposition of distinct static images, as when we are shown a series of temporally related photographs; by transforming temporal properties into spatial ones (as in Filippo Lippi's tondo in the Pitti Palace, wherein events earlier in the life of the Virgin are represented deeper within the picture space); by special techniques such as blurring and multiple exposure. But these possibilities do not constitute grounds for calling painting and still photography arts of time in the way that cinema is, for with them time is not represented by means of time.[11]

Illusionism

Having said that film is realistic in that it deploys our natural recognitional capacities, it may seem as if I am thereby committed to illusionism. If a cinematic image of a horse triggers my horse recognition capacity, doesn't that mean that I take the image to be a horse, thereby falling victim to an illusion? No. I say that my horse recognition capacity and my capacity to judge whether there is a horse in front of me (rather than, say, an image of one) are two different things. Indeed, they operate at different cognitive levels. Judging that there is a horse in front of me is something I do; it takes place at the *personal* level. Having my horse recognition capacity triggered—by a horse or by an image of one—is something that goes on in me, at some level within my visual processing system; it is a *subpersonal* process. Once we distinguish between these capacities and the levels at which they operate, we can be perceptual realists without falling into the trap of illusionism.

So I may be a perceptual realist and deny that film is illusionistic, which I do deny. I do not deny that it is *possible* for film to engender this sort of an illusion on the part of a viewer; on a liberal enough view of possibility, it is possible for anything to create an illusion of anything else. But this mere possibility is not what is at issue when people claim that film is illusionistic. Rather, they claim that the standard mechanism by means of which film engages the audience is illusionistic, that the creation of an illusion of reality is a standard feature of the transaction between film and viewer.[12] That is what I deny.

The claim that film creates an illusion of the reality of the fiction it presents can take a number of forms. So far as I can see, film theorists have tended to opt for a particularly strong version of that claim. They have tended to say that the illusion is not merely that the fictional events are real, but that the viewer is present at those events, observing them from within the world of the fiction, thinking of him- or herself as placed where the camera is, experiencing those events with the visual perspective of the camera. There are other, more moderate versions of illusionism one might hold to, but I believe that in the end we shall find no more use for them than for the strong version. Anyhow, it is the strong version I shall concentrate on here.

There are two serious objections to the idea that film induces the illusion that fictional events are real and that the viewer is directly witnessing them. The first derives from a functionalist view about the nature of beliefs: that beliefs are, essentially, states apt to cause certain kinds of behavior.[13] Of course we know that there is no simple, invariant correlation between having a certain belief and engaging in a certain kind of behavior. But we can say this: there are certain kinds of beliefs which are such that, where they are not accompanied by the relevant behavior, their disconnection from behavior is to be explained by appeal to other, countervailing beliefs. Someone who believes herself in danger may take no evasive action, but that will be explained by reference to some other belief: that evasion will have unacceptable costs in terms of peer appraisal, that staying put will be the best way to avoid the danger, and so on. Now film watchers do not behave like people who really believe, or even suspect, that they are in the presence of ax murderers, world-destroying monsters, or nuclear explosions, which is what the films they see frequently represent. And in their cases, appeal to the sorts of countervailing beliefs just mentioned sound rather hollow. The real reasons people stay in movie theaters or in front of videos during frightening films are, for example, because they want to see the rest of the film, or because they have paid their money, or because they want to experience the sensations of fear. None of these explanations sits comfortably with the view that patrons believe, even partially or "with part of the mind," as people sometimes say, that they are really in the presence of dangerous, catastrophic, or tragic events. Explanations of our responses to cinematic fictions in terms of belief work only so long as we do not take the notion of belief, and its connection with behavior, seriously.[14] Of course we do need a psychological explanation of our sometimes very intense responses to film. In the absence of an explanation in other terms, an explanation that appeals to belief can seem attractive, for all its evident drawbacks. Elsewhere I have given an explanation of our responses to fictions, in terms of imagining.[15] I shall say here only that I believe this account applies as well to cinematic as to other kinds of fictions.

The second objection to Illusionism is that it is at odds with much of the experience of film watching.[16] Consider what would be involved in the film viewer believing that she is watching real events. The viewer would have to suppose that her perspective is that of the camera, that she is positioned within and moves through the film space as the camera is positioned and moved. Indeed, there have been elaborate attempts to argue that the viewer does identify with the camera, and Christian Metz has gone so far as to assert that without identification there would be no comprehension of film.[17] But this is psychologically implausible. Identification with the camera would frequently require us to think of ourselves in peculiar or impossible locations, undertaking movements out of keeping with the natural limitations of our bodies, and peculiarly invisible to the characters. None of this seems to be part of the ordinary experience of film watching. In the attempt to associate the camera with some observer within the world of the action with whom the viewer can in turn identify, film theorists have exaggerated the extent to which shots within a film can be thought of as point-of-view shots, and have sometimes postulated, quite ad hoc, an invisible narrator from whose position the action is displayed and with whom the viewer may identify. For example, Jacques Aumont asserts very confidently that ". . . the frame in narrative cinema is always more or less the representation of a gaze, the auteur's or the characters."[18] Here, I believe, we are in the grip of a manifestly false theory. It would be better to acknowledge that cinematic shots are only rarely from a psychological point of view, and to abandon the thesis that the viewer identifies with an intelligence whose point of view is the camera.

A variant of Illusionism, and one which might be thought to take some account of the objections just propounded, says that the situation of the film watcher approximates to that of a dreamer. During our dreams we remain physically passive, yet we are convinced of the reality of the dream. In that case the camera would correspond to a supposed "inner eye" by means of which we perceive the images of dreams. This analogy has been a powerful stimulus to the development of psychoanalytic theories of film and film experience. In fact, as Noël Carroll has shown, the analogy with dreaming proceeds by systematically failing to compare like with like.[19] Dreamers, like film watchers, usually are physically passive while watching or dreaming. But the *experience* of dreaming is usually one that involves action—sometimes ineffectual—on the dreamer's part, while the experience of film watching, our reflex responses aside, rarely moves us to physical action. And it is the experience of film watching and the experience of dreaming that are claimed by the advocates of the dream/film analogy to be alike. The fact that both dreaming and film watching typically take place in the dark is another irrelevant consideration often raised, since darkness is not typically part of the experience of dreaming, though it does typically accompany the experience of film watching. There are other notable dissimilarities between film watching and dreaming. In dreams, our own actions and sufferings are of central concern to us, but the experience of film watching makes us largely forgetful of ourselves while we concentrate on the fate of the characters. Perhaps in some way film watching is like dreaming; perhaps everything is in some way like everything else. There does not seem to be any substantial, systematic likeness between film experience and dreaming that holds out promise of serious explanatory gains.

Cognitive and Perceptual Illusions

The version of Illusionism I have been considering so far is a very strong one; it commits the Illusionist to saying that film viewers are systematically caused to have false beliefs. It is interesting to argue that a strong view is true, but less interesting to argue that it is false, as I have done. By definition, strong views are more *likely* to be false than weak ones. Might there be some weaker, apparently more plausible, version of Illusionism? If so, and if we could show that this weaker version is also wrong, that would be a result of considerable interest. I believe that there is a weaker, more plausible version of Illusionism, and I shall argue against it.

First I need to distinguish between two kinds of illusions: cognitive and perceptual illusions. I mean by a cognitive illusion a state of mind essentially involving a false belief. Thus if someone sees an oasis in the desert and there is no oasis there (at least not where it seems to be), and comes thereby falsely to believe that there is an oasis there, she is subject to a cognitive illusion. Similarly, when someone sees two lines of equal length, but provided with "arrowheads" pointing in different directions so that the lines seem to be of different lengths, she might believe the lines to be of different lengths. This person is also suffering a cognitive illusion. But not all illusions are cognitive. You may know that the two lines are of equal length and still be subject to the so-called Muller-Lyer illusion which I have just described: the lines just *look* as if they are of different lengths. Zenon Pylyshyn has introduced the term "cognitively impenetrable" to describe mental processes which operate independently of our beliefs. For example, if someone moves his fist quickly toward your face you will recoil even though you know he won't hit you. Visual illusions involve processes which are cognitively impenetrable: belief doesn't make any difference to the way the illusory phenomenon looks.

An illusion of this kind, which is what I am going to call a perceptual illusion, occurs when experience represents the world as being a certain way, when in fact the world is not that way and the subject knows it. And experience may represent the world as being a way it isn't, as when it represents the two lines as being of unequal length, even though the subject knows that experience is misrepresenting the world.[20]

Now someone might claim that cinema is illusionistic in this perceptual sense, and not in the cognitive sense I have been considering up until now. My arguments so far presented against Illusionism are ineffective against Perceptual Illusionism, because they are arguments designed to show that we lack the beliefs necessary to underwrite the claim of Cognitive Illusionism. So I need quite different arguments if I am going to oppose Perceptual Illusionism. I shall provide some. But we should bear in mind a point I have already made: that Perceptual Illusionism is a distinctly weaker thesis about cinema than Cognitive Illusionism, and one with quite different consequences. There has been, I think, a tendency to assume that the truth (the alleged truth) of Perceptual Illusionism somehow supports the claim of Cognitive Illusionism. Perhaps Perceptual Illusionism is the Trojan horse by means of which advocates of Cognitive Illusionism hope to gain their victory. It needs to be said, therefore, that Perceptual Illusionism, even if true, does not in itself provide an argument for Cognitive Illusionism, though of course it might provide such an argument in conjunction with other premises. So it is not essential to my case against Cognitive Illusionism that I oppose Perceptual Illusionism as well. Nonetheless, I am inclined to oppose Perceptual Illusionism. I do not claim to be able to refute it; at most I shall sow the seeds of doubt about it.

What merely perceptual illusion is cinema said to create? A very common view is that the technical mechanism that film employs is itself productive of an illusion—this supposed illusion being that the viewer sees a moving image or sequence of such images, when in fact there is no moving image to be seen. All there "really" is is light projected through an aperture against which are laid, in quick succession, a series of still photographs (the standard rate of succession being 24 frames per second). So what we see is a series of projected static images, and not the moving image that we seem to see. Francis Sparshott writes that "A film is a series of motionless images projected onto a screen so fast as to create in the mind of anyone watching the screen an impression of continuous motion"—an impression Sparshott goes on to call "the basic illusion of motion."[21] On this view, our experience when watching a film represents the world as containing movement of a certain kind: movement of images. And this is an illusion, according to Sparshott and others, because the world in fact contains no such movement of images; there is, to repeat, only a succession of static images.

I had better clarify exactly what I mean when I speak of "moving images." Strictly speaking, the cinematic image is the whole area of illumination on the screen during projection. We all agree, I take it, that this does not move, unless the projection equipment starts to shift around. What moves, on my account, is a part or parts of this image; if we are watching a shot of a man walking along a street, the part of the image which represents the man will move from one side of the screen to the other. Movement of this kind, which is what I am concerned with here, needs to be distinguished from the movement which occurs as a result of a continuous change in the position of the camera during a single shot. This latter kind of movement introduces somewhat complex considerations which I shall not attempt to deal with here. Also, the movement with which I am concerned here is to be distinguished from the radically discontinuous movement which might be said to occur across shots: we see the image of the man in one place on the screen in one shot, and in another place on the screen in the next shot. All I am claiming here is that there really is movement within a single shot taken from a fixed perspective. That, obviously, is enough to contradict the claim that movement in film is an illusion produced by the juxtaposition of static images.

Someone might argue that this supposed illusion of cinematic motion is a cognitive, and not merely a perceptual illusion, because most people who watch films actually believe that they are watching moving images; it is only when one reflects on the technical mechanisms of cinema that one realizes that this is not the case. That may be true, but the fact is that the appearance of cinematic motion does not go away for those people who convince themselves that it is, indeed, an illusion. If cinematic motion is illusory, then it is essentially a perceptual illusion and only incidentally a cognitive one. That is why I shall treat it simply as a cognitive illusion.

Before I consider the case for Perceptual Illusionism, a word on metaphysical background. Arguments about motion, and about change generally, sometimes raise deep questions about what motion and change actually are. There are two basic and mutually incompatible positions on this. One, which I shall call three dimensionalism, says that change takes place when a thing has a property at one time which it, that very same thing, lacks at another time. The other view, four dimensionalism, says that change occurs when a certain temporal stage possesses a property, and another temporal stage lacks that property, where those temporal stages are so related to constitute temporal stages of the same object. I don't myself believe that there is anything in our common belief about change which decides one way or the other between these two theories, and nothing I shall say about cinematic movement here is intended to prejudge which is correct.[22] So while I shall speak of our cinematic experience as representing to us that an image moves from one place to the other, this is to be taken as neutral between the view that there is one thing which is in one place at one time and in another place at another time, and the view that there are distinct but suitably related temporal parts that are in different places. Obviously, both construals are inconsistent with the view that there is, literally, no movement of an image on the screen.

One way to argue that there is real movement of cinematic images would be to adopt very liberal criteria of reality. In particular, if we could persuade ourselves that there is no clear distinction between what it is useful for us to say and what it is true to say, we would find it relatively easy to establish the reality of cinematic movement. After all, there is undeniable utility in describing a film by reference to the movement of the images it presents us with. Daniel Dennett has recently advocated a kinder, gentler realism that allows us to say that all sorts of things are real on account of their usefulness.[23] A and B claim to detect different patterns in the same array, the differences between them being accounted for in the different signal-to-noise ratios they claim to detect in the array; both do fairly well in predicting extensions of the array, chalking up their different patterns of failure to their respective assumptions about noise. Who is right? Both, says Dennett, and so is anyone else who can do comparably well by detecting yet another pattern in the array. It's no good saying: "Yes I know they are all making money out of their systems, but who's got the right pattern?" That, for Dennett, is symptomatic of the outmoded, inflexible, and unforgiving realism he wants to supersede—we might call it, "first-strike realism." I can't do justice here to the complexity, and certainly not to the brilliance, of Dennett's argument. I can say only that at the end of it I still wanted to retain a distinction between usefulness and truth in areas where it seemed to me Dennett blurs the distinction. I shall not, therefore, be arguing for the reality of the movement of cinematic images simply on the grounds that it is useful for us to think and speak as if there really were such movement, though the usefulness of this way of thinking and speaking is certainly the reason why we are interested in the question of whether this kind of movement is real. So I remain a first-strike realist. As we shall see, even we hawks are capable of ontological generosity.

So my thesis is just that a certain, restricted kind of apparent motion in cinema is, in fact, not merely apparent, but real. I shall call that motion simply "cinematic motion." But I shall not be looking for a positive argument in favor of the reality of cinematic motion. In debates over whether some type of experience is illusory, it seems to me that the burden of proof, or perhaps merely of argument, lies with the party who asserts that the experience in question is illusory, just as it does with someone who asserts that a certain belief is false. In both cases—belief and perception—we have grounds for treating veridical and nonveridical states asymmetrically, since states of belief and perception are states we have *because* they tend to be veridical. In that case, we should hold that cinematic experience of movement is veridical unless there is a significant weight of evidence and argument against that view.

What is the argument for saying that the experience of cinema involves a perceptual illusion of movement? I have the impression that the argument sometimes appeals to the fact that there is no movement on the cinematic film roll itself, that there is just here just a sequence of static images. This is true, but it does nothing to establish the unreality of cinematic movement. After all, when we listen to a tape or other kind of sound recording, there is no sound literally *on the tape itself;* what is on the tape is just a pattern of selective magnetization, or whatever. But we would not conclude from this that when we listen to a tape recording of music, we are subject to an auditory illusion. The claim of Perceptual Illusionism is the claim that there is no movement *on the screen,* for this, after all, is where we seem to see movement.

An argument which might seem to favor Perceptual Illusionism is the following: the supposed movement that there is on the screen is the product of our perceptual system, and cannot be thought to exist independent of it. Suppose you described the goings-on on the screen from the kind of objective viewpoint we try to occupy in physical science: you exhaustively describe the impact of particles or waves of light on the screen, and you therefore describe all the relevant physical goings-on at that surface. But you do not describe any movement of the kind we claim to observe there; you do not describe any object as moving from one place on the screen to another. So there simply isn't any movement here, since the objective description comprehends all the relevant physical facts but describes no movement. It is only when you take a subjective point of view, and include in the description the viewer's subjective experience of the screen, that movement enters your description.

I hope that by now warning bells are going off all over the place. This argument is parallel to a class of other arguments that would establish the illusory nature of all our experience of what are called secondary qualities. Consider the case of color: we describe the object from a physical point of view exhaustively, including everything about the spectral reflectance profile of its surface, but we say nothing about the way it looks; color enters our vocabulary only when we include the observer's subjective point of view in the story. Now there are those, like Paul Boghossian and J. David Velleman, who relish this conclusion, and say that the experience of color is indeed illusory; experience represents things as having color properties when in fact they do not have them.[24] But on the whole philosophers resist such starkly revisionist conclusions, and I go along with them. What a realist about color should say is what we have already said: colors and other secondary properties are real, response-dependent properties of things. Perhaps, then, the "apparent motion" of projected film is not merely apparent; perhaps it is real, response-dependent motion.

One common and natural thought in response to this proposal is that the proposal can succeed only at the cost of destroying the distinction between real and merely apparent phenomena, or that it will, at the very least, intolerably expand the class of phenomena we shall have to count as real. It is worth seeing that this is not so. First of all, someone might claim that, by an argument parallel to the one I have given for the reality of cinematic motion, we can establish that the experience induced by the Muller-Lyer phenomenon is veridical. Just say that in those cases of experience singled out as exemplifying the Muller-Lyer illusion, what experience represents is the holding, between two lines, of the relation *being longer * than,* where length * is not the metrical property of objects we measure with rigid rods, but rather a response-dependent length: a length that stands to metrical length as the response-dependent movement I have been describing stands to the movement we measure by tracking physical objects across space. In that case there is no illusion involved in the Muller-Lyer phenomenon, but merely the veridical experience of one line being longer * than another.

This objection fails. Our experience in the Muller-Lyer illusion represents the lines as standing in the relation longer than, not the relation longer * than. The visible appearance of the lines suggests that, were you to measure them in the conventional way, the result would be that one was measurably longer than the other. That is why this is genuinely a case of an illusion, rather than a veridical experience of a response-dependent property. With the experience of screen watching, however, it is doubtful whether the movement that our experience represents as taking place is of a kind that would be undermined by independent checks analogous to the measuring check we can carry out in the case of the Muller-Lyer illusion. For example, I do not think that our experience of screen watching is an experience which has as its representational content: There are reidentifiable physical objects moving in front our our eyes. Rather, its content is: There are *images* of reidentifiable physical objects moving in front of our eyes. In this respect the experience seems not to be undercut by information from other sources, and therefore to be crucially different from that induced by the Muller-Lyer setup.

Someone might also object that my appeal to response-dependence in the filmic case has the false consequence that there is no illusion involved in our perception of the movement of a wave. Our perception of wave phenomena suggests that there is something, namely a wave, which moves outward from the center of disturbance. But if we examine the matter closely we discover that there is no physical object—no single, reidentifiable body of water that spreads outward when wave motion occurs. All there is is the transfer of energy from one molecule to the next, as can be established by placing a free-floating object on the wave surface and seeing it remain stationary with respect to the horizontal axis. But it would seem that my argument for the reality of the movement of the cinematic image applies equally to the movement of the wave, in which case we should have to say that there is after all no illusion of movement in the case of the wave, and that seems wrong.

But there is a difference, on my account, between the case of the cinematic image and the case of the wave. In the case of the wave, but not in the case of the cinematic image, there is a physical object, namely a body of water, which perception represents to us as moving outward as the wave "spreads." But our perception of the motion of cinematic images does not suggest that there is some particular physical object which moves when a cinematic image does. That is why there is a perceptual illusion, or at least a perceptual error, in the case of the perception of wave motion and not in the case of the perception of cinematic images.

There are a number of other apparent motions which are normally classed as merely apparent and which retain their status as mere appearances on my account. For example, psychologists speak of *induced* motion, a phenomenon noticeable when we see clouds drifting across the face of the moon; if the clouds drift slowly to the left, the moon appears to be drifting to the right. And tall buildings viewed from below against a background of moving clouds seem to be falling.[25] In these and like cases we have a perceptual illusion of movement: experience represents something moving which is not moving. But these cases, I shall argue, are unlike the case of cinematic motion. And there are kinds of motion which cinema sometimes gives us and which are or can be illusory, rather than real motions. For example, films in 3-D display an illusion of depth; our experience of watching 3-D is one in which objects are represented as moving toward or away from the viewer when in fact no object is moving toward or away from the viewer. The cinematic motion I claim to be real belongs to the kind which psychologists call "motion in the frontal plane."

But even within this restricted class of motion phenomena I can make distinctions, for not all motion in the frontal plane will count as real by my lights. It is well known, for example, that if one looks at a point light source in an otherwise darkened environment, the point of light will seem to shift around, when in fact the light source remains steady. The explanation seems to be that the appearance of movement is produced by random eye movements which are uncompensated for because the viewer has no visible frame of reference other than the light source itself. Now suppose that, instead of looking directly at the light source, the viewer looks at the image of the light source projected on a screen. Then the projected image will seem to move around, just as the light source itself would. And this, I claim, is a case of illusory rather than of real motion on the screen. For the following is a necessary condition for there to be genuine movement of an image: that at each place on the screen occupied by the image as it moves, there should be illumination at that place (and at the relevant time) on the screen. But in the case we are presently considering, there will be only one fixed and unchanging place on the screen which is illuminated, and at many places on the screen where the image seems to be, there will be no illumination. So here, we seem to see movement of an image, but in fact there is no movement of an image. But in the case of what is conventionally called the moving image of film, where the image seems to move, there really is illumination on the screen.[26]

So I say that part of the content of cinematic experience is that there is movement of images, and there really is such movement. We see the cinematic image of a man, and we see that it is in one place on the screen, and we later see that it is in another; indeed, we see—really see—that image move from one place to another on the screen. That image is not to be identified with some particular physical object. It is not like the image in a painting which consists of a certain conglomeration of physical pigments, at least relatively stable over time. It is an image sustained by the continuous impact of light on the surface of the screen, and no particular light wave or particle is more than minutely constitutive of it. Nonetheless, that image is a particular, reidentifiable thing, and a thing which moves.

At a minimum, motion involves change over time in the position of a reidentifiable object (or, for four dimensionalists, the location of distinct temporal parts of an object at distinct places). If cinematic motion is real, it must be possible to reidentify cinematic images over time. How? One initially plausible answer is that images get their identity conditions from their causal antecedents. This image and that one are both cinematic images *of* the same man, so they are the same image (or on the four-dimensionalist view, they are temporal parts of the same image). But this answer strikes me as unsatisfactory. First of all, I would make the same claim for the reality of movement in animated cartoons, and there the argument from sameness of causal antecedents will not allow us to reidentify images over time: cartoon images do not have the kind of causal antecedents required to make the argument from common causal origin work. The better criterion for the identity of cinematic images across time is their relation to the mental states of the viewer. This image is the same as that one because both are identified by normal viewers in normal conditions as being images of the same individual. Here again, as with color, the concept we appeal to is response-dependent. Identity between images is itself a response-dependent concept, because questions about how to reidentify images across time are answered by appeal to facts about the psychological responses of the viewer to those images. But just as with colors, this response-dependence is perfectly compatible with the reality of the images concerned.

In arguing against perceptual illusionism, I have been insisting that cinematic motion is real, using that term to contrast, naturally enough, with "illusory." You may think this taxonomy is insufficiently refined. After all, we commonly contrast reality with appearance; my dichotomy will then have us identify that which belongs to the realm of mere appearances with that which is illusory. That seems hard on appearances. There ought to be room for a position which says that colors and other secondary properties belong to the realm of appearances, but which denies that the experience of color is illusory. (Perhaps in the end this position will turn out to be incoherent; I just don't want to rule it out at this stage.) On that view, the real contrasts with the illusory and with the apparent. Equivalently, we could say there are two senses of "real": a weak sense, which has as the complement of its extension the illusory, and a stronger sense, which has as the complement of its extension the illusory and the apparent, which we can then lump together under the heading "antirealism." If we adopt that labeling system, my view is simply that cinematic motion is real in the weak sense. I can then agree that in a strong, metaphysical sense we ought to be antirealists about cinematic motion, and perhaps about color as well. But we shall need to make a distinction between, on the one hand, antirealist concepts, for the application of which we are in the realm of mere appearances, and, on the other, antirealist concepts for the application of which we are in the realm of illusion. Whatever your view on color, there is surely a difference, for example, between ascribing blueness to a U.S. mailbox, and ascribing greenness to the (actually white) stripes displayed in a McCullough aftereffect experiment. The difference, I submit, is that in the second case but not in the first, you are subject to an illusion. So, if my parallel between cinematic motion and color does not persuade you to be a strong realist about cinematic motion, it may still be enough to undermine illusionism about cinematic motion.

To underline this last point, let us notice a feature of response-dependent concepts sometimes thought to be grounds for being an *antirealist* about such concepts. Realists sometimes emphasize the radical fallibility of our beliefs about a domain to which they claim realism applies; if it's possible, even under epistemically ideal circumstances, for us to be mistaken in our beliefs about that domain, that is a sign that we are in the realm of reality. But with certain kinds of response-dependent concepts, radical fallibility is ruled out.[27] If a normal observer in normal circumstances judges that something is red, it is red; similarly, if a normally sighted person, sitting in a darkened cinema at the appropriate distance and attending to the screen as the projector rolls, judges that the cinematic image is moving, then it is. That, as I say, might be grounds for rejecting metaphysical realism about color, and about cinematic motion. But it cannot be grounds for thinking that cinematic movement is an illusion. Where there is no possibility of error, there can be no illusion.

Conclusion

Grand theories of film—like grand theories of anything else—are always prone to catastrophic error: get the basic conceptual priorities and relations wrong, and the whole system collapses. That, I believe, is how it has been with semiotically and psychoanalytically oriented film theories. These theories have simply presupposed that film is in some way or other an illusionistic medium. I have argued here that the concept of illusion is in fact entirely irrelevant to understanding the nature and function of film. It is realism, not illusionism, that needs to play a central role in film theory. But the realism we need is not just anti-illusionistic, it is anti-absolutist as well; the realist need not believe that the world is fully describable without taking into account subjective points of view.

The conclusions of this paper go beyond film theory to embrace general metaphysics. It is traditional to regard motion as a paradigmatically primary quality, to be contrasted with those secondary qualities which are in some sense observer-dependent, like color. If what I have said here about cinematic motion is correct, we shall have to acknowledge a kind of motion which takes its place among the secondary qualities.

NOTES

Earlier versions of this paper were read at the Adelaide-Flinders Research Seminar, March 1994 and at a symposium on philosophy and film at the American Philosophical Association Central Division Annual Meeting in Kansas City, in May 1994. I thank the audiences on both occasions for their critical comments. Special thanks are owed to David Bordwell, Noël Carroll, Marty Davies, and Brian Medlin.

1. See, for example, André Bazin, *What Is Cinema?* vol. 1, trans. and ed. Hugh Gray (Berkeley: University of California Press, 1971). For an analysis of Bazin's view and of other relevant aspects of the history of film theory, see Noël Carroll, *Philosophical Problems of Classical Film Theory* (Princeton: Princeton University Press, 1988).

2. Kendall Walton, "Transparent Pictures: on the Nature of Photographic Realism," *Critical Inquiry* 11, 2 (1984): 246–77. For Walton, and also for Bazin, the transparency of film is a consequence of its mechanicity, a thesis which Walton explicates in terms of patterns of counterfactual dependence between the photograph and the photographed scene which are independent of the photographer's mental states. For an analysis of the argument from mechanicity to transparency, see my "Photography, Painting, and Perception," *Journal of Aesthetics and Art Criticism* 49 (1991): 23–29.

3. Christian Metz, for example, discusses how film creates "a certain degree of *belief* in the reality of an imaginary world" (*The Imaginary Signifier: Psychoanalysis and the Cinema* (Bloomington: Indiana University Press, 1982), pp. 118 and 72; emphasis in the original). This view is by now more or less standard; see for example, Robert B. Ray, *A Certain Tendency of the Hollywood Cinema* (Princeton: Princeton University Press, 1985), p. 38. Metz's formulation suggests a certain hesitancy about exactly how much belief there really is here, a hesitancy displayed in other remarks of his on the same subject: "somewhere in oneself one believes that [the events of the fiction] are genuinely true" (*Imaginary Signifier,* p. 72).

4. See my "Photography, Painting, and Perception."

5. I think Noël Carroll was the first person to give this characterization of realism. See his "The Power of Movies," *Daedalus* 114, 4 (1985): 79–103. See also Flint Schier, *Deeper into Pictures* (New York: Cambridge University Press, 1986).

6. For more on this see my "The Long Goodbye: On the Imaginary Language of Film," *British Journal of Aesthetics* 33 (1993): 207–19.

7. See, for example, Patrick Ogle, "Technological and Aesthetic Influences on the Development of Deep-Focus Cinematography in the United States," in *Movies and Methods,* vol. 2, ed. Bill Nichols (Berkeley: University of California Press, 1985.

8. Richard Dawkins, *The Blind Watchmaker* (Harlow: Longman Scientific and Technical, 1986).

9. See Kathleen A. Akins, "What Is It Like to Be Boring and Myopic?" in *Dennett and His Critics: Demystifying Mind,* ed. B. Dalhbom (Oxford: Basil Blackwell, 1993).

10. The term "response-dependence" is due to Mark Johnston. See his "Dispositional Theories of Value," *Proceedings of the Aristotelian Society*, supplementary volume, 63 (1989): 139–74. See also Philip Pettit, "Realism and Response-Dependence," *Mind* 100 (1991): 587–623; and Mark Johnston, "Objectivity Refigured," and Crispin Wright, "Order of Determination, Response-Dependence and the Eurythro Contrast," both in *Realism and Reason*, ed. J. Haldane and C. Wright (Oxford: Basil Blackwell, 1992).

11. See my *Image and Mind: Film, Philosophy, and Cognitive Science* (New York: Cambridge University Press, forthcoming), chapter 3; and Jerrold Levinson and Philip Alperson, "What Is a Temporal Art?" in *Midwest Studies in Philosophy*, vol. 16, *Philosophy and the Arts*, ed. P. French, T. Uehling, and H. Wettstein (Notre Dame: Notre Dame University Press, 1991).

12. "The predominant myth of cinema, fostered by cinema itself, is that its images and sounds present reality" (John Ellis, *Visible Fictions: Cinema, Television, Video* [London: Routledge and Kegan Paul, 1982], p. 77). ". . . conditions of screening and narrative conventions give the spectator an illusion of looking in on a private world" (Laura Mulvey, "Visual Pleasure and Narrative Cinema," in *Film Theory and Criticism* 4th ed., edited by Gerald Mast, Marshall Cohen, and Leo Baudry [Oxford: Oxford University Press, 1992] p. 749). "The camera becomes the mechanism for producing an illusion of Renaissance space" (ibid., p. 757).

13. Functionalism in the philosophy of mind is best viewed as the successor to behaviorism. The behaviorists said that mental states are items of behavior or, on a more sophisticated conception, dispositions to behave. Functionalism rejects this idea, but holds to the idea that behavior is still constitutive of mental states. For example, a (grossly simplified) functionalist definition of pain might say that pain is the mental state which is typically caused by bodily damage and typically causes avoidance behavior.

14. Many writers on film emphasize the partial nature of the illusion that film creates, and how it competes with our knowledge that it is an illusion. Jean-Louis Comolli, for example, says that "We want to be . . . both fooled and not fooled [by cinema]" ("Machines of the Visible," in *Film Theory and Criticism*, p. 759). See also Metz's qualifications, n. 4 above. But such admissions do little to make the illusionist view more plausible. Film viewers do not behave like people who even partially believe in the reality of what they see, or who are torn between belief and disbelief. See Kendall Walton, "Fearing Fictions," *Journal of Philosophy* 75 (1978): 5–27.

15. See my *The Nature of Fiction* (New York: Cambridge University Press, 1990), chapter 5, and my "Imagination and Simulation: Aesthetics Meets Cognitive Science," in *Mental Simulation*, ed. M. Davies and A. Stone (Oxford: Basil Blackwell, 1994). See also Kendall Walton, *Mimesis as Make-Believe: On the Foundation of the Representational Arts* (Cambridge: Harvard University Press, 1990).

16. On this, see also William Rothman, "Against 'The System of the Suture,'" in *Movies and Methods*, vol. 1, ed. Bill Nichols (Berkeley: University of California Press, 1976).

17. ". . . [the viewer] certainly has to identify . . . if he did not the film would become incomprehensible" (Metz, *The Imaginary Signifier*, p. 46). See also Nick Brown, *The Rhetoric of Filmic Narration* (Ann Arbor, Mich.: UMI Research Press, 1976), chapter 1.

18. Jacques Aumont, "The Point of View," *Quarterly Review of Film and Video* 11 (1989), p. 2. On shot/reverse-shot editing as a means of maintaining the illusionism of film, see Kaja Silverman, *The Subject of Semiotics* (New York: Oxford University Press, 1983), p. 202.

19. Noël Carroll, *Mystifying Movies: Fads and Fallacies in Contemporary Film Theory* (New York: Columbia University Press, 1988).

20. See Christopher Peacocke, *Sense and Content: Experience, Thought, and Its Relations* (Oxford: Clarendon Press, 1983), pp. 5–6.

21. "Basic Film Aesthetics," in *Film Theory and Criticism*. See also Haig Khatchadorian, "Remarks on the 'Cinematic/Uncinematic Distinction in Film Art," in his *Music, Film, and Art* (New York: Gordon and Breach, 1985), p. 134: "a film . . . is necessarily a sequence of visual images that create the illusion of movement."

22. See Frank Jackson, "Metaphysics by Possible Cases," in *1992 ANU Metaphysics Conference,* ed. Brian Garrett and Peter Menzies. Working Papers in Philosophy no. 2, Research School of Social Sciences, Australian National University (Canberra, 1992).

23. "Real Patterns," *Journal of Philosophy* 88 (1991): 27–51. I am grateful to Jerrold Levinson for drawing my attention to his work and for valuable discussion of the topic of this paper.

24. Paul A. Boghossian and J. David Velleman, "Colour as a Secondary Quality," *Mind* 98 (1989): 80–103.

25. Stuart Anstis, "Motion Perception in the Frontal Plane," in *Handbook of Perception and Human Performance,* vol. 1, ed. K. Boff, L. Kaufman, and J. Thomas (New York: Wiley, 1986).

26. Thanks to Dan Gilman and Sue Feagin for helping me to see this point. The illusion described above is called autokinetic movement. See E. L. Brown and K. Deffenbacher, *Perception and the Senses* (New York: Oxford University Press, 1979), pp. 412–15.

27. See Richard Holton, "Intentions, Response-Dependence, and Immunity from Error," in *Response-Dependent Concepts,* ed. Peter Menzies (Research School of Social Sciences, Australian National University: Canberra, 1991).

PSYCHOLOGY
OF FILM

In preceding sections, several authors have spoken of the contributions that cognitive and perceptual psychology might make to debates in film studies. Consequently, a section devoted exclusively to such psychology seems apposite. Included in this section are a series of technical essays in psychology which not only address perennial topics of film theory, such as the nature of film perception, but which have ramifications for new directions in reception studies.

In "The Case for an Ecological Metatheory," Barbara and Joseph Anderson attempt to make the language of the psychologist J. J. Gibson available for film studies. Their leading idea is that Gibson's vocabulary, including notions like invariance and affordance, can supply film theorists with a metatheory that will enable them to deal with such issues as the way in which viewers perceive and comprehend film.

In contrast, "Movies in the Mind's Eye," by Julian Hochberg and Virginia Brooks, examines related topics from a non-Gibsonian viewpoint, exploring the viewing experience in terms of various hypotheses about the processes of recognition and construction that audiences may employ in organizing the visual array. They place special emphasis on the role that the identification of behaviors play in comprehending and storing film imagery. They also advance the tantalizing proposal that something rather like comic-book narration may be the best way in which to represent what goes on at the level of mental processing in film viewers. In this respect, their essay has suggestive implications for film notation and publishing.

In "Notes on Audience Response," Richard Gerrig and Deborah Prentice offer a characterization of the role of the audience as what they call *side-participants*. Exploiting insights from the theory of conversation, they offer an account of the way in which viewers are drawn into films and inclined toward rhetorically determinate responses. Their work has important implications for debates about film identification and about the nature of our emotional responses to films. At the same time, their sensible experimental method should suggest a worthwhile model for future research in film reception.

In his introductory piece to this volume, Noël Carroll pointed out that cognitivism is not a theory, but a stance. One reason for this is that there are important disagreements even among cognitivists. For not only do Anderson and Anderson, and Hochberg and Brooks disagree on methodological points, but given their use of the notion of illusion, Anderson and Anderson also disagree with authors like Currie in the preceding section. In this regard, it is perhaps helpful to reiterate that it is not the intention of this book to paper over differences, but to afford a space where disagreement can flourish.

16

The Case for an
Ecological Metatheory

Joseph Anderson and Barbara Anderson

Introduction

Hugo Münsterberg predicted in 1915 that the "photoplay" would "become more than any other art the domain of the psychologist who analyzes the working of the mind."[1] As it turned out, he couldn't have been more wrong. Psychologists have actually had little effect upon either filmmaking or film theory. In the case of the latter there has been an almost unanimous rejection of Münsterberg's psychology and of his scientific approach.[2] Film theorists have preferred to look elsewhere for support for their theories of film.

In the case of film *making*, Münsterberg's identification of the "chief task" of moving pictures—to "bring entertainment and enjoyment and happiness to the masses"—proved far more prescient than his prediction concerning the role of psychologists.[3] Filmmaking became the province not of the psychologist but of the entrepreneur. Moviemaking quickly became a major economic enterprise. It fit well within the pattern required by a free market system, raising capital to produce a product (with the attendant assumption of risk), the production of that product, the marketing of the product (resulting in the consumption of the product), and finally the return of capital to investors. Moviemaking can be said to have thrived within capitalism; indeed, it thrives today. In such a system the success of a particular motion picture was and is largely measured by the number of tickets it sells at the box office. And most important for our purposes, in such a system the incentives are greatly weighted in the direction of making movies which will appeal to a wider and wider audience.

A fundamental determinant of just how wide that appeal might be is accessibility. That is, audiences both at home and abroad are more likely to buy tickets to movies that are accessible to them—accessible in the most fundamental ways, such as whether a potential viewer can perceive the fictional events that occur on the screen and follow the basic story line. Apart from the obvious problem of language differences, which can be greatly alleviated by subtitles or dubbing, the problems of accessibility are problems of perception. Perceptual problems are of course the domain of the psychologists to whom

Münsterberg alluded, but we know that the direction filmmaking took in America was controlled not by psychologists but by entrepreneurs, studio executives, marketing people, producers, directors; few, if any, had any training in perceptual psychology. These people were driven by the forces of economics to create a product of greater and greater accessibility, and they proceeded in the only way available to them—by trial and error. Purely by trial and error, the moneymen, the technicians, and the artists who made up the American film industry succeeded in developing a style of filmmaking that was potentially accessible to every human being on earth. Whatever its shortcomings, the Hollywood style became more universally accessible than that of any of its competitors, and it remains so today.

We are interested in accessibility as a theoretical, not a political, issue.[4] It is not our purpose to argue for a privileged status for the classical Hollywood style, but to point out that the problem of accessibility in motion pictures is not merely a matter of culture. It is more fundamentally a matter of perception, and the horde of contemporary cultural relativists who have attempted to deal with the problem otherwise have made little headway. The problem of accessibility, along with an even more basic problem—that of the inherent power of motion pictures to engage us—have eluded most contemporary film writers.

Cognitive Science

Hugo Münsterberg predicted that film would become the province of the psychologist because as a psychologist/film theorist he understood that motion pictures are designed to interact directly with the mind of the viewer, and it was precisely the interaction of the motion picture with the human mind that fascinated him. For the film scholar who would today address such questions as that of the fundamental power of the motion picture to engage us, and specifically which films or portions of the films are accessible to which audiences and why, there exist resources far beyond those of Münsterberg's day and very likely far beyond anything he could have imagined. Contemporary film scholars may be the beneficiaries, if they choose to be, of the prodigious output of thinkers, researchers, and writers who have been engaged for the latter half of this century in what has been called the "Cognitive Revolution."

What these investigators have in common, beyond the audacity to ask how the human mind works, is a shared confidence in the scientific method. Underlying the method itself, of course, is the assumption that the universe is real and that we can know it, that our knowledge is derived from observations, be they direct or indirect, carried out in ways that are open and repeatable. And though claims can never be proven unequivocally true, unfounded claims can often be demonstrated to be false. This adherence to the basic demands of scientific procedure, while inquiring into the processes of the mind, allows the resulting output to be called "cognitive science" rather than "cognitive belief" or "cognitive metaphor."

Metatheory

In the early 1970s when we made our first attempts toward applying perceptual psychology to questions of film spectatorship, we found the task daunting, very nearly impossible. The knowledge about seeing and hearing that could be gained from the literature of psychology just didn't fit the issues of film spectatorship raised in the literature of film. Over the next several years we slowly came to understand that we needed a metatheory. A metatheory is quite simply a theory designed to explain or deal with another theory. What we needed was a metatheory which could encompass perceptual theory and inform our construction of film theory.

David Marr, one of the most insightful and influential cognitive theorists of our time, offered a similar insight when faced with the problem of building a machine capable of visual recognition. Marr argued that before one can describe or define the process of visual perception, one must have what he called a "computational theory" (in the sense of a theory stating what it is that is being computed), a metatheory, if you will, of the human perceptual system, an overview that answers the question, What is the goal of the system?[5] Marr observed that in the field of visual perception the closest anyone had come to a computational theory was J. J. Gibson, and though he by no means agreed with every aspect of Gibson's theory, he found it possible to accept Gibson's fundamental concept of an ecologically driven approach to visual perception.[6]

In 1982 Eleanor Gibson described how J. J. Gibson had come to his insight.[7] During World War II Gibson, as a young psychologist, was given the task of helping pilots fly and land airplanes. He quickly discovered that his training in perception had not prepared him adequately. What he had been taught had come largely from experiments in visual perception carried out in laboratories, usually with subjects' heads held rigid and their eyes fixed upon a point. While much had been learned in this way about the physics of light and vision, there was very little to help one understand how a pilot might actually use his sense of vision to increase his chances of landing an airplane safely. Gibson realized that the major difference was that airplane pilots were not sitting immobile in a laboratory but were moving rapidly through the air above the ground; their problem was to make sense of a visual world that was rushing past them at astonishing speeds. Clearly, problems of perception were subject to one's relationship to one's environment.

The ecological approach to visual perception emphasizes the information contained in the changing patterns of light available to the eye (or as Gibson called it, the ambient optic array). The changes in the optic array contain invariant properties that persist through changes in illumination and point of view, and these "invariants" specify objects or events in the world, which in turn inform action on the part of the viewer. In this ecological approach perception and action are "tightly interlocked and mutually constraining."[8]

Gibson's recognition of the reciprocity of perceiver and environment has found some acceptance in the communities of psychology and artificial intelligence. It is also, unfortunately, the source of many claims by cultural relativists to Gibsonian patronage. The claims are unfortunate because Gibson was anything but a relativist. He warned of the "danger of falling into the ridiculous pit of solipsism,"[9] of "concluding that we can know nothing but our perceptions. . . . Once having made this argument, a theorist is trapped in a circle of subjectivism and is diverted into futile speculations about private worlds."[10]

Gibson was careful to distinguish between a present situation and the organism's ecological niche within the larger ecological reality, which includes evolutionary development.[11] Realizing the importance of this distinction, psychologist James Cutting observed: "The underlying appeal of Gibson is to the ecology of the perceiver. But it is a particular ecology, deeply and fundamentally *biological.*"[12] The recognition of evolutionarily wrought biological constraints on contemporary perception places Gibson in direct opposition to cultural relativism in all of its forms. It is upon the implications of the biological foundation of all human capacity that Gibson's theory of perception rests, and that an ecological theory of film must rest, for whether one is attempting to understand the landing of airplanes or the viewing of movies the problem is precisely that of an organism interacting with a contemporary situation using a perceptual system developed in another time for another purpose.

The theory accounting for how our perceptual systems, indeed all biological systems, developed was set forth by Charles Darwin in his *Origin of the Species* in 1859. His theory of evolution cleared up a lot of confusion at the time, and, even with the explosion of knowledge in the fields of genetics and molecular biology in our own time, which has led to much elaboration and some correction of specifics, Darwin's theory still underpins biological science today. In Darwin's time there was an active industry in livestock breeding and quite a bit was known about the subject. There was also the theory advanced by Jean-Baptiste de Monet de Lamarck some fifty years earlier that biological organisms had a built-in drive toward perfection achieved in part by the passing on to offspring of acquired characteristics.[13] Darwin's theory contained no need for a grand plan of perfection, and accounted for change in a species without the inheritance of characteristics "acquired" by progenitors. He proposed a theory based upon the principles of *diversity* and *natural selection.* Although he did not know precisely why, he had observed during his five-year voyage to the Galapagos Islands that in any given population individuals were not exactly alike; that, in fact, diversity existed in populations of the same species. Furthermore, his observations led him to the conclusion that the small differences that existed between individuals were heritable. He chose the term *natural* selection to make the point that nature can and does perform the task that breeders of livestock performed in the process of *artificial* selection. Livestock breeders were quite accustomed to selecting certain animals that exhibited specific characteristics that the breeders considered desirable—such as finer wool, or faster running speed, or greater milk capacity. Darwin's point was that in nature, the environment "selects" individuals for breeding by allowing to survive to breeding age those who can, for example, withstand the climate, avoid predators, and find, ingest, and digest a food supply. According to Darwin, species (not individuals) change and develop through chance diversity and natural selection, and are thus shaped by the contingencies of their environment.[14] The process of evolution is slow, oblivious to any eventual outcome, and, above all, relentless.

With the fundamentals of biological evolution clearly in mind, let us focus upon the human perceptual system and pose for that system Marr's question for understanding any system: What is the goal of the system? Taking care not to make the Lamarckian error of assuming an ultimate and preordained purpose, we might ask in retrospect, what during the millions of years of development of our perceptual systems constituted adaptation?

Biological organisms exist in environments which are not static, and which may in fact be in a state of continual and sometimes rapid change. For the individual organism some changes are potential dangers and some are potential opportunities. Any information about such changes in the environment is potentially useful, for the organism could theoretically act in its own interest with regard to each particular change. Such acts could so increase an individual organism's chances of survival that "selection" for capacities for gaining information would take place. For example, a creature that could detect the presence of light could perhaps position itself more favorably with regard to it. And a creature that could differentiate between the presence and absence of light could perhaps detect the looming shadow of an approaching predator and avoid the fate of its less aware cousins. In this way even a simple sea-dwelling creature could extract information from an array of light and act upon its meaning. (And we should note that arriving at this "meaning" and taking appropriate action is no intellectual feat, no act of inference; it is a response of a simple organism to a pattern of light and dark in its world.)

Information useful to a perceptual system could consist of changes in light, that is, patterns of electromagnetic radiation in a narrow frequency band. Information could also exist in patterns of compression and rarification of molecules in the air or water, or the presence in such a medium of molecules of various chemical compounds, or changes in the temperature. Any anatomical or physiological change in an organism which increased its capacity to access such information would thereby increase the organism's chances of surviving and producing offspring. The answer to Marr's question concerning the goal of the perceptual system is that it developed in the direction of extracting information from the environment which could inform action.

There is another important point to be made with regard to the development of sensory systems which process information from the environment in the service of informing action: the perceived information must not lead the organism to take the wrong action. If an organism often moves in the wrong direction, or at the wrong speed, or at the wrong time, its chances of surviving long enough to reproduce are greatly diminished. This will be true whether the organism is merely inept in its actions or is getting inaccurate information. Negative selection for both types of failure can be expected. What remains amounts to a positive selection for physical skill and for perceptual *veridicality*. The clear implication is that even for complex perceptual systems such as our own, the contingencies of our evolution favored the development of a capacity for perceptions which were consistently veridical—that is, accurate enough to act upon, literally accurate enough to bet one's life upon.

If the "goal" of the perceptual system is to inform action in the world, and information for the system is contained in patterns of electromagnetic radiations, molecular disturbances in the air, the chemical makeups of gases and plants, and the like, then it is reasonable to ask how the information, which exists out there in the world, comes to inform the internal actions of an organism. This is the issue that separated Marr and Gibson. Gibson said that information exists in the environment and the perceiver has but to "resonate" to it, to pick it up directly. Marr countered that perception is a complex multilevel process, and not the simple act that Gibson described.

In Gibson's defense, it seems fair to say that he was not arguing that perception is simple, as Marr seems to imply, but that perception need not necessarily involve higher-level cognitive processes that presumably only humans possess. His ecological approach to perception made him well aware that the lowliest of creatures somehow extract information from their environment and act upon it. In discussing visual attention, for instance, Gibson writes:

> The parts of the array must be fixated in succession; there must be exploration and selection of certain items of interest to the neglect of other items. . . . Exploration makes possible a better overall registration of ambient light, but only over time, since the simultaneous registration of the whole array has been sacrificed. This temporal integration has been considered a puzzle. If it is conceived as a process of remembering retinal images, the process is made to seem an advanced intellectual achievement. It is surely not that, for it began in the fish.[15]

The roots of the controversy over direct or indirect, mediated or unmediated, perception run deep in the field of perceptual psychology. Hermann von Helmholtz in 1850 achieved fame for measuring the rate at which a signal is propagated along a nerve path. His studies of the visual and the auditory systems taught him that sensory signals travel rather slowly, and that they are processed by the brain even more slowly. He hypothesized that a great deal of processing was going on in all that time, and that the sensory signals had meaning only in relation to associations built up by learning. For him perception was definitely *learned*, but not necessarily *conscious*—it was a process of "*unconscious inference.*"

Classical perceptual psychology since Helmholtz has held that ". . . our sensory receptors analyse the energies provided by the physical world into independent, simple, but unnoticeable sensations, and the world teaches us to perceive those objects and events."[16] The idea is that from impoverished sensations perceptions are somehow "constructed," presumably through a process of "unconscious inference." But Gibson rejected both of the idea of "construction" and that of "unconscious inference."

While finding no fault with Helmholtz's description of the basic physiology, Gibson found the notion of inference, conscious or not, unpalatable. He questioned who was making the inference, and suggested that the concept of inference led to an infinite regress. He was fond of saying that there is no homunculus, no little green man in the brain making judgments or looking at pictures. For Gibson perception was direct; it needed no mediation, no interpretation.

The schism between Gibson's theory of perception and that of traditional perceptual psychology runs right along the boundary between direct perception and mediated perception, and it becomes an open chasm over the notion of representation.[17] Even for a theory of film one might ask whether one's perception of a film is a representation or perhaps an illusion (Gibson, by the way, was interested in neither concept.) If a scene in a movie is a representation of a fictional world, does perception then construct a representation of the representation?

The argument over representation revolves around the question of mediation in perception: Is it necessary to form an internal representation of the object/event in the world in order to perceive it? Unfortunately, the term "representation" is often not clearly defined, and it is not used consistently in the literature of perception. As perceptual psychologists Vicki Bruce and Patrick Green have noted, the term "is used to refer to any symbolic description of the world—whether this is the world as it has been in the past (as in stored 'memories'), as it is now (the 2½-D sketch or structural descriptions), or as it might be in the future (as in certain kinds of imagery). It is also used by 'connectionist' theorists to refer to nonsymbolic patterns of activation in simple networks, which, nevertheless *represent* some object, feature, distance or other property of the surroundings."[18]

If one considers representations to be nonsymbolic patterns of activity in networks of neurons, "representational" theorists and "ecological" theorists may find themselves on common ground. Moreover, it is possible to interpret some of the computational theories (even those that are avowedly representational) as providing a series of algorithms that describe the processes taking place in ecological perception. It is only when the "representation" becomes a symbolic conceptual entity that there is something to argue about, but the debate is furious, ongoing, and complex.[19]

Fortunately it is not necessary that we resolve the issue of representation or even that we agree upon a precise definition of the term in order to begin to forge a theory of film informed by a metatheory based on Gibson's ecological optics. One of the advantages of an ecological metatheory is that it explicitly allows the development of a theory of perception and, by extension, a theory of film which largely circumvents the problems raised by representation.

An ecological theory of film not only avoids the problems raised by the notions of representation, but illuminates problems for which traditional psychology and the film theories built upon it have no viable solutions. For example, the problems of continuity editing (that is, why some cuts cause jumps and others do not and why some combinations of camera placements work better than others),[20] the so-called "constancies" of size, shape, and distance, or the apparent paradox of being able to view a film satisfactorily from any seat in the house in spite of the retinal distortions that inevitably occur in the projection of the image upon the retina. But let us not rush ahead, let us begin at the beginning.

Illusions

We possess a visual system forged over millions of years of evolution to extract information from patterns of light.[21] And even though film theorists, psychologists, and neurophysiologists do not yet completely understand the processes by which the perceptual system transforms information contained in patterns of light into potential for action in the world, we have good evidence that the transformation results in veridical perception. But what about those instances in which the perceptual system follows its own internal procedures for processing the array of light before it and the resulting perception is in error? Such errors in perception we call illusions.

Illusions occur occasionally in our interaction with the natural environment, yet they are rare, and apparently have played no role in evolution. For this reason Gibson tended to dismiss the significance of illusions, but we shall not be so quick to do so.

It is important to note that illusions occur when the perceptual system is functioning normally. When nonveridical perceptions occur due to a malfunctioning of the perceptual system, say from the effects of drugs or disease, we call the resulting perceptions hallucinations. And of course, when nonveridical perceptions occur during sleep we call them dreams. A visual illusion occurs when a normal visual system following its own internal rules processes the patterns of light before the eyes (Gibson's "ambient optic array"), and yet the resulting perception is nonveridical—that is, by some external procedure it can be demonstrated that perception is at considerable variance with physical reality and is therefore not a reliable basis for action. But why should such perception occur in normal healthy vision?

Given a normally functioning perceptual system, there are at least two types of circumstances that will result in nonveridical perceptions. First, there are those so-called illusions that have been constructed explicitly to take advantage of the limitations of a visual system developed by evolution to extract information from a natural environment, and for which the process of evolution could not possibly have prepared the viewer. For example, there was no way that the forces of evolutionary development could have anticipated that humans sometime in the future would go to all the trouble to construct a full-sized room as contorted as an Ames room in order to test visual illusions, or to construct an entire fictional world composed only of patterns of light as in a motion picture. When faced with such constructions, the visual system simply processes them as it would the natural world; it has no alternative. In such cases the processing is not in error, it is just that the resulting perceptions when compared to physical reality inevitably turn out to be illusions.

For purposes of illustration, let us examine a viewer's experience of the Ames room. The Ames room is constructed with a floor that tilts and walls that do not form square corners, with the result that the back wall is much closer to the viewer at one end that at the other (Fig. 16.1). But when one views the room from a certain point it appears to be rectangular. Furthermore

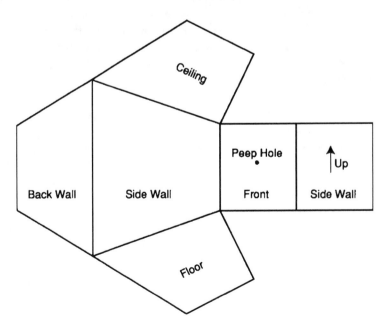

Fig. 16.1. An Ames-like room construction. (This can be enlarged on a copier and folded together.)

Fig. 16.2. Photograph of an Ames room, with human figures seen from the position of the peephole.

when two people stand opposite each other in the far corners, one person appears much larger than the other (Fig. 16.2). One explanation of the phenomenon is that the initial perception of the room through the peephole is an illusion because the viewer is accustomed to a carpentered world in which floors are level and perpendicular to vertical walls, and that the people standing in the room are distorted in size because of the assumption of regularity on the viewer's part.

We are skeptical of such an explanation because there is a much simpler one: the room appears rectangular because it was carefully constructed by the rules of projective geometry to appear rectangular from the peephole in spite of its deformations. The visual system has the capacity to extract from a visual array via projective geometry all the information that is available from a given point. The potential for the extraction of information based on projective geometry existed from the moment the eye changed from an open pit into a closed chamber with a hole (or lens) in it; and evolution refined the capacity. The Ames room is constructed to provide the information, by the rules of projective geometry, that the floor is level and that all the surfaces are perpendicular to each other. The information available via projective geometry (the positions of feet and heads relative to floor and ceiling) also indicates that one of the figures is larger than the other. In the absence of any other information than that of projective geometry, the visual system perceives it in exactly that way.

Yet when one explores the dimensions of the room physically, for example with a stick, the room and the people it contains are perceived more accurately. This isn't surprising, since the whole purpose of perception is to gain information, and exploring distances with a stick provides information that one could have gained by viewing from another position had one been allowed to do so. There is no need to have had experience with a carpentered world in order to experience the illusion of the Ames room, including the illusion of size difference when human figures are placed within it. One need only possess a visual system forged to extract information from the projective geometry inherent in lensed viewing.

A motion picture differs from the Ames room in that it is constructed not of plywood and paint but entirely of patterns of light playing across a reflective screen. Yet the basic problems of perception are similar. In both cases the viewer is presented with an array of light consisting of patterns that are coherent from a certain viewing point, that is, from a peephole and from the position of the camera lens, respectively. The patterns are coherent in that they contain all the information about the nature of objects and the relationships between them that is inherent in projective geometry. In the case of the motion picture, the array of light from a point is displayed upon a large screen and the viewer is spared the inconvenience of keeping one eye to a peephole, and may sit anywhere in the theater. Why this is possible is itself something of a puzzle. It is possible to view a movie image from any seat in the theater, even though viewing the image from any angle other than the original camera position (the center of the theater) results in some distortion of the image upon the viewer's retina.[22] James Cutting argues that our capacity to perceive a motion picture correctly from any angle is not a matter of our familiarity with slanted screens and of taking into account the distortions and then constructing the true shape at some cognitive level of mental activity, but that "in the human visual system, local measurements of objects are apparently made according to projective geometry; in those measurements, small amounts of certain distortions in projection are tolerated."[23]

Neither the illusion of the Ames room nor the basic illusion of the motion picture require cultural explanations, nor do they rely upon higher-level mental processing such as inference and deduction. They can be accounted for by lower-level processes such as the built-in capacity of the visual system to access the information from an array of light under the constraints of projective geometry. And both the Ames room and motion pictures are manmade constructions designed to exploit the fact that the sense of vision is locked into the ecological niche within which it developed.

A second set of circumstances that gives rise to illusions also has to do with the processing capacities built into the visual system through evolution, but deals more specifically with the program (to employ a computer metaphor) of visual processing itself. Vilayanur Ramachandran and Stuart Anstis proposed that at a very fundamental level the visual system makes "assumptions" about the physical world in order to facilitate processing. They identified three such "assumptions" from a series of experiments on apparent motion: (1) that objects tend to remain in continuous existence, and if in motion tend to move along a straight path; (2) that objects are rigid, that is, all their parts tend to move together; and (3) that a moving object will progressively cover and uncover portions of the background[24] (Fig. 16.3).

Ramachandran and Anstis maintain these "shortcuts" are taken by the visual system in order to make the relatively slow neural processing more effi-

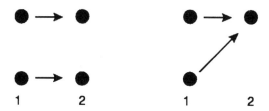

cient, and that in general the "assumptions" made by the system are constant.
For example, by the first rule, if one sees a leopard running across a field and
it disappears behind a bush, one "assumes" at the most basic levels of visual
processing that the leopard emerging from the other side of the bush is the
same leopard. If one catches sight of a few spots on the leopard's coat leaping
across a chasm, one "assumes" that the other spots leapt also, by the rule of
rigidity; and by the third rule, that of occlusion, that as the leopard walks, the
grass through which he passes will continually disappear at the edges of his
head and shoulders and continually reappear at the edges of his hind legs and
tail. To test each "rule," the researchers devised situations to induce apparent motion, such as dots displaced spatially and flashing sequentially on a
screen.

What they found was that indeed the rules were followed in visual processing even if what was seen was not veridical, and even if the viewer knew
that what he was seeing was not what was really happening. For example, two
dots were placed on the screen one over the other in one frame, and then in
the next frame the two dots were displaced slightly to the right. The result,
when shown in succession, as we would expect, was apparent motion—the
dots seemed to move to the right. However, when the bottom dot in frame
two was removed, the two dots from frame one were seen to converge on the
remaining top dot in the second frame. That is, the bottom dot in frame one
was seen to move in a diagonal path to the remaining dot at the top of frame
two. More peculiarly, when a piece of tape was placed on the screen in the
position of the bottom dot that had been removed, the two dots once again
moved horizontally with the bottom dot seeming to "hide" behind the piece
of tape. Clearly, the rules were being followed even though what was seen
was nonveridical, that is, the bottom dot did not move at all. This is an illusion, one of those instances when the built-in "shortcuts" led to nonveridical
perceptions.

In "hiding" the missing dot behind the piece of tape stuck to the screen,
the visual system is doing more than merely filling in the missing dots between
two points. It "assumes" that the dot "hid" from view behind the piece of

tape rather than allow that the dot ceased to exist. Apparently, in the presence of a plausible occluder, the *continuity of existence* "rule" operates to form a percept which is nonveridical. (There is no second dot.)

One might be tempted to conclude that the making of such "assumptions" and the attribution of "hiding" to the behavior of a dot would require the involvement of higher-level cognitive processes, but more likely such processing is carried out at a low level in the visual system by neurons that programmatically excite and inhibit other neurons, not by the logic of language, but by the computational strategies built into the system itself. Ramachandran and Anstis are specific on this point. Their experiments, they write, ". . . were designed to eliminate the effects of high-level cognition; specifically, we flashed images at speeds too rapid to allow the brain to make thoughtful decisions about what it was seeing. Our results therefore suggest that low-level processes can, on their own, control the perception of apparent motion during the early stages of visual processing."[25] Seeing the dot move behind the piece of tape and then move back to its original position is an illusion, an instance when the visual system, following its internal program, creates a nonveridical perception, and thus reveals the program itself.

We have attempted to demonstrate that visual illusions can occur in a normal healthy visual system. They occur when visual processing, following its own internal program, produces a nonveridical perception of the world. With regard to motion pictures, the visual system simply processes the visual array before it. Having developed in a natural environment in which the patterns of light in one's visual field were usually made up of direct reflections from surfaces, the visual system developed processes for "resonating" (to use Gibson's word) with the information contained in these patterns. The system was designed to extract information from the natural environment. There was no other environment; there was no need to develop an additional or different way of processing man-made constructions of light patterns as in a motion picture. Since the visual system has a program for processing only the environment within which it developed, then everything is processed according to that program.

Film Theory

We are now in a position to address the status of the motion picture. The information contained in the dancing patterns of light specifies an entire fictional world. And that is just the point: that the dancing, flickering patterns of light *specify* rather than symbolize that world. If we take symbols to be more or less arbitrary vehicles for conventional meanings, then we can state emphatically that our perception of motion pictures is not symbolic. The motion picture does not symbolize a fictional world, it allows the patterns of light and therefore the information for a fictional world to be substituted for the ambient optic array of the real world. And since evolution has provided no special capacity for processing patterns of light from a constructed fictional world, the visual system processes the information which specifies such a world as it processes information specifying the real world. Herein lies the key to the compelling impression of reality we feel when viewing a motion picture.

If the patterns of light reflected from a movie screen are processed by the visual system as though they were reflected directly from the surfaces of physical reality, then film theory is in a position to benefit enormously from Gibson's theory of ecological optics. He has identified the patterns of light that constitute the common denominator for all perception—that of the real world or of motion pictures. "The optical information for distinguishing the various events," Gibson writes, "can only be various disturbances of the local structure of the optic array. . . . Nevertheless, strange to say, they are what we are visually most sensitive to, all of us, animals, babies, men, women, and moviegoers."[26]

To avoid any confusion, let us quickly note that the patterns of light that reach our eye from a theater screen contain not only information about the fictional world of the movie, but also information about the screen itself. In Gibson's terms there is information for both "scene and surface," and our attention alternates between the two sets of information. But let us concentrate upon the set of information that defines a fictional world. It is here that Gibson's concepts of invariants, direct perception, and affordances are of most use to us.

Gibson went to considerable effort to describe in detail the various kinds of surfaces and textures that exist in the world and differentially reflect light. Any information we may get from viewing these surfaces is contained not in ourselves to be projected upon such surfaces, but in the patterning of light, the optic array itself, as it is reflected from them. Our part is in the detection of "invariants" within the array which specify objects in the environment. The patterns of light are continually shifting as we move through our environment, and as the patterns change, some aspects of the visual array vary and some stay the same. Those that do not vary as the light changes and as we change our point of view constitute "invariants" in Gibson's terminology, and specify objects in the world. Evolution has given us the capacity to process for such invariants. We learn where one object ends and another begins by walking around and looking at it or observing the object (or individual) as it moves. Those invariant patterns of light specify the object. Similarly, patterns observed during movement (of parts of the array or of oneself) provide information about the relationships of those objects to each other. If an object, for instance, is behind another object, it will be systematically covered or uncovered as movement progresses. Information, then, consists of patterns of actual relationships between objects in the world. It is not something added or deduced or inferred from raw data. The information contained in these patterns of light is encountered directly by the visual system and processed immediately and ongoingly without the necessity of high-level logical or linguistic constructions which only humans might be able to perform, for after all perception is not unique to humans—it began with the fish. This is what Gibson meant by "direct perception."

The concepts of invariants and direct perception begin to define a theory, or as James Cutting has suggested, a metatheory, of perception which is both parsimonious and consistent with what we know of biological evolution. But it is Gibson's conception of affordance that is truly useful, for it connects the perception of objects with their meaning. Gibson coined the term "affordance" because no such term or concept existed. "The affordances of the environment are what it offers the animal, what it provides or furnishes, either for good or ill. . . . It implies the complementarity of the animal and the environment."[27] The ground affords walking upon, an overhanging ledge affords shelter, an apple may afford eating.

The concept is radical and more difficult to grasp than it may seem. Film theorists, even cognitively oriented film theorists, might have reservations about the concept of affordances. They might consider it inadequate to account for the perception of complex culturally defined relationships such as those found in a fictive film, or they might fear that it opens the gate to unbridled relativism. It offends once by placing what has previously been thought to be higher-level meaning at the level of animal perception, and again by defining meaning as a relationship between the perceiver and the object of perception.

Yet one may find that these reservations are greatly diminished by the very elegance of Gibson's conception: it is in the very act of seeing an object that one perceives its affordance. One sees not simply the ground, a ledge, or an apple, but ground to walk upon, a ledge to hide under, an apple to eat. An affordance thus defines a relationship embedded in perception. Different objects may provide the same affordance to an individual, and different individuals may see different affordances in the same object.

But if cognitivists remain ill at ease with the idea of affordances, cultural relativists cannot take much comfort either, for affordances are constrained on the one end by physical reality (that is, the environment) and on the other by human capacity (cognitive architecture). Thus, in practical terms, actual objects and events often turn out to provide a rather small number of affordances.

If we take an affordance to be a relationship or perhaps even a potential relationship between ourselves and our environment, then we might reasonably ask what happens when we learn something about the environment that changes our relationship to it. Do the affordances change also? And what about things that have little meaning outside a cultural context? Does Gibson's concept of affordance apply to such cultural phenomena?

Ulric Neisser asked these questions, and in answering them pointed out, as

Gibson had, that there is more information in the world than we could ever process; that the task of perception is not to build up perceptions from scant, insufficient data, but to select patterns of information from the plethora of information that normally exists in our environment. This is a basic distinction between the traditional view of perception and an ecological perspective. If one considers the visual field to be filled with rays of light impinging upon the retina, then one might posit a degraded or impoverished retinal image which must be somehow filled in or enriched, or one might posit a retina over-whelmed by so many rays of light and requiring a filtering mechanism that allows only certain sensations to reach consciousness as a percept. With an ecological approach, however, one considers the visual array to consist of pat-terns of information contained in the ambient light, and perception becomes a process of selection. It is not that we "see" everything out there and have to filter out what is unwanted, but that we select certain of the patterns that are available to perception.

It is our knowledge, our perceptual schema, that informs our selection. This is not to say, however, that we see only what we know. It is rather, in Neisser's words, that "we can see only what we know how to look for."[28] And, as neurophysiologist Michael Gazzaniga reminds us, our capacities for learning what to look for are themselves subject to biological constraints: "Evolutionary processes have probably not conferred upon the human being all possible capacities to learn all kinds of strange things. There must be phe-nomena in the world that totally elude us because we do not have a capacity for considering their meaning."[29] Again, there is more information in the world that any one creature can possibly have the capacity to use.

Neisser presents an example of the interaction of knowledge and percep-tion when viewing the highly abstracted, culturally defined array of chessmen on a chessboard:

> The chess master quite literally *sees* the position differently—more adequately and comprehensively—than a novice or a non-player would. Of course, even a novice or a non-player sees a great deal: the chessmen are of carved ivory, the knight resembles a horse, the pieces are (perhaps) arrayed with a certain geomet-ric regularity. A young child would see still less: that the piece would fit into his mouth, perhaps, or could be knocked over. A newborn infant might just see that "something" was in front of him. To be sure, he is not mistaken in this: some-thing *is* in front of him. The differences among the perceivers are not matters of truth and error but of noticing more rather than less.[30]

Let us hasten to note that it would be a mistake to conclude from Neisser's chess example that all perception of a chessboard is relative in the broadest use of the term "relative," that the possible affordances to an individual are in no way constrained. Within the game of chess itself the rules rigidly constrain the possible moves and define success and failure for an individual making a series of choices regarding moves. Outside the game, that is, for nonplayers, the affordances of chess are subject to a number of constraints, some physical, some cultural.

To answer the questions posed above: Clearly, learning about our environment does change its affordances for us. And we would expect that the more we know of an environment, the more affordances it would hold for us, since at each successive level of knowledge we gain potential affordances, and those of the previous levels do not necessarily go away. Even the chess master sees that something is in front of him just as the infant does. And yes, the concept of affordance applies to a highly abstract and perhaps symbolic cultural phenomenon like chess playing as well as to natural phenomena.

But, of course, our interest is in motion picture viewing, and it might be instructive at this point to compare Neisser's view of the perception of a chessboard to the perception of motion pictures. As with chess, certain dimensions of a motion picture are highly conventionalized. Within the information specifying a fictional world, for example, there may indeed be embedded information concerning conventions of dress, behavior, speech, and even filmic construction. And the film expert, like the chess master, will see affordances (meanings) in all this. An unsophisticated viewer might see only the events of the story, that such and such happened to the people inhabiting the fictional world of the film. A child might see only people moving about doing things. The analogy holds, as far as it goes, but there are some fundamental differences between viewing a chessboard and viewing a motion picture.

The chessboard may be taken as an abstract representation of a battlefield, with the various chessmen symbolizing a complex social hierarchy. By no stretch of the imagination could the chessboard be defined as an illusion of an actual battlefield, or the chessmen as illusions of the people who may together constitute a society. It is important to make such a distinction, for while it seems absurdly obvious to note that the squares of a chessboard do not comprise an illusion of a battlefield but a symbol of one, the other side of the analogy has not been so obvious—that a battlefield in a motion picture *is* an illusion of a battlefield. And although the chessboard may stand for a battlefield as we plan abstract battle strategies, to our visual system it cannot stand in for an actual battlefield. In a motion picture an illusion of a battlefield can present much of that same information in the same terms—patterns of light—as the actual physical battlefield. Our visual system processes the information contained in the patterns of light in the same way it would process information contained in the patterns of light actually reflected from a physical surface (an actual battlefield).

A similar argument can be made with regard to the chessmen on the chessboard and the characters in a movie. The king and queen, the knights, the bishops are all symbolized by carved pieces of ivory and ebony, or perhaps marble or molded plastic. There is no illusion here. In a motion picture, however, the king and queen, the entire entourage, have the appearance of reality. Their appearance is illusory, of course, but they serve as surrogates to our perception of a real royal court. They and their entire world may be fictional, but we can process their appearances and the sounds of their voices as though they were real.

We perceive the affordances of the fictional world in terms of affordances to specific characters. And even in a fictional world the affordances for particular characters are constrained. In fact the makers of the movie work very hard to limit the number of implications for each of the characters. Possible affordances for the characters and ultimately meanings for viewers must be constrained and they must be plausible. We demand intelligibility and plausibility. Even in the fictional world of a motion picture we are unable to accept an arbitrary affordance for a character; we demand that a potential affordance, provided for a character by that character's relationship to an object or event, be plausible within the constraints of the fictional world inhabited by the character. This should not be surprising, for nature has simplified the problem of perception by "assuming" a stable lawful natural world. We expect no less of a fictional one.

Conclusion

As we have suggested, film theorists, even cognitive film theorists, may have difficulty seeing how Gibson's concepts of invariants and affordances can account for the complex, often culturally defined activities involved in film viewing. The process is indeed complex. Yet we should not be too quick to conclude that a perceptually based theory has no place in an explanation of the complex and abstract components of human behavior. Gibson was aware of this perceived weakness in his ecological theory and was careful to caution against assuming untenable dichotomies:

> Culture evolved out of natural opportunities. The cultural environment, however, is often divided into two parts, "material" culture and "non-material" culture. This is a seriously misleading distinction, for it seems to imply that language, tradition, art, music, law, and religion are immaterial, insubstantial, or intangible whereas tools, shelters, clothing, vehicles, and books are not. . . . But let us be clear about this. . . . No symbol exists except as it is realized in sound, projected in light, mechanical contact, or the like. All knowledge rests on sensitivity.[31]

The extent to which higher-level cognitive activities are inextricably tied to perception is one of the issues addressed by cognitive psychologist Ulric Neisser in his work on conceptualization and categorization. Neisser suggests that, in the fundamental act of categorization, there may be a link between the perception of affordance and higher-level processes possibly involving deduction and inference. He posits three illustrative levels of categorization drawn from the work of Eleanor Rosch: a basic level, and both superordinate and subordinate levels. A chair might belong in a basic-level category, with "furniture" and "rocking chair" in superordinate and subordinate categories respectively. Categorization begins with the basic level categories, categories which are defined by appearance and function. Items in the basic-level categories tend to look alike, and our interaction with them tends to be similar.[32]

Gibson's concepts of invariants (aspects of the visual array that persist through changes in illumination and point of view) and affordances (relationships between an organism and its environment) apply directly to the process of basic-level categorization, where objects are categorized according to their affordances on the basis of appearance. For example, one might while taking a walk see in the trunk of a fallen tree the affordance of sitting. The perception of such an affordance does not require language; it is not a matter of naming; one has simply perceived a place to sit, which we may for the purpose of discussion call a "seat." It is a seat because it looks like a place one could sit, that is, by appearance and affordance. One could bring a portion of the tree home and use it to sit upon; at this point we might name it, perhaps calling it a chair. It is perhaps an intellectual leap to link a chair to other items such as tables, beds, and chests of drawers into a superordinate category (furniture). Such a leap might require inference and a level of abstraction available only to humans. And of course assigning a name to such a category requires language.

It is, then, from the basic, ecologically driven act of perception and categorization that we proceed, by way of inference, deduction, abstraction, and so on, to other levels of categorization—the superordinate or subordinate categories. Such hierarchies, according to Neisser, "often have more than three levels . . . but there is always at least one basic level near the middle." [33]

This basic level category is central to our perception of motion pictures, where it is, after all, the appearances of objects and events that are recorded by the camera. As Neisser recognizes, "These principles apply even to the perception of television images and movies and (recently) holograms, where optical structure is made to appear without any real environmental substrate. No objects are actually present in such displays, but in a sense perception is still direct." [34]

In viewing a movie, we bring everything we know to the experience—what we know about other movies and movie conventions, our cultural knowledge, our specific background and education. We make inferences; we put things together and draw conclusions; we go through all of the higher-level mental activities we as humans are capable of. But all of this we might do in a discussion of film.

What makes the viewing of a film different from a discussion is the visual array which makes possible the direct perception of the fictional world presented on the screen. This perceptual basis is the common denominator, shared even cross-culturally when viewing a motion picture. The objects and events and affordances for film characters can be perceived by each viewer at the basic level.

Of course movies can and do go beyond basic-level categorization. Yet it is the perceptual basis of the film-viewing experience that allows these intellectual and cultural abstractions to be incorporated into our understanding and our emotion as well. Most theories of film spectatorship, even those that are cognitively based, tend to address the so-called higher-level processes while ignoring the basic perceptual processes altogether. What is needed is a consistent and coherent metatheory that can incorporate both, and make clear the crucial role played by perception in the film-viewing experience. An ecological metatheory fills this need, and it does so within the constraints imposed by our evolution as a species.

In addressing issues such as the role of emotion in film spectatorship, the process of narrative comprehension, character recognition and identification, the creation and maintenance of diegetic space, the hierarchical nature of film structure, the nature of film editing practices, we must always be aware that in the motion picture/mind interface the former is our construction and the latter a construction of evolutionary processes. And while we are perfectly free to change the structure of motion pictures at will, we do not yet have the power to change the basic structures of the human mind. As film theorists our most adaptive strategy might be to adopt a willingness to be both informed and constrained by our knowledge of that biological system in our theoretical speculations about the nature and functioning of motion pictures.

NOTES

This work was supported by University of Kansas General allocation #3242-20-0038.

1. Hugo Münsterberg, "Why We Go to the 'Movies,'" *Cosmopolitan*, December 1915, p. 31.

2. Rudolf Arnheim, whose approach to film studies was most certainly informed by his training in gestalt psychology, was a notable exception. In his only work devoted to the cinema, *Film as Art* (Berkeley: University of California Press, 1966) Arnheim's focus is on a defense of film as a form of art and not on developing a coherent and consistent theory of film based on gestalt psychology.

3. Münsterberg, "Why We Go," p. 22.

4. For a more extensive discussion of the general accessibility of movies, see Noël Carroll, "The Power of Movies," *Daedalus* 114, 4 (Fall 1985): 79–103.

5. See David Marr, *Vision* (New York: W. H. Freeman, 1982), pp. 27–29.

6. Ibid., pp. 29–31.

7. Eleanor J. Gibson, Foreword to *Reasons for Realism: Selected Essays of James J. Gibson*, ed. Edward Reed and Rebecca Jones (Hillsdale, N.J.: Lawrence Erlbaum, 1982), pp. x–xi.

8. Vicki Bruce and Patrick R. Green, *Visual Perception: Physiology, Psychology, and Ecology*, 2d ed. (Hillsdale, N.J.: Lawrence Erlbaum, 1990), p. 224.

9. James J. Gibson, "New Reasons for Realism," in *Reasons for Realism*, p. 382.

10. James J. Gibson, "Perception as a Function of Stimulation," in *Psychology: A Study of Science*, vol. 1, ed. S. Koch (New York: McGraw-Hill, 1959), pp. 462–63n.

11. James J. Gibson, *The Ecological Approach to Visual Perception* (Boston: Houghton Mifflin, 1979), pp. 128–29.

12. James E. Cutting, "Perceptual Artifacts and Phenomena: Gibson's Role in the Twentieth-Century," in *Foundations of Perceptual Theory*, ed. S. C. Main (New York, 1993), p. 236.

13. Jean-Baptiste Pierre Antoine de Monet de Lamarck, *Philosophie zoologique* (Paris, 1909. Reprint, Weinheim, 1960).

14. For a discussion of evolution from a contemporary perspective, see John Rennie, "DNA's New Twists," *Scientific American* 26, 3 (March 1993): 122–32.

15. James J. Gibson, *The Senses Considered as Perceptual Systems* (Boston: Houghton Mifflin, 1966), p. 175.

16. Julian Hochberg, "Gestalt Theory," in *The Oxford Companion to the Mind*, ed. Richard L. Gregory (Oxford: Oxford University Press, 1987), p. 288.

17. The schism runs through the middle of most of the disciplines that make up cognitive psychology. For example, in artificial intelligence (AI) there is the "symbolic processing" approach and the "situated action" approach, with proponents of the latter generally claiming lineage to Gibson, even though one might question whether there is sufficient appreciation of the biological (as opposed to merely environmental) basis of Gibson's theory in that claim.

18. Bruce and Green, *Visual Perception*, p. 382.

19. There is yet another level of the representation debate, to which Bruce and Green referred in listing the use of the term "representation" to describe the world as it has been in the past—that is, representation as a relatively long-term memory that allows individuals to reconstruct spatial layouts of places "seen" sometime in the past. These "representations" have sometimes been called cognitive maps. Gibson preferred to situate a discussion of this kind of behavior in the context of orientation of the observer to his environment and denied the need for "mapping" of any sort. See Gibson, *Ecological Approach*, pp. 198–200.

20. See, for example, Joseph Anderson, "A Cognitive Approach to Continuity," *Post Script* 13, 3 (Fall 1993): 61–66; and Noël Carroll, "Toward a Theory of Point-of-View Editing," *Poetics Today* 14, 1 (Spring 1993): 123–41.

21. We are making our argument in terms of vision; a similar argument could be made for sound.

22. James Cutting has called this phenomenon "La Gournerie's paradox" after the man who first addressed the problem of slanted images in 1859. See James E. Cutting, "Rigidity of Cinema Seen from the Front Row, Side Aisle," *Journal of Experimental Psychology: Human Perception and Performance* 13, 3 (1987): 323–34.

23. Ibid., p. 323.

24. Vilayanur S. Ramachandran and Stuart M. Anstis, "The Perception of Apparent Motion," *Scientific American* 254, 6 (June 1986): 102–9.

25. Ibid., p. 109.

26. Gibson, *Ecological Approach*, Houghton Mifflin, p. 110.

27. Ibid., p. 127.

28. Ulric Neisser, *Cognition and Reality* (New York: W. H. Freeman, 1976), p. 20.

29. Michael S. Gazzaniga, *Nature's Mind* (New York: Basic Books, 1992), p. 95.

30. Neisser, *Cognition and Reality*, pp. 180–81.

31. Gibson, *Senses Considered*, p. 26.

32. See Ulric Neisser, "From Direct Perception to Conceptual Structure," in *Concepts and Conceptual Development*, ed. Ulric Neisser (Cambridge: Cambridge University Press, 1987), pp. 11–24.

33. Ibid., p. 14.

34. Ibid., p. 13.

17

Movies in the Mind's Eye

Julian Hochberg
and Virginia Brooks

Most writers on film, and most filmmakers, need no science. But any serious discussion of whether the medium was used effectively or artistically in any instance requires some understanding of how we perceive and remember moving pictures, and that must derive from research: introspection will not serve. Scattered aspects of cognitive science have begun to appear, therefore, in recent writings on film.[1] On the other side of the aisle, students of perception and visual memory cannot afford to ignore moving pictures, but until recently they have mostly confined their attention to low-level motion phenomena, as have introductory film texts. The latter, if they write at all about perception, still proclaim that we perceive motion from successive still frames because of (heavens protect us!) "persistence of vision."[2] In any case, stroboscopic motion is only a small part of the perception of visual events, which is what film is about.

In this essay we reexamine the cognitive systems that contribute to the visually informative and artistically important characteristics of film and tape, trying to keep both the science and the art in view.

Depicting Events in Moving Pictures

There are three steps to the depiction of events in moving pictures: low-level vision, relational parsing, and action schemas. We will look at each separately.

Movement as Primitive Sensory Response

A continuous motion in the world is, of course, captured by successive displaced images on film (or their video equivalent). For most events, these displacements are small, and within the range of the low-level sensory receptors of the visual system; these respond identically to the small displacements on the screen and to the differences provided from one moment to the next by smooth physical motion in the world. Recent studies of this system offer an increasingly important window on the underlying neurophysiology, and reveal some surprising phenomena (for example, reversals of direction).[3] This low-level response is preemptive and "unintelligent." Notably, it occurs between nearby successive contours regardless of what objects they belong to (see, for example, Fig. 17.3A), thereby causing many "bad cuts" (which result from this fundamental displacement-detection mechanism, rather than some violation of cinematic "grammaticality"). Many techniques aimed at achieving "seamless" editing work by avoiding such unwanted apparent motion between noncorresponding objects. In the time of Eisenstein, however, and especially in the New Wave, such visual jolts became desirable, although (or because) they slow the viewer's comprehension and make the medium itself more intrusive.

Although vision psychologists and neurophysiologists sometimes write as though these low-level mechanisms account "directly" for perceiving motion, which would, if it were true, make it easy to explain and predict what people will see, it is simply not true: we usually perceive movements very different from the displacements in the eye or on the screen. Indeed, were it not for these differences, films as we know them would not be possible, as we see next.

Framework-Relative Paths of Motion

We perceive (approximately) the framework-relative paths of motion, and not the displacements on the screen which determine low-level motion.

An object may be *perfectly stationary* on the screen and yet it will appear irresistibly to move if given a moving framework (Fig. 17.1Ai) or background (Fig. 17.1Aii), and the actual motions of the frameworks or backgrounds themselves are often not noticeable. This is part of a rich body of phenomena known as *induced motion*.[4] Something akin to Fig. 17.1Ai happens outside of the laboratory when the eye tracks a moving object in a *pursuit movement* or when a camera acts similarly in a *pan* or *track* shot (Fig. 17.1Aiii).[5] Thanks to this phenomenon, a continuous motion can be presented over a space *s'* that may be many times larger than the screen, in the same way that the movements of the viewer's head and eyes provide a wider prospect than the limits of gaze within any glance. The screen would be stage-bound, were it not for this resource. Similarly, the parts of an object or group of objects moving in one direction on the screen may instead be irresistibly seen as moving in another (Fig. 17.1Bi, 17.1Bii).

Neither of these demonstrations is only about dots in the laboratory. The phenomenon of Fig. 17.1A reappears in Fig. 17.1C: The rightward movement of a dancer across the screen (M2) is lost if filmed in limbo (with little

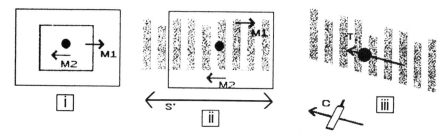

Fig. 17.1A. *i.* Although it is perfectly stationary on the screen (indicated by the outermost rectangle), the black dot appears very strongly to move leftward (M2) if a large object, the background, or the framework actually moves rightward (M1). *ii.* If the background continues to enter on the left edge of the screen and scroll off the right edge, for a total distance (s') that is larger than the screen, the induced movement (M2) can continue as long as the filmmaker wishes it to. *iii.* Such scenes are usually made by moving the camera, C, in synch with the target, T, in a tracking or pan shot.

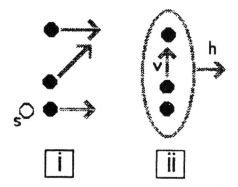

Fig. 17.1B. With three dots moving on the screen, as shown by the arrows in *i*, a very different event is perceived, especially if only the dots are visible (that is, white dots in limbo). *ii.* the center dot is seen in vertical motion (arrow *v*) between the two end dots. If the surroundings are not completely featureless (that is, if the edges of the projection screen are dimly discernible, or there is a stationary dot, like that at *s*), the entire set of dots may be detected as moving horizontally (arrow *h*).

or no framework), as in Fig. 17.1Ci. Indeed, the movement is perceived as *leftward* (M4) if the corps, as background, moves rightward on the screen (Fig. 17.1Cii). The phenomenon of Fig. 17.1B reappears in Fig. 17.1D: At (i), we show the first and last frames in a dance movement across the stage; without a strong background, the curve that the lifted dancer's arm describes across the screen in Fig. 17.1Di is not perceived, and only the arm's movement relative to framework provided by the moving body is perceived. Intermediate frames are shown at (ii), in which the curved movement is essentially lost in any case because the dancers are kept centered by a pan shot.

In analyzing a narrative fiction film, such a microscopic approach makes it difficult to get back to the macroscopic content; in films of dance, and other

choreographed spectacles, and indeed in any film in which the visual content
is defined by the subject, the camera and the editing are at once relatively open
to visual study and critical to an appreciation of the film, such detailed study
of the movements seems as important to an understanding of the film as it is
to our understanding of cognitive process.

And that leads us to ask: If the movements we perceive may thus be very
different from those we can measure on the screen, how can we say in advance
what they will be? As part of a more general solution, it has been argued that
the background is specified as stationary in the world because it remains otherwise invariant while moving as a whole, and that the relative motion between object and surround is attributed to the eye or camera. If that is true,
then a layout of space equal to $s' = m1 \times t$, where s', m are as labeled in
Fig. 17.1A and t is m's duration, is also specified, as is the apparent velocity
$m2$ of the target (although really stationary on the screen). A similar explanation has been offered for Fig. 17.1Bii, in terms of the vector that remains
after subtracting the component, h, that is shared by all the moving dots.[6]

This sounds like an automatic prescription, but it cannot serve as such. For
one thing, there is always a stationary visible framework—the edge of the
screen—which by the preceding analysis should restrict our perceived motions to the physical displacements within that framework. But we have seen
that that does not happen. Indeed, under normal viewing conditions (that is,
not in limbo), both on stage and on the screen, the viewer sees the graceful
curve as well as the body-relative movement (in Fig. 17.1Di), in some manner
hard to describe and even harder to measure. The distinction between these
two motions is analogous to the distinction between the 3-D spatial layout
represented in a picture, and its pictorial composition: the former is view-

Fig. 17.1C. *i.* A dancer or actor actually moving rightward in space (M2) against a
weak or featureless background, but tracked by the camera so as to remain
stationary on the screen, will in fact appear stationary. *ii.* The same dancer, against
a background (here, the corps) with a net rightward screen movement (that is, M3
> M4), will appear to move leftward (M4), against its true direction of movement
in space.

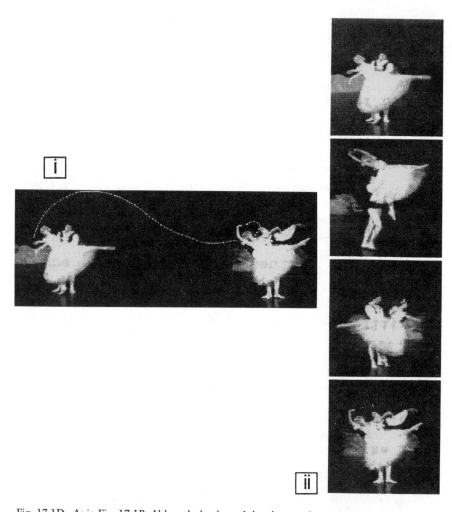

Fig. 17.1D. As in Fig. 17.1B: Although the dancer's hand traces the curve across the screen as drawn in *i*, that curve is not seen if there is no background; the hand movements relative to the body (intermediate frames are shown in *ii*) are seen instead.

point-independent, whereas the latter, which greatly affects the feeling and aesthetics of the view, depends very much on the viewpoint of eye or camera.

Which movement actually predominates in any filmed passage seriously affects the aesthetics of the passage. The balance depends, among other things, on where the viewer attends. For example, a stationary background spot aligned as at *s* with the diagonal motion in Fig. 17.1Bi will, if the viewer stares at it, make the diagonal movement much more visible.[7] The filmmaker learns by trial and error—not by any principles in the production handbook—how to obtain the desired effect.

How can we know in advance what will occur and why?

A set of perceptual theories, each of which uses quite different terms (unconscious inference, perceptual logic, internalization of the laws of physics, and ecological realism), are all versions of Helmholtz's likelihood principle[8]: *we perceive that which would in our normal life most likely have produced the effective sensory stimulation we have received.*

That principle must surely be at least approximately true, or we could not survive. It is probably a good source of intuitions for filmmakers and other visual artists. But within this set of theories lie two extremely different subsets. Theories of the first class assert that some internal mental representation of the event or scene is formed within the viewer's mind, in response to the movements on screen and in the eye; such theories are frequently accused of being uneconomical and mentalistic (a term with pejorative overtones). To us, a more damaging aspect is that such theories are not predictive, because they have not addressed the nature of the representations they postulate in general; or the nature of what those representations are like in the case of moving pictures in particular.

A second kind of theory of visual perception and cognition seems much more hard-headed, specific, and based in the real world (that is, more "behaviorist"), referring only to the information offered the viewer, and to what that information specifies about the world: the extent of surface defined in Fig. 17.1Bii, for example, or when and where we will make contact with an approaching surface or a thrown ball. In this class of theory, it may be thought that we as scientists or as moving picture craftsmen need only to know the relevant principles of physics to know what people will perceive.[9]

Don't count on it. Whether or not such nonmentalistic or physics-specific theories will ever be good or useful replacements for their mentalistic counterparts for any purposes (and we do not think they will), they fail us here for two reasons that should tell us much about visual cognition quite generally. First, they work by defining motion in a space-time coordinate system, with time as a dimension. It is easy to do this when discussing physical events that can be predicted by physical laws, such as the distance s' traversed in Figure 17.1Aii. But after some brief time, the space and movement of film gone by can exist only in a fallible viewer's limited working memory, and they do not remain unchanged somewhere simply because they had been "specified" by information that has flowed past on the screen. Second, motions that follow simple physical laws that we can hope to formulate do not make up much of moving pictures in any case.

Consider the first point, that is, the role of perceptual memory as opposed to physical specification. In situations like Fig. 17.1Aii, in which a motion $m1$ brings some offscreen surface into view, viewers can judge when remembered objects, currently beyond the screen, will come into sight. Yet experimental measures show that such space in the mind's eye is compressed when out of sight, that is, $s' < m \times t$.[10] Studies in which an object moving at some velocity goes out of view for some brief period t, and the viewer reports whether it was early or late when it reappeared (like testing the timeliness of the return from a cutaway, or of a strolling actor's reappearance from behind an occluding object), found the ability lost within 1,200 msec.[11] In describing what the viewer gains from a moving picture, both of these kinds of study reveal mental representations (effective memories) of motion and of constructed space, rather than merely the specified physical variables. The former is thus not merely a more mystical phrasing of the latter: they have different properties. But it is even more important to us that represented movements and extents do not long outlast their presentation on the screen.

This means that, very shortly after it has occurred, the representation of an event, or of a part of an event, is different from the perception obtained during the event itself. Some specific physical information about space and time is lost with time. We assume that such losses occur as well after each change in direction or speed, or after each cutaway or change in scene. That is, unless the viewer has available some mental structure or schematic event into which the segments take their place, *and from which they can be regenerated when needed,* the continual movement in space becomes indeterminate in memory.

This, in turn, is what gives the second point—that most moving pictures are not assemblies of simple physical trajectories—its theoretical and practical importance.

Beyond Physical Trajectories: Represented Goals and Intentions

The fact is that we must parse most of the motion patterns we encounter in terms of purposeful acts, not in terms of physically specifiable trajectories. They are not the same, in that the identical act can be expressed and represented by very different physical motions. In Fritz Heider and Marianne Simmel's film (Fig. 17.2), a triad of geometric figures interact in a rich social narrative, across more different trajectories than viewers can remember if they try to do so in terms of geometric paths, but which they can remember far better as purposive acts within a story structure.[12]

The story structure encodes the too-numerous trajectories as a smaller number of more distinctive and familiar, purposeful actions. These are the same units by which the motions of people and animals achieve recognizable organization (and which are perhaps learned by infants even before they learn simpler physical motion). All of the unrelated movements are immediately meaningful if the viewer has undertaken to construe them as purposeful and expressive actions.

The Heider and Simmel film itself was an explicit request for a new look at social psychology, at narrative, and at visual cognition. Since it appeared in 1944, social psychologists have shown that viewers agree consistently about the *breakpoints* (the bounds of staged purposive actions); they have also

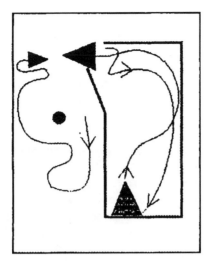

Fig. 17.2. Motion paths of an animated
story film by Heider and Simmel. Cast:
small circle, large and small triangles (the
gray triangle marks a particularly lengthy
pause).

shown that sequences assembled from breakpoints alone are better comprehended than those assembled from intermediate stills. (For this reason, films
seem a natural joint venture for film theory and social psychology.)[13]

The physically defined (nonmentalistic) approaches to visual cognition say
nothing about such animate events. But even if they did, we should have to
abandon these approaches, designed to make mentalistic accounts unnecessary, when we consider how cuts are used in moving pictures.

Cuts, Story Structure, and the Nature
of Movies in the Mind's Eye

It is not clear that any of the more mentalistic likelihood theories can be put
in working order as theories about the mind. In general, although after the
fact they can plausibly explain why something was seen as it was, they cannot
successfully say *in advance* what movement will be perceived, or what the
mental representations are like. The worst failure is that virtually all likelihood
theorists (mentalistic *or* physicalistic)[14] depend on the *rigidity principle*, that
is, that we perceive just that rigid 3-D object which fits the changing 2-D
pattern of light in the eye or on the screen. This assumption can make it relatively easy to predict what surfaces or jointed structures (like people and animals) should be perceived, and why they are perceived; but the assumption is
wrong. It has long been contradicted by laboratory demonstrations.[15] And it

really does not apply to normally viewed moving pictures, in which changes in camera lens (close-up, long shot, and so on) and audience seating make it almost certain that *only a nonrigid and deforming object* could provide a geometrical fit to the moving image on the screen.[16] (Indeed, it seems likely to us that familiar animate bodily movements, and perhaps others as well, are perceived as opportunistic and therefore elastic fits to the motions of the extremities, rather than as rigid motions anchored at their joints, as has been claimed.[17])

There are many other problems that current accounts of mental representation leave unaddressed.[18] That is unfortunate, because as we see next the use of cuts in moving pictures poses a clear need for a theory that is specific about the nature of mental representations of events.

We take one last stab at a nonmentalistic account, and then a first step toward a mentalistic one.

Overlapping and Nonoverlapping Cuts

In most film and video, events and layouts are conveyed by both motion-based information and by discontinuous shots. Either could be used exclusively, but that is only rarely done. The Heider-Simmel film (like the scenes in Hitchcock's *Rope*) lies at one extreme, a single continuous shot, with no change in camera viewpoint. At the other extreme, Chris Marker's *La Jetée* (1964) consists of cuts between some 424 separate shots in 27 minutes, *all but one of which contains no subject movement at all.* (There are a few camera movements within still pictures.) It is an engrossing visual narrative, despite the absence of movement. What is important to us is that *it is essentially a normal film in immediate memory, even as one watches it.* And it is hard to see how one might hope to discuss an event or a layout as communicated in this way without assuming some contribution by the viewer, some mental representation.

Overlapping cuts (Fig. 17.3A) might conceivably challenge this assumption because they potentially specify physically how the camera or eye has moved relative to the scene as a whole. This physically specified factor might in fact contribute to how we combine our successive saccadic glances at the world,[19] but it fails to predict what viewers actually perceive in overlapping cuts. Both low-level and high-level processes can subvert the technique (when indeed it has any effects at all). Depending on spacing, the low-level mechanisms mentioned earlier can provide misleading apparent motion between noncorresponding objects in successive views: for example, in Fig. 17.3A, because each letter in the second shot (*ii*) is just rightward of noncorresponding letters in the first shot (*i*), a rightward jump is seen instead of the true leftward displacement of the letters. This is a common cause of bad cuts and affects the course of looking at filmed narrative.[20] In Figs. 17.3Bi and 17.3Bii, a high-

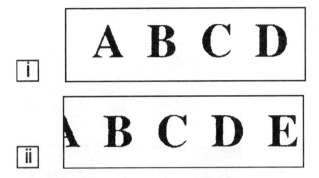

Fig. 17.3A. The overlap between shots *i* and *ii* specifies that *ii* is leftward of *i* in relation to eye or camera, but strong *rightward* motion is instead seen between the noncorresponding letters, thanks to low-level motion-detection mechanisms.

level cue as to what will come next, that is, the direction of the actors' gaze, overcomes the overlap between views (compare the long shot in Fig. 17.3C) and causes the second view (*ii*) to appear to lie rightward of the first (*i*), in the space beyond the screen.

For all we know at present, therefore, even overlapping cuts may work not because their overlap automatically "specifies" anything at all, but because overlap, like an actor's gaze, *acts as a cue about what to expect.*

In any case, however, moving pictures also routinely use *non*overlapping cuts. Such shots, by themselves, cannot convey anything about events or layouts beyond their boundaries. Admittedly, they can be individually remembered, to a degree. After being shown a rapid sequence of unrelated skills (in laboratory research), viewers can recollect information about some of the individual shots, and they show some signs of having visual expectations about what will come next. There is also evidence of a visual buffer that stores some small number of views;[21] indeed, we know that a great many briefly viewed pictures will be recognized on a second viewing as having been seen before. But recognition memory does not of itself provide the viewer with coherent events in rememberable sequence (or a rememberable place larger than the separate shots). Fig. 17.4Ai represents a stationary circular aperture on the screen (in the laboratory), through which the corners of a geometrical figure (a cross) are shown in sequence. Such sequences are not remembered. But if first shown a long shot as at Fig. 17.4Aii(1), the viewer can then test each successive view as to whether it fits the remembered cross in some regular order, and the sequence is then much better distinguished from other sequences.[22]

Without a mental structure in which to place the series of shots—their order as parts of an event, or as sample views of some spatial layout—the series is not rememberable. But it is rememberable given such a structure and the effort to apply it (that is, the attentional resources[23]). That argues that mental

Fig. 17.3B. *i, ii.* Two successive shots, predominantly seen as a camera move from left to right.

Fig. 17.3C. A more inclusive shot.

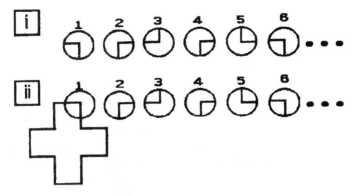

Fig. 17.4A. *i.* The first six shots in a sequence in which the corners of a cross are successively shown through a single stationary aperture. *ii.* The same sequence, with the entire cross shown in the first shot.

structure is involved in the process of event-perception itself, and we must therefore try to say more about what such structure is like.

Mental Representations and Story Structures

Something like this idea is found in many traditional cognitive theories, which take the testing of mental structures as central to the perceptual process.[24] To some filmmakers, good editing poses first a visual question and then a visual answer.[25] In experimental studies of film or video cutting, using short acted or animated scenes, both the visual question posed (as in Figs. 17.3Bi–iv) and the larger story structures within which the shots are presented significantly affect how the edited shots are comprehended.[26] But we must be more explicit about such mental structures if they are to be considered seriously.

Deciding what they *cannot* be like may help us to think of what they *may* be like. The mental structures fitted to our successive glimpses at the screen and at the world cannot have the characteristics of the world itself (despite assertions that they do).[27] Movements as we remember or anticipate them do not continue to run off in time, nor do remembered or anticipated layouts continue to extend in space. As we saw earlier, we start to lose extended time and space when the supporting input ceases. In any case, it certainly does not take some ninety minutes to review in our minds the average movie's representation.

We therefore simply cannot take either the moving picture or the events and space it represents as a faithful model for the film's mental representation. It is often hard to avoid doing just that, or to avoid making the opposite error by turning to the abstract story structure instead. There are plausible theories about written story structure, in the form of hierarchical analyses which account for much of readers' memories of the story's contents.[28] Bordwell has given narrative film a related approach, which explicitly deals with cuts, distinguishing the time covered by the story from the actual screen time after editing.[29] Despite some experimental applications suggested by this approach,[30] such analyses describe the structure of the narrative film itself, as we argue next, and not the viewer's mental representation while viewing the events on the screen.

Online Perception vs. Leisurely Analysis

Even with written stories, readers probably do not normally construct detailed representations while reading: After they have read that Mary stirred her cup, sensitive tests reveal no trace of a spoon in the readers' minds.[31] Nor is the entire story kept in mind and used on-line: subjects who were interrupted at reading regained their speed much faster after a brief review of the last few lines than they did after reviewing the preceding story structure.[32] While reading on-line, therefore, events that are distant in the narrative may go unconsulted, and unmentioned details are not filled in, so long as no inconsistency is encountered.[33]

When someone watches a film or tape unfold at its own pace, it seems even more likely that no filling in is done and no overall structure is consulted, so long as the new input is consistent with the immediately preceding or local context. And a well-made film, intended like most films in history for a single viewing, must therefore in general be *locally* comprehensible. In Fig. 17.4B, *i–iv* are sketches of shots 12–15 of *La Jetée*, stills of 1.27-2.0-, 1.0-, and 1.12-second durations, respectively. In watching the sequence, their relationship is evident without effort. Shot *i* poses a question, *ii* answers it (with an overlap that surely doesn't amount to physical specification); *iii* and *iv* are evidently looking at *ii*, following the principle in Fig. 17.3B. Using a continuous pan to connect the shots (as in Fig. 17.1) would have invited explanation in terms of relative motion detectors and invariants, but such explanations do not apply here (or to cutting in general). Giving the viewer appropriate acquaintance with the film prior to these shots would invite explanation in terms of story structure, but such reliance on overall structure would obscure the

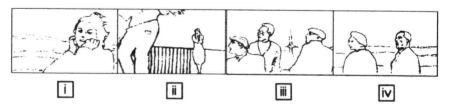

Fig. 17.4B. *i–iv*. Sketches of shots 12–15 in *La Jetée*, all stills, by Chris Marker.

purely local comprehensibility of the shot sequence. We do not know whether the local meaning depends on the actors' gaze as a cue (perhaps by directing the viewer's attention), or whether it reveals a relatively autonomous Gricean process of construal (for example, "why else are we being shown actors looking to the left?"). The final story structure will be *essentially the same* in any case. Only the films will differ, and the perceptual and cognitive processes by which their equivalent stories are achieved will differ too. That may be important for aesthetic reasons (pacing, affective cutting tone, attentional load, looking maintenance); it will be important for comprehension as well if the motions themselves are the film's subject, as in any filmed dance; and it is certainly important in any attempt to understand the perceptual processes at work in watching moving pictures. For many purposes, one might always patch such local analyses into the more conventional overall narrative analysis. But to do so one would first have to know about these local determinants, and whether they were in fact effective in the present instance.

As Thompson[34] has pointed out, there are many appropriate approaches from which to analyze film. To know what there is to comprehend in the film, to know what will arouse expectations early in the film that may later be fulfilled, to know what echoes and resonances are potentially effective, indeed to know what will be a misleading local reading of some stretch of the filmed narrative—these purposes and more require analyses in terms of overall narrative structure. Such analyses necessarily stand outside of the time flow of the film. To us, however, it is important to consider the film as it is experienced in the course of its first viewing (which for many a film will be its only viewing), thereby addressing what is most characteristic of the medium. Such an approach will distinguish one particular moving picture from another whose narrative might be summarized identically but which is very different in its moment-by-moment presentation. And such an approach scrutinizes the act of viewing itself, forcing us to attend to the rich mix of processes by which that act proceeds, and by which a mental representation of the narrated event is achieved, even though most of the steps along the way fade quickly in the course of the viewing.

In fact, considering how rapidly a filmed narrative can advance through brief and partial glimpses of previously unseen objects and events, perhaps at least three kinds of mental structure, each with different time scales and consequences, should be experimentally separated from story structure and from each other. First, there is the answer or confirmation to be obtained by the next glance. Second, there are the next expected features or landmarks, not immediately imminent, implied by the current action. Third, the viewer has a set of abstract readinesses, primed by previous events, for whatever may come afterward. Then, if a contradiction or some appeal by the film itself requires it, the viewer can consult and revise the story structure as far as it has developed. (Such appeals are very frequent. Why is that glass of milk so bright in *Suspense?* Why do we keep cutting away from the two combative adults to the rapt child in the *Third Man?* And why does the same child reappear among the crowd to stare accusingly at the camera/protagonist?) But this process will probably incur some cost in attentional resources, and escape the more passive viewer. The filmmaker, knowing the story structure, can only hope that the viewer can and will make the effort and draw the right conclusions.

It seems unlikely that, aside from the endorsement of some small repertory of local determinants (like that in Fig. 17.3B), such a detailed on-line analysis would be helpful to the narrative filmmaker. It seems likely that with all its limits, our storage capacities (as in speech) allow us to reconstrue earlier segments in the light of later information. But such analysis will certainly be helpful in extending present perceptual psychology, which is still largely confined to the study of the individual event, into the sequence of perceptual consequences with which it must deal in real-world behavior. It will probably be helpful in the programming of interactive (and virtual-reality) media. And it will certainly be helpful where the narrative itself is of a specific visual event, as in recording some dance performance, in which different cuts and camera angles may provide totally different visual (and audiovisual) experiences.

This brings us to the last point that emerges from our argument that the motions on the screen are not simply stored intact and subject to replaying. The story structure, as it is usually laid out by film scholar or cognitive psychologist in words and tree diagrams, also differs from what the viewer perceives and remembers, or can reconstruct, in that it is not visual. We need a notation system better fitted by visual displays than by words. Perhaps it should consist of brief high points or action features economically sampled from the flow of events; it will be relatively schematic, since details are not normally maintained unless needed; it will be mostly ego-centered, or camera-centered, with a definite viewpoint and 2-D composition as distinguished from an object-centered layout specified in 3-D coordinates; and the amount of information that it can store depends on how redundant the viewer finds the film. Remember that striking images, regardless of their place in the story hierarchy, are sure to be recognized when next viewed, and that can itself affect the story; a shot very similar to that of Fig. 17.4Bi reappears to great effect at the end of that film.

Comic strips and their predecessors[35] are a good approximation (although some frames serve only to hold dialogue); so is the filmmaker's storyboard, especially if it follows Eisenstein's shot scripting.[36] DeWied's ingenious recent version of Bordwell's analysis, combining storyboard, breakpoints, and tree structure, seems close to what is needed.[37]

Comic strips may be popular because they approximate the ways in which we think of the visual world. *La Jetée* may differ little in retrospect from what it would have been with full movements. Perhaps even a visual passage that exists only for its specific flow of movements, like a nonnarrative dance, remains with the viewer as an annotated "shot script." That representation may be hierarchical, in the limited sense that the knowledgeable viewer can, *if nec-*

essary, reconstruct and insert additional boxes between the major break points; it may be that specific continuous motions are noted briefly where they are important (as in Figs. 17.1C, 17.1D); and it may even be that viewers can, when needed, reenvision those movements in real time.[38] Nevertheless, we take the mental representation that is approximated by this notation to be *in general* nonredundant and therefore static and discontinuous.

This is intended as first step at a description of the mental representation of visual events. The next step would seem to be close analysis and experimental research with moving pictures.

NOTES

1. Joseph Anderson and Barbara Anderson, "The Myth of Persistence of Vision Revisited," *Journal of Film and Video* 45 (Spring 1983): 3–12, and "Motion Perception in Motion Pictures," in *The Cinematic Apparatus,* ed. Teresa DeLauretis and Stephen Heath (New York: St. Martin's Press, 1980), pp. 76–95; David Bordwell, *Narration in the Fiction Film* (Madison: University of Wisconsin Press, 1985); Virginia Brooks, "Film, Perception and Cognitive Psychology," *Millennium Film Journal* 14/15 (Fall/Winter 1984–85): 105–26.

2. There seems to be no way to put this to rest. The latest version appears in J. Cantine, S. Howard, and B. Lewis, *Shot by Shot: A Practical Guide to Filmmaking* (Pittsburgh: Pittsburgh Filmmakers, 1993). For recent criticisms, see Anderson and Anderson, "Motion Perception"; Julian Hochberg and Virginia Brooks, "The Perception of Motion Pictures," in *Handbook of Perception,* vol. 10, ed. Edward C. Carterette and Morton P. Friedman (New York: Academic Press, 1978), pp. 259–304. For detailed history of where this incurable silliness started, see Olive Cook, *Movement in Two Dimensions* (London: Hutchinson, 1963) and Hugo Münsterberg, *The Film: A Psychological Study* (1916; reprint, New York: Dover, 1970).

3. There has been a recent explosion of work in this area. For discussion of short-range and longer-range motion mechanisms in relation to moving pictures, see Anderson and Anderson, "Myth of Persistence of Vision," and for a survey of research on the mechanisms and on the viability of the distinction, see Julian Hochberg and Virginia Brooks, "Perception of Moving Pictures Revised," in *Handbook of Perception,* ed. Edward C. Carterette and Morton Friedman, rev. ed. (in press).

4. Karl Duncker, "Über insuzerte Bewegung," *Psychologische Forschung* 12 (1929): 180–259. For a recent review, see Arien Mack, "Perceptual Aspects of Motion in the Frontal Plane," in *Handbook of Perception and Human Performance,* vol. 1, *Sensory Processes and Perception,* ed. Kenneth R. Boff, Lloyd Kaufman, and James P. Thomas (New York: John Wiley, 1986), chapter 17, pp. 1–38.

5. The question of what visuomotor information the viewer takes into account when making pursuit movements, as when tracking a target in the world, and the complexities involved when a moving stationary viewer regards a stationary object against a moving background on a stationary motion picture screen, are more involved than we can treat here. See Hochberg and Brooks, "Perception of Moving Pictures Revised."

6. Gunnar Johansson, *Configurations in Event Perception* (Uppsala, Sweden: Almqvist and Wiksells, 1950). For a discussion of recent work on this phenomenon, see Hochberg and Brooks, "Perception of Moving Pictures Revised." For demonstrations that the effect is not simply the result of the eye's tracking *h,* leaving *v* as the only

384 Part Three: Psychology of Film

motion on the retina, see Julian Hochberg and Peter Fallon, "Perceptual Analysis of Moving Patterns," *Science* 194 (1976): 1081–83.

7. With the stationary dot at either of the two corners which are not aligned with the diagonal, the vertical motion remains predominant, as reported by Julian Hochberg and Jeremy Beer, "Alternative Movement Organizations: Findings and Premises for Modeling (Abstract)," *Proceedings of the Psychonomic Society* (1990), p. 25; and as discussed in Hochberg and Brooks, "The Perception of Moving Pictures Revised."

8. Helmholtz's rule is compressed and rephrased from his *Treatise on Physiological Optic,* vol. 3, ed. and trans. J. P. C. Southall, from the 3rd German ed. (1909–11) (Rochester, N.Y.: The Optical Society of America, 1924–25), pp. 4–13. See Julian Hochberg, "Visual Perception," in *Stevens' Handbook of Experimental Psychology,* vol. 1, ed. R. Atkinson, R. Herrnstein, G. Lindzey, and D. Luce (New York: John Wiley, 1988), pp. 295–75. For work by current advocates of that position, see Richard Gregory, *The Intelligent Eye* (London: Weidenfeld and Nicolson, 1970); Irvin Rock, "The Logic of 'The Logic of Perception,'" (*Giornale italiano di psychologia* 20 (1994): 841–67; and Roger N. Shepard, "Ecological Constraints on Internal Representation: Resonant Kinematics of Perceiving, Imagining, Thinking, and Dreaming," *Psychological Review* 91 (1984): 417–47.

9. The strongest claim that perception is a direct response to stimulus information, not involving contribution from any mental representation, came from James J. Gibson, *The Ecological Approach to Visual Perception* (Boston: Houghton Mifflin, 1979). Without pursuing that claim, many visual scientists have pursued his goal of uncovering the rich, mathematically specifiable information about the world that is available to a moving observer (or one watching movies). Their recent work relevant to moving pictures is reviewed in Hochberg and Brooks, "Perception of Moving Pictures Revised." For somewhat opposing views of the information about movement into depth (a phenomenon relevant to the viewer's perception of dolly shots), see W. Warren and K. Kurtz, "The Role of Central and Peripheral Vision in Perceiving the Direction of Self-Motion," *Perception and Psychophysics* 51 (1992): 443–54; and James Cutting, *Perception with an Eye for Motion* (Cambridge: MIT Press, 1986). For a sophisticated study of how movement provides information about surface structure (for example, slopes, peaks, depressions), see J. S. Lappin and T. D. Wason, "The Perception of Geometrical Structure from Congruence," in *Pictorial Communication in Virtual and Real Environments,* ed. S. R. Ellis, M. K. Kaiser, and A. J. Grunwald (London: Taylor and Francis, 1991), pp. 425–48.

10. Jeremy M. A. Beer, "Perceiving Scene Layout through an Aperture during Visually Simulated Self-Motion," *Journal of Experimental Psychology: Human Perception and Performance* (in press).

11. Lynn A. Cooper, "Mental Models of the Structure of Three-Dimensional Objects," in *Object Perception: Structure and Process,* ed. B. Shepp and S. Ballestreros (Hillsdale, N.J.: Lawrence Erlbaum, 1989), pp. 91–119.

12. Fritz Heider and Marianne Simmel, "An Experimental Study of Apparent Behavior," *American Journal of Psychology* 57 (1944): 243–59.

13. D. Newtson and G. Enqvist, "The Perceptual Organization of Ongoing Behavior," *Journal of Experimental and Social Psychology* 12 (1976): 436–50; D. Newtson, J. Hairfield, J. Bloomingdale, and S. Cutino, "The Structure of Action and Interaction," *Social Cognition* 5 (1987): 121–237.

14. See Irwin Rock, "The Logic of 'The Logic of Perception'" and Shepard, "Ecological Constraints on Internal Representation" for mentalistic theories, and see Gib-

son, *Ecological Approach to Visual Perception;* G. Johansson, "Visual Space Perception through Motion," in *Tutorials on Motion Perception,* ed. A. H. Wertheim, W. A. Wagnaar, and H. W. Liebowitz (New York: Plenum, 1982); and Stephen Ullman, *The Interpretation of Visual Motion* (Cambridge: MIT Press, 1979) for physicalistic theories.

15. Strong evidence that rigidity is not the fundamental constraint that allows us to recover three-dimensional structure from changing images, to the exclusion of static pictorial depth information, is reported by M. L. Braunstein and G. J. Andersen, "Testing the Rigidity Assumption: A Reply to Ullman," *Perception* 15 (1986): 641–44; Julian Hochberg, "Machines Should Not See as People Do, But Must Know How People See," *Computer Vision, Graphics, and Image Processing* 37 (1987): 221–37; B. J. Schwartz and G. Sperling, "Non-Rigid 3D Precepts from 2D Representations of Rigid Objects," *Investigative Ophthalmology and Visual Science,* ARVO Supplement, 24 (1983): 239 (abstract). The strategic value that the rigidity constraint offered direct theories of perception was that it made static pictorial depth cues unnecessary to any account of the perception of moving pictures, or of the perception of the world by a moving observer. Once we know that rigidity does not make the depth cues unnecessary, it becomes very hard to dispense with mental representations in one's theoretical account.

16. See Julian Hochberg and Virginia Brooks, "Perception of Still and Moving Pictures," in *International Encyclopedia of Communications,* ed. Erik Barnouw (New York: Oxford University Press, 1989); Julian Hochberg, "Representation of Motion and Space in Video and Cinematic Displays," in *Handbook of Perception and Human Performance,* vol. 1, ed. Kenneth R. Boff, James P. Thomas, and Lloyd Kaufman (New York: John Wiley, 1986), pp. 1–64.

17. For their explanation of the well-known film of actors made visible only by small lights at their joints, see G. Johansson and G. Jansson, "Perceived Rotary Motion from Changes in a Straight Line," *Perception and Psychophysics* 4 (1986): 165–70.

18. See Julian Hochberg, "Perceptual Theory and Visual Cognition," in *Cognitive Approaches to Human Perception,* ed. S. Ballesteros (Hillsdale, N.J.: Lawrence Erlbaum, 1994), pp. 269–89.

19. This was suggested by J. J. Gibson, *Perception of the Visual World* (Boston: Houghton Mifflin, 1950). It is the only explicit purely visual explanation offered for how glances combine, and it has some recent experimental support. (See D. F. Irwin, J. L. Zacks, and J. H. Brown, "Visual Memory and the Perception of a Stable Visual Environment," *Perception and Psychophysics* 47 [1990]: 35–46.) But it has also allowed Gibson and his followers to argue that the entire optic array, which remains invariant under the changing glance of eye or camera, is the effective stimulus on which perception is based—an argument that has no experimental support and much to oppose it. (See Hochberg, "Visual Perception.")

20. Julian Hochberg and Virginia Brooks, "Film Cutting and Visual Momentum," in *Eye Movements and the Higher Psychological Functions,* ed. J. W. Senders, D. F. Fisher, and R. A. Monty (Hillsdale, N.J.: Lawrence Erlbaum, 1978), pp. 293–313; G. D'Ydewalle and M. Vanderbeeken, "Perceptual and Cognitive Processing of Editing Rules in Film," in *From Eye to Mind: Information Acquisition in Perception, Search, and Reading,* ed. R. Groner, G. d'Ydewalle, and R. Parham (Amsterdam: North Holland, 1990), pp. 129–39.

21. The experimental study of montages of unrelated stills deserves more attention in film studies than it has received. For its start, see M. Potter and E. Levy, "Recognition Memory for a Rapid Sequence of Pictures," *Journal of Experimental Psychology* 81

(1969): 10–15. For a recent review and analysis of what the data imply as to mental representations and the normal integration of our successive glances, see H. Intraub, R. Bender, and J. Mangels, "Looking at Pictures But Remembering Scenes," *Journal of Experimental Psychology: Learning, Memory, and Cognition* 18 (1992): 180–91; and H. Intraub, "Contextual Factors in Scene Perception," in *The Role of Eye Movements in Perceptual Processes,* ed. E. Chekaluk and K. R. Llewellyn (Amsterdam: North Holland, 1992), pp. 47–72, respectively.

22. As described in Hochberg, "Representation of Motion and Space in Video and Cinematic Displays," pp. 58–60.

23. Although we know of no experimental research to this point, it is clearly a demanding task, requiring both intention and concentration.

24. Such structure testing underlies the general formulations offered by psychologists and philosophers of the past and present centuries, starting with John Stuart Mill and von Helmholtz.

25. Karel Reisz and Gavin Millar, *The Technique of Film Editing,* 2d ed. (New York: Focal Press, 1968).

26. R. N. Kraft, "The Influence of Camera Angle on Comprehension and Retention of Pictorial Events," *Memory and Cognition* 25 (1987): 291–307; P. S. Cowen, "Manipulating Montage: Effects on Film Comprehension, Recall, Person Perception, and Aesthetic Responses," *Empirical Studies on the Arts* 6 (1988): 97–115; R. N. Kraft, "Light and Mind: Understanding the Structure of Film," in *Cognition and the Symbolic Processes: Applied and Ecological Perspectives,* ed. R. R. Hoffman and D. S. Palermo (Hillsdale, N.J.: Lawrence Erlbaum, 1991), pp. 351–70; d'Ydewalle and Vandebeeken, "Perceptual and Cognitive Processing."

27. Rock, "The Logic of 'The Logic of Perception'"; Shepard, "Ecological Constraints."

28. G. Bower, J. Black, and T. Turner, "Scripts in Memory for Text," *Cognitive Psychology* 11 (1979): 177–220; J. M. Mandler, "A Code in the Node: The Use of a Story Schema in Retrieval," *Discourse Processes* 2 (1978): 14–35; J. M. Mandler and N. S. Johnson, "Remembrance of Things Parsed: Story Structure and Recall," *Cognitive Psychology* 9 (1977): 111–51.

29. Bordwell, *Narration in the Fiction Film.* When Bordwell's distinctions between the various scales of narrative time in moving pictures are placed against the limited resources of working memory, something like the mental shot script we discuss below seems an unavoidable attribute of on-line mental representation.

30. M. A. de Wied, "The Role of Time Structures in the Experience of Film Suspense and Duration: A Study on the Effects of Anticipation Time upon Suspense and Temporal Variations on Duration Experience and Suspense" (Ph.D. diss., University of Amsterdam, 1991).

31. B. A. Dosher and A. T. Corbett, "Instrument Inferences and Verb Schemata," *Memory and Cognition* 10 (1982): 531–39.

32. M. Glanzer, B. Fischer, and D. Dorfman, "Short-Term Storage in Reading," *Journal of Verbal Learning and Verbal Behavior* 23 (1984): 467–86.

33. G. McKoon and R. Ratcliff, "Inference during Reading," *Psychological Review* 99 (1992): 440–66.

34. Kristin Thompson, *Breaking the Glass Armor: Neoformalist Film Analysis* (Princeton: Princeton University Press, 1988).

35. E. H. Gombrich, *Art and Illusion: A Study in the Psychology of Pictorial Representation* (Princeton: Princeton University Press, 1961).

36. Vladimir Nizhny, *Lessons with Eisentein,* trans. and ed. Ivor Montagu and Jay Leyda (New York: Hill and Wang, 1962), pp. 62–92.

37. De Wied, "Role of Time Structures."

38. Beer, "Perceiving Scene Layout"; Cooper, "Mental Models"; Lynn A. Cooper, "Demonstration of a Mental Analog of an External Rotation," *Perception and Psychophysics* 19 (1976): 296–302.

18

Notes on Audience Response

Richard J. Gerrig and Deborah A. Prentice

In the movie *Lethal Weapon II*, the identity of the bad guys is known almost from the beginning: they are diplomatic representatives of South Africa. Because they have diplomatic immunity, they can commit crimes with no fear of punishment (or so the movie leads us to believe). As Joss Ackland, playing the chief criminal, puts it in a harsh Afrikaans accent, "My dear fellow, you could not even give me a parking ticket." By the end of the movie, Ackland and his associates have severely tested their diplomatic immunity by murdering virtually all of the police personnel who have been involved in the effort to undo their drug operations. The only two officers who remain living are Danny Glover (playing Roger Murtaugh) and Mel Gibson (playing Martin Riggs). As the movie speeds toward its climactic scenes, Glover and Gibson share an emotional telephone conversation. Gibson, who is visibly maddened by the need for revenge mumbles, "I'm not a cop tonight, Roger, it's personal. I'm not a cop." At the end of the conversation, Glover removes his police badge and puts it in his desk drawer.

Although they are more than a bit bloodied by the effort, Gibson and Glover methodically eliminate their enemies. In the movie's final scene, Glover calls out to Gibson, "Hey Riggs, you okay?" Just after they exchange "okay" gestures, shots ring out and the view changes to show Ackland firing repeatedly into Gibson's body. As soon as it becomes clear that Ackland's gun is empty, the focus shifts to Danny Glover who raises his gun, points it toward Ackland (who is at a reasonable distance away), and shouts, "Drop it, asshole." The camera shifts to a close shot of Ackland, who flips up an ID and asserts, with rankled smugness, "Diplomatic immunity." The focus returns to Glover and his raised gun. Just briefly we see emotion playing over Glover's face, but quickly the focus draws back to the gun, with Glover blurring in the background, and finally all that fills the screen is the gun in perfect focus.

How do audience members respond to this moment's hesitation? If they have been sufficiently drawn into the world of the story, it seems almost inevitable that the little voices inside their heads will call out "Do it!" or "Pull the trigger!" If this is the case, the voices will be satisfied. Just a moment later, a shot rings out and, as the view quickly shifts again, a burst of blood appears from Ackland's forehead. He crumples. We now see Glover's face again as he intones, "It's just been revoked."

There is, of course, no sense in which the viewers' preference—"Pull the trigger!"—affects the movie's outcome. Nor do we believe that any viewer, if given an appropriate opportunity to reflect on the question, would maintain that his or her response *did* affect the movie's outcome. Nonetheless, this essay will be devoted to what we will call the participant theory of audience response:

- Under appropriate circumstances, experiencers of narrative produce psychological responses *as if* they were really participating in the events.
- Formal properties of film—and particularly, the ability of film to fix the focus of attention—make it especially likely that such *as if* responses will occur.

We initiate our support for this pair of assertions by setting out Alfred Hitchcock's own thoughts on audience participation. We take our cue from this expert to argue against the link between silence and passivity in audience response to film. We then present some preliminary empirical support for our theoretical perspective. Finally, we explore some special properties of film.

Hitchcock on Participation

In 1962, Alfred Hitchcock took part in a series of conversations with François Truffaut about his life and his movies. When Truffaut asked Hitchcock to explain suspense, Hitchcock explicitly invoked the notion of audience participation:

> We are now having a very innocent little chat. Let us suppose that there is a bomb underneath this table between us . . . and the public *knows* it, probably because they have seen the anarchist place it there. The public is *aware* that the bomb is going to explode at one o'clock and there is a clock in the decor. The public can see that it is a quarter to one. In these conditions this same innocuous conversation becomes fascinating because the public is participating in the scene. The audience is longing to warn the characters on the screen: "You shouldn't be talking about such trivial matters. There's a bomb beneath you and it's about to explode!"[1]

Somewhat later in the conversations, Hitchcock analyzes his own movie *Psycho* to explain how he gets the public "participating in the scene":

> You know the public always likes to be one jump ahead of the story; they like to feel they know what's coming next. So you deliberately play upon this fact to control their thoughts. The more we go into the details of the girl's [Janet Leigh, as Marion] journey, the more the audience becomes absorbed in her flight. That's why so much is made of the motorcycle cop and the change of cars. When

Anthony Perkins [as Norman Bates] tells the girl of his life in the motel, and they exchange views, you still play upon the girl's problem. It seems as if she's decided to go back to Phoenix and give the money back, and it's possible the public anticipates by thinking, "Ah, this young man is influencing her to change her mind." You turn the viewer in one direction and then in another; you keep him as far as possible from what's actually going to happen. . . .

Psycho has a very interesting construction and that game with the audience was fascinating. I was directing the viewers. You might say I was playing them, like an organ.[2]

What we have learned from Hitchcock is that he had explicit theories of how his films achieved their effects—by eliciting certain types of predictable responses from his audience. To the extent that Hitchcock succeeded in manipulating the viewer, we must give him credit for being a brilliant intuitive psychologist: not just in the sense of intuiting the fears buried in the collective unconscious but, perhaps more importantly, in the sense of understanding how those fears could best be exploited with respect to the architecture of human cognitive processes. That is our central concern: what features of the structure of human psychological processing enabled Hitchcock to achieve his effects? Our answer will lie chiefly in the direction of participation—Hitchcock's own metaphor—and *as if* responses. We begin by exploring exactly what the metaphor of participation might mean.

Participation in Film

What does it mean for viewers to participate in a film? We need to give an account of participation that is constrained by the hard reality that filmgoers do not actually imagine themselves to be able to direct a character's attention to an anarchist's bomb. We need, that is, to define a form of participation in film that affords a comfortable dissociation between intention and action. To do so, we will draw on phenomena of ordinary conversation. We claim that the skills individuals acquire through conversation are exactly those required by film.

Viewing as Side-Participation

On first pass, it might seem that conversation provides a faulty model for film going. Conversations seem to have *speakers* and *addressees* and viewers clearly do not address the characters on the screen nor, in any coherent sense, do the characters on the screen directly address the viewers. However, let us look to an excerpt from *Casablanca* to see why "speaker" and "addressee" do not exhaust the repertory of conversational roles. Humphrey Bogart, playing Rick, is trying to convince Ingrid Bergman, playing Ilsa, that she must board the waiting airplane with her husband. Although the camera is focused only on Rick and Ilsa, the viewer knows that Claude Rains, playing Captain Louis Renault, is listening in the background. Rick says:

"Now, you've got to listen to me. Do you have any idea what you'd have to look forward to if you stayed here? Nine chances out of ten we'd both wind up in a concentration camp. Isn't that true, Louis?"

For the bulk of this speech, Rick could properly be called the *speaker* and Ilsa the *addressee*, but in what conversational role has Louis been cast? Rick's "Isn't that true, Louis?" makes it clear that Rick has the strong expectation that Louis will have been attending and understanding his utterances even though it is only Ilsa he is trying to persuade. In this way, Louis is a *side-participant* because, although Rick didn't expect Louis himself to be persuaded to get on the plane, he did expect him to be *informed* that he was trying to persuade Ilsa.[3] In this film moment Louis is both literally and psychologically off to one side, but he is entirely prepared to utter the response, "I'm afraid Major Strasser would insist."

The defining criterion for possession of Louis's conversational role is that the speaker formulated his or her utterance with the specific intention that the side-participant be informed. Given the evidence in this scene, we can believe that Rick took into account the common ground of both Ilsa and Louis, and produced a series of utterances that faithfully conveyed his intentions to both of them. The situation would be different if, for example, Rick had chosen to make use of the special knowledge he shared with Ilsa to exclude Louis from his meaning—as he does, for example, when he reminds Ilsa that "We'll always have Paris. We didn't have . . . We, we'd lost it until you came to Casablanca. We got it back last night." In this case Louis is an *overhearer*.[4] He has been excluded either by design—Rick has performed a series of utterances that purposefully mystify the uninitiated—or happenstance—Rick has performed utterances without any particular intentions toward an individual who was neither the addressee nor a side-participant. This example makes it clear that Rick, and speakers in general, control the distribution of non-addressees into the categories of side-participant or overhearer. When, however, parties to conversations have been cast in the role of side-participant, the speakers' intention is that they be duly informed by the speech acts being directed to the addressees.

What is most important for current purposes is that conversationalists have an extraordinary amount of experience being side-participants. In any conversation involving more than two people, it will regularly be the case that language users are accustomed to being informed by utterances for which they are not formally the addressee. They are also, therefore, accustomed to being held responsible for the contents of those utterances by which speakers intended them to be informed. Louis is not surprised, that is, that Rick took for granted that he would know what assertion Rick had made to Ilsa. We can generalize Louis's sangfroid to the claim that conversationalists are also quite skilled at generating responses that are appropriate to the information they receive as side-participants. To the extent that these observations capture everyday experience, we can draw the important conclusion that competence in conversation requires individuals to be in possession of cognitive processes that enable them to function smoothly as side-participants.

We are moving toward the conclusion that those cognitive skills of side-participation are applied to the experience of film. The next step in our argument is to show how this characterization accords well with the experience of reading a fictional or nonfictional narrative. Traditional theories of reading, particularly of reading fiction, have been unable to offer a satisfying account of the relationship of the reader to the text. Speech act theories, for example, have been entirely hamstrung by the necessity of reconciling the patent non-addressee-ness of readers with the definitional speaker-addressee dichotomy. By importing the category of "side-participant"—which doesn't feel like a particularly brave move given its naturalness for conversation—we have a way of making sense of what readers are. In particular, readers bring the accustomed cognitive skills of side-participation to the task of reading, and are appropriately informed by the texts that they read.[5]

The corollary to this claim is that authors most often treat readers as if they are side-participants. They most often, that is, design the utterances of narratives such that readers will have appropriate knowledge to be accurately informed by those utterances.[6] This does not mean that each narrative utterance must be entirely transparent. Authors also have the power to make overhearers of their readers. They may choose, for example, to design utterances that only take on their full implications as the narrative unfolds. Such instances are unproblematic because this fluidity of roles is also present in everyday experience—as we illustrated earlier, Rick rendered Louis a side-participant and an overhearer at different moments of the same conversation. The cognitive skills to navigate between side-participation and overhearing are in place, and may effectively be applied to reading.

The move to film is now straightforward. We claim that viewers of film also assume the role of side-participant. What that means is that we, the viewers, are also informed by Rick's utterance. The intention to inform us is, of course, not Rick's—he doesn't know we exist. Instead, we, the film theorists, must invoke the script writer or director as the ultimate source of the intention. Even so, as we, the viewers or film theorists, watch the movie we behave as if Rick has intentions with respect to us—and so we are informed by his utterances. The basic premise, once again, is that viewers have a superabundance of practice—before they've ever seen a movie—experiencing stories from a bit off to the side. Practice, on our view, implies cognitive psychological preparedness.

Our account of viewers as side-participants helps explain why in the experience of film—even more than in the experience of texts—individuals are likely to lose track of the fact that they can't *really* participate. Why does the impulse to yell a warning arise? Why offer cheers of congratulation? Why boo the villain? We suggest that each of these responses is normal for side-participants—or, at least, the cognitive processes that undergrid side-participation provide an important causal component to these responses. Thus, we can get a good start toward forging a theory of audience response to film by understanding how side-participation works.

The Potential of Silence

We are now in a position to sort out what is essential about audience participation from what is optional. We claim that the cognitive processes that allow the experience of film are the cognitive processes of the side-participant: side-participation, therefore, is an inescapable feature of audience response.[7] We have not, however, arrived yet at a demonstration that "experiencers of narrative produce psychological responses *as if* they were really participating in the events." We believe that this special sort of response occurs against the important background of side-participation—but the occurrence of *as if* responses will depend on both the inclinations of the viewer and the structure of the film. In this section, we will once again illustrate the types of cognitive processes we believe to be critical to the repertory of film viewers. Here, however, we are defining processes that are optionally, rather than obligatorily, applied.

What are viewers doing when they sit in the silence of darkened theaters? There has been a tendency in film theory to characterize viewers as necessarily passive—the claim, in a variety of forms, has been that film psychologically immobilizes viewers and makes of them unknowing victims of ideology.[8] We have no doubts that for all individuals at some times, and for some individuals at all times, such passive viewing takes place. Most members of the audience, for example, are likely to be merely swept up in the beauty of the scenery as the camera pans at the outset of *The Sound of Music* rather than wondering what danger lurks among the wildflowers. However, it is almost impossible to imagine that viewers, later in the movie, would not mentally cry out for Rolf not to reveal the von Trapps' hiding place to the Nazis. To support this assertion, we will illustrate ordinary instances of conversation that break the link between silence and passivity.

The structure of conversation dictates, for example, that some people be silent at all times—each speaker has at least one addressee as well as, potentially, side-participants and overhearers. For conversation to function smoothly, however, some subset of those individuals must clearly be preparing responses. Consider the process whereby a conversational participant makes the transition from addressee to speaker.[9] In their analysis of the rules governing turn-taking in conversation, Harvey Sacks, Emanuel Schegloff, and Gail

Jefferson observed that "transitions (from one turn to a next) with no gap and no overlap are common."[10] An important reason that gap-free-ness predominates is that addressees can only become speakers by capturing the floor, and—if the current speaker has not explicitly designated the next—the way to capture the floor is to be the first to speak. One analysis of "gap length" found that 34 percent of all transitions took less than 0.2 seconds.[11] This figure is important because 0.2 seconds is about as fast as the quickest voluntary response humans can emit. The implication is that there would be far too little time for an addressee to listen to a speaker, process her message, and then plan a response. Rather, to capture the floor, each addressee must be generating reasonably accurate expectations about the speaker's likely words so that he can begin his own utterance with split-second timing. It would be a great mistake, therefore, to imagine that the people doing the listening in conversations are merely passive recipients of information.

We can, however, say more than that. Speakers and addressees are collaborating partners in the construction of meaning.[12] Speakers do not simply deliver their utterances into a passive void. A speaker and an addressee share the responsibility of ensuring that the speaker's intention has been successfully communicated (to some appropriate conversational criterion). We can see active collaboration in a final excerpt from *Casablanca*. This interchange occurs during the first scene in which Rick and Ilsa are reunited at Rick's Café.

> ILSA: Let's see, the last time we met . . .
> RICK: . . . was La Belle Aurore.
> ILSA: How nice, you remembered.

Rick has anticipated the memory Ilsa wishes to evoke, and successfully completed her utterance. Ilsa herself has not stumbled—it is almost like a test for Rick. We see here that being momentarily cast in the silent conversational role implies no stoppage of cognitive processes. To the contrary, evidence converges on the conclusion that addressees have the capacity—and the experience—to be forever vigilant.

What of the viewer? If one is seeing *Casablanca* for the first time, it is unlikely that one could be anything but passive with respect to this single exchange ("the last time we met . . ."). If, however, one has seen the film before, it is more than likely that one *could* be ready to chime in with at least "Paris."[13] In real conversation we would be prepared to provide this information, with split-second timing. When viewing a film, we know that we *should* not jump in (although sometimes people do), but inaction cannot be taken as a sign of a lack of preparation. We know exactly how to prepare ourselves to participate, even as we wait in silence.

Let us sort out what we claim to be essential and optional in the experience of film. Viewers, we believe, fall naturally into the role of side-participants when the movie starts up. At that point, however they have some control over how hard they wish to work. We suspect that idiosyncratic properties of individual films will determine the extent to which the modal viewer becomes not only a side-participant, but one who is ready to plunge in to participate and respond at any given moment. The viewer has all the requisite skills: local circumstances will determine the extent to which they are put to use. We will now demonstrate how the use of these cognitive skills leads to *as if* responses.

As If Responses and *As If* Emotions

To put *as if* responses in an appropriate context, we will begin by offering a sketch of a taxonomy of the types of responses viewers may have as side-participants. Let us imagine a situation in which a character in a film—someone to whom we've become at least a bit attached—is in a taxi, trying to make it to an airport in time for an important flight. In what variety of ways does the viewer respond to this moment?

A Taxonomy of Audience Responses

A first type of viewer response, *inferencing,* will arise in part because the camera picks and chooses which aspects of the scene are kept in focus. We might, for example, have a sequence that alternates roughly between showing the passenger encouraging the cab driver to hurry, and a long shot of the taxi in traffic. To unite these alternations of shots, viewers will have to be capable of drawing appropriate inferences about continuity. Some categories of inferences will be familiar from other domains of cognitive processing: viewers wouldn't be particularly surprised if a waiter appeared in a scene set at a restaurant or if blood spurted from the chest of a criminal at whom a gun was fired. Other types of inference processes might be put to greater use in film circumstances, as in our example of two views of a speeding taxi. Although inferential processing is essential, we don't imagine it to be a major aspect of the phenomenology of film going: viewers will rarely have conscious access to their experiences of filling gaps.

We would, by contrast, claim regular conscious access to a second category of responses, *participatory responses.* David Albritton and Richard Gerrig coined this phrase, and *p-responses* for short, to stand in opposition to the category of inferences.[14] Many of the responses readers and viewers produce do not fill gaps—witness "Pull the trigger!" Film seems a particularly potent medium for eliciting p-responses because there are so many junctures at which, for example, the director can control point of view to warn us that danger lurks nearby—"Don't go in the water!" "Don't go through that door!" If we have in mind what a frantic drive to an airport could be like, we could imagine that our experience of the scene would be filled with mental cries of "Look out for that truck!" and "Why didn't you run that red light?" and "Quick, jump out of the cab!"

Within this category of p-responses, we can specially separate out *as if* responses. By *as if* responses we will mean those that approximate the types of responses viewers would have were they really participating in the film's events. All the examples of p-responses we have given so far meet this criterion. We might be more likely to let the voice be more than mental if we had a real-life opportunity to yell, "Don't go through that door," but the impulse has an identical origin in both circumstances.

Not all p-responses are *as if* responses. Some are comments by the viewer on the experience of the movie—"This would be a better film if John Williams's score weren't so grandiose" or "How come the good guy is able to outrun the machine guns?" In these cases, the viewer is functioning as a critic, addressing the question, "How could this movie be changed to enhance my experience?" In a sense, these other types of p-responses are comments on the film's ability to generate and sustain *as if* responses. They reflect participation in the experience of the narrative—a more distanced stance—rather than participation directly in the narrative.[15] When a film actively engenders such p-responses, it may, in fact, be quite difficult for viewers to sustain their *as if* participation.

Whenever a film is of sufficient quality that the viewer is not driven from the narrative world, *as if* responses will be a major category of audience response. As we shall now see, *as if* responses yield discernible emotional experiences.

The Origins of *As If* Emotions

Return again to the hero hurtling toward the airport. How upset will you feel on his behalf if he misses his plane? Clearly this is an unpleasant outcome, but what emotion is added to the situation by seeing it unfold over time? Consider this scenario:

> Mr. Crane and Mr. Tees were scheduled to leave the airport on different flights, at the same time. They traveled from town in the same limousine, were caught in a traffic jam, and arrived at the airport 30 minutes after the scheduled departure time of their flights.
> Mr. Crane is told his flight left on time.
> Mr. Tees is told his flight was delayed, and just left five minutes ago.
> Who is more upset?[16]

When college students were asked this question, 96 percent of them responded that Mr. Tees would be more upset. To explain this result, Daniel Kahneman and Amos Tversky invoked the *simulation heuristic*. They suggested that "there appear to be many situations in which questions about events are answered by an operation that resembles the running of a simulation model."[17] The point, in this context, is that readers can imagine things that might have been different, such that Mr. Tees could have made his airplane. Here, then, we have a dissociation between an emotion attendant on an outcome and an emotion attendant on the unfolding of that outcome.

We can see this dissociation even more forcefully in circumstances in which there is a discrepancy between the objective valence of outcomes and how readers imagine characters who experience those outcomes would feel. Consider a study in which subjects read scenarios that ended with near-positive and near-negative outcomes. Joel Johnson invented stories in which characters went through a series of events.[18] In one story, a character came very close to a desirable, positive outcome:

> Chris learned that his family had just won a grand prize in the sweepstakes, but later discovered that the letter informing them of the prize was fraudulent and had been disclaimed by sweepstakes officials. To compensate for the inconvenience, however, sweepstakes officials sent the family $25.00 and a certificate for a free dinner at a local Mexican restaurant.[19]

In another version, Chris narrowly escaped a tragic, negative outcome:

> Chris was stricken with a critical illness, from which his doctors believed that full recovery was doubtful. Two days later, however, he was "resting comfortably in his hospital bed," recovering fully from what was finally diagnosed as food poisoning. He was informed that he had "escaped death by a hair."[20]

Johnson asked his subjects (each of whom read one version of the story) to imagine themselves in these situations and to rate how lucky, happy, and satisfied they would feel. On all three dimensions, subjects who assumed Chris's role gave higher ratings after near-negative outcomes than after near-positive outcomes. These ratings were clearly more sensitive to the unfolding of the events than to the actual polarity of the outcome.

We would expect film viewers often to experience emotions related to the value of an outcome. We define *as if* emotions, however, to be the special emotional experiences that arise as a function of participating, of generating *as if* responses, in the unfolding of the action toward a particular outcome. The experimental data we have just cited support the claim that we will often not be able to predict the exact form of the *as if* emotion by only knowing the outcome. Thus, in circumstances in which we feel prompted to yell, "Don't go in the water," we may feel fear, because we worry that the skinny-dippers will not survive their frolic, or anger, because they go ahead and take the plunge, or superiority, because we believe that the narrative will soon provide evidence that our advice ought to have been heeded.[21] If the skinny-dippers are saved, fear can turn into relief; if they meet a great white shark, superiority could turn quickly to guilt. In this way, a whole series of emotions can result from participation, rather than from an outcome itself.

Some Preliminary Data

We have begun to gather empirical evidence to support our account of *as if* responses and emotions. Earlier research on simulation has not focused on the unfolding of an outcome. We wished to demonstrate more directly the emotional consequences of participation. For practical reasons, we have begun by using written rather than film materials. We sought to create a situation in which readers could be made to provide evidence of a psychological response that would be most likely to arise only if they were acting as if they had actively participated in narrative events. We turned to the emotion of *guilt* as our target response. Our prediction was straightforward: Readers who committed themselves to wishing for an action that (later) had unfavorable consequences would manifest *as if* guilt about that preference.

Our experimental materials were based on a short story by Thom Jones. Participants in the experiment were given the following instructions:

> The following pages provide excerpts from Thom Jones's short story "The Pugilist at Rest." Please read each excerpt and then answer the accompanying questions.

They then read the first excerpt from Thom Jones's story, given in Table 18.1.

Table 18.1. Experimental Materials

First Excerpt

["Hey Baby" obtained his nickname because his Marine sergeant read a letter to his girlfriend aloud that began "Hey, Baby!"]

Hey Baby was not in the Marine Corps for very long. The reason for this was that he started in on my buddy, Jorgeson. Jorgeson was my main man, and Hey Baby started calling him Jorgepussy and began harassing him and pushing him around. He was sort of down on Jorgeson because whenever we were taught some sort of combat maneuver or tactic, Jorgeson would say, under his breath, "You could get *killed* if you try that." Or, "Your ass is *had* if you do that." You got the feeling that Jorgeson didn't think loving the American flag and defending democratic ideals in Southeast Asia were all that important. But even when I was pissed at Jorgeson, I still knew he'd save *my* ass if it came to that.

But Hey Baby just thought "Jorgepussy." And then, about two weeks before boot camp was over, when we were running out to the parade field for drill with our rifles at port arms, all assholes and elbows, I saw Hey Baby give Jorgeson a nasty shove with his M-14. Jorgeson nearly fell down as the other recruits scrambled out to the parade field, and Hey Baby gave a short, malicious laugh. Hey Baby was a large and fairly tough young man who liked to displace his aggressive impulses on Jorgeson, but he wasn't as big or as tough as I.

Second Excerpt

I ran past Jorgeson and caught up to Hey Baby; he picked me up in his peripheral vision, but by then it was too late. I set my body so that I could put everything into it, and with one deft stroke I hit him in the head with the butt of my M-14. It was not exactly a premeditated crime, although I had been laying to get him. My idea before this had simply been to lay my hands on him, but now I had blood in my eye. I was a skilled boxer, and I knew the temple was a vulnerable spot; the human skull is otherwise hard and durable, except at the base. There was a sickening crunch, and Hey Baby dropped into the ice plants along the side of the company street.

The entire platoon was out on the parade field when the house mouse screamed at the assistant D.I., who rushed back to the scene of the crime to find Hey Baby crumpled in a fetal position in the ice plants with blood all over the place. There was blood from the scalp wound as well as a froth of blood emitting from his nostrils and his mouth. Blood was leaking from his right ear. Did I see skull fragments and brain tissue? It seemed that I did.

We intended the first part of this story, as perhaps did Jones, to make it very likely that readers would want Hey Baby to be punished in some way. Roughly one hundred subjects were explicitly asked what we will call the *commitment question* after reading this first excerpt:

Would you like to see the narrator help Jorgeson get back at Hey Baby?

Subjects were asked to circle a number on a scale of 1 to 9, ranging from "definitely no" to "definitely yes." A second group of one hundred readers responded on the same scale to a *neutral* question:

From what you've read so far, do you think Jorgeson will make an effective Marine?

Readers were pretty much neutral on the question of Jorgenson's fitness, with a mean response at 5.06 on the 9-point scale, but were more interested in seeing revenge accomplished, with a mean response of 6.47. Recall that these ratings were given just after readers read the first story excerpt.

As the second excerpt in Table 18.1 shows, the subjects who voted for action were rewarded—but with the unexpected negative consequence that Hey Baby was done extraordinary harm (in fact, we amended Jones's story in this excerpt to make it a little *less* vicious than the original). What kinds of responses might readers have now? If our hypothesis is correct, readers who committed themselves to wanting revenge will feel guilty, in a way, given how badly things turned out. We might expect to be able to capture that guilt, by comparison to the neutral readers, by asking them a question that allows emotions to hold sway.

After they read the second excerpt, we asked the readers three questions that were designed to assess their perceptions, opinions, and feelings about the story events. On the perception and opinion questions, the two groups did not differ. When asked, How likely do you think it is that Hey Baby will recover?, the commitment group responded on average 2.37 and the neutral group 2.46 (1 = highly unlikely; 9 = highly likely). When asked, Do you approve of what the narrator did?, the commitment group responded 2.67 and the neutral group 2.79 (1 = definitely no; 9 = definitely yes). In this latter case, there was a modest but reliable correlation ($r = 0.26$) between responses on the commitment question and responses on this opinion question—indicating that readers who had voted more strongly for revenge were also more likely to approve of the narrator's actions.

A difference between the two groups' ratings emerged forcefully, as we expected it would, when we looked at reports of feelings. Both groups were asked to respond to the question, How much do you hope that Hey Baby will recover (1 = not at all; 9 = very much)? To this question, the commitment group gave responses that were reliably higher, 6.24, than the neutral group, 4.97. Our explanation for this result is straightforward. We believe that readers who had committed themselves to revenge felt guilty when the narrator's actions had such dire consequences. When assessed on an emotional dimension, "hope," that guilt produced a more polarized response.

Note that we do not have direct evidence for this mediation through guilt. We can only safely conclude that something about explicitly considering the possibility of revenge led our commitment readers to hope more for Hey Baby's recovery. In the vaguest terms, *something* about participating changed their emotional reactions. At the same time, if we are correct that the commitment readers *were* feeling guilt, then that feeling of guilt was not merely inherited from the narrator via identification. Inspection of the second story excerpt in Table 18.1 will confirm that the narrator seems rather pleased with the injury he caused: "Did I see skull fragments and brain tissue? It seemed that I did." This hint of glee may shock readers, and may, in fact, contribute to overall feelings of negative emotionality. Because, in any case, there is no model for guilt within the story, to the extent that readers *do* experience guilt they are doing so on their own account. We would expect to find exactly such dissociations among the emotional responses, for example, of real-life conversationalists. We believe, therefore, that these data support the general contention that readers produce emotions that mimic those they might feel were they bona fide side-participants.

What seems less than optimal about this preliminary study, however, is that we had to ask our readers for an explicit commitment. If our account of *as if* emotions is correct, we would expect that the story itself would put each reader in a frame of mind in which he or she would be primed for revenge. It is, in fact, possible that the neutral group did wish for Hey Baby's comeuppance. We cannot test this assertion because we have no appropriate baseline with which to compare their "hope" ratings (that is, we would need a group who, perhaps, had been otherwise made to hope that the revenge would not take place). In fact, a much more elegant way to test our hypothesis would be with film. We turn now to that claim.

How Film Commands Commitment

Let us return to the climactic moments of *Lethal Weapon II*. What the camera shows us at the critical juncture is a full-screen view of the gun: a finger on a trigger. Earlier we claimed that the modal filmgoer would feel compelled to, at least, think very loudly, "Pull the trigger!" But why? We claim that the sequence of shots brings about a type of commitment. We can evaluate this claim with respect to two possible alternate versions of the sequence:

- Imagine that at the first instant we saw Glover and his gun, he pulled the trigger. The viewer would have insufficient time to develop the preference, "Pull the trigger!"
- Imagine that the image's focus stayed directly on Glover's face. Viewers might still think about what Glover was thinking about (that is,

whether to shoot the bad guy), but it seems much less likely that they would formulate a thought as specific as, "Pull the trigger!"

In the first instance, the director manipulates timing—something that is easy to do in a film, but relatively hard to do in a novel—to allow or disallow a certain range of thoughts. In the second instance, the director manipulates the specificity of focus—again, something that is done easily in film—to increase or decrease the probability that the audience will have specific thoughts. The timing and focus of the original sequence in *Lethal Weapon II* appear to be designed exactly so that viewers will commit themselves to a preference that Glover fire the gun.

As a final vantage point on this claim, let's consider one other alternative reality:

• Imagine that, after the original sequence of shots, Glover *did not* pull the trigger. Wouldn't viewers be shocked, and perhaps even angry?

Once again, we can decompose this putative response of anger into two different sources. We would suspect, first, that viewers would be angry because Glover had failed to do the right thing. That is, the anger attaches to the outcome. Second, we would expect viewers to be angry because Glover did not do what they wanted him to do. This latter type of anger attaches to participation in the making of the outcome and is the *as if* emotion. Given the actual ending—Glover pulls the trigger—we would claim that the modal viewer felt both outcome satisfaction and *as if* satisfaction.

The purpose of our experiment was, of course, to tease apart the two types of emotion—by having the desired outcome lead to negative consequences. It should now be clear how film would allow us to improve on our original design. Rather than stopping our readers and requiring them to make a commitment or not, we could change the sequence or timing of shots so that viewers would be led with more or less force to entertain the thought "Revenge!" As experimental psychologists, we would almost certainly still want to stop the movie and ask the viewers how much they hoped Hey Baby would recover. Were we, instead, gifted auteurs we could likely think of a way to exploit the *as if* guilt to draw the viewer more deeply into our narrative world.

We can turn back to a final excerpt from one such gifted auteur's words to provide a second example of the power of the camera to command commitment. Hitchcock is describing the way in which the climax of *Young and Innocent* unfolds:[22]

Toward the end of the picture the young girl is searching for the murderer, and she discovers an old tramp who has seen the killer and can identify him. The only clue is that the man has a nervous twitch of the eyes.

So the girl dresses up the old tramp in a good suit of clothes and she takes him to this big hotel where a *thé dansant* is in progress. There are lots of people there, and the tramp says, "Isn't it ridiculous to try to spot a pair of twitching eyes in a crowd of this size."

Just then, right on that line of dialogue, I place the camera in the highest position, above the hotel lounge, next to the ceiling, and we dolly down, right through the lobby, into the big ballroom, and past the dancers, the bandstand, and the musicians, right up to a close-up of the drummer. The musicians are all in blackface and we stay on the drummer's face until his eyes fill the screen. And then, the eyes twitch. The whole thing was done in one shot.

The viewers now know who and where the murderer is. If they are participating in the movie in the ordinary way, they are committed to passing on the knowledge the camera has allowed them to acquire. Hitchcock, by his own description, provides a rich set of circumstances in which this commitment can be played out: the twitching murderer is smoking in an alley when the police hurry by; his nervousness leads to telltale difficulties keeping rhythm with his drum; he faints and the heroine begins to administer first aid. In each instance, we can imagine the viewer's internal voice crying out "The smoking man is the murderer!" or "Listen to the telltale drumming" or "You've got to notice his twitching eyes!" As each cry is ignored, we would expect the viewer to have a striking *as if* experience of powerlessness. The murderer's unmasking should satisfy the viewers both because goodness has triumphed and because their knowledge has finally been vindicated.

Conclusions

Viewers bring some range of cognitive processes to the experience of film. Our intention has been to characterize those processes in two ways. First, we developed analogies from conversation to suggest that viewing engages at least the processes of side-participation and potentially other processes of active silence. Second, we described the products of these processes, most specifically the *as if* responses that give texture to the claim that viewing means participating. When our inner voice call out "Pull the trigger!" it does not take that commitment lightly.

NOTES

1. François Truffaut, *Hitchcock*, rev. ed. (New York: Simon and Schuster, 1984), p. 73.
2. Ibid., p. 269.
3. A theory of side-participation in conversation is given by Herbert H. Clark and Thomas B. Carlson in "Hearers and Speech Acts," *Language* 58 (1982): 332–73.
4. Ibid.
5. A detailed case for reading as side-participation is given in Richard J. Gerrig, *Experiencing Narrative Worlds* (New Haven: Yale University Press, 1993).
6. Authors, of course, will sometimes be wrong—or become wrong as a work ages—in their expectations about readers' knowledge. They might also have accurate expectations that some, but not all, members of their audience will be accurately informed of their intentions.

7. Once again we caution that the viewers' general (tacit) expectations that they are side-participants does not preclude the possibility that the film will occasionally make overhearers of them. We are not, in any sense, suggesting that the meaning of films is always transparent. We are, instead, making a claim about the general repertory of cognitive processes that viewers bring to the experience of film.

We suspect, in any case, that film viewers will experience smaller numbers of circumstances in which they will *never* know the true meaning of utterances than will ordinary conversationalists. Consider a scene in which some unknown woman rushes in and says, to a second stranger, "I did it!" In real life it is quite possible that you'll never know what she did. In a film, it seems likely that, over time, the identity of her deed will be revealed.

8. For a review and thorough critique of these positions see Noël Carroll, *Mystifying Movies: Fads and Fallacies in Contemporary Film Theory* (New York: Columbia University Press, 1988).

9. Side-participants and overhearers also can become speakers. We will refer solely to addressees only for ease of exposition.

10. Harvey Sacks, Emanuel A. Schegloff, and Gail Jefferson, "A Simplest Systematics for the Organization of Turn-Taking for Conversation," *Language* 50 (1974): 708.

11. G. W. Beattie and P. J. Barnard, "The Temporal Structure of Natural Telephone Conversations (Directory Assistance Calls)," *Linguistics* 17 (1979): 213–29.

12. For several essays on collaboration in conversation see Herbert H. Clark, *Arenas of Language Use* (Chicago: University of Chicago Press, 1992).

13. We are assuming that the film viewer is not sufficiently familiar with *Casablanca* to have simply memorized the dialogue.

14. David W. Allbritton and Richard J. Gerrig, "Participatory Responses in Prose Understanding," *Journal of Memory and Language* 30 (1991): 603–26.

15. Gerrig, *Experiencing Narrative Worlds.*

16. Daniel Kahneman and Amos Tversky, "The Simulation Heuristic," in *Judgment under Uncertainty: Heuristics and Biases,* ed. Daniel Kahneman, Paul Slovic, and Amos Tversky (New York: Cambridge University Press, 1982), p. 203.

17. Ibid., p. 201.

18. Joel T. Johnson, "The Knowledge of What Might Have Been: Affective and Attributional Consequences of Near Outcomes," *Personality and Social Psychology Bulletin* 12 (1986): 51–62.

19. Ibid., pp. 54–55.

20. Ibid., p. 55.

21. It is often the case that viewers' advice appears to be heeded. When, for example, we (mentally) warn a character not to go through a door and he or she subsequently turns back, it will feel as if the character paid attention. In this light, *as if* responses, and participation in general, can be highly reinforcing.

22. Truffaut, *Hitchcock,* p. 114.

PART FOUR

HISTORY AND ANALYSIS

Since the 1970s, many energetic scholars have revised our thinking about the history of cinema. This section presents eight essays which reflect the richness of contemporary historical research. In each case, the author poses concrete questions which open onto broader theoretical or historiographic issues.

The section begins with two essays on the American film industry. Douglas Gomery's "Toward a New Media Economics" outlines several obstacles to understanding the structure and conduct of the Hollywood studios over history and particularly in the present. His call for a performance-based study of corporate activity is answered by Tino Balio's study of Columbia pictures. Balio traces how Columbia, in an effort to become a major company, acted carefully, systematically devoting resources in ways which would make it competitive with more prosperous studios.

While Gomery and Balio examine industry conduct on a large scale, the two following essays show how particular films can be illuminated by historical research. Richard Maltby's study of ambivalences within a key scene of *Casablanca* lead him to exhume studio production documents, reconstruct debates with the Hays Office, and conjecture how different spectators, then and now, handle gaps and indeterminancies presented by classical films. From another perspective, Donald Crafton questions the canard that *The Jazz Singer*, as the "first talking feature," was a stupendous success. Crafton also reflects upon how, facing a fragmentary record and the agendas of popular journalism, the historian can make inferences about audience response.

The four essays which conclude the book consider problems of writing national and international histories of cinema. Michael Walsh critically examines Fredric Jameson's account of cinema as a manifestation of postmodernity. Walsh suggests that a more adequate history will be sensitive to the specificity of cultural processes and of particular filmmaking traditions. Such a specificity also forms the object of Donald Kirihara's attention in his discussion of Japanese cinema of the 1930s. By reviewing the literature on Japanese cinema and by scrutinizing a key passage in Mizoguchi's *Story of the Last Chrysanthemum*, Kirihara arrives at a proposal for considering national cinema traditions as varied, norm-bound practices.

The possibilities of national filmmaking also form the basis of Mette Hjort's essay. How well, she asks, do current conceptions of identity politics capture the efforts of "minor cinemas" to gain wide audiences? Hjort explores the prospects for films which "leverage" themselves to international prominence while still retaining cultural specificity. Finally, Vance Kepley discusses how studies of historically situated reception can enrich our understanding of cinema as a social process. In the course of his essay, he meshes a critique of "apparatus theory" with detailed examination of the routines of film exhibition in the bustling, occasionally rowdy atmosphere of Soviet workers' clubs.

19

Toward a New
Media Economics

Douglas Gomery

Hollywood has just undergone a complete reorganization. Since 1984 we have seen new owners purchase the six major studios and begin to tackle the vexing problem of how best to deal with the coming electronic superhighway. These and other industrial changes prompt us to look back and reexamine how scholars have treated Hollywood as an industry. The contemporary emergence of media conglomerates yields fresh ways to examine not only the immediate past but also the entire history of Hollywood. If we do so, we notice certain trends at work that were not apparent to earlier generations of historians—trends which led up to the state of the industry today.

In addition, we can better account for some of the features about the past that were ignored or misunderstood. We should aim to understand not just Wall Street financing, industry structure, and corporate behavior, but also proper performance. In the spirit of David Hackett Fischer, I want to identify and remove five important roadblocks which stand in the way of our understanding of the long-powerful Hollywood film industry. Only by removing these long-held myths can we proceed to a truly general understanding of cinema. We can do better; we should cease blundering about our business; we should establish better arguments for something as important as the Hollywood industry.[1]

Myth Number I

"The history of the U.S. film industry is best understood apart from the developments in other mass media industries, such as popular music, radio, and television."

The year 1930 marked the end of the industry's manufacture of a single product. For more than sixty years Hollywood corporations have done more than produce money-making movies. During the late 1920s Hollywood companies took over the popular music business. In the 1950s they added television production and theme parks. For more than a generation Hollywood corporations have operated as diverse industrial operations.

We should cease lamenting the coming of television and recognize that for nearly a half century most people have watched most films on television. We may regret the inferior image, but to Hollywood the coming of television has proven to be the most significant technical addition in industry history.

Indeed, the emergence of various forms of television has greatly expanded revenues. Since 1955 the portion of total monies entering the system from theatrical box office has been constantly shrinking. In the United States today, the expected revenues from box office sales account for less than one-fifth of total revenues. Yet because the data for revenues generated from presentations on television are difficult to come by, we regularly ignore the "other" 80 percent and focus our attention on theatrical box-office take.

The Hollywood feature film can be run and rerun. A library of features offers a stream of revenues long after the cost of creation has been fully written off, meaning that with little in the way of added cost, any new revenues generate pure profit.

The Hollywood feature film of the late twentieth century can create a popular culture phenomenon. This is so-called ancillary merchandising: toys to theme parks, recorded music to books, stores in shopping malls to sports teams. (Disney named its Anaheim hockey franchise the Mighty Ducks after a motion picture from its studio.) With a blockbuster, revenues from these ancillary markets alone can top the revenues from the now various theatrical and TV sources and seemingly go on forever.

A motion picture can become a billion-dollar asset. There is no reason to think that the new world of technology might change that; it can only add to the value of the successful blockbuster. And since all blockbusters begin in movie theaters, then it would seem, ironically, that the world of five hundred channels only enhances the value of movie theaters. Figures from first-run theaters serve as rough predictors of future revenues, and because of that "voting booth" function, the movie theater will never disappear.

At the heart of all the billion-dollar mergers which have created today's Hollywood stands the realization that this land rush for the takeover of five hundred channels begins at Hollywood's doorstep. The new wonderland of video will make money for those who own the means of production. Without libraries of moving images and regular creation of new visual narratives, the promised electronic superhighway will simply be like fancy plumbing without water.

Myth Number 2

"The studio system of the 1930s and 1940s offers us the most important era for industry study. Then filmmaking was pure, not confused and compromised by that evil of all evils—television."

The studio era was important, but it represents only one of four fundamental eras in the history of the Hollywood cinema industry. The activities during the 1930s and 1940s were important, but we ought to be careful not to overestimate the typicality of one epoch, unless we spell out useful criteria by which to demonstrate that one era was indeed superior to another.

The motion picture industry in the United States grew from its origins during the final years of the nineteenth century to an oligopolistic consolidation amidst the coming of sound in the late 1920s. This is the first era, and much new and exciting research has illuminated this period, but it has sometimes been tainted by an overlay of sadness; in the end the industry prevented what "might have been"—a working-class audience served by progressive filmmakers. Instead capitalist Hollywood took an overt profit-maximizing structure.

Next came the era of the studio system. This epoch has been valorized and well analyzed because here Hollywood functioned as a unified system. David Bordwell, Janet Staiger, and Kristin Thompson have carefully examined aspects of this system.[2] So have I.[3]

Yet what we have done is "easy" when compared to examining the origins of the Hollywood industry or analyzing later industrial developments. The studio era had a defined beginning, middle, and end. The industry was logically organized, transformed only by intrusions from the outside. The studio era began with the coming of sound, an innovation developed outside the industry. Sound caused a crest in attendance. This surge was followed by a decline in demand caused by the Great Depression. The studio era came to a close after World War II. The Hollywood industry was transformed by the Paramount antitrust decrees of 1948, (suburbanization, the baby boom), and the emergence of a moving-image rival, television. Hollywood was turned upside down. By 1960 filmmaking was an ancillary business; Hollywood had become the world's television factory.

The third era starts with the coming of television; that much seems clear enough. But when did it end? If ever? This issue of closure presents a vexing problem. Let me take a stand. The three-network world of television began to change with the coming of cable television and home video; then we began the fourth era of industrial history. I date this from the mid- to late 1980s. During the mid- to late 1980s we saw a transformation of ownership. I argue that outsiders recognized a new industrial era and bought in. The owners and operators of the third era, led by Lew Wasserman at Universal, cashed in and let others grapple with the future new world of video, of five hundred cable TV channels, of movies-on-demand.

This fourth era might be said to have commenced in 1986 when Rupert Murdoch took over Twentieth Century Fox (and dropped the hyphen), at the same moment Michael Eisner, Frank Welles, and Jeffrey Katzenberg began to transform and rebuild the Walt Disney Corporation. At the end of the 1980s Japan invaded: Sony took over Columbia Pictures, and Matsushita acquired MCA. Time and Warner merged. Viacom took over Paramount. Thus early in

1994 all six of the major Hollywood studios had changed ownership and had begun to position their companies for the expected battle over the information and entertainment electronic superhighway.

This fourth era has seen even tighter control by fewer Hollywood studios. The studio era of the 1930s and 1940s is called one of near monopoly, but the situation of control by a handful of corporations more accurately describes the market structure of today. During the past decade we have seen a number of small Hollywood enterprises challenge the major studios, only to lose millions of dollars and declare bankruptcy. The corporate shells of Orion and New World are now marginal at best. Even once powerful MGM/United Artists is poised to go out of business.

The Hollywood industry today consists of but six multinational media conglomerates: Disney, Fox's Twentieth Century Fox, Matsushita's MCA/Universal, Viacom's Paramount, Sony's Columbia, and Time-Warner's Warner Bros.

Myth Number 3

"The Hollywood industry, past and present, is controlled by financial institutions. There is no reason to do any further analysis. As with all aspects of capitalism in the United States, the mass media industries are shaped by forces found in the investment banking community, commonly known as Wall Street."

This argument, known as "finance capitalism," addresses the important trend of long-term industrial concentration. And this version of Wall Street control provides an important and vital hook by which Marxists frequently assume direct linkage to the economic base. No work necessary; the Hollywood industry simply functions as another part of capitalism controlled by Wall Street. This said, the analyst is able to move on to considerations of individual films and filmmakers.

In the Hollywood industry by the mid-1930s it became J. P. Morgan and John D. Rockefeller who held "the balance of power within the eight major studios and their affiliated theater and distribution channels."[4] F. D. Klingender and Stuart Legg, in their 1937 book *Money behind the Screen*, popularized the "Morgan and Rockefeller" hypothesis. Klingender and Legg appropriated the analysis from Anna Rochester's *Rulers of America: A Study in Finance Capitalism*, published in February of 1936. Rochester's research on the Hollywood industry was based on examination of data generated from studies by the U.S. government, principally commissioned for helping set in place the regulatory mechanisms of the National Recovery Act.[5]

Anna Rochester was inspired by very important writings in the Marxist tradition. Rudolph Hilferding's *Das Finanzkapital*, which was published in 1910, led V. I. Lenin to write, in *Imperialism: The Highest Stage of Capi-*

talism, that in decadent capitalism, banks and financiers had taken control. Indeed for Lenin, on the eve of the Russian Revolution, financial control provided one of the five pillars of modern capitalism. Rochester skillfully translated this to mean Morgan and Rockefeller, and so she was able to mesh the Hollywood industry with mainstream American capitalism and affix the blame for the Great Depression on it.[6]

Yet it seems to me that even Marxists do not believe in finance capitalism any more. "Finance capitalism" is a theoretical product of history, a proposed explanation of the first years of the twentieth century. Contemporary work suggests that applying finance capitalism to modern economics in the United States is no longer helpful. Furthermore, I maintain that finance capitalism only misleads us in analyzing Hollywood in the 1930s.

Marxist economists Paul Baran and Paul Sweezy have argued that the Great Depression signaled the close of the era of finance capitalism and the commencement of a corporate hegemony. The dominant Hollywood corporations have long outlived their bankers. Baran and Sweezy argue that after the 1930s bankers took on more and more secondary roles in the economy of the United States. I agree; from the studio era onward, the principal unit for study of the Hollywood industry ought to be the corporation.[7]

There is sometimes corporate cooperation. We find this in the case of the Motion Picture Association of America. This is a classic trade association. In this forum, when the members of the oligopoly define a common interest, they act as one. We can appreciate the successes of the Motion Picture Association of America by watching the Hollywood oligopolists working together for the 1993 GATT talks, just as they cooperated sixty years earlier to form the "Hays Code." Indeed, successful industrial cooperation commenced with the negotiations required by the National Recovery Act.[8]

It is when the corporations do not act together and seem to compete that they offer the analyst a complex case. Neither a pure neoclassical model nor a Marxist model of financial capitalism is able to successfully reduce the case of the Hollywood industry to something straightforward and simple. The study of the Hollywood industry is as complex a case study as can be found in industrial economics: the modern corporation in an oligopolistic industrial setting.

Myth Number 4

"At least the locus of analytical action is straightforward. It rests in a single site, the Detroit of the movie business—Hollywood, California."

This has never been the case. This argument reduces the film industry from three functions (production, distribution, and presentation) to one, filmmaking. While production was largely centered in California, finance and distribution and exhibition operated far more widely. Yes, there have been instances of vertical integration, as with the case of extensive theater ownership during the 1930s and 1940s. But even then the vast majority of movie houses (more than 80 percent) were owned by independents based throughout the United States. Hollywood companies manifested control by owning the two thousand or so picture palaces, but few of the remaining twenty thousand motion picture theaters.

Taking the city of Hollywood as the single industrial center badly misleads. Since the close of World War I, power of the (Hollywood-based) U.S. film industry has rested principally with its absolute control over international distribution. Taking advantage of sizable economies of scale, the U.S. industry has long dominated bookings around the globe. Enterprising film companies have taken on the "Hollywood" colossus, often backed by their central governments, but the major firms continue to rule. Ask any filmmaker outside the United States.

The companies secure another enormous advantage because they can distribute films around the world at relatively low costs. With economies of scale Hollywood corporations have long been able to spread out over dozens of films and amortize multimillion dollar production budgets and the expenses of maintaining a global network of offices. That makes the per-film distribution costs far lower than competitors'.

Moreover, abroad Hollywood companies can formally work together free of the antitrust threats they face in the United States. Through various alliances individual foreign film companies do not simply face a Warner Bros. or Twentieth Century Fox, but the two companies (sometimes three or more) working in tandem. Book films from us, under our terms, or lose the chance at any Hollywood blockbuster.

Since the 1920s Hollywood has held on to its considerable economic power through control and exploitation supported by worldwide distribution. And all this power is accumulated far from the studios in Southern California.

Yet recognizing a fundamental truth and studying it are two different matters. Proportionately few scholars have been inspired to research the core of Hollywood's power: its international control of distribution. Sadly, distribution is the least analyzed part of the industry; there are no fascinating movies to consider, only dry dull figures, both numerical and executive, defining and producing raw power. We need more of the important kind of work that Kristin Thompson and Ian Jarvie have given us.[9]

There is a third sector of the film business—the presentation of films. This too stretches far outside Los Angeles. Films appear in thousands of theaters and on millions of television sets around the world. Hollywood strives to make films that will appeal to people in all nations. The executives recognize that the monies that make cinema production possible enter the system through theaters and television.

And this presentation sector has seen considerable change in recent years in the United States. In 1972 Time introduced HBO and set off a revolution in cable TV. Today, with American Movie Classics, Turner Network Television, and a dozen more channels viewers can see Hollywood feature films twenty-four hours a day. In the 1980s came home video; people in the United States now rent an average of twenty thousand titles per day. Both these innovations threatened, experts told us, to kill the movie theater. Not so. Today more people are watching more films than ever in history, only through a variety of means of presentation. And the Hollywood conglomerates collect the bulk of these new revenues.

Today the Hollywood system is a center for media conglomerates, with positions in nearly all forms of mass media. Viacom's Paramount division, with its Simon and Schuster and Prentice-Hall units leading the way, is one of the leading book publishers in the world. MCA, Warner, and Sony are all leading producers of recorded music—in cassettes, compact discs, and whatever new forms will come. Time Warner is the world's leading publisher of magazines. Disney pioneered theme parks; MCA and Viacom's Paramount are industry leaders today as well. As part of Rupert Murdoch's News, Inc. empire, Fox is allied with leading newspapers around the world. And so on.

More media convergence is on the way. The U.S. media conglomerates presently stand at the center of the new world of video, computers, and interactivity. Within a decade our homes and workplaces will be wired with fiber optics and in will pour more of Hollywood's products, making the six media conglomerates more diversified and more powerful. As was the case with the coming of the videocassette recorder, the battle for control of the five hundred cable TV channels will be won by Hollywood. In the end the U.S. companies create what people around the world have long desired, and there is no reason to think that a new wire into the home will change that.

Myth Number 5

"Of course the major firms are as powerful as you say. The Hollywood industry has long ranked as one of the central industries in the United States economy."

As an industry, Hollywood has never been as important as we think it is. Yes, famous stars come from its studios, and we spend hours upon hours watching its visual narratives. Yet Hollywood has always been a small, albeit efficient, set of enterprises. The belief that it is a major industry is a product of Hollywood's own hype.

During the first historical era Hollywood did grow quickly, seemingly overnight. Studio leaders, impressed with their new fame and fortune, were soon claiming that they ran the fourth largest industry in the United States. They might have ranked this high with respect to the amount self-promoting publicity churned out, but not by more traditional measures. *Variety* told anyone who would listen that "Some fool, back in 1927 put it in the bonnet of the [United States] Chamber of Commerce that pictures were the fourth largest [industry in the United States]. Of course that is ridiculous."[10]

With the advent of the NRA in 1933, the U.S. government was required to name the top ten industries in the United States. The impartial experts at the NRA's Washington, D.C., headquarters figured the list (in no particular order) this way: textiles, coal, petroleum, steel, automobiles, lumber, garments, wholesale trade, retail trade, and construction. They ranked motion pictures fortieth! The NRA based its ranking on total revenues. In terms of total assets, the other common measure of industrial activity, the film industry ranked below number 50.[11]

In terms of economic scale, it took television to transform Hollywood. And as television has expanded to include cable TV and home video, the financial figures on Hollywood's balance sheets finally soared into the billions and billions of dollars.

Television expanded Hollywood's possible audiences. During the studio era there were an estimated twenty thousand movie houses with a capacity of ten to twelve million seats. Today there are ninety-five million homes with television sets plus twenty-five thousand video stores and twenty thousand movie screens. Virtually everyone has a television set; most of us have two or more. There are nearly 200 million television sets in use—at the beach, in automobiles, even strap-on models to accompany joggers.

As a business, television represents the core of a multibillion dollar stream of revenues. Yearly figures are impressive. Total advertising on television in the United States weighs in at over $30 billion. We correctly associate the bulk of television's business with the four major networks, which take in about $4 billion from prime time and billions more from morning, soap opera, news, and late-night offerings. Cable television chips in advertising revenues in excess of $3 billion, and we paid $2 billion for the privilege of watching the dozens of channels on cable TV.

And certain moments of television commerce generate mind-boggling financial figures. For example, advertisements during the 1993 Super Bowl (which NBC sold out a month in advance of kickoff) sold for $28,000 per second. Pepsi, Budweiser, and Gillette, among others, gladly paid this extraordinary tab because that annual spectacle gathers so many viewers in front of television sets that few billion-dollar corporations can pass up the chance to introduce new products to them. Apple successfully introduced its Macintosh personal computer during the 1984 game.

Television shows provide one of the biggest positive exports for a U.S. economy with a sizable trade deficit. The surplus figure reaches in excess of $4 billion per year, second only to the aerospace industry. Buying and selling television shows was a $25 billion business last year, principally in the domain of the major Hollywood studios.

Film figures, even with blockbusters, pale in comparison. The total U.S.

box-office take is a mere $5 billion, with a similar amount coming from overseas theaters. Again, it is with television that the numbers pile up. For example, in 1975 Hollywood's take from home video rental was nothing. By the 1990s total video rental topped $10 billion, with billions more from sales. The six major Hollywood studios share in the bulk of that new money.

The confusion over the true economic power of Hollywood comes with ownership. The movie studios totally control the production and distribution of feature films, and they control a sizable number of theaters. Yet even these empires generate revenue figures that pale beside a truly big business such as Exxon or General Motors. For as poorly as IBM has done in the 1990s, it could still take in all of Hollywood, and the mighty media conglomerates would remain but a small division.

True, Hollywood's products have always taken up large portions of our leisure time. Persons in the United States watch a lot of television and film, and once we pile up all those minutes into eight hours a day, the time commitment comes to 250 billion hours per year. If we take the average hourly wage in the United States to be about $10, we come to a couple of trillion dollars of time invested. But we do not pay that amount for this pleasure, and so the Hollywood industry remains a mid-sized, highly profitable set of enterprises.

Conclusion

Since about 1920 a handful of huge corporations have controlled the Hollywood industry, principally by maintaining a stranglehold on international distribution and skillfully adapting to new technologies for delivery. Today the mass media industry, controlled by a few diversified media conglomerates, is alive and well, a powerful but not overwhelming industrial force.

Above I have tried to position prior work. I end with a plea: we should move the study of the media industry to the center of our scholarly labors.

Forget the past. Marxist "critical studies" and "free market" empiricism both lack appeal because both ask us to analyze a subject when we already "know" a predetermined answer. Many leftist critics of the mass media assume an all-encompassing conspiracy of media monopolies. Yet a cursory examination of the contemporary radio and magazine industries undercuts such a monolithic image. There is no media monopolist in radio and magazines. Entry into those two industries is relatively cheap and easy. And this was also the case with cable TV, home video, and even film at the beginnings of those industries.

By contrast, conservative "free market" advocates assume that efficient operation represents the paramount and only goal for any enterprise, even one so vital to democracy and quality of life as mass communication and mass entertainment. Studying the economics of mass media as though one were simply dealing with ever-identical products offers far too narrow a perspective.

The new media economics needs to have at its core the study of changing conditions of industrial performance. In performance, ideology and the production of meaning intersect with Hollywood corporations. I favor a model for media economic analysis that not only examines questions of who owns the media (economic structure) and how these corporations make money (media conduct), but also looks closely at how well they do (industry performance). We should define the basic conditions of an industry, then seek to establish its major players (structure), then analyze the behavior governed by this structure (conduct), and finally evaluate the core questions of industry performance.

Simply listing "who owns the media" is not enough. One needs to understand how a particular form of industrial structure leads to certain corporate conduct. Recognizing that single-firm industries (for example, monopolies) are ruthless or that competitive industries lead to greater choice and more far-reaching expression offers only the first step in a long journey. We need a system for media economic analysis that moves from industrial structure to industrial conduct to industrial performance and back again. But in the end, understanding the performance of the mass media industries ought to be the ultimate step in our analysis.

For example, many lament that a handful of companies seem to forever dominate movie making in the United States. With a half dozen today, there is little room, many critics sadly note, for independent visions. This is a challenge on the level of performance. But we need then to analyze what techniques of corporate conduct and conditions of market structure led to this performance. It is one thing to recognize what we do not like, yet another to understand why this situation has come about.

The first step is simple enough: recognize what industry we are talking about. It may seem that we are approaching a world of "one mass medium," yet in economic reality there exist three defined types of media businesses. We should stop separating industries by technology (television vs. film and so on) and move to understand how they gather money.

On one hand there, are *direct payment* industries. For books, popular music, movies in theaters, and pay-per-view TV we as consumers pay for a product and the industry sells its wares directly to the public. On the other hand, there is the world of *indirect payment*. Here advertisers buy audiences. Over-the-air television and radio have long seemed to be "free" to the consumer. Of course they are not. Advertisers pay and that is why popular shows often go off the air and less-than-popular programming continue long runs.

Finally, there are the hybrids. These are mass media which have a small initial charge (for example, the subscription price of a newspaper or magazine), but rely upon advertising fees to generate the bulk of the revenues. Indeed, cable television is the current hot medium because we as consumers pay up front and then the cable companies also collect for advertising.

One important distinction emerges here for the study of industrial mass media conduct. With direct-payment industries customers are able to tele-graph their preferences directly. We can signal interest in certain specific products through bidding up prices and adding to the accumulation of total take.

For advertising-supported mass media, the client is the advertiser, not the viewer or listener or reader. Advertisers seek out mass media that can best help sell products or services; advertisers desire placement in mass media that can persuade customers who can be convinced to change their buying behavior and have the means to execute new purchases.

This three-part organization can help transform our understanding of Hollywood historiography. For example, the era of silent film seemed "pure" because there was no advertising. Apparently, if a motion picture was popular, then it was a hit. Today the industry seems far more "corrupt" because advertising plays a vital role; ads are inserted in cable TV showings and even at the beginning of the videotape version. A theatrical showing is not regularly interrupted by advertising; today's TV versions are, constantly.

We can now better deal with the bulk of Hollywood history, a history that since mid-century has had to deal with television and advertising. Surely it is no bold prediction that the five-hundred-channel-cable TV universe will be filled with advertising for its motion picture presentations. And it is through advertising that Hollywood links to nonmedia corporate America, moving beyond any simple assumption of moviemaking purity. Through advertising Hollywood interacts with and promotes true big business in the United States.

But throughout all eras of different revenue formation, Hollywood has survived and thrived. Given this success, it would seem that we will almost always have to choose among a handful of powerful mass media corporations. Idealists will never find that world of small direct-revenue creative entrepreneurs; nor will we have to long put up with a single evil monolith. Analysis of the mass media industry through time tells us that we ought to seek to understand corporate oligopolists and then find a way, through governmental action, to prod them to optimal performance. To hope for more is to hope for a world which will never come to be, for performance that will never happen.

NOTES

1. David Hackett Fischer, *Historians' Fallacies: Toward a Logic of Historical Thought* (New York: Harper and Row, 1970).

2. David Bordwell, Janet Staiger, and Kristin Thompson, *The Classic Hollywood Cinema* (New York: Columbia University Press, 1985).

3. Douglas Gomery, *The Hollywood Studio System* (New York: St. Martin's Press, 1986).

4. See the classic summary of this statement made by Lewis Jacobs in *The Rise of the American Film* (New York: Harcourt, Brace, 1939), p. 421. I do not single out Jacobs; many (including Jean Mitry, Arthur Knight, and Stephen Heath) have made this claim.

5. See F. D. Klingender and Stuart Legg, *Money Behind the Screen* (London: Lawrence and Wishart 1937), and Anna Rochester, *Rulers of America: A Study in Finance Capitalism* (New York: International Publishers, 1936).

6. See Rudolph Hilferding, *Finance Capital: A Study of the Latest Phase of Capitalist Development*, ed. Tom Bottomore, trans. Morris Watnick and Sam Gordon (London: Routledge and Kegan Paul, 1981), and V. I. Lenin, *Imperialism: The Highest Stage of Capitalism* (Peking: Foreign Language Press, 1975).

7. See Paul M. Sweezy, *The Theory of Capitalist Development* (New York: Monthly Review Press, 1970), and Paul A. Baran and Paul M. Sweezy, *Monopoly Capital* (New York: Monthly Review Press, 1966).

8. See, as a case study of how simple it is to examine the Hollywood industry when the dominant corporations work together, Douglas Gomery, "Hollywood, the National Recovery Administration, and the Question of on Monopoly Power," *Journal of the University Film Association* 31 (Spring 1979): 47–52.

9. See Kristin Thompson, *Exporting Entertainment: America in the World Film Market, 1907–1934* (London: British Film Institute, 1985); and Ian Jarvie, *Hollywood's Overseas Campaign: The North Atlantic Movie Trade, 1920–1950* (Cambridge: Cambridge University Press, 1992).

10. *Variety* (27 June 1933): 5.

11. See Daniel Bertrand's governmental reports: *The Motion Picture Industry—National Recovery Administration Evidence Study 25* (Washington, D.C., 1935), and *The Motion Picture Industry—National Recovery Administration Works Materials 34* (Washington, D.C.: Government Printing Office, 1936).

20

Columbia Pictures: The Making
of a Motion Picture Major,
1930–1943

Tino Balio

Starting out in Poverty Row, Columbia Pictures survived the battle for the theaters, the conversion to sound, and the Great Depression to emerge as a full-fledged member of the Hollywood establishment by 1934. In that year, giant film companies such as Paramount, Fox, and RKO had been dragged down by their theater chains into receivership or bankruptcy, but little Columbia won the respect of Wall Street by earning over $1 million in profits. In 1934, Columbia also won accolades from the critics by releasing two surprise hits, Victor Schertzinger's *One Night of Love,* a modern-dress operetta starring soprano Grace Moore, and Frank Capra's *It Happened One Night,* a screwball comedy starring Claudette Colbert and Clark Gable. *It Happened One Night* had the distinction of sweeping the top five Academy Awards—an achievement that has occurred only one other time in the history of the Oscars.[1]

The economic arena Columbia operated in was a virtual oligopoly dominated by the so-called Big Five—Loew's Inc. (MGM), Paramount Pictures, Warner Bros., Twentieth Century-Fox, and RKO. These companies were fully integrated—that is, they produced practically all the top-quality pictures, operated worldwide distribution networks, and owned large affiliated theater chains. Columbia, Universal Pictures, and United Artists were the Little Three. Columbia and Universal produced and distributed mostly low-budget pictures that played on the bottom half of double bills; United Artists functioned solely as a distributor for a small group of elite independent producers. These eight companies constituted the majors.

Although Columbia's role in the business during the studio system era is well established, the company's entrée into the Hollywood establishment has never been fully explored.[2] A definitive account of Columbia's escape from Poverty Row must wait until the studio opens its corporate records to researchers, but even without the benefit of primary sources much can be inferred about Columbia's development from articles in the trade press, movie reviews, and the occasional piece in business magazines. Using these sources,

I have isolated the goals that Columbia met in becoming a major motion picture company, which were: volume production, national distribution, first-run exhibition, a roster of one or two stars, and a few hits.

These goals were consonant with the business practices of the American film industry as it entered the era of big business in the twenties.[3] And as Columbia's entrée into the majors will demonstrate, these goals were mutually dependent. In practice, they had to be targeted pretty much in succession. As a result, this case study has certain implications for understanding the history of the film industry. First, the major studios had no preordained right to succeed. Each company had to acquire the pragmatic skills to carve a niche for itself in the market, to stabilize its operations, and to generate profits. Second, production had to be tailored first and foremost to the paying public. Producing films to suit the personal tastes of studio moguls, boards of directors, or financiers would have ruined a company. Third, the market presented companies with an array of options. All motion picture companies had the goal of profit maximization, but they chose different means to achieve that end.

To place some perspective on Columbia's maneuverings, I have compared its strategies to those of United Artists and Eagle-Lion Pictures. At first glance, such comparisons might seem odd; after all, UA was founded in 1919 by Mary Pickford, Charles Chaplin, Douglas Fairbanks, and D. W. Griffith exclusively as a distributor of high-quality independent productions, while Eagle-Lion didn't get started until after World War II and functioned partly as a distributor of British films. But a closer look will reveal that Columbia, United Artists, and Eagle-Lion confronted similar problems but solved them in different ways.

Poverty Row Beginnings

Columbia Pictures got its start as CBC Film Sales Company, which was founded by Jack Cohn, Joe Brandt, and Harry Cohn in 1919 to produce and market novelty shorts.[4] Jack Cohn and Joe Brandt handled sales and managed the business affairs of the company in New York, while Harry Cohn handled the production end in Hollywood where he operated out of a rented studio in Poverty Row. The American film industry had entered the era of big business during the twenties and CBC had to expand or perish. Gradually branching out into Westerns, comedies, and even a few inexpensive features, CBC signaled its growing aspirations by incorporating as Columbia Pictures on January 10, 1924.[5] The immediate objective was to take control of its own distribution. Severing its ties to states'-rights operators, Columbia acquired its first exchange in 1925; by 1929 it had established a national distribution network and by 1931 it had branched out into foreign markets. Meanwhile, Columbia shored up its feature film production by purchasing a small studio on Gower Street in Hollywood in 1926 and by signing new directors, most notably Frank Capra, soon after.

Despite such moves, Columbia found itself in a bind. The quality of its features was not good enough to secure regular bookings in the affiliated theater chains, and the quantity of its output could not meet the needs of smaller independent theaters. That Columbia overcame these barriers to entry was largely the handiwork of Harry Cohn. Columbia underwent a management shakeup in 1931 when Jack Cohn and Joe Brandt attempted to oust Harry Cohn from the company. The details of the attempted coup are unclear, but when Columbia financier A. H. Giannini of the Bank of America threw his support to Harry Cohn, Brandt retired from the company and sold his interest to Harry Cohn. Harry Cohn took over the presidency of the company while retaining his job as chief of production, which made him the only executive in the business to hold the two posts; Jack Cohn moved up to executive vice-president in charge of distribution and remained in New York. Harry and Jack Cohn retained most of the equity and voting stock in the company and operated Columbia as a family-run business throughout the studio system era.[6]

Reorganizing Production

Columbia, with its limited financial resources, could not compete with the Big Five in important first-run situations, but it could hope to tap the low end of the market by servicing unaffiliated theaters that changed bills up to three times a week. In contrast, United Artists targeted the high end of the market by distributing high-quality independent productions. During the thirties, UA released the films of Charles Chaplin, Samuel Goldwyn, Alexander Korda, Howard Hughes, and Twentieth Century Pictures, a production company operated by Joseph Schenck and Darryl Zanuck. All specialized in "prestige pictures," although not exclusively. Prestige pictures, by far the most popular production trend of the decade, did not constitute a genre. The term implied production values and treatment—a big-budget special based on a presold property, often as not a literary "classic," and tailored for top stars.[7] For Goldwyn, prestige meant adaptations of Pulitzer Prize winners (*Street Scene* [1931]) or novels written by Nobel laureates (*Arrowsmith* [1932]); for Korda, it meant historical biopics (*The Private Life of Henry VIII* [1933] and *Catherine the Great* [1934]); for Howard Hughes, it meant spectacular action films (*Hell's Angels* [1930]). United Artists released relatively few pictures each year, from fifteen to twenty, but the pictures earned the company a reputation as the Tiffany's of the industry.

To service the low end of the market, Columbia continued its policy of marketing shorts and Westerns. Columbia's roster of shorts was immense and consisted of Walt Disney's Mickey Mouse cartoons and Silly Symphonies, Krazy Cat cartoons, Eddie Buzzell's Bedtime Stories, Scrappy cartoons,

Screen Snapshots, and Sunrise Comedies, among others; its roster of Westerns included the Buck Jones and Tim McCoy series. Since the demand for these types of pictures was seemingly limitless, they provided a stable financial base for the company.

On this base, Columbia expanded feature film production. Harry Cohn modified studio operations in 1931 by converting from the central producer system to the producer-unit system and by delegating the day-to-day details of production to a group of associate producers.[8] Columbia released around thirty features a year from 1930 to 1934, when output rose to forty-three. The cause of this jump is not known exactly, but double features no doubt played a role.

Showing two pictures for the price of one was an old business practice. The shortage of talking pictures during the conversion to sound and the higher rentals they commanded stemmed the practice for a while, but the Depression gave double-featuring a boost. Independent theaters adopted the practice to break down the barriers of booking protection, which is to say, excessive clearances enjoyed by first-run theaters. Indies reasoned that if they could not present hit pictures in a timely manner to their patrons, they would offer quantity instead. Although the affiliated theater chains initially fought the practice, they too soon fell into line and by 1934, nearly every theater in competitive situations—the markets that generated the bulk of the box-office gross—showed double features. Double features essentially doubled the demand for product. Since the production facilities and talent of the Big Five limited the number of pictures they could produce, a gap existed that was soon filled by Columbia, Universal, and Poverty Row studios.

Surveying Columbia's releases from 1930 to 1934 reveals that the studio specialized in low-budget pictures having ordinary contemporary settings. Of the more than 150 features produced in this period, approximately 50 were dramas, 20 were crime/gangster pictures, 18 were mysteries, 10 were comedies, 9 were women's films, and 8 were action/adventures. In addition, the studio produced 15 Buck Jones and 7 Tim McCoy series Westerns. It is significant that the studio's roster included only 3 musicals and 2 horror films—genres that are expensive to produce because of their technical demands and special effects.

In its quest for profits, Columbia's policy was to produce economy models of class-A pictures. This meant following trends closely and relying heavily on remakes. Concerning the quality of a typical Columbia release, *Variety* had this to say: "Nothing new in a familiar story" (*Fugitive Lady* [1934]); "Makes no pretense of being above the split-week grade" (*The Sky Raiders* [1931]); and "Just a western with airplanes instead of horses" (*Air Hostess* [1933]). Concerning Columbia's cost-cutting techniques, *Variety* said of *Murder on the Roof* (1930): "The obvious inexpensive manner in which Columbia produced this all-talker won't be noticed by lay audiences. When a producing company can turn one out like this on this kind of dough, that company is bound to make money with it. So are the theatres playing it—certain theatres." Occasionally, a Columbia picture generated special appeal. *Variety* described *By Whose Hand?* (1932) as follows: "This Columbia [picture] is the answer to the grind house exhib's prayer. It is a vigorous melodrama, loaded with climaxes and speed, trimly played and expertly produced for the lesser grade house."[9] Occasionally, pictures like *By Whose Hand?* might qualify as programmers, which meant they could fill either the top or bottom half of a bill, depending on the genre, location of the theater, and audience.[10]

Expanding Distribution

Expanding feature film production required an efficient distribution system, since the two areas were interdependent. Branching out into distribution after incorporating had been expensive, but Columbia no longer had to pay commissions to states'-rights exchanges. A national distribution system also meant that Columbia could coordinate domestic release patterns, control advertising and publicity at every level of the market, and set prices for its pictures—requirements if the company ever expected to release class-A pictures.

Columbia's B production operated on tight margins and it was crucial for the company to wring every possible dollar in film rentals from the market. Columbia's B features cost from $50,000 to $100,000 to produce; in contrast, the majors spent as much as $300,000 on B films and Poverty Row as little as $10,000. Regardless of cost, Columbia's routine films were sold in blocks on a flat-fee basis following industry custom.

Although block booking had been harshly attacked by federal agencies, independent theaters, and citizen's groups, the trade practice persisted throughout the thirties as a form of wholesaling which permitted studios to peddle their entire season's output to exhibitors on an all-or-nothing basis. Block booking offered distributors several advantages, among them the scale economies of selling in bulk and the guarantee that every picture released by the company would find a market regardless of quality.[11] Unlike percentage terms used for class-A pictures, flat fees prevented a distributor from capturing the extraordinary profits of an unexpected hit; on the other hand, flat fees had the advantage of generating predictable returns, so that if a studio kept costs within limits, its pictures could earn a profit. Since Harry Cohn was a notorious penny-pincher, we can assume that Columbia's conservative spending habits and its control over distribution helped secure a steady flow of financing from its principal backer, the Bank of America.

The Case of United Artists

To get some perspective on Columbia's operations thus far, we can take a closer look at the way United Artists structured its operations.[12] United Artists was founded by Mary Pickford, Douglas Fairbanks, Charles Chaplin, and

D. W. Griffith in 1919 as a distribution company to be owned and operated by stars. The founders had risen through the ranks of the business to become prominent independent producers. They had obtained financing and had released their pictures through leading firms such as Famous Players-Lasky and First National, but the founders decided to team up in response to the merger movement in the film industry which promised, among other things, to contain the skyrocketing salaries of big-name talent like themselves.

The founders of UA gained control of a key element of the film business. As independent producers, the founders controlled the making of their pictures. By forming UA, they could oversee the sales, promotion, and advertising of their pictures as well. Under this plan, UA's founders had to secure their own financing, but UA would reduce the risks of production financing by selling pictures individually on a percentage basis rather than in blocks and by charging producers a modest distribution fee for its services. United Artists was supposed to operate at just above breakeven and to funnel most of the distribution gross to its independent producers, thereby permitting them to pay off the production loans on their pictures promptly and to reach profits sooner. In other words, the founders decided to forgo the profits of the middleman—that is, the profits from owning a distribution company—in the hope of maximizing profits as independent producers.

To function efficiently—that is, to meet the overhead expenses of maintaining a sales staff in the principal markets of the world—United Artists required a larger volume of quality pictures than the founders as a group could provide. UA hoped to attract other stars and big-name directors to the fold; however, the thought of leaving the paternalistic care of the studio system appealed to few Hollywood luminaries and UA faced a chronic product shortage from the start.[13]

UA found a way out of its dilemma by aligning itself with a different type of independent—the creative producer. Unlike Chaplin, Fairbanks, and Pickford, who were actor-producers, the creative producer, typified by Joseph Schenck and Samuel Goldwyn, was an entrepreneur who operated in much the same way as the head of a studio, only on a much smaller scale. Schenck and Goldwyn chose suitable properties for the stars they had under contract, oversaw the development of their scripts, secured the financing, and supervised production. Every prominent producer who released through United Artists from 1930 to 1950 functioned in this manner. And only this type of independent could be relied on to deliver enough pictures on a regular basis to keep UA's distribution pipeline full. However, because UA did not have the financial resources to provide production financing, it remained the smallest of the eight majors.

What lessons could Columbia have learned from United Artists? None really, since during the early thirties Columbia had precious little money to devote to any class-A production. And besides, Harry Cohn was not about to entrust the studio's most important projects to outside producers. Columbia eventually opened its doors to independent producers, but not until the breakdown of the studio system after World War II.

Strengthening Exhibition

Having acquired a studio and exchanges, Columbia's next objective was to gain access to first-run theaters. Unlike the Big Five companies, which were completely integrated, the Little Three did not own theater chains. (Universal owned a small chain for a while but was forced to sell it during the Depression.) An analysis of Columbia Pictures by *Barron's* magazine, a national financial weekly, noted that the studio's financial health in 1935 resulted partly from its steadfast refusal to own theaters.[14] The magazine made this observation during the depths of the Depression when Paramount, Fox, and RKO seemed hopelessly mired in red ink as a result of their investments in real estate. With the return of prosperity, however, the assessment of *Barron's* would no longer be valid. Ownership of theaters, first-run houses in particular, would become the tool that enabled the Big Five to maintain control of the market. Columbia, Universal, and United Artists remained in a subservient position vis-à-vis the Big Five precisely because they did not own important theater chains.

Columbia released its pictures primarily to two types of theaters. Most were subsequent-run houses, typically small independent operations; less numerous were first-run houses, typically affiliates of the majors. Since the studio had meager financial resources, it could only occasionally produce a contender and only then did the studio want access to first-run houses. (As I will discuss later, Columbia would be relegated to subsequent-run venues until it had big-name stars on its roster.) First-run playing time meant longer runs—usually a week—in large, prestigious theaters and the opportunity of renting a picture on a percentage-of-the-gross basis. Thus if a release struck the public's fancy, the studio could enjoy a substantial share of the box-office take.

United Artists had gained access to first-run houses not only because it handled quality pictures, but also because the company had indirectly gone into exhibition. Alarmed by the battle for theaters, UA's owners, with the exception of Chaplin, invested $1 million to form United Artists Theatre Circuit in 1926. With an additional $4 million from a public stock issue, the Theatre Circuit constructed and/or purchased first-run theaters in key cities. What linked United Artists to United Artists Theatre Circuit was a ten-year franchise that granted the theater chain the preferential right to exhibit UA's pictures. The maneuver worked, with the result that affiliated theater chains recognized United Artists as a forceful competitor and booked its pictures.

How did Columbia gain access to first-run theaters? Reviews in *Variety* reveal that Columbia signed a franchise agreement with RKO in 1930 granting the theater chain first call on Columbia's releases. Unlike the other members of the Big Five, RKO was a relative newcomer to the business. Founded by RCA in 1928 to complete head on with AT&T in the sound recording and playback field, RKO merged Joseph P. Kennedy's Film Booking Office, the Keith-Albee-Orpheum circuit of vaudeville houses, and RCA's Photophone sound system into a vertically integrated firm containing three hundred theaters, four studios, and $80 million in working capital.

Despite RKO's impressive pedigree, the company faced the same challenges breaking into the market that Columbia did, plus one more—choice attractions to fill the playing time of its theaters. Since the Big Five had their own interests to protect, RKO turned to independent producers and the Little Three for help. The terms of RKO's franchise agreement with Columbia are not known, but if they are similar to the terms of RKO's franchise agreements with United Artists, the deal probably went something like this. RKO agreed to exhibit a specific number of better-quality pictures each year in selected theaters and to pay a film rental for each engagement based on the production cost of the picture and on the overhead expense of the respective theater.[15] In practice, RKO made a down payment based on a sliding scale that measured the relative production cost of the picture (the higher the production cost, the higher the down payment) and then split the box-office gross fifty-fifty after deducting the overhead expenses of the theater. These terms constituted a variation of the percentage of the gross form of rental and enabled Columbia to receive remuneration in relation to the box-office performance of its pictures.

The RKO franchise agreement may have been a turning point for Columbia. It provided both an incentive to produce higher quality pictures and a venue for their exhibition. If this assumption holds good, having a Frank Capra on the lot gains significance. A talented director, a star or two, and a few acceptable literary properties provided the leverage to lift Columbia into the majors.

After joining the studio in 1927, Capra quickly earned Harry Cohn's confidence and was awarded the task of handling the studio's occasional class-A picture. Capra responded by directing a series of inexpensive but well-received comedies. Going into the thirties, Capra's stature as a director grew with each successive release. By the time he made *American Madness* in 1932, critics were referring to him as "one of Hollywood's best."[16] Capra's *The Bitter Tea of General Yen* (1932) was chosen as the first feature presentation of RKO's new Radio City Music Hall in New York. After *It Happened One Night* swept the Academy Awards in 1934, Capra literally became a star and received top billing in Columbia's ads. Beginning with *The Bitter Tea of General Yen,* all the pictures Capra made for Columbia received a Music Hall send-off. Since his pictures received royal handling in New York, we can assume that a similar treatment awaited them in first-run situations around the country.

The fate of Columbia's other class-A products in this period is more difficult to assess. What is clear, however, is that simply having one Frank Capra was not enough to maintain Columbia's status as a member of the Little three. All of Columbia's competitors relied not only upon masterful directors but also upon stars. Star vehicles typically enjoyed a ready-made market, reduced the risk of production financing, and commanded the best rental terms.[17] Could a substitute be found for stars in the making of class-A pictures?

The Case of Eagle-Lion

A glance at Eagle-Lion Films suggests how one studio pursued such a strategy.[18] Eagle-Lion was a short-lived venture founded in 1946 by American industrialist Robert R. Young. The owner of Producers Releasing Corporation (PRC), a Poverty Row studio that specialized in cheap Westerns starring Buster Crabbe, Tim McCoy, Al "Lash" LaRue, and others, Young wanted nothing less than to create a new motion picture company. An alliance with British film magnate J. Arthur Rank, who was trying to break into the U.S. exhibition market, seemed an excellent way to begin.

At the end of World War II, Rank dominated all branches of the film business in Great Britain. Outside Great Britain, Rank owned or controlled theaters in France, Canada, and Australia and had close ties with exhibitors throughout the British Commonwealth. Although Britain was the most important overseas market for American films, it was not large enough to support indigenous production. Rank therefore had to export to survive, but getting playing time in the affiliated theater chains of the Big Five proved daunting. Rank had no other choice but to deal with the second tier of the American film industry. Universal agreed to distribute part of the Rank line in return for a reciprocal favor from Rank in Great Britain and in other markets. Since Rank produced more pictures than Universal could comfortably handle alone, he also agreed to collaborate along similar lines with Robert Young.

The alliance with Rank provided Young with instant prestige and access to important theaters overseas—a passport out of Poverty Row, or so it was thought. To comply with the agreement, Young spent over $12 million of his own money to form a vertically integrated operation, Eagle-Lion Films, a distribution company, and Eagle-Lion Studios, a production company. The former had offices in New York and had as its goal doing business with a higher-grade exhibitor; the latter operated out of the PRC studio in Hollywood, which was upgraded at a cost of $1 million, and had as its goal the making of class-A pictures.

But Eagle-Lion faced formidable barriers to entry in the American market, not the least of which was an industrywide recession. All the optimistic predictions about the postwar prosperity for the movies soon began to ring hollow. Although the domestic box office rose steadily to peak in 1946, late in 1947 it began a steady decline that would last ten years. Producing a roster of lackluster pictures its first year, Eagle-Lion found itself shut out of first-run theaters. Much had to do with Eagle-Lion's stars. Unlike Columbia, Eagle-Lion could not borrow stars from the majors for the simple reason that the majors would never entrust one of their valuable properties to a Poverty Row studio, or in this case a studio without an established track record. Because Eagle-Lion did not have the resources to develop stars, the studio limped along for a while using aging leading men on their way down (that is, George Brent and Louis Hayward) and a few young people working their way up (that is, Richard Basehart, June Lockhart, and Scott Brady).

Neither strategy succeeded and to stay afloat Eagle-Lion developed a radical production policy that substituted action, color, natural locations, and authenticity for the usual combination of stars and pre-sold stories. The result was a form of product differentiation—a string of film noir pictures that put Eagle-Lion, albeit temporarily, in the limelight. Produced on low budgets, these pictures included Anthony Mann's *T-Men* (1947), a semidocumentary based on Treasury Department cases; Crane Wilbur's *Canon City* (1948), a reenactment of a jailbreak at the Canon City, Colorado, state penitentiary that was shot on the site; and Alfred Werker's *He Walked by Night* (1948), a thriller depicting a brilliant psychotic killer. All made money and all received favorable press. For example, *Canon City,* which introduced Scott Brady as one of the prison busters, grossed $1.2 million on a budget of $424,000 and was cited by *Life* and *Look* as one of the top pictures of the year.

The postwar recession at the box office proved fatal to Eagle-Lion. Since the market for B films had declined, the company could not use this type of picture to create a firm financial base. With audiences becoming selective in their moviegoing tastes, even class-A features found the going rough. Had conditions been better, Eagle-Lion's product differentiation strategy might have saved the company. Regardless, the studio demonstrated that an alternative existed to expensive star-studded pictures. But this option was not a viable one for Columbia. For one thing, location shooting just was not practical until new technology was introduced after World War II. For another, censorship forces during the early thirties were up in arms over the depiction of violence and crime in the movies.

Acquiring Stars

Columbia therefore had no choice but to adopt the star system if it wanted to produce class-A pictures. Commenting on Columbia's star power in the period from 1930 to 1934, *Barron's* said, "Another factor in [Columbia's] success has been the avoidance of onerous long-term contracts with stars, the long-term appeal of which is bound to be uncertain. It has followed a policy of signing artists and directors for a few pictures a year or of borrowing actors and actresses from other companies, a program that makes for economy and flexibility of production cost."[19] This assessment needs qualification; Columbia would have been fortunate indeed to have had real stars under long-term contract. Because *Barron's* assessment was likely based in part on interviews with company executives, it has the ring of a rationalization for the studio's lackluster roster.

Concerning star development, a studio had three options: (1) It could develop stars by casting players in different roles and testing audience reaction; (2) it could borrow stars from other studios; or (3) it could pretend it had stars and hope that exhibitors and the public would play along. The first option obviously consumed the most time and money; the second was feasible only for studios that had already achieved major status; the third required the most chutzpah.

During the early thirties, Columbia had the chutzpah to "star" veteran actor Jack Holt in over a dozen pictures. A typical Holt picture was an action story containing "love interest, melodramatics, outdoors and he-man stuff," said *Variety*. In its review of *The Woman I Stole* (1933), *Variety* said, "Jack Holt has been making pictures like this for years and has prospered. There's nothing especially distinguished in the output, but it is all eminently saleable material. Factory product, but factory product of a successful kind, with a ready market and satisfactory returns."[20] Columbia's supporting male players were Ralph Graves and Ralph Bellamy. That was it. Columbia had one true female star under contract—Barbara Stanwyck—but Columbia saw her name in lights only briefly. Stanwyck got her big break as the leading lady in Frank Capra's *Ladies of Leisure* (1930). *Variety* said that Stanwyck saved the picture "with her ability to convince in heavy emotional scenes," but that she had "small gifts for graceful comedy."[21] After testing her in several roles, Columbia gave her star billing in Frank Capra's *The Miracle Woman* (1931). Her biggest hit and final Columbia release was Capra's *The Bitter Tea of General Yen* (1933). Afterward, Stanwyck departed for Warner Bros., leaving Columbia temporarily with only one female personality of any magnitude on its roster—opera singer Grace Moore.

To bolster class-A production, Columbia had to exploit the second star-based tactic: reliance on loan-outs from other studios. The majors loaned talent to one another on a regular basis. Try as they might, studios found it impossible to keep high-priced players busy all the time. Since an idle star was a heavy overhead expense, loan-outs could spread the costs. Studios devised various formulas to determine loan-out fees: the most common one was to charge a minimum fee of four weeks salary plus a surcharge of three weeks; another was to charge the basic salary for however long the star was needed plus a surcharge of 25 percent.[22]

The Big Five, having large stables of stars, would consider loan-outs to the Little Three, including the top-ranked independent producers associated with United Artists. Myth has it that the majors used loan-outs to discipline stars and to keep difficult people in line. But this argument does not make much sense, because it implies that a studio would risk its investment in a star by allowing him or her to appear in an inferior picture produced by a second-rate company. Actually, most stars were on the lookout for challenging parts and wanted the opportunity to play them anywhere. Given Columbia's lowly status in the early thirties, most of the loan-outs to the studio were on their way down. Claudette Colbert and Clark Gable were in lulls when Columbia borrowed them from Paramount and MGM, respectively, to star in *It Happened One Night;* the picture revitalized both their careers, but their home studios, not Columbia, enjoyed most of the benefits.

Producing Hits

By demonstrating the ability to produce the occasional hit, Columbia met its final goal. Columbia could have existed as a Poverty Row studio without hits, but the company needed a winner or two each year as a major to strengthen its financial reserves, to retire its debt, and to retain the interest of Wall Street. Yet producing a box-office winner has always been a difficult task. As *Barron's* pointed out, "Gauging the box-office appeal of a play or motion picture before production has, in the long run, proved to be . . . as hazardous as guessing the results of a horse race. Public taste is fickle, and the mere success of a single 'movie' offers no assurance that its type—gangster, biography, musical comedy, etc.—will maintain its appeal. 'Will they buy it?' is the nightmare of the producer of every theatrical production, and the answer can never be accurately foretold."[23] Therefore, producing hits not only generated profits, but also established a studio's credibility in the marketplace.

At Columbia, the task of producing winners fell mainly to Frank Capra. Columbia produced only three big hits from 1930 to 1934: Frank Capra's *Lady for a Day* in 1933 (Columbia's first release to make it to *Film Daily's* Ten Best pictures list), Victor Schertzinger's *One Night of Love,* and Capra's *It Happened One Night* (both in 1934). The latter two pictures enabled Columbia to generate profits of $1,009,000 in 1934, nearly equaling the company's peak pre-Depression earnings of $1,030,000 in 1929.

The question is: what strategy did the studio use to produce hits? Let's examine *It Happened One Night.* This picture and two other 1934 comedy hits—Howard Hawks's *Twentieth Century* (Columbia) and W. S. Van Dyke's *The Thin Man* (MGM)—have traditionally been regarded as initiating the screwball cycle in the thirties. However, contemporaneous sources saw *It Happened One Night* as a continuation of ongoing trends. Noting that Robert Riskin's screenplay about a runaway heiress who falls in love with a tough reporter was based on a short story in *Cosmopolitan* by Samuel Hopkins Adams entitled "Night Bus," *Variety,* saw the picture as "another long distance bus story," a variation on MGM's *Fugitive Lovers* and Universal's *Cross Country Cruise,* which had been released a month earlier.[24] Others considered the picture a "traveling hostelry" film similar to *Grand Hotel* and such spin-offs as Fox's *Transatlantic* (1931), Paramount's *Shanghai Express* (1932), and Columbia's own *American Madness* (1932).[25] Seen from this perspective, *It Happened One Night* did not materialize out of nowhere, but from Columbia's strategy of following trends.

Capitalizing on the success of *It Happened One Night,* Columbia decided to specialize in screwball comedies. Again, Capra carried most of the burden and produced three hits, *Mr. Deeds Goes to Town* (1936), *You Can't Take It with You* (1938), and *Mr. Smith Goes to Washington* (1939). If one line of screwball comedy featured the madcap adventures of wealthy heroines in comedies of remarriage, the Capra pictures, which were written in collaboration with either Robert Riskin or with Sidney Buchman, followed another line by depicting "utopian fantasies" where the little guy always comes out on top.[26] To play the heroes of these pictures, Columbia borrowed Gary Cooper from Paramount for *Mr. Deeds* and James Stewart from MGM for the other two. Jean Arthur, Columbia's only contract star, costarred in all three.

Capra's stature as a director had grown enormously after *It Happened One Night* and, beginning with *Mr. Deeds,* Columbia placed Capra's name above the title of his pictures. The three Capra comedies were named to *Film Daily's* Top Ten and won numerous awards, including special honors for Capra. *You Can't Take It with You,* the most acclaimed of the group, was hailed by *Time* as "the Number 1 cinema comedy of 1938" and received Academy Awards for best picture and best direction.

The returns on these pictures was another matter. Columbia budgeted $500,000 for *Mr. Deeds,* double the amount it spent on *It Happened One Night* and made a prudent investment. But Columbia permitted the budgets for Capra's subsequent productions, including his prestige picture *Lost Horizon* (1937), to escalate well beyond $1.5 million. The pictures did well at the box office, but as a group they barely recouped their production costs. Few pictures in the thirties could support such investments, with the result that Capra's pictures enhanced the reputation of the studio but earned modest profits.[27]

Columbia's other attempts at exploiting the screwball cycle fared less well. The studio borrowed Claudette Colbert from Paramount a second time to produce Gregory La Cava's *She Married Her Boss* (1935), a comic variation of the traditional "sob-and-hanky" melodrama. The picture did only so-so business. Columbia then designed two vehicles for Irene Dunne. Dunne had previously made a name for herself at other studios performing in melodramas and musicals, but Columbia offcast her in Richard Boleslawski's *Theodora Goes Wild* (1936) and Leo McCarey's *The Awful Truth* (1937). In the former, Dunne played a "female Mr. Deeds" opposite Melvyn Douglas in a "distaff version" of Capra's *Mr. Deeds Goes to Town,* noted a review. In the latter, she played opposite Cary Grant in a comedy of remarriage. Neither picture made it to *Variety's* annual list of box-office champions, although *The Awful Truth* won considerable acclaim by being named to *Film Daily*'s Ten Best pictures list and by winning the best direction Oscar for McCarey.

Lacking a roster of stars and a large financial cushion, Columbia was forced to concentrate mainly on one production trend as a source of its class-A pictures during the second half of the thirties. The Big Five, on the other hand, had the resources to spread risks by focusing on a range of production cycles and by producing pictures with trend-setting possibilities. And as owners of first-run theaters, the Big Five profited from any picture that struck the public's fancy regardless of which studio released it. Members of the Little Three would not secure an equal footing with the Big Five until the *Paramount* decrees went into effect beginning in 1948.

This case study has plotted a "bottom-up" course of development for Columbia Pictures as it struggled to become a member of the motion picture establishment. I have thereby rejected the conventional portrait of the studio era as a mature oligopoly in which Columbia, along with the other members of the Little Three, were somehow consigned by the Big Five to the second tier of the majors. In its place, this case study has offered a more dynamic account of industrial behavior depicting how one company successfully pursued a series of mutually dependent goals and objectives. Comparing Columbia to United Artists and Eagle-Lion adds perspective to the account by revealing how other small studios attempted to solve similar problems. Each choice affected the fortunes of the respective companies and as a consequence the ways in which they made their pictures.

NOTES

1. *One Flew Over the Cuckoo's Nest,* a United Artists release, swept the top Academy Awards in 1975. Producers Saul Zaentz and Michael Douglas received the Best Picture Oscar; the other winners were director Miloš Forman, actor Jack Nicholson, actress Louise Fletcher, and screenwriters Laurence Hauben and Bo Goldman.

2. Douglas Gomery's concise overview of Columbia Pictures in *The Hollywood Studio System* ([New York: St. Martin's Press, 1986], esp. pp. 161–72) is the most authoritative account of the studio currently available; Edward Buscombe's essay, "Notes on Columbia Pictures Corporation, 1926–1941" (*Screen* 15 [Autumn 1975]: 65–82) suggests a relationship between the financing of Columbia's pictures and the ideology of Capra's films; and Joel Finler's chapter on the studio in his *The Hollywood Story* ([New York: Crown, 1988], pp. 68–87) contains a wealth of data on the studio's releases and personnel.

3. See, for example, Halsey, Stuart & Co's prospectus, "The Motion Picture Industry as a Basis for Bond Financing" (27 May 1927) in *The American Film Industry,* rev. ed., ed. Tino Balio, (Madison: University of Wisconsin Press, 1985), pp. 195–217.

4. Gomery, *The Hollywood Studio System,* p. 162. Anthony Slide's *The American Film Industry: An Historical Dictionary* ([New York: Greenwood Press, 1986], p. 70) states that CBC was founded in 1922; David Bordwell, Janet Staiger, and Kristein

Thompson's *The Classical Hollywood Cinema: Film Style and Mode of Production to 1960* ([New York: Columbia University Press, 1985], p. 403) gives 1918 as the founding date.

5. Temporary National Economic Committee, *The Motion Picture Industry—A Pattern of Control* (Washington, D.C.: U.S. Government Printing Office, 1941), p. 62.

6. Warner Bros. was the only other major that continued to be run by its founders, the others having passed into the hands of professional managers during the twenties.

7. For a discussion of the importance of the prestige film as a production trend, see Tino Balio, *Grand Design: Hollywood as a Modern Business Enterprise, 1930–1939* (New York: Charles Scribner's Sons, 1993), pp. 179–211.

8. Bordwell, Staiger, and Thompson, *The Classical Hollywood Cinema*, p. 321.

9. *Variety Film Reviews* (New York: Garland, 1983—). See the entries for the following dates: 11 December 1934; 2 June 1931; 24 January 1933; 29 January 1930; 16 August 1932.

10. Brian Taves, "The B Film: Hollywood's Other Half," in *Grand Design: Hollywood as a Modern Business Enterprise, 1930–1939:* pp. 317–18.

11. For a contemporaneous discussion of block booking, see Howard T. Lewis, *The Motion Picture Industry* (New York: D. Van Nostrand, 1933), pp. 142–80, and TNEC, *The Motion Picture Industry*, pp. 21–33.

12. Tino Balio, *United Artists: The Company Built by the Stars* (Madison: University of Wisconsin Press, 1975).

13. Gloria Swanson was the only other big star to join United Artists during the twenties. Unfortunately, Miss Swanson's decision proved disastrous to her career since she failed to learn the skills to oversee both the business and artistic sides of independent production. See Balio, *United Artists*, pp. 82–84.

14. "Unique Motion Picture Enterprise," *Barron's* 15 (25 March 1935): 14.

15. Balio, *United Artists*, pp. 65–66.

16. Charles Wolfe, *Frank Capra: A Guide to References and Resources* (Boston: G. K. Hall, 1987), p. 11.

17. A fuller discussion of the economics of the star system is found in Cathy Klaprat, "The Star as Market Strategy: Bette Davis in Another Light," in *The American Film Industry*, pp. 351–76.

18. Tino Balio, *United Artists: The Company That Changed the Film Industry* (Madison: University of Wisconsin Press, 1987), pp. 11–39.

19. "Unique Motion Picture Enterprise," *Barron's*, p. 14.

20. *Variety Film Reviews*, 4 July 1933.

21. *Variety Film Reviews*, 28 May 1930.

22. "Less Than 2,000 Players Work," *Variety*, 7 September 1938, p. 2.

23. "Unique Motion Picture Enterprise," *Barron's*, p. 14.

24. *Variety Film Reviews*, 27 February 1934.

25. Heidi Kenaga, "Studio Differentiation of 'Screwball' Comedy" (unpublished paper, University of Wisconsin, Department of Communication Arts, 1990).

26. Wolfe, *Frank Capra: A Guide*, p. 22.

27. Finler, *The Hollywood Story*, p. 75.

21

"A Brief Romantic Interlude": Dick and Jane go to 3½ Seconds of the Classical Hollywood Cinema

Richard Maltby

I

"Can I tell you a story, Rick?"
"Has it got a wow finish?"
"I don't know the finish."
—Ilsa Lund (Ingrid Bergman) and
Rick Blaine (Humphrey Bogart)
in *Casablanca* (1942)

"Don't worry what's logical. I make it so fast no one notices."
—Director Michael Curtiz,
during the production of *Casablanca*

Three quarters of the way through "America's most beloved movie,"[1] Ilsa Lund comes to Rick Blaine's rooms to try to obtain the letters of transit that will allow her and her Resistance leader husband, Victor Laszlo (Paul Henreid), to escape Casablanca to America. Rick, the disillusioned romantic, refuses to hand them over. She pulls a gun and threatens him. He tells her, "Go ahead and shoot, you'll be doing me a favor." She breaks down and tearfully starts to tell him the story of why she left him in Paris. By the time she says, "If you knew how much I loved you, how much I still love you," they are embracing in close-up. The movie dissolves to a 3½-second shot of the airport tower at night, its searchlight circling, and then dissolves back to a shot from outside the window of Rick's room, where he is standing, looking out, and smoking a cigarette. He turns into the room, and says, "And then?" She resumes her story. . . .

This essay circles around this moment in *Casablanca* as an example of the intricate and intimate relationship between movies and their viewers in classical Hollywood cinema. The conventional assumptions of Post-Structuralist textual criticism assert that "mainstream Hollywood narrative, so indebted to literary realism, strives toward clear representation, the resolution of ideological contradiction, and a full revelation of the 'truth.'" In this paradigm, the critic's task is to "deconstruct the central elements of . . . Hollywood storytelling [and] the narratological/ideological premises of the studio-controlled world."² In discovering textual contradiction and ambiguity, Post-Structuralist criticism claims to stage a liberation of the text from earlier, repressive "readings" of it.³ This textual liberation, however, takes place at the expense of the movie's audience, archetypally dismissed by Jean-Loup Bourget as those "women [who] ply their handkerchiefs at Sirk's films" while missing their ironic intent. More conventionally, textual criticism dismembers the audience into an aggregation of singular but not individual spectators "positioned" or "cued" by the text. Both psychoanalytic and cognitive analyses construct the spectator as a concept, not a person. Whether understood as a unified subject position or a viewing competence, the spectator in both approaches is represented as a singular hypothetical identity capable of executing operations delineated by the text, but not as an individual agent.

Accounts of spectatorial agency that begin with the text seem destined to follow the road taken by Umberto Eco, who proposes that the author foresees a Model Reader, able to "deal interpretively with the expressions in the same way as the author deals generatively with them." This reader's competence is responsive: imaginatively active, perhaps, but not proactive; it accommodates the reader to the world of the text. Superman comics or James Bond novels pull "the reader along a predetermined path, carefully displaying their effects so as to arouse pity or fear, excitement or depression at the due place and at the right moment." Unlike the critic, who inhabits an alternative sphere of analytic liberty in which the fissures of the text are exposed and its sutures unsewn, Eco's "average reader" is a good bourgeois, never seeking to occupy a position from which it might disrupt the text.⁴

In *A Practical Manual of Screen Playwriting*, Lewis Herman describes a similar scenario for Hollywood, in which the "well planned, well plotted, holeless story leaves the audience with the feeling that they have witnessed a completely unified, satisfying tale of events that could have happened to anyone, even themselves":

> Everything in any story must be completely understandable to the audience, at least after the denouement. . . . Care must be taken that every hole is plugged; that every loose string is tied together; that every absence is fully explained . . . that no baffling question marks are left over at the end of the picture to detract from the audience's appreciation of it.⁵

Herman's rhetorical ambition of absorbing the spectator within the perfectly closed text is, however, at odds with the norms of audience experience. It takes little account of the promiscuous nature of the commercial Hollywood movie, of what Parker Tyler called "its will to make indiscriminate numbers of people indiscriminately happy." Classical Hollywood deals in economies of pleasure rather than the aesthetics of organic forms. Its criticism might usefully address the effects of the consumption practice of single viewings of movies by undifferentiated audiences. In every Hollywood movie there are coincidences, inconsistencies, gaps, and delays, which are registered by the audience as digressions or as opportunities for what Pauline Kael calls the most intense pleasure of moviegoing, the "non-aesthetic one of escaping from the responsibilities of having the proper responses required of us in our official (school) culture." This ordinarily irresponsible pleasure extends to using movies "to learn how to dress or how to speak more elegantly or how to make a grand entrance or even what kind of coffee maker we wish to purchase, or to take off from the movie into a romantic fantasy or a trip."[6]

Hollywood has less commercial interest in producing coherent interpretations of a movie than in promoting what Barbara Klinger calls "multiple avenues of access" to it, so that it will "resonate as extensively as possible in the social sphere in order to maximize its audience." A movie's "consumable identity," the promotional values by which it is identified as a commodity, may distract the viewer into selecting some aspect of the movie other than its story to entertain us: performance, mise-en-scène, star biography, or the conspicuous display of budget and technical wizardry.[7] In the process the movie's producers must surrender a significant amount of control over the meanings of a text. So must its critics, for the identity of a text:

> cannot be eternally secured on the basis of its internal features, when these features themselves are subject to diverse constructions by practices which accompany the text throughout the course of its circulation. Popular genres in mass culture are subject to such reconstruction as a condition of their existence.[8]

For instance, when Harry Burns (Billy Crystal) meets Sally Albright (Meg Ryan) for the first time, they discuss their own relationship by arguing over *Casablanca*. Harry refuses to believe that Sally would prefer a passionless marriage to living "with the man you've had the greatest sex of your life with just because he owns a bar." Sally explains that any woman in her right mind would choose to be "the first lady of Czechoslovakia. . . . Women are very practical, even Ingrid Bergman, which is why she gets on the plane at the end of the movie." "I understand," responds Harry. "Obviously, you haven't had great sex yet." I want to consider the moment of *Casablanca* that I have described at the beginning of this essay as an example of the way in which Hollywood movies presuppose multiple viewpoints, at multiple textual levels, for their consuming audience. Then, by looking at the material history of the production and consumption of what Eco has called "the heavy industry of dreams in a capitalistic society," I hope to account for why this happens.

2

Paradoxically, the more exactly we describe the narration, the more fragmented it becomes.
—Edward Branigan, *Narrative Comprehension and Film*

"The less time to think, the easier for all of us. Trust me."
—Rick to Ilsa

The sequence under discussion is not, strictly speaking, ambiguous, but it is paradoxical. Viewers interpret what happens in this scene in at least two mutually conflicting ways. Half the audience insists that the scene must be understood to be suggesting that Bogart and Bergman had slept together. The other half deny it with as much vehemence. Few viewers acknowledge any uncertainty about what has—or has not—happened, or argue that the movie hints that Rick and Ilsa *might* have slept together *or* they *might not* have. In the *Casablanca* that half the audience watched, they did, and in the *Casablanca* the other half watched, they didn't. The sources of information on which these interpretations depend contradict each other, and their disparities cannot be resolved. On one side, the dissolve suggests at most only a brief ellipsis, and this is reinforced by the continuity of Bergman's storytelling—plus, of course, the fact that they both look perfectly unruffled. On the other hand, Bogart is smoking the standard-issue postcoital cigarette, the airport tower is recognizably phallic, and the shot sequence of embrace/dissolve away from scene/return is a conventional device for signaling an offscreen—a censored—significant act. Seldom do either of these arguments persuade adherents of the other interpretation to change their minds.

One way of expressing the paradox at the center of this scene is to suggest that it is both underdetermined and overdetermined. The evidence is slight, inconclusive, a matter of inference and hypothesis, but it is also excessive and contradictory. To maintain either understanding of the plot event, a viewer must ignore or discard some of the interpretative clues he or she is offered. In order for the scene to permit both interpretations of its action, the evidence for each interpretation must be present in the text. Rather than ambiguity, this "excessively obvious" sequence presents contradiction: Rick and Ilsa *must* have slept together, *and* they *can't* have done so. Viewers infer, hypothesize, and from that moment on, the two halves of the audience find themselves watching the unfolding of different stories.

In Rick's final exchange with Laszlo at the airport, the movie returns self-consciously to the issue:

RICK: You said you knew about Ilsa and me?
VICTOR: Yes.
RICK: You didn't know she was at my place last night when you were . . . she came there for the letters of transit. Isn't that true, Ilsa?
ILSA: Yes.
RICK: She tried everything to get them and nothing worked. She did her best to convince me that she was still in love with me. That was all over long ago; for your sake she pretended it wasn't and I let her pretend.
VICTOR: I understand.

What that means is, literally, anybody's guess, but it also demonstrates Hollywood's contradictory refusal to enforce interpretive closure at the same time that it provides plot resolution. The movie neither confirms nor denies either interpretation. Instead, it provides supporting evidence for both outcomes while effectively refusing to take responsibility for the story some viewers may choose to construct. Edward Branigan has offered a general explanation of Hollywood's "excessive obviousness": rather than appearing ambiguous or encouraging multiple interpretations, Hollywood narrative is chameleon-like, "adaptable, resilient and accommodating. It will try to be what the spectator believes it to be." Moreover, "it will congratulate the spectator for his or her particular selection by intimating that that selection is uniquely correct."[9] As an alternative to Branigan's organic metaphor, we might identify this moment in the story of *Casablanca* as an antinomy: a contradiction resulting from the formulation of discrepant but apparently logical conclusions.

Knowing whether Rick and Ilsa have consummated their renewed, regenerative passion or not is obviously quite important to how any individual viewer understands *Casablanca*. Or at least, it is if the viewer decides it is, if he or she seeks to comprehend *Casablanca* as a closed text, and chooses to include a sexual component in his or her comprehension of their romance. For such viewers, the scene in question may even amount to the movie's most significant plot event. Arguments about scenes such as this are often constructed around an opposition between "sophistication" and "innocence." "Sophisticated" viewers, who "read into" the sequence an element of off-screen sexual behavior, regard those who do not as "naïve" or "innocent" viewers. Through this terminology of self-approbation they reward themselves for their skill in reading a second order of signification within the scene. All the textual evidence for presuming that nothing has happened between the characters across the dissolve is conveyed at a level of interpretation concerned with the surface description of events and a commitment to linearity in narrative development. Because there is no *obvious* event, because the dissolve contains no obviously relevant plot information, the "innocent" viewer can understand it as if it were not there, as if it were not an ellipsis, as if, that is, nothing had happened. On the other hand, all the information implying that something has happened is available only to those "sophisticated" (in another terminology, "competent") enough to read the conventions through which it is presented: either the conventions of the tower's symbolism, or the conventions of the visual presentation of the sequence, or the conventional role of cigarettes in adult sexual behavior.

Although these interpretations can be distinguished by identifying one as "innocent" and the other as "sophisticated," the antinomian presentation of the scene makes it impossible to hierarchize them in terms of an adequacy to the text, to the psychology of the characters, or to some or other external notion of verisimilitude.[10] As a text, the movie has it both ways—They Did *and* They Didn't—and Dick and Jane Viewer can argue about it afterward for as long as they like. *Casablanca* presupposes multiple interpretations in its consumption: Jane can just as firmly insist that Ingrid Bergman would never do that sort of thing as Dick can protest, "What do you think the tower stood for, then?"

Allow me to introduce you to Dick and Jane. Since my discussion of *Casablanca* begins with textual analysis it finds itself, like all textual analyses, in need of an equivalent to Eco's Model Reader, or the spectator of other theories. In fact, I need two such figures, who disagree about what they saw. Since my essay is also concerned with social audiences, I want to envisage Dick and Jane as social beings, white adolescents, gone to *Casablanca* on a date. I would prefer you not to think of them as gendered subject positions any more than they should be considered "real people." We might call them cultural hypotheses, or the names of viewing and interpretative procedures, but I prefer to imagine them as fictional characters, discussing the resolution of ideological contradiction over a post-movie soda in Sullivan, Indiana, in 1943. In later life, perhaps, they became one of the couples who describe their own romance in *When Harry Met Sally* (1989). As creatures of my analytic imagination, Dick and Jane have much in common with the hypothetical entities of other critical approaches occupying the universally uncertain ground Judith Mayne calls spectatorship, "where 'subjects' and 'viewers' rub against each other." They are, however, incomplete, unavailable for ethnographic inquiry, and at times no more than stereotypes. Since they are only fictional characters, we can know no more about them than we do, for instance, about Rick ("cannot return to America, the reason is a little unclear") or Ilsa ("we said no questions"). My intention in constructing them as fictional characters is to lay bare the device of "the spectator," and consider the textual implications of the suggestion that each viewer is "a multiple intersection of variables . . . a complex and contradictory construction of . . . self-identities," not all of them readily available to the critic.[11] As fictional representations of *Casablanca*'s original audience, however, Dick and Jane inhabit some of the expectations of patriarchy and moviegoing, circa 1943. Believing himself to be "sophisticated," Dick thinks Jane "innocent." As we shall discover, Jane knows better.

The "innocent" interpretation of the scene is in one sense logically prior: it is consumed first, and consumed by everyone. The "sophisticated" story is constructed only by viewers equipped to consume in an already "knowing" way. But the "sophisticated" interpretation assumes a priority once it is raised as a possibility, because the "innocent" viewer, to whom it never occurred that Rick and Ilsa might have slept together, is now forced to defend her opinion that "nothing" happened. During Jane's first viewing, there was no ellipsis, because temporal continuity was established by the extra-diegetic music and the sense that nothing was missing from the action or dialogue. Confronted with Dick's alternative account of the sequence that insists that the dissolve on the image track conceals *something*, Jane is now forced to explain away the presence of an absence she didn't know was (or wasn't) there, against the assertion that the absence is significant and the accusation that she has been naïve in ignoring it. Watching *Casablanca* on a date, Dick and Jane are, like Harry and Sally, themselves in a social situation where questions of "how far to go" may be uppermost in their minds. Jane's "innocent" interpretation may be an act of resistance to Dick's assertion that it is "sophisticated" to understand everything sexually, insisting that his interpretation is merely salacious, and that such things did not happen in Hollywood movies. At the same time, her response increases her vulnerability to his accusations of sexual naïveté.[12]

Beyond the trivialities of adolescent fantasizing, the scene raises questions about Hollywood's hermeneutics. Richard deCordova has argued that, in a "dynamic of secrecy and confession, concealment and revelation," the star system accords sexuality "the status of the most private, and thus the most truthful, locus of identity." In its quest for the Oedipal master plot, psychoanalytic criticism overlaps knowledge and sexuality, so that "sexuality becomes the site of questions about what can and cannot be known." The femme fatale described by Mary Ann Doane as the appearance that deceives was identified by an earlier generation of psychoanalytic critics, writing not long after *Casablanca*'s release, as a "good-bad" girl, a character who created hermeneutic and epistemological unease by embodying within her person contradictory traits. Apparently promiscuous or guilty of a serious crime, the good-bad girl remains a figure of uncertain moral character for most of the movie, until the hero's suspicions of her are disproven. "What the man sees turns out to be illusory; what the woman tells him is true. Deceptive circumstances have been substituted for the deceiving woman." In *Movies: A Psychological Study*, Martha Wolfenstein and Nathan Leites treat *Gilda* (1946), for example, as a typical instance not just of the good-bad girl, but of the more general phenomenon of the drama of false appearances.[13]

Wolfenstein and Leites describe a recurrent situation in both Hollywood comedies and melodramas in which the hero and heroine are placed in a compromising position, either over their sexual behavior or over a crime. Their actions are observed by a character "who sees things mistakenly," identifying "illicit implications in the innocent behavior of hero and heroine." Wolfenstein and Leites argue that comedies characteristically "prove the nonoccurrence of sexual happenings," just as melodramas prove their heroes innocent of the crime of which they are accused. Plots frequently revolve around the protagonists' increasingly convoluted attempts to assert their innocence. But they seldom achieve this by forcing a reinterpretation of existing evidence: the demonstration that someone else is guilty relieves the hero of trying to get people to believe his story, or a final mistaken impression makes everything turn out well for the victims of previous misleading appearances. The on-looker, who caused all the trouble, is paid off by remaining deceived. In *Bachelor Mother* (1939), for example, Polly Parrish's (Ginger Rogers) at-tempts to prove that she is not the mother of the baby she found outside an orphanage are complicated by the attempts of David Merlin (David Niven) to prove that he is not its father. Only when they succumb to the pressures of romantic convention and the expectations of other characters by falsely ac-knowledging their parenthood and creating themselves as a couple can David discover the proof of his bride's innocence—an event which, of course, takes place offscreen, after the end of the movie. The audience's enjoyment in large part derives from our omniscience, which allows us to take pleasure in the mistakes of Freddie (Frank Albertson), *Bachelor Mother*'s comic onlooker. But Freddie also performs an essential service in the movie's expression of cen-sored thoughts, allowing the viewer to see the hero and heroine enact forbid-den wishes, but escape any penalty, since we know that despite false appear-ances, nothing has happened.[14]

In our fictional viewing of *Casablanca,* Jane can place Dick as the comic onlooker, but deceived by the familiar Hollywood drama of false appearances. Jane is not only an "innocent" spectator; she is also a knowledgeable one. She knows what does and does not happen in Hollywood. If Jane's position im-plies an interpretive naïveté assigned to women under patriarchy—"a ten-dency to deny the processes of representation, to collapse the opposition be-tween the sign (the image) and the real"—that is perhaps because Jane understands that Hollywood's fragile morality depends upon Ingrid Bergman (and therefore Ilsa Lund) remaining inviolate. Jane knows that the moral sense of the movies is hinged around what Parker Tyler called the "blushlessly journalistic" question of "whether the act of fornication did or did not take place." The temporal constraints of a Hollywood movie concentrate its plot's attention on dramatic turning points of sexual conduct. The morality of char-acters is determined by whether they give in to their socially unsanctioned desires or sublimate them. Tyler called this the Morality of the Single In-stance. An iron law of sexual decency requires that whatever the mutual temp-tation, the hero and heroine—the Chosen Pair—keep closed the floodgates of desire, preserve their honor, and ensure that they—the actors, and there-fore the characters—do not "become committed to any irretrievable act whose consequences they must bear." Under this constraint, Hollywood movies maintain what Tyler called "a grammar of sex," as indispensable to their expressive organization as good photography and articulate speech: "a form of etiquette practiced by ladies and gentlemen of fiction, aided and abetted by actors and actresses of Hollywood."[15] The Morality of the Single Instance was, perhaps, most cogently articulated by another fictional character, F. Scott Fitzgerald's Monroe Stahr, explaining to his scriptwriters how the audience is to understand their heroine's motivation:

> At all times, at all moments when she is on the screen in our sight, she wants to sleep with Ken Willard. . . . Whatever she does, it is in place of sleeping with Ken Willard. If she walks down the street she is walking to sleep with Ken Willard, if she eats her food it is to give her enough strength to sleep with Ken Willard. *But* at no time do you give the impression that she would even consider sleeping with Ken Willard unless they were properly sanctified.[16]

Understanding all this, Jane, like the hero and heroine of almost every movie she watches, can consciously deny and be "absolved from guilty impulses," secure in the knowledge that the movie will demonstrate (as it does) "that mere wishes are harmless and that one should not feel guilty for them."[17] In *Casablanca,* Jane will patiently explain, Ilsa, Rick, and even Captain Renault (Claude Rains) sacrifice their sexual ambitions for a higher cause. The movie she has seen has been about the process of sublimation, and its avocation of the nobility of sacrifice for that cause is one of the most overt satisfactions it offers, as well as being indispensable to the politics of *Casablanca.*

3

Even as children we knew how much of what we were seeing was untrue, wishful, escapist. What were we—idiots? I am always astonished at how so much writing about old movies assumes that the audience believed everything in them. Of course we didn't . . . We chose what we temporarily wanted to pretend was true, and when real experience didn't provide a yardstick, we cautiously wondered and questioned. We grew to understand and accept a great secret of the Hollywood films: its ambivalence, its knowing pretense. You were a fool to believe any of it, but you were a fool if you didn't. It didn't matter, because movies were only about one thing: a kind of yearning. A desire to know what you didn't know, have what you didn't have, and feel what you were afraid to feel.
                                        —Jeanine Basinger, *A Woman's View*

One obvious sense in which we might identify two separate viewing activities is in relation to the interplay among genres that goes on in this movie, and in most movies. Much genre criticism presumes that genres are monolithic, misrecognizing the essential opportunism of Hollywood's creative practice.

The majority of Hollywood movies support two different and mutually irreducible *fabulae*, the most obvious instance being that nine of every ten Hollywood movies take a heterosexual romance as their main plot or subplot, but also provide a second sub- or main plot as a consumable alternative. *Casablanca* is a case in point: the romance and the adventure-war story coexist as separable commodities, encountering each other oddly, and we (plural, social audiences) tolerate the oddities in "the way that characters change mood, morality, and psychology from one moment to the next" precisely because we recognize that this story takes place within the particular discursive universe we call Hollywood. It is, of course, possible to invent an interpretation of *Casablanca* that reconciles these elements into an integrated fictional whole. But it is not necessary to do so, nor is it required for a satisfactory (that is to say satisfying) act of viewing/consumption.[18]

Movie attendance at the classical Hollywood cinema was a social activity, undertaken by couples, families, or other groups of both sexes. The assumptions under which the industry operated suggested that not only did women on the whole attend more frequently than men, but that the decision about which movie to attend was more likely to be made by the female members of the potential audience.[19] In a patriarchal culture given to the simplistic ascription of gender roles, the frequency of plots concerning heterosexual romance might be explained by their marketing function in appealing to the dominant consumer group—the female audience—while the function of the adventure-war story plot was to satisfy those male members of the audience dragged along by their spouses to see the latest Ingrid Bergman movie. According to such an account, *Casablanca* quite deliberately constructs itself in such a way as to offer distinct and alternative sources of pleasure to two people sitting next to each other in the same cinema. Under such circumstances, even tidy narrative resolution has only a limited merit, to the extent that it does not interfere with the supply of multiple audience satisfactions.

A movie's inclusion of contradictions, gaps, and blanks allowed it to be consumed as at least two discrete, even opposing stories going on in the same text. The rationale for such strategies is, of course, economic. Such a movie (the antinomian text), would play to undifferentiated audiences. In this typical instance, the uncertainty meant that *Casablanca* could play to both "innocent" and "sophisticated" audiences alike. The alternative, which the studios resisted staunchly until 1968, was to differentiate movies and audiences through a rating system. They resisted ratings because it would disrupt their patterns of distribution, because it would change the nature of the place that the movie theater was—especially in small towns and suburban areas—and, to a lesser extent, because it would involve admitting that some of their products were not suitable for everyone. Instead, production of the antinomian text meant that the studios could make movies that "sophisticated" and "innocent" audiences alike could watch at the same time, without realizing that they were watching different movies. This capacity was constructed into the movies as a necessity of their commodity function, to sell the same thing to two or more audiences at the same time.

This practice of textual construction severely interferes with the ideological project commonly (and correctly) ascribed to Hollywood movies, since it postulates and exploits (in economic terms) an unpredictable audience. *Casablanca* has one overt ideological project: to overcome its audience's "latent anxiety about American intervention in World War II" through its consistent criticism of prewar American isolationism: "If it's December 1941 in Casablanca, what time is it in New York?"[20] *Casablanca* also has a collection of implicit ideological projects, in reinforcing cultural assumptions about gender roles, sexuality, monogamy, heroism, and educating its audience into such roles. To some extent, this contradiction between textual construction and ideological project, between economic efficiency and ideological affect, is contained by the way in which alternative possibilities are subsumed within relatively crude binary categories, of which my division of audiences by gender would be a case in point. To some extent, it is also contained by its location within an ideology of pluralism manifested in the notion of the undifferentiated movie audience. And it is of course further contained within the highly ideologically overdetermined notion of entertainment, which offers its audiences capitalism's fifth freedom, the freedom of inconsequential choice among equal commodity forms: in this case, that once you have made the commercial transaction of buying your ticket, you may be entertained by whatever you choose to be.

These observations are inevitably intertextual. Jane has, after all, brought Dick to the movies to see Ingrid Bergman, not Ilsa Lund, and the fictional character with whom Jane sustains a relationship is the Swedish actress, not the future first lady of Czechoslovakia. She pays less attention to the quality of Bergman's *acting* than to the appropriateness of her *casting:* it is not so much a matter of whether the actress turns in a good performance as whether the role is right for the actress. In observing that Ingrid Bergman wouldn't have done that sort of thing, Jane is constructing a commonplace but complex relationship between the fictional character Ilsa Lund and the fictional intertextual persona of Ingrid Bergman, a relationship that is entirely consistent with her understanding of how and why she watches movies. Jane's ability to construct this intertextual relationship is dependent on her sources of knowledge external to the movie—her reading of fan magazines, for example. Any Hollywood movie, exploiting the star system, is almost bound to employ some notion either of tension or recognition between character and star persona. Bergman, however, projects a particularly poignant version of the star-character symbiosis, in that it was her persona, rather than a character she played, that enacted the postwar drama of a scandalous female sexuality requiring punishment.

In *Hollywood's Wartime Women,* Michael Renov suggests that an explanation for the recurrence of the "evil woman" figure in film noir may be found in a more general cultural "crisis of female self-image produced by sudden adulation and its reversal at war's end." The scandal surrounding Bergman's affair with Roberto Rossellini—beginning in 1949 and resulting in her being "barred" from American movies for seven years—staged the punishment inflicted on the women in film noir in the public arenas of the American press and the U.S. Congress. In March 1950 Senator Edwin C. Johnson of Colorado accused Bergman of perpetuating "an assault upon the institution of Marriage" and being "a powerful influence for evil." He speculated that his former favorite actress, "a sweet and understanding person with an attractive personality which captivated everybody on and off the screen," might be suffering from "the dreaded mental disease schizophrenia," or else be the victim "of some kind of hypnotic influence" exerted by "the vile and unspeakable Rossellini." Whatever the cause of her moral aberration, however, Johnson proposed that her self-imposed exile be officially confirmed, since "under our law no alien guilty of turpitude can set foot on American soil again." Johnson and many others appeared to understand Bergman's adultery as an act of betrayal against them: as she summarized her mail, "some of the letters from America were impossible to answer. How could I do this to *them? They* had set me on a pedestal, put me up as an example to *their* daughters. Now, what were they going to tell their daughters? I fall in love with an Italian and they don't know what to tell their daughters."[21]

4

[Josef] von Sternberg . . . made a gesture of reasonableness. "At this point, of course," he said, "the two principals have a brief romantic interlude." . . .

"What you're trying to say," fumed Breen, "is that the two of them hopped into the hay. They fucked."

"Mr. Breen, you offend me."

. . . "Oh, for Christ's sake, will you stop the horseshit and face the issue. We can help you make a story about adultery, if you want, but not if you keep calling a good screwing match a 'romantic interlude.' Now, what do these two people do? Kiss and go home?"

"No," said the director, getting the point, "they fuck."

"Good!" yelped Breen, pounding the desk, "now I can understand your story."

The director completed his outline, and Breen told him how he could handle it in such a way as to pass the Code. The picture eventually made a lot of money, and the director was grateful to Breen for life.

—Jack Vizzard, *See No Evil*

Dick finds himself addressing a different issue from Jane's. In recognizing the conventions by which he is convinced that Rick and Ilsa have had "a brief romantic interlude," Dick will also recognize why the interlude is represented in such heavily conventionalized disguise. That second recognition obliges him to understand the liaison as an impossible plot event. The world of *Casablanca* cannot conceive of Rick and Ilsa sleeping together, because events in the world of *Casablanca* are regulated by the Production Code, which did not permit of unpunished adultery. Dick has registered the movie's antinomy. In order for him to keep up his belief in the liaison, he has to construct a parallel *Casablanca,* in which everything that happens in the *Casablanca* Jane has been consuming happens, except that the characters are not bound by the moral regulation of the Production Code. Like Jane, Dick thinks of Rick and Ilsa as Humphrey Bogart and Ingrid Bergman, and tries to liberate the desires of these two complex characters from the censorship of convention. As Parker Tyler explained it, Dick's resolution of the ambiguity of an event in the story unfolding before him is an act of willful participation in the story's creation, "wrestling it from its makers, and molding it, at least in this all-important detail, to suit our desires." [22] Dick understands the Morality of the Single Instance, in the sense that he recognizes why the story event is presented ambiguously. But he also believes that the parallel *Casablanca* he has discovered under the repressive surface of the text is the story the producers intended, and he finds enough evidence in some of the movie's textual significations to encourage him in his belief.

This moment in *Casablanca* embodies an almost ideal version of Hollywood's solution to the censorship of sexuality. The industry's decision not to classify its products carried with it an obligatory investment in codes of representation that made its principal product—entertainment—accessible to all. Driven by the ideological presupposition of a universal, undifferentiated audience, the industry invested in the apparatus of the Production Code and its administration as a codification of representational strategies intended to render "the objectionable unobjectionable." [23] Having chosen not to divide its audience, Hollywood was obliged to devise a system that would allow "sophisticated" viewers to read whatever they liked into a formally "innocent" movie, so long as the producers could use the mechanics of the Production Code to deny that the sophisticated interpretation had been put there in the first place. Much of the work of self-regulation in the 1930s and 1940s lay in the maintenance of this system of conventions, which operated, however perversely, as an enabling mechanism at the same time that it was a repressive one. As PCA director Joseph Breen persistently argued, the Production Code was not so much a system of censorship as an alternative to one: a system by which—as in the anecdote at the head of this section—censurable content could be coded and codified so as to avoid censorship. Like Roland Barthes, the Code's administrators recognized the institutions of representation as systems for the production of subjective pleasure through the projection and fulfillment of desire on the part of the viewer or reader. They also recognized the need to contain "sophistication" at the same time that it was catered to. The primary site of private pleasure to be simultaneously concealed and disclosed in public was sexuality, and Hollywood developed particularly intricate strategies of ambiguity and antinomy in its expression and repression. The early sound period in which the Production Code was developed was of central importance to this process. Those charged with administering the Code worked in cooperation with the studios to devise such strategies, clearly recognizing the role of ambiguity in addressing more than one audience at the same time. Explicit declarations of this purpose can be found in abundance in the early records of the PCA. They occurred less frequently later, because the ground rules of "delicate indication" became better and more tacitly understood between producers and regulators. A letter that Breen wrote to Jack Warner during the scripting of *Casablanca* illustrates this mutually cooperative understanding:

> With a view to removing the now offensive characterization of Renault as an immoral man who engages himself in seducing women to whom he grants visas, it has been agreed with Mr. Wallis that the several references to this particular phase of the gentleman's character will be materially toned down, to wit:
> Page 5: the line in scene 15 "The girl will be released in the morning" will be changed to the expression "will be released later." . . .
> Page 75: The word "enjoy" in Renault's line is to be changed to the word "like." "You like war. I like women."[24]

On the one hand the Production Code strove to eliminate any moral ambiguity in a movie's narrative progression through the increasingly rigid imposition of a deterministic plot line, ascribing every character a position on a fixed moral spectrum. But at the same time, precisely the same forces obliged movies to construct strategies of ambiguity around the details of action—the spectacle, the cinema's erotic performance—which they were not permitted to present explicitly. What was ambiguous was also deniable, and as the agencies of the Production Code developed, they constructed mechanisms by which they might deny responsibility for whatever "sophisticated" stories some viewers chose to construct. This "deniable" mode of narrative construction provided a satisfactory economic solution to the problem of censoring sexuality. In providing pictures that, as the trade paper *Film Daily* put it, "won't embarrass Father when he takes the children to his local picture house," it accommodated both the sophisticated and the "innocent" viewer at the same time. So long as the story remained comprehensible at the "innocent" level, innocence was protected, because "innocent" viewers were not educated into sophistication by being forced into some half-understood suggestive interpretation. On the other hand, a "sophisticated" audience willing to play a game of double-entendre could find hidden, "subversive," or "repressed" meanings in almost any movie by supplying "from its own imagination the specific acts of so-called misconduct which the Production Code has made unmentionable." They might in the process supply more plausible motivations for the behavior of characters in scenes that had been designed, according to Elliot Paul, to "give full play to the vices of the audience, and still have a technical out" as far as the Production Code was concerned. In the case of adaptations from novels, the repressed of the text might often be the original story, the "unsuitable" or "objectionable" elements of which had been removed in the process of adapting it to the screen.[25]

Late 1930s movies achieved a particular "innocence" by presenting a deadpan level of performance that acted as a foil to the secondary "sophisticated" narrative constructed within the imaginations of some viewers. The innocence of the discourse on sexuality in the screwball comedies or Astaire-Rogers musicals was a highly sophisticated innocence, in which only the characters remained innocent of the suggestiveness that typically underpinned their social relations. What could not be shown was graphic, explicit, unambiguous, unmistakable, sexual behavior. Instead what could be shown was mistakable sexual behavior, the presence of which could always be denied. The more the movie world diverged from what audiences knew went on in the real world, the more the movies took on a comic sophistication of their own. They gained a wit, a knowingness that audiences could take pleasure in, because it revealed and rewarded their own sophistication.[26]

The 3½ seconds of *Casablanca* over which Dick and Jane have been puzzling were, in fact, the invention of Joe Breen. On June 18, 1942, he wrote to Warner about the scene in Rick's apartment:

> The present material seems to contain a suggestion of a sex affair which would be unacceptable if it came through in the finished picture. We believe this could possibly be corrected by replacing the fade-out on page 135, with a dissolve, and shooting the succeeding scene without any sign of a bed or couch, or anything whatever suggestive of a sex affair. . . . If shot in this way, we believe the finished scene would be acceptable under the provisions of the Production Code. However, great care will be needed to avoid anything suggestive of a sex affair. Otherwise it could not be approved.[27]

The crucial word in the above passage is "suggestive." Suggestion was in part a matter of appearances—the "sign of a bed"—and in part a matter of timing. By replacing a fade with a dissolve, Breen deprived *Casablanca* of the temporal opportunity to suggest Rick and Ilsa's affair. Instead, it was represented as a "missed opportunity," which nevertheless appeared to characters and audience alike as "a relief, like being provided with a good excuse for getting out of an examination."[28]

What Wolfenstein and Leites called "the drama of false appearances" extended the strategy of the double entendre in the fields of visual and narrative structure. In this dramatic arena characters are constantly engaged in deciphering "the intentions, desires, and weaknesses of other characters," and viewers, of course, must do the same. Eventually, the plot unfolds a process of proof, and a deceptive appearance is replaced by an exonerating reality.

Gilda (Rita Hayworth) "turns out to be a faithful and devoted woman who has never loved anyone but the hero." As the understanding detective explains, "She didn't do any of those things. It was just an act." In the drama of false appearances, however, our favorite characters spend so much of their time looking and acting guilty that the forbidden wishes we have for them are not necessarily dispersed by the declaration of their innocence—which, after all, we knew all along. For Wolfenstein and Leites, this is the Return of the Repressed: "the content of what is projected and denied tends to reappear." More poetically, Tyler describes Dick's continuing struggle to transgress the plot's preordained logic and its conventionalized, generic morality: "as the words go on, as the routine proceeds, as these human beings obey all the conventions of art, manners, and their sexual natures . . . we are tempted to contradict it all, to unmake history, to stop the film." The critic, reflecting on the text in ahistorical tranquillity, experiences less anxiety in refusing to believe that appearances are false, and through analysis, releasing the repressed, subversive subtext. Mary Ann Doane, for instance, recognizes that the narrative of *Gilda* enacts the logic of the "good-bad" girl as a form of striptease, "peeling away the layers of Gilda's disguises in order to reveal the 'good' woman underneath." But, she suggests, in *Gilda* "the logic slips": the ending lacks credibility because Gilda performs her act of false appearance too well. Likewise, Larry Vonalt remakes *Casablanca* into a noir shadow of itself, as Rick betrays appearances in the final scene, and pays Ilsa back for having abandoned him, rejecting her as he believes she had rejected him: "there is a hint of cruelty in his putting her through such emotional turmoil to get her to confess her love for him and then tossing her over to Laszlo."[29]

To a large extent, at issue in these descriptions is the relationship between the boundaries of the text and the boundaries of interpretation. In the scene Dick and Jane have been arguing over, Rick changes his mind, and hence the direction of the plot, but whatever it is that changes his mind happens offscreen. Most of the pivotal changes in the movie occur either offscreen, or in moments without dialogue—usually in close-ups of Bogart's face. *Casablanca*'s invocation of offscreen space invites its audiences to imagine narrative events not represented by the text. Some of these events lie outside the permissible sphere of textual representation; as "offensive ideas" their presence can only be indicated by drawing our attention to an absence. We must, for example, decide what Annina (Joy Page) means when she talks of doing "a bad thing." It may be that a strictly textual criticism cannot imagine what these events are, but much of the work in the narration of any Hollywood movie involves offering the audience incentives to "read into" or activate these absences in ways that open up an intertextual field of possible meanings not explicitly articulated by the movie-as-text. In this sense, *Casablanca* presents an incomplete narrative requiring of its viewers a good deal of basic work in hypothesis-forming and -testing before the movie's story can be constructed—and, importantly, providing considerable autonomy to individual viewers to construct the story as they please—that is, the story which provides each individual viewer with a maximum of pleasure in the text.

5

"It's still a story without an ending . . ."
—Rick

Nothing is impossible for a brilliantly perverse mind.
—Umberto Eco, *The Role of the Reader*

For both popular and academic audiences, *Casablanca* is recognized as a perfected instance of classical Hollywood narrative. But it is also one of relatively few classical Hollywood movies accorded "cult" status. Like critics, cult audiences are prone to aberrant decodings, believing "that only they can see certain qualities or resonances in a film, which have simply been overlooked or missed by mainstream viewers, often because those mainstream viewers look in such a conventional, *single* way." As "Classic Hollywood's most representative film," *Casablanca* is perhaps too popular to be a cult object, but if Timothy Corrigan is correct to suggest that cult audiences engage in a radical bricolage, wrenching representations "from their naturalized and centralized positions," *Casablanca*'s cult status has been effectively commodified both by its capacity to generate other texts and by the folklore describing its production as "an accumulation of accidents." [30] *Casablanca* has been the site of a multiplicity of alternative narratives, from the unproduced play on which it was based, *Everybody Goes to Rick's* ("revived" for six weeks as *Rick's Bar, Casablanca* in London in 1991),[31] to the unmade versions starring Ronald Reagan or George Raft or Ann Sheridan, to two television series in 1955 and 1983 and several unsuccessful attempts at a musical version, to Woody Allen's *Play It Again, Sam* (which enacts the ritual relationship between cult spectator and film: "It's from *Casablanca*. I've waited all my life to say it"), to Robert Coover's "You Must Remember This," a piece of *Playboy* postmodernism that inserts four sex acts and a paralipsis into the 3½ seconds I have been discussing.[32]

From Andrew Sarris's assertion that *Casablanca* was "the happiest of happy accidents, and the most decisive exception to the *auteur* theory," the idea of the movie's "nearly accidental creation" pervades its critical assessment, by popular and academic critics alike. Umberto Eco's account of the film's genesis follows a general trend: those who tell production anecdotes call it "a fairly ramshackle affair with—as was admitted—a narrative-line which seems to have been made up as it went along." The importance given to hermeneutic structures in classical Hollywood narrative is emphasized by anecdotal accounts of the script being rewritten and doctored day by day so that "the suspense built into the film was natural," because "nobody from Hal Wallis and Michael Curtiz on down had decided exactly how the film should end." Bergman remembered her discomfort with shooting "off the cuff" as an uncertainty about "how the movie was going to end. Would she stay with Bogart or fly away with Henreid?" Subsequent criticism has more kindly suggested that her uncertainty about who she was supposed to be in love with was the "essential point" of her character, and that her anxiety "gave her portrayal of Ilsa a marvelously distraught quality." More generally, Otto Friedrich suggests "that the unhappiness of the whole cast was what made *Casablanca* such a triumph." [33]

Eco's engaging analysis of the movie as "a hodgepodge of sensational scenes strung together implausibly" out of mannered performances and psychologically incredible characters, is oddly reliant on this mythology:

> One is tempted to read *Casablanca* as T. S. Eliot read *Hamlet,* attributing its fascination . . . to the imperfection of its composition. . . . Forced to improvise a plot, the authors mixed a little of everything, and everything they chose came from a repertoire that had stood the test of time. When only a few of these formulas are used, the result is simply kitsch. But when the repertoire of stock formulas is used wholesale, then the result is an architecture like Gaudi's *Sagrada Familia:* the same vertigo, the same stroke of genius. . . . Nobody would have been able to achieve such a cosmic result intentionally. Nature has spoken in place of men.

There is considerable slippage in Eco's account between the deconstructive practice of his analysis and his claim that the pleasure of *Casablanca* lies in "its glorious ricketiness." To achieve the status of a "cult" object, Eco argues that a movie, unlike a book, "must be already ramshackle, rickety, unhinged in itself. . . . It should display not one central idea but many. It should not reveal a coherent philosophy of composition." What constitutes cult status remains uncertain, but Eco uses the claim to it as a means to avoid clarifying his own project. Suggesting that "perhaps the best deconstructive readings should be made of unhinged texts (or that deconstruction is simply a way of breaking up texts)," he conveniently camouflages the distance between object and analysis, and denies *Casablanca* textual coherence by the same maneuver that he claims a space for infinite critical experimentation. The film is "a great example of cinematic discourse, a palimpsest for future students of twentieth-century religiosity, a paramount laboratory for semiotic research into textual strategies. [*Casablanca*] is not *one* movie. It is 'movies.'" [34]

For Eco the purpose in viewing *Casablanca* as a cult movie is to allow himself this critical freedom by dehistoricizing the object of his inquiry. He describes "the normal situation of a cult movie" as being one in which members of the audience "find in the movie even memories of movies made after *Casablanca.*" Such ahistorical criticism is seldom disconcerted by pedestrian accounts of the material history of production and consumption, but it is important to note that Eco's acceptance of the mythology of *Casablanca*'s production allows him to claim that the movie, as fortuitous accident, works "in defiance of any aesthetic theory." The disingenuousness of such faux naïveté may be a form of postmodern playfulness that loses something in the translation to the colder, more Calvinist climate in which I write. The cult object *Casablanca* that Eco constructs is both like and unlike the movie I am familiar with. In my *Casablanca*, too, the clichés talk among themselves, but the palimpsest runs alongside a text assembled according to a quite rigidly constructed formal framework that is in no sense "accidental," any more than the movie's ending was made up at the last minute. Perhaps the faux naïveté conceals a genuine naïveté about the engineering principles of "the heavy industry of dreams," or perhaps simply a disregard of its productive processes in favor of the greater rewards of critical prestidigitation.

Casablanca is *both* sutured and rickety. Moreover, it is both sutured and rickety for a coherent set of reasons that relate to its functional effectiveness as an object of consumption inside the institution of entertainment, and thus it is typical of other, comparable objects of consumption. Its incoherence and fissures can, therefore, not only be savored as "the extreme of banality allow[ing] us to catch a glimpse of the Sublime," or interrogated for their revelation of ideological function. They can also be understood as part of the performative work of the movie in communicating with its multiple audiences.

The idea that the story was being made up as it went along is delightful nonsense, of course, but it is revealingly delightful nonsense. *Casablanca* must end as it does, with "the start of a beautiful friendship," but its constant references to itself as being "still a story without an ending" encourage the imagining of other narratives. Despite the fact that, like Rick, we have all heard a lot of stories that began, "Mister, I met a man once . . . ," the production anecdotes have helped to sustain these alternatives. On the one hand, a number of critics have demonstrated the textual coherence of *Casablanca* in pursuit of its anti-isolationist ideological project, to which the movie was as institutionally committed as it was to its observance of the Code.[35] Robert Ray suggests that the movie's borrowing of the structure of the "reluctant hero" mythology from the Western also fixes its narrative trajectory: "as a disguised western intent on demonstrating the impermanence of all interventions in society's affairs, *Casablanca* could have not conceivably allowed its outlaw hero to keep the girl." For Ray, the ending derives its force from the coincidence between the official morality of the Production Code and the ideological need for sacrifice.[36] On the other hand, production anecdotes are used by other critics as evidence of a narrative divergence or hesitation in the "text." Thus, Dana Polan argues:

> In *Casablanca* . . . the conversion narrative is in tension with an oedipal narrative. It may not be insignificant that the screenwriters report their confusion all through the days of production as to which ending to use (should Rick stay with

Ilsa or not? Should desire or duty triumph?); their hesitation is the hesitation of the Hollywood machine at this moment, the hesitation of narrativity itself at this moment.[37]

The conversion Polan is discussing is Rick's; strangely, he situates it at the end of the movie, when the conversion enacted is Renault's. I cite Polan here as another instance of a critic who has been watching a different movie from the *Casablanca* I saw. But as Larry Vonalt's account of yet another *Casablanca* suggests, the familiarity that cult or canonic status brings to a text invites the imagination of other versions, what Robin Wood has called the "awareness of the suppressed, ghostly presence of an alternative film saying almost precisely the opposite, lurking just beneath the surface.[38]

Casablanca's production anecdotes preserve a sense of alternative possibilities, of other versions of the movie, the imagination of which is given a kind of legitimacy by their allegedly having been imagined in production: one recent account of the movie's production suggests that the strength of Bogart's performance led producer Hal Wallis to consider other possible endings: "Rick takes Ilsa off to Lisbon; Ilsa stays with Rick in Casablanca; Rick is killed helping the Laszlos escape; Victor is shot, leaving the two lovers together. . . . Word of these discussions must have gotten to the actors, because they were beginning to express some anxiety over how the film would end." The charm and power of this production mythology lies in the possibility of transgression provided by the anecdote: that an alternate ending was possible, one that did not remind its audience that classical Hollywood cinema was a rigidly controlled Jesuitical universe and that its products were inevitably trivially conventional; an ending, that is, that permitted the escape of repressed desire (the desires viewers projected onto the actors or the characters) from the confining closure of a deterministic narrative. It is, of course, important to understand that given the ideological configuration of the movie, all these endings were impossible: only with Laszlo dead can Rick and Ilsa be united, and to have the Nazi villain kill a Resistance leader who has "succeeded in impressing half the world" would undermine the movie's overt ideological project. While it might succeed in satisfying the sophisticated viewers of the movie's entirely deniable sex scene, any outcome that united Rick and Ilsa would be at the expense of the movie's essential premise. In every version of the script, as well as in its source, Rick sends Ilsa to Lisbon with Victor; in every version, the Laszlos leave, Rick kills Strasser and banters with Renault; in every version, Ilsa has no active part to play in her destiny, any more than Bergman did in the fate of her character.[39]

The evidence of the Warner Bros. production files makes it clear that the rewriting was a matter of how to maneuver the plot convincingly to its required outcome, not in any sense what that outcome was going to be.[40] What was under discussion was not the movie's plot, but its performance, how to make "the sacrifice ending" work.[41] Perhaps Ingrid Bergman, making only her fifth Hollywood film, did not sufficiently understand the functional control of the Production Code over plot development. Perhaps her stories merely reflect her irritation at being unable to construct a coherent characterization from a finished script.[42] Everyone else involved in spreading these anecdotes, however, knew better. But since it is a Hollywood story, the production narrative insists just as much as the movie plot on the discourse of the happy accident and the serendipitous coincidence, repeating the passage of a classical Hollywood narrative in taking the most improbable route ("the unhappiness of the whole cast") to reach the inevitable outcome ("a triumph"). Being the best of all possible worlds, in Hollywood everything works out for the best.

To a large extent, unravelling *la vrai histoire* from these entangled discourses is irrelevant. "When the legend becomes fact, print the legend." What has happened in these accounts is that the anecdotes about script rewrites—a common enough Hollywood procedure that clearly ran somewhat more out of hand than usual on this occasion—have been converted into a much better story, in which the plot of *Casablanca* was "made up as they went along." This story echoes an "innocent" experience of viewing narrative as unconstructed, a childhood fantasy of cinema in which the actors invent their own dialogue and make up stories by acting them out. Accounts of Hollywood in its "age of innocence" similarly repeat fictions of "the days when they shot off the cuff and there wasn't any script." The production anecdotes surrounding *Casablanca* appeal so strongly and intensify our pleasure in the text because they offer us a sophisticated version of our innocent assumptions about where movies come from. In some versions, for instance, the most memorable lines are attributed to the invention of the performers: on no evidence other than appropriateness, Charles Francisco attributes both "Here's looking at you, kid," and "of all the gin joints . . ." to Bogart.[43] These stories are not absolutely naïve in that they have penetrated the veils of illusion far enough to recognize that the characters are not people but actors; but they do not penetrate the industrial process any deeper than the level of the individual text.

The experience of cinema puts the audience in the position of inventing a movie's narrative as the film passes before them. What transpires in the anecdotes of production is an act of transference, by which the audience chooses to describe and attribute its own activity to some other party, whether it identifies that party as actor, auteur, or text. This allows the audience to experience the movie not as a simple transparency, but as a complex one. Classical Hollywood movies have determinate narrative structures. Convention, whether in the form of generic predictability or the Production Code, dictates order, morality, and outcome. In the journey that a conventionally sophisticated audience takes in a classical Hollywood narrative, they always know where they are going, and they never know the route. Imagining that it is "being made up as they go along" is the intertextually innocent response to this combination of a determinate outcome and an unpredictable progression. The "sophisticated" viewing of a movie, on the other hand, can be an act of fatalistic, doomed resistance to the inevitability of its moralistic ending. In the early days of the Production Code, reformers often, if unfairly, castigated the industry for having "invented the perfect formula—five reels of transgression followed by one reel of retribution."[44] But as the implementation of the Code developed, it insisted on an ever more coherent narrative, the very interrelatedness of which provided a defence against accusations of promoting immorality. Audiences "viewing against the grain" found themselves also viewing against the "stair-step" construction of narrative causation. And yet such pleasurably aberrant viewings were always possible within classical Hollywood cinema, because the narrative determinism was overlaid with, or even constructed from, plot implausibility, character inconsistency, melodramatic coincidence—all opportunities for audiences to distance themselves from the movie, to allow the repressed of the text to return in some parallel imagined version, no less implausible than the one on the screen.

NOTES

This essay developed out of discussions with students taking courses on Hollywood Cinema at the University of Exeter, and was completed during a University Study Leave. I am grateful to my students, my colleagues in the School of English and American Studies, and the University Research Committee for their support. It has benefited from the advice and suggestions that have followed a number of public airings, including the Text and Theory Seminar at Exeter. I want particularly to thank David Bordwell, Kate Bowles, Lyn Browne, Ian Craven, Mick Gidley, Jo Seton, and Michael Wood. My greatest debt, intellectual and much more, is to Ruth Vasey, who shared this essay's gestation and tempered its worst excesses. Of all the gin joints in all the towns in all the world . . .

1. Entry for *Casablanca, Cinemania Interactive Movie Guide* (1992).

2. R. Barton Palmer, "The Metafictional Hitchcock," *Cinema Journal* 25, 2 (Winter 1986): 10.

3. See, for example, Lucretia Knapp, "The Queer Voice in *Marnie*," *Cinema Journal* 32, 4 (Summer 1993): 7, 11.

4. Jean-Loup Bourget, "Sirk and the Critics," *Bright Lights* 6 (Winter 1977–78): 8; David Bordwell, *Narration in the Fiction Film* (Madison: University of Wisconsin Press, 1985), p. 29; Mary Ann Doane, "Response," *Camera Obscura* 20–21 (1990): 143; Umberto Eco, *The Role of the Reader: Explorations in the Semiotics of Texts* (Bloomington: Indiana University Press, 1979), pp. 7–8.

5. Lewis Herman, *A Practical Manual of Screen Playwriting for Theater and Television Films* (New York: World, 1974), pp. 87–88. The assertion is a commonplace of screenwriting manuals. See, for instance, Eugene Vale, *The Technique of Screenplay Writing* (New York: Crown, 1944, 1973), 171.

6. Parker Tyler, *The Hollywood Hallucination* (New York: Simon and Schuster, 1994), p. 10; Pauline Kael, "Trash, Art, and the Movies," in *Going Steady* (Boston: 1970), p. 101.

7. Barbara Klinger, "Digressions at the Cinema: Reception and Mass Culture," *Cinema Journal* 28, 4 (Summer 1989): 10, 14, 16.

8. Barbara Klinger, "Much Ado About Excess: Genre, *Mise-en-Scène* and the Woman in *Written on the Wind*," *Wide Angle* 11, 4 (1989): 20.

9. Edward Branigan, *Narrative Comprehension and Film*, (London: Routledge, pp. 98, 149.

10. The published script, which does not describe its source, describes the action as follows: "Rick has taken Ilsa in his arms. He presses her tight to him and kisses her passionately. She is lost in his embrace. Sometime later, Rick watches the revolving beacon at the airport from his window. There is a bottle of champagne on the table and two half-filled glasses. Ilsa is talking. Rick is listening intently" (Howard Koch, *Casablanca: Script and Legend* [Woodstock, N.Y.: Overlook, 1973], p. 156).

11. Judith Mayne, *Cinema and Spectatorship* (New York: Routledge, 1993), p. 37; Janet Staiger, *Interpreting Films: Studies in the Historical Reception of American Cinema* (Princeton: Princeton University Press, 1992), pp. 26, 13.

12. With multiple viewings, there are more variations. Under social pressure to deny her innocence on a subsequent viewing, Jane may respond, as a student did in one seminar discussion, that the last time she saw the movie they hadn't slept together, but this time, they had.

13. Richard deCordova, *Picture Personalities: The Emergence of the Star System in America* (Urbana: University of Illinois Press, 1990), p. 143; Mary Ann Doane, *Femmes Fatales: Feminism, Film Theory, Psychoanalysis* (London: 1991), p. 1; Martha Wolfenstein and Nathan Leites, *Movies: A Psychological Study* (Glencoe, Ill.: Free Press, 1950), pp. 29, 35.

14. Ibid., pp. 243–44, 247, 250–51.

15. Doane, *Desire to Desire*, p. 1; Tyler, *Hollywood Halluciation*, pp. 37, 46, 49, 52, 54; Wolfenstein and Leites, *Movies*, p. 301.

16. F. Scott Fitzgerald, *The Last Tycoon* (Harmondsworth, England: Penguin, 1960), pp. 51–52.

17. Wolfenstein and Leites, *Movies*, pp. 87, 109.

18. David Bordwell, Kristin Thompson, and Janet Staiger, *The Classical Hollywood Cinema: Film Style and Mode of Production to 1960* (London: Routledge, 1985), p. 16; Virginia Wright Wexman, *Creating the Couple: Love, Marriage, and Hollywood Performance* (Princeton, N.J.: Princeton University Press, 1993), pp. 3–5; Umberto Eco, "*Casablanca:* Cult Movies and Intertextual Collage," in *Travels in Hyperreality*, trans. William Weaver (San Diego: Harcourt, Brace, 1987), p. 209. One site in which coherence is frequently lacking is in a movie's lighting plot. In *Casablanca*, for instance, variations in lighting are visible in several scenes in Rick's bar. For an elaboration of Hollywood as a generic cinema rather than a cinema of genres, see chapter 3 of Richard Maltby and Ian Craven, *Hollywood Cinema: An Introduction* (Oxford: Blackwell's, 1995).

19. This conventional industry wisdom was unchallenged until 1942, when George Gallup presented survey evidence indicating that 51 percent of the movie audience was male. That evidence was subjected to a withering critique by Lou Pollock, former advertising and publicity manager for Universal, who articulated the industry's conventional wisdom that most of the audience attending a successful movie "will be formed by mixed pairs, the females of which had previously announced to their males: 'Let's go to see *Mrs. Miniver* tonight. Or it might have been *Rebecca* or *Yankee Doodle Dandy* or *Gone with the Wind*. And the men said, 'Okay, honey,' and they stumbled

along—little suspecting that they were going to mislead a lot of bright, young statisticians into thinking that it was their idea in the first place." Had Pollock been writing a year later, he would in all probability have used *Casablanca* as his principal example. Quoted in Thomas Doherty, *Projections of War: Hollywood, American Culture, and World War II* (New York: Columbia University Press, 1993), p. 152.

20. Robert Ray, *A Certain Tendency of the Hollywood Cinema* (Princeton, N.J.: Princeton University Press, 1985), p. 90. See also Richard Maltby, *Harmless Entertainment: Hollywood and the Ideology of Consensus* (Metuchen, N.J.: Scarecrow, 1983), pp. 193–210.

21. Michael Renov, *Hollywood's Wartime Women: Respresentation and Ideology* (Ann Arbor: UMI Research Press, 1988), p. 228: Ingrid Bergman and Alan Burgess, *Ingrid Bergman: My Story* (New York: Delacorte, 1980), pp. 298–99, 317–18. Bergman's return to American respectability came, appropriately enough, when she played an amnesiac refugee in *Anastasia* (1956), a performance for which she won her second Oscar.

22. Tyler, *Hollywood Hallucination*, pp. 69, 40.

23. For discussion of a particular instance of this policy in practice, see Richard Maltby, " 'To Prevent the Prevalent Type of Book': Censorship and Adaptation in Hollywood, 1924–1934," *American Quarterly* 44, 4 (December 1992): 554–83.

24. Joseph Breen to Jack Warner, June 5, 1942, PCA *Casablanca* file, quoted in Rudy Behlmer, *Inside Warner Bros. (1935–1951)* (New York: Viking, 1985), p. 212.

25. Harold J. Salemson, *The Screen Writer*, (April 1946), quoted in Ruth Inglis, *Freedom of the Movies: A Report on Self-Regulation from the Commission on Freedom of the Press* (Chicago: University of Chicago Press, 1947), pp. 183–84; Elliot Paul and Luis Quintanilla, *With a Hays Nonny Nonny* (New York: Random House, 1942), 63–64.

26. Ruth Vasey, *Diplomatic Representations: The World According to Hollywood, 1918–1939* (Madison: University of Wisconsin Press, forthcoming).

27. Breen to Warner, June 18, 1942, PCA *Casablanca* file, quoted in Harlan Lebo, *Casablanca: Behind the Scenes* (New York: Simon and Schuster, 1992), p. 105.

28. Wolfenstein and Leites, *Movies*, p. 90.

29. Doane, *Desire to Desire*, p. 72; Wolfenstein and Leites, *Movies*, pp. 300–301, 28, 177; Tyler, *Hollywood Hallucination*, pp. 67, 73; Doane, *Femmes Fatales*, 107–8; Larry Vonalt, "Looking Both Ways in *Casablanca*," in *The Cult Film Experience: Beyond All Reason*, ed. J. P. Telotte (Austin: University of Texas Press, 1991), p. 64.

30. Vonalt, "Looking Both Ways," p. 65; Ray, *Certain Tendency*, p. 89; Timothy Corrigan, *A Cinema without Walls: Movies and Culture after Vietnam* (Rutgers, N.J.: Rutgers University Press, 1991), pp. 83, 91. Colin McArthur calls *Casablanca* "possibly the richest generator of other texts in the past fifty years" (Colin McArthur, *The Casablanca File* [London: Half Brick Images, 1992], p. 5). By 1977, *Casablanca* had become the movie most frequently screened on U.S. television (Aljean Harmetz, *Round Up the Usual Suspects: The Making of Casablanca—Bogart, Bergman, and World War II* [New York: Hyperion 1992], xiii, 346).

31. It was produced under the title *Casablanca* in Newport, Rhode Island, in 1946 (Charles Francisco, *You Must Remember This: The Filming of Casablanca* [Englewood Cliffs, N.J.: Prentice-Hall, 1980], p. 205).

32. Robert Coover, "You Must Remember This," in *A Night at the Movies or, You Must Remember This* (London: Paladin, 1989), 185–86. Coover also makes Ilsa, who used once to be an American called Lois, German. In 1988 Howard Koch "suggested

a sequel in which Rick's son by Ilsa—she must have gotten pregnant during that dissolve in Rick's apartment—goes to Morocco to find out what happened to his father" (Harmetz, *Round Up*, p. 339).

33. Andrew Sarris, *The American Cinema: Directors and Directions* (New York: E. P. Dutton, 1968), p. 176; James Card, "Confessions of a *Casablanca* Cultist," in Telotte, *The Cult Film Experience*, p. 71; Tom Hutchinson, *Screen Goddesses* (London: 1984), p. 84; Francisco, *You Must Remember This*, p. 172; Friedrich, *City of Nets: A Portrait of Hollywood in the 1940s* (New York: Harper & Row, 1987), pp. 137–38.

34. Eco, "*Casablanca*," pp. 201–2, 197, 208–9.

35. Warner Bros. produced an eight-page "justification" of *Casablanca* for the Office of War Information, demonstrating how the movie conformed to the ideological goals established by the OWI's Government Information Manual for the Motion Picture Industry. See Harmetz, *Round Up*, pp. 297, 309.

36. Actually, an interpretation of *Casablanca*'s precise ideological project turns out not to be quite so simple, either. The movie's New York premiere was sponsored by Free French War Relief with a parade and a recruiting booth in the theater. Although the coincidence of its release with the invasion of North Africa made *Casablanca* fortuitously timely, it failed to reflect U.S. policy toward the Free French, who were not accorded diplomatic recognition until October 1944. According to Richard Raskin, at the time of the movie's release, "men like Victor Laszlo were being arrested by the police of the administrators the U.S. supported in North Africa." Raskin suggests that the movie might have been intended to alter American attitudes toward the Free French, but that, paradoxically, by "conferring unlimited prestige to the Free French and militant anti-fascism, *Casablanca* contributed to a blurring of public awareness of the essentially anti-Free French orientation of U.S. policy and of American support of Vichy leaders in North Africa." The differences between American foreign policy and *Casablanca*'s representation of Vichy were sufficient to affect the movie's foreign release. Although approved for general overseas showing, the Office of War Information withheld it from shipment to North Africa "on the advice of several Frenchmen within our organization who feel it is bound to create resentment on the part of the natives." See Ray, *A Certain Tendency*, p. 110; Richard Raskin, "*Casablanca* and United States Foreign Policy," *Film History* 4, 2 (1990): 161; Harmetz, *Round Up*, p. 286.

37. Dana Polan, *Power and Paranoia: History, Narrative, and the American Cinema, 1940–1950* (New York: Columbia University Press, 1986), p. 156.

38. Robin Wood, *Personal Views: Explorations in Film* (London: Fraser, 1976), p. 129.

39. Frank Miller, *Casablanca: As Time Goes By . . .* (Atlanta: Turner, 1992), p. 140. See also Behlmer, *Behind the Scenes*, p. 170; Lebo, *Behind the Scenes*, p. 77; Harmetz, *Round Up*, p. 228, 232.

40. In a preproduction memo to Hal Wallis, uncredited scriptwriter Casey Robinson described the scene in which Ilsa comes for the visas, and breaks down, "absolutely helpless in the great passionate love she has for him. She knows that she's doing wrong . . . that in a way it is a violation of all the high idealism and honor of her nature . . . but she can't help herself. This is a great scene for a woman to play. . . . Now you're really set up for a swell twist when Rick sends her away on the plane with Victor. For in doing so, he is not just solving a love triangle. He is forcing the girl to live up to the idealism of her nature, forcing her to carry on with the work that in these days is far more important than the love of two little people" (Behlmer, *Behind the Scenes*, p. 167).

41. "There were two major problems: how to make Ilsa's leaving the man she loved

seem believable and what to do with Rick after she leaves" (Harmetz, *Round Up,* p. 228; Behlmer, *Inside Warner Bros.,* p. 213).

42. However, *Casablanca*'s production schedules indicate that Bergman filmed several of her scenes with Bogart and Henreid, including the one under discussion, after the final scene had been shot (Miller, *As Time Goes By,* p. 154).

43. Fitzgerald, *Last Tycoon,* p. 191; Francisco, *You Must Remember This,* p. 163.

44. "Virtue in Cans," *The Nation,* (16 Apr. 1930): 441.

22

The Jazz Singer's
Reception in the Media and
at the Box Office

Donald Crafton

There has been a discernible shift in film theory from propositions about production to ones involving reception. Films tend to be regarded less as industrial and formal artifacts made by studios and filmmakers, and more as consumer goods. To determine their function and value, scholars are examining such issues as the psychology and perceptual activities of spectators and the identification of audiences and social formations. These topics are supplementing authors and texts as the principal objects of study.

As an ancillary project in the study of reception, one increasingly prominent tool has been the recovery and analysis of original texts surviving from the time of distribution. The circulation of these journalistic writings have made us more aware of the debates surrounding film "readers." But generally speaking, there has not been a corresponding increase in awareness about actual audiences. A good example might be Janet Staiger's discussion of *Zelig*. She collates published reviews of Woody Allen's film into categories of response; for example, critics influenced by their religion and those who write for a cultural elite.[1] There is a presumption that these authors speak both to and on behalf of real audiences. This is a welcome departure from accounts that ignore viewer/listeners altogether or, paraphrasing her, preconstitute their identity. And her approach is materialist in the sense that she has researched actual artifacts, the published documents that record how some viewers "received" the film. Yet these audiences are not specified except in broad terms like "Jews in America" and "cultural elite." Typical of many reception studies, this seems to be the limit. Beyond it we apparently do not know much more about who was watching *Zelig*. Nor is there an indication of the degree to which the journalists cited are representative of other viewers. The implication is that they are the voice of constituencies and that the diversity of their utterances is metonymical for viewers without voices. The interpretations of a few become the index of the film's general reception.

In a slightly different context, Staiger acknowledges that studying journalists' reports is not indicative of social formations in general: "Such an unspoken mass [of moviegoers] deserves as much attention as does the popular press—if not more. How to do this for historical readers in a responsible scholarly way, however, is a very real problem."[2] She is referring to the representation of non-Anglo-Saxon–American viewers, but isn't the problem even more universal? Should we scrutinize our faith in the popular press to speak for all (or any) audiences?

It is not a trivial question. One of the most trenchant areas of film studies has been the exploration of the public sphere, the larger social, political, and aesthetic context into which cinema gradually inserted itself during the first third of the twentieth century. This theoretical approach to film history, which descends from the Frankfurt School, has developed in tandem with the ready availability of reprinted texts published during periods of intensified conflicts between film and society. The anthologies edited by Anton Kaes; Ludwig Greve, Margot Pehle, and Heidi Westhoff; and Richard Abel help reconstitute a public sphere of cinema reception in Germany and France.[3] The editors have assembled and categorized articles from the early entertainment trade press and mass-circulated magazines and newspapers that document the prevailing arguments. Indirectly, these tracts give us a sense of a struggle to define and tame a medium not yet integrated into a social hierarchy. These articles and reviews are taken to be chronicles of the expectations and anxieties that consumers experienced about the most popular form of entertainment.

But there are many problems with media analysis as a historical method. One is veracity; the standards of journalists generations ago are not the modern academic standards of accuracy and source citation. Plenty of fabrication could be introduced into the public record. There was not always a separation between opinion and fact.

Another problem is responsibility: to whom does the author answer? It would be a mistake to assume that a journalist's or a trade reviewer's audience is the same audience the films addressed. The constituent audience of the writer is more likely to be subscribers to the periodical than the attenders of cinema. There may be a certain overlap, of course, but common sense suggests that reviewers' and films' audiences are not identical.

Journalists and writers about culture often profess allegiance to a mass audience, sharing its desire for quality entertainment. Conversely, in American popular writing of the 1920s, several authors adopted an elitist attitude influenced by H. L. Mencken, scorning the middle class and their lowbrow entertainments in general. Throughout the period, these cultural mandarins generally held Hollywood films and their public in low esteem. The former were judged to be not living up to their cinematic potential (exemplified by European imports, notably *The Last Laugh* [*Der Letzte Mann*]); the latter were represented as passive, aesthetically indiscriminate crowds. We should not assume that writers from either camp have a privileged insight into the "popular" or the "arts," or that their real motives are necessarily as stated. For one thing, their opinions are frequently formed by outside editorial pressures that have little to do with film audiences. Publishers, advertisers, film producers, distributors, exhibitors, publicity departments, and press agents have been instrumental in trying to shape films' critical evaluations.

And there is the question of relevance: the author may not be addressing an issue that pertains to audiences. His or her response to a film may be uniquely determined by personal opinions and idiosyncratic concerns.

These questions have not blocked the wish of many analysts to construct detailed agendas concerning the reception of films. The result is that reception has come to mean interpretation, and reception study becomes imputing hermeneutic readings to hypothetical readers based on the remarks of a few professional readers.[4] But it is reasonable to suggest that building a social context for cinema must encompass a constant reevaluation of available information concerning those who actually went to the films.[5] Otherwise the reception being theorized is not that of film audiences, but that of those who are laying claim to those audiences.

The problem is, of course, that we know very little about the physical composition of movie attenders—even current ones, despite the expenditure of enormous sums by studios, banks, and networks on demographic research. As we go further back in time, the ceiling of obtainable knowledge becomes lower and the evidence of original reception becomes more precious. Nevertheless, as media analysis as a tool for understanding audiences becomes more pervasive, I think it is time to interject a note of caution about its use.

While I researched a history of the transition to sound in Hollywood,[6] I encountered an apparent discrepancy as reported by journalists and as measured by box-office receipts. The discrepancy concerns the popularity of a key film from the early sound period: *The Jazz Singer*. My preliminary findings demonstrate that referential methods of assessing audience reaction, in this case media analysis, are important, but that they must be correlated with direct evidence.

By referential methods I mean evidence that is supposed to "incorporate by reference"[7] information about the audience. For instance, several press anecdotes suggest that in the pre-talkie period chatting during films and reading the titles aloud were commonplace behaviors. How do we know that audience-generated noise was normal? The multiple occurrences of this information in print suggests that different authors are citing a common phenomenon. But it is also possible that one author is simply repeating the other. We also, however, have artifacts in the form of "Quiet Please!" lantern slides which are evidence that a behavior was taking place which the management sought to control. Taken together, we can make inferences about the existence of these specific behaviors. But without direct evidence, questions like how widespread a certain behavior was will remain unanswered. Did audience sounds vary by city or geographical region? By the social-ethnic background of the community? By proximity to legitimate theaters or vaudevilles which might have had different norms for audience participation? By the content of the film program? By the presentation context of the theater, for example, amount of ambient light on the audience during projection? By the size of the audience? It would be rare to find direct evidence to answer these questions, but sometimes, as in Mary Carbine's study of music in Chicago's black theaters, we can find statements that specify precisely what behaviors were taking place.[8] On the legal side, ordinances proscribing distracting or unsafe behaviors, restricting exhibition, or establishing censorship norms can be extrapolated to yield information about audience activity.

Journalist discourse has been the kind of referential information that is easiest to access because of its status as a public record. Historical spectators have vanished and film prints have deteriorated, but articles claiming to reflect and mold public opinion about film have been preserved in libraries.

When we read published accounts of *The Jazz Singer*'s New York premiere we form an impression of its sparkling critical and popular triumph and its fabulous yet unexpected success at the Broadway box office—a success so great that other reluctant moguls were convinced to convert to sound.

The question is, how successful was *The Jazz Singer* when measured against contemporary silent and sound films? We get two answers depending on whether we use reports in the popular media or rely on available box-office data, inadequate though they may be.

Media Analysis

The newspaper and magazine reports of the time consistently regarded *The Jazz Singer* as a breakthrough, turn-around motion picture for Warner Bros. and the genesis of the talkies. Curiously, the authors tended to repeat themselves in trying to express the film's importance. For example, the May 1928 issue of the influential monthly magazine *The American Mercury*, published an account of the film's success:

> Al Jolson made his appearance in *The Jazz Singer*, singing both "Mammy" and the Kol Nidre, beside conversing with his Ghetto Mamma. The celebrated Irving Berlin wept at this première and other hard-hearted gentlemen of Broadway admitted that Mr. Jolson was never better. The film coined money. At the time it was released, there were but 400 theatres wired with the talking film apparatus. It went into everyone of them and broke record after record. In New York, Chicago, Boston, Baltimore, Kansas City, and Los Angeles, it entertained the public for week after week.[9]

One finds this article's narrative of the premiere and its statistics echoed in *The Independent and Outlook* in December:

> After a few of these [synchronized sound effects] feelers they [Warners] produced their great *coup*, *The Jazz Singer*, which starred Al Jolson, and which is

credited with having been the biggest box office success released in 1927, even though less than four hundred theatres were then wired for sound. It was at that point that the other producers began to scratch their heads and wonder.[10]

Another persistent story was that Jolson had aided Warner Bros. by deferring his salary:

> At the Motion Picture Club, on Broadway, which is the clearing house for news and gossip about the business, it is generally agreed that Al Jolson's picture, *The Jazz Singer,* was the turning point for sound pictures. . . .
> [The Warners] admitted that they didn't have enough money to pay [Jolson] what they thought he would demand, but the story was his story and he said, "I'll go out to Hollywood and see what comes of it."
> There are tales to the effect that during the making of the picture the Warners were so low in funds that Jolson did not draw all of his salary until weeks later. Some say that he even loaned them money to pay the other actors. So interested was he in the production that he was determined that it should be finished if he had to pay for it himself. . . .
> *The Jazz Singer* opened in New York, and at eleven o'clock that night the leaders of the motion picture industry, who stood cheering in the theater, knew that their business had been turned upside down. All the leaders were there.[11]

A few months later the anecdote was retold: "As the story goes, Mr. Jolson, in his sentimental interest in the tale, even made unprecedented concessions in his price."[12] Robert L. Carringer has documented other versions of the legend of Jolson's concessions. Yet the contract with Warner Bros. is unambiguous. Jolson's pay was $75,000, but it was to be disbursed in installments.[13] By ascribing the information to preexisting narrative forms (the tale, the story), these articles implicitly acknowledge that they are circulating fictions. Perhaps this was believed to provide a mantle of libel protection, but it also functioned to aggrandize Jolson's stardom and the Warner brothers' business acumen.

Two articles appeared in April 1929 that used an identical, unexpected metaphor:

> That October [1927], Warner Brothers brought Al Jolson to New York in tins and *The Jazz Singer,* a film and sound version of a stage play. . . .
> [Jolson] had hoisted the infant talkie upon his blackamoor shoulder and waded across a stream every pioneer must ford. In Julius Caesar's day they called it Rubicon.
> Theater records were broken by *The Jazz Singer.* Towns where a release was doing excellent business if it ran for three days held a print for weeks.[14]

The figure of crossing the Rubicon must have been appealing. Whether a coincidence or inspired by a common, as yet unidentified source, another author wrote of Jolson's first talking part:

> It wasn't much. A mere "bit"—and the picture was rolling on in its silent, sentimental way. But, to forty million movie fans, that act of Al Jolson's—his crossing the room to get at his piano—was a more important historical event

than Caesar's crossing of the Rubicon. It meant that the screen had shaken off the shackles of silence.[15]

All these articles retroactively transformed the release of *The Jazz Singer* into a cultural, industrial, and personal monument. We can point to these elements in the journalistic construction of the film's reputation: spoken dialogue was a novelty; film executives in the audience were immediately convinced of the profitability of sound production; *The Jazz Singer* played in all the theaters then wired; it was the big hit of 1927, making huge sums for Warners; and Al Jolson had a personal stake in the film's production.

The repetitions in the accounts suggest that the authors are either borrowing from each other—by no means an uncommon practice—or that they have been inspired by common sources. These might have been items from the journalists' rumor mills, or an institutionalized source of misinformation: press releases from Warner Bros. What direct methods are available for verifying these journalists' accounts of this signal moment in film history? For that matter, what kind of evidence is now available for learning about any audience in the 1920s?

While the modern researcher may feel hampered in trying to discover what original audiences thought about films, contemporary observers would have felt similar futility. The primary means of communication about audiences during the pre-talkie era was oral. The exhibitor or his representative (the house manager) would watch the film with the crowd and notify his superiors and the distributors about the house reaction. This would happen by phone or in a sales meeting, resulting in no "paper trail" for researchers to pick up. Some exhibitor box-office report forms provided space for audience reactions along with other relevant variables such as meteorological conditions, local holidays, special presentations at other theaters, and competing attractions (auto shows were especially feared). Few of these documents exist.[16]

For primary cinemas in a few large cities, stringers for the trade magazines such as *Variety, Moving Picture World,* and *Motion Picture Herald* reported on audience reactions in their weekly review of box-office receipts. Some of these reports might have been based on direct observation of audiences, but frequently they were just the impressions of the theater managers. Anyway, these comments were subjective, not analytical. A manager might note that a film appealed to the "feminine crowd" or that the plot was confusing. In small towns the theater operators sometimes wrote to their trade journals to express their audience's reactions to films.

Most large cities had regular newspaper reviewers who covered film along with theater and the local art scene. The writers varied widely in their professionalism, and many seem to have taken advantage of the studio publicity departments' press books—preassembled information and boilerplate reviews which made it easy to fabricate a few columns without ever attending a screening. We tend to suppose that reviewers watched the films, but even this assumption is not unassailable. And if they did, they probably saw it at a preview screening, where the audience was composed primarily of other journalists. Or reviewers might have viewed the film at an opening night gala for which the producers had distributed free tickets to presumably sympathetic spectators. There are some reviews that indicate the author watched the film alone in the projection booth. No doubt the institutionalized practices of press-kit distribution, press screenings, and the premiere helped to create a gap between the critical perception of a film's merits and the experience of audiences.

Producers, distributors, and exhibitors—at least as early as the teens—began asking audiences their opinions as they left the theater and sometimes asked them to put their thoughts down in writing.[17] At least some theaters conducted polls by distributing picture postcards. One surviving specimen has a scene from *The Squall* (1926) on the obverse. The reverse asks the patron to, "Be your own critic and tell your friends the TRUTH about *The Squall*. An attendant will collect—stamp and mail this card for you."[18] The audience member's sentiment would be noted by the management before the cards were posted. The customer received a free greeting to a friend; the producers, for two-cent stamps, could glean viewers' opinions.

On other survey cards the questions were similarly open-ended: Did you like this picture? Who was your favorite actor? Did you like the ending? Responses to questions like this strike us now as being very general and difficult to quantify. What surveys there were seem crude in retrospect. For example, apparently the sole finding of a 1927 survey of sixty theaters revealed that the average audience was 55 percent male and 45 percent female.[19] Fan magazines, newspapers, and women's magazines conducted polls of their readers who mailed in responses to questions like "Who is your favorite star?" Viewers also wrote unsolicited letters to fan magazines, and these are interesting primary documents. These polls and letters were unscientific (and possibly rigged by agents). But at least they were published and are relatively accessible. Hollywood's use of "scientific" public opinion testing developed gradually and was not adopted by the major studios until the late 1930s.[20]

Some modern researchers have interviewed people who attended early sound film screenings, but these oral histories must be used with circumspection. Memories are fallible; experiences might have been atypical. The same cautions are in order concerning biographies and memoirs, for example those of William Fox, George Jessel, Al Jolson, and Eddie Cantor. In addition, there are the possibilities of self-serving distortions and ghost writers' modifications.

The audience votes with its feet. This aphorism of stage and screen managers translates into a formula that should equate attendance with the audience's appreciation of a film. But really, the number of people going to a film tells us nothing about how the audience perceived its meaning or whether they even liked the show. Attendance is notoriously fickle. It would be affected by the appeal and penetration of the promotional campaign, the popularity of stars, and knowledge of the literary source of the story. If a film was exceptionally good or bad entertainment, then word-of-mouth advertising might be an influence. External factors also affected attendance: transportation disruptions, the weather, and the season (moviegoing peaks during the week before Christmas).

To further complicate things, attendance figures were seldom published; perhaps they were not even tallied. The important cipher was the account of weekly gross receipts, which might have combined two or more features. Houses were "scaled"; that is, admissions varied according to the time of day, place in the theater, and the age of the patron, making it difficult to estimate attendance based on the weekly gross.[21] Certainly we can tell the hits from the flops, but using the box office as a subtle barometer of popularity has only limited usefulness.

Even if we could know reliably how many people attended, we still would not know who they were. Many assumptions about audiences are based on the geographical location of theaters. But with a population that took pride in its mobility, we should not assume a demographic correlation between a theater and its locale.[22] In fact, common sense suggests a rule of thumb: the larger the metropolitan region, the greater the diversity of the total audience. Nothing illustrates this better than Broadway.

In the 1920s, the Broadway-Times Square theater district attracted a spectrum of customers ranging from upper- and middle-class patrons of the legitimate stage to itinerant moviegoers. Besides the locals, there were tourists from all over the country and military personnel and businessmen from all over the world.

Because of such diversity, it is risky to infer why audiences attended, what they thought or whether their reaction in the theater was uniform. Even if there were some corroboration, the results would probably be valid for one theater at one time. Analysts would expect significant variations in responses by time of day, day of the week, and length into the run. A film that played well in New York might do poorly in another city. It is also becoming clear that going to see the film being projected was not necessarily the main motivation for going to the movies; financial, social, and other pressures, as well as constantly changing tastes in entertainment, were at work. For instance, one aspect of theater design in the 1920s was the incorporation of arcade shops—distant ancestors of shopping malls.

So supposedly "direct" sources of knowledge about the audiences of the 1920s also have flaws. Still, can enough empirical knowledge about movie attendance be discovered to support or challenge the claims in the referential discourse about what happened during the initial Broadway run of *The Jazz Singer*?

Box-Office Analysis

One should feel nervous about equating a film's income with its popularity. Nevertheless, the box-office gross receipts may be the best way to judge how many viewers attended films in the 1920s, accepting certain inherent limitations.

Even if detailed records of box-office receipts were preserved in studio archives, the numbers would not be totally reliable. "Hollywood accounting" practices applied to the exhibition as well as to the production end of the business. Distributors resorted to audits, numbered tickets, and field observations to monitor their exhibitors' and managers' honesty. The actual figures were guarded as business secrets and were probably known accurately to only a few financial insiders. The theaters' announced revenue must be taken with a grain of salt, but for now it is the best available source for directly measuring a real, not hypothetical audience.

The data in my study are *Variety*'s copyrighted weekly box-office reports published for each preceding week. They purported to be unbiased, but they were also clearly identified as unaudited, rounded estimates. Since the weekly receipts were transmitted by managers, the report may have been adjusted to suit the house's own needs. Occasionally the editor will note that the figure supplied is "generous," suggesting that his visual observations were out of line with the income reported by the management.

Since the box-office gross was an estimation, several factors might influence its accuracy. For example, as a run extended, the producers regularly handed out free passes in order to augment the audience. These viewers are just as important as the paying audience, of course, but their presence distorts the estimate of gross, since the producer was in effect paying for these customers in order to enhance the illusion of a competitive film. In addition, theatrical agencies sold tickets to the most popular films. There was also a thriving scalper's market. These "ticket specs," as they were then called, resold tickets at a premium to sold-out performances. So it is difficult to know how, if at all, these nonbox-office receipts were figured into the gross numbers.

But, caveats aside, by an estimation, *The Jazz Singer* was an immediate hit. But was it the monumental success of its journalistic legend? Not quite. A comparison to the New York market shows that the film was by no means the most flourishing movie either in terms of gross or in length of run.

Fig. 22.1 slices four representative weeks from the 1927 run of *The Jazz Singer*. It shows gross weekly receipts from near its opening (two weeks ending 15 October) and from its tenth and eleventh weeks (ending 17 December). The averaged receipts of the Warner's Theater were in the middle ranking of Broadway's fourteen important movie houses. But notice how the theater district was dominated by the three huge pictures palaces: the new Roxy (6,250 seats), the Capitol (5,450), and the Paramount (4,000). What were these popular movies that were competing with Warner's part-talkie? In fact, they were low-budget, forgettable "programmers." The theaters drew customers for their live stage presentations, not their films. As Douglas Gomery has emphasized, the live-action stage show that preceded films at most large theaters attracted huge audiences.[23]

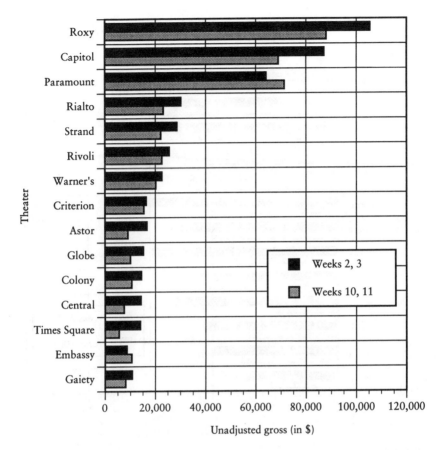

Fig. 22.1. Four representative gross weekly receipts from the 1927 run of *The Jazz Singer.*

The summer and fall of 1927 were especially significant because the popularity of jazz music was just beginning to be reflected at the theaters. The Roxy had switched to a "jazz policy" shortly before the Warner Bros. film opened there, and other new policy theaters were reporting markedly increased attendance, presumably by jazz fanatics who came for the live performances. Al Jolson was by far the most popular jazz vocalist. His chief rival as a stage act was Paul Whiteman's jazz band.

At the Warner's Theater, of course, there was no live prologue; it was the original Vitaphone concept to provide a substitute for these increasingly expensive (and some producers and critics were saying, distracting) performances. Instead, Vitaphone went head-to-head against the live jazz competition with musical shorts like *Red Spike's Band* (1927). *Variety*'s box-office review for the week which included *The Jazz Singer*'s premier is revealing. It was not Thursday's new talkie that was hailed, but rather the Capitol Theater's switch to a jazz orchestra: "Most of the excitement centered over the

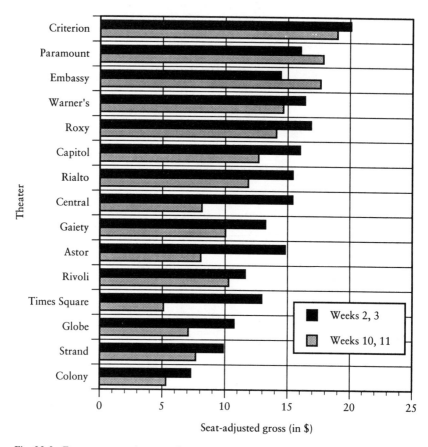

Fig. 22.2. Four representative seat-adjusted gross weekly receipts from the 1927 run of *The Jazz Singer*.

week-end and around the Capitol, where a new policy was inaugurated."[24] In early October it was showing *The Big Parade* in second run and taking in about $60,000 per week. After adopting its "new headline presentation act policy"—jazz acts and low-budget films—its weekly gross jumped to over $95,000.

The gross receipts data also distort the popularity of the programs because of discrepancies in theater size. The capacity of the Roxy, for example, was more than ten times that of the Embassy. Perhaps a more meaningful comparison is what we shall call the "seat-adjusted" gross, a ratio obtained by dividing the receipts by the capacity.

Fig. 22.2 displaying the combined receipts over four selected weeks, shows how calculating the amount of money a theater was able to get for each of its seats strikingly alters our picture of the public's preferences. The Criterion, showing *Wings*, jumps to the head of the class, consistently getting about $20 per week for each of its 812 seats. The Strand drops from fifth to next-to-last place (showing *When a Man Loves* in third run). Despite its 2,900 seats, it was getting less than $10 for them weekly. These differences are factors of the number of shows presented each week, the admission price, and the ability of the house to fill its seats to capacity. The seat-adjusted gross seems to be a better indicator of popularity than either the straight gross or simple attendance because it represents marketability—what people were willing· to pay for a certain show expressed in terms of the demand for seats.

Now the performance of *The Jazz Singer* looks more impressive. It trails the Publix stage presentation at the Paramount, but noses out Rothapfel's extravaganza at the Roxy and the jazz band at the Capitol. No picture, however, comes close to *Wings*, already running for more than ten weeks at $2 a ticket. In December the Embassy's fortunes were elevated by the release of *Love*. Starring Garbo, the sensational adaptation of *Anna Karenina* immediately garnered a higher seat-adjusted gross than *The Jazz Singer* and, for a couple of weeks, even surpassed *Wings*.

A traditional measure of popularity has been how long a film plays on Broadway. Fig. 22.3 compares the seat-adjusted gross of *The Jazz Singer*'s

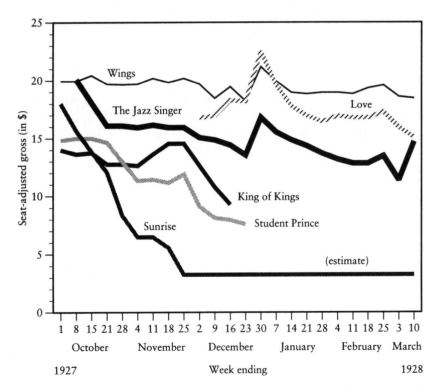

Fig. 22.3. Seat-adjusted gross weekly receipts from the Broadway runs of *The Jazz Singer*, and five competing movies, from October 1927 to March 1928.

most important competitors during the length of its first-run booking at the Warner's Theater. Again, the strength of *Wings* is evident; it steadily outperformed other films and would remain at the Criterion until October 1928. The trajectories of *King of Kings* and *The Student Prince* were typical of the course of a normal run—strong films that began to fade after about six weeks. But the precipitous drop in gross receipts for *Sunrise* is noteworthy and will be discussed below.

Why did the studio not move *The Jazz Singer* to a larger house? Of course they owned the Warner's Theater so they saved some lease money, but given the film's success, theater rental cost would not have been an important consideration. They had previously played their films at the Colony and the Roxy. It is possible that all the big prestige houses were already committed, but we don't have any information that might verify this hypothesis. It is probable, even likely, that the studio was content to play the film in its smaller house as a means of sustaining enthusiasm and extending the run.

Playing to a full house was an important promotional strategy. Producers liked seeing long lines at the box office and even turning away a reasonable number of customers because the attendant word-of-mouth advertising would help fortify the public image of an extremely desirable attraction. Attendance for *The Jazz Singer* did not begin to slip until the nineteenth week, when the gross dropped below $18,000 for the first time. A month later Warner Bros. moved the film into the Roxy for a two-week run where it took in $117,000 and $109,500 respectively. Much of this increased income reflects what might be called the Roxy premium: Many out-of-towners visited the mammoth picture palace just to experience the theater (it was less than a year old); and its capacity made high grosses the norm. The average weekly take was $104,000. By comparison, *What Price Glory?* when it was bumped into the Roxy, made $144,200 and $126,000 during its two-week run. It was followed by *Seventh Heaven*, which grossed $123,000 and $109,000.[25] So *The Jazz Singer*'s performance at New York's showcase movie house was very good, but did not consistently fill the big theater to capacity. It did about the same as *Loves of Carmen*.

We conclude that while the Warner's film was among New York's top entertainment attractions, it did not match Paramount's aerial saga or Garbo and Gilbert's clinches. *The Jazz Singer*'s Broadway run of twenty-three weeks was good but not exceptional.

But how did it measure up to other "sound" films? From the New York audience's perspective, seeing a film with synchronized music, sound effects or even dialogue, as in *The Jazz Singer*'s famous singing and "talking" scenes, was no novelty. For months moviegoers had been hearing music played through phonographic instruments to accompany films nonsynchronously and, not coincidentally, to eliminate the band in the orchestra pit. DeForest's Phonofilm acts had been around for years, and Fox had begun screening talking shorts with *What Price Glory?* in January. In the spring of 1927, aviator Charles Lindbergh's takeoff and his return ceremonies generated increased excitement, which was exploited by DeForest's and Fox's synchronized sounds and speech.[26] Although the Fox Movietone newsreel did not officially begin until December 1927, the company's talking shorts had been screened sporadically at the Roxy since 30 April and had begun playing regularly with *Seventh Heaven* back in June, at the Harris Theater.

By far the most important influence on the reception context of *The Jazz Singer* was undoubtedly the Vitaphone features and shorts that preceded it. In addition to *Don Juan*, which had opened at the Warner's in August 1926, the company had released three other synchronized features and launched a production program to make one-reel musical shorts to play with Warner Bros. silents and Vitaphone specials. Most of the shorts were "singing" and a few, for example, *Willie and Eugene Howard in "Between the Acts at the Opera,"* were "talking." A review of the seat-adjusted gross receipts for these first Vitaphone programs reveals that the first two features outperformed the *Jazz Singer* at the Warner's Theater box office.

Analyzed at comparable moments in their first runs in Table 22.1, we see that *Don Juan* ran consistently ahead of the Jolson film and *The Better 'Ole* began its run a little better than *The Jazz Singer.* (One factor in its appeal might have been the accompanying short, *Al Jolson in a Plantation Act.*) Less successfully, *Old San Francisco* grossed only about half as much per seat as *Don Juan; The First Auto* took in about one third as much and was pulled after a month. Again, the gross receipts for *The Jazz Singer* were unexceptional by Vitaphone standards, but what of its rival from Fox?

F. W. Murnau's *Sunrise,* with a synchronized Movietone soundtrack, opened on 16 September 1927, two weeks before the Warner's film. As with the early Vitaphone features, there was no recorded dialogue, only a score. The film immediately won critical raves and several honors including *Film Daily Yearbook's* "ten best" list. But on Broadway, it sank like a stone. Apparently the meaning of the film was obscure. In a front-page *Film Daily* review, the editor, Maurice Kann, wrote, "It is an amazing film. It gets over to the

Table 22.1. Seat-adjusted box-office gross

Title (theater)	Week in run			
	2nd	3rd	10th	11th
Don Juan (Warner's)	21.48	21.48	18.79	18.79
Jazz Singer (Warner's)	16.67	16.09	14.86	14.42
Better 'Ole (Colony)	17.19	16.79	11.52	11.17
Sunrise (Times Square)	18.01	15.65	3.24e	3.24e
First Auto (Colony)	6.41	5.81	—	—

Sources: *Variety* Key City Grosses©; *Film Daily Yearbook*
Notes: e   estimate (report not available)
— film no longer in first run

audience an indefinite something; just what, it is difficult to describe."[27] But two positive attractions were singled out: the quality of the recorded score, and the Movietone shorts on the same program.

Kann continued his review, "In tonal range and quality, Movietone has demonstrated its superiority in the field of synchronized sound and action films." The *Variety* reviewer also commented, "Nor should be neglected credit as a detail contributing vastly to a satisfying whole, the accompaniment of the Movietone. . . . The musical accompaniment was reproduced with flawless delicacy and under absolute control, merging into the entertainment and apparently disappearing as a separate element."[28] There were also two new Movietone subjects, the Vatican choir and a statement by Mussolini delivering in English what producer Winfield R. Sheehan called "a message of friendship." *Variety* attributed much of the *Sunrise* program's popularity to the shorts: "Thus far regarded as a draw. Getting all the barbers in five boroughs to hear Ben Mussolini speak his piece."[29]

But the popularity of *Sunrise* soon wore off. Though its opening seat-adjusted gross was higher than that of *The Jazz Singer* or any of the Vitaphone features (except *Don Juan*), by the third week its returns had entered a strong downward trend. By week nine the seat-adjusted gross was around $5 per week; after that the theater no longer reported figures, although *Variety* revealed that there were days when the Times Square Theater (1,080 seats; admission $1.00–$1.50) took in less than $400.

Despite what must have been a huge loss to Fox, the film continued to play first run for twenty-three weeks until 4 April 1928.[30] One explanation for this might have been a policy we can call "buying Broadway." Jerome Beatty described the practice:

> *Sons of Destiny* [a hypothetical movie] would run at a Broadway theater for twenty-six weeks. It would be lavishly advertised as a tremendous success. The best seats would sell for two dollars at evening performances and at Saturday, Sunday and holiday matinées. Perhaps the price would be boosted to $2.50 for Saturday and Sunday nights. Toward the end of the run free tickets would be passed around liberally, so as to keep the theater well filled. . . . "A riot on Broadway," the advertising to the trade would read, and the general impression would be that *Sons of Destiny* was making a lot of money at the [hypothetical] Columbine Theater. Yet, when the final accounting was made, the [hypothetical studio] Amalgamated would "go in the red" for $26,000.

Only a few pictures, according to Beatty, actually made money during their Broadway runs—*The Jazz Singer* and *Wings* were among them. Most lost thousands of dollars but the studios wrote off the cost in their "exploitation" budgets, viewing the run as necessary to secure national audiences. "Even a flop," Beatty reports, "will earn more money with a Broadway run back of it."[31] He also described the strategy of an unnamed producer:

> He was determined that the show should have half a year on Broadway. . . . Special salesmen were sent from house to house to sell tickets at half price. Or-

ganizations of all kinds were solicited and offered special group rates. School children were given slips which entitled the bearer to two tickets for the price of one. Passes by the hundreds were distributed in offices and department stores. In spite of this, some matinées played to as few as twenty-five persons, and the gross receipts one week were $2450.

The people demonstrated with a pathetic thoroughness that they just didn't want to see this man's show. The Broadway run cost the producer nearly $100,000. When he took the picture outside of New York City, however, it played to enormous business.[32]

Whether this incident involved William Fox, Cecil B. DeMille, or some other showman is unknown; but it probably explains the rationale for playing *Sunrise* to near-empty houses for almost six months. The practice also highlights the dangers of relying on any one measure, such as length of run, to determine popularity. Meanwhile, *Sunrise* opened in December at a gala five-dollar premiere at the Carthay Circle in Los Angeles. Its initial seat-adjusted gross was $8.84 per week and it performed respectably for ten weeks. Whether its West Coast success benefited from "buying Broadway" cannot be verified.

When *The Jazz Singer* opened it joined a cast of films which have since become legendary: *The Big Parade, Wings, King of Kings, The Student Prince,* and *Sunrise.* Yet when judged on the basis of its actual box-office record, it was far behind the most popular films. *The Big Parade* lasted on Broadway for two years and grossed a then-record $1.75 million just in New York. By comparison, *The Jazz Singer's* total domestic gross income was $1.97 million.[33] *Wings* had opened nine weeks before *The Jazz Singer* and continued to sell out almost every performance through the spring of 1928. The box office reported steady income of from $15,000 to $16,000, good for the small Criterion Theater. In show business jargon, *Wings* had legs.

Warner Bros. withheld *The Jazz Singer* from national release until mid-November 1927, when the film opened in Philadelphia at the Locust, a Fox theater with 1,800 seats. By delaying, Warner Bros. was practicing a form of buying Broadway and building up anticipation for the film outside of its New York venue. The preview trailer that the studio produced for *The Jazz Singer* might have been part of this suspense-generating strategy. It showed throngs outside the Warner's Theater but teasingly refrained from including scenes with Jolson speaking or singing. Predictably, the film did well in Philadelphia, opening with a $14,000 gross. But earlier in the year *What Price Glory?* had opened there with $20,000 and *Seventh Heaven* with $14,500, so *The Jazz Singer* was not a blockbuster. It had an eight-week run, but the other films had enjoyed runs of thirteen and eight weeks, respectively. The film opened New Year's Day 1928, in Los Angeles, St. Louis, Seattle, and Washington, D.C., with good, but not record, receipts.

Table 22.2 characterizes the early pattern of the film's national release. At the Orpheum in Chicago, *The Jazz Singer* was outgrossed throughout its run by the Vitaphone talking feature *Tenderloin.* In Los Angeles, *Wings* in second

Table 22.2. Unadjusted gross

Title	Week ending	Orpheum, Chicago		
		1st week	2nd week	6th week
Jazz Singer	3 March 1928	12,200	9,500	7,300
Tenderloin	14 April 1928	13,400	11,000	8,200

Title	Week ending	Criterion, Los Angeles		
		1st week	2nd week	5th week
Jazz Singer	7 Jan. 1928	19,600	14,400	8,600
Wings	9 Sept. 1928	21,200	16,800	12,000

Title	Week ending	Embassy, San Francisco		
		1st week	2nd week	4th week
Jazz Singer	18 Feb. 1928	20,200	21,000	18,000
Lights of New York	4 Aug. 1928	24,000	22,000	20,000

run at the Criterion outperformed *The Jazz Singer* in its first run. *Lights of New York* did better than *The Jazz Singer* at the Embassy, in San Francisco. In summary, in its national first-run release, *The Jazz Singer* did well, judged by box-office receipts and the length of its runs, but it was in a distinct second tier of attractions compared to the most popular films of the day and even with other Vitaphone talkies.[34]

Conclusions

If *Variety*'s data are accurate, then the "unprecedented success" of Warner Bros.' first part-talking feature was more of a retrospective creation of the media than a box-office reality. Eventually *The Jazz Singer* went on to become a huge national success—grossing nearly $2 million was an achievement in 1927–28—but the best available direct evidence also indicates that *The Jazz Singer* was not a Broadway smash.

Our finding that the Broadway statistics do not corroborate the legend of the film's initial success does not necessarily disqualify the use of popular journalism as a source of historical documentation about audiences. It would be overly simple to say that the popular version of the story is wrong, and the revisionist historian is right. Legends are also historical documents. The misleading nature of the journalistic version should make us look more closely at why the *Jazz Singer* legend developed the way it did.

One explanation, inspired by Hayden White, is that historiography traditionally has followed its own narrative conventions—causality, closure, and other rationalizing principles. Certainly the popular version written by the journalists tends to apply a simple conceptual grid to scattered events whose relationships might otherwise be difficult to discern. As the case of the referential discourse about the *Jazz Singer* illustrates, it is more "efficient" for a historical discourse to have a "turning point"—a Rubicon to cross—in lieu of a slow, convoluted, somewhat irrational development, as was the case with the coming of sound. This rewriting of events as a drama with the loose ends erased is helpful in retelling a complicated process as a conventionalized, thus comprehensible, narrative. It is also a strategy to monumentalize phenomena: the coming of sound can be collapsed into *The Jazz Singer*, creating a mnemonic that provides a date, a studio, and a star to epitomize a whole history.

Classical narratives often rely on personal deeds and motives, and our media analysis of *The Jazz Singer*'s reputation shows how historiography too may be influenced by personality. Accounts of the film are intertwined with Jolson's persona, implying that it was he who was responsible not only for its production, but for the success of the talkies altogether. For example:

> Al Jolson started the trouble. Yes, trouble is the word, unless you think it is no trouble to rebuild twenty or thirty studios, reorganize the fourth—or is it the second?—largest industry in America and equip every theatre in the country with sound-producing gadgets. A few short-reel novelties—and then *The Jazz Singer* by Warner-Vitaphone.
>
> Thousands of people had heard Jolson's songs on the phonograph, and though they enjoyed them enormously, there were many who could not understand the singer's great personal popularity in the big cities where he was known. Now, however, they heard his songs in direct contact with his own magnetic personality, and they instantly joined in the metropolitan applause.[35]

This and similar extracts from early commentators lead us to emphasize several components of the *Jazz Singer* which have not been sufficiently factored into the history of the early talkies. One is the popularity of recorded music and the novelty of hearing it in a theater. Koszarski has surmised that "Few of the Vitaphone first-nighters had ever heard an electrically recorded and reproduced phonograph record, and none had ever experienced theater-quality sound."[36] Specifically, the fad for jazz both as musical expression and as a sign of a modern urban lifestyle must have attracted many viewers to the talkies.

Another component is the audience's intensive psychic investment in the star system. Increasingly throughout the decade the screen personae of Chaplin, Fairbanks, Valentino, Menjou, and Garbo became idolized by millions of adoring fans. Though kindled by studio publicity, fan magazines, and numerous promotional activities, the growth of star-worship appears to be a genuine populist phenomenon of massive proportions in the 1920s. Parallel to cinema, the worlds of music, sports, and current events developed indigenous fan cultures of perhaps unprecedented secular scope. Jolson's "pull" as a performer cannot be underestimated. Even such unlikely public figures as Lindbergh, Mussolini, and George Bernard Shaw became Movietone "stars." (One editor quipped, "Shaw 'registers' so well that one regrets a lost film actor.")[37]

A catalyst for stardom was radio, which was commercially bound up with the film industry. Fans had heard voices and seen faces—Jolson had been broadcast nationally several times since 1922—but the talkies imparted to the stars' speaking images the sense of realistic presence that many felt to be the cinema's essence.[38]

When media analysis is checked against available direct evidence the conclusions may be similar or, as seems to be the case with the opening of *The Jazz Singer*, they may diverge. When the direct evidence does not corroborate the referential evidence, then we should wonder why the discrepancy exists. Sometimes not having facts available may explain journalists' misinformation. With *The Jazz Singer* this can be ruled out because timely box-office figures (the same ones we have used) were disseminated. Evidently, the print media were more interested in writing a "story" than reciting facts.

The popular press bowdlerized certain aspects (less-than-record grosses for *The Jazz Singer* and box-office failure for *Sunrise*) while embroidering others (the former's commercial and the latter's artistic triumph). What does this discovery tell us about the prospects of media analysis for reception study? For one thing, we should not take the information contained in the press at face value. Facts should be challenged routinely. But it also shows that there may be a pattern to the modifications and omissions that suggest a censoring mechanism at work that itself may be analyzed. A consistent bias or "spin" in coverage suggests that the media are reworking events for some pragmatic reason, perhaps due to some external influence, perhaps to narrativize history more efficiently. There is usually logic behind the legend.

A fully engaged history of film reception would examine not only the institutional milieu of cinema and the interpretations of commentators, but also the actual audiences insofar as their traces can be retrieved. Our research shows how factual information must also be provisional and it emphasizes that retrieving numbers tells us nothing about individual or group interpretations. But I've also suggested that the critics may have had little connection with popular discourses about films.

This seems to leave us in a quandary. If we think of "historical reception" as a recoverable fact, then we will always be disappointed because of the oblique nature of journalistic discourse. But if we try to anchor our findings on knowledge of actual audiences, then we inevitably will be frustrated by the unattainability of reliable direct evidence.

Alternatively, we might regard reception theory itself as an ideal construction incorporating both referential and direct documentation. Like history writing, it may be a kind of fiction in its own right. But if the study of reception were based on and consistent with specific known details of audience identity and behavior, understood to be fragmentary and revisable, then it would be a useful historical tool and more than an interpretation of interpretations.

NOTES

1. Janet Staiger, *Interpreting Films: Studies in the Historical Reception of American Film* (Princeton: Princeton University Press, 1992), pp. 206–8.
2. Staiger, *Interpreting Films,* p. 211.

3. *Kino-Debatte: Texte zum Verhältnis von Literature und Film, 1909–1929,* ed. Anton Kaes (Munich: Deutscher Taschenbuch-Verlag; Tübingen: Niemeyer, 1978); Deutsches Literaturarchiv (exhibition catalogue), ed. Ludwig Greve, Margot Pehle, Heidi Westhoff, *Hätte Ich das Kino! Die Schriftsteller und der Stummfilm* (Stuttgart: Kösel, 1976); *French Film Theory and Criticism: A History/Anthology 1907–1939* 2 vols.; ed. Richard Abel (Princeton: Princeton University Press, 1988).

4. Staiger proposes that this aspect of reception can be turned to an advantage by applying Bakhtin's dialogic model of text and audience interaction: "Such an observation also suggests that while the dialogic may be 'in' the text, the text's *significance* derives from the contextual determination of the reader's interpretation as a process of reception" (*Interpreting Films,* p. 209).

5. Donald Crafton, "Audienceship in Early Cinema," *Iris* 11 (Spring 1990): 1–12.

6. Donald Crafton, *History of the American Cinema,* vol. 4: *The Talkies* (New York: Charles Scribner's Sons), forthcoming.

7. Incorporation by reference is a legal term meaning that a secondary document is designated part of a primary document by specifying it.

8. Mary Carbine, "The Finest Outside the Loop: Motion Picture Exhibition in Chicago's Black Metropolis, 1905–1928," *Camera Obscura* 23 (May 1990): 9–42. This special issue of the journal, edited by Lynn Spigel, is devoted to "Popular Culture and Reception Studies."

9. Robert F. Sisk, "The Movies Try to Talk," *American Mercury* (August 1928, 492–93.

10. Helena Huntington Smith, "The Movies Speak Out," *Outlook and Independent,* 5 December 1928, 1270.

11. Jerome Beatty, "The Sound Investment," *Saturday Evening Post,* 9 March 1929, 129.

12. Wesley Stout, "Lend Us Your Ears," *Saturday Evening Post,* 15 June 1929, 50.

13. Robert L. Carringer, "Introduction," *The Jazz Singer* (Madison: University of Wisconsin Press, 1979), pp. 18–19.

14. Robert E. MacAlarney, "The Noise Movie Revolution," *World's Work* (April 1929): 50.

15. Frederick L. Collins, "Now They Talk for Themselves," *Delineator,* April 1929, 21.

16. Some exhibitor reports may be preserved in the Warner Bros. Archives at the Doheny Library, University of Southern California, but that material has yet to be catalogued at the time of this writing.

17. Richard Koszarski, *History of the American Film,* vol. 3: *An Evening's Entertainment: The Age of the Silent Feature Picture, 1915–1928* (New York: Charles Scribner's Sons, 1990), discusses some polls of the 1920s on pps. 25–34.

18. Author's collection. This particular card advertised a screening at the 48th Street Theater, in New York City. The message reads: "Dear Aunt Marie, Peach of a show"—a favorable review.

19. *Variety,* 21 September 1927, 5. Unfortunately, no further details were published so the source of the survey is unknown. The paragraph notes an exception: the audience for Colleen Moore's *Naughty But Nice* was composed of 55 percent females and 45 percent males. This reference makes us suspect the behind-the-scenes influence of a self-serving studio or press agent.

20. Susan Ohmer, "Who's Watching? The Industry, the Audience, and Market Research," unpublished paper, Society for Cinema Studies Conference, New Orleans, 12 February 1993.

21. In a recent listing of the twenty-five most popular Best Picture winners, the editor noted: ". . . records for *Wings* (1927), the first film to receive the Academy's award, proved too sketchy to estimate attendance reliably" (Lawrence Cohn, "The Box Officer," *Premiere,* April 1994, 88).

22. The obvious exception is racial composition. Actual and de facto segregation was still prevalent in the United States during this period. See Douglas Gomery, *Shared Pleasures: A History of Movie Presentation in the United States* (Madison: University of Wisconsin Press, 1992), pp. 155–80.

23. Ibid., pp. 50–53.

24. *Variety,* 12 October 1927, 7.

25. *Seventh Heaven* receipts from *Variety,* 21 September and 28 September 1927. The Roxy's statistics were published in *Variety,* 12 October 1927. The theater's average overhead, including film rental, was $84,000 per week; profit was $20,000; average ticket was 90 cents. The Roxy sold out on the average 20.5 times each week.

26. DeForest Phonofilms of Lindbergh's New York and Washington reception played at the Capitol; Fox's played at the Roxy and Paramount during June 1927.

27. Maurice D. Kann, "*Sunrise,*" *Film Daily,* 25 September 1927, 1.

28. Rush, *Variety,* 28 September 1927, 21.

29. *Variety,* 19 October 1927, 23.

30. The *Jazz Singer*'s first run was also 23 weeks—coincidence?

31. Jerome Beatty, "The Red [*sic*] to Profits," *Saturday Evening Post,* 16 February 1929, 15.

32. Ibid., p. 154.

33. Warner Bros. Pictures, Inc., "Comparison of Negative Costs and Gross Income on 1927–28 Productions to August 31st, 1944," Warner Bros. Archives, University of Southern California. I am grateful to Ned Comstock and Bill Whittington, curator, for supplying this information.

34. Robert C. Allen and Douglas Gomery report that *The Jazz Singer*'s greatest success came later in 1928, and that it played best in medium-size towns (*Film History: Theory and Practice* [New York: Alfred Knopf, 1985], p. 121). I have not researched the film's box office for this later period.

35. Rob Wagner, "Silence Isn't Golden Any More," *Collier's,* 25 August 1928, 12.

36. Richard Koszarski, "On the Record: Seeing and Hearing the Vitaphone," in Mary Lea Bandy, ed., *The Dawn of Sound* (New York: Museum of Modern Art, 1989), p. 16.

37. Anonymous, "American Debut of G.B.S.," *Literary Digest,* 28 July 1928, 21.

38. In his extensive "Radiography," Herbert G. Goldman cites four broadcasts before the *Jazz Singer*'s premiere. Jolson's own program ran on N.B.C. in 1932–33 (fifteen broadcasts) and he was a frequent guest on other programs throughout the 1930s and 1940s. An adaptation of *The Jazz Singer,* starring Jolson, was aired on the C.B.S. "Lux Radio Theatre" on June 2, 1947 (*Jolson: The Legend Comes to Life* [New York: Oxford University Press, 1988], pp. 372–74).

23

Jameson and "Global Aesthetics"

Michael Walsh

Fredric Jameson is one of a number of theorists from diverse fields who have turned their attention to the cinema as they have moved toward making more general claims about cultural production. Given that academic film studies has developed as the cuckoo in other disciplinary nests, it has a history of being receptive to these kinds of interventions. Consequently a lot of film theory and criticism has developed as an eclectic mix of literary theory, Marxism, psychoanalysis, and other things. Generally the aim of such work is to show how films either cause or exemplify some wider social phenomena. With two collections of writing on films (*Signatures of the Visible* [1990] and *The Geopolitical Aesthetic* [1992]) published within the space of two years, Jameson has concentrated on the cinema as a major force in securing the dominance of the postmodern. In *The Political Unconscious* (1981) he refers to film as "the hegemonic formal expression of late capitalist society."[1] By the time of *Postmodernism or, the Cultural Logic of Late Capitalism* (1991), however, he has backed away from this, stating that, although film contains instances of the postmodern, it is no longer a "privileged symptomatic index of the zeitgeist."[2] As can be seen from these two remarks, his primary critical interest is not so much in studying films as aesthetic objects but rather in locating the aesthetic as serving a function within a larger historical framework.

One key to Jameson's writings on film is to look at them in the light of the reasons often cited for the breakup of the Lacanian psychoanalytic paradigm. Two major criticisms were leveled against this line of theorizing by those who were nevertheless sympathetic to its aims and who wished to preserve something of its methods. First, they claimed that it posited a motivating cause—the Symbolic Order—which was so broad and totalizing as to be both idealistic and finally, ahistorical. Second, critics objected that in using psychoanalysis to foreground sexual difference, these theories had no effective way of talking about other forms of difference such as race or class. Just as Jameson describes the persistence of older literary paradigms even after their original historical stimuli have been leached away,[3] his own work can best be seen as an attempt to adapt the totalizing theoretical practices that had become such an important part of contemporary film theory, while attempting to deal with the criticisms I have mentioned. Ideology and Symbolic order are replaced as motivating causes by a specific, material mode of production, capitalism, which is then further historically nuanced by the use of Ernest Mandel's distinction of a three-stage evolution to its "late," or transnational, version.[4] The use of a Marxist framework, as updated by Mandel's emphasis on transnational forces, leads Jameson to focus on issues of social domination and resistance within, but particularly between, societies. The central mechanism of his theoretical practice is the attempt to link the historical changes in mode of production to the production of aesthetic discourses and the attendant production of subjectivities.[5]

My interest here will be in tracing the outlines of Jameson's theory from its general premises to its specific applications to film and then in assessing the coherence and value of his work in this area. Although Jameson comes to film via broader concerns, his work does rely on an ontology of film, as well as a history and a "geography" of the medium. He characteristically concentrates on framing large-scale periods into which he slots films in order to find their social and historical significance. This project raises a number of questions—about the value of such large-scale periodization as a preliminary to the analysis of artworks, about the way in which the periods are defined, and about the way in which Jameson writes his film analysis and film history to fit with them.

Jameson on History and His History of Film

Ernest Mandel has proposed that capitalism has passed through the three historical phases of market capitalism, monopoly or imperialist capitalism, and late or transnational capitalism. Jameson bases his work on the idea that these three phases are related to three major aesthetic macrostructures: realism, modernism, and postmodernism. Adopting a Gramscian perspective, Jameson maintains that none of these will be an all-embracing force but rather a "cultural dominant," occupying the hegemonic high ground within a given society at a historical moment.

Within this large-scale framework of economic context and cultural response, Jameson argues that realism in art corresponds to the unified subject position demanded by early capitalism, while modernism's relation to monopoly capitalism is more ambivalent. His earlier writings stress modernism as a counterpart to mass culture; both express the fragmentation of subjectivity under capitalism. Yet if both tendencies had this same function, the force of postmodernism's eventual collapse of the distinction between the high and the low culture would be less striking. Therefore Jameson has more recently emphasized the negativity of modernism in culture. The formal experiments of modernism are not simply a response to modernity but also often a reaction against modernizing capitalist economies.[6]

Postmodernism corresponds to the economic sphere's entry into late capitalism. Institutions such as the museum and the university have canonized and commodified art works, even the most radically avant-garde ones of modernism. The breakdown of unified subject positions, which began under modernism, has now become a cultural dominant. The resultant cultural formation is one of fragmentation, of sheer signification without reference or any notion of originality, expressivity, or affect (for who would be the subject of these?), of commodification and reification and, most crucially, of the loss of any kind of genuinely historical thinking. For Jameson, in late capitalist society the victory of culture over nature is complete. Now that there is no old there can be no relational position of the new and so, in this sense, industrialized Western capitalist societies have moved beyond modernity.

Mandel describes late capitalism as a phenomenon of the postwar period, its "original point of departure" being "the defeats of the working class by fascism and war."[7] Due to the semi-autonomy of cultural forms, however, postmodernism emerged as a dominant only after the cultural upheavals of the late 1960s cleared its passage. The reconfiguration of capital into a global system means that Nature, which had previously functioned as the cultural Other, has now moved offshore into the Third World. According to Jameson, the hegemony of the postmodern era is grounded in the way oppositional positions are themselves included within the logic of postmodernism. Any kind of social dissent is based on the fragmented collectivity of the localized group rather than the historically significant model of class.

The relations between the cultural sphere and the economic sphere are analogous and, in some degree, causal. They are analogous in that both capitalism and the arts are seen as progressing through a series of discontinuous phases. Discontinuities in one sphere are lined up with discontinuities in the other. Yet Jameson insists that the relation of the economic sphere to the cultural sphere is not simply one of base-superstructure reflection or functionalism. He sees the cultural as a *transcoding* of the dominant mode of production, an attempt to mediate the economic realm and respond to its demands in complex ways. He assumes varying degrees of autonomy within the two spheres. What this means in practice is that cultural systems are semiautonomous *in relation to the mode of production,* so that the relation between the two remains the central issue of his aesthetic theory. Sooner or later changes in the social structuring of the mode of production will lead to some sort of complementary alteration in the macrostructures of cultural production. This assumes that cultural production is best described in terms of these dominant structures, such as realism and postmodernism, with the latter replacing the former in relations of dominance via the intermediate phase of modernism. This large-scale epochal framework allows Jameson to track the kinds of historical changes which he sees as fundamental and profoundly determining.

A standard criticism of reflectionist approaches is that they reduce the diversity of artworks to the same thing. A better way of putting this in relation to Jameson is that finally only one question is asked of films: How do they respond to the prevailing global situation? For Jameson the aesthetic object is finally necessary because History itself is equivalent to the Lacanian Real, which is graspable only through discursive mediation. It is not the text that is important so much as what it can merely gesture toward. The major interest for Jameson's criticism is in seeing how the artwork will activate these gestures in responding to the conditions laid down by the historical context. The considerable range and complexity of his criticism are contained within a model of art as response.[8]

Since Jameson stresses his project as a historical one in linking the economic and the aesthetic, we need briefly to examine the model of history with which he is working. He is openly Hegelian in generating a narrative based around the teleology of a primary agent—capital taking the role of *geist*. He sees the advantage of Marxism as its ability to locate specificities (of the present, of individual artworks) within a grounding totality (a materialist conception of history). The starting point of any discussion of Jameson's theorizing is generally this insistence on seeing both economic and cultural production within a totalizing system, the "absolute horizon" of a Marxian view of history.[9]

He has been criticized for this by Post-Structuralist critics who proclaim the end of transcendent metanarratives.[10] He has, though, a number of defenses against such objections. First, his insistence on the complex semiautonomy of cultural forms saves him from charges of vulgar Marxism. He also refines his notion of a totalizing system to make it something of a negative concept. The historical moment does not simply dictate what must be said; rather, it provides a set of external circumstances to which there can be varied responses, but responses within limits. Jameson describes the activity of totalizing as a "playing with the boundary."[11] Finally, he employs a psychoanalytic analogy to preserve his own totalizing narrative in the face of his claim that postmodernism has meant the end of grand narratives. Postmodernism has not meant the end of grand narrative; rather, it has driven such narratives underground. The narration of history becomes the great repressed, the political unconscious.

The cinema is close to Jameson's concerns in that its popularity can be taken as a sign of cultural dominance. Film's basis in visual imagery also situates it centrally in relation to Guy Debord's oft-cited formulation of a "society of the spectacle." Debord's initial contention is that under the current mode of production "all of life presents itself as an immense collection of spectacles" where the term spectacle is understood as "a social relation among people mediated by images."[12] Jameson sees the fragmentation of the senses under modernity as linked to a privileging of the visual, which is then used to mediate social relations at the same time as it masks the reality of them from its subjects.

When Jameson turns his attention to the cinema, he advances on two conceptual fronts. The first is his large-scale historical schema, within which there is lodged a theory of film which harks back to classical theorizing. His ontology of film is dominated by the visual, which in turn is conceived of as an aggressive mastering gaze intent on physically possessing its objects. Film offers us objects in the way postmodern culture leads us to think of the world— as a collection of isolated objects. "Such reduction to the body is clearly a function of film as a medium."[13] Pornography and violence, both "reductions to the body," are thus seen as an intrinsic proclivity of the cinema ("the visual is essentially pornographic"[14]), one which is encouraged within our cultural regime.[15] This is a kind of negative adaptation of the Barthesian position which finds a jouissance in the visual excess of the image. At several points in his writings Jameson draws on Heidegger for a distinction between the World (read as History, the attempt to produce meaning out of experience) and the Earth, the inertia of sheer matter.[16] Film's ontological basis in the visual gives it an affinity with the Earth but its ability to represent the World (historical relations) is more problematic. Following Althusser, Jameson sees History as the absent cause, while film's visual basis is rooted only in what is present.

His second line of analysis is that cinema does not just produce visual spectacle but crucially, spectacle in the form of narrative. It is through narrative that Jameson can reconcile film to his historical hermeneutic. Thus narrative film will always represent, at least symptomatically, the political unconscious of its historical moment. By necessity films, like dreams, must never be about what they seem to be about (at least in late capitalist societies).[17] It is interesting to compare Jameson to Siegfried Kracauer on this point. For Kracauer it is the visual richness of the image which allows it to exceed conscious intention and register the social unconscious.[18] For Jameson, on the other hand, the visual simply stops meaning and needs to be buttressed or even counteracted by its incorporation into narrative. So visual "glossiness" will count against Hollywood films and lead to the valorization of rougher visual forms.

Jameson's narrative of film history is patterned by his broader narrative of the expansion of capital. Not surprisingly this history can be broken into three fundamental stages—realism, modernism, and postmodernism, which can be related to market, monopoly, and late capitalism. However, the relationship is not a simple one. As film is semiautonomous in relation to these wider changes in mode of production, its trajectory through the three stages will be a distinctive one. In fact Jameson goes so far as to assert that film has two histories: one for the silent film, in which there is a progression from realism to modernism, then a truncation with the introduction of sound.[19] This begins the process over from scratch, moving from an interlocking system of classical Hollywood genres (realism) to the modernism which comes to the fore in both practice and criticism (auteurism) in the 1950s with the end of the classical studio film, to full postmodernism, which emerges after the 1960s exploit the cultural conditions of postwar late capitalism. Brian DePalma, for example, is referred to as the first American postmodernist director.[20]

At the level of criticism, a good deal of the difficulty in Jameson's writing is that he writes *around* the films that he discusses more than he writes about them. In locating a film within the larger schema of modernism and postmodernism, he opens it up to intertextual references. These are drawn from a range of aesthetic, economic, and political practices as well as from a prodigious range of theorists. This dispersal of the artwork into a variety of historical contexts is in keeping with the Post-Structuralist distinction between work and text, in which the latter term signifies a nodal point where different discourses coalesce. Jameson's arguments depend not so much on the analysis of individual films, novels, or paintings as on their emplotment within his broader narrative. Typically, his analysis of a film's social position and function demonstrates that the qualities it exhibits are responses to the social moment. *The Terrorizer* (1986) is simply described as a modernist film produced within an increasingly postmodern context. As such, Jameson's interest is not so much in the modernist strategies employed by Edward Yang as in the way these strategies have a different historical significance from those of an analogous modernist, Andre Gide, whose modernism was situated in a different social context.

As Jameson argues at length in *The Political Unconscious,* the critic should read texts symptomatically, looking for the repressed expression of the historical moment out of which they have been generated. His critical method is grounded in a Freudian interpretive tradition that, in film studies at least, has antecedents such as Kracauer's use of psychoanalysis and sociology to produce claims about a collective social unconscious which generates both artworks and political events. More recently, the idea of a national or cultural imaginary has been used as a way of broaching similar issues. Jameson does not go this far, locating unconscious meaning as an attribute of the text rather than as a socially existent entity. He is also quite close to critical approaches generated by feminist film theory of the 1970s in the way he offers two directions to the theorist/critic. The first is the symptomatic reading of the cultural object produced under the dominant ideological system, and the second is the valorization of objects which reject or struggle against the dominant. Where the avant-garde largely fulfilled this latter function for 1970s psychoanalytic feminist criticism, Jameson turns to films from the Third World, and to a lesser extent, Eastern Europe. These represent the possibilities of a cultural practice which provides an external perspective on contemporary capitalism as well as expressing utopian collective impulses. The important metaphor here is that of Nature: "(T)he 'culture industry' or the consciousness industry, penetrates one of the two surviving pre-capitalist enclaves of Nature within the system— namely the Unconscious. (The other one is the pre-capitalist culture of the Third World.)"[21] This two-part strategy—the symptomatic within the system, and the Natural which resists it from outside—provides the format for *The Geopolitical Aesthetic.* Here Hollywood film is identified with the encroaching totality of the late capitalist superstate while other cinemas exemplify various "circumnavigations" of this totality. Under the latter rubric, Jameson discusses a range of national cinemas and the ways in which they have registered the global impulses of late capitalism. On the one hand the globalization of capital is seen as giving the international market precedence over the nation-state.[22] At the same time Jameson is conscious that "there is no late capitalism in general but only this or that national form of the thing."[23] The pressures of the transnational expansion of capital are exerted on preexisting historical structures and consequently there will be a range of response. These national variations are not simply felt between First and Third Worlds. Jameson tells that Jürgen Habermas's national situation in Germany is an important context for understanding his position on modernism and postmodernism, that *Klute* exhibits "American therapeutic overtones," and that North Americans have a "generalized ideological incapacity" to imagine collective processes.[24]

Still, pressures on the sphere of national culture will be felt more dramatically in the Third World. Jameson's best known piece on the Third World deals with literature rather than film but as both media share narrative, the material of the political unconscious, Jameson can transfer his ideas from one to the other.[25] Art in the Third World, by virtue of its putative links to Nature, holds out the possibility of a release from our "imprisonment in the present of postmodernism," giving us an external perspective on our own cultural experience. The totalization of Jameson's hermeneutic reappears with a vengeance when he tells us that "all third-world texts are necessarily . . . national allegories."[26] In a move that is reminiscent of Russian Constructivism, he tells us that the Third World text pushes the personal over into the historical. This is in contrast with the way that the First World text recontains its libidinal energies through the idealization of psychologism, which encourages us to see the world in terms of "the co-existence of individual monads."[27]

The Problems of Periodization

A response to Jameson's work can usefully be divided into two sections: the issues raised by his general theory of culture, history, and the postmodern, and then the way those ideas are applied to film analysis and history. Given that many analyses of Jameson's general ideas exist, I will pass over these fairly quickly and spend more time looking at his work on film.[28] Here questions can be raised about his ontology of film, the value of his periodizations, the effects of them on his critical practice, his narrative of film history, and his geography of national cinemas.

Jameson's tripartite divisions are often as unwieldy and as obstructive to the historian as the Symbolic Order proved to be. He wants to claim a broad explanatory power as the justification for his reliance on epochal periodizations, but it is purchased at the cost of a certain historical precision. If it is a commonplace to say that no two theorists of postmodernism agree on when it begins, there is a similar vagueness about the invocation of late capitalism. Mandel himself cautions that "late capitalism is not a new epoch of capitalist development. It is merely a further development of the imperialist, monopoly-capitalist epoch."[29] Anton Kaes, for instance, has written of the way that the cinema, *from its very inception,* was a product of late capitalism.[30] These periodized economic and aesthetic schemas are broad generalizations which seek to capture large-scale changes. There are frequently going to be problems in applying them to specific cases as the starting point for critical and historical practice.

There are also difficulties of internal consistency in the application of Jameson's periodizations. For example, once Jameson grants modernism a critical, negative function, he then has to deny that modernism was ever culturally dominant, since presumably what the modernist artwork negates is the dominant affirmative culture. This incompatibility hinders his initial effort to correlate modernism with the sovereignty of monopoly capitalism.[31] Elsewhere, when he claims that under postmodernism Nature has become located in the Third World, he also asserts that late capitalism involves the establishment of "internal third-worlds" within the First World.[32] It is hard to see how Jameson can put forward both claims while still maintaining that Nature has been banished from the First World.

In all, Jameson's very large-scale method of description needs broad and vague generalizations to get off the ground. An example of this is the apparently self-evident contention that culture has now banished Nature. Similarly, if within the new cultural dominant of postmodernism the subject is dissolved, we can greet such an assertion with a high degree of scepticism. He is asserting that a massive and basic change has taken place within contemporary society, but where is the evidence of this? Some contemporary theory and avant-garde practice may well set out to problematize the stability of certain conceptions of subjectivity offered within certain types of discourse in Western society, but to claim this as evidence of a new cultural dominant is to conflate limited sectors of artistic and intellectual practice with both the broader range of cultural production and with the overall range of practices of everyday life. Even Jameson remarks that he has only "pretended to believe that the postmodern is as unusual as it thinks it is."[33]

Jameson wants to link the cultural sphere to the dominant mode of production, but one might ask about the exact nature of the link between late capitalism and postmodernism. Realism has a functional role in relation to its accompanying mode of production in that it supplies ideologically unified subjects, while modernism problematizes this by opening up a negative stance in the face of the growing contradictions of monopoly capitalism. Postmodernism is seen as a return to functionalism in its effacement of historicity and its accentuation of commodification and reification. Yet the question remains as to why late capitalism, whose distinctiveness from the previous phase of capitalism is in its transnational nature, should require this new form of subjectivity—which turns out to be the dissolution of subjectivity altogether.

The causal mechanisms that bring this phenomenon into being must be questioned. In what ways has the change to late capitalism, if we are to read this as increased transnationalism, helped to bring about a new cultural regime? Here, Jameson's criteria for defining late capitalism seem to shift to something more akin to more generalized versions of "the image society" without a sustained connection to the economic. This is to point to other questions that have been raised consistently against Jameson and other theorists of the postmodern: namely, whether postmodernism is a distinctively different cultural phenomenon, and whether it can be neatly (or even messily) periodized in relation to a history of changes in the mode of production.

Jameson's historical and aesthetic periodizations go hand in hand with large-scale concepts whose multiple, shifting criteria provide the analyst with a lot of room for maneuver. With the burgeoning of analyses of the postmodern, analysts have a great range of criteria at their fingertips. Some criteria can be produced in some cases while being held in abeyance in others. One film, for instance, can be held to be postmodern through its use of pastiche, another because it dismantles fictional subjectivities, a third simply because its commodity status obscures the relations of production it represents. Similarities can be cited as evidence of the postmodern and so can differences, because these point to cultural fragmentation. Postmodernism can be mobilized as an explanatory device across a widely varying range of films because it can be so many different things at so many different moments.

Although the traces of postmodernism can be identified using a very diverse range of criteria, they then become grist for one interpretive mill. While Jameson's contention that historical context delimits the possibilities open to the artist may seem unobjectionable as an account of cultural production, it raises problems if we attempt to apply it to critical practice. Here the untranscendable horizon of history (read "mode of production") seems to demand that the critic privilege certain hermeneutic strategies (allegory) and direct those strategies toward certain predetermined meanings (the mode of production). The hermeneutic exercise becomes a circular one in which the critic lines the text up against the aesthetic dominant, which is understood as being linked to the historical mode of production, so that it speaks of that same mode of production. In other words, the critic finds what he or she sets out to find. It is difficult to see how Jameson will read a Taiwanese film such as Edward Yang's *The Terrorizer* as finally dealing with anything but Taiwan's position in the transnational economy.

The individual film is fitted into the narrative of history by sacrificing a good deal of its own complexity. Like Kracauer before him, Jameson has to rework the films to make prominent those aspects which can be allegorized most easily. For example, on the basis of very slim evidence Jameson argues that the doctor in *The Terrorizer* functions as the central protagonist of that film. He can then be converted into a figure who allegorizes Taiwan's position in the emerging global economy. Although Jameson acknowledges that the film is "polyvocal," he believes that the doctor should be privileged because he offers the best "key to interpretation." [34] In the following chapter Jameson has to quickly assert, on the basis of no stronger evidence than that of an "ad hoc or experimental imperative" that Jerzy is not the protagonist of Godard's *Passion* (1986) so that this film can be allegorized in terms of the decentered collective.[35] In both cases the conclusion becomes the basis for defining the evidence that will prove the conclusion.

One of the arguments Jameson uses in the defense of totalizing systems is that this is the best alternative that is available if we are to fully realize the complexities of the artwork. To refuse a Marxist-Hegelian historical narrative is seen by Jameson as leading to an empiricist fragmentation, which is clearly in line with his sense of the logic of postmodernism. If we return his argument against empiricism to the terrain of critical practice, the equivalent position which is attacked in film theory is formalism. He finds attempts to encounter films as empirical objects to be lacking in explanatory power because they render the object as having a false autonomy, severing its relational aspects and giving only a "first reading" strongly conditioned by the visual, while refusing a second, ultimately defining historical meaning. William Rothman's book on Hitchcock is taken to task for just such a limitation.[36] While one might agree with Jameson's criticism of a formalism which seeks to cede the artwork an empirical autonomy, most self-consciously formalist film study does not actually do this, but rather tries to consider the historical, social, and authorial aspects of formal systems.[37]

Careful formal analysis does not necessarily revert to a position of traditional aesthetic objecthood—the autonomous work rather than the dispersed text. Even though Jameson is not interested in the aesthetic as an autonomous realm of endeavor, he still needs to be responsible and precise in formal analysis, since form is putatively where ideology flourishes. While Jameson agrees that form is important as a marker of ideology, there are some fairly severe limitations on what he fits into the category of film form. He is interested in the visual on an ontological level, but his film analysis does not contain much precise visual detail from the films he analyzes, nor is there much on editing or sound. The result is that he offers very little discussion of large sections of what most film theorists would regard as formal elements.

Jameson's reliance on an ontological theory of film, drawn from Stanley Cavell, is one reason for the limitations on his study of film as a set of formal processes. When he writes of form in film he is almost exclusively interested in reducing this to a consideration of the pro-filmic material. The most striking example of this is in his analysis of *All the President's Men* (1976). Here he refers in passing to work published in *Screen* on spatial organization in Hollywood films, but then goes on: "Most often, however, the thesis of some spatialization of a spatial medium like film amounts to little more than a pretentious way of drawing attention to the extended place of architecture as such within the medium in question." [38] He uses this as a way of switching into a discussion of the architecture in the film. Similarly, in referring to the

use of space in *The Terrorizer,* he limits himself to simply discussing the locations in the film.[39] Jameson's critique seems to be a willful misreading of research which attempts to establish that the visual form is more complex than
he wants to allow. Such research points to the way in which the visual is more
than just an element of physical reproduction, but that it can also establish the
conditions through which we apprehend narrative.

The reduction of space to its pro-filmic components also serves Jameson's
broader allegorical hermeneutic. It is easier to allegorize modern buildings in
Taipei as signifying something about the role of capital than it is to allegorize
depth, shot scale, and editing strategies. At one point, he notes that Pakula
has a great liking for the close-up, but uses this as a way of getting back to the
pro-filmic, to a discussion of the importance of faces, whereas one might have
expected that he would want to discuss the way a film like *The Parallax View*
(1974) uses close-ups rather than establishing shots as a way of disorienting
the spectator and undermining mainstream conceptions of cinematic space.[40]

Jameson has a lot invested in the term "space," but his use of it is primarily
a metaphorical one. His rather dismissive view of analyses of film space is in
the service of his larger point that postmodern culture, in abolishing historical
thinking, has abolished the category of the temporal and therefore the spatial
must provide the primary means of contemporary analysis. At a broader level,
the temporal can be identified with diachronic analysis. The spatial then
stands as the term for synchronic analysis, which for Jameson primarily means
the disposition of social groups in relation to the mode of production. He
acknowledges that his major spatial concept, cognitive mapping, really refers
to class consciousness.[41] Research which stresses the ways in which dominant
film styles characteristically articulate space so that it gives the appearance of
being unambiguous (and even produces unified subject positions for viewers,
according to suture theorists) is going to be at odds with Jameson's prized
example of the Bonaventure Hotel and the spatial disorientation that it induces.[42] Although he wants to understand spatial analysis in metaphorical
terms, Jameson does want to retain some literal level in order to get from text
(literal space) to history (metaphorical space). Postmodern architecture is the
privileged field here; hence his comments about film analysis and architecture.
I suspect that if he were to look for strategies of spatial disorientation in the
cinema, he would be forced to associate this much more with modernism than
postmodernism, returning us to the earlier problems of periodization.

If postmodernism involves the sheer play of the signifier, the reduction to
the surface, Jameson remains committed to a putatively oppositional practice
of reading through the signifier to underlying meaning, reading the text only
as a symptom which lays bare an unconscious. The result is that the manifest
signifier (at least when he is discussing film) is finally of very little interest to
him: "This kind of analysis resembles Freud's mainly in the way in which,
when successful, it liquidates the experiences in question and dissolves them
without a trace; I find I have no desire to see again a movie about which I

have written well."[43] Jameson's distrust of the visual and the limitations of his formal analysis also stem from the epistemology of his theory of film. For him the visual "has its end in rapt, mindless fascination."[44] He sees film as overwhelmingly sensory, experienced in the body. He argues that this strong sensory appeal of the visual "seals up the crevices in the form"[45] and ensures that the "naïve viewer" never experiences films in terms of shots or frames.[46] He quotes Stanley Cavell to the effect that one's memory of a film (or lack of it) is more to the point than the film itself. As an argument against formal analysis, this will be familiar to most film studies teachers as coming from their disgruntled undergraduates. However, it should be noted that Jameson's ideas of the lack of historicity and the political unconscious are based precisely on trying to alter the responses of the naïve viewer. If we accept his arguments that one can analyze politics and history in terms which are not immediately grasped by the subject of experience, we should also be able to analyze artistic form at the same level.

Just as Jameson is more interested in the Visual than in visual detail, as a film historian he is much more interested in History in a broad Hegelian sense than in doing history in the way that most contemporary film scholars would recognize. He clearly believes that history moves forward in large leaps rather than small increments. In his attempt to link the economic and the aesthetic spheres he ignores a whole intermediate level of description. Much of the theoretical thrust of contemporary film history has been generated out of the recognition that economic forces do not exert themselves in sweeping and unconflicted ways but are mediated through the influence of competing institutions, which include those of the state as well as of commerce. This is a level of description that is completely missing from Jameson's work. Beyond his categorization of the three stages of capitalism, there is really very little economic detail in his work. He understands the economic largely as "a grand patterning system."[47] When discussing individual films he will refer in passing to the crisis in the U.S. film industry in the 1950s or the present-day pressures of transnational films, but there is little industrial history in his writings or in his footnotes. Rather than seeing the economic as operating through a range of mediations and fluctuations, he concentrates simply on the broad outline of his grand narrative of the expansion of capital.

When Jameson moves away from large-scale historical narration to specific historical details concerning film, problems quickly arise. For example, he asserts rather than argues for the division between silent and sound film, and we are left to speculate on the primacy assigned to the split. My sense is that Jameson would explain the difference in terms of the change in the physical presence of the medium with the addition of diegetic sound. He sees this as enhancing the physicality of the visual, the Cavellian sense of the presence of the pro-filmic in the absence of the spectator. This is a step back from the fragmentation of sensory experience which advancing capitalism demands and modernism begins to register.

Whatever the reasoning, Jameson's narrative of film history turns out to be strongly reminiscent of classical figures such as Lewis Jacobs or Rudolf Arnheim. The silent film is seen as beginning from a position of reproduction, which is replaced by an emphasis on visual artistry which is then overturned (and not for the better) by the introduction of the sound film.[48] Jameson's history might seem to be suggestive in the way it traces a movement from Lumière to Constructivism-Expressionism-French avant-garde and then explains the disappearance of these latter movements.

But surely this is a historical narrative which few if any film historians would still accept. This standard historical narrative has long been undermined at both ends, if not in the middle as well. The enormous volume of work done over the past fifteen years on the early cinema, pointing to what Tom Gunning has called the cinema of attractions, has, if anything, reversed Jameson's narrative sequence. Gunning shows that the early cinema could be considered closer to modernist textual practices and in fact moved away from them as it was codified around the foregrounding of narrative over the course of the silent cinema. Similarly, David Bordwell has demonstrated that within a couple of years of the introduction of sound, the visual systems introduced during the silent Hollywood cinema had been adapted to sound with only minimal change.[49]

The Jamesonian may dismiss the analyses of Gunning or Bordwell as formalist and hence empiricist. Yet it must be recognized that Jameson is himself making claims that can be subjected to empirical inquiry—for instance, that one dominant replaced another within the cultural system of the cinema. If he is trying to explain the disappearance of modernist movements within the European cinema, he may have some case to argue about the introduction of sound, although most historians of German film would want to claim that German expressionism had died out well before sound and that the *Neue Sachlichkeit* realist movement was much more prominent at the end of the silent period. (At the other extreme, arch-empiricist Barry Salt even argues that German Expressionism consisted of only six films.[50]) It is important to stress that Jameson does not claim that modernist cinema was simply a set of formal features, but a set of formal features which occupied a social position, if not of dominance, then at least of some importance as a major collective response to the economic sphere at a given historical moment. Yet he makes no attempt to show that these Europeans movements came remotely close to challenging the social dominance of the mainstream narrative film.

This is to return to an earlier criticism of Jameson: he claims cultural dominance, if not for modernism, then certainly for postmodernism in their respective historical moments; but the major way in which he argues these claims is through a commentary on texts without any consideration of how valid it is to generalize from these texts to the cultural sphere as a whole.[51] For example, when we discuss the rise of the art cinema in the 1950s as an ascension of modernism, it needs to be kept in mind that this was a viable way of positioning films in niche markets. Presumably some mass-cultural counterpart of modernism was the cultural dominant of the moment, though Jameson has little interest in this domain. He does, however, set up the historical context with a number of statements that are either generalized past any useful sense of historical writing or just plain wrong. Even though Hollywood was ailing in the 1950s and again in the early 1970s, it has remained a hegemonic force whose textual strategies are more easily explained in terms of historical continuity than rupture. To say that genres were repudiated by the mainstream cinema, as Jameson does, is demonstrably not true.[52]

Similarly, recent films such as *Die Hard* (1988) or *Sleepless in Seattle* (1993) may appear to embody postmodern aspects by some sets of criteria (quotation, self-consciousness) but, although they reference Westerns and romantic melodramas, they arguably succeed in creating the same coherent subject positions for their audiences as do their forerunners. It might be countered that, in order to highlight the emergence of new trends, one may need to deemphasize similarity and bring out the differences that Jameson is trying to get at; that perhaps one needs to play along with the pretense that postmodernism is as important as its theorists think it is. Still, such unsupportable assertions as "capitalist countries today are now in a field of stylistic and discursive heterogeneity without a norm"[53] cannot be seen as mere polemic. They must be at the basis of Jameson's whole enterprise in order for him to establish the criterion of cultural dominance. If the economic is central and the cultural is a response to the conditions of the economic, then the cultural responses must be made out to be central as well. It might also be pointed out that historians, or theorists who claim that history needs to be taken more seriously, ought not to be in the business of pretense.

Although Jameson presents a history of mainstream film in which traditional genres crumble in the 1950s to be replaced by the modernist organizing principle of the auteur, most of his own work on contemporary American film is based on genres (forcing him into the ungainly formulation "postgeneric genre films"[54]). The genre of nostalgia film is particularly important to his idea of the postmodern because it replaces true historicity by a spurious historicism of mere images. Jameson sees nostalgia as the reconstruction of the past in terms of surface imagery or simulacra. On the face of it, this seems an extremely suggestive insight, explaining how popular reconstructions of periods privilege isolated signifiers as a kind of pure style while omitting and depoliticizing vast areas of cultural experience. It also casts light on the dissatisfaction of many with current incarnations of the "cinema of quality": Merchant-Ivory films or the beautifully designed and photographed Australian period films that followed the international success of *Picnic at Hanging Rock* and *My Brilliant Career*. However, many of the problems of film theory have been caused by generalizing from ideas that seem to have suggestive power. Things became more problematic when one looks closely at the theoretical underpinnings which sustain and differentiate such categories as the nostalgia film.

Jameson distinguishes the nostalgia film from what he calls its non-postmodern analogue, the magic realist film, on the basis of a visual glossiness in which color is employed in such a way that it "smears objects together" to create a homogeneous field which excludes the libidinal energy of the magic realist film.[55] The criterion of distinctiveness must be raised here. Hollywood films have been criticized for glossiness as long as there have been Hollywood films, and Truffaut will remind us that the "cinema of quality" and its discontents have been around for quite a while.[56] Also, when have films with historical settings ever been historically accurate? There is very little mention of economic depressions of the 1890s in a 1940s Fox Alice Faye "gay nineties" film.

Jameson's major room for maneuver is in the vagueness of his criteria, but this makes his classifications open to empirical dispute. For example, his prime example of the nostalgia film is *The Conformist* (1970), which is certainly visually striking, but still retains (to my mind) an immediacy or direct energy in its use of color. (Think of the use of white in the asylum scene.) As such criteria—postgeneric genres, smeared objects, glossy color—accumulate in Jameson's writing, questions arise about their internal coherence. We are told in *Signatures of the Visible* that postmodern imagery is marked by homogenization and a lack of energy, whereas in his original postmodernism essay, he claims that postmodernism is marked by fragmentation, pastiche, and schizophrenic intensities.[57] (The distinction he borrows from Lyotard between feelings and intensities does not help either, as it is precisely the lack of intensity that Jameson identifies in the glossy nostalgia film.) For all the complexity of his intertextual referencing, Jameson will frequently resort to vague critical practices to line films up with the place he has prepared for them in the larger scheme of things.

Jameson's other major postgeneric genre, the conspiracy film (the most impressive example being *The Parallax View*), is seen as a response to postmodern social fragmentation. Here the individual is lost in social, technological, and economic systems that have spiraled beyond his or her cognitive powers. The narrative of the conspiracy theory is seen as an allegory for the process of cognitive mapping that Jameson puts at the heart of his critical practice—the elaboration of a symbolic, spatialized model to give social subjects a sense of the scope of the social totality of capitalism. One is led to ask again whether there is anything particularly postmodern about this. If we are to say in a meaningful way that in postmodernism social subjects cannot conceptualize the social totality, then we must posit some historical moment when social subjects could comprehend the social systems under which they lived. But when has this ever been the case? I am not disputing Jameson's reading of the genre so much as the historical specificity of the significance he attributes to this reading. In Jameson's sense, cognitive mapping and the role of art in this process long predate any period of postmodernity Similarly, the conspiracy film is not an invention of the 1970s but a subgenre within the detective genre. True, Jameson is aware of this objection and gives a number of grounds for the distinctiveness of the subgenre. These include the stress laid on technology, the collectivization of the villain, and the detective's loss of privileged distance. Once again, the points are quite suggestive, but consider the ways in which Jameson refuses to discuss these films. He is resolutely opposed to seeing them in terms of the assassinations of the 1960s or Watergate, which he regards as localized manifest material which one needs to get beyond if one is to see the hand of Capital (the only real form of agency) at work at a latent level. In the context of mainstream First World films he wants to reject reflectionism and the localized context as an explanatory mechanism which is too close to an irrelevant political "consciousness." (He asserts that after the 1960s electoral politics are no longer meaningful.[58])

He does, however, want to reconfigure the conscious/unconscious metaphor differently in a Third World context. Within the First World, political allegory is present, to be sure, but it is unconscious; the manifest level of the film deals with characters understood in terms of individuated psychologies. The paradox here is that while, on the one hand, Jameson sees the postmodernist text as dealing with the dissolution of subjectivities, he simultaneously sees it as attempting to preserve the traditional capitalist position of the autonomous individual through its stress on psychologism as an explanatory mechanism. In contrast, Jameson sees Third World political allegory as both conscious and overt. In trying to establish a set of binary oppositions between First and Third Worlds, between unconscious and conscious, between fragmentation and unity, he has located an essentialized cultural practice and subjectivity in the Third World.

Part of Jameson's explanation for the overt consciousness he attributes to Third World filmmakers is that artists who are "outside the centre or the superstate itself" are placed so as to be intensely aware of "the dilemmas of national subalternity" produced by global capitalism.[59] When we attempt to relate this to film, it can be seen as an argument that needs to be restated with a good deal more refinement to recognize, if not the autonomy, then at least the specificity of the film industry. In what ways is it useful to cite the transnationalism of contemporary Hollywood in relation to postmodernism when transnationalism has been a vital component in the film industry since its very inception? The global nature of film production and distribution, from the Lumières onward, is certainly no new phenomenon. We therefore require a much broader framework than a recent evolution in capitalism to contextualize it.[60] There are also a good many filmmakers in the Third World (in India, for example) who, because of the regional nature of their production, are less threatened by Hollywood than are, say, French filmmakers. Another variable that needs to be taken into account is the role of the state in creating and supporting film industries, thereby insulating them to a greater extent than many other industries from the logic of comparative advantage and large-scale global encroachment. It is in such mediating institutional factors that the semiautonomy of cultural forms needs to be grounded.

Part of the problem here is the reliance on a unified cultural dominant to describe a national cinema. The concept of a cultural dominant is meant to acknowledge the existence of a range of practices, but in Jameson's hands it tends to become a way of subsuming that range under a single description. Stephen Crofts provides a much more useful means of analysis by setting out a taxonomy of seven different models for conceiving of national film industries and acknowledging that any given national cinema will generally contain several of these models within it.[61]

Aijaz Ahmad has most notably taken Jameson to task over his early formulations of Third World art, charging him with suppressing the multiplicity of cultural expression in these countries.[62] He argues that Western analysis is usually skewed because only certain types of Third World authors are available in translation. In a comparable way, Jameson considers only films from the international festival circuit without reference to the vast numbers of popular Indian, Hong Kong, and Egyptian films whose lack of allegorical overtness may cause problems for his assertions. Ahmad's major criticism, however, is directed at the whole project of what he calls Three Worlds Theory, arguing that capitalism, socialism, and the experience of a kind of colonialism are all found within what we commonly refer to as the Third World and that consequently the nations that we commonly refer to as being part of the Third World are not "suspended outside the modern systems of production" in the way that Jameson's identification of the Third World as the last bastion of Nature implies.[63]

Jameson has responded to this critique by increasingly considering the impact of global capitalism on national cinemas in both Asia and Eastern Europe, and by making reference to the idea of a Third World proletariat within the "superstates" of the United States, Japan, and Western Europe. If postmodernism is predicated on the basis of the crumbling of the nation-state as a source of explanatory power, it has been necessary to bring back the concept of the superstate to serve some of its purposes when dealing with global relations. (If we can have post-generic genres, this is the equivalent position of a post-national state.) Given that one of the tenets of postmodernism is the collapse of distance within global culture, Jameson needs some way of maintaining conceptual boundaries if he wants to continue to talk about the unequal relations of geographically defined groups. But then without the geographic component—that is, if we simply accept the contention that the First World has fostered a Third World within itself—geopolitics may become dissolved into the need for a general class consciousness.

Homi Bhabha has recently tried to adapt Jameson's ideas for an analysis of postcolonial aesthetic production through reading in his work not so much a binary opposition between First and Third World cultures, but rather a radical gap or discontinuity between them. Bhabha concentrates on the ways in which postcolonial cultural production can be read in terms of the currently popular concept of liminity, which he refers to as "third space."[64] This has its counterpart in formulations such as "Third Cinema," which has been a point of debate for some time among film theorists.[65] The dangers here are either of essentializing discursive practices and subjectivity (as something like "the Natural"), or of defining the Third World if not as sheer difference, then at least still within the terms of First World critical theory rather than in terms of its own specificities, discontinuities, and complexities. The question remains as to whether Jameson's global apparatus of modernism and postmodernism is of much use here, especially for writers from these emerging countries for whom the historical specificities of their localized situations need greater acknowledgment than the terms of a modernist/postmodernist debate will allow. There are fairly severe limitations to being thought of as a "circumnavigation."

One can finally return this discussion to the same terrain as Jameson's work on film history. In using the individual artwork to get to the large-scale totalizing periodization or conceptualization, Jameson fails to describe the artwork precisely and often ignores the more localized relations. He builds his analysis from the outside in, from epochal context to artwork, which then in turn sends us back toward the large historical context. The problem in this is that the conclusion sets the terms of the analysis of the films. Jameson wants to get from the artwork to a complex series of relations, but if the analysis of the artworks is done so selectively or if the artworks are not representative of the range of cultural production, then our belief in the relations he proposes cannot be maintained.

One criticism of psychoanalytic theory was that, in its attempts to provide answers to large questions, it described something we can talk about in fairly precise terms (a rhetorical process) in terms of something we can only talk about in vague and tentative ways (the unconscious). In maintaining this focus on large questions, Jameson has suggested a political content for the unconscious, but in the process he has certainly not escaped the terms of this criticism. If anything, the epochal periodizations he has added to the psychoanalytic analogy have significantly increased the vagueness of his critical and historical practice.

NOTES

1. Fredric Jameson, *The Political Unconscious: Narrative as a Socially Symbolic Act* (Ithaca, N.Y.: Cornell University Press, 1981), p. 160. Hereafter cited as *PU*.

2. Fredric Jameson, *Postmodernism: or, the Cultural Logic of Late Capitalism* (Durham, N.C.: Duke University Press, 1991), p. 69. Hereafter cited as *PCL*.

3. *PU*, pp. 151, 186.

4. Ernest Mandel, *Late Capitalism*, trans. Joris de Bres (London: New Left Books, 1975).

5. *PCL*, p. xiv.

6. Ibid., p. 307.

7. Mandel, *Late Capitalism,* p. 9.

8. *PCL,* p. 164.

9. *PU,* p. 17.

10. See R. Radhakrishnan, "Postmodernist Poetics: Towards a Theory of Coalition," in *Postmodernism/Jameson/Critique,* ed. Douglas Kellner (Washington, D.C.: Maisonneuve, 1989), pp. 301–33.

11. *PCL,* p. 363.

12. Guy Debord, *Society of the Spectacle,* rev. trans. (Detroit: Black & Red, 1983), unpaginated. Quotations from sections 1 and 4.

13. Fredric Jameson, *Signatures of the Visible* (New York: Routledge, 1990), p. 148. Hereafter cited as *SV.*

14. Ibid., p. 1.

15. Ibid., pp. 3, 147.

16. *PCL,* p. 7, and "The Synoptic Chandler" in *Shades of Noir,* ed. Joan Copjec, ed., *Shades of Noir* (London: New Left Books, 1993), pp. 48–50.

17. Fredric Jameson, *The Geopolitical Aesthetic: Cinema and Space in the World System* (Bloomington: Indiana University Press, 1992), p. 67. Hereafter cited as *GA.*

18. Siegfried Kracauer, *From Caligari to Hitler: A Psychological Study of the German Film* (Princeton, N.J.: Princeton University Press, 1947), p. 7.

19. *SV,* p. 157.

20. Ibid., p. 55.

21. Fredric Jameson, "Pleasure: A Political Issue," *Formations of Pleasure,* ed. Tony Bennett et al. (London: Routledge and Kegan Paul, 1983), p. 3.

22. Anders Stephanson, "Regarding Postmodernism—A Conversation with Fredric Jameson," *Social Text* 17 (Fall 1987): 29–54; and *PCL,* p. 412.

23. *PCL,* p. xx.

24. Ibid., p. 59; *GA,* pp. 54, 41.

25. Fredric Jameson, "Third World Literature in the Era of Multinational Capitalism," *Social Text* 15 (Fall 1986): 65–88.

26. Ibid., p. 69.

27. *PU,* pp. 221–22.

28. See Kellner, *Postmodernism/Jameson/Critique* for a bibliography. See also *Diacritics* 12 (Fall 1982).

29. Mandel, *Late Capitalism,* p. 10.

30. Anton Kaes, "The Debate about Cinema: Charting a Controversy (1909–1929)," *New German Critique* 40 (1989): 10.

31. *PCL,* p. 318.

32. Ibid., pp. 150, 159.

33. Ibid., p. xiii.

34. *GA,* p. 145.

35. Ibid., p. 166.

36. *SV,* pp. 99–127.

37. The historical poetics which David Bordwell calls for at the end of *Making Meaning: Inference and Rhetoric in the Interpretation of Cinema* (Cambridge: Harvard University Press, 1989) is an attempt to ground the study of form in its historical context, the difference being that he seems to see history in terms of smaller-scale, more immediate influences.

38. *GA,* p. 74.

39. Ibid., p. 154.

40. Ibid., p. 64.

41. Jameson, "Afterword: Marxism and Postmodernism," in *Postmodernism/Jameson/Critique,* p. 387.

42. *PCL,* pp. 39–44.

43. *SV,* p. 4.

44. Ibid., p. 1.

45. Ibid., p. 5.

46. Ibid., p. 100.

47. *GA,* p. 212.

48. *SV,* pp. 155–57.

49. Tom Gunning, "An Unseen Energy Swallows Space: The Space in Early Film and Its Relation to American Avant-Garde Film," in *Film before Griffith* ed. John Fell (Berkeley: University of California Press, 1983), pp. 355–66; Noël Burch, *Life to Those Shadows* (Berkeley: University of California Press, 1990); David Bordwell, Janet Staiger, and Kristin Thompson, *The Classical Hollywood Cinema* (New York: Columbia University Press, 1985), pp. 298–308.

50. Barry Salt, "From Caligari to Who?" *Sight and Sound* 48, 2 (Spring 1979): 119.

51. See Douglas Kellner, "Jameson, Marxism, Postmodernism," in *Postmodernism/Jameson/Critique,* ed. Douglas Kellner, pp. 1–52.

52. *SV,* p. 177.

53. *PCL,* p. 17.

54. *GA,* p. 5.

55. Ibid., pp. 139, 142.

56. François Truffaut, "A Certain Tendency of the French Cinema," in *Movies and Methods,* ed. Bill Nichols (Berkeley: University of California Press, 1976), pp. 224–36.

57. Fredric Jameson, "Postmodernism, or the Cultural Logic of Late Capitalism," *New Left Review* 146 (July–August 1984): 52–92.

58. *GA,* p. 48.

59. Ibid., p. 110.

60. Jim Collins has also pointed out that at the level of aesthetic macrostructures, it is modernism rather than postmodernism that reacts most strongly against the national (*Uncommon Cultures: Popular Culture and Post-Modernism* [New York: Routledge, 1989], p. 122).

61. Stephen Crofts, "Reconceptualizing National Cinema/s," *Quarterly Review of Film and Video* 14, 3 (April 1993): 49–67.

62. Aijaz Ahmad, "Jameson's Rhetoric of Otherness and the 'National Allegory,'" *Social Text* 17 (Fall 1987): 3–25.

63. Ibid., p. 13.

64. Homi K. Bhabha, *The Locations of Culture* (London: Routledge, 1994): pp. 212–23.

65. See *Questions of Third Cinema,* ed. Jim Pines and Paul Willemen (London: British Film Institute, 1989).

24

Reconstructing Japanese Film

Donald Kirihara

In a scene from Kenji Mizoguchi's *The Story of the Last Chrysanthemum* (1939), Kiku, the young ward of a famous Kabuki acting clan, meets the family nursemaid walking a baby late at night. He rides up in a rickshaw (Fig. 24.1), gets out, and begins walking with her. The camera tracks with them as they talk, but neither comes closer nor moves farther away (Figs. 24.2–24.4). After a 5-minute, 12-second shot, the scene ends when the couple pauses under a streetlamp, then walks out of the frame (Fig. 24.5).

This is a remarkable shot, representative of Mizoguchi's long take style of the late 1930s and indicative of his films of the 1950s like *Sansho the Bailiff* and *Chikamatsu Monogatari:* films that created fabulous worlds of feudal settings, richly detailed mise-en-scène, and transcendent suffering. They are films that can evoke "the world of reality as the essence of a tragic dream," as Parker Tyler said of Mizoguchi's *Ugetsu*.[1] For some it may also be a quintessentially Japanese moment, not only in theme, but *materially* in its unusual handling of space and time. We are reminded here of Donald Richie's remark that for many Western viewers, Mizoguchi's films represent what Japanese films are supposed to look like.[2]

The scene is a moment that is supremely strange, but is it also uniquely Japanese? What constitutes that uniqueness? How is Japanese film style so different? These are difficult questions, since they direct us toward an examination of film style in history: What is it different from and what are the specifics of that difference? In what follows I wish to examine the importance of culture in explaining film style, particularly how and why it affects film style's development. My area of interest is Japanese cinema because in recent years it has received considerable attention for the ways in which culture mediates film practice and film viewing. This seems an appropriate moment to reexamine Noël Burch's work on Japanese film as an attempt to address the ways in which cultures collide in film practice.

To begin with, there remain some overlapping assumptions film historians use to explain what makes a Japanese film Japanese. For us they provide a convenient point of departure for arguing why Japanese film commands the attention of Western film scholarship.

We assume Japanese film is different because of its isolation. Part of our view

Fig. 24.1. *The Story of the Last Chrysanthemum.*

Fig. 24.2. *The Story of the Last Chrysanthemum.*

Fig. 24.3. *The Story of the Last Chrysanthemum.*

Fig. 24.4. *The Story of the Last Chrysanthemum.*

Fig. 24.5. *The Story of the Last Chrysanthemum.*

of Japan is influenced by the country's self-imposed social quarantine from the 1600s to the mid-1800s. It bloomed late as an industrialized nation, and it competed fiercely to catch up. In this view, Japanese cinema followed that legacy, remaining from the late 1910s to the 1980s one of the world's few countries where American films did not dominate the screens. Japanese film production was also relatively unknown internationally until the early 1950s, when films like *Rashomon* and *The Life of Oharu* dazzled art cinema audiences. By comparison, *The Story of the Last Chrysanthemum* won awards in Japan at its release but was unseen in the West for twenty years. Yet at the same time Japan is home to one of the world's oldest film industries, with the origins of the vertically integrated Nikkatsu (an often-dissolved, often-revived company) dating back to 1912, and one of today's major companies, Shochiku, founded in 1920. Studios in Tokyo and Kyoto cranked out four to five hundred films per year in the 1920s and 1930s, a frantic output that rivaled the Hollywood studios of the same era. And Japan was anything but deprived of foreign movies, constituting a significant market for European and American films continuously from the beginning of the century to the bombing of Pearl Harbor in 1941.

We assume Japanese cinema is different because the creators (and to a lesser extent, the viewers) have a different aesthetic sense. This "temperamental" approach is taken by the most influential presentation of Japanese cinema to the West, Joseph L. Anderson and Donald Richie's *The Japanese Film*. For them, a different style is accounted for by a creator's personal intervention. Mizoguchi uses camera movement, long takes, and long camera-to-subject distance because they better allow him to create the precious and rarefied atmospheres that are important to his films. This authorial explanation is made difficult because usually the particulars of a filmmaker's style change over time. Mizoguchi's long takes, for example, do not become a consistent part of his films until *The Story of the Last Chrysanthemum*, about sixteen years and sixty-one films after the beginning of his directing career. In other words, it is not an explanation that helpfully accounts for historical specificity or stylistic change.

We assume Japanese cinema is different because Japanese culture is a non-Western culture. This is at least on the surface a more plausible explanation, if an unwieldy one. Acknowledging that, say, Kabuki theater is different from American musical comedy is not the same as saying *The Story of the Last Chrysanthemum* is like Kabuki, or for that matter different from *Young Mr. Lincoln* (also released in 1939). This is, nonetheless, the starting point for Noël Burch's inquiry on Japanese film.

Culture and Codes

My approach is, of course, historical in every sense.
—Noël Burch, *To the Distant Observer*

Burch's *To the Distant Observer,* published in 1979, is the most ambitious attempt to date to explain the uniqueness of Japanese cinema through its cultural heritage. He states at the outset that his is "not a history of the Japanese cinema but rather a reading of a body of Japanese film in the light of Japanese history." [3] This reading involves considering Japanese cinema within two contexts: an institutional mode of representation associated with Western filmmaking practices after 1907, and premodern Japanese aesthetics.

What is a mode of representation? Burch is vague about this in *To the Distant Observer,* but elsewhere Thomas Elsaesser has attempted to summarize it:

> Burch's mode of representation embraces: historically pertinent media and spectacle intertexts (optical toys, dioramas, vaudeville, variety theatre, operetta, stage melodrama); formal parameters (staging, shot relations, kinds of closure, editing, inserts); the social parameters (spectatorial foreknowledge of story material, ethnic appeal, class and respectability, gender and morality); and finally, the recognition that changes in film style and film technique are determined not by acts of God or individual genius, but by an interaction of several, often unevenly operating pressures or constraints.[4]

The imposing breadth of Burch's concept, as Elsaesser notes, attempts to recast film style historically, accounting for stylistic change by examining the films closely for their use of particular devices and by situating the cinema experience in a cultural context which reaches beyond the film toward the parties and forces that produced and consumed it. What Burch calls the Institutional Mode of Representation (IMR) developed in the United States and Europe between 1907 and 1928, with an emphasis on psychologically motivated characters and continuity. It was inextricably linked with the rising dominance of bourgeois preferences, not just in what they wanted depicted, but how they wanted it shown. Moreover, after the imposition of synchronized sound in 1928 contributed to the constriction of formal and political experimentation in the European art cinemas, the possibilities for alternative modes effectively ended and the IMR attained a self-sustaining dominance.

The Japanese mode of representation, on the other hand, is an interesting study for Burch because it represents a viable and popular alternative to the IMR. Burch asserts that the Japanese, influenced by film imports from the West, adopted the Western mode until around 1912. At that point the Japanese cinema experienced a problem similar to that experienced in the United States in 1907—a sudden growth in the popularity of films coinciding with consolidation in the industry, embodied by the incorporation of the vertically integrated Nikkatsu. This economic crisis in the industry created a representational crisis that the *benshi* helped resolve. After 1912, the growing popularity of these accompanists who stood beside the screen and added dialogue and explanation helped promote a means of developing a cinema experience that did not depend upon a self-sufficient narrative supplied by the producer. In the West, this practice of a human accompanist at the screening had largely disappeared by 1910.[5]

Burch notes that as a medium introduced by Western entrepreneurs, the cinema initially invited the Japanese to be very aware of Western industrial and filmmaking practices. Some directors, like Ozu and Mizoguchi in the early 1920s, quickly mastered the classical continuity editing system. But Japanese audiences continued to prefer their own benshi-accompanied films after 1920. Why? Because they preferred those arts in which the narrative element was not dominant. Drawing from Roland Barthes' observations on the Kabuki and doll theater, Burch argues that the narrative in those forms is "isolated, set apart from the rest of the theatrical substance, *designated as one function among others.*"[6] This separation of functions emphasizes an aesthetic preserved from premodern practices, particularly from the Heian period (A.D. 794–A.D. 1185), in which the process of production is inscribed in the performance, granting them a "presentational" character. In the Japanese cinema, the benshi "removed the narrative burden from the images," and in so doing deconstructed the artifice of the illusionist Hollywood codes. "The most 'transparently' representational film, whether Western or Japanese, could not be read as transparent by Japanese spectators, because it was already being read as such *before* them, and had irrevocably lost its pristine transparency."[7] The West, on the other hand, has insisted on a "narrative saturation" in its novel, theater, and cinema since the eighteenth century, in which a "representational" condition of the illusionistic "diegetic effect" operates.[8]

In effect, Burch argues that the norms by which Japanese films were viewed and constructed shifted in this period (roughly 1912–15), away from those models that typified films initially imported into the country and toward representational systems identified with earlier periods of traditional Japanese arts. The popularity of the benshi helped to stave off a complete takeover of Japanese screens by American films during the 1920s, and prepared audiences and filmmakers for the blossoming of a "golden age" of the 1930s, well after the IMR ossified in the West. A determining factor in this development was the rise of militarist nationalism during this decade, which encouraged both a reaction against Western values and filmmaking practices that turned inward toward traditional norms and values. Furthermore, the delayed diffusion of synchronized sound into the mid-1930s helped prolong the influence of the benshi, making that decade "a period in which the aesthetic values of Japan's past came to be fully reincarnated in cinema."[9]

What happens after the 1930s? No golden age lasts forever, and for Burch its end for Japanese film came with the surrender to the Americans in 1945 and the subsequent U.S. occupation. The democratic liberals of the occupation not only helped retool the Japanese economy in the image of the United States—thus intensifying class struggle in Japan—but also encouraged adoption of the IMR to further that development. "What could better favour the implantation of such a system than a benevolent Occupation by that cultural power which had been instrumental in developing, disseminating and consolidating it on a world-wide scale?"[10] The Hollywood codes, held off by a war that was as much cultural as political, finally win out, forcing even uncommon stylists like Mizoguchi (whose techniques become "academically decorative") and Ozu (whose work suffers a "gradual fossilization") to depart from their innovative work of the 1930s.

Burch uses this historical account to explain why Japanese films of the 1930s look so unconventional. The films of this decade generally exhibit a "dialectical symbiosis of abstraction and narrative" that works to fulfill the distancing effects once achieved by the benshi.[11] Although Burch never undertakes a full-blown analysis of this dialectic as it works in one film, we can get some idea of it from his analysis of the scene mentioned at the outset of this essay.

The scene from *The Story of the Last Chrysanthemum* is for Burch the clearest instance of a "scroll shot" in Mizoguchi's career. Burch likens the effect of the shot to viewing an ancient painted hand scroll (*e-makimono*): the camera movement is lateral; the movement of figures in the shot is also lateral rather than toward the foreground or background, the figures remain comparatively small in the frame throughout the shot, and the backdrop parallels the direction of the camera movement. This produces a series of "tableaux which appear as both discrete and inter-penetrating," replicating a major effect of the *e-makimono*. Burch finds Mizoguchi's handling of this scene even more remarkable for its centrality to the story: it is the first we see of the maid Otoku, who will play a determining role in Kiku's career, and it is the couple's first meeting. Not only is the scene an example of a style that forwards its own materiality in a manner comparable to a traditional aesthetic practice (through sheer length of take and staging), but it is also indicative of a willingness to distance the most narratively pertinent aspect of the scene, the couple's conversation. Burch notes, "it is remarkable that the *presence* of the characters is in fact ensured by voice alone."[12]

Burch's book is ambitious and sweeping in its aim of finding cultural antecedents for Japanese film practices, but it has come under scrutiny for the verifiability of his assertions. While acknowledging these problems, I wish to focus on what Burch's approach has to offer the study of stylistic change in Japanese film. In trying to emphasize the positive aspects of his approach, however, I think it worthwhile to examine two related difficulties in his discussion of Japanese film style. One has to do with his notion of codes and the other with the nature of their impact on Japanese film.

Burch's "materialist semiology" assumes that modes of representation like the IMR owe their longevity to "codes." He cites a linguistic-based, dictionary definition for codes: "a system of signals—or signs or symbols, which by pre-established convention, is intended to represent or to transmit information between the origin or transmitter of the signals and the destination or receiver."[13] Despite the formality of this definition, however, his use of the term varies widely. For Burch codes are "basic systems" of a mode (at times his shorthand for the IMR is "the Codes"). They may include techniques as specific as "'three-dimensional' lighting/composition, developed chiefly during the 1920s," synchronized sound, and "Griffith codes of editing." But codes may also be as broad as "codes of genre" and "shot-size codes." Codes may be wrapped within other codes, as "The 'editing codes' are in fact part of the foundation supporting the more complex codes of the dominant system" (that is, the IMR).[14] Putting aside for now the problem of scope, it is clear that Burch wishes to use codes in a historical sense: they are systems with traceable lineages and specific characteristics.[15] Why do codes take the shape that they do? Burch would say that the interests of the dominant class account for the eventual composition of codes. Thus, the "illusionist" codes of the IMR are both consistent with earlier representational forms familiar to bourgeois audiences and components of economic and ideological systems that enrich that class.

Burch's codes are by design historical, but they are only as good as the histories that he constructs for them. To a great degree, the bulk of his work after *To the Distant Observer* has been dedicated toward constructing this history for the IMR. But for Japanese cinema Burch relies upon secondary sources, particularly Joseph Anderson and Donald Richie's *The Japanese Film,* a synoptic history written in the late 1950s and itself drawing considerably from Junichiro Tanaka's *Nihon Eiga Hattatsu Shi.*[16] The thinness or lack of supporting facts cause many of his assertions to fall short of actual arguments. How do we know whether a 1930s Japanese moviegoer would have adequate knowledge of many of the ancient viewing protocols that Burch describes? What if the failure of "American-style" photoplays was not the complete rejection that Burch (after Anderson and Richie) suggests? What confirmation do we have that Burch accurately characterizes the benshi's function? Burch's reluctance to return to Japanese film since publication of *To the Distant Observer* may indicate the difficulty of answering questions like these using verifiable data.

There is another reason to doubt the historicity of Burch's codes. How can they be subject to development if they are indeed historical? For instance, once codes reach a certain point of equilibrium—which Burch implies occurs with the Hollywood codes between 1906 and 1920—are they then unchangeable standards, like rules? Or, to put it differently, do codes change and if so, how? Given Burch's polemical stance, it is difficult for him to say that they change in any way but in the interests of the dominant class. As many writers have indicated, this gives his findings a deterministic flavor.[17]

Burch does, however, allude to another way of accounting for change in the codes. He notes that codes depend upon "pre-established convention" and that "it is reasonable to postulate the existence of codes of expectation with regard to the established procedures of editing, for example."[18] This seems to prompt Burch's claim that the Japanese were willing to use the

Codes as the basis for a series of "displacements and condensations" in their "transformation" of the Codes.[19] However, rather than using this to systematically examine the nature of these borrowings (by, say, studying the function of a device like shot-reverse shot within a system of devices in a single film) he uses the notion of transformation to further his polemic.

For example, *The Scarlet Bat* (1931) uses swish pans and other devices as "polyvalent signifiers" to indicate a variety of temporal and spatial transitions, and in doing so undercuts and "radicalizes" the thriftiness of the IMR's bourgeois illusionism. The film "does not simply substitute one code for another but constitutes, on this narrow but significant level, a challenge to the very notion of the code."[20] In a manner similar to "advanced" Western filmmakers like Dreyer and Vertov, the Japanese worked oppositionally against the Codes, challenging their dominance. But this does not argue for an alternative or even modified system of representation embodied by Japanese cinema. To effectively argue that, Burch would have to widen his study from one of devices (particularly editing devices, which serve as the focus of most of the book's examples) and also show how the sum of the codes as a system was modified by the codes as used in an individual text.

This "compulsive return," as Phil Rosen calls it, to comparisons between the IMR and Japanese film, informs what I think is a second problem in Burch's approach. It is fundamentally negative with regard to the Japanese cinema. By attempting to reach far back into premodern (for Burch, pre-Western-influenced) Japanese aesthetic traditions for his argument, Burch also seems to regard the Japanese mode of representation as an autonomous system—not an alternative to a Western mode, but its antithesis. "What was a mass cultural attitude in Japan was a deeply subversive vanguard practice in the Occident."[21] Here Burch's tendency to describe Japanese cinema as epistemologically distinct resembles a similar strategy at work in his description of a primitive mode of representation, with similar problems.[22] For Burch, Japanese cinema is the anti-illusionist negation of the IMR: in trying to define what the IMR is, we are left only with what Japanese cinema is not. Through the many scenes that he analyzes in detail in the book, Burch constructs a body of films filled with examples of the parameters that he articulates in *The Theory of Film Practice*.[23] To a certain extent the examples help us better understand what he means by the IMR—for example, the benshi is a useful tool in understanding the function of the lecturer in European and American cinema[24]—but leaves Japanese film comparatively impoverished. One could ask after Burch: if Japanese cinema of the 1930s is so anti-illusionist, then why are its films so readable?

Should Burch's approach be scrapped? In one sense, Burch's attempt to frame Japanese film simultaneously within a "Japanese" cultural context and a "Western" cultural context is a significant step forward from crudely conceptualizing that cinema as either the product of a hermit kingdom, different and strange because of its supposed isolation from the rest of the world, or as a film practice that mindlessly parroted the commercialism of Hollywood in construction and appeal. Phil Rosen has noted that Burch's overall analysis attempts to see the IMR as a constant background for Japanese film, with the two intertwining in unpredictable and sometimes contradictory ways but without the smoothness that problematizes his account of the transition from a primitive mode of production to the IMR.[25] The Japanese reacted to many Western film practices—like German Expressionist lighting and set design, classical continuity editing, or wide-screen formats—quickly and with unusual inventiveness. They reacted to others—like synchronized sound—with measured deliberation. While positioning Japanese cinema as a deconstructive antidote to Hollywood hegemony may be unsupportable, it is one of Burch's enduring points that Japanese cinema can only be seen in relation to dominant film practices, and that Japan's reaction to those practices was anything but passive or predictable.

To understand how styles develop and the difference that Japanese film makes, I think we need to better understand the norms at work in particular periods, as well as the norms at work in particular films. Burch is instructive in this regard, for he implicitly uses the IMR as the cinematic basis for comparison with Japanese cinema. But because his conception of the IMR is so all-encompassing, so rigid, and more to the point here, so *Western*, the nuances of the Japanese film's interaction with Western practices are often lost in oversimplified oppositions (for example, wipes were abandoned by Western directors because they self-consciously drew attention to the edit, and embraced by Japanese directors for exactly the same reason). Similarly, but perhaps more interestingly, his argument for a resuscitation of Heian aesthetic devices in 1930s films presents an alternative set of norms that may have been available for filmmakers. For example, it can be argued that Heian—or at least premodern—culture was publicly embraced and financially supported by the Japanese government in the late 1930s through such vehicles as nonfiction, nationalistic "cultural films."[26]

For Burch, norms are synonymous with codes, but here we may wish to refine the term so that it is different from Burch's codes or some set of inflexible rules. We might consider a norm as a social fact, established by practice and holding collective validity. To develop this point further, and without "correcting" Burch, it may be useful to conceptualize an artwork not as Western and Japanese, or ancient and modern, but as Jan Mukařovský called it, a "complex tangle of norms" in a "dynamic equilibrium."[27] An artwork can seldom be considered as contained within a single tradition; it can partly obey and partly contradict existing norms at the same time. For a viewer confronting an artwork, norms provide precedents against which we can measure deviations that stray from our expectations. Since any artwork represents an unstable equilibrium of norms, it will not usually exhibit simple antithesis.

Instead, deviations will be seen as they relate to many standards that converge upon the work, a complex process calling attention to the intermix of norms within the work.

For Japanese cinema of the 1930s, Heian devices may have been a pertinent set of norms operative in the construction and viewing of a film, but that represents only one category of norms, what Mukařovský called an "aesthetic" norm drawn from another representational system. A norm might be "technical," drawing from established traditions like genres. "Practical" or nonaesthetic norms gain resonance from social or political realms, while "material" norms of film construction work from assumptions about space, time, and causality. Furthermore, because an artwork's instability is dynamic, norms can potentially change with each actuation, but seldom so radically that the new state is totally unfamiliar from the old. Individual artworks or artistic personalities do not arrive at some magic moment to change things. To paraphrase Mukařovský, they appear when things are already prepared for a turn.

Mukařovský's theory of norms effectively establishes an art like film as a living, progressive system (or structure) within a broader system of culture. Perhaps one way to get at what is different about Japanese cinema is not to ask how Japanese cinema deconstructed the IMR, but how the Japanese "mode" actually functioned within the hierarchy of structures that Mukařovský proposes. To answer this, we need to recreate the norms of the age in question as well as examine the internal norms as they are constructed and manipulated within the system of an individual film. This means, I think, asking questions that are more limited, more specific, and more positive.

Tradition and Expectations

During their long collaboration, Mizoguchi used to implore his scriptwriter Yoshikata Yoda to rewrite his work again and again to add nuance and complexity to the stories. "Thickening" is what Mizoguchi called it, and he performed much the same sort of exercise in taking Yoda's scripts and thickening them day by day during production. We might demand the same of some of Burch's theses about Japanese film, without being quite as vague as Mizoguchi and without abandoning Burch's efforts to find cultural justification for what makes Japanese film different. In the remainder of this essay I would like to suggest some ways in which this could be done.

We can, I think, make limited and useful comparisons between Japanese film and the aesthetic norms of other arts, such as traditional Japanese arts. One way would be to compare the cues given viewers to construct depth in films to those offered in other representational systems. For example, the parallel perspective of woodblock prints organizes space as a system of parallel lines in which orthogonals do not converge toward a vanishing point, as with central perspective.[28] There are multiple "nodes" of interest, or areas of structural density, instead of a center of interest as in "one point" central perspective. Where central perspective contains the space within the frame, the oblique axes of parallel perspective produce a space without beginning or end. The viewer's gaze moves across such prints unguided by a vanishing point, and his or her expectations for anticipating the occurrence, positioning, and movement of items of interest are much different in this system than in "one point" central perspective. By positioning the camera at extreme high angles and using wide-angle lenses, Mizoguchi's films of the 1930s sometimes attempted to achieve similar relationships in depth (Figs. 24.6–24.7).

Fig. 24.6. *Taki no Shiraito.*

Fig. 24.7. *The Story of the Last Chrysanthemum.*

But to what end? One possibility would be to self-consciously "quote" an earlier form as a transtextual reference. In Mizoguchi's *The 47 Ronin* (1941– 42) it may be to offer a view reminiscent of a woodblock print to better bring out the flavor of a highly "traditional" story told in a monumental fashion, as Darrell Davis has proposed.[29] In *Five Women around Utamaro* (1946) it may be to refer to the work of the actual artist or to insert backgrounds that refer to the floating world of the story (Fig. 24.8).[30] Films with a "pictorial" tendency toward polished mise-en-scène, like the *gendai-geki* (films of modern

Fig. 24.8. *Five Women around Utamaro.*

life) melodramas of Nikkatsu where Mizoguchi began his career in the 1920s, seem to have been particularly inclined toward inserting these culturally charged moments of "Japaneseness" in their films.[31] Such quotations of practical norms are not limited to those from Japanese antiquity. James Peterson has shown how Kinugasa's 1926 *Page of Madness* used both European and Japanese avant-garde literary works as reference points in its construction.[32]

Even allowing for these transtextual references, large-scale comparisons between ancient traditions and modern film practice remain problematic, not the least because the modern world seems to get in the way. Describing the remnants of ancient culture as they appear in films remains a desirable task for critics, but as Kristin Thompson has shown in criticizing interpretations of cultural conservatism in Ozu's *Late Spring*,[33] it is appropriate that we inscribe that culture in the structure of the moment, attending to the more direct influences that may have affected the films' construction. The emphasis that Burch gives to premodern aesthetics and his inadequate reference to twentieth-century culture are, I think, the bases for criticisms that his analysis falls into a trap of orientalist essentialism. Not only does he make broad and unsubstantiated assertions about what Japanese in 1930 liked, wore, patronized, or thought, but he also seems to present an arbitrarily constructed, utopian dream, different from the West but similar enough to pique an "avantgarde" interest.[34]

Here it may be appropriate to return to what Burch refers to as "codes of expectation" as they relate to the technical norms that constituted classical film style. Burch admits that Western films, particularly those from the United States after 1917, had a formative influence upon Japanese filmmakers. Elsewhere I have shown how widespread that impact actually was during the 1920s and 1930s, from adoption of organizational models in the film industry, to reliance upon Western technology like cameras and film stock, to careful scrutiny of the latest foreign film techniques.[35] Furthermore, there is ample evidence that foreign films remained wildly popular in Japan through the 1920s and 1930s and up to Pearl Harbor, and that Japanese studios counted on their popularity in formulating their own exhibition strategies. Japanese cinema of the 1930s, far from turning inward toward ancient traditions (as perhaps governmental and intellectual institutions wished it to do), was the site of an extraordinarily rich international film culture in which foreign films played an important role at every level of the film industry.

From this we may wish to propose that pre–World War II Japanese film transformed classical cinema, but not exactly in the ways that Burch suggests. The popularity and pervasiveness of classical films presented filmmakers and audiences with expectations of a domestic film practice that followed in fundamental ways the goals of classical cinema, even if it diverged somewhat in its strategies. To see this we can review two areas which are relevant for Burch in how film styles change in prewar Japanese cinema: the function of the ben-shi and the construction of the films themselves.

Did the benshi materially affect the production and exhibition of Japanese films, as Burch argues? There now seems little doubt that they did. Filmmak-ers boasted of pacing their films for their favorite benshi, and in the 1920s theaters remained smallish to accommodate the benshi, factors which alone had significant impact on the Japanese industry's mode of production.[36] But it is a jump from this assertion to one which argues for the benshi as an "anti-illusionist" presence at film showings. What was the benshi's role in con-structing a film for a viewer?

To understand the benshi's function we first must reconstruct a more de-tailed context for his work. Burch argues the benshi were instrumental both in resisting Hollywood codes during the 1920s and in delaying the implemen-tation of synchronized sound technology in Japan until the mid-1930s. Re-garding the latter, I have argued elsewhere that the benshi may have helped delay the coming of sound due to their numbers and organization, but that more specific reasons such as shortcomings in industrial cooperation toward a technological standard in Japan, poor box office and labor difficulties experi-enced by most Japanese studios at the time, and the high costs of foreign sound equipment contributed more to the delay.[37] While the benshi had im-portant creative and economic functions within the film industry during the 1920s, the profitability of the industry did not rest solely upon the vigor of the benshi, and the film experience was not reducible to their role.

The benshi drew from aesthetic norms of the time—popular oral storytell-ing traditions more than the expensive Kabuki and Bunraku puppet thea-ters—and they were subject as well to the practical norms of the time, being licensed and censored by the government. What evidence exists indicates that they worked within the technical norms of film form and style of 1920s and 1930s Japan, not contradicting the projected images with sounds or forward-ing aural techniques to challenge the narrative, but embellishing the images with their performance. The benshi could integrate explanatory and dialogue intertitles, commentary on the images and events in the film, and characters' voices, providing greater or lesser distance from the action. The benshi facili-tated the telling of the story, creating a unique, but not unclassical cinema. In most instances the function of the benshi may be best seen as an emotional overlay upon the essential classicism of the film screened (the obvious excep-tions would be nonclassical films like *Page of Madness* and Mizoguchi's *The Downfall of Osen* [1935][38]).

The classicism that the benshi embellished was a familiar mode of film con-struction for filmmakers and audiences in Japan during the 1920s and 1930s. From the 1920s Japanese filmmakers closely studied classical style, construct-ing narratives hooked together by causal chains and propelled by goal-directed protagonists. Contemporary accounts, reminiscences by creative personnel, and surviving films all point to principles of story construction and the supportive role of style that were standardized in Hollywood style by 1917.[39]

The difference, which helps to further explain the benshi's popularity and function, was the willingness in Japan to support a more overt narrational presence as a way of differentiating the domestic product from the foreign and also to signify polish and virtuosity within the industry. As David Bordwell has shown, practices such as occasional subjective point-of-view shots, meandering camera movements, or rapid-fire editing maintained the centrality of character-centered causality and the overall supportive function of film style, while seeking to differentiate their product through stylistic "flourishes."[40] Like the benshi's embellishments within a fundamentally supportive role for the narrative, the decorative tendency of Japanese film style transformed expectations already resident in the culture of the time to differentiate Japanese film practice. As a variant of classical film style, the Japanese cinema of the 1930s was distinct and familiar at the same time, a particularly opportunistic nest of norms.

So if most Japanese films are classical, readable, familiar films for the most part, what about moments like that in *The Story of the Last Chrysanthemum?* What about the really strange films? Here too, Burch is helpful in providing leads. As noted earlier, his work on Japanese cinema explores the possibility of a film practice in which narrative is only one paramater among many, capable of being set aside for other systems. In this he supports the work of David Bordwell and Kristin Thompson, who since 1976 have argued for such a separation of the narrative system and the system of stylistic techniques in Ozu's films.[41]

Burch, however, wishes to say that this inclination characterized prewar Japanese cinema as a whole—that Ozu and Mizoguchi, for example, are only representatives of widespread practices in Japanese cinema of the 1920s and 1930s. He can hardly argue otherwise, given his argument for fundamental cultural differences between Japan and the West. Still, this may be the weakest assertion in his book, mainly because he does not seem to believe it himself. Most of his examples are drawn from atypical films (like *Souls on the Road, Page of Madness, A Star Athlete*) and he is most interested in the work of specific filmmakers already known in the West like Ozu, Mizoguchi, Naruse, Kurosawa, and Oshima, and some directors "discovered" in the course of his research like Hiroshi Shimizu and Tamizo Ishida. Many of these filmmakers, like Ozu and Mizoguchi, were seen by their peers within the industry as atypical and original.

From Burch's distillation of devices, shots, and scenes it is evident that filmmakers like Ozu and Mizoguchi do something more, "decentering" classical practice to create films that are readable, but in which the narrative is syste-

matically set aside so that other systems of techniques may rise to our attention. Stressing the importance of reconstructing the norms does not mean
stopping at simply describing classical Japanese cinema. These are works of
matchless precision and innovative strategies that depart from normative practices of Japanese film in the 1930s, and Burch touches upon many of them in
To the Distant Observer. But to show that within this strange cinema there are
even stranger films we need to go significantly beyond the itemization of devices to examine the structure of the individual text, or the individual text as
system.

Let us take the scene described at the outset of this essay once more (see
pp. 507–9). As Burch indicates, the characters remain distant from the camera
throughout the shot, which appears at one level like a scroll. But there is
more. We can describe the construction of the shot more precisely.[42] The
couple talks as they walk, generally with the maid behind Kiku so that they do
not look at each other. This tactic, which appears in other Mizoguchi films of
the 1930s (like *Naniwa Elegy* [1936], leaves the conversation without the
compositional center that a face-to-face chat would afford and contributes to
the dispersive mise-en-scène characteristic of the film. Their postures also
contribute to the disembodied quality of the scene that Burch notes. With the
figures not only distant but turned from each other, their dialogue—the primary carrier of story information in this scene—seems oddly detached from
the visuals. The coordinated timing of figure and camera movements is special
as well. Movement in Mizoguchi's films of the period is often tied to a particular trajectory plotted across a shot's duration.[43] In this shot the couple
stops at a vendor to buy a wind chime to quiet the baby (Fig. 24.2). The
tracking stops when they stop. Couple and camera begin moving again until
Otoku starts to criticize Kiku's acting. Kiku stops and turns (Fig. 24.3), and
as the conversational center is established between them the camera continues
past them and pivots (Fig. 24.4), keeping them in frame but presenting their
figures in relief as the camera moves around them.

Camera placement and lens selection also contribute to the creation of this
odd space and further earlier experimentation by Mizoguchi with spatial distortion through cinematography. The low camera angle of the shot, combined with the wide-angle lens, exaggerate the height and width of the building facades, so that they loom behind the couple. Cameraman Minoru Miki
and Mizoguchi realized that use of a wide lens with a low camera angle would
deform vertical lines during a lateral tracking shot. In this shot the buildings
in the background seem to bend inward as the couple move by, and passing
lampposts twist crazily as they pass through the frame. Altogether, figure
movement, camera placement and movement, and lens selection combine to
give the shot an ethereal quality of depth, but they do so through strategies
and not simply through devices.

This is far more complex than the embellishments of most pictorially inclined Japanese filmmakers of the time, and is made more so because Mizoguchi uses such strategies systematically throughout the film, setting up internal norms within the film and then developing and varying them in remarkable patterns. When Mizoguchi begins using long takes in systematic fashion in *The Story of the Last Chrysanthemum*, it is in a manner that tests and revises our expectations about duration, frequency, and order—in other words, about time itself.

Thus, Mizoguchi was quite different from his contemporaries, and setting his films against the material norms of his time helps explain how the filmmaker can be simultaneously recognized as a singular stylist and—as Richie's remark summarizes—the very representative of what makes Japanese film Japanese. He, and his colleagues, used a range of traditions with considerable facility, building off classical practices (as did the benshi) rather than opposing them. For Mizoguchi the deviation was both more systematic and more extreme, and Burch is helpful in seeing how this occurs in the structure of an individual film, even if here *Theory of Film Practice* is more useful than *To the Distant Observer*.

Like many others, Burch found Japan an inviting place to study the contradictions of twentieth-century culture and his work serves to remind us that representation is a social process. He has continued asking how and why culture intervenes through cinema, although it has remained for others to examine that process in Japan. Writers like the ones I have mentioned in this essay have constructed histories that develop the specificity of Japanese cinema, pairing careful textual analyses with focused investigations of historical phenomena. In doing so many have developed "structures of style" in a historical sense, seeking to better explain a cinema and a culture that continues to fascinate distant observers—distant in period as well as geography—for its material richness and its ability to defamiliarize.

NOTES

I wish to thank David Bordwell, Noël Carroll, and Vance Kepley, Jr., for their suggestions and criticisms of earlier versions of this essay. I am also grateful for the support of the Vice President for Research at the University of Arizona, Michael Cusanovich.

1. Parker Tyler, "Ugetsu," in *Classics of the Foreign Film: A Pictorial Treasury* (New York: Citadel, 1962), p. 209.

2. Donald Richie, "Kenji Mizoguchi," in *Cinema: A Critical Dictionary*, vol. 2, ed. Richard Roud (New York: Viking, 1980), p. 697.

3. Noël Burch, *To the Distant Observer: Form and Meaning in Japanese Cinema*, rev. and ed. Annette Michelson (Berkeley: University of California Press, 1979), p. 16.

4. Thomas Elsaesser, "Introduction" in *Early Cinema: Space, Frame, Narrative*, ed. Thomas Elsaesser and Adam Barker (London: British Film Institute, 1990), pp. 406–7. See also Burch's *Life to Those Shadows*, trans. and ed. Ben Brewster (Berke-

ley: University of California Press, 1990) for his most sustained explanation of the development of the institutional mode. For another discussion of Burch's IMR and its relationship to Japanese cinema, see David Bordwell, "The Power of a Research Tradition: Prospects for Progress in the Study of Film Style," *Film History* 6, 1 (Spring 1994): 69–73.

5. For a discussion of the film lecturer in the West, see André Gaudreault, "Showing and Telling: Image and Word in Early Cinema," in *Early Cinema*, pp. 274–81.

6. Burch, *To the Distant Observer*, p. 98. For Barthes, see *Empire of Signs*, trans. Richard Howard (New York: Hill and Wang, 1982); "Lesson in Writing" in *Image/ Music/Text*, trans. Stephen Heath (New York: Hill and Wang, 1977), pp. 170–78; and "The Three Scripts," trans. Sandy Macdonald, *The Drama Review* 15, 3 (Spring 1971): 76–80.

7. Burch, *To the Distant Observer*, p. 79.

8. Ibid., pp. 67–74, 98–99.

9. Ibid., p. 147.

10. Ibid., p. 274.

11. Noël Burch, "Akira Kurosawa," in *Cinema: A Critical Dictionary*, vol. 1, ed. Richard Roud (New York: Viking, 1980), p. 572.

12. Burch, *To the Distant Observer*, pp. 99, 228–29, 234.

13. Ibid., p. 20. The definition is drawn from *Dictionnaire de linguistique* (Paris: Librarie Larousse, 1973), p. 92.

14. Ibid., p. 20.

15. Here Burch seems to combine the notions of code and subcode as formulated by Christian Metz. For an analysis of this distinction in Metz, see David Bordwell, "Textual Analysis, Etc." *Enclitic* 5, no. 2/6 no. 1 (Fall 1981/Spring 1982): 125–29.

16. Joseph L. Anderson and Donald Richie, *The Japanese Film: Art and Industry* (Tokyo: Tuttle, 1959); Jun'ichiro Tanaka, *Nihon Eiga Hattatsu Shi*, 4 vols. (Tokyo: Chuo Koronsha, 1957).

17. See Elsaesser, 407–8; Kristin Thompson and David Bordwell, "Linearity, Materialism, and the Study of Early American Cinema," *Wide Angle* 5, 3 (1983): 4–15; David Bordwell, review of *To the Distant Observer*, *Wide Angle* 3, 4 (1980): 70–73; Geoffrey O'Brien, "The Ghost Opera," *New York Review of Books* 38 (30 May 1991), p. 6.

18. Burch, *To the Distant Observer*, p. 20.

19. Ibid., p. 111.

20. Ibid., p. 115.

21. Ibid., p. 115.

22. Elsaesser, "Introduction," pp. 407–8. See also Donald Kirihara, "Critical Polarities and the Study of Japanese Film Style," *Journal of Film and Video* 39, 1 (Winter 1987): 16–25.

23. *Theory of Film Practice*, trans. Helen R. Lane (Princeton: Princeton University Press, 1981). Originally published as *Praxis du cinéma* (Paris: Editions Gallimard, 1969).

24. Elsaesser, "Introduction," p. 167.

25. Phil Rosen, "History, Textuality, Nation: Kracauer, Burch, and Some Problems in the Study of National Cinemas," *Iris* 2, 2 (1984): 78–79, 82–83.

26. See Takao Itagaki, "Cultural Films," *Cinema Year Book of Japan 1938* (Tokyo: Kokusai Bunka Shinkokai, 1938), pp. 44–46. See also Gregory J. Kasza, *The State and the Mass Media in Japan, 1918–1945* (Berkeley: University of California Press, 1988).

27. Jan Mukařovský, "The Aesthetic Norm," in *Structure, Sign, and Function: Selected Essays by Jan Mukařovský*, trans. and ed. John Burbank and Peter Steiner (New Haven: Yale University Press, 1977), p. 52.

28. See Donald Kirihara, *Patterns of Time: Mizoguchi and the 1930s* (Madison: University of Wisconsin Press, 1992), p. 86; David Bordwell, *Narration in the Fiction Film* (Madison: University of Wisconsin Press, 1985), pp. 104–10; Rudolf Arnheim, *The Power of the Center: A Study of Composition in the Visual Arts* (Berkeley: University of California Press, 1982), pp. 180–81, 186; Donald L. Weismann, *The Visual Arts as Human Experience* (Englewood Cliffs, N.J.: Prentice-Hall, 1970), p. 188.

29. D. William Davis, "*Genroku Chūshingura* and the Primacy of Perception," in *Cinematic Landscapes: Observations on the Visual Arts and Cinema of China and Japan*, eds. Linda C. Ehrlich and David Desser (Austin: University of Texas Press, 1994), pp. 199–210. See also D. William Davis, "Picturing Japaneseness: Monumental Style and National Identity in Prewar Japanese Film," Ph.D. diss., University of Wisconsin-Madison, 1990.

30. See Donald Kirihara, "'L'assimilation Mizoguchi/Utamaro est évidente': *Five Women Around Utamaro* and the U.S. Occupation of Japan," *East-West Film Journal* 8, 1 (1994): 3–23.

31. Kirihara, *Patterns of Time*, pp. 65–68; David Bordwell, *Ozu and Poetics of Cinema* (London: British Film Institute, 1988), pp. 23–24.

32. James Peterson, "A War of Utter Rebellion: Kinugasa's *Page of Madness* and the Japanese Avant-Garde of the 1920s," *Cinema Journal* 29, 1 (Fall 1989): 36–53.

33. Kristin Thompson, "*Late Spring* and Ozu's Unreasonable Style," in *Breaking the Glass Armor: Neoformalist Film Analysis* (Princeton: Princeton University Press, 1988), pp. 317–52.

34. See David Bordwell, "Our Dream Cinema: Western Historiography and the Japanese Film," *Film Reader* 4 (1979): 45–62; Brett de Bary, review of *To the Distant Observer, Journal of Japanese Studies* 8, 2 (1982): 405–10; Mitsuhiro Yoshimoto, "The Difficulty of Being Radical: The Discipline of Film Studies and the Postcolonial World Order," in *Japan in the World*, ed. Masao Miyoshi and H. D. Harootunian (Durham, N.C.: Duke University Press, 1993), pp. 338–53. This is also a criticism of Barthes' *Empire of Signs*. See Yoshimoto's essay and Rob Wilson, "Theory's Imaginal Other: American Encounters with South Korea and Japan," in *Japan in the World*, p. 332.

35. Most of the following is drawn from Kirihara, *Patterns of Time*, chapter 4.

36. Joseph L. Anderson, "Spoken Silents in the Japanese Cinema; or, Talking to Pictures: Essaying the *Katsuben*, Contexturalizing the Texts," in *Reframing Japanese Cinema: Authorship, Genre, History*, ed. Arthur Nolletti, Jr., and David Desser (Bloomington: Indiana University Press, 1992), pp. 277–79.

37. Kirihara, "A Reconsideration of the Institution of the Benshi," *Film Reader* 6 (1985): 42–45.

38. Kirihara, *Patterns of Time*, pp. 60–61. Joseph L. Anderson also asserts that film narratives after 1920 could stand alone without a benshi's narration, although their popularity, indeed their perceived necessity in a film program, made it unlikely until the early 1930s. See Anderson, "Spoken Silents," p. 273.

39. Kirihara, *Patterns of Time*, pp. 58–65.

40. David Bordwell, "A Cinema of Flourishes: Japanese Decorative Classicism of the Prewar Era," in *Reframing Japanese Cinema*, pp. 328–46.

41. Kristin Thompson and David Bordwell, "Space and Narrative in the Films of

Ozu," *Screen* 17, 2 (Summer 1976): 41–73. See also Kristin Thompson, "Notes on the Spatial System of Ozu's Early Films," *Wide Angle* 1, 4 (1977): 8–17; and Bordwell, *Ozu and the Poetics of Cinema*.

42. For a more detailed discussion of this film, see Kirihara, *Patterns of Time,* pp. 137–57.

43. For a concentrated discussion of this, see David Bordwell and Kristin Thompson, *Film Art: An Introduction,* 4th ed. (New York: McGraw-Hill, 1993), pp. 236–37. See also Kirihara, *Patterns of Time,* chapter 8.

25

Danish Cinema and the
Politics of Recognition

Mette Hjort

I propose to examine the relation between film and its publics in a particular context of cinematic production, one where reflection on this connection, or lack thereof, is ongoing and urgent on account of prevailing hierarchies of cultural production. The context I have in mind is that of Danish cinema. I will thus be raising questions about the ways in which the meanings of "cinema" and "nation" circulate and mutate—especially as these terms are combined in that key component of a coverage model of cinema studies: national cinema.

I would like to suggest that Danish cinematic production contributes to what many think of as a minor culture. The classification of a culture as minor has serious consequences, the most important of which may well be the ongoing exposure of a nation's citizens to the overpowering effects of major cultures. This point is best substantiated by a consideration of the ways in which certain European nations have responded to the cultural imperialism that affects them most directly: that of the United States. Attempts to create a strong national culture form one such response, and this in turn raises the question of how a Danish cinema is or should be defined. I want to argue that the creation of a Danish cinema cannot simply be a matter of appealing to local audiences. Indeed, as we shall see, within certain discourses of a nationalist bent, cultural specificity is systematically linked to ideas about international publics. While this connection may seem puzzling at first, it begins to make sense once we understand the ways in which the creation of a national cinema is part of a politics of recognition. It is important to note, however, that the strategy best suited for achieving the desired recognition of Danish cinema and culture differs substantially from the one typically employed by marginal groups situated, however uneasily, within major cultures.

It is my conviction that the recognition of Danish cinematic culture depends on the extent to which filmmakers are able simultaneously to appeal to multiple audiences. Since I am interested in the cinematic strategy that is most likely to generate the desired recognition, my descriptive account is necessarily selective. The mixed strategy that I identify and discuss in detail here is by no means the only one adopted by Danish filmmakers, but I do believe that pragmatic considerations make it the best choice. Other strategies could no doubt be devised in moments of scholarly reflection, but such thought experiments would tend to be so far removed from ongoing practices as to have little prescriptive force. My argument, then, combines descriptive and prescriptive elements in a spirit of pragmatic realism.

Hierarchies of Culture

Aspects of Danish cinematic production and reception are determined by existing cultural hierarchies, and the immediate task at hand is to examine the elements mobilized within certain comparisons, as well as the rationale governing attributions of superior and inferior worth. Cultures, we know, can be variously classified and hierarchized. Pierre Bourdieu, for example, speaks of low-brow, middle-brow, and high-brow tastes, thereby evoking a set of prevalent cultural distinctions operative within nations where agents use aesthetic judgments strategically to construct and negotiate social hierarchies.[1] Gilles Deleuze and Félix Guattari, on the other hand, introduce a distinction between major and minor cultures as they imagine the features of a "minor literature" capable of subverting the dominant language or culture of a given nation-state.[2] Although Deleuze and Guattari restrict their analysis to the cultural politics of Franz Kafka's Czechoslovakia, the idea of major and minor cultures can be readily and usefully mobilized within an analysis of an international politics of culture.

The relative worth of cultural products is determined only partially, if at all, by comparative assessments of intrinsic features such as the aesthetic qualities of the work. The salience of certain cultural objects within an international cultural sphere is in large measure a function of economic, demographic, and geopolitical factors, although that salience is easily taken by members of dominant cultures as an indication of cultural superiority and as a justification for a division of cultures along major and minor lines. In extreme cases cultural salience becomes a form of intense monologia, capable of exiling diverse forms of cultural expression from the public sphere.

To be a member of a minor culture is to encounter the problematic nature of publics, for inferior status within a hierarchy of cultures is directly linked to attitudes of public indifference or overt disdain. It would appear that in the case of minor cultures, lack of interest is expressed, not by one, but by multiple publics, only some of which are located outside the boundaries of the nation-state. In small countries such as Denmark, directors of art films must contend with local audiences who prefer light comedies featuring blondes frollicking in haystacks to "serious" art. Although this situation may not be peculiar to small nations, it is exacerbated by other factors which clearly are. More specifically, the cultural imperialism engaged in by large nation-states tends to monopolize not only markets but publics. For example, during the

GATT negotiations a French politician pointed out that it was impossible at the moment to see a European film in a public cinema anywhere in Portugal. This saturation of markets entails processes of acculturation, which the French, in a critical spirit, are calling *mondialisation;* a public obliged to see only films such as *Working Girl* and *Jurassic Park* acquires tastes at odds with indigenous modes of cultural expression.

The monologic nature of certain international publics dominated by a small number of major cultures or nations makes it particularly difficult for members of small nations to express themselves in anything resembling an authentic voice. International publics are frequently intensely monolingual, with participation hinging on fluency in the tongue favored by the dominant culture. Whereas members of minor cultures must be multilingual if they are to be part of an international public, members of major cultures need rely only on their mother tongues. In certain contexts all traces of national specificity—accents, foreign tongues, and even subtitles—appear only as so many uncanny and displeasing departures from what is dominant and seemingly natural.

The difficulties encountered in attempts to secure national and international audiences for Danish films are by no means recent, nor are they specific to this one European nation. In the Danish case, however, the problem of publics is experienced all the more intensely, since the current situation can be contrasted with memories of a bygone golden age of Danish cinema. As is well-known, the advent of sound—and a politics of language favoring only certain tongues—undermined what until World War I was a thriving Danish silent film industry, one recognized internationally for the technical and realistic as well as erotic qualities of its products.[3]

Responding to Cultural Imperialism

The flooding of the European market with American films during the cold-war period has been admirably documented by Thomas H. Guback, as have some of the European responses.[4] That European attempts, from 1925 onward, to counter American cultural imperialism by means of restrictions on imports, distribution, and screen time have been anything but successful is amply evidenced by recent GATT negotiations. Whereas the ideological role of exporting American film on a large scale was acknowledged in 1945,[5] French and other opponents of a globalized American culture now find themselves challenging an equation of culture and commerce, a conception of culture as somehow culturally neutral. At the same time, it is a matter of insisting on the necessity of creating the conditions under which particular national and cultural identities can survive, and this in the context of free-market negotiations indebted to a tradition of liberal thinking that refuses to arbitrate between different substantive conceptions of the good life. In foregrounding the need to continue to subsidize the French film and television industry,

Jacques Toubon and others do, however, continue to build on earlier attempts to stem the influx of American products.

The European Economic Community has been seen by some as a means
of counteracting the Americanization of European publics. Indeed, in 1990
the EEC launched the so-called MEDIA project, the principal purpose of
which was to promote European film and television by means of improved
production and distribution networks, technical training, and film archives.
The strategy of international cooperation is also evident within the more narrow context of the Nordic countries, where Scandinavian coproductions are
becoming increasingly common. Examples include Bille August's *Pelle the
Conqueror* and Max von Sydow's *Katinka*, both of which are Swedish-Danish
coproductions. The budget for a Swedish-Danish coproduction may be almost twice that of an exclusively Danish or Swedish film, since coproductions
draw on financial support from two, rather than one, of the state-funded national film institutes. Coproductions thus provide a means of imbuing Scandinavian films with the kind of high-cost production values that colonized
Scandinavian publics appear to crave.

Yet the strategy of international cooperation, be it European or Scandinavian, may create as many problems as it potentially resolves. The strategy in
question speaks directly to the indifference of national publics, but overlooks
one of the key motivations behind attempts to counteract the internationalization of culture in the image of certain dominant or major cultures. The
motivation in question is, of course, a desire for cultural reciprocity, which is
possible only if cultural specificity is somehow maintained. The point, as Anthony Smith has argued in his "National Industry and the idea of European
Unity,"[6] is that national or established cultures may well be inimical to the
creation of a cosmopolitan culture, which is clearly what coproductions are.
What underwrites the idea of coproductions as an expression of cultural policy
is a belief in the existence of a European or Scandinavian identity understood
in terms of notions of shared language groups, religions, economies, and so
on. However, we need only recall the initial Danish rejection of the Maastricht
Accord in a national referendum to understand just how problematic it is to
presuppose an existing European identity that might be expressed in film.
Similarly, the idea of a Scandinavian identity may well be one that seems cogent primarily to non-Scandinavians. In this respect it is interesting to note
that Hans Kohn's remarks about the dissolution of the nineteenth-century
Pan-Scandinavian movement foreground the very same issues mentioned by
a Danish film critic reflecting on the ways in which coproductions can fail.
Kohn attributes the demise of the Pan-Scandinavian movement to the fact
that the countries in question "jealously preserved their national sovereignty,
policy, and personality, achieving separation (Norway from Sweden; Iceland
from Denmark), not integration."[7] Lene Nordin, on the other hand, uses
culinary metaphors to highlight the need for cultural specificity within coproductions. In so doing she identifies the very element most readily mobi-

lized within a separatist discourse capable of undermining the creation of a cosmopolitan culture involving international cooperation: "In the case of Northern co-productions, as well as those involving other countries, the nations in question must have a natural place within the film's action, if the stew is to have any flavor at all and to be more than a pretty arrangement."[8]

Defining Danish Cinema

One refrain within discourses on cultural imperialism emphasizes the need to strengthen national cultures and cinemas. Although the tone in many cases is one of urgency, it remains unclear what exactly is being urged. For what, one might ask, *is* a national cinema? How are we to understand the relation between nations and film? Is it a matter, for example, of promoting a nationalist cinematic culture? Interestingly, cinema as a public sphere accommodates a number of different responses to these questions, including what might be called a "culturally minimalist" definition of Danish cinema. According to the law, a film is Danish if it qualifies for financial support from the state-funded Danish Film Institute. Following one definition, then, a feature-length film is Danish if at least 25 percent of its actors and technical crew are Danish. We note that eligibility for financial backing in no way depends on use of the Danish language or on the film's being shot in Denmark. Curiously, then, films directed by other nationals outside Denmark are potentially Danish. Although the legal definition of Danish film grows out of a concern to support a national culture, it remains largely indifferent to the linguistic and territorial factors associated with concepts of nationhood. Yet, as Bille August has argued, the contribution of the cultural policy in question is by no means negligible.[9] Essentially, this policy enables Danish directors to make films that have no commercial viability, films, that is, for which no public, be it local or international, can be identified in advance.

The minimalist definition of Danish film is but one of several conceptions circulating within the public sphere, for there are alternative understandings that rely on a thicker, more substantive view of culture. More specifically, there is an assumption that a film's Danishness depends on more than simply meeting certain quotas dictating minimal levels of participation by Danish nationals. Statements by actors, filmmakers, critics, and spectators suggest the existence of a network of mutual beliefs characterizing properly Danish films, for the same elements are emphasized time and again by the supporters of a strong national cinematic culture.

Language is one such element, for genuinely Danish films are widely believed to employ the Danish language as an authentic mode of expression. Of interest in this respect is August's adaptation of the first part of the canonized socialist novel by Martin Andersen Nexø, *Pelle Erobreren*. In an interview August underscores his understanding of important links between language and national culture: "Various coproduction partners in the U.S. and Canada offered to back the film if we shot in English, but it is a Danish national classic and it is important to retain the different languages of Swedish and Danish of the characters."[10] August's film depicts the adventures of a young boy, Pelle, who leaves his native Sweden with his father, Lasse, to seek a brighter future in Denmark. Swedish, then, is the language spoken by the impoverished immigrants eking out a meager existence on a large Danish farm overseen by a ruthless and bigoted foreman. August's decision not to have the actors speak English in the film suggests a view of Danish as the only acceptable language for adaptations of national classics, except, that is, in cases in which the action of these texts require the presence of another tongue, such as Swedish.

A recurrent feature of films considered properly Danish is the translation into the cinematic medium of cultural monuments that are part of a canonized, national culture. It is noteworthy in this regard that Carl Theodor Dreyer had attempted earlier to acquire the rights to adapt Nexø's novel. Unfortunately, Dreyer's project was blocked by Nexø's descendants and by bureaucrats in the former German Democratic Republic, where the leftist author had settled. Dreyer did, however, clearly establish the connections between a properly Danish cinema and certain cultural icons, including "literary classics," in a short article.[11] Here he calls for a film about "our great national author," Hans Christian Andersen, whom he also refers to as "one of the greatest literary assets in the world."[12] Dreyer envisages a film made in such a way as to elicit the "blessings of the Danish people."[13] The film, that is, would present Andersen in a manner consonant with Danish perceptions of the author and his work. What is more, as a result of its cultural specificity, the film could function abroad as a form of "cultural propaganda for Denmark."[14]

Danish films are further understood to explore the shared practices of an imagined community located within the borders of the nation-state.[15] They are assigned the important task of thematizing this community's past and of projecting its future. Speaking of the relation between *Pelle* and present-day Denmark, August says: "Immigrants are treated as second class citizens. I wanted to try to establish an understanding of their lives and their struggles, as well as their feelings and qualities."[16] The harsh treatment of Swedish immigrants in nineteenth-century Denmark thus becomes a means of reflecting on the choices facing Danes as their society becomes increasingly multicultural due to reconfigurations of the European and other political landscapes.

Interestingly, the representative statements, examined above, about what constitutes a properly Danish cinema, focus on elements that can be derived directly from shared beliefs about a national culture. That is, notions of cinematic specificity are systematically subordinated to ideas of cultural specificity. Although the statements in question by no means rule out the possibility of a Danish national cinema having certain characteristic aesthetic or formal properties, the emphasis falls squarely on concepts derived from the discourses of nationhood, rather than from the terms of cinema studies.

Cultural Specificity and
International Publics

Reflections on the need to foster a Danish national cinema inevitably raise the question of audiences or publics. A common argument, for example, is that the emphasis on cultural specificity has a dual purpose. The aim, we are told, is not simply to create a truly national culture, but to bring about the conditions under which international recognition of the relevant cultural products can occur. Speaking once again of *Pelle,* August establishes a direct connection between a film's cultural specificity and its international appeal: "What pleases me enormously about the movie is that it is so Nordic. I feel that by making films that maintain a strong national identity, we succeed in making them international. When we try to imitate say, American action films, we end up with products which ultimately have no identity at all." [17] In articulating his hopes for a film about Hans Christian Andersen, Dreyer makes a similar point: "It is a misunderstanding to think that we enhance a film's foreign appeal by letting it emerge as an international factory product. On the contrary, it will win greater interest the more we show our own face and the less we grovel for foreign taste." [18] Only if we show a face with distinctive features can we hope to be recognized by others. Trying to appeal directly to perceived standards of international taste is a losing game in at least three respects. To do so is to undermine a commitment to authentic self-expression and to invite recognition on the wrong terms. The likelihood of properly grasping and meeting the standards in question is small if one is embedded within a minor culture. And, finally, only rarely does the imitative capacity to produce products resembling those of a dominant culture meet with applause.

The fact that talk about national specificity provokes thoughts about international audiences suggests that Guback's understanding of the purpose of a national cinema remains incomplete in important ways. "The purpose," he says, "is not to compete in the making of films for international audiences, but to use the cinema to present or clarify the problems, lives, and aspirations of peoples." [19] The aim, as Guback claims, is indeed to give expression to a national culture. However, it is also imperative that the corresponding identity be *recognized* by publics outside the nation-state. The task, then, becomes one of specifying why international recognition is crucial. At the same time, it is important to determine how international recognition can be achieved without thwarting the desire for authentic self-expression.

It has been suggested that the internationalist bent of Danish national cinema can be partially explained in terms of the role played by the state in the process of cinematic production.[20] As the principal producer of Danish films, the state has an interest in expanding the number of publics for its products. Although financial support is granted to individual directors and producers in the form of loans, the conditions of repayment are extremely lenient. Indeed, most Danish films fail to generate the level of profit beyond which repayment becomes an obligation. Although it is no doubt interesting to reflect on the role played by the state in processes of internationalization, it seems unlikely that the desire, expressed by members of the film industry, to have certain films circulate within an international public sphere, can be adequately explained along these lines. A more plausible explanation, I believe, is to be found in what Charles Taylor has called "the politics of recognition."[21]

The Politics of Recognition

A key claim made by Taylor is that identities are elaborated dialogically, in conversation with or at least in relation to others. An agent's sense of self, for example, is importantly shaped by the moral sources of the group to which he or she belongs. Yet, as Taylor points out, agents are also oriented toward "significant others,"[22] that is, toward groups whose collective identities are quite different. In an important attempt to explain this other-directedness, Taylor posits a human need for recognition. This need, claims Taylor, is the motivating force behind the increasingly influential discourses of subaltern or minority groups, be they black, feminist, gay, or lesbian. Once we understand that agents need recognition, it becomes clear that a failure to recognize or affirm certain individual or collective identities can be a form of violence.

Recognition, claims Taylor, becomes an issue with the transition from the premodern to the modern period. In contexts where identities are "socially derived," fixed, and stable, recognition is automatic. However, as hierarchies of being collapse, allowing for an "inwardly" rather than a socially derived identity, the conditions arise "in which the attempt to be recognized can fail."[23] On this view, then, the problematic nature of recognition flows directly from aspects of modernity.

Agents experiencing the harmful effects of misrecognition, or the absence of recognition, can make recognition a political issue. According to Taylor the politics of recognition practiced by minority groups combines elements from two strands of modern thought. A discourse of authenticity, traceable to the Romantics, supports the idea that it is the value of an inwardly generated, authentic self that must be acknowledged. If we owe the idea of authenticity to the Romantics, we are indebted to Enlightenment thinkers, such as Kant, for our modern notions of equality and dignity. These are the notions informing discourses of human rights, which are bent on an equalization of rights and entitlements. When these two strands of thought combine, as they do in a politics of recognition, it becomes a matter of claiming that it is an individual's basic human right to demand that his or her particular mode of authentic self-expression be recognized as having at least the same value as other forms of self-expression. The criterion of universalizability governing a politics of equal rights is thus held also to pertain to the area of authentic self-expression. Taylor argues persuasively that this tendency to conflate questions of dignity and authenticity is problematic, though for reasons that need not concern us here.

North American postcolonial and multiculturalist discourses have been most effective in promoting a politics of recognition, for these discourses focus intensely on the value of culture produced by groups lacking economic and political power. In North America the demand for recognition is thus explicitly linked to a project of political empowerment. Interestingly, this focus on the link between cultural and political power makes it difficult for North American discourses to grasp the need for a politics of recognition in contexts in which economic and political power is distributed with greater equality among citizens. Nor can these theories readily comprehend the multiculturalist aspirations of citizens belonging to nations lacking the kind of ethnic diversity characteristic of North America. In the Danish case, for example, economic and social privilege does little to alleviate the nation's cultural marginality within international contexts. What contemporary theories overlook, then, is the way in which relations between major and minor cultures necessitate a politics of recognition oriented toward international, rather than only national publics.

How, then, can directors rooted in minor cultures win international audiences? One strategy is to appeal directly to international tastes and to construe cultural specificity as an obstacle that must be overcome. Lars von Trier, for example, demonstrates little or no attachment to Danish culture in films such as *Element of Crime* and *Europa*.[24] The characters in these films speak American, English, or German, rather than Danish, and their actions are depicted in a manner that resuscitates images associated with Sternberg, Hitchcock, Welles, and Tarkovsky, as well as certain European and American comic books. Now, it could be argued that von Trier effaces the traces of national identities in order to raise questions about the viability of collective, European identities. The absence of cultural specificity need not, then, bespeak an indifference to problems of identity. However, if the goal is to clarify the nature of a politics of recognition specific to minor cultures, then a quite different strategy for securing international publics needs to be considered.

Leveraging as a Strategy

Danish directors adopt a leveraging strategy when they mobilize certain international elements in order to ensure foreign recognition of Danish culture. This strategy is, I believe, a feature of what Benjamin Lee refers to as cross-writing, as well as of what might be called cross-filming. To use the term "cross" in this context is to point to the ways in which certain directors self-consciously orient their films toward different and to some extent irreconcilable publics. In order to understand how this dual orientation supports a minor culture's politics of recognition, it is necessary to focus on what can be called the opaque, translatable, and international nature of certain cinematic elements. More precisely, it is a matter of grasping how the distance created by some of these elements can be bridged by others. In developing these points, it is helpful to refer to a couple of films by Bille August, a director intensely attuned to the risks and advantages of cross-filming.

Cinematic elements are opaque when they are so firmly rooted within a given national imaginary that international audiences cannot be expected to understand their meaning without the help of native informants. An example is the sequence of events involving the Danish town, Svendborg, in one of August's early films, *Twist and Shout*. The action of the film is generated in part by the amorous relation between two adolescents, Bjørn and Anna. Early on in their relationship, Anna announces that she will be going away for a few days. Bjørn's desperate response is rendered all the more comic to Danish audiences when Anna announces her journey's destination: Svendborg. Svendborg is not that far from Copenhagen, although inhabitants of the capital think of it as a distant, provincial town. The film goes on to explore Bjørn's anxieties concerning the separation. Thus, for example, he imagines farmers gathering in a barn in the depth of winter to experience a little warmth generated by a striptease performed by Anna. Members of international audiences cannot fail to notice the importance that characters in the film attribute to a place called Svendborg. What they cannot fathom, however, is that August uses distances separating cosmopolitan and provincial cultures to create a series of effects that local publics will consider particularly humorous.

The situation is quite different in the case of translatable elements. Although such elements have a distinctly Danish flavor, their cultural specificity does not prevent members of foreign audiences from grasping the relevant meanings. In *Pelle the Conqueror*, for example, Lasse repeatedly articulates his conception of a good life, which includes having coffee in bed on Sundays and roast pork with raisins instead of herring on Christmas eve. Although members of foreign audiences may eat neither roast pork with raisins nor herring on Christmas eve, the significance of these foods is accessible to anyone capable of mobilizing distinctions between festive and workaday temporalities. In other words, processes of intercultural translation become possible when certain categories of social experience are shared by cultures that are significantly different in other respects.

In addition to their opaque and translatable elements, many Danish films—including August's *Pelle*, Gabriel Axel's *Babettes Gaestebud* (*Babette's Feast*), and Dreyer's *Gertrud*—have a certain international dimension. The text by Martin Andersen Nexø on which August's *Pelle* is based is not only a Danish classic, but a work canonized by an international socialist movement. In the early part of the twentieth century, Nexø's *Pelle* was widely translated and distributed in serial form. Lenin, for example, is said to have recommended a Russian translation of the work after having read the third volume in the French Communist Party's newspaper, *L'Humanité*.[25]

Inasmuch as Pelle and Erik dream of emigrating to America—the land of hope and opportunity—*Pelle* evokes the waves of emigration that connect Denmark to other nations, particularly the United States. Interestingly, August has claimed that to some extent America is constitutive of various European identities: "It is important to remember that the United States is the crucible in which all European nations have been combined. As a result, different cultures have been more or less subtly integrated. To some extent we are all at home in America."[26]

Underwriting August's *Pelle* is an assumption that, if correct, helps secure an international audience for the film: much as concepts of America have shaped European identities, so have visions of Europe contributed to the self-understandings of American citizens.[27] International elements in *Pelle* help viewers construe Denmark as a land having personal relevance for members of American publics. Nor is this relevance limited to Americans of Danish or Scandinavian ancestry, for within the internationalist rhetoric of the film Denmark becomes representative of other countries of origin. That is, the dismal conditions that cause Erik and Pelle to dream of America may well have existed in Denmark, but they existed elsewhere too.

How, then, do the elements discussed above relate to the question of a minor culture's publics and to that of a politics of recognition practiced by citizens of small nations? Although the seduction of national audiences depends on all three elements, it relies particularly on the opaque features of Danish films. More specifically, cinematic opacity contributes to a kind of mirroring effect, for it helps persuade local audiences that they, through their language, humor, and specifically Danish practices, are central to, or at least represented in, a given film. The interest of international publics, on the other hand, is provoked, not by a perception of cultural difference or specificity, but by the already internationalized elements of a film. International elements, then, become the lever enabling various forms of cultural specificity to appear before, and to be recognized by, international publics.

The central role played by a leveraging strategy in the internationalization of Danish film suggests key differences between a politics of recognition motivated in part by a desire to rectify political and economic imbalances, and a politics of affirmation generated primarily by indifference to the cultural production of small nations. An *explicit* emphasis on cultural difference is only viable as a strategy of recognition if the specificity in question is linked, as a matter of common knowledge, to political and economic injustices that a given society is committed, in theory or practice, to effacing. Leveraging, on the other hand, becomes necessary when cultural difference is associated with economic prosperity and a well-functioning political democracy, as it is in the case of Denmark. To replace leveraging and mediation with appeals to a public sense of injustice would be to suggest that Danes are victimized by foreign indifference to their culture. And, although this indifference does inflict a form of harm, the claim cannot be fully vindicated on account of the prosperity that most Danes enjoy. Danes, to put it simply, make unlikely victims. I have been focusing on what I take to be the effective means of creating a viable, national cinematic culture capable of commanding international recognition. This strategy is clearly already being used, but should perhaps be more widely employed and better understood. Of course, this strategy may have its limitations. For example, it may well be the case that key aspects of a national culture simply cannot be linked to the international elements needed for leveraging to occur. If that is so, as I suspect it is, then it would be imprudent in the long run to engage only in leveraging at the expense of other modes of engaging local and international audiences. Nonetheless, as it stands, Danish filmmakers, including August, can only learn from the successes of films such as *Twist and Shout, Pelle,* and *The Best Intentions.* Indeed, it could be argued that August courted disaster in his latest film, *House of the Spirits,* precisely because he set aside the mixed strategy characteristic of his earlier work.

NOTES

I would like to thank my research assistant, Brian Lynch, who spent many hours tracking down recent discussions of Danish cinema. The Social Sciences and Humanities Research Council of Canada provided generous financial support for this project, as did the Fonds pour la Formation de Chercheurs et l'Aide à la Recherche. I am grateful to my colleague, Peter Ohlin, for sharing his thoughts on Swedish cinema with me.

1. See Bourdieu's *Distinction: A Social Critique of the Judgement of Taste,* trans. Richard Nice (Cambridge: Harvard University Press, 1984).

2. "What Is a Minor Literature?" in *Kafka: Toward a Minor Literature,* trans. Dana B. Polan (Minneapolis: University of Minnesota Press, 1986).

3. See Ron Mottram, *The Danish Cinema before Dreyer* (Metuchen, N.J.: Scarecrow, 1988).

4. Thomas H. Guback, "Hollywood's International Market," in *The American Film Industry,* ed. Tino Balio (Madison: University of Wisconsin Press, 1976), pp. 387–409.

5. According to Guback, the Motion Picture Export Association "launched its postwar distribution campaign with the blessing and indeed the support of the government" (*ibid.,* p. 396).

6. *International Affairs* 68 (1992): 55–76.

7. Hans Kohn, "Nationalism," *International Encyclopedia of the Social Sciences,* vol. 2, ed. David Sills, (New York: Macmillan, 1968), pp. 63–69, 68.

8. "Men med nordiske, såvel som co-produktioner med andre lande, gaelder det, at de forskellige nationaliteter skal have en naturlig plads i filmens handling, hvis den sammenkogte ret skal smage af noget og ikke blot blive en flot anretning." "80ernes danske film fra A til Z," *Kosmorama* 33 (1987): 38–43, 41.

9. "The policy of appointed film institute consultants and state-produced films [the state collaborates with private producers, but provides most of the financing] protects

the industry from having to make only commercially viable products." Cited by Jytte Jensen in "Bille's Feast," *The Village Voice* (7 June 1988): 59.

10. "'Pelle' to Play N.Y. and Coast in December via Miramax Films," Lawrence Cohn, *Variety* (12 October 1988): 6.

11. "New Roads for the Danish film," in *Dreyer in Double Reflection*, ed. Donald Skoller (New York: Dutton, 1973), pp. 81–89.

12. Ibid., pp. 81, 86.

13. Ibid., p. 81.

14. Ibid., p. 82.

15. I am drawing here on Benedict Anderson's influential *Imagined Communities* (London: Verso, 1983). Peter Ohlin demonstrates the utility of Anderson's concept for cinema studies in his unpublished manuscript, "Language, Discourse, Identity: The Swedishness of Swedish Films."

16. Jensen, "Bille's Feast," p. 59.

17. Ibid., p. 59.

18. Dreyer, "New Roads for the Danish Film," pp. 81–82.

19. Guback, "Hollywood's International Market," p. 406.

20. "80ernes danske film fra A til Z": 40. Andrew Higson makes the profit motive a central feature of national cinema as such: "Histories of national cinema . . . are histories of business seeking a secure footing in the market-place, enabling the maximisation of an industry's profits while at the same time bolstering a nation's cultural standing. At this level, the politics of national cinema can be reduced to a marketing strategy, an attempt to market the diverse as, in fact, offering a coherent and singular experience." "The Concept of National Cinema," *Screen* 30 (1989): 36–46, 37–38.

21. See his chapter by that title in *Multiculturalism and "The Politics of Recognition,"* ed. Amy Gutmann (Princeton, N.J.: Princeton University Press, 1992), pp. 25–73.

22. Ibid., p. 32.

23. Ibid., p. 35.

24. It is no accident that Daniel Sauvaget should claim that "Le Danemark est décidément un pays trop petit pour Lars von Trier." See "Lars von Trier ou les délices de l'ambiguïté," *La Revue du Cinéma* 476 (1991): 69.

25. Palle Schantz Lauridsen, "Fra Brønshøj til Bornholm: Pelle Erobreren er blevet en kraftfuld og stor film," *Kosmorama* 182 (1987): 9.

26. "Mais il ne faut pas perdre de vue que les États-Unis sont un creuset dans lequel toutes les nations européennes sont venues se fondre. Ce qui fait que les différentes cultures ont été intégrées de façon plus ou moins subtile. Nous sommes tous un peu chez nous en Amérique." Yves Alion, "Bille August: Entretien," *La Revue du Cinéma* 443 (1988): 43.

27. Historical support for this assumption is readily found in the statistics on emigration, which indicate, for example, that 300,000 Danes made their way to America between 1870 and 1914. See Stewart Oakley, *A Short History of Denmark* (London: Faber, 1972), p. 195.

26

Whose Apparatus? Problems of
Film Exhibition and History

Vance Kepley, Jr.

The premise of Edwin Porter's *Uncle Josh at the Moving Picture Show* (1902) is a rube's susceptibility to cinematic illusion. The title character is so thoroughly taken in by the images projected on screen that he thinks he can intervene in the fictional world they represent. In his awkward, frenetic efforts to do so, however, he merely tears down the movie screen, betraying the presence of a projector and, thereby, the source of the deception.

Does this film challenge cinematic illusionism by revealing the processes of the cinematic apparatus which so readily deceives spectators? Perhaps. Apparently at least some modern theorists would seem to think so.[1] Nevertheless I'm prepared to believe—call it a hunch—that virtually every adult who ever watched this film, including members of the original 1902 audience, knew something about film projection and were not especially surprised to discover that a machine supplied the images which so mystified poor Uncle Josh. Indeed, the film's joke depends on the gap between Josh's naïveté about the cinematic apparatus and the spectator's understanding of same.[2] The film's spectators knew enough about the institution, in fact, to enter into a rational social contract with it, giving up time and money to extract particular pleasures from its processes. Film spectators have done so for an entire century, now, in different lands and in *different circumstances of projection and reception*. Some *Uncle Josh* fans may even have watched this film in a venue where the projector resided in full view and offered a mechanical clatter that was downright distracting.

Yet the assumption that there is a single, privileged situation for watching movies—the legendary dream world of the darkened theater with its processes discreetly hidden—underpins much of our thinking about spectatorship. Film viewers supposedly enter a darkened chamber, thereby losing material contact with the "real" world outside; there they settle into a passive state to receive the sights and sounds emanating from the screen; and, having no opportunity to test the impressions presented in this artificial environment, they succumb to the power of its projected fictions. They surrender their rational faculties and social identities and enter into the illusions presented for them. This characterization of movie viewing is common enough in popular literature about the "dream world" of cinema, to be sure. But it has just as salient a presence in scholarly thinking about film spectatorship, thanks to the fact that it was given theoretical validity in the literature of psychoanalysis.

The most cogent and influential theoretical account of this situation resides in Jean-Louis Baudry's theory of the cinematic apparatus. In two seminal essays published in the 1970s, Baudry not only brings the conditions of film viewing into the domain of film theory and psychoanalysis, he contends forcefully that the power of illusion in cinema resides less in the content of films than in the instruments and institutions which make and exhibit them. "Ideological Effects of the Basic Cinematographic Apparatus" and "The Apparatus: Metaphysical Approaches to the Impression of Reality in Cinema" speak to related questions of spectatorship, identification, subjectivity, and ideology that were taken up during film theory's "psychoanalytical turn" of the 1970s.[3] The essays proved timely and instrumental to the development of psychoanalytical and ideological film theory by virtue of the fact that Baudry took issues from those domains and extended them to the whole institution of cinema. His contribution was such that David Rodowick, in his critical history of modern film theory, could confidently assert that "[o]ne cannot overestimate the impact of Baudry's work in this period."[4] Likewise Judith Mayne, in assessing work on film spectatorship, refers to Baudry's apparatus model as crucial to the "ground-breaking work of the early and mid-1970s" and as a source of continuing influence.[5]

The essence of Baudry's contribution is his contention that the machinery and institutions of cinema cannot be thought of as neutral transmitters of information. They are fundamentally implicated in ideology and forms of social control by their very design. Much of the force of the argument derives from the literary skill with which Baudry extends the term "apparatus" through a series of elegant analogies.[6] It encompasses the actual hardware of filmmaking and projection, the institutions which bring spectators into contact with films. It also refers to the viewer's psychological "machinery" which is engaged when that contact comes about. It even takes up the "ideological state apparatus" which allegedly shapes subjects' understanding of the world. By finding a set of parallels among film viewing, dream work and the unconscious, and ideological manipulation, Baudry could add film viewing to categories of experience treated by Freudian and Lacanian psychoanalysis and by Althusserian social theory.

Although the literal act of film viewing is not the only issue treated in Baudry's theory of the cinematic apparatus, it is central to his explanation of how movies manipulate spectators. The conditions of exhibition, according to Baudry, evoke the conditions of dreaming and virtually assure that spectators will abandon their critical faculties. Spectators remain immobile, in the dark, with no means to orient themselves physically or to test the reality of the images projected on screen. What is more, the movie screen provides the equivalent of the "dream-screen" upon which dreamers are said to observe dream imagery. The combination of these conditions forces the spectator to regress to a state of primitive narcissism in which the distinctions between oneself and one's environment, and between perception and representation, are lost. The spectator would thus be hard-pressed to resist the apparently superreal images and sounds presented as the only stimuli in this hermetic environment.

And any reader of Baudry would be equally hard-pressed to conclude that he does not portray the spectator as a victim: "Projection and reflection take place in a closed space, and those who remain there, whether they know it or not (but they do not), find themselves chained, captured, and captivated."[7] Even if one does understand that there is technology in this environment providing fictional images, the apparatus works somewhat like the unconscious: one can more or less know that it is there and surrender to its power nevertheless.

The sealed, darkened chamber may be the most important ingredient making possible the causal sequence which Baudry says produces illusion, and it is the source of the analogies he uses to extend his argument. One sits alone in the dark, imbibing stimuli someone else has designed and presented. Whether the theater is crowded or virtually empty, whether a given spectator is attending the film with a group of peers or alone, once the lights go down, the spectator is forced to interact with the film as a single, isolated psyche. All sights and sounds from the real world (as opposed to the fictional world of the film) are omitted from the spectator's experience until the final credits finally come up on the screen. Baudry's stress on the hermetic quality of this setting is so strong that he analogizes it with Plato's cave and even with the womb. The spectator resides in a controlled environment, one that sustains illusion through its physical design.

And whereas the prisoners of Plato's cave chose to remain and watch the flickering images even after their chains were removed, Baudry suggests that this illusion-filled environment for film viewing is as much a fulfillment of the spectator's deeply repressed desires as it is a condition imposed on him or her. Humans, it would seem, have long sought to find a material situation that would evoke the dream experience. The technological invention in the late nineteenth century of film projection provided the long-delayed equivalent of the conditions under which dreams are experienced. "What desire was aroused, more than two thousand years before the actual invention of cinema . . . ?"[8] Baudry asks rhetorically to suggest that the invention of the darkened movie theater with its single lit screen was predicted by humankind's own machinery of desire. It seems that we all waited through the millennia for the Lumières finally to decide to turn down the lights and throw a projection beam on a screen. One might well ask: Was the entire history of public entertainment prior to the theatrical exhibition of movies merely a prelude? And what does one make of the fact that, after craving so long for psychic satisfaction in darkened movie theaters, so many members of industrialized societies casually abandoned that perfect fulfillment of psychic need when television came along to offer an alternative visual experience—one that is commonly realized, it should be noted, in a fully lighted room filled with ancillary sounds and activities?

I submit these purposely flippant counter-questions in order to raise the issues of history and actual social practice. Apparatus theory takes account of neither matter in its description of the conditions of film viewing. Rather, it appeals to an ostensible archetype: first by suggesting that the movie theater is merely a modern incarnation of primordial archetypes (the cave, the womb), and then by making one particular version of film exhibition into the archetype for the whole experience of film viewing. It treats a particular type of film exhibition—one that may have been prominent in certain industrialized societies for a period of years in the early to mid-twentieth century—as though it were a universal.

It does not ask, for example, about alternative ways of seeing movies: were open-air showings at amusement parks and fairgrounds not to be counted as cinema since spectators would doubtless have taken in other sights and sounds while watching movies? It does not ask about the social practices of audiences watching films in the classic situation of the darkened chamber: did/do spectators actually sit quietly in the dark? It does not ask what social pleasures (as opposed to psychic drives) might be satisfied by going to the movies, pleasures which might have little or nothing to do with a desire to return to the womb: might spectators find forms of social companionship, for example, by attending movies with friends and peers? Finally (and importantly), it does not ask about the ways in which practices of film viewing changed over time and from society to society: is it possible that a Russian villager in the 1920s saw movies in circumstances that were materially different from those of a French intellectual in the 1970s and that those conditions produced different effects?

Such questions might complicate one's understanding of the moviegoing experience, and they most assuredly would complicate the archetypal image of exhibition that was given such theoretical force by apparatus theory.[9] That added complexity could be measured, in part, as historical specificity.

The prominence of Baudry's apparatus is attributable to psychoanalysis, or more accurately to film theory's celebrated appropriation of psychoanalysis in the 1970s. That period also witnessed the beginnings of another, more modest scholarly enterprise which has continued for the past two decades and which has provided salutary alternatives to psychoanalytical film theory's reified account of film viewing. Several American historians, few of whom would have considered themselves to be part of a sustained scholarly project, began researching the history of film exhibition in cautious, measured steps. The signature quality of the work has been the apparent modesty of each historical enterprise. Such historians posed deceptively simple questions about who went to the movies in particular situations, why they went, and under what circumstances. The researchers then offered limited, even tentative conclusions about specific historical situations. The narrow case study, rather than the totalizing intellectual construct, has constituted the principal rhetorical genre of the work. It has concentrated on finite terrains: Boston in the nickelodeon era, Manhattan in the early 1910s, Chicago's black neighborhoods in the 1920s. And the findings were not always transferable to other settings: Chicago's African-American residents did not necessarily follow a pattern established by New York's immigrants.

Since the outcome of the research has been a series of discrete findings rather than a comprehensive record, this historiographic movement (if that is the right term) can only be characterized by adduction, by finding some related features among a selection of the projects. The movement does not offer itself to etiology. One cannot easily locate a point of intellectual origin, an initial inspiration, which set in motion the research in exhibition history. In tracing the course of this research, one can only note a selection of those essays which seem to have encouraged other historians and which have shown some staying power. Even an incomplete survey of the research, however, promises to generate some dissatisfaction with apparatus theory's reified version of exhibition history.

To the extent that one might speak of origins, research on nickelodeons undertaken in the 1970s might warrant attention, notably Russell Merritt's and Robert Allen's initial case studies.[10] Each exploited demographic information about American cities to make some claims about the social status of early film audiences. Merritt's account of nickelodeon theaters in Boston used the locations of theater and the geography of working-class and middle-class neighborhoods to refine our sense of the class identity of the nickelodeon audience. Allen took account of these methods and adapted them in his study of Manhattan. He also appealed to urban geography to describe early movie audiences demographically, and he added the variable of immigration patterns among New York's various ethnic groups to give that audience a somewhat more precise identity. Thus, group-based patterns of social affiliation, deriving from class and ethnic identity, allowed Merritt and Allen to take a seemingly amorphous entity ("the audience") and to give it more specific historical markings. And a by-product of their research is the suggestion that those social identities actually were reinforced by the practice of moviegoing.

Other researchers took stronger account of temporal dynamics such as urban development or evolving forms of social behavior. Those concerns were evident in early studies by such historians as Garth Jowett and Douglas Gomery.[11] Jowett's treatment of the first American film audiences invoked turn-of-the-century patterns of expanded leisure time for the American labor force, increased spending on amusements, and the emergence of a general leisure industry in the American economy. These dynamics provided explanations for the social development of film and could offer some indications of how film viewing fit into other consumerist practices. Gomery looked to urban growth patterns and the movement of populations within cities. By noting such issues as the designs of mass transit systems and how they anticipated new housing and business patterns, he could track the demographic evolution of an urban movie audience over time. Such efforts suggested ways to add temporal change to studies of audiences and exhibition.

The foregoing accounts exploited the demographic data which proved readily available for major urban markets. Any possible urban research bias from that data was offset by case studies of medium-sized cities and small towns. Studies of such communities as Austin, Texas, and Winona, Minnesota, for example, extended the cross section, and they revealed still new variables.[12] More than neighborhood and ethnic identity, film exhibition in smaller towns answered to conditions which encompassed the entire community. As David Thomas's account of Winona showed, moviegoing fit into patterns of behavior which were designed to enhance the town's general sense of community.

Specialized, regional exhibition was studied in Diane Waldman's account of the "company theater" of Rockefeller's Colorado Fuel and Iron Company.[13] Waldman's research offers particular promise since it ventures into the realm of alternative, noncommercial cinema and because of its innovative procedure for describing the social consequences of film viewing. The CF&I movie service was provided to miners in the 1910s as part of the company's effort to forestall union activity and to promote a sense of welfare capitalism. It extended corporate influence into the leisure hours of employees, and Waldman explored the effects of that practice on the miner population, an effort troubled by the dearth of written records by the miners themselves. Through a series of careful steps, Waldman established correlations between CF&I's identifiable corporate ideologies and the institutional practices of the theater service. Without benefit of statements from the miners, Waldman could nevertheless describe the conditions under which the films were seen, and she could offer a plausible conclusion about the extent to which corporate interests were served by the theater's operation.[14]

Such an effort raises the issue of how to discuss the social effects of film viewing. Moviegoing is certainly a practice which has a consequence in individual lives. Yet one cannot assume that audience members will leave behind a comprehensive or even representative record of their experiences for the convenience of historians. Some historians have dealt with this issue by looking at the activity of moviegoing in the context of other noncinema social practices that could be documented. Elizabeth Ewen's and Judith Mayne's accounts of immigrant women and early cinema found that film attendance was a part of an ongoing process of acculturation.[15] The movie theater provided a venue where one could have access both to peers and to images of American society, and movie attendance served as one of an array of social practices which helped immigrant groups adjust to new circumstances. Ewen in particular showed how the moviegoing ritual helped younger immigrant women establish an identity separate from that of the family and its traditions. The movie theater provided a space away from the influence of family where one could interact with one's social peers and find images of the modern industrial society. Her work suggests how members of a class, in particular historical circumstances, could use movie theaters to shape their social identities.

Recovering information about the actual activity of film viewing—what went on inside the building—has typically meant appealing to the records the institution has left behind. Industry discourse and surviving institutional records have provided historians a sense of the material conditions in which movies were seen and that evidence, in turn, has offered some sense of what spectators must have experienced once they entered the hall. Such basic issues as architecture and interior design betoken the range of impressions available to audiences. Research into the design history of film venues—from fairground booths to picture palaces—has confirmed the variety of conditions under which movies were consumed, and such research should undermine any confidence that there is a single, archetypal situation in which spectators saw films.[16]

Information on programs and their presentations also provides alternative models. Indeed, several accounts of film programs establish that any number of events on programs would contradict the archetypal image of the audience sitting passively in the dark staring at a lighted screen. For example, the heterogeneous programs of early cinema—a mix of films, live acts, sing-alongs, and so on, that carried over from vaudeville and music hall traditions—have been well documented in the literature.[17] Such eclectic forms would hardly permit a sustained period of illusion. Nor would the general atmosphere of the hall, which was frequently noisy, crowded, and full of distractions. In some circumstances, it may have been the case that one's interaction with one's companions in the hall was as important as one's identification with the images on the screen.[18]

Whether the same can be said of the more comfortable surroundings of larger, more formal theaters of a later generation is not (to my knowledge) well established by the historical research.[19] But there are intriguing findings about audience behavior in alternative venues. In her research on Chicago's African-American theaters in the 1920s, Mary Carbine found that spectators identified more with events taking place in the auditorium than with the fictional world of the film.[20] Drawing from such sources as reviews in Chicago's black press, Carbine found an apparent tension between the musical performances, which were often provided by black jazz bands, and the Hollywood films on the programs. Audiences were more engaged with the culturally indigenous music than with the films, and the movie theater took on the exuberant atmosphere of a club, with an energetic give and take between audience and orchestra.

The legacy of such research is not to establish that the archetypal exhibition situation described by Baudry could not have happened historically; rather it is to suggest that there may have been more exhibition variants in heaven and earth (earth, at least) than in all his analogies. My frankly cursory and ruthlessly selective review of this historical research on exhibition should at least prove sufficient to establish that exhibition practice varied substantially from period to period and from social situation to social situation.[21]

The researchers cited above—none of whom would have considered themselves to be part of an effort to challenge the archetypal model and few of whom would have perceived themselves to be part of any coordinated effort—provide the beginnings of an inventory of social factors which can be taken into account in future reflections on exhibition practice. The work raises such questions as how ethnic, class, and gender distinctions figure into the moviegoing experience and mediate the meaning of that experience; how one's social situation motivates one's habits of film attendance; how one's social identity could be shaped and reshaped by the various activities taking place in and around the exhibition venue; and how one's interaction with other members of the audience may have been as important as one's identification with the fictions presented on screen. One's acquired social status and experience are not likely to be surrendered at the theater entrance along with the cost of admission. And they are not likely to be negated when the lights go down. Indeed, in some situations described above, they may have been enhanced, a process which is hard to reconcile with Baudry's contention that spectators regress to primitive narcissism.

The archetypal image of exhibition will likely suffer additional encumbrance as research on the history of American exhibition progresses. But what about film exhibition in non-American settings? It's a big world, after all.

It so happens that the most vigorous and sustained research on exhibition has concentrated on the American situation, a consequence, no doubt, of the centrality of American cinema to film studies generally. Ongoing research on other national settings will doubtless confirm the extent to which culturally specific conditions shape exhibition practices. As accounts of non-American exhibition practices accumulate, we can anticipate encountering even more alternatives to the archetypal image of the sealed chamber and additional problems with the essentialism of Baudry and the attendant psychoanalytical film theory.

My own research on early film exhibition in Soviet Russia has profited enormously from the legacy of several of the historians cited above. Their procedure of approaching the audience through the exhibition institution, their effort to recreate the viewing experience by describing the institution's physical environment and protocols, and their practice of linking moviegoing to other social behaviors, have provided me with salutary methodological antecedents. Their findings, however, cannot be simply replicated in the Russian situation—which is precisely the point. One cannot afford to assume that particular forms of exhibition are somehow transferable from one national setting to another. A summary of some of my findings on early Soviet exhibition can provide a complement to the American situation that others have explored, and it can suggest the extent to which exhibition practices answer to local conditions.[22]

The formation of a national exhibition network in the U.S.S.R. involved a sustained developmental effort through the 1920s. The effort was viewed by Soviet leaders as a precondition to making cinema into a genuinely mass medium, and it was treated as a matter of some urgency, to the extent that official discourse on cinema rang with calls to "cinefy" the countryside. The effort was necessitated by the fact that prerevolutionary cinema did not reach rural areas, where the bulk of the population resided.[23] The effort to develop a nationwide exhibition network in the 1920s had to rely heavily on market forces since the state lacked resources to build an entire exhibition infrastructure through direct investment. And to the extent that it was feasible, Soviet leaders looked to Western (especially American) commercial cinema for organizational models.

We thus have a case study of a national exhibition system that was built more or less from scratch on a state initiative and which had the American model available. To some extent, the act of moviegoing was being invented through state-managed procedures because so much of the population had no prior contact with cinema. What is most telling, even in the circumstance, is the extent to which the effort was controlled by social conditions that long predated the cinefication program. If anything, the system that finally emerged simply inserted moviegoing into established social practices, and the viewing protocols that developed bore the strong traces of local tradition. Moviegoing in Soviet Russia became a practice that accommodated prior social behaviors.

In its broadest structure, the system answered to the sharp class and geographical distinctions of Soviet Russia's diverse population. The distinctions included: the urban middle class, which was beginning to prosper in the general economic recovery of the 1920s; the industrial proletariat of the major cities and industrial towns; and the peasantry, who represented almost 80 percent of the U.S.S.R.'s population and who were geographically dispersed in thousands of isolated villages. Those class identities were sufficiently clear that no single exhibition formula could be imposed on each population. Clearly, for example, the large but scattered peasantry, which had virtually no prior history of film viewing, could not be served by institutions modeled on Moscow's commercial theaters. The problem was to develop variants that would conform to the social conditions of each group.[24]

The system that emerged involved three complementary exhibition types. Commercial theaters were revived in the major cities to serve urban populations. A more specialized network of worker clubs developed in response to the particular needs of the industrial labor force, and itinerant exhibition procedures were innovated to reach the scattered peasant populations. Each exhibition service (as we shall see) adopted practices that were endemic to its particular constituency.

This trifurcated system had important practical qualities, not the least of which was financial feasibility. The costs of maintaining the alternative exhibition forms of worker clubs and rural exhibition had to be sustained by urban commercial houses since the clubs and villages could not afford the burden. The commercial houses consequently had to generate sufficient profits to subsidize the other two domains. To this end, a variant of the Western commercial system of staggered runs and clearances developed. City commercial houses received the prime product (including popular foreign films) in first run. They were then allowed to charge high prices, from 25 kopeks to 1.5 rubles (or roughly 12 to 75 cents). These rates in turn provided a margin which permitted the clubs and village cinemas to operate at costs and to hold ticket prices down for their audiences: 12–15 kopeks in clubs and 5–8 kopeks (or gratis) in villages. The profitability of the commercial houses was protected by staggered runs. Films were allowed to play for at least one month in commercial houses before they became available to clubs, and that "window" assured that discount club cinemas would not undercut commercial venues in the same city. Films did not make it to the village circuit until as much as one year after their commercial release, and then the inventory of films for the villages was restricted. Soviet Russia thus implemented a version of the run and clearance policies (complete with a pricing hierarchy) that a Hollywood executive might have recognized, but the Soviets modified it to fit their situation; the measures not only drew income to first-run houses but provided subvention to the alternative, noncommercial services for clubs and villages.[25]

Most Soviet commercial theaters were revived from prerevolutionary days. The tradition of moviegoing was well established in Russian cities by the 1910s. Urban movie theaters built their business by appealing to a casual, walk-up trade. Continuous programs with no specified starting times were the norm through the early 1910s. Even after feature-length films and announced starting times became common in the middle 1910s, the theaters continued to appeal to impromptu walk-ups. The houses thus exploited the habit of many Russians of making a casual evening on the town by strolling with friends through a town or through a city's entertainment neighborhoods with no set itinerary. Such self-made entertainment might end up in a cafe or tavern, or possibly a movie theater.[26]

These traditions apparently carried into the Soviet era and affected urban commercial cinemas. Commercial houses continued to appeal to the walk-up patrons through the 1920s. Theater managers, for example, were advised to put posters around pedestrian thoroughfares and streetcar exchanges to catch the eye of passersby. They were especially encouraged to poster the immediate neighborhood of the theater on the assumption that someone noticing a flyer would spontaneously drop in at a nearby theater. Managers were discouraged from advertising in newspapers on the contention that moviegoers were not likely to preplan movie attendance by reading the daily paper. And although movies had announced starting times, this spontaneity sometimes meant that spectators might drop into a film at any time.[27] The atmosphere inside could be equally casual. Foyers with buffets were part of the design of most commercial establishments, and patrons typically snacked during the screening. And although musical accompaniment by an organ or small orchestra was standard in commercial houses, there was not a particularly strong etiquette of silence in the audience. It seems that spectators chatted among themselves during screenings. Moreover, the screening was rarely an uninterrupted event. Most houses had dual-system projection; but mid-reel breakdowns were a constant problem, and one projector might simply be out of service for extended periods. Breaks in the continuity of the program represented such an abiding issue that managers were coached on how to come into the auditorium during a hiatus and chat with audience members. The immediate incentive was to prevent patrons from leaving during interruptions (and possibly requesting a refund), but the consequence of such practices would have been to create a somewhat extemporaneous quality to the program.[28] Indeed, to the extent that any of these conditions obtained—patrons materializing on the spur of the moment, interruptions of the projection, conversations during projection or during gaps—the screening may have represented a more open-ended experience than the archetypal model would permit.

Club cinema exhibition departed even more radically from the archetype. The club network was developed under the Soviets to offer sites of relaxation and cultural enlightenment for proletarians. Clubs were organized by labor unions or attached to factories and typically included such amenities as libraries, game rooms, and cafeterias, and they hosted any number of group activities, including lectures, concerts, and amateur sporting events. Most clubs had a main auditorium for group events, and it would have been equipped with a single projector for movies, which were offered two nights per week.

The fact that the clubs existed at all derived from a hard, abiding fact of Russian urban life: the chronic housing shortage that was particularly endured by the industrial proletariat. Workers often lived in cramped, communal apartments or even in barracks-like settings. In such conditions, the apartment was not so much a home as merely a place to sleep; one went out to spend one's leisure hours, and one found relaxation with one's peers in public spaces. Before the revolution, the tavern, dance hall, and music hall were among the favored venues. These locations provided a noisy but convivial atmosphere with social interaction among the patrons representing the primary appeal. This was even true of the music hall performances favored by workers; audience members did not sit quietly taking in the stage shows but interacted with performers and with each other. These qualities carried over to the Soviet worker clubs in the 1920s. Indeed, some club organizers even complained of rowdy behavior at the clubs' public events.[29]

Film screenings, if anything, were designed to take this apparent audience energy and channel it into the event itself. The screenings sometimes had the quality of an open, participatory meeting as much as a film performance. Few clubs could afford musical accompaniment for movies and were likely to substitute lectures or ongoing discussions during the movies. Someone would address the audience while the film was underway, commenting on the events in the film and, very frequently, fielding questions and comments from audience members. Since clubs lacked dual-system projection, breaks for reel changes were planned parts of the event, not to mention the inevitable mid-reel breakdowns in the equipment. Such gaps were filled with audience discussions or even songs. And anecdotal information from clubs suggests that spectators discussed the films (among other things) during the performance. They apparently commented on details of the film among themselves, and some read intertitles out loud for the benefit of nonliterate companions. Parts of the official mandate of the clubs was to reinforce a sense of class solidarity among workers. The community dynamic within the hall may have served that end as much as any of the movies projected up on the screen.[30]

Such informality was even more characteristic of village exhibition, which consisted of a system of itinerant cinemas. A traveling projectionist would visit individual villages as part of a circuit and set up a portable apparatus for a day or two in a public space. Such sites included schools, churches, town halls, and even village squares in good weather. In these makeshift arrangements, audience members might gather in all manner of configurations around the projector, some on benches and many on the floor (or on the ground). The only formal practice was to rope off a section for smokers so as to lessen the possibility of nitrate fires, but even this policy may have been honored in the breach as well as the observance. In these circumstances, the projection apparatus not only was not hidden, it was often the object of attention, its presence offering an occasion for a public gathering. It was even common for projectionists to demonstrate the machine's features to all curious spectators as part of the film service.[31]

Long-standing routines of peasant life shaped the film service. Peasant families tended to live in relative isolation in scattered hamlets and to gather in central village locations on regular occasions for community events such as holidays, market days, and religious observances. Such events were important to affirming a sense of community, and they were used as opportunities to create entertainments with a strong participatory quality, such as feasts and carnivals. Traveling theater companies also brought stage entertainments to villages with heterogeneous programs of songs, skits, acrobatic acts, and the like. The programs could be modified on the spot to suit the local constituency, and audience input was encouraged. Spectators might call out to the

Fig. 26.1. A portable projection apparatus being demonstrated to villagers. From *Film und Volk* (November 1928).

stage and have their remarks worked into the performance, and group songs were common program items.[32]

Movie showings were built into such routines. Projectionists tried to plan itineraries so they could schedule movies on dates when villagers would gather for community activities. The sense of the audience as participating in the event was encouraged in the informal atmosphere of the screenings. Typically a speaker (a local teacher, a party official) was recruited to comment on films during showings. Peasants were inclined to talk throughout the program in any event, and speakers tried to turn this into an ongoing discussion of the material depicted in the film. If the program included an informational documentary—and that represented the most prominent genre of the rural film service—the speaker might encourage extended discussion of the relevant topics. A local doctor might appear for a documentary on disease prevention and discuss preventive measures with audience members before or after the showing. Such practices suggest that movies may have represented one of several forms of community interaction that were part of the fabric of village life, albeit with an added educational strand.[33]

This summary of some features of 1920s exhibition practice notes distinctions among exhibition types and how the practices seem to answer to established social patterns. A survey extending beyond Soviet Russia to include the ethnically distinct Soviet republics would doubtless reveal even more local variants. Nevertheless, even in my brief account, one can identity alternatives to the American experience others have researched.

How and why people have chosen to gather in the presence of a movie projector over the years are issues historians are still exploring. Apparatus theory skipped over such basics in the course of appropriating one type of exhibition and assigning it the status of an archetype. It might be argued that there is a useful distinction to be maintained between the "theoretical spectator" postulated by psychoanalysis (and developed by Baudry) and the "empirical spectator," which is somehow understood to be the separate domain of historians. The ahistorical nature of apparatus theory is thus thought to be justifiable since it creates a model which is not limited to particular historical periods. If anything, however, apparatus theory simply extrapolated from a historically limited situation. It took the kind of exhibition most familiar to its author (and presumably to its immediate readership), the kind practiced in first-run theaters in postwar Europe, for example, and it assigned that model to the whole of cinema. If anything, apparatus theory was unwittingly a product of history and thus is as limited in its useful applications as any of the empirical accounts in the literature.

Perhaps apparatus theory was simply intended to provide a heuristic, something that did not exist in pure form but aided in understanding the process of cinematic illusion. But even the universality of that process can be questioned. One issue which keeps coming back in the research I have summarized is that some audiences often treated films as occasions to experience pleasures not explained by the concept of cinematic illusion. Some even created the atmosphere in the hall through their own interactions. There are apparently forms of social intercourse and companionship available in many exhibition venues which are not accurately described by the image of the psychologically isolated spectator sitting in the dark and identifying with images flickering on a screen.

It would seem that interconnected social factors, independent of psychological identification, can explain a lot of what it means to watch a movie. This statement should be recognized as self-evident. It should constitute a truism of film studies. But in the aftermath of psychoanalytical film theory, it can still be offered as a mild corrective.

NOTES

1. See, for example, Stephen Heath, *Questions of Cinema* (Bloomington: Indiana University Press, 1981), pp. 4–5; and Judith Mayne, *Private Novels, Public Films* (Athens: University of Georgia Press, 1988), pp. 83–84.

2. Indeed, the film's premise seems to have been fairly common in early cinema; see Charles Musser, *Before the Nickelodeon: Edwin S. Porter and see the Edison Manufacturing Company* (Berkeley: University of California Press, 1991), p. 192.

3. The two essays are published in English in (respectively), *Film Quarterly* 28, 2 (1974–75), trans. Alan Williams, and *Camera Obscura* 1 (1976), trans. Jean Andrews and Bertrand Augst. Both essays are reprinted in *Film Theory and Criticism*, 4th ed., ed. Gerald Mast, Marshall Cohen, and Leo Braudy (New York: Oxford University Press, 1992), pp. 302–13 and 690–707 (respectively). Subsequent citations are from this volume.

4. Rodowick, *The Crisis of Political Modernism* (Urbana: University of Illinois Press, 1988), p. 89.

5. Mayne, *Cinema and Spectatorship* (New York: Routledge, 1993), pp. 41, 44–52. The quotation is from p. 41.

6. As Mayne has noted, however, the English translations of Baudry use the English word "apparatus" for two distinct French terms, *appareil* and *dispositif* (ibid., p. 47).

7. Baudry, "Ideological Effects," p. 309.

8. Baudry, "Apparatus," p. 696.

9. The main thrust of my argument, as should be apparent by now, is to question that part of apparatus theory which purports to describe the nature of film exhibition. My emphasis is on the ahistorical nature of Baudry's construct. I do not take it upon myself to treat the overall value of Baudry's theory. An impressive critique of Baudry's theory, one that identifies both flawed premises and internal contradictions, has already been mounted by Noël Carroll (*Mystifying Movies: Fads and Fallacies in Contemporary Film Theory* [New York: Columbia University Press, 1988], pp. 13–32).

10. Russell Merritt, "Nickelodeon Theaters, 1905–1914: Building an Audience for the Movies," in *The American Film Industry*, ed. Tino Balio (Madison: University of Wisconsin Press, 1976), pp. 59–79; Robert Allen, "Motion Picture Exhibition in Manhattan, 1906–1912: Beyond the Nickelodeon," *Cinema Journal* 18, 2 (1979): 2–15.

11. Garth Jowett, "The First Motion Picture Audiences," *Journal of Popular Film* 3, 1 (1974): 39–54; Douglas Gomery, "The Picture Palace: Economic Sense of Hollywood Nonsense?" *Quarterly Review of Film Studies* 3, 1 (1978): 23–36, and "Movie Audiences, Urban Geography, and the History of American Film," *The Velvet Light Trap* 19 (1982): 23–29.

12. Burnes St. Patrick Hollyman, "The First Motion Picture Shows: Austin, Texas, 1884–1913," *Journal of the University Film Association* 29, 3 (1977): 3–8; David O. Thomas, "From Page to Screen in Small Town America: Early Motion Picture Exhibition in Winona, Minnesota," *Journal of the University Film Association* 33, 3 (1981): 3–13.

13. Diane Waldman, "Toward a Harmony of Interests: Rockefeller, the YMCA, and the Company Movie Theater," *Wide Angle* 8, 1 (1986): 41–51.

14. She also found some fragmentary but intriguing evidence of worker resistance, especially in areas where union activities were strongest (ibid., pp. 48–49).

15. Judith Mayne, "Immigrants and Spectators," *Wide Angle* 5, 2 (1982): 32–41; Elizabeth Ewen, "City Lights: Immigrant Women and the Rise of the Movies," in Elizabeth and Stuart Ewen, *Channels of Desire: Mass Images and the Shaping of American Consciousness* (Minneapolis: University of Minnesota Press, 1992), pp. 53–74.

16. See for example Charlotte Herzog, "The Archeology of Cinema Architecture: The Origins of the Movie Theater," *Quarterly Review of Film Studies* 9, 1 (1984): 9–31; and Douglas Gomery, *Shared Pleasures: A History of Movie Presentation in the United States* (Madison: University of Wisconsin Press, 1992), esp. chapters 7–9.

17. See for example, Merritt, "Nickelodeon Theaters," pp. 60–62.

18. See for example Ewen, "City Lights," p. 65.

19. For example, Gomery's admirable history of American exhibition gives due attention to the major theater chains and the palaces of American cinema's classical era, but his research says little about the conduct of patrons (*Shared Pleasures,* chapters 3–4).

20. Carbine, "'The Finest Outside the Loop': Motion Picture Exhibition in Chicago's Black Metropolis, 1905–1928," *Camera Obscura* 23 (1990): 10–41.

21. My brief review of this research does not do justice to many important studies or even acknowledge others. The reader may wish to consult Dan Streible, "The Literature of Film Exhibition: A Bibliography on Motion Picture Exhibition and Related Topics," *The Velvet Light Trap* 25 (1990): 80–119. Robert Allen provides a more theoretical account of this research on exhibition history in "From Exhibition to Reception: Reflections on the Audience in Film History," *Screen* 31, 4 (1990): 347–56. His essay traces (and advocates) a movement from researching exhibition per se to the larger problem of film reception. In reception studies information about the material conditions of exhibition would be subordinated to the question of how audiences responded to particular films. In such studies, exhibition conditions provide the contexts to explain "the myriad readings of individual texts among viewers and over time" (ibid., p. 353). This move has been important to film studies, to be sure, though it is not my central concern here. An example of this kind of work is Janet Staiger's *Interpreting Films: Studies in the Historical Reception of American Cinema* (Princeton: Princeton University Press, 1992).

22. This summary derives from research I have done on a related set of articles: see my "Cinema and Everyday Life: Soviet Worker Clubs of the 1920s," in *Resisting Images: Essays on Cinema and History,* ed. Robert Sklar and Charles Musser (Philadelphia: Temple University Press, 1990), pp. 108–25; "'Film Seance': The Role of Speech in Soviet Film Exhibition of the 1920s," *Wide Angle* 15, 1 (1993): 7–27, and "'Cinefication': Soviet Film Exhibition of the 1920s," *Film History* 6, 2 (1994): 262–77.

23. By one estimate, peasants made up less than 10 percent of the prerevolutionary film audience despite that fact that they represented almost 80 percent of the national population (Iu. Kalistratov, *Ekonomika i organizatsiia kinoseti* [Moscow: Goskinoizdat, 1948], p. 26).

24. E. Lemberg, *Kinopromyshlennost' SSSR* (Moscow: Teakinopechat', 1930), p. 138; A. Katsigras, *Kino-rabota v derevne* (Moscow: Kinopechat', 1926), pp. 19–20.

25. Lemberg, *Kinopromyshlennost',* pp. 101–2, 277–79; *Film Daily Yearbook—1927,* ed. Maurice D. Kann (New York: Alicoate, 1928), pp. 949–50; *Film Daily Yearbook—1930,* ed. Maurice D. Kann (New York: Alicoate, 1931), p. 1043.

26. Yuri Tsivian, "Early Russian Cinema and Its Public," *Historical Journal of Film, Radio, and Television* 11, 2 (1991): 105–16; Richard Stites, *Russian Popular Culture: Entertainment and Society Since 1900* (Cambridge: Cambridge University Press, 1992), pp. 9–12.

27. M. Boitler, *Kino-teatr—organizatsiia i upravlennie* (Moscow: Kinopechat', 1926), pp. 7–8, 23–32.

28. Ibid., pp. 12–22, 36–43.

29. E. H. Carr, *A History of Soviet Russia,* 14 vols. (New York: Macmillan, 1954–78), vol. 10: 612–15, 958; Stites, *Russian Popular Culture,* pp. 10–22; John Hatch, "The Politics of Mass Culture: Workers Communists and Proletkul't in the Development of Workers' Clubs, 1921–25," *Russian History/Histoire Russe* 13, 2–3 (1986): 141–45.

30. V. Filippov, *Kino v rabochem klube* (Moscow: VTsSPS, 1926), pp. 21–32, 53–

73; A. V. Troianovskii and R. I. Egiazarov, *Izuchenie kino-zritelia* (Leningrad: Gosudarstvennoe izdatel'stvo, 1928), pp. 66–68.

31. Katsigras, *Kino-rabota,* pp. 25–26, 51–70.

32. Stites, *Russian Popular Culture,* p. 17; Helmut Altrichter, "Insoluble Conflicts: Village Life between Revolution and Collectivization," in *Russia in the Era of NEP,* ed. Sheila Fitzpatrick, Alexander Rabinovitch, and Richard Stites (Bloomington: Indiana University Press, 1991), pp. 195–99.

33. Katsigras, *Kino-rabota,* pp. 57–69.

Selected Bibliography
Index

SELECTED BIBLIOGRAPHY

Allen, Robert. "From Exhibition to Reception: Reflections on the Audience in Film History." *Screen* 31, 4 (1990): 347–56.

Allen, Robert C., and Douglas Gomery. *Film History: Theory and Practice.* New York: Knopf, 1985.

Althusser, Louis. *For Marx.* Translated by Ben Brewster. London: Allen Lane, 1969.

Balio, Tino. *Grand Design: Hollywood as a Modern Motion Picture Enterprise, 1930–1939.* New York: Charles Scribner's Sons, 1993.

Balio, Tino. *United Artists: The Company Built by the Stars.* Madison: University of Wisconsin Press, 1975.

Balio, Tino. *United Artists: The Company That Changed the Film Industry.* Madison: University of Wisconsin Press, 1987.

Baran, Paul A., and Paul M. Sweezy. *Monopoly Capital.* New York: Monthly Review Press, 1966.

Barkow, Jerome H., Leda Cosmides, and John Tooby, eds. *The Adapted Mind: Evolutionary Psychology and the Generation of Culture.* New York: Oxford University Press, 1992.

Basinger, Jeanine. *A Woman's View: How Hollywood Spoke to Women, 1930–1960.* New York: Knopf, 1993.

Baudry, Jean-Louis. "The Apparatus: Metamphysical Approaches to the Impression of Reality in the Cinema." In *Film Theory and Criticism,* 4th ed., edited by Gerald Mast, Marshall Cohen, and Leo Braudy, pp. 690–707. New York: Oxford University Press, 1992.

Baudry, Jean-Louis. "Ideological Effects of the Basic Cinematographic Apparatus." In ibid., pp. 302–12.

Bordwell, David. "A Case for Cognitivism." *Iris* 9 (Spring 1989): 11–40.

Bordwell, David. "A Case for Cognitivism: Further Reflections." *Iris* 11 (Summer 1990): 107–12.

Bordwell, David. "Cognition and Comprehension: Viewing and Forgetting in *Mildred Pierce*." *Journal of Dramatic Theory and Criticism* 6, 2 (Spring 1992): 183–98.

Bordwell, David. "Historical Poetics of Cinema." In *The Cinematic Text: Methods and Approaches,* edited by R. Barton Palmer, pp. 369–98. New York: AMS Press, 1989.

Bordwell, David. *Making Meaning: Inference and Rhetoric in the Interpretation of Cinema.* Cambridge: Harvard University Press, 1989.

Bordwell, David. *Narration in the Fiction Film.* Madison: University of Wisconsin Press, 1985.

Bordwell, David. *Ozu and the Poetics of Cinema.* Princeton: Princeton University Press, 1988.

Bordwell, David. "The Power of a Research Tradition: Prospects for Progress in the Study of Film Style." *Film History* 6, 1 (Spring 1994): 59–79.

Bordwell, David, and Kristin Thompson. *Film Art: An Introduction.* 4th ed. New York: McGraw-Hill, 1993.

Bordwell, David, Janet Staiger, and Kristin Thompson. *The Classical Hollywood Cinema: Film Style and Mode of Production to 1960*. New York: Columbia University Press, 1985.

Boruah, B. H. *Fiction and Emotion*. Oxford: Clarendon Press, 1988.

Boudon, Raymond. "The Freudian-Marxian-Structuralist (FMS) Movement in France: Variations on a Theme by Sherry Turkle." *The Tocqueville Review* 2, 1 (Winter 1980): 5–23.

Branigan, Edward. *Narrative Comprehension and Film*. London: Routledge, 1992.

Branigan, Edward. *Point of View in the Cinema: A Theory of Subjectivity in Classical Film* (New York: Mouton, 1984).

Brecht, Bertolt. *Brecht on Theatre*. Translated and edited by John Willett. London: Methuen, 1964.

Brooks, Virginia. "Film, Perception and Cognitive Psychology." *Millennium Film Journal* 14/15 (Fall/Winter 1984–85): 105–26.

Brown, Donald E. *Human Universals*. Philadelphia: Temple University Press, 1991.

Brown, Royal S. *Overtones and Undertones: Reading Film Music*. Berkeley: University of California Press, 1994.

Bruce, Graham. *Bernard Herrmann: Film Music and Narrative*. Ann Arbor, Mich.: UMI Research Press, 1985.

Bruce, Vicki, and Patrick R. Green. *Visual Perception: Physiology, Psychology, and Ecology*. 2d ed. Hillsdale, N.J.: Lawrence Erlbaum, 1990.

Bryant, Jennings, and Daniel R. Anderson, eds. *Children's Understanding of Television: Research on Attention and Comprehension*. New York: Academic Press, 1983.

Bryant, Jennings, and Dolf Zillmann, eds. *Responding to the Screen: Reception and Reaction Processes*. Hillsdale, N.J.: Lawrence Erlbaum, 1991.

Burch, Noël. *Theory of Film Practice*. Translated by Helen R. Lane. Princeton: Princeton University Press, 1981.

Burch, Noël. *To the Distant Observer: Form and Meaning in the Japanese Cinema*. Revised and edited by Annette Michelson. Berkeley: University of California Press, 1979.

Carroll, Noël. "Cognitivism, Contemporary Film Theory, and Method: A Response to Warren Buckland." *Journal of Dramatic Theory and Criticism* 6, 2 (Spring 1992): 199–219.

Carroll, Noël. "Film." In *The Postmodern Moment*, edited by Stanley Trachtenberg, pp. 100–133. Westport, Conn.: Greenwood, 1985.

Carroll, Noël. "Film, Rhetoric, and Ideology." In *Explanation and Value in the Arts*, edited by Salim Kemal and Ivan Gaskell, pp. 215–37. Cambridge: Cambridge University Press, 1993.

Carroll, Noël. "From Real to Reel: Entangled in Nonfiction Film." *Philosophic Exchange* 14 (1983): 5–45.

Carroll, Noël. "The Image of Women in Film: A Defense of a Paradigm." *Journal of Aesthetics and Art Criticism* 48, 4 (1990): 349–60.

Carroll, Noël. "The Moral Ecology of Melodrama: The Family Plot and *Magnificent Obsession*." *New York Literary Forum* 7 (1980): 197–206.

Carroll, Noël. *Mystifying Movies: Fads and Fallacies in Contemporary Film Theory*. New York: Columbia University Press, 1988.

Carroll, Noël. *Philosophical Problems of Classical Film Theory*. Princeton: Princeton University Press, 1988.

Carroll, Noël. *The Philosophy of Horror; or, Paradoxes of the Heart*. New York: Routledge, 1990.

Carroll, Noël. "The Power of Movies." *Daedalus* 114, 4 (Fall 1985): 79–104.

Carroll, Noël. "Toward a Theory of Film Suspense." *Persistence of Vision* 1 (Summer 1984): 65–89.

Carroll, Noël. "Toward a Theory of Point-of-View Editing: Communication, Emotion, and the Movies." *Poetics Today* 14, 1 (Spring 1993): 122–41.

Cavell, Stanley. *Pursuits of Happiness: The Hollywood Comedy of Remarriage.* Cambridge: Harvard University Press, 1981.

Chatman, Seymour. *Coming to Terms: The Rhetoric of Narrative in Fiction and Film.* Ithaca, N.Y.: Cornell University Press, 1990.

Cherchi Usai, Paolo. *Burning Passions: An Introduction to the Study of Silent Cinema.* Translated by Emma Sansone Rittle. London: British Film Institute, 1994.

Clark, Herbert H. *Areas of Language Use.* Chicago: University of Chicago Press, 1992.

Clover, Carol J. *Men, Women, and Chain Saws: Gender in the Modern Horror Film.* Princeton: Princeton University Press, 1992.

Cole, Peter. *Radical Pragmatics.* New York: Academic Press, 1981.

Collins, Jim. *Uncommon Cultures: Popular Culture and Post-Modernism.* London: Routledge, 1989.

Collins, Richard, et al., eds., *Media, Culture, and Society: A Critical Reader.* London: Sage, 1986.

Collins, W. Andrew. "Children's Comprehension of Television Content." In *Children Communicating,* edited by Ellen Wartella, pp. 21–52. Beverly Hills: Sage, 1979.

Collins, W. Andrew. "The Developing Child as Viewer." *Journal of Communication* 25, 4 (1975): 35–44.

Cook, Mallorie. "Criticism or Complicity? The Question of the Treatment of Rape and Rape Victim in Jonathan Kaplan's *The Accused.*" *CineAction!* 24/25 (1991): 80–85.

Currie, Gregory. "Impersonal Imagining: A Reply to Levinson." *Philosophical Quarterly* 43 (1993): 79–81.

Currie, Gregory. "Visual Fictions." *Philosophical Quarterly* 41 (1991): 129–43.

Cutting, James E. "Rigidity in Cinema Seen from the Front Row, Side Aisle." *Journal of Experimental Psychology: Human Perception and Performance* 13, 3 (1987): 323–33.

De Sousa, Ronald. *The Rationality of Emotion.* Cambridge: MIT Press, 1990.

De Wied, Minet. *The Role of Time Structures in the Experience of Film Suspense.* Ph.D. diss., University of Amsterdam, 1991.

Doane, Mary Anne. *The Desire to Desire: The Woman's Film of the 1940s.* Bloomington: Indiana University Press, 1987.

Dosse, François. *Histoire du structuralisme.* 2 vols. Paris: La Découverte, 1992.

Erlich, Victor. *Russian Formalism: History—Doctrine.* 2d ed. New Haven, Conn.: Yale University Press, 1981.

Feagin, Susan L. "Imagining Emotions and Appreciating Fiction." *Canadian Journal of Philosophy* 18 (1988): 485–500.

Fischer, David Hackett. *Historians' Fallacies: Toward a Logic of Historical Thought.* New York: Harper and Row, 1970.

Fiske, John. *Television Culture.* London: Methuen, 1987.

Flinn, Caryl. *Strains of Utopia: Gender, Nostalgia, and Hollywood Film Music.* Princeton: Princeton University Press, 1992.

Freeland, Cynthia A. "I Spit on Your Gaze." *Afterimage* 20, 1 (March 1993): 12–13.

Freeland, Cynthia A. "Realist Horror." In *Philosophy and Film*, edited by Cynthia Freeland and Thomas E. Wartenberg. New York: Routledge, 1995.

Friedberg, Anne. "A Denial of Difference: Theories of Cinematic Identification." In *Psychoanalysis and Cinema*, edited by E. Ann Kaplan, pp. 36–45. New York: Routledge, 1990.

Gardner, Howard. *The Mind's New Science: A History of the Cognitive Revolution*. New York: Basic Books, 1985.

Gerrig, Richard J. *Experiencing Narrative Worlds*. New Haven: Yale University Press, 1993.

Gever, Martha, John Greyson, and Pratibha Parmar, eds. *Queer Looks: Perspectives on Lesbian and Gay Film and Video*. London: Routledge, 1993.

Gibson, James J. *The Ecological Approach to Visual Perception*. Boston: Houghton Mifflin, 1979.

Gibson, James J. *Reasons for Realism: Selected Essays of James J. Gibson*, edited by Edward Reed and Rebecca Jones. Hillsdale, N.J.: Erlbaum, 1982.

Gibson, James J. *The Senses Considered as Perceptual Systems*. Boston: Houghton Mifflin, 1966.

Goldman, Alvin. "Empathy, Mind, and Morals." *Proceedings and Addresses of the American Philosophical Association* 66 (November 1992): 17–41.

Gombrich, E. H. *Art and Illusion: A Study in the Psychology of Pictorial Representation*. Princeton: Princeton University Press, 1961.

Gombrich, E. H. *The Image and the Eye: Further Studies in the Psychology of Pictorial Representation*. Ithaca, N.Y.: Cornell University Press, 1982.

Gombrich, E. H. *The Sense of Order: A Study in the Psychology of Decorative Art*. Ithaca, N.Y.: Cornell University Press, 1979.

Gombrich, E. H., Julian Hochberg, and Max Black. *Art, Perception, and Reality*. Ithaca, N.Y.: Cornell University Press, 1972.

Gomery, Douglas. "Hollywood, the National Recovery Administration, and the Question of Monopoly Power." *Journal of the University Film Association* 31 (Spring 1979): 47–52.

Gomery, Douglas. *The Hollywood Studio System*. New York: St. Martin's Press, 1986.

Gomery, Douglas. *Shared Pleasures: A History of Movie Presentation in the United States*. Madison: University of Wisconsin Press, 1992.

Gorbman, Claudia. *Unheard Melodies: Narrative Film Music*. Bloomington: Indiana University Press, 1987.

Gordon, Robert. "Folk Psychology as Simulation." *Mind and Language* 1 (1986): 158–71.

Grossberg, Lawrence, Cary Nelson, and Paula Treichler, eds. *Cultural Studies*. New York: Routledge, 1992.

Hall, Stuart et al., eds. *Culture, Media, Language: Working Papers in Cultural Studies, 1972–79*. London: Hutchinson, 1980.

Harding, D. W. "Psychological Processes in the Reading of Fiction." In Harold Osborne, ed. *Aesthetics in the Modern World* (New York: Weybright and Talley, 1968), pp. 300–317.

Heath, Stephen. "Lessons from Brecht." *Screen* 15, 2 (Summer 1974): 103–8.

Hobbs, Renée. "Television and the Shaping of Cognitive Skills." In *Video Icons and Values*, edited by Alan Olson, Christopher Parr, and Debra Parr, pp. 33–44. Albany, N.Y.: SUNY Press, 1991.

Hobbs, Renée, Richard Frost, Arthur Davis, and John Stauffer. "How First-Time

Viewers Comprehend Editing Conventions." *Journal of Communications* 38, 4 (1988): 50–60.

Hochberg, Julian. *Perception*. 3d ed. Englewood Cliffs, N.J.: Prentice-Hall, 1987.

Hochberg, Julian. "Representation of Motion and Space in Video and Cinematic Displays." In Kenneth R. Boff, Lloyd Kaufman, and James P. Thomas, eds. *Handbook of Perception and Human Performance*, vol. 1: *Sensory Processes and Perception*, chapter 22. New York: John Wiley, 1986.

Hochberg, J., and V. Brooks. "Film Cutting and Visual Momentum." In *Eye Movements and the Higher Psychological Functions*, edited by J. W. Senders, D. F. Fisher, and R. A. Monty, pp. 293–313. Hillsdale, N.J.: Erlbaum, 1978.

Hochberg, J., and V. Brooks. "Integration of Successive Cinematic Views of Simple Scenes." *Bulletin of the Psychometric Society* 4 (1974): 263.

Hochberg, J., and V. Brooks. "The Perception of Motion Pictures." In *Handbook of Perception*, edited by E. C. Carterette and M. Friedman. vol. 10, pp. 259–302. New York: Academic Press, 1978.

Hochberg, J., and V. Brooks. "Pictorial Recognition as an Unlearned Ability: A Study of One Child's Performance." *American Journal of Psychology* 75 (1962): 624–28.

Hollis, Martin, and Steven Lukes, eds. *Rationality and Relativism*. Cambridge: MIT Press, 1982.

Jackson, Leonard. *The Poverty of Structuralism: Literature and Structuralist Theory*. London: Longman, 1991.

Jacobs, Lewis. *The Rise of the American Film*. New York: Harcourt, Brace, 1939.

Jameson, Fredric. *The Geopolitical Aesthetic: Cinema and Space in the World System*. Bloomington: Indiana University Press, 1992.

Jameson, Fredric. *The Political Unconscious: Narrative as a Socially Symbolic Act*. Ithaca, N.Y.: Cornell University Press, 1981.

Jameson, Fredric. *Postmodernism; or, the Cultural Logic of Late Capitalism*. Durham, N.C.: Duke University Press, 1991.

Jameson, Fredric. *Signatures of the Visible*. New York: Routledge, 1990.

Jarvie, Ian. *The Philosophy of Film: Epistemology, Ontology, Aesthetics*. New York: Routledge, 1987.

Jay, Martin. *Downcast Eyes: The Denigration of Vision in Twentieth-Century French Thought*. Berkeley: University of California Press, 1993.

Johnson-Laird, P. N. *Mental Models: Towards a Cognitive Science of Language, Inference, and Consciousness*. Cambridge: Harvard University Press, 1983.

Kahneman, Daniel, Paul Slovic, and Amos Tversky, eds. *Judgment under Uncertainty: Heuristics and Biases*. New York: Cambridge University Press, 1982.

Kalinak, Kathryn. *Settling the Score: Music and the Classical Hollywood Film*. Madison: University of Wisconsin Press, 1992.

Kaplan, E. Ann, ed. *Psychoanalysis and Cinema*. New York: Routledge, 1990.

Kepley, Vance, Jr. "'Cinefication': Soviet Film Exhibition of the 1920s." *Film History* 6, 2 (1994): 262–77.

Kepley, Vance, Jr. "Cinema and Everyday Life: Soviet Worker Clubs of the 1920s." In *Resisting Images: Essays on Cinema and History*, edited by Robert Sklar and Charles Musser, pp. 108–25. Philadelphia: Temple University Press, 1990.

Kepley, Vance, Jr. "'Film Seance': The Role of Speech in Soviet Film Exhibition of the 1920s." *Wide Angle* 15, 1 (1993): 7–27.

Kirihara, Donald. *Patterns of Time: Mizoguchi and the 1930s*. Madison: University of Wisconsin Press, 1992.

Kitcher, Patricia. *Freud's Dream: A Complete Interdisciplinary Science of Mind*. Cambridge: MIT Press, 1992.

Kivy, Peter. *Music Alone: Philosophical Reflections on the Purely Musical Experience*. Ithaca, N.Y.: Cornell University Press, 1990.

Kozloff, Sarah. *Invisible Storytellers: Voice-Over in American Fiction Film*. Berkeley: University of California Press, 1988.

Kristeva, Julia. *Powers of Horror: An Essay on Abjection*. Translated by Léon Roudiez. New York: Columbia University Press, 1982.

Kuhn, Annette. *Women's Pictures: Feminism and Cinema*. London: Routledge, 1982.

Lakoff, George. *Women, Fire, and Dangerous Things: What Categories Reveal about the Mind*. Chicago: University of Chicago Press, 1987.

Lerdahl, Fred, and Ray Jackendoff. *A Generative Theory of Tonal Music*. Cambridge: MIT Press, 1983.

Levinson, Jerrold. "Making Believe." *Dialogue* 32 (Summer 1993): 359–74.

Levinson, Jerrold. "Seeing, Imaginarily, at the Movies." *Philosophical Quarterly* 43 (January 1993): 70–78.

Macey, David. *Lacan in Contexts*. London: Verso, 1988.

Maltby, Richard. *Harmless Entertainment: Hollywood and the Ideology of Consensus*. Metuchen, N.J.: Scarecrow, 1983.

Maltby, Richard. "*Baby Face* or How Joe Breen Made Barbara Stanwyck Atone for Causing the Wall Street Crash." *Screen* 27, 2 (March–April 1986): 22–45.

Maltby, Richard. "'To Prevent the Prevalent Type of Book': Censorship and Adaptation in Hollywood, 1924–1934." *American Quarterly* 44, 4 (December 1992): 554–83.

Maltby, Richard, with Ian Craven. *Hollywood Cinema: An Introduction*. Oxford: Blackwell's, 1995.

Mandel, Ernest. *Late Capitalism*. Translated by Joris De Bres. London: New Left Books, 1975.

Marr, David. *Vision*. New York: W. H. Freeman, 1982.

Mayne, Judith. *Cinema and Spectatorship*. New York: Routledge, 1993.

Merquior, J. G. *From Prague to Paris: A Critique of Structuralist and Post-Structuralist Thought*. London: Verso, 1986.

Messaris, Paul. "To What Extent Does One Have to Learn to Interpret Movies?" In *Film/Culture*, edited by Sari Thomas, pp. 168–83. Metuchen, N.J.: Scarecrow, 1982.

Messaris, Paul. *Visual Literacy: Image, Mind, and Reality*. Boulder: Westview Press, 1994.

Metz, Christian. *L'Énonciation impersonnel ou le site du film*. Paris: Klincksieck, 1991.

Metz, Christian. *The Imaginary Signifier: Psychoanalysis and the Cinema*. Translated by Celia Britton, Annwyl Williams, Ben Brewster, and Alfred Guzzetti. Bloomington: Indiana University Press, 1982.

Modleski, Tania. "The Terror of Pleasure: The Contemporary Horror Film and Postmodern Theory." In *Studies in Entertainment: Critical Approaches to Mass Culture*, edited by Tania Modleski, pp. 155–66. Bloomington: Indiana University Press, 1986.

Mulvey, Laura. "Visual Pleasure and Narrative Cinema." In *Visual and Other Pleasures*, pp. 14–26. Bloomington: Indiana University Press, 1990.

National Conference on Visual Information Processing. *Report to the National Institute of Education*. Washington, D.C.: Government Printing Office, 1974.

Neisser, Ulric. *Cognition and Reality*. New York: W. H. Freeman, 1976.

Nichols, Bill. *Representing Reality*. Bloomington: Indiana University Press, 1991.

Noletti, Arthur, Jr., and David Desser, eds. *Reframing Japanese Cinema: Authorship, Genre, History*. Bloomington: Indiana University Press, 1992.

Novitz, David. *Knowledge, Fiction, and Imagination*. Philadelphia: Temple University Press, 1987.

Odin, Roger. *Cinéma et production de sens*. Paris: Armand Colin, 1990.

O'Sullivan, Tim, John Hartley, Danny Saunders, Martin Montgomery, and John Fiske. *Key Concepts in Communication and Cultural Studies*. 2d ed. London: Routledge, 1994.

Peacocke, Christopher. "Depiction." *Philosophical Review* 96 (1987): 383–410.

Peterson, James. *Dreams of Chaos, Visions of Order: Understanding the American Avant-Garde Cinema*. Detroit: Wayne State University Press, 1994.

Peterson, James. "A War of Utter Rebellion: Kinugasa's *Page of Madness* and the Japanese Avant-Garde of the 1920s." *Cinema Journal* 29, 1 (Fall 1989): 36–53.

Pinker, Steven. *The Language Instinct: How the Mind Creates Language*. New York: William Morrow, 1994.

Plantinga, Carl. "Defining Documentary: Fiction, Nonfiction, and Projected Worlds." *Persistence of Vision* 5 (Spring 1987): 44–54.

Plantinga, Carl. "The Mirror Framed: A Case for Expression in the Documentary." *Wide Angle* 13, 2 (Summer 1991): 40–53.

Prince, Stephen. "The Discourse of Pictures: Iconicity and Film Studies." *Film Quarterly* 47, 1 (Fall 1993): 16–28.

Ramachandran, Vilayanur S., and Stuart M. Anstis. "The Perception of Apparent Motion." *Scientific American* 254, 6 (June 1986): 102–9.

Renov, Michael, ed. *Theorizing Documentary*. New York: Routledge, 1993.

Rock, Irwin. *The Logic of Perception*. Cambridge: MIT Press, 1983.

Rodowick, D. N. *The Difficulty of Difference*. New York: Routledge, 1991.

Rosch, Eleanor, and Barbara B. Lloyd, eds. *Cognition and Categorization*. Hillsdale, N.J.: Lawrence Erlbaum, 1978.

Rosen, Philip, ed. *Narrative, Apparatus, Ideology*. New York: Columbia University Press.

Roudinesco, Elisabeth. *Jacques Lacan & Co.: A History of Psychoanalysis in France, 1925–1985*. Translated by Jeffrey Mehlman. Chicago: University of Chicago Press, 1990.

Ryan, Michael, and Douglas Kellner. *Camera Politica: The Politics and Ideology of Contemporary Hollywood Film*. Bloomington: Indiana University Press, 1988.

Schier, Flint. *Deeper into Pictures: An Essay on Pictorial Representation*. Cambridge: Cambridge University Press, 1986.

Silverman, Kaja. *The Subject of Semiotics*. New York: Oxford, 1983.

Silverman, Kaja. *The Acoustic Mirror: The Female Voice in Psychoanalysis and Cinema*. Bloomington: Indiana University Press, 1988.

Sitney, P. Adams. *Visionary Film: The American Avant-Garde, 1943–1978*. New York: Praeger, 1974.

Solso, Robert L. *Cognition and the Visual Arts*. Cambridge: MIT Press, 1994.

Soper, Kate. *Humanism and Anti-Humanism*. La Salle, Ill.: Open Court, 1986.

Sperber, Dan, and Dierdre Wilson. *Relevance: Communication and Cognition*. Cambridge: Harvard University Press, 1986.

Staiger, Janet. *Interpreting Films: Studies in the Historical Reception of American Cinema*. Princeton: Princeton University Press, 1992.

Stam, Robert, Robert Burgoyne, and Sandy Flitterman-Lewis. *New Vocabularies in*

Film Semiotics: Structuralism, Post-Structuralism, and Beyond. New York: Routledge, 1992.

Stillings, Neil A., et al. *Cognitive Science: An Introduction.* Cambridge: MIT Press, 1987.

Streible, Dan. "The Literature of Film Exhibition: A Bibliography on Motion Picture Exhibition and Related Topics." *The Velvet Light Trap* 25 (1990): 80–119.

Tallis, Raymond. *In Defence of Realism.* London: Edwin Arnold, 1988.

Tallis, Raymond. *Not Saussure: A Critique of Post-Saussurean Literary Theory.* London: Macmillan, 1988.

Tan, Ed S.-H. "Constraint and Convention in Psychological Film Aesthetics." In *Proceedings of the Conference on Film Pragmatics: Amsterdam, March 1992,* edited by Jurgen Müller. Münster: Nodus (forthcoming).

Tan, Ed S.-H. "Film-Induced Affect as a Witness Emotion." *Poetics Today* (forthcoming).

Tan, Ed S.-H., and Inge J. M. van den Boom. "Explorations in the Psychological Affect Structure of Narrative Film." In *Reader Response to Literature: The Empirical Dimension,* edited by Elaine F. Nardocchio, pp. 57–94. Berlin: Mouton, 1992.

Thompson, Kristin. *Breaking the Glass Armor: Neoformalist Film Analysis.* Princeton, N.J.: Princeton University Press, 1988.

Thompson, Kristin. *Exporting Entertainment: America in the World Film Market, 1907–1934.* London: British Film Institute, 1985.

Tyler, Parker. *The Hollywood Hallucination.* New York: Simon and Schuster, 1944.

Van Dijk, Teun A., and Walter Kintsch. *Strategies of Discourse Comprehension.* New York: Academic Press, 1983.

Vasey, Ruth. *Diplomatic Representations: The World According to Hollywood 1918–1939.* Madison: University of Wisconsin Press, forthcoming.

Walton, Kendall. *Mimesis as Make-Believe: On the Foundation of the Representational Arts.* Cambridge: Harvard University Press, 1990.

Walton, Kendall. "Transparent Pictures: On the Nature of Photographic Realism." *Critical Inquiry* 11, 2 (December 1984): 246–77.

Weis, Elisabeth, and John Belton, eds. *Film Sound: Theory and Practice.* New York: Columbia University Press, 1985.

Whittock, Trevor. *Metaphor and Film.* Cambridge: Cambridge University Press, 1990.

Williams, Linda. "Film Bodies: Gender, Genre, and Excess." *Film Quarterly* 44 (Summer 1991): 2–13.

Williams, Linda. "When the Woman Looks." In *Re-Vision: Essays in Feminist Film Criticism,* edited by Mary Ann Doane, Patricia Mellencamp, and Linda Williams, pp. 83–99. Frederick, Md.: University Press of America/American Film Institute, 1984.

Wilson, George. *Narration in Light: Studies in Cinematic Point of View.* Baltimore: Johns Hopkins University Press, 1986.

Wolfenstein, Martha, and Nathan Leites. *Movies: A Psychological Study.* Glencoe, Ill.: The Free Press, 1950.

Wollen, Peter. *Signs and Meaning in the Cinema.* Bloomington: Indiana University Press, 1969.

Wollheim, Richard. "Imagination and Identification." In *On Art and the Mind,* pp. 54–83. Cambridge: Harvard University Press, 1974.

Wollheim, Richard. *The Thread of Life.* Cambridge: Cambridge University Press, 1984.

Zimmerman, R., and J. Hochberg. "Responses of Infant Monkeys to Pictorial Representations of Learned Visual Discriminations." *Psychonomic Science* 18 (1970): 307–8.

INDEX